Good Wine Guide 2002

Robert Joseph

A DORLING KINDERSLEY BOOK

LONDON, NEW YORK, MUNICH,
MELBOURNE, DELHI

A PENGUIN COMPANY

Produced by RJ Publishing Services

Editor • Robert Joseph
Deputy Editors • Susie Barrie, J.D. Haasbroek
Photography • Steve Gorton, Ian O'Leary

DORLING KINDERSLEY
Senior Editor • Edward Bunting
Senior Art Editor • Anna Benjamin
Managing Editor • Sharon Lucas
Senior Managing Art Editor • Derek Coombes
DTP Designer • Sonia Charbonnier
Production • Sarah Coltman

Fourth Edition published 2001
by Dorling Kindersley Limited
80 Strand, London WC2R 0RL

2 4 6 8 10 9 7 5 3 1

A CIP catalogue record of this book is
available from the British Library.

ISBN 07513 3512 6

Text film output by Personality, London
Colour reproduced by Colourscan, Singapore
Printed and bound in Italy by Graficom

See our complete
catalogue at
www.dk.com

CONTENTS

INTRODUCTION

Welcome to the 17th edition of the Robert Joseph *Good Wine Guide,* and the first to feature details and descriptions of 1,000 great and great value wines from the 2001 International Wine Challenge, the world's biggest wine competition.

The addition of this new section helps to make the *Good Wine Guide* a wine drinker's companion that is really four books in one. In the first section – *The Basics* – you'll find all the grounding you need to get through a dinner party among wine buffs, with guidance on styles, flavours, vintages, and ideal marriages between food and wine. There is also a feature on wine on the web, and a larger-than-ever section on wine and health.

The following section – *The A–Z of Wine* – is an encyclopedia of some 3,000 wines, terms, regions, and producers, recommended examples, and the best way to pronounce the names of all those wines. So, you'll never have to pause before ordering a bottle of Ngatarawa from New Zealand.

Next come those International Wine Challenge wines – the 226 Gold Trophy Winners and medallists and some 780 other Great Value award winners across a wide range of styles, and chosen for the flavour and character they deliver for the price tag they bear.

Having chosen your wine, you won't have to search to find it. Simply turn to the fourth section of the book – *Retailers* – where you will find over 250 wine merchants, ranging from quirky one-man-bands, auctioneers, and fine-wine traditionalists to wine clubs, mail-order specialists, high-street chains, and supermarkets.

Taken as a whole, the *Guide* should (as a reviewer wrote of a previous edition) be the "only wine book you need" when choosing, buying, or drinking wine in 2002.

This year's *Guide* owes a great deal to stalwart deputy editors Susie Barrie, who juggled work on the book with her commitments as the host of a television wine programme, and the unflappable J.D. Haasbroek who, once again, almost single-handedly kept the book on track. Lavinia Sanders' organizing skills saved me from the asylum, and Charles Metcalfe and Anthony Downes provided much moral support. I also have to thank Piers Russell-Cobb and, at Dorling Kindersley, Derek Coombes, Sonia Charbonnier, and Anna Benjamin. Richard Davies and Jane Brown at *WINE* magazine and Kim Murphy at the Wine Institute of Asia were all indulgent as ever. All of these people share any credit for this book; the criticism should, as ever, fall on my shoulders alone.

THE
BASICS

PALATES IN WONDERLAND

SIZE MATTERS

Just paint a picture in your mind, if you will, of a winemaker. What do you see? An old beret-wearing, French vigneron who, with the help of his family tends a small patch of vines planted by his grandfather and crushes the grapes picked from them into a ruby-hued liquid with which he will manually fill his bottles one by one. Or a young man in a white coat, at the controls of high-tech equipment that looks as though it might, with a little tinkering, be adapted for inter-planetary travel?

The reality behind both images can be found throughout the world, if you go looking for it. I've visited one-man-band operations in Australia producing great wine using old-fashioned basket presses that were discarded in France a generation ago. And I've seen shiny 21st century wineries in Europe that could put the most ambitious efforts of the Napa and Barossa Valleys to shame.

The old and new, big and small are, however, increasingly united, whether they like it or not, by the market place in which they have to sell their wines – a domaine where branding, marketing, and physical distribution are increasingly of equal and sometimes greater importance than the quality and individual character of the stuff in the bottle.

Over the last year, the takeover mania has accelerated across the planet. So the Australian Fosters-owned giant Mildara Blass took over Beringer in California – and became Beringer Blass – while its competitor BRL Hardy launched a joint venture with Constellation, the US leviathan that recently swallowed such wineries as Franciscan, Simi, and Sonoma Cutrer. In another clever deal, Rosemount, the dynamic family-owned firm that had already set up its own joint venture with Mondavi, virtually took over the far larger publicly quoted Southcorp (owner of Penfolds, Lindemans, Seaview, Seppelt, Coldstream Hills, etc.) in a move to protect it from multi-national predators like Allied Domecq. New Zealand had fewer such defences to call on when that same UK-based firm launched its bid for Montana, the producer that, since its takeover of its smaller rival Corbans, is now responsible for over two thirds of New Zealand's wine.

Soon it seems a few big firms like these may well control the whole industry. Who'd have guessed, a few years ago, that one company, LVMH – and its boss – would now direct the destinies of Krug, Newton Vineyards, Moët & Chandon, Cape Mentelle, Ruinart, Cloudy Bay, Veuve Clicquot, Mountadam, and Châteaux d'Yquem and Cheval Blanc?

And who'd have foreseen the arrival of "global wines" such as the Mondavi Woodbridge range, which includes similarly labelled wines from France and California, and E&J Gallo's Garnet Point wines that are now produced in California and in Australia?

A large number of modern wine drinkers evidently care as little about the precise origin of the stuff in their glass as they do about the whereabouts of the factory that produced their Bosch washing machine, their Marks & Spencer shirt, or their children's Barbie and Action Men dolls. And, if the wine tastes good, who's to blame them?

"Garage" wines can come from traditional cellars – if quantities are small enough.

GARAGE SALES

Perhaps inevitably, there's another side to the coin: wines produced in tiny quantities from very specific plots and hyped on the basis of their intrinsic rarity. These recently launched, critically well-received, "garage" wines – so-called because they were often produced in parts of private houses that were intended for automobiles rather than barrels –

now sell for far more than wines from estates with track records that go back for hundreds of years. One bottle of Screaming Eagle from California or Valandraud from St. Emilion would, for example, buy you three or more of a great, classic Médoc wine such as Château Léoville-Barton or Lynch-Bages, or of a great Burgundy or Barolo. But just remember when you're tempted to pay the asking price for one of these instant superstars that the true value of anything tends to emerge with time. Give them a few years, and you might just find that cost of the pricier garage wines could follow the same downward course as the shares you bought in Yahoo! and Amazon.com.

Organic grapes – the fruit of the future?

Bug Watch

Just a few years ago, California's vineyards were devastated by a louse called phylloxera devastatrix – the same all-American creature that had crossed the Atlantic a century earlier to do similar damage to Europe's wine industry. The only way to protect vines from phylloxera is to plant them on resistant rootstock, which is what the Europeans did and many ill-advised Californians, sadly, initially did not. California phylloxera has now been consigned to the history books, and the Napa, Sonoma, and Central valleys are carpeted with freshly replanted resistant vines.

So all is well. Or at least it would be if it weren't for another pest, colourfully known as the glassy-winged sharpshooter, which threatens even worse damage than phylloxera – simply because, unlike phylloxera, this insect spreads a disease called Xylella fastidiosa or Pierce's Disease, for which there is no known remedy. Estimates of the insect's progress vary, but some fear that it may already be spreading throughout California's vineyards. If this pessimistic view is correct, the cost to the wine industry could run into billions of dollars.

Going Green

One of the more interesting responses to the sharpshooter problem is to deploy a parasitic, stingerless wasp that has been imported from Mexico. This natural approach is in direct contrast to the belief of some experts that the only effective way to beat the sharpshooter will be to plant vines that have been genetically modified to be impervious to it. The debate between the two camps, and the enthusiasm for the wasps, illustrates a growing support throughout the wine world for organic agriculture. Once a sideline associated with the hippier fringe of the winemaking world, natural – or as some prefer to call it, sustainable – grape farming and winemaking is now firmly moving into the mainstream. The large Californian winery Fetzer was an early pioneer in the US, and its successful Bonterra brand is still probably the world's most prominent organic brand. But others who are following in Fetzer's tracks include world famous giants such as Robert Mondavi and E&J Gallo in California, and Penfolds and BRL Hardy in Australia. All of them acknowledge that the routine use of once-popular chemical insecticides, fungicides, and strong fertilizers is no longer acceptable. Among the band of higher profile, smaller European producers who now also make their wine in this way, or follow the even stricter biodynamic rules, are Chapoutier in the Rhône, Dr. Loosen in Germany, Gaston Huët in the Loire, and such illustrious Burgundy domaines as Leflaive, Lafon, and Leroy.

So far, there has been little effort to promote organic winemaking commercially on wine labels, but given the investment that has gone into it over the last few years and the impending wine glut, there is every likelihood that wine advertising will soon take on a decidedly green hue.

Enough is as Good as a Feast

Wine promotion and price cutting will become a lot more aggressive in 2002 as the industry acknowledges that it is facing the first ever surplus of decent quality wines. These will have been made from grapes grown in recently planted vineyards by the highly professional growers and wineries who between them have, for example, more than doubled the annual production of both Australia and California in under a decade. Given the restructuring and modernization of vineyards in France, Spain, and Italy, it's hardly surprising that the price of Chardonnay grapes, for instance, has already dropped in some regions by half in less than three years. Nor is it that surprising the marketing men are busily trying to launch "White Merlot" produced from recently planted vines in California's Central Valley.

The good news for wine drinkers is that the price of daily-drinking wine is unlikely to rise and may well fall. The bad news is that the crisis – and that's what I foresee – may favour bigger producers with deep pockets. Which helps to explain why so many inexpensive wines now taste pleasant but decidedly short of character.

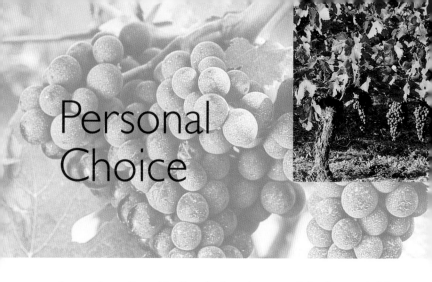

Personal Choice

An unashamedly quirky list of wines that, out of the thousands I have tasted this year, have caught my attention. Prices are rounded off to the nearest pound. Stocks of many of these are limited, so it is likely that in some cases, the vintage mentioned may become unavailable during the lifetime of this Guide.

REDS FOR DAILY DRINKING

1998 Chateau Thézannes Corbières (£5 Co-op) Southern France is really beginning to show that it can compete with the New World, with rich, characterful wines like this that combine berries and earthy, regional character.

2000 Garnet Point Australia Shiraz-Cabernet Sauvignon (£5 widely available) And here's an Aussie version made by Yalumba in the Barossa Valley for the US giant, E&J Gallo, for you to compare it with. Juicy, peppery, and very easy to drink

2000 Terramater Zinfandel Shiraz (£5 Asda) A Chilean blend of grapes usually associated with California and Australia. Spicy, smoky wine with flavours of soy sauce and blueberry.

2000 A Mano Primitivo (£5 Oddbins) Made from the same grape in Southern Italy (where the Zinfandel is known as the Primitivo), this is gorgeous, mouth-filling wine with chocolatey, berry flavours.

1999 Alamos Ridge Malbec (£5 Bibendum) A peppery, plummy wine made in Argentina from a grape that used to be part of the blend for red Bordeaux.

2000 Barbera d'Asti Contea di Castiglione (£5 virginwines.com) Plummy wine made from one of Italy's most characterful grape varieties. Bursting with wild berry flavour..

1998 Casillero del Diablo (£5 Safeway) From French Merlot to one from Chile. Delicious plummy wine with a fresh but soft texture.

REDS FOR SPECIAL OCCASIONS

1999 Knappstein Lenswood Vineyards Pinot Noir (£17 Berkmann Wine Cellars) Fresh, intensely berryish Pinot from recently-planted vineyards high in the Adelaide hills above the sunbathing vines of the Barossa Valley.

1998 Clos De Tart (£50 Harrods) Grand Cru red Burgundy from an underrated vintage that will take time to mature. Be patient though, and you'll be rewarded with lovely complex layers of raspberry, chocolate, and oak.

1998 Kent Rasmussen Winery Carneros Pinot Noir (£10 Berry Bros & Rudd) From one of the most reliable Pinot producers in California, this is beautiful, stylish wine, with plummy richness.

1995 Chateau la Mission Haut Brion (£35 Farr Vintners) Often traditionally overshadowed by its neighbour Haut-Brion, this estate has been growing in stature with every vintage. Lovely maturing, blackcurranty wine.

1998 The Aviator, Alpha Domus (£20 Noel Young) A new name to watch from New Zealand – and a new Bordeaux blend, with delicious bright flavours.

1999 Kaapzicht Steytler Pinotage (£15 Seckford Wines) Really good Pinotage is a rarity – this South African variety is not an easy grape to get right – so don't let this spicy, peppery example pass you by.

1996 Cain Five (£30 Harvey Nichols) The traditional Bordeaux blend produced here in vineyards on some of the best, highest slopes in the Napa Valley. Blackcurranty Bordeaux style and Bordeaux quality.

1998 Guelbenzu Lautus (£17 Moreno Fine Wine) Spain's new-wave winemakers are improving with every vintage, and this Navarra red blend of Tempranillo, Merlot, and Cabernet is a top-class juicy, toffeeish effort.

1999 Cumaro Rosso Conero (£16 Valvona & Crolla) From the Marche region in Eastern Italy, this rich, impeccably-made, deep plummy, herby wine has the luxurious quality more usually associated with much more highly priced reds from Tuscany.

1998 Nero d'Avola Santa Cecilia, Planeta (£18 Waitrose) The superstar Sicilian winery does it again – this time with a wine made from a traditional southern Italian grape. Drink this dark, modern, oaky wine with a plateful of prosciuto.

1999 Penfolds Koonunga Hill Shiraz Cabernet (£7 widely available) Ludicrously underpriced for its quality, and ludicrously easy to find, this is a really classic example of rich Aussie red with spice and deep berry fruit to spare. Well worth keeping, but I doubt anyone will.

WHITES FOR DAILY DRINKING

2000 Palo Alto Chardonnay (£5 Wine Cellar) A Chilean Chardonnay made in a cactus-bestrewn region better known for pisco spirit than wine. Its appeal depends on its passion-fruity flavour rather than oak.

2000 Oxford Landing Chardonnay (£5 Majestic) Bearing one of Australia's most reliable labels, this is attractive, easy going wine with pineapple and mango flavours..

1999 Soave Classico, Vigneto Colombara, Zenato (£5 Waitrose) An unusually classy example of what can be a woefully dull style. Lovely, cream wine, with flavours of almonds and brazil nuts. Great with food.

2000 Jacob's Creek Dry Riesling (£5 widely available) Pretentious wine drinkers will walk past this popular Aussie label, but they'll be missing a lovely bottle of appley, peary, easy-to-drink wine. Hide the label and serve it at a party.

2000 Deen de Bortoli Vat 6 Verdelho (£6 Adnams) Marvelous, fresh, limey wine made from a grape variety that is rarely found outside the fortified wines of Madeira and still wines like this of Australia.

2000 Santa Julia Viognier (£5 Thresher) Bored with Chardonnay? Try this Argentine wine which offers a lovely yellow-plummy, floral taste of the Viognier grape at less than a third of the price of many less impressive examples from California.

2000 Spice Trail White (£4 widely available) Good, simple, refreshing, and dangerously easy to drink, this Hungarian blend of Pinot Gris and the grapey local Irsay Oliver, offers a welcome example of the new face of Eastern European wine.

1999 Sanctuary Chardonnay (£5 Sainsbury) Good enough for a special occasion, but very fairly priced, this is a fresh, tropically fruity wine from New Zealand with lovely passion fruit flavours.

2000 Tesco's Finest Hunter Valley Semillon (£5 Tesco) Bored with Chardonnay? Try this classic Australian wine made (by Rosemount) from a grape that's usually at home in Bordeaux. Rich, ripe and both peachy and savoury.

2000 Caballo de Plata Torrontes (£4 Safeway) A great chance to taste a wine style that's rarely found outside Argentina. Made from that country's "own" white grape, the Torrontes, it's deliciously fresh and grapey, but surprisingly dry.

2000 Gentilini Classico (£6 Oddbins) New-wave Greek wine, with fascinating, herby, fennel-like flavours, coupled with citrus freshness and a creamy texture.

WHITES FOR SPECIAL OCCASIONS

1998 Clos la Chance Santa Cruz Mountain Chardonnay (£15 Berry Bros & Rudd) A match for any self-satisfied Napa Valley Chardonnay, this is a classy wine with the ripe fruity appeal of California and a texture that reminds me more of Burgundy than some of the sweet efforts from that better-known region.

1998 Planeta Chardonnay (£18 Waitrose) The Sicily superstar's impressive white, demonstrating that even on this sunny southern island, well-sited vines can produce lovely, fresh, peachy white wine.

1999 Chablis, Brocard (£10 Oddbins) Punching way beyond its weight, this is a complex, dry, mineral-rich Chablis that could easily be passed off as a Premier Cru selling at a far higher price.

1999 Chassagne-Montrachet Morgeots, Gagnard Delagrange (£25 Anthony Byrne) Impeccable white burgundy with a lovely rich texture. This needs time, though, to show what it can do.

1998 Leeuwin Estate "Art Series Chardonnay" (£25 Domaine Direct) From Margaret River vineyards originally chosen by Robert Mondavi (for an unrealized project), this is a supreme Australian wine with the class of top Burgundy. Old vintages prove how well it can age.

1999 Eitelsbacher Karthaüserhof, Riesling Spätlese (£16 OW Loeb) One of the bargains of the wine world: appley, floral Riesling with the slatey backbone that is the hallmark of the Mosel-Saar-Ruwer. Tempting to drink now, but well worth keeping.

1999 Domaine Weinbach Gewürztraminer Cuvée Théo (£20 Justerini & Brooks) Less oily and heady than some examples of this grape, but just as perfumed. Delicious, lingering, hedonistic wine.

1997 Condrieu, Coteaux de Vernon, Georges Vernay (£20 Yapp Bros) From the king of Condrieu, this is great, typically apricoty wine with heady spice notes, too.

1985 Domaine du Chevalier Blanc (£30 Farr Vintners) Nearly two decades old, but still fresh, with peachy, figgy flavours to spare, balanced by a note of lemony acidity.

1998 Pouilly Fumé Silex, Didier Dagueneau (£20 Harvey Nichols) Loire Sauvignon with real mineral character – that comes from the soil. Fresh gooseberry and pear fruit, too – from the skill of the winemaker.

2000 Wither Hills Marlborough Sauvignon Blanc (£8 Pont de ka Tour) A glloriously typical example of this grape from New Zealand with gooseberry, plus asparagus. Irresistably pungent and mouthwatering. Great value too, especially when compared to certain better-known, climatically-named wines from this region.

SPARKLING WINES AND ROSÉ

The Co-op Cava (£5) Spain's fizz has often been dull stuff in the past, but newer examples, like this, are among the bargains of the wine world. Fresh, easy-going, party fare.

1996 Jansz of Tasmania Premium Non Vintage Brut Cuvée (£10 Oddbins) Quite serious fizz from Tasmania, where conditions are quite similar to those in Champagne. Creamy, mouth-filling, and very convincingly Champagne-like.

Seaview Brut (£8 widely available) A bargain from Down Under. Mouth-filling and fruity but dry. Look out for the same winery's even more impressive Blanc de Blancs.

Domaine Ste. Michelle Cuvée Brut (£10 Harvey Nichols) A recent discovery for me, this Washington State winery's sparkling wine is fresh, and creamy, and very easy to drink.

Mumm Cuvée Napa Rosé Brut (£11 Oddbins) Still more impressive than the once-starry white, this pink fizz offers California's best bargain bubbles.

1995 Cuvée William Deutz (£50 Berkmann Wine Cellars) Made by a sister company to the better-known Roederer, this is classy, nutty Champagne that will last.

1985 Charles Heidsieck Champagne Charlie (£80 Wine Rack) Still fresh after 17 years, this is really great Champagne with wonderful intense, complex layers of nutty, toasty flavors.

1995 Champagne H Blin et Cie (£16 Oddbins) From a small producer, this has the quality character of Champagne from any of the bigger houses. Chocolatey, appley, and mouth-filling.

1990 Dom Pérignon Rosé (£140 Fortnum & Mason) Ludicrously pricy, but so's a Ferrari, and this has a racy, luxurious feel to it too. This is great, rich but subtle raspberryish Champagne to drink with food.

ROSÉ

2000 Geoff Merrill Grenache Rosé (£7 Oddbins) Aussie pink wine to make any Provence rosé maker blush. Peppery, plummy, and wonderfully refreshing. Drink with a plateful of charcuterie.

2000 Amethystos Rosé (£5 Oddbins) Greek wines are making an extraordinary comeback in red, white, and, yes, pink. This is a beautifully herby, floral wine to sip at by itself.

2000 Colegiata Toro Rosé, Bodegas Farina (£6 Laymont & Shaw) Spanish rosé is often, dull, bronze-colored stuff, but it doesn't have to be, as this example from one of the most progressive producers in Toro brilliantly proves.

SWEET AND FORTIFIED WINES

1995 Vin Santo de Capezzana Riserva (£15 everywine.co.uk)
Good Vin Santo is a rarity: most is merely a liquid with which to wash down the ameretti biscuits. This, though, is the real, nutty, raisiny, sherryish thing, made by one of the best producers in Tuscany.

1997 Chateau Climens Barsac (£35 Justerini & Brooks) A bargain – like all top sweet white Bordeaux this is great, peachy, honeyed wine that really ought to be kept for a decade or so. But it's very tempting to pull the cork now.

1997 Château la Variére, Bonnezeaux (£30 Pont de la Tour) Top class late harvest wine from some of the best vineyards in the Loire. Appley, honeyed, and intense, with just enough dried-apricot intensity.

1996 Disznòkö Tokaji Aszù 5 Puttonyos (£12 for 50cl Harrods) Made by Frenchmen in Hungary, this is delicious intense wine with flavours of fried apricots and traditional marmalade.

2000 Noble One Botrytis Sémillon (£15 for 37.5cl Berry Bros & Rudd) Rich, luscious, honeyed, peachy and apricoty Aussie late-picked wine that has, in previous vintages, beaten some very big name Sauternes in blind tastings.

1998 Alois Kracher Chardonnay Welschriesling Trockenbeerenauslese No. 7 Nouvelle Vague (£22 for 37.5cl Noel Young) An unusual mixture of grapes, and a rare chance to taste late harvest Chardonnay. Creamy, peachy, and long.

Fortified

Valdespino Inocente Fino Sherry (£8 Morrisons) Characterfully, "salty" dry sherry with a lemony bite and toasty richness. Drink with smoked salmon.

Florio Terre Arse Marsala Vergine (£11 Harrods) Most Marsala is aimed directly at the saucepan, but this deep, raisiny example is a delight to drink – or more accurately, to sip at.

Warre's Otima Ten Year Old Tawny Port (£10 for 50cl, Oddbins) Beautifully packaged wine that has nothing to do with the traditional image of port. Nutty, marmaladey, and very seductive.

1997 Burmester Vintage Port (£25 Heyman Barwell & Jones) From a smaller port house, this is top-class, deep, plummy wine that's built to last. Complex stuff to be laid down for at least a decade.

15 Year Old Verdelho, Henriques & Henriques (£25 Lea & Sandeman) Why is Madeira so unfashionable? Try this green-bronze hued, rich, limey-marmaladey dry wine, and you'll probably wonder the same thing. Wine for individualists.

Wine on the Web

BURSTING THE BUBBLES

Rome, as they say, wasn't built in a day. So, maybe we shouldn't be too surprised that, despite the seductive appeal of the internet, the new technology has taken longer than a year or so to persuade millions of people to change the way they buy their wine.

The past 12 months have not been a happy time for the pioneers of vinous e-commerce. Most dramatically, in the US, the giant wine.com has been absorbed by a rival and shed large numbers of its staff. The blame for wine.com's woes was laid by some observers at the door of the archaic rules that restrict the way wine is sold in America. There's no question that the inability to ship wine to individuals in 31 states has not helped. Nor have the accusations that e-commerce sites market alcohol to minors, which effectively stopped Ebay from including wine in its auctions.

But wine-on-the-net has hardly been a roaring success in countries with more favourable conditions. The most notable failure outside the US involved the Australian-based wineplanet.com, the pioneering UK arm of which gave up selling wine in 2001, despite the backing of the brewery giant Fosters. Another well-funded Australian-based global site, winepros.com (for which I write), has also given up plans to retail wine overseas and has evolved into an online publisher.

As elsewhere on the net, everyone is now talking about "Clicks-and-mortar" – retail websites set up by established

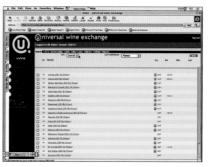

Bidding for bottles at uvine.com.

Information and chat at Robin Garr's Wine Lovers' Page.

terrestrial companies such as Berry Bros & Rudd (bbr.com). Even more enterprisingly, in the UK two leading retailers, Sainsbury and Oddbins, have combined forces with an interactive TV broadcaster to launch the Destination Wine Co. that sells wine off the page and the screen. I'll bet that others will soon successfully follow their example. An American initiative that will be copied elsewhere is wineaccess.com, which directs browsers to local retailers who can supply the precise wine they seek.

I'd predict that winebid.com., the online auctioneer, will continue to do well, as will uvine.com, which allows serious buyers direct – but anonymous – access to wines offered by equally anonymous sellers. Wine producers and organizations will make increasing use of the net. Château Haut Brion (hautbrion.com), Robert Mondavi (mondavi.com), and Penfolds (penfolds.com) are all well-established online pioneers, but the decision by Bordeaux merchants to publish their own impressions of the 2000 vintage on the net was a definite novelty.

Lastly, there's the democratic strand. Sophisticated independent informative sites such as Jamie Goode's wineanorak.com, Robin Garr's wineloverspage.com, and Tom Cannavan's wine-pages.com will flourish – as will sites for people with an interest in particular aspects of the wine world. Freethegrapes.com, for example, was set up by wine lovers in the US who are lobbying for the freedom to buy bottles across state boundaries, while my own corkwatch.com counters the big-budget spin doctoring of the manufacturers of corks and alternative closures by allowing professionals and amateurs to air their views on the subject.

For a full list of recommended wine-related websites, see page 395

Tasting and Buying

Saint-Emilion
* CH. LAPRADE   1998   5c
  Côtes de Francs
* CH. DE ROUGERIE 1998   65
  Bordeaux Supérieur 100% Merlot
* CH. DE TUSSET   1997   70
  Montagne St Emilion
* CH. MOUTON 1998   80
  Bordeaux Supérieur
* LES AILES DE BERLIQUET 1996 90
  Saint Emilion grand cru
* ESPRIT DE CHEVALIER 1996   160
  Pessac leognan 2ème Vin du Dom. de Chevalier
* CH. GRAND TAYNE 1996   255
  St Emilion grand cru classé

SPOILED WITH CHOICES

Buying wine today has often become just like buying a gallon of paint. Just as the manufacturer's helpful chart can be daunting with its endless shades of subtly different white, the number of bottles and the information available on the supermarket shelves can make you want to give up and reach for the one that is most familiar, or most favourably priced.

If you're not a wine buff, why should you know the differences in flavour between wines made from the same grape in Meursault in France, Mendocino in California, and Maipo in Chile? Often, the retailer has helpfully provided descriptive terms to help you to imagine the flavour of the stuff in the bottle. But these too can just add to the confusion. Do you want the one that tastes of strawberries or raspberries, the "refreshingly dry", or the "crisp, lemony white"?

Arm yourself with a good corkscrew.

I can't promise to clear a six-lane highway through this jungle but, with luck, I will give you a path to follow when you are choosing a wine, and one from which you can confidently stray.

THE LABEL

Wine labels should always reveal the country where the wine was produced (see page 24), and possibly the region and grape variety (see page 48) from which it was made. Both region and grape, however, offer only partial guidance as to what you are likely to find when you pull the cork.

Bear in mind the following:

1 Official terms such as Appellation Contrôlée, Grand or Premier Cru, Qualitätswein, and Reserva are often as trustworthy as official statements by politicians.

2 Unofficial terms such as Réserve Personnelle and Vintner's Selection are, likewise, as trustworthy as unofficial statements by the producer of any other commodity.

3 Knowing where a wine comes from is often like knowing where a person was born; it provides no guarantee of how good the wine will be. Nor how it will have been made (though there are often local rules). There will be nothing to tell you, for instance, whether a Chablis is oaky nor whether an Alsace or Vouvray is sweet.

4 "Big name" regions don't always make better wine than supposedly lesser ones. Cheap Bordeaux is far worse than similarly priced wine from Bulgaria.

5 Don't expect wines from the same grape variety to taste the same: a South African Chardonnay may taste drier than one from California. The flavour and style will depend on the climate, soil, and producer.

6 Just because a producer makes a good wine in one place, don't trust him or her to make other good wines, either there or elsewhere. The team at Lafite Rothschild produces less classy Los Vascos wines in Chile; Robert Mondavi's inexpensive Woodbridge wines bear no relation to the quality of his Reserve wines from Napa.

7 The fact that there is a château on a wine label has no bearing on the quality of the contents.

8 Nor does the boast that the wine is bottled at that château.

9 Nineteenth-century medals look pretty on a label; they say nothing about the quality of the 20th- or 21st-century stuff in the bottle.

10 Price provides some guidance to a wine's quality: a very expensive bottle may be appalling, but it's unlikely that a very cheap one will be better than basic.

A WAY WITH WORDS

Before going any further, I'm afraid that there's no alternative to returning to the thorny question of the language you are going to use to describe your impressions.

When Washington Irving visited Bordeaux 170 years ago, he noted that Château Margaux was "a wine of fine flavour – but not of equal body". Lafite on the other hand had "less flavour than the former but more body – an equality of flavour and body". Latour, well, that had "more body than flavour." He may have been a great writer, but he was evidently not the ideal person to describe the individual flavours of great Bordeaux.

Michelangelo was more poetic, writing that the wine of San Gimignano "kisses, licks, bites, thrusts, and stings...". Modern pundits say wines have "gobs of fruit" and taste of "kumquats and suede". Each country and generation comes up with its own vocabulary. Some descriptions, such as the likening to gooseberry of wines made from Sauvignon Blanc, can be justified by scientific analysis, which confirms that the same aromatic chemical compound is found in the fruit and wine.

Then there are straightforward descriptions. Wines can be fresh or stale, clean or dirty. If they are acidic, or overly full of tannin, they will be "hard"; a "soft" wine, by contrast, might be easier to drink, but boring.

There are other less evocative terms. While a watery wine is "dilute" or "thin", a subtle one is "elegant". A red or white whose flavour is hard to discern is described as "dumb". Whatever the style of a wine, it should have "balance". A sweet white, for example, needs enough acidity to keep it from cloying. No one will enjoy a wine that is too fruity, too dry, too oaky, or too anything for long.

The flavour that lingers in your mouth long after you have swallowed or spat it out is known as the "finish". Wines whose flavour – pleasant or unpleasant – hangs around, are described as "long"; those whose flavour disappears quickly are "short".

Finally, there is "complex", the word that is used to justify why one wine costs 10 times more than another. A complex wine is like a well-scored symphony, while a simpler one could be compared to a melody picked out on a single instrument.

TASTING

Wine tasting is surrounded by mystery and mystique. But it shouldn't be – because all it really consists of is paying attention to the stuff in the glass, whether you're in the formal environment of a wine tasting or drinking the house white in your local bar. The key questions are: do you like the wine? And is it a good example of what it claims to be? Champagne costs a lot more than basic Spanish Cava, so it should taste recognizably different. Some do, some don't.

See

The look of a wine can tell you a lot. Assuming that it isn't cloudy (which if it is, send it back), it will reveal its age and hint at the grape and origin. Some grapes, like Burgundy's Pinot Noir, make naturally paler wines than, say, Bordeaux's Cabernet Sauvignon; wines from warmer regions have deeper colours. Tilt the glass away from you over a piece of white paper and look at the rim of the liquid. The more watery and brown it is, the older the wine (Beaujolais Nouveau will be pure violet).

Swirl

Vigorously swirl the wine around the glass for a moment or so to release any reluctant smells.

Sniff

You sniff a wine before tasting it for the same reason that you sniff a carton of milk before pouring its contents into coffee. The smell can tell you more about a wine than anything else. If you don't believe me, try tasting anything while holding your nose, or while you've got a cold. When sniffing, take one long sniff or a few brief ones. Concentrate on whether the wine seems fresh and clean, and on any smells that indicate how it is likely to taste.

What are your first impressions? Is the wine fruity, and, if so, which fruit does it remind you of? Does it have the vanilla smell of a wine that has been fermented and/or matured in new oak barrels? Is it spicy? Or herbaceous? Sweet or dry? Rich or lean?

Sip

Take a small mouthful and – this takes practice – suck air between your teeth and through the liquid. Look in a mirror while you're doing this: if your mouth looks like a cat's bottom and sounds like a child trying to suck the last few drops of Coke through a straw, then you're doing it right. Hold the wine in your mouth for a little longer to release as much of its flavour as possible.

Focus on the flavour. Ask yourself the same questions about whether it tastes sweet, dry, fruity, spicy, herbaceous. Is there just one flavour, or do several contribute to a "complex" overall effect?

Now concentrate on the texture of the wine. Some – like Chardonnay – are mouth-coatingly buttery, while others – like Gewürztraminer – are almost oily. Muscadet is a good example of a wine with a texture that is closer to that of water.

A brief look, then swirl the wine around the glass to release the aromas.

Does the wine smell fresh and inviting? Simple or complex?

Reds, too, vary in texture; some seem tough and tannic enough to make the inside of one cheek want to kiss the inside of the other. Traditionalists rightly claim tannin is necessary for a wine's longevity, but modern winemakers distinguish between the harsh tannin and the "fine" (non-aggressive) tannin to be found in wine carefully made from ripe grapes. A modern Bordeaux often has as much tannin as old-fashioned examples – but is far easier to taste and drink.

Spit

The only reason to spit a wine out – unless it is actively repellent – is simply to remain upright at the end of a lengthy tasting. I have notes I took during a banquet in Burgundy at which there were dozens of great wines and not even the remotest chance to do anything but swallow. The descriptions of the first few are perfectly legible; the 30th apparently tasted "very xgblorefjy". If all you are interested in is the taste, not spitting is an indulgence; you should have had 90 per cent of the flavour while the wine was in your mouth.

Pause for a moment or two after spitting the wine out. Is the flavour still there? How does what you are experiencing now compare with the taste you had in your mouth? Some wines have an unpleasant aftertaste; others have flavours that linger deliciously in the mouth.

SHOULD I SEND IT BACK?

Wines are subject to all kinds of faults, though far less than they were even as recently as a decade ago.

Acid

All wines, like all fruit and vegetables, contain a certain amount of acidity. Without it they would taste flabby and dull and go very stale very quickly. Wines made from unripe grapes will, however, taste unpalatably "green" and like unripe apples or plums – or like chewing stalky leaves or grass.

Bitter

Bitterness is quite different. On occasion, especially in Italy, a touch of bitterness may even be an integral part of a wine's character, as in the case of Amarone. Of course, the Italians like Campari too.

Cloudy

Wine should be transparent. The only excuse for cloudiness is in a wine like an old Burgundy whose deposit has been shaken up.

Corked

Ignore any cork crumbs you may find floating on the surface of a wine. Genuinely corked wines have a musty smell and flavour that comes from mouldy corks. Some corks are mouldier, and wines mustier, than others, but all corked wines become nastier with exposure to air. Around 8% of wines – irrespective of their price – are corked.

Crystals

Not a fault, but people often think there is something wrong with a white wine if there is a layer of fine white crystals at the bottom of the bottle. These are just tartrates that fall naturally.

Maderized/Oxidized

Madeira is fortified wine that has been intentionally exposed to the air and heated in a special oven. Maderized wine is stale, unfortified stuff that has been accidentally subjected to warmth and air.

Oxidized is a broader term, referring to wine that has been exposed to the air – or made from grapes that have cooked in the sun. The taste is reminiscent of poor sherry or vinegar – or both.

Sulphur (SO_2/H_2S)

Sulphur dioxide is routinely used as a protection against bacteria that would oxidize (qv) a wine. In excess, sulphur dioxide may make you cough or sneeze. Worse, though, is hydrogen sulphide and mercaptans, its associated sulphur compounds, which are created when sulphur dioxide combines with wine. Wines with hydrogen sulphide smell of rotten eggs, while mercaptans may reek of rancid garlic or burning rubber. Aeration or popping a copper coin in your glass may clear up these characteristics.

Vinegary/Volatile

Volatile acidity is present in all wines. In excess, however – usually the result of careless winemaking – what can be a pleasant component (like a touch of balsamic vinegar in a sauce) tastes downright vinegary.

Reading
the Label

INTRODUCTION

Labels are an essential part of the business of wine nowadays, but even a century ago they barely existed. Wine was sold by the barrel and served by the jug or decanter. Indeed, the original "labels" were silver tags that hung on a chain around the neck of a decanter and were engraved with the word "claret," "hock," "port," or whatever.

Today, printed labels are required to tell you the amount of liquid in the bottle, its strength, where it was made, and the name of the producer or importer. Confusingly, though, labelling rules vary between countries and between regions. Labels may also reveal a wine's style – the grape variety, oakiness, or sweetness, for example. And lastly, they are part of the packaging that helps to persuade you to buy one wine rather than another. The following examples should help you through the maze.

CHAMPAGNE

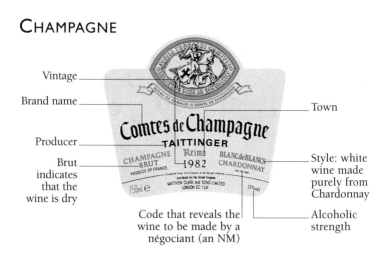

Vintage

Brand name

Town

Producer

Brut indicates that the wine is dry

Style: white wine made purely from Chardonnay

Code that reveals the wine to be made by a négociant (an NM)

Alcoholic strength

WHITES

Alcoholic strength

Producer

Region

Volume of contents

Address of importer

Brand

Grape variety

State of origin

Region

Village

Appellation

Grape variety

One of more than 50 individual vineyards granted superior status

Rich, sweet "botrytized" wine from specially selected grapes

Vintage

Producer

Town/ Region

Year firm was founded

Vineyard

Village

Quality level

Producer

Vintage

Grape

Sweetness

Volume of contents

Region

Official identity number

REDS

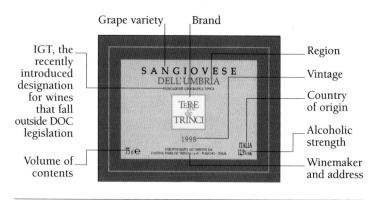

Grape variety — Brand

IGT, the recently introduced designation for wines that fall outside DOC legislation

Region

Vintage

Country of origin

Alcoholic strength

Winemaker and address

Volume of contents

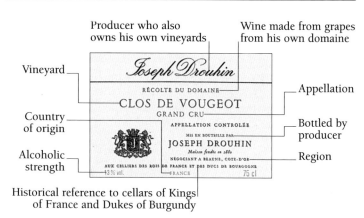

Producer who also owns his own vineyards

Wine made from grapes from his own domaine

Vineyard

Appellation

Country of origin

Bottled by producer

Alcoholic strength

Region

Historical reference to cellars of Kings of France and Dukes of Burgundy

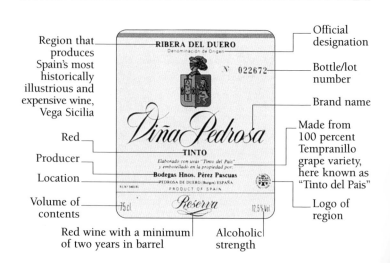

Region that produces Spain's most historically illustrious and expensive wine, Vega Sicilia

Official designation

Bottle/lot number

Brand name

Red

Made from 100 percent Tempranillo grape variety, here known as "Tinto del Pais"

Producer

Location

Volume of contents

Logo of region

Red wine with a minimum of two years in barrel

Alcoholic strength

SWEET AND FORTIFIED

Paste made from
"nobly-rotten" grapes

Wine name

A *puttonyo* is
the "hod" of
Aszú sweet
grape paste
used to
sweeten tokaji
– the number
of puttonyos
indicates the
sweetness of
the wine

Volume of contents –
smaller than standard
wine bottle size

Producer

Producer's
crest

Country
of origin

Alcoholic
strength

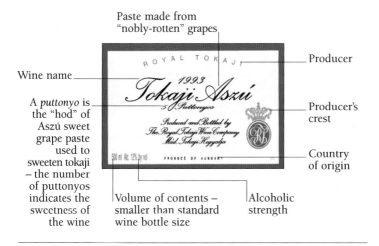

Style of
sherry, Old
Amontillado

Produced
and bottled in
principal sherry
town, Jerez

Producer's
crest

Producer

Brand name

Producer

History and
credentials
of producer

Vintage

LBV ports
bottled 4 to 6
years after the
vintage (rather
than 2 for
vintage port)

Alcoholic
strength

"Traditional"
means "unfiltered,"
like real vintage
port. Other late
bottled vintage is
filtered so as to
remove the need
for decanting

Unlike
"tawny,"
which is
matured
in barrels

Bottling
date –
obligatory
for LBV
labels

Company's name
and address

Volume of
contents

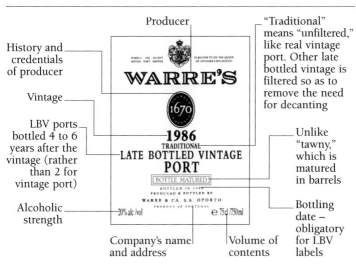

Countries

WHERE IN THE WORLD?

Whatever the grape variety, climate, and traditions, the local tastes of the place where a wine is made still largely dictate its style. Let's take a whirlwind tour of the most significant winemaking nations. (For more information on grapes, terms, and regions, see the A–Z, starting on page 97).

AUSTRALIA

Reading the label: Late harvest/noble harvest – *sweet.* Show Reserve – *top-of-the-line wine, usually with more oak.* Tokay – *Australian name for the Muscadelle grape, used for rich liqueur wines.* Verdelho – *Madeira grape used for limey, dry wines.* Mataro – *Mourvèdre.* Shiraz – *Syrah.* Tarrango – *local success story – fresh, fruity, and Beaujolais-like.*

Twenty or so years ago, Australian wines were the butt of a Monty Python sketch. Today, these rich and fruity wines are the reliable vinous equivalent of Japanese hi-fi and cameras. It is hard to explain how this switch happened, but I would attribute much of the credit to the taste the Australians themselves have developed for wine. Having a populace that treats wine the way many Americans treat milk or beer has provided the impetus for two of the best wine schools in the world – and for a circuit of competitions in which even the humblest wines battle to win medals.

Another strength has been the spirit of exploration which led to the establishment of areas like the Barossa and Hunter valleys, and which is now fuelling the enthusiastic planting of vines in new regions such as Orange, Robe, Mount Benson, Young, and Pemberton.

Remember these names; they are already appearing on a new generation of subtler Australian reds and whites that will make some of today's stars look like amateurs. And look out too for unconventional blends of grape varieties, as well as delicious new flavours none of us

SOUTHEAST AUSTRALIA

Darling
Macquarie
Lachlan
Murrumbidgee
Murray

Port Macquarie
Upper Hunter Valley
Mudgee
Hunter
Orange
Cowra
Lower
Hunter Valley
● NEWCASTLE

Clare Valley/
Watervale
MORGAN
Adelaide Plains
Riverland
Mildura
Murrumbidgee
Irrigation Area
● SYDNEY

ADELAIDE ●
Barossa Valley Eden
Adelaide Hills
Murray Valley

Southern Vales/
Langhorne

Padthaway
Great Western
Pyrenees
Bendigo
Yarra Valley
Goulburn Valley
Northeast
● CANBERRA
Coonawarra
Ballarat
Gippsland
Canberra
GEELONG ●
Geelong
● MELBOURNE
Mornington
Peninsula

TASMAN
SEA

WESTERN
AUSTRALIA
Gingin
Swan Valley
● PERTH
Coastal Plains
Margaret River
Great Southern
ALBANY ●

LAUNCESTON ●
TASMANIA
HOBART ●

has ever tasted. Australia is the only region or country to have drawn up a master plan to dominate the world's premium wines within 25 years. Judging by what's been achieved so far, I think the Australians may just be on track to achieving their ambitions.

AUSTRIA

Reading the label: Ausbruch – *late-harvested, between Beerenauslese and Trockenbeerenauslese.* Erzeugerabfüllung – *estate bottled.* Morillon – *Chardonnay.* Schilfwein – *made from grapes dried on mats.*

Austrian winemakers are riding high with wonderful, late harvest wines, dry whites, and increasingly impressive reds. Names to look out for include Alois Lang, Kracher, and Willi Opitz.

CANADA

Reading the label: VQA (Vintners Quality Alliance) – *local designation seeking to guarantee quality and local provenance.*

Icewines, made from grapes picked when frozen on the vine, are the stars here, though Chardonnays and other light reds are improving fast.

EASTERN EUROPE

After a bright start in the 1980's, the Eastern European wine industry is now coming to terms with life under capitalism surprisingly slowly.

Bulgaria

The pioneer of good Iron Curtain reds, Bulgaria remains a reliable source of inexpensive, ripe Cabernet Sauvignon and Merlot, as well as the earthy local Mavrud. Whites have been helped by visiting Australian winemakers.

Hungary

Still best known for its red Bull's Blood, Hungary's strongest hand today lies in the Tokajis, the best of which are being made by foreign investors. Reds are improving, as are affordable Sauvignons and Chardonnays.

Romania, Moldova, and Former Yugoslavia

Even if former Yugoslavia had escaped its recent turmoil, rebuilding a wine industry founded on exports of cheap Lazki Rizling would be a tough call. Romania has inexpensive Pinot Noir, and Moldova produces aromatic white.

ENGLAND AND WALES

Despite an unhelpful climate and government, the vineyards of England and Wales are using recently developed German grape varieties to make Loire-style whites; high-quality, late harvest wines; and good sparkling wines. There are reds, too, but these are only really of curiosity value and are likely to remain so until global warming takes effect.

FRANCE

Reading the label: Appellation Contrôlée (or AOC) – *designation covering France's (supposedly) better wines.* Blanc de Blancs/Noirs – *white wine made from white/black grapes.* Cave – *cellar.* Cave des Vignerons de – *usually a cooperative.* Cépage – *grape variety.* Château – *wine estate.* Chêne – *oak barrels, as in Fûts de Chêne.* Clos – *(historically) walled vineyard.* Côte(s)/Coteaux – *hillside.* Crémant – *sparkling.* Cuvée – *a specific blend.* Demi-sec – *medium sweet.* Domaine – *wine estate.* Doux – *sweet.* Grand Cru – *higher quality, or specific vineyards.* Gris – *pale rosé, as in* Vin Gris. Jeunes Vignes – *young vines (often ineligible for* Appellation Contrôlée). Méthode Classique – *used to indicate the Champagne method of making sparkling wine.* Millésime – *year or vintage.* Mis en Bouteille au Château/Domaine – *bottled at the estate.* Moelleux – *sweet.* Monopole – *a vineyard owned by a single producer.* Mousseux – *sparkling.* Négociant (Eleveur) – *a merchant who buys, matures, bottles, and sells wine.* Pétillant

– *lightly sparkling.* Premier Cru – *"first growth", a quality designation that varies from area to area.* Propriétaire (Récoltant) – *vineyard owner/manager.* Réserve (Personelle) – *legally meaningless phrase.* Sur Lie – *aged on the lees (dead yeast).* VDQS (Vin Délimité de Qualité Supérieur) – *"soon-to-be-abolished" official designation for wines that are better than* Vin de Pays *but not good enough for* Appellation Contrôlée. Vieilles Vignes – *old vines (could be any age from 20–80 years), should indicate higher quality.* Villages – *supposedly best part of a larger region, as in* Beaujolais Villages. Vin de Pays – *wine with regional character.* Vin de Table – *basic table wine.*

Still the benchmark, or set of benchmarks, against which winemakers in other countries test themselves. This is the place to find the Chardonnay in its finest oaked (white Burgundy) and unoaked (traditional Chablis) styles; the Sauvignon (from Sancerre and Pouilly Fumé in the Loire, and in blends with the Sémillon in Bordeaux); the Cabernet Sauvignon and Merlot (red Bordeaux); the Pinot Noir (red Burgundy and Champagne);

FRANCE

the Riesling, Gewurztraminer, and Pinots Blanc and Gris (Alsace). The Chenin Blanc still fares better in the Loire than anywhere else, and despite their successes in Australia, the Syrah (aka Shiraz) and Grenache are still at their finest in the Rhône.

France is handicapped by the unpredictability of the climate in most of its best regions and by the unreliability of winemakers, some of whom are happy to coast along on the reputation of their region and on *Appellation Contrôlée* laws that allow them to get away with selling poor quality wine.

Alsace

Reading the label: Sélection de Grains Nobles – *Sweet wine from noble rot-affected grapes.* Vendange Tardive – *late harvested.* Edelzwicker – *blend of white grapes, usually Pinot Blanc and Sylvaner.*

Often underrated, and confused with German wines from the other side of the Rhine, Alsace deserves to be more popular. Its odd assortment of grapes make wonderfully rich, spicy wine, both in their customary dry and more unusual late harvest styles. This is my bet to follow the success of its spicy red counterparts in the Rhône.

Bordeaux

Reading the label: Chai – *cellar.* Cru Bourgeois – *level beneath Cru Classé, but possibly of similar quality.* Cru Classé – *"Classed Growth", a wine featured in the 1855 classification of the Médoc and Graves, provides no guarantee of current quality.* Grand Cru/Grand Cru Classé – *confusing terms, especially in St. Emilion, where the former is allocated annually on the basis of a sometimes less-than-arduous tasting, while the latter is reassessed every decade.*

For all but the most avid wine buff, Bordeaux is one big region (producing almost as much wine as Australia) with a few dozen châteaux that have become internationally famous for their wine.

Visit the region, or take a look at the map, however, and you will find that this is essentially a collection of quite diverse sub-regions, many of which are separated by farmland, forest, or water.

Heading north from the city of Bordeaux, the Médoc is the region that includes the great communes of St. Estèphe, Pauillac, St. Julien, and Margaux, where some of the finest red wines are made. The largely gravel soil suits the Cabernet Sauvignon, though lesser Médoc wines, of which there are more than enough, tend to have a higher proportion of the Merlot. For the best examples of wines made principally from this variety, though, you have to head eastward

BORDEAUX

- SOULAC-SUR-MER

Gironde

Médoc

St. Estèphe
PAUILLAC •   Côtes de Blaye
St. Julien
Margaux   • BLAYE
Listrac   Côtes de Bourg
Moulis   • BOURG

Garonne   Dordogne

Haut-Médoc   Fronsac   Pomerol
  • LIBOURNE   Libournais
  St. Emilion
  Côtes de Francs
BORDEAUX •   Côtes de Castillon

Premières Côtes
Pessac-Léognan   de Bordeaux

Graves   Entre-Deux-Mers

Cérons   Loupiac
Barsac   Ste. Croix-du-Mont
LANGON •
Sauternes

– – – AOC Bordeaux

to St. Emilion and Pomerol and the regions of Bourg and Blaye where the Merlot is usually blended with the Cabernet Franc.

To the south of Bordeaux lie Pessac-Léognan and the Graves, which produce some of Bordeaux's lighter, more delicate reds. This is also dry white country, where the Sémillon and Sauvignon Blanc hold sway. A little farther to the southeast, the often misty climate provides the conditions required to produce the noble rot required for the great sweet whites of Sauternes and Barsac.

Each of these regions produces its own individual style of wine. In some years, the climate suits one region and/or grape variety more than others. The year 2000, for example was better for the Médoc than for St. Emilion. So beware of vintage charts that seek to define the quality of an entire vintage across the whole of Bordeaux.

BURGUNDY

Chablis
AUXERRE ●
Sauvignon de St.-Bris
Irancy

Serein
Armançon
Seine

DIJON ●
Côte de Nuits
Gevrey-Chambertin
Côte d'Or
Vosne-Romanée   Clos de Vougeot
Nuits-St. Georges
Volnay   ● BEAUNE
Côte de Beaune
Pommard   Meursault
Puligny-Montrachet
● CHALON-SUR SAONE

Côte Chalonnaise

Mâconnais

● MACON
Juliénas
Chénas   St. Amour
Fleurie
Morgon
Moulin-à-Vent   Beaujolais
● VILLEFRANCHE-SUR-SAONE

Coteaux du
Lyonnais   ● LYON

Saône

– – – – AOC Burgundy

Burgundy

Reading the label: Hospices de Beaune – *wines made and sold at auction by the charitable* Hospices de Beaune. Passetoutgrains – *a blend of Gamay and Pinot Noir.* Tasteviné – *a special label for wines that have passed a tasting by the* Confrérie des Chevaliers de Tastevin.

The heartland of the Pinot Noir and the Chardonnay and Chablis, Nuits-St.-Georges, Gevrey-Chambertin, Beaune, Meursault, Puligny-Montrachet, Mâcon Villages, Pouilly-Fuissé, and Beaujolais. The best wines theoretically come from the Grands Crus vineyards; next are the Premiers Crus, followed by plain village wines and, last of all, basic Bourgogne Rouge or Blanc.

The region's individual producers make their wines with varying luck and expertise, generally selling in bulk to merchants who are just as variable in their skills and honesty. So, one producer's supposedly humble wine can be finer than another's pricier Premier or Grand Cru.

Champagne

Reading the label: Blanc de Blancs – *white wine from white grapes, i.e.,
pure Chardonnay.* Blancs de Noirs – *white wine made from black grapes.*
Brut Sauvage/Zéro – *bone dry.* Extra-Dry – *(surprisingly) sweeter than Brut.*
Grand Cru – *from a top-quality vineyard.* Négociant-manipulant (NM) –
buyer and blender of wines. Non-vintage – *a blend of wines usually based on
wine of a single vintage.* Récoltant manipulant (RM) – *individual estate.*

Top-class Champagne has toasty richness and subtle fruit. Beware of cheap
examples, though, and big-name producers who should know better.

Loire

Reading the label: Moelleux – *sweet.* Sur Lie – *on its lees (dead yeast),
usually only applied to Muscadet.* Côt *local name for the Malbec.*

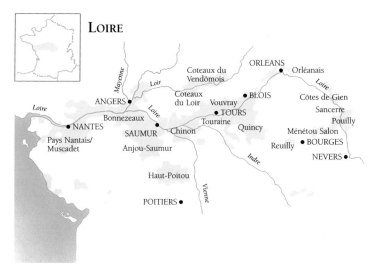

This is the heartland of fresh, dry Sauvignons and honeyed, sweet Vouvray,
Quarts de Chaume, and Bonnezeaux, sparkling Saumur and Vouvray, and
blackcurranty red Chinon and Bourgeuil. Careless winemaking can give
wines – particularly sweet ones – an unpleasantly "woolly" character.

Rhône

Reading the label: Vin Doux Naturel – *fortified wine, such as Muscat de
Beaumes de Venise.* Côtes du Rhône Villages – *wine from one of a number
of better sited villages in the overall Côtes du Rhône appellation, and thus,
supposedly finer wine than plain Côtes du Rhône.*

Côte Rôtie

Condrieu   VIENNE

Rhône

Côtes-du-
Rhône

Hermitage

St. Joseph   Crozes-
Hermitage

Cornas

● VALENCE

Drôme   Clairette
de Die

Rhône   Chatillon-
en-Diois

● MONTELIMAR

Côtes du   Coteaux du
Vivarais   Tricastin

Côtes-du-Rhône-
Villages

Béaumes-de-Venise

● ORANGE

Châteauneuf- Gigondas
du-Pape   Vaqueyras

Tavel   ● CARPENTRAS

● AVIGNON

Côtes du Ventoux   Coteaux de
                           Pierrevert

Durance

RHÔNE

Côtes du Lubéron

Even if US guru Robert Parker were not an avowed Rhône fan, this area would probably have become just as fashionable as it has over the past few years. Today, red wine drinkers throughout the world want the kind of ripe, spicy flavours that the Syrah and Grenache grapes reliably provide in the warm climate of this region. As the star of basic Bordeaux falls, I'll bet that Côtes du Rhône will climb further up the hit parade to take its place.

The Southwest

Reading the label: Perlé or Perlant - *gently sparkling, used in Gaillac.*

THE SOUTHWEST

Côtes de / Haut-   ● PERIGUEUX
Montravel   Bergerac

                                    Dordogne

● BORDEAUX   Pécharmant   ● BERGERAC
             Côtes de   Monbazillac
             Duras   RODEZ ●

ARCACHON   Lot

Côtes du   Cahors
Marmandais

Côtes du
Buzet   ● AGEN   Aveyron

MONT-DE-MARSAN   Armagnac   ● ALBI
                         MONTAUBAN ● Gaillac

Adour   Côtes du
                                     Frontonnais

Madiran Côtes de
● BAYONNE St. Mont   ● AUCH   ● CASTRES
Béarn   ● TOULOUSE
                                     MAZAMET ●
BIARRITZ

PAU ●   CARCASSONNE ●
Irouleguy Jurançon ● TARBES
                                     Limoux

Garonne

This conservative corner of France is the home of sweet and dry Jurançon, Gaillac, Cahors, and Madiran. Despite their fame among French wine buffs, these were often pretty old-fashioned, in the worst sense of the term.

Today, a new wave of winemakers is learning how to extract fruit flavours from grapes like the Gros and Petit Manseng, the Tannat, Mauzac, and Malbec. These wines are worth the detour for anyone bored with the ubiquitous Cabernet and Chardonnay and dissatisfied with poor claret.

The South

Reading the label: Vin de Pays d'Oc – *country wine from the Languedoc region. Often some of the best stuff in the region.* Rancio – *woody, slightly volatile character in Banyuls and other fortified wines that have been aged in the barrel.*

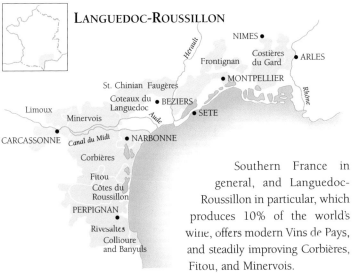

LANGUEDOC-ROUSSILLON

Southern France in general, and Languedoc-Roussillon in particular, which produces 10% of the world's wine, offers modern Vins de Pays, and steadily improving Corbières, Fitou, and Minervois.

The combination of an ideal climate and increasingly dynamic winemaking is raising the quality here and in Provence, where classics such as Cassis and Bandol now attract as much attention as the ubiquitous rosé.

Eastern France

Reading the label: Vin de Paille – *sweet, golden wine from grapes dried on straw mats.* Vin Jaune – *sherry-like, slightly oxidized wine.*

Savoie's zingy wines are often only thought of as skiing fare but, like Arbois' nutty, sherry-style whites, they are characterfully different, and made from grape varieties that are grown nowhere else.

GERMANY

Reading the label: Amtliche Prüfungsnummer (AP number) – *official identification number*. Auslese – *sweet wine from selected ripe grapes*. Beerenauslese – *luscious wines from selected, riper grapes (Beeren), hopefully affected by botrytis*. Erste Gewächs – *top vineyard*. Erzeugerabfüllung – *bottled by the grower/estate*. Halbtrocken – *off-dry*. Hock – *British name for Rhine wines*. Kabinett – *first step in German quality ladder, for wines that fulfill a certain natural ripeness*. Kellerei/Kellerabfüllung – *cellar/producer/estate-bottled*. Landwein – *the equivalent of a French Vin de Pays*. QbA (Qualitätswein bestimmter Anbaugebiete) – *basic quality German wine*. QmP (Qualitätswein mit Prädikat) – *QbA wine with "special qualities" subject to (not very) rigorous testing. The QmP blanket designation is broken into five ripeness rungs, from Kabinett to Trockenbeerenauslese plus Eiswein*. Schloss – *literally "castle," the equivalent of Château, designating a vineyard or estate*. Sekt – *basic, sparkling wine*. Spätlese – *second step in the QmP scale, late harvested grapes, a notch drier than Auslese*. Staatsweingut – *state-owned wine estate*. Tafelwein – *table wine, only the prefix "Deutscher" guarantees German origin*. Trocken – *dry*. Trockenbeerenauslese – *wine from selected botrytis-affected grapes*. Weingut – *estate*. Weinkellerei – *cellar or winery*. VDP – *the emblem of a group of quality-conscious producers*.

Ignore the sugar-water sold as Liebfraumilch, Piesporter Michelsberg, and Niersteiner Domtal. Ignore, too, the big-name estates that get away with sub-standard fare. For real quality, look for Mosel Rieslings from producers like Dr. Loosen and Richter, and new wave Rhine wines made by Künstler, Müller Catoir, and Kurt Darting, not to mention the occasional successful red from Karl Lingenfelder. Avoid dry "Trocken" Kabinett wines from northern Germany unless you want the enamel removed from your teeth.

ITALY

Reading the label: Abboccato – *semi-dry*. Amabile – *semi-sweet*. Amaro – *bitter*. Asciutto – *bone dry*. Azienda – *estate*. Classico – *the best vineyards at the heart of a DOC*. Colle/colli – *hills*. DOC(G) Denominazione di Origine Controllata (e Garantita) – *designation, based on grape variety and/or origin*.

Dolce – *sweet*. Frizzante – *semi-sparkling*. IGT, Indicazione Geografica Tipica – *new designation for quality* Vino da Tavola. Imbottigliato nel'origine – *estate-bottled*. Liquoroso – *rich, sweet*. Passito – *raisiny wine made from sundried grapes*. Recioto – *strong, sweet (unless designated Amarone)*. Vino da Tavola – *table wine. Now replaced by IGT for top wines.*

Three facts about Italy. 1) It is more a set of regions than a single country. 2) There is a tradition of interpreting laws fairly liberally. 3) Style is often valued as highly as content. So when it comes to wine, this can be a confusing place. Producers do their own frequently delicious thing, using indigenous and imported grape varieties and designer bottles and labels in ways that leave legislators – and humble wine drinkers – exhilarated and exasperated in equal measure.

NEW ZEALAND

This New World country has one of the most unpredictable climates, but produces some of the most intensely flavoured wines. There are gooseberryish Sauvignon Blancs, Chardonnays, and innovative Rieslings and Gewürztraminers, and impressive Pinot Noirs.

Hawke's Bay seems to be the most consistent region for reds, while Gisborne, Marlborough, Auckland, and Martinborough share the honours for white wine (though the last, like Central Otago, produces classy Pinot Noir).

NORTH ISLAND

Northland

Auckland
● AUCKLAND

Bay of Plenty
Waikato

Gisborne/
Poverty Bay

Hawke's
Bay

Wairarapa/
Martinborough
● WELLINGTON

Nelson
Marlborough

Waipara

PACIFIC OCEAN

TASMAN SEA

Canterbury ● CHRISTCHURCH

SOUTH ISLAND

Central Otago

● DUNEDIN

NEW
ZEALAND

STEWART ISLAND

NORTH AFRICA

Islamic fundamentalism has done little to encourage winemaking of any description in North Africa. Even so, Algeria, Morocco, and Tunisia can all offer full-flavoured, old-fashioned reds that will probably delight people who liked Burgundy when it routinely included a slug of Algerian blackstrap.

PORTUGAL

Reading the label: Adega – *winery*. Branco – *white*. Colheita – *vintage*. Engarrafado na origem – *estate-bottled*. Garrafeira – *a vintage-dated wine with a little more alcohol and minimum ageing requirements*. Quinta – *vineyard or estate*. Reserva – *wine from a top-quality vintage, made from riper grapes than the standard requirement*. Velho – *old*. Vinho de Mesa – *table wine*.

Like Italy, Portugal has grapes grown nowhere else in the world. Unlike Italy, however, until recently the Portuguese had done little to persuade foreigners of the quality of these varieties.

But now, thanks to a new generation of innovative producers like Luis Pato in Bairrada and Jose Neiva, with a bit of help from Australians like David Baverstock and Peter Bright we can see what the native grapes can do.

Try any of Pato's Bairradas, Bright's new-wave Douro reds, and Baverstock's tasty Quinta do Crasto red wines from the Douro.

PORTUGAL

SOUTH AFRICA

Reading the label: Cap Classique – *South African term for Champagne method.* Cultivar – *grape variety.* Edel laat-oes – *noble late harvest.* Edelkeur – *"noble rot," a fungus affecting grapes and producing sweet wine.* Gekweek, gemaak en gebottel op – *estate-bottled.* Landgoedwyn – *estate wine.* Laat-oes – *late harvest.* Oesjaar – *vintage.* Steen – *local name for Chenin Blanc.*

Until recently, too many wines have had the "green" flavour of over-cropped and underripe grapes, grown on virused vines. Wineries like Boekenhoutskloof, Thelema, Saxenburg, Plaisir de Merle, Rust en Vrede, Rustenberg, Naledi/Sejana, Zandvliet, Vergelegen, and Fairview show what can be done, while Grangehurst, Kanonkop, and Vriesenhof support the cause for South Africa's own spicy red grape, the Pinotage. Chardonnays and Sauvignons are often very European in style – as are late harvest and sparkling wines.

THE CAPE

Andalusia

UPINGTON
Orange River Valley
Vaal
KIMBERLEY
Orange
Groenwater
Douglas
Riet

Olifants River

Doring

NORTHERN CAPE

Piketberg

Swartland
Tulbagh
Worcester
Klein Karoo
OUDTSHOORN
MALMESBURY
Paarl
Groot
Durbanville
Robertson
GEORGE
CAPE TOWN
Stellenbosch
Brak
Swellendam
Riviersondeerena
Breëde
MOSSELBAAI
Constantia
Overberg

SOUTHERN CAPE

SOUTH AMERICA

BOLIVIA

• BRASILIA

• LA PAZ

BRAZIL

Paraná

PACIFIC
OCEAN

PARAGUAY

RIO DE JANEIRO

SAO PAULO •

Salta *Teuco*

Catamarca Tucamán

Salado

La Rioja

ASUNCION

ATLANTIC
OCEAN

Aconcagua San Juan • CORDOBA URUGUAY

Casablanca Mendoza • ROSARIO

Rapel •SANTIAGO BUENOS •

Curicó Maipo AIRES MONTEVIDEO

Maule ARGENTINA La Pampa

Itata *Colorado*

Bio Bio Rio
Negro

CHILE *Negro*

Chico

SOUTH
AMERICA

Argentina

Reading the label: Malbec – *spicy red grape*. Torrontes – *grapey white*.

As it chases Chile, this is a country to watch. The wines to look for now are the spicy reds made from the Malbec, a variety once widely grown in Bordeaux and still used in the Loire. Cabernets can be good too, as can the grapey but dry white Torrontes.

Chile

Reading the label: Envasado en Origen – *estate-bottled*. Carmenère/ Grand Vidure – *grape variety once used in Bordeaux*.

One of the most exciting wine-producing countries in the world, thanks to ideal conditions, skilled local winemaking, and plentiful investment. The most successful grape at present is the Merlot, but the Cabernet, Chardonnay, Pinot Noir, and Sauvignon can all display ripe fruit and subtlety often absent in the New World.

SOUTHEASTERN EUROPE
Greece
Finally casting off its image as supplier of Europe's worst wines, Greece is beginning to show what can be done with "international" grapes and highly characterful indigenous varieties. Prices are high (so is demand in chic Athens restaurants), but as the new-wave wines trickle out into the outside world, producers like Château Lazaridi, Gentilini, and Hatzimichali are set for international success.

Cyprus
Still associated with cheap sherry-substitute and dull wine, but things are changing. Look out for the traditional rich Commandaria.

Turkey
Lurching out of the vinous dark ages, Turkey has yet to offer the world red or white wines that non-Turks are likely to relish.

Lebanon
Château Musar has survived all the tribulations of the last few years, keeping Lebanon on the map as a wine-producing country.

Israel
Israel's best Cabernet and Muscat now comes from the Yarden winery in the Golan Heights – a region that may soon lose its Israeli nationality as part of a new peace agreement.

SPAIN

Reading the label: Abocado – *semi-dry*. Año – *year.* Bodega – *winery or wine cellar.* Cava – *Champagne method wine.* Criado y Embotellado (por) – *grown and bottled (by).* Crianza – *aged in wood.* DO(Ca) Denominacion de Origen (Calificada) – *Spain's quality designation, based on regional style. Calificada (DOC) indicates superior quality.* Elaborado y Anejado Por – *made and aged for.* Gran Reserva – *wine aged for a designated number of years in wood; longer than for Reserva.* Joven – *young wine, specially made for early consumption.* Reserva – *official designation for wine that has been aged for a specific period.* Sin Crianza – *not aged in wood.* Vendemia – *harvest or vintage.* Vino de Mesa – *table wine.* Vino de la Tierra – *designation similar to the French "Vin de Pays".*

Spain used to be relied on for a certain style of highly predictable wine: soft, oaky reds with flavours of strawberry and vanilla, and whites that were either light, dry, and unmemorable (Marqués de Cáceres Rioja

Blanco), oaky and old-fashioned (traditional Marqués de Murrieta Rioja), or sweet and grapey (Moscatel de Valencia). Suddenly, however, like a car whose driver has just found an extra gear, Spanish wines have begun to leap ahead – into often largely uncharted territory. The first region to hail the revolution was Penedés, where winemaker Miguel Torres made a speciality of using both traditional and imported grape varieties.

Others have overtaken Torres in regions like Somontano, Rueda, and Navarra. In Rioja itself experiments are quietly going on to see whether the Cabernet Sauvignon can improve the flavour of this traditional wine. There are traditionalists who would prefer to stop all this pioneering business, but the wine genie is out of the Spanish bottle and there seems little chance of anyone forcing it back inside again.

SWITZERLAND

> **Reading the label:** Gutedel, Perlan, Fendant – *local names for the Chasselas.* Grand Cru – *top designation which varies from one canton to the next.* Süssdruck – *off-dry, red wine.*

The only place in the world where the Chasselas produces anything even remotely memorable – and the only one sensibly to use screwcaps for many of its wines. Other worthwhile grapes are the white (Petite) Arvigne and Amigne (de Vétroz) and the red Cornalin, as well as the Gamay, Syrah, Pinot Noir, and Merlot, a variety that is used to make white wines here.

USA

Reading the label: Blush – *rosé*. Champagne – *any sparkling wine*. Fumé – *oak-aged white wine, especially Sauvignon (Blanc Fumé)*. Meritage – *popular, if pretentious, name for a Bordeaux blend (white or red)*. Vinted – *made by (a vintner, or winemaker)*. White Grenache/Zinfandel, etc – *refers to the unfashionable rosé, slightly pink wines, sometimes also referred to as "blush"*.

California

These are busy days for the best-known winemaking state of the Union. After 20 years of almost single-minded devotion to the Chardonnay and Cabernet Sauvignon, and to the Napa Valley, the focus has broadened to take in a wide range of grapes (particularly Italian and Rhône varieties) and regions (Sonoma and Santa Barbara, especially for the Pinot Noir, plus San Luis Obispo, Santa Cruz, Mendocino, and Monterey).

CALIFORNIA

Within the Napa Valley, too, where vineyards are being replanted in the wake of the damage caused by the phylloxera louse, there is growing acknowledgment that some sub-regions produce better wines than others. Carneros is already famous for its Pinot Noir, Oakville for its Chardonnay, while Rutherford and Stag's Leap are known for their Cabernet. But try other worthwhile areas, such as Mount Veeder and Howell Mountain.

The Pacific Northwest

Outside California, head north to Oregon for some of the best Pinot Noirs in the US (at a hefty price) and improving, but rarely earth-shattering, Chardonnays, Rieslings, and Pinot Gris. Washington State has some Pinot, too, on the cooler, rainy, west side of the Cascade Mountains. On the east, irrigated vineyards produce great Sauvignon and Riesling, as well as top-notch Chardonnay, Cabernet Sauvignon, and impressive Syrah and Merlot.

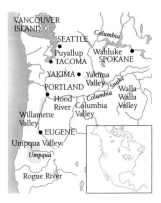

New York and Other States

Once the source of dire "Chablis" and "Champagne," New York State is now producing worthwhile wines, particularly in the microclimate of Long Island, where the Merlot thrives. The Finger Lakes are patchier but worth visiting, especially for the Rieslings and cool-climate Chardonnays. Elsewhere Virginia, Missouri, Texas, Maryland, and even Arizona are all producing wines to compete with California and indeed some of the best that Europe can offer.

The Grapes

BLENDS OR SINGLE VARIETIES?

Some wines are made from single grape varieties – e.g. red or white Burgundy, Sancerre, German Riesling, most Alsace wines and Barolo – while others, such as red or white Bordeaux, California "Meritage" wines, port, and Châteauneuf-du-Pape, are blends of two or more types of grape. Champagne can fall into either camp, as can New World "varietal" wines, which, though generally labelled as "Chardonnay," "Merlot," "Shiraz," etc., can often – depending on local laws – contain up to 25 per cent of other grape varieties. Blends are not, per se, superior to single varietals – or vice versa.

WHITE WINE GRAPES

CHARDONNAY

The world's most popular and widely planted premium white grape variety, and the one whose name has become almost a synonym for dry white wine, is surprisingly hard to define. The flavour of any example will depend enormously on the climate, soil, and the particular type of clone. Burgundy and the best California examples (Kistler, Peter Michael, Sonoma Cutrer), taste of butter and hazelnuts; lesser New World efforts are often sweet and simple and often very melony (a flavour which comes from the clone). Australians range from subtle buttery pineapple to oaky tropical fruit juice. Petaluma, Giaconda, Coldstream Hills, and Leeuwin show how it can be done. New Zealand's efforts are tropical too, but lighter and fresher (Te Mata, Cloudy Bay).

Elsewhere, Chile is beginning to hit the mark, as is South Africa (Jordan). In Europe, look around southern France (James Herrick), Italy (Gaja), Spain, and Eastern Europe, but beware of watery cheaper versions.

Chenin Blanc

Loire variety with naturally high acidity that makes it ideal for fresh sparkling, dry, and luscious honeyed wines; also raw stuff like unripe apples and, when over-sulphured, old socks. Most California Chenins are semi-sweet and ordinary. South Africans call it the Steen and use it for cheap dry and luscious sweet wines. There are few good Australians (but try Moondah Brook) or New Zealanders (try Millton).

Gewürztraminer

Outrageous, oily-textured stuff that smells of parma violets and tastes of lychee fruit. At its best in Alsace (Zind Humbrecht, Schlumberger, Faller), where identically labelled bottles can vary greatly in their level of sweetness. Wines that guarantee luscious sweetness will be labelled as either *Vendange Tardive* or – the intensely sweet – *Sélection de Grains Nobles*. Try examples from Germany, Chile, New Zealand, and Italy too.

Marsanne

A classic, flowery, lemony variety used in the Rhône in wines like Hermitage (from producers like Guigal); in Australia – especially in Goulburn in Victoria (Chateau Tahbilk and Mitchelton); in southern France (from Mas de Daumas Gassac); in Switzerland (late harvest efforts from Provins); and in innovative wines from California. At its best young or after five or six years.

Muscat

The only variety whose wines actually taste as though they are made of grapes, rather than some other kind of fruit or vegetable. In Alsace, southern France, and northeast Italy it is used to make dry wines. Generally, though, it performs best as sparkling wine (Moscatos and Asti Spumantes from Italy, and Clairette de Die Tradition from France) and as sweet fortified wine. Look out for Beaumes de Venise and Rivesaltes in southern France, Moscatel de Setúbal in Portugal, Moscatel de Valencia in Spain, and Liqueur Muscat in Australia (Morris, Chambers, Yalumba).

Pinot Blanc/Pinot Bianco

As rich as Chardonnay, but with less fruit. At its worst – when over-cropped – it makes neutral wine. At its best, however (also in Alsace), it can develop a lovely cashew-nut flavour. When well handled it can also do well in Italy, where it is known as Pinot Bianco (Jermann), and in Germany (especially in Baden), where it is called Weissburgunder.

Pinot Gris/Pinot Grigio

An up-and-coming Alsace variety also known as Tokay but unrelated to any other Tokay. Wines can be spicy, and sweet or dry. The perfumed, aromatic qualities are associated with later-harvest examples. In Italy it is called Pinot Grigio, and in Germany, Grauerburgunder. Look for examples from Oregon (Eyrie), California, and New Zealand.

Riesling

The king of white grapes. Misunderstood – and often mispronounced as Rice-ling rather than Rees-ling – it is often mistaken for cheap German wine made from quite different grapes. At its best, it makes dry and sweet, grapey, appley, limey wines that develop a spicy, gasoline character with age. Quality and character depend on soil – ideally slate – more than climate, and while the best examples come from Germany, in the Mosel (Maximin Grünhaus) and Rhine (Schloss Johannisberg), and Alsace (Zind-Humbrecht, Faller), this variety can perform well in such different environments as Washington State, Australia (Grossett, Tim Adams), and New Zealand (Matua Valley). Not to be confused with unrelated varieties such as Lazki, Lutomer, Welsch, Emerald, or White Riesling.

Sauvignon Blanc

The grape of Loire wines, such as Sancerre and Pouilly Fumé, and white Bordeaux, where it is often blended with Sémillon. This gooseberryish variety performs wonderfully in Marlborough in New Zealand (where

Muscat

Sauvignon Blanc

the flavours can include asparagus and pea-pods), in South Africa (Thelema), and in Australia (Shaw & Smith, Cullen). Chile has good examples (from Casablanca) and Washington State can get it right, as can California (Cakebread, Frog's Leap), but many examples are sweet or overburdened by oak. Oaked US versions, wherever they are produced, are usually labelled Fumé Blanc, a term first coined by Robert Mondavi. Only the best of these improve after the first couple of years.

SÉMILLON

In Bordeaux – in blends with the Sauvignon – this produces sublime dry Graves and sweet Sauternes. In Australia there are great, long-lived dry pure (often unoaked) Sémillons from the Hunter Valley and (more usually oaked) Barossa Valley. Good "noble" late harvest examples have also been produced (by de Bortoli) in Riverina. Elsewhere in Australia the grape is sometimes blended with the Chardonnay. Progress is being made in Washington State and South Africa (Boekenhoutskloof), but most examples from California, New Zealand, and Chile are disappointing.

VIOGNIER

A cult grape, the Viognier was once only found in Condrieu and Château Grillet in the Rhône, where small numbers of good examples showed off its extraordinary perfumed, peach-blossomy character, albeit at a high price. Today, however, it has been widely introduced to the Ardèche, Languedoc-Roussillon, and California (where it is sometimes confused with the Roussanne), and made with loving care (and often over-generous exposure to oak barrels) in Eastern Europe, Argentina, and particularly Australia (where Yalumba makes several good examples).

While examples of affordable Viognier are welcome, most lower-priced efforts are disappointing because this is a variety that performs poorly when asked to produce too much wine per acre. Clones of this grape vary widely too. Buy with care.

Sémillon

Viognier

RED WINE GRAPES

BARBERA

A widely planted, wild-berryish Italian variety at its best in Piedmont, where it is increasingly successful in blends with the Nebbiolo and Cabernet (look out for Elio Altare, Bava, and Roberto Voerzio). Good in Argentina; making inroads into California and Australia (Brown Bros).

CABERNET SAUVIGNON

A remarkable success, associated with the great red wines of the Médoc and Graves (in blends with the Merlot) and the best reds from the New World, especially California, Chile, and Australia. Eastern Europe has good value examples (Bulgaria), as does southern France (Vin de Pays). Spain is rapidly climbing aboard (in the Penedès, Navarra, and – though this is kept quiet – Rioja). The hallmark to look for is blackcurrant, though unripe versions taste like a blend of weeds and bell peppers. There are some great Cabernets in Italy, too. Good New World Cabernets can smell and taste of fresh mint but, with time, like the best Bordeaux, they develop a rich, leathery "cigar box" character.

GRENACHE/GARNACHA

Freshly ground black pepper is the distinguishing flavour here, sometimes with the fruity tang of sweets. At home in Côtes du Rhône and Châteauneuf-du-Pape, it is also used in Spain (as the Garnacha) in blends with the Tempranillo. There are good "Bush" examples from Australia.

MALBEC

Another refugee from Bordeaux, this lightly peppery variety is used in southwest France (for Cahors), the Loire, and Italy, where it generally produces dull stuff. It shines, however, in Argentina (Zuccardi, Catena) and is finding a new home in Chile and Australia.

Cabernet Sauvignon   *Malbec*

MERLOT

The most widely planted variety in Bordeaux and the subject of (enthusiastic over-) planting in California. In Bordeaux where, in some vintages it performs better than Cabernet Sauvignon, it is at its best in Pomerol, where wines can taste of ripe plums and spice, and in St. Emilion, where the least successful wines show the Merlot's less lovable dull and earthy character. Wherever it is made, the naturally thin-skinned Merlot should produce softer, less tannic wines than the Cabernet Sauvignon (though some California examples seemed to contradict this rule).

NEBBIOLO/SPANNA

The red wine grape of Barolo and Barbaresco in Piedmont now, thanks to modern winemaking, increasingly reveals a lovely cherry and rose-petal character, often with the sweet vanilla of new oak casks. Lesser examples for earlier drinking tend to be labelled as Spanna.

PINOT NOIR

The wild-raspberryish, plummy, and liquoricey grape of red Burgundy is also a major component of white and pink Champagne. It makes red and pink Sancerre, as well as light reds in Alsace and Germany (where it is called Spätburgunder). Italy makes a few good examples, but for the best modern efforts, look to California, Oregon, Australia, Chile, South Africa, and, especially, New Zealand (Martinborough, Felton Road).

PINOTAGE

Almost restricted to South Africa, this cross between the Pinot Noir and the Cinsaut can, in the right hands, make berryish young wines that may develop rich gamey-spicy flavours. Poorer examples can be dull and "muddy"-tasting. Try Kanonkop, Grangehurst, and Vriesenhof.

Nebbiolo

Pinot Noir

SANGIOVESE

The grape of Chianti, Brunello di Montalcino, and of a host of popular IGT wines in Italy, not to mention "new wave" Italian-style wines in California and Argentina. The recognizable flavour is of sweet tobacco, wild herbs, and berries.

SYRAH/SHIRAZ

The spicy, brambly grape of the Northern Rhône (Hermitage, Cornas, etc.) and the best reds of Australia (Henschke Hill of Grace and Penfolds Grange), where it is also blended with the Cabernet Sauvignon (just as it once was in Bordeaux). Marqués de Griñon has a great Spanish example, and Isole e Olena has made an unofficial one in Tuscany. Increasingly successful in California and Washington State and, finally, in South Africa. Surprisingly good, too, in both Switzerland and New Zealand.

TEMPRANILLO

Known under all kinds of names around Spain, including Cencibel (in Navarra) and Tinto del Pais (in Ribeira del Duero), the grape gives Spanish reds their recognizable strawberry character. Often blended with the Garnacha, it works well with the Cabernet Sauvignon. So far, little used in the New World, but watch out for examples from Argentina and Australia.

ZINFANDEL

Until recently thought of as California's "own" variety, but now proved (by DNA tests) to be the same variety as the Primitivo in southern Italy. In California it makes rich, spicy, blueberryish reds (see Ridge Vineyards), "ports", and (often with a little help from sweet Muscat), sweet pink "White Zinfandel". Outside California, Cape Mentelle makes a good example in Western Australia.

Syrah

Zinfandel

OTHER GRAPES

WHITE

Albariño/Alvarinho Floral. Grown in Spain (delicious examples from Rias Baixas in Galicia) and Portugal, where it is used for Vinho Verde.

Aligoté Lean Burgundy grape, well used by Leroy.

Arneis Perfumed variety in Piedmont.

Bouvier Dull variety, used for late harvest wines in Austria.

Colombard Appley, basic; grown in S.W. France, US, and Australia.

Furmint Limey variety, traditionally used for Tokaji.

Grüner Veltliner Limey. Restricted to Eastern Europe and Austria.

Kerner Dull German grape. Can taste leafy.

Müller-Thurgau/Rivaner Occasionally impressive variety, grown in Germany (where as Rivaner it is brilliantly made by Müller-Cattoir) and England. Can have a similar "cat's pee" character to Sauvignon.

Roussanne Fascinating Rhône variety that deserves more attention.

Scheurebe Potentially impressive, grapefruity grape grown in Germany. Best in late harvest examples. Known as Samling in Austria.

Silvaner/Sylvaner Earthy, non-aromatic variety of Alsace and Germany.

Torrontes Grapey, Muscat-like variety of Argentina.

Ugni Blanc/Trebbiano Basic grape of S.W. France and Italy.

Verdelho Limey grape found in Madeira and Australian table wine.

Viura Widely planted, so-so Spanish variety.

Welschriesling Basic. Best in late harvest Austrians. Like Lutomer and Laszki and Italico "Riesling"s, not related to the genuine Riesling.

RED

Cabernet Franc Kid brother of Cabernet Sauvignon, grown alongside it in Bordeaux and by itself in the Loire and Italy.

Carmenère/Grand Vidure Peppery variety making waves in Chile.

Cinsaut/Cinsault Spicy Rhône variety; best in blends.

Carignan Toffeeish non-aromatic variety widely used in S. France.

Dolcetto Cherryish Piedmont grape. Drink young.

Dornfelder Successful, juicy variety grown in Germany.

Gamay The Beaujolais grape; less successful in the Loire and Gaillac.

Gamay Beaujolais/Valdiguié Pinot Noir cousin, unrelated to Gamay.

Mourvèdre (Mataro) Spicy Rhône grape; good in California and Australia, but can be hard and "metallic".

Petit Verdot Spicy ingredient of Bordeaux. Now being used on its own.

Petite-Sirah Spicy; thrives in California and Mexico. Durif in Australia.

Ruby Cabernet Basic Carignan-Cabernet Sauvignon cross.

Tannat Tough variety of Madiran. Better in Uruguay.

Styles

STYLE COUNCIL

Wine can be separated into easily recognizable styles: red, white, and pink; still and sparkling; sweet and dry; light and fortified. To say that a wine is red and dry says little, however, about the way it tastes. It could be a tough young Bordeaux, a mature Rioja, or a blueberryish Zinfandel.

Knowing the grape and origin of a wine can give a clearer idea of what it is like, but it won't tell you everything. The human touch is as important in wine as it is in the kitchen. Winemakers vary as much as chefs. Some focus on obvious fruit flavours, while others – in France for example – go for the *goût de terroir* – the character of the vineyard.

In a world that is increasingly given to instant sensations, it is perhaps unsurprising that it is the fruit-lovers rather than the friends of the earthy flavour who are currently in the ascendant.

NEW WORLD/OLD WORLD

Until recently, these two philosophies broadly belonged to the New and Old Worlds. Places like California and Australia made wine that was approachably delicious when compared with the more serious wine being produced in Europe, which demanded time and food. Today however, there are Bordeaux châteaux with a New World approach and South Africans who take a pride in making wine as resolutely tough and old-fashioned as a Bordeaux of a hundred years ago.

Flying Winemakers

These changes owe much to the "flying winemakers" – mostly Australians – who are contracted to produce wine all over the world. Today, you can choose between a white Loire made by a Frenchman – or one bearing the fruity fingerprint of a winemaker who learned his craft in Coonawarra or the Barossa Valley.

Fruit of Knowledge

European old timers like to claim that the Australians use alchemy to obtain those fruity flavours. In fact, their secret lies in the winemaking process. Picking the grapes when they are ripe (rather than too early); preventing them from cooking beneath the midday sun (as often happens in Europe while work stops for lunch); pumping the juice through pipes that have been cleaned daily rather than at the end of the harvest; fermenting at a cool temperature (overheated vats can cost a wine its freshness); and storing and bottling it carefully will all help a wine made from even the dullest grape variety to taste fruitier.

COME HITHER

If the New Worlders want their wines to taste of fruit, they are – apart from some reactionary South Africans and Californians – just as eager to make wine that can be drunk young. They take care not to squeeze the red grapes too hard, so as not to extract bitter, hard tannins, and they try to avoid their white wines being too acidic.

Traditionalists claim these wines do not age well. It is too early to say whether this is true, but there is no question that the newer wave red Bordeaux of, say 1985, have given more people more pleasure since they were released than the supposedly greater 1970 vintage, whose wines often remained dauntingly hard throughout their lifetime. A wine does not have to be undrinkable in its youth to be good later on; indeed, wines that start out tasting unbalanced go on tasting that way.

ROLL OUT THE BARREL

Another thing that sets many new wave wines apart has nothing to do with grapes. Wines have been matured in oak barrels since Roman times, but traditionally new barrels were only bought to replace ones that were worn out and had begun to fall apart. Old casks have little flavour, but for the first two years or so of their lives, the way the staves are bent over flames gives new ones a recognizable vanilla and caramel character.

Winemakers once used to rinse out their new casks with dilute ammonia to remove this flavour. Today, however, they are more likely to devote almost as much effort to the choice of forest, cooper, and charring (light, medium, or heavy "toast") as to the quality of their grapes. Winemakers who want to impress their critics take pride in using 100 percent new oak to ferment and mature their wine. Or more. Some pricey, limited-production red Bordeaux actually goes through two sets of new oak barrels to ensure that it gets enough rich vanilla flavour.

Oak-mania began when Bordeaux châteaux began to spend the income from the great vintages of the 1940s on replacements for their old barrels – and when New World pioneers like Mondavi noticed the contribution the oak was making to these wines. Ever since, producers internationally have introduced new barrels, while even the makers of cheaper wine have found that dunking giant "teabags" filled with small oak chips into wine vats could add some of that vanilla flavour too.

If you like oak, you'll find it in top-notch Bordeaux and Burgundy (red and white), Spanish *Crianza, Reserva,* or *Gran Reserva,* and Italians whose labels use the French term *"Barrique."* The words *"Elévé en fût de Chêne"* on a French wine could confusingly refer to new or old casks. Australian "Show Reserve" will be oaky, as will Fumé Blanc and "Barrel Select" wines.

Red Wines – Fruits, Spice, and... Cold Tea

If you enjoy your red wines soft and juicily fruity, the styles to look for are Beaujolais, Burgundy, and other wines made from the Pinot Noir; youthful Côtes du Rhône; Rioja, and reds from Spain; inexpensive Australians; young Pomerol and St. Emilion from Bordeaux; and Merlots from almost anywhere. Look too for Barbera and Dolcetto from Italy, and Nouveau, Novello, and Joven (young wines).

The Kitchen Cupboard

Italy's Sangiovese is not so much fruity as herby, while the Syrah/Shiraz of the Rhône and Australia, the peppery Grenache and – sometimes – the Zinfandel and Pinotage can all be surprisingly spicy.

Some Like it Tough

Most basic Bordeaux, and all but a few wines from St. Estèphe and Listrac in Bordeaux, are more tannic, as are most older-style wines from Piedmont, California, and most traditional South African Cabernets and Pinotages. The Cabernet Sauvignon will almost always make tougher wines than the Merlot or Pinot Noir.

White Wines – Honey and Lemon

If dry wines with unashamedly fruity flavours are what you want, try the Muscat, the Torrontes in Argentina, basic Riesling and Chardonnay, and New World and Southern French Sauvignon Blanc.

Non-Fruit

For more neutral styles, go for Italian Soave, Pinot Bianco, or Frascati; Grenache Blanc; Muscadet; German or Alsace Silvaner; and most traditional wines from Spain and Southern France.

Riches Galore

The combination of richness and fruit is to be found in white Burgundy; better dry white Bordeaux; and in Chardonnays, Semillons, and oaked Sauvignon (Fumé) wines from the New World.

Aromatherapy

Some perfumed, spicy grapes, like the Gewürztraminer, are frankly aromatic. Also try late-harvest Tokay-Pinot Gris – also from Alsace. Other aromatic varieties include Viognier, Arneis, Albariño, Scheurebe, and Grüner Veltliner.

Middle of the Road

Today, people want wine that is – or says it is – either dry or positively sweet. The Loire can get honeyed *demi-sec* – semi-sweet – wine right. Otherwise, head for Germany and Kabinett and Spätlese wines.

Pure Hedonism

Sweet wine is making a comeback at last. The places to look for good examples are Bordeaux, the Loire (Moelleux), Alsace (Vendange Tardive or Sélection des Grains Nobles), Germany (Auslese, Beerenauslese, Trockenbeerenauslese), Austria (Ausbruch), the New World (late harvest and noble late harvest), and Hungary (Tokaji 6 Puttonyos).

All of these wines should have enough fresh acidity to prevent them from being cloying. Also, they should have the characteristic dried-apricot flavour that comes from grapes that have been allowed to be affected by a benevolent fungus known as "botrytis" or "noble rot".

Other sweet wines such as Muscat de Beaumes de Venise are fortified with brandy to raise their strength to 15% or so. These wines can be luscious too, but they never have the flavour of "noble rot".

PINK

Tread carefully. Provence and the Rhône should offer peppery-dry rosé, just as the Loire and Bordeaux should have wines that taste deliciously of blackcurrant. Sadly, many taste dull and stale. Still, they are a better bet than California's dire sweet "white" or "blush" rosé. Look for the most recent vintage and the most vibrant colour.

SPARKLING

If you find Champagne too dry, but don't want a frankly sweet grapey fizz like Asti Spumante, try a fruity New World sparkling wine from California or Australia. If you don't like that fruitiness, try traditional Spanish Cava, Italian Prosecco, and French Blanquette de Limoux.

Storing

LAYING DOWN FOR BEGINNERS

THE RESTING PLACE

Not so long ago, when winemaking was less sophisticated and there were fewer ways to counter tricky vintages, there were two kinds of wines: the basic stuff to drink immediately, and the cream of the crop that was left in the barrel and/or bottle to age. So, a good wine was an old wine. And vice versa. Young wine and old wine had as much in common as hamburgers and haute cuisine.

Today there are plenty of wonderful wines that never improve beyond the first few years after the harvest, and are none the worse for that. On the other hand, some wines – German Riesling, fine red Bordeaux and top Australian Shiraz, for example – by their very nature, still reward a few years' patience in the cellar.

While many of us live in homes that are ill-suited for storing wine, one can often find an unused grate or a space beneath the stairs that offers wine what it wants: a constant temperature of around 44–60°F (never lower than 40°F nor more than 68°F), reasonable humidity (install a cheap humidifier or leave a sponge in a bowl of water), sufficient ventilation to avoid a musty atmosphere, and, ideally, an absence of vibration (wines stored beneath train tracks – or beds – age faster). Alternatively, invest in a fridgelike Eurocave that guarantees perfect conditions – or even adapt an old freezer.

RACKS AND CELLAR BOOKS

Custom-built racks can be bought "by the hole" and cut to fit. Square chimney stacks can be used too. If you have plenty of space, simply allocate particular racks to specific styles of wine. Unfortunately, even the best-laid cellar plans tend to fall apart when two cases of Australian Shiraz have to be squeezed into a space big enough just for one.

If the size of the cellar warrants it, give each hole in the rack a cross-referenced identity, from A1 at the top left to, say, Z100 at the bottom right. As bottles arrive, they can then be put in any available hole and their address noted in a cellar book, in which you can record when and where you obtained it, what it cost, and how each bottle tasted (is it improving or drying out?). Some people, like me, prefer to use a computer programme (Filemaker Pro or Microsoft Excel).

To Drink or Keep?

A guide to which corks to pop soon and which bottles to treasure for a few years in the rack:

Drink as Soon as Possible

Most wine at under £7.50, particularly basic Chardonnay, Sauvignon Blanc, Merlot, Cabernet, and Zinfandel. French Vins de Pays and all but the best white Bordeaux; cheap red Bordeaux and most Beaujolais. Nouveau/Novello/Joven reds, Bardolino, Valpolicella, light Italian whites, almost all "blush" and rosé.

Less than 5 Years

Most moderately priced (£5–10) California, Chilean, Argentine, South African, and Australian reds and whites. Petit-Château Bordeaux and Cru Bourgeois, and lesser Cru Classé reds from poorer vintages (such as 1997); basic Alsace, red and white Burgundy, and better Beaujolais; Chianti, Barbera, basic Spanish reds; good mid-quality Germans. All but the very best Sauvignon from anywhere.

5–10 Years

Most Cru Bourgeois Bordeaux from good years; better châteaux from lesser vintages; all but the finest red and white Burgundy, and Pinot Noir and Chardonnay from elsewhere; middle-quality Rhônes; southern-French higher flyers; good German, Alsace, dry Loire, and finer white Bordeaux; most mid-priced Italian and Portuguese reds; most Australian, California, and Washington State; South African, Chilean, and New Zealand Merlots and Cabernets on sale at under £15. Late harvest wines from the New World and medium-quality Sauternes.

Over 10 Years

Top-class Bordeaux, Rhône, Burgundy, and sweet Loire from ripe years; top-notch German and Bordeaux late harvest, Italian IGT, Barolo, and the finest wines from Tuscany; best Australian Shiraz, Cabernet, Rieslings, and Semillon; and California Cabernet and finest Merlot and Zinfandel.

Serving

THE RULES OF THE GAME

"The art in using wine is to produce the greatest possible
quantity of present gladness, without any future depression."

The Gentleman's Table Guide, 1873

The Romans used to add salt to their wine to preserve it, while the Greeks
favoured pine resin (which explains the popularity of pine-flavoured
Retsina today). Burgundians often refer to Napoleon's taste for Chambertin,
but rarely mention that he diluted his red wine with water. A century ago,
the English used to add ice to red Bordeaux – and in winter, in Europe
today, skiers drink hot "mulled" wine, adding sugar, fruit, and spices.
Today, Chinese wine drinkers apparently prefer their Mouton Cadet with a
dash of Sprite. And why not? Millions of American wine drinkers got their
first taste of wine in the form of a "cooler", – a blend of wine, sugar, and
flavoured soda. I'm sure the addition of soda pop would do many a skinny
Bordeaux a world of good – it's just a pity when it's added to a classier glass
of Médoc or St. Emilion. It's well worth questioning accepted rules –
especially when they vary between cultures. Have no fear, the advice that
follows is based on common sense and experience – and offered only to
help you to decide how you enjoy serving and drinking wine.

SOME LIKE IT HOT

Particular styles of wine taste better at particular temperatures. At many
restaurants, though, white and sparkling wine are more often served too
cold than too hot. Paradoxically, it is the reds that suffer most from
being drunk too warm. Few of the people who serve wines at "room
temperature" recall that, when that term was coined, there wasn't a lot
of central heating. Be ready to chill a fruity red in a bucket of ice and
water for five to 10 minutes before serving.

Red Wine

When serving red, focus on the wine's flavour. Tough wines are best slightly warmer. The temperatures given are a rule-of-thumb guide:

1 Beaujolais and other fruity reds: 50–57°F (an hour in the fridge).
2 Younger red Burgundy and Rhônes and older Bordeaux, Chianti, younger Rioja, New World Grenache, and Pinotage: 58–62°F.
3 Older Burgundy, tannic young Bordeaux, Rhônes, Zinfandel, bigger Cabernet Sauvignon, Merlot, Shiraz, Barolo, and other bigger Italian and Spanish reds: 62–67°F.

Rosé

Rosé should be chilled at 54–57°F, or for five to 10 minutes in a bucket of ice and water.

White Wine

The cooler the wine, the less it will smell or taste. Subtler, richer wines deserve to be drunk a little warmer.

1 Lighter sweeter wines and everyday sparklers: 39–46°F (two or three hours in the fridge or 10–15 minutes in ice and water).
2 Fuller-bodied, aromatic, drier, semi-dry, lusciously sweet whites; Champagne; simpler Sauvignons; and Chardonnays: 46–53°F.
3 Richer dry wines – Burgundy, California Chardonnay: 54–57°F.

Don't cook your reds – or freeze your whites...

THE PERFECT OUTCOME

The patented Screwpull is still the most reliable way to get a cork out of a bottle. The "waiter's friend" is the next best thing, especially the modern versions with a hinged section designed to prevent corks from breaking. Whatever corkscrew you choose, avoid the models that look like a large screw. These often simply pull through old corks. These fragile stoppers are often most easily removed using a two-pronged "Ah So" cork remover. I find these really tiresome for younger wines, however.

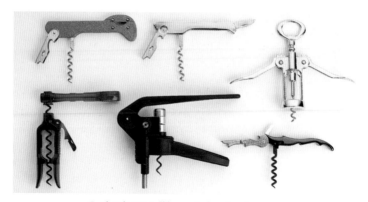

Good corkscrews all have spirals rather than screws.

WHICH GLASSES?

On occasions when no other glass was available I have enjoyed great wine from the glass in my hotel bathroom. I suspect, though, I'd have gotten more out of the experience if something a bit more stylish had come to hand.

Glasses should be narrower across the rim than the bowl. Red ones should be bigger than white because whites are best kept chilled in the bottle rather than warming in the glass. If you like bubbles in your sparkling wine, serve it in a flute rather than a saucer from which they will swiftly escape. Schott, Spiegelau, and Riedel are among a number of companies that now produce attractive glasses that are specially designed to bring out the best in particular styles of wine.

Wines definitely benefit from custom-designed glasses like these.

TO BREATHE OR NOT TO BREATHE?

After what may well have been a fairly lengthy period of imprisonment in its bottle, many a wine can be a bit sulky when it is first poured. Giving it a breath of air may help to banish the sulkiness and bring out the flavour and richness, which is why many people tend to remove the cork a few hours before the wine is to be served. This well-intentioned action, however, is almost a complete waste of time (the contact with oxygen offered by the neck of the bottle is far too limited). If you want to aerate a wine, you'd be far better off simply pouring it into a jug and back into the bottle just before you want to drink it. Broad-based, so-called "ship's decanters" not only look good, but also facilitate airing wine as it flows down the inside of the glass in a fine film. Alternatively, small devices are now available that bubble air into wine to mimic the effect of decanting.

As a rule, young red and – surprisingly perhaps – white wines often benefit from exposure to air, especially when the flavour of a white has been temporarily flattened by a heavy dose of sulphur dioxide. Older red wines, however, may be tired out by the experience and may rapidly lose some of their immediate appeal.

Mature red Bordeaux, Rhône, and port, for example, may need to be decanted in order to remove the unwelcome mudlike deposit that has dropped to the bottom of the bottle. This initially daunting task is far easier than it seems.

Simply stand the bottle for up to a day before decanting it. Pour it very slowly, in front of a flashlight or candle, watching for the first signs of the deposit. Coffee filters suit those with less steady hands.

Decant red – or white – wine to bring out the flavour.

ORDER OF SERVICE

The rules say that white wines and youth respectively precede red wines and age; dry goes before sweet (most of us prefer our main course before the dessert); the lighter the wine, the earlier. These rules are often impossible to follow. What are you to do, for example, if the red Loire is lighter-bodied than the white Burgundy? Can the red Bordeaux follow the Sauternes that you are offering with the foie gras? Ignore the absolutes but bear in mind the common sense that lies behind them. Work gently up the scale of fullness, "flavoursomeness," and quality, rather than swinging wildly between styles.

Investing

LIQUID ASSETS

Wine and dot.com shares have one thing in common: the prices they command may have little to do with their true worth or potential. For a brief, heady moment, baby dot.coms were valued more highly than firms with established track records. Similarly, 1997 claret, though undeniably inferior to the 1996, sold for higher prices *en primeur* – in the barrel – as producers took advantage of the wine boom in Asia. Trendy wine buyers today pay four times as much for a hyped California Cabernet from a recently launched winery than for a wine from an old Bordeaux château – simply because of its rarity. 1996 Bordeaux now sells for more than mature 1986, which may well taste better now and live longer.

SUPPLY AND DEMAND

New money has new tastes. Today's buyers want limited-production, young wine, with powerful, immediately attractive, oaky-fruity flavours they find easy to understand. So, apart from the "blue chips" (Latour, Cheval Blanc, Pétrus, etc.) with a guaranteed following, the Bordeaux that are attracting the greatest interest are wines from small estates (such as l'Eglise Clinet) and recently launched "microwines" – or "garage" wines produced in tiny quantities, such as le Pin and Valandraud. This enthusiasm for rarity is also evident in the unprecedented growth of interest in rare wines from Burgundy, the Rhône, California (Harlan Estate, Screaming Eagle), and Australia (Clarendon Hills). It remains to be seen whether some of these wines will sustain their ludicrously high prices any more successfully than the NASDAQ.

My guess is that, quite often, they won't. The few surviving older bottles may well prove that some of the new stars are fundamentally not as fine as some of the older ones. We'll see. In the meantime bear the following rules in mind.

The Rules

1) The popularity and value varies from one country to another. 2) Wines are not like works of art; they don't last forever. 3) Tread carefully among microwines which have yet to prove their potential. 4) When buying futures, deal with financially solid merchants. 5) At auction, only buy wines that have been carefully cellared. 6) Store your wines carefully – and insure them. 7) Follow their progress – read critics' comments and watch auction prices. 8) Even in an age of internet auctions, wine is tougher to sell instantly than stocks or a piece of jewellry. 9) Beware of falling reputations: the 1975 Bordeaux was soon eclipsed by the 1970 and 1982 vintages.

France
Bordeaux
Châteaux l'Angélus, Ausone, Cheval Blanc, Cos d'Estournel, Ducru-Beaucaillou, Eglise-Clinet, Figeac, Grand-Puy-Lacoste, Gruaud-Larose, Haut-Brion, Lafite, Lafleur, Latour, Léoville Barton, Léoville Las Cases, Lynch Bages, Margaux, la Mission-Haut-Brion, Montrose, Mouton-Rothschild, Palmer, Pétrus, Pichon Lalande, Pichon Longueville, le Pin, Rauzan Ségla, Valandraud. Vintages: 1982, 1983 (for Margaux), 1988, 1989, 1990, 1995, 1996, 1998, 1999 (top properties only), 2000.

Burgundy
Drouhin Marquis de Laguiche, Gros Frères, Hospices de Beaune (from négociants such as Drouhin or Jadot), Méo-Camuzet, Romanée-Conti (la Tâche, Romanée-Conti), Lafon, Leflaive, Leroy, Denis Mortet, de Vogüé.

Rhône
Chapoutier, Chave, Guigal (top wines), Jaboulet Aîné "La Chapelle."

Portugal (Port)
Cockburn's, Dow's, Fonseca, Graham's, Noval, Taylor's, Warre's.

California
Beaulieu Private Reserve, Diamond Creek, Dominus, Duckhorn, Dunn, Harlan Estate, Howell Mountain, Grace Family, Heitz Martha's Vineyard, (varied in the late 1980s and early 1990s), Matanzas Creek, Robert Mondavi Reserve, Opus One, Ridge, Spottswoode, Stag's Leap.

Australia
Armagh, Clarendon Hills, Ch. Tahbilk 1860 Vines Shiraz, Henschke Hill of Grace, Cyril Henschke, Mount Edelstone, Penfolds Grange and Bin 707, Petaluma Cabernet, "John Riddoch," Virgin Hills, Yarra Yering.

Vintages

TIME WILL TELL

Twenty-five years ago, good wine was only produced when the climate was just right. Man had yet to develop ways – physical, chemical, and organic – of combating pests and diseases. Really disastrous years are a rarity now, however, but some places are naturally more prone to tricky vintages than others. Northern Europe, for example, suffers more from unreliable sun and untimely rain than more southerly regions, let alone the warm, irrigated vineyards of Australia and the Americas. A dependable climate does not necessarily make for better wine; grapes develop more interesting flavours in what is known as a "marginal" climate – which is why New World producers are busily seeking out cooler, higher-altitude sites in which to plant their vines.

IT'S AN ILL WIND

Some producers can buck the trend of a climatically poor year – by luckily picking before the rainstorms, carefully discarding rotten grapes, or even using equipment to concentrate the flavour of a rain-diluted crop. In years like these, well-situated areas within larger regions can, in any case, make better wines than their neighbours. France's top vineyards, for example, owe their prestige partly to the way their grapes ripen. The difference in quality between regions can, however, also be attributed to the types of grapes that are grown. Bordeaux had a fair-to-good vintage for red wine in 1997, but a great one for Sauternes. Similarly, there are vintages where, for example, the St. Emilion and Pomerol châteaux have already picked their Merlot grapes in perfect conditions before rainstorms arrive to ruin the prospects of their counterparts' later-ripening Cabernet Sauvignon in the Médoc, only a few miles away.

The following pages suggest regions and wines for the most significant vintages of this and the past century.

OVER 50 YEARS OF WINE...

2001 (SOUTHERN HEMISPHERE)

Quantity generally is lower, with both Chile and South Africa seeing a considerable drop, but quality is generally high. There are plenty of highlights from New Zealand, and Australia saw a record harvest.

2000

Bordeaux, especially the Médoc had a very good-to-great vintage, while red Burgundy, Sauternes, and most of Northern France fared less well. Spain saw one of its largest harvests ever; and although quantity was down in Portugal, quality was up. Italy saw its best results in the south and also in the whites of the northeast, while 2000 was not as spectacular as 1999 in Germany. South Africa's wines were high in alcohol, and in Oz, Western Australia and the Hunter Valley were best.

1999

A patchy year, with great Sauternes, but red Bordeaux was very variable. There were great red and white Burgundies and worthwhile Rhônes, Loires, and Alsaces. Look out for top Italians – especially Chianti – and German wines from the Mosel-Saar-Ruwer. The vintage in Spain was good rather than great. Australia's stars were from Coonawarra and Victoria. New Zealand, Chile, and Argentina did well.

1998

Untimely rain made for a mixed vintage throughout the northern hemisphere. There were some great red Bordeaux (St. Emilion, Pomerol, and top Medoc and Graves), lovely Sauternes and Alsace, and fine white Burgundies (especially Chablis) and ports. California reds were varied.

1997

Bordeaux produced light reds and brilliant sweet whites, and Burgundy had great whites and variable reds. Elsewhere in Europe, Alsace, Italy, Germany, and Austria made terrific wines, as did the port houses of the Douro and producers in the US, Australia, and New Zealand.

1996

A classic vintage for Bordeaux (especially the Médoc, Graves, and Sauternes) and for white Burgundy and the Loire. Alsace and the Rhône were patchy. Germany made austere Kabinett and Spätlese wines, while Italy, Spain, and Portugal had a fair vintage. California, New Zealand, and Australia produced top-class red and white wines.

1995

Attractive, approachable, classy red Bordeaux and white Burgundy. Italian and Loire reds, Rhône, Alsace, German, Rioja, and Ribera del Duero are all worth buying, as are wines from Australia, New Zealand, South Africa, and North and South America.

1994

Unripe red Bordeaux, fine northern Rhône reds, fading red Burgundy, and great Vintage port. Average-to-good Italian reds and Germans; California had a great vintage, and Australians were good to very good.

1993

Red Bordeaux is tiring now. There are excellent Tokaji, Alsace, and Loires (red and white), good red Burgundy and top-class whites. Wines were better in South Africa and New Zealand than in Australia.

1992

Bordeaux was poor, but white Burgundy was good. Red Burgundy is for early drinking. Taylor's and Fonseca produced great vintage port. California Cabernets are fine – finer than efforts from Australia.

1991

Maturing Bordeaux and good Northern Rhône reds. Fine port and good wines from Spain, South Africa, California, New Zealand, and Australia.

1990

Great red and white Bordeaux, Champagne, German Rieslings, Alsace, Loire whites, red Rhônes, Burgundies, Australians, Californians, Barolo, and Spanish reds, especially from the Duero.

1985–1989

1989 Top-class, juicy ripe red and good white Bordeaux and Champagne. Stunning German wines (from Kabinett to TBA) and excellent Alsace. Outstanding Loires (especially red), good red and superb white Rhône, good red Burgundy. **1988** Evolving red Bordeaux, fine Sauternes and Champagne, long-lasting Italian reds, Tokaji, German, Alsace, Loire reds and sweet whites, good red and white Rhône, and red Burgundy. **1987** Fading red Bordeaux and Burgundy. **1986** Fine red and white Bordeaux, Australian reds, white Burgundy. **1985** California reds, red Bordeaux, vintage port, Champagne, Spanish and Italian reds, Alsace, sweet Loire, red Rhône, Burgundy.

1980–1985

1984 South African and Australian reds, and Rieslings. **1983** Red Bordeaux, red Rhône, Portuguese reds, Sauternes, Madeira, vintage port, Tokaji, Alsace. **1982** Red Bordeaux, Australian, Portuguese and Spanish reds, Italian reds, Burgundy and Rhône. **1981** Alsace. **1980** Madeira, port.

1970–1979

1979 Sassicaia, sweet Austrians. **1978** Rhône, Portuguese reds, Bordeaux, Burgundy, Barolo, Tuscan and Loire reds. **1977** Port, sweet Austrians. **1976** Champagne, Loire reds and sweet whites, sweet Germans, Alsace, Sauternes. **1975** Top red Bordeaux and port, Sauternes. **1974** California and Portuguese reds. **1973** Napa Cabernet, sweet Austrians. **1972** Tokaji. **1971** Bordeaux, Burgundy, Champagne, Barolo and Tuscan reds, sweet Germans, red Rhône, Penfolds Grange. **1970** Port, Napa Cabernet, red Bordeaux, Rioja.

1960–1969

1969 Red Rhône, Burgundy. **1968** Madeira, Rioja, Tokaji. **1967** Sauternes, Châteauneuf-du-Pape, German TBA. **1966** Port, Burgundy, red Bordeaux, Australian Shiraz. **1965** Barca Velha. **1964** Red Bordeaux, Tokaji, Vega Sicilia, Rioja, sweet Loire, red Rhône. **1963** Vintage port, Tokaji. **1962** Top Bordeaux and Burgundy, Rioja, Australian Cabernet and Shiraz. **1961** Red Bordeaux, Sauternes, Champagne, Brunello, Barolo, Alsace, red Rhône. **1960** Port, top red Bordeaux.

1950–1959

1959 Red Bordeaux, Sauternes, Tokaji, Germans, Loire, Alsace, Rhône, Burgundy. **1958** Barolo. **1957** Madeira, Vega Sicilia, Tokaji. **1956** Yquem. **1955** Red Bordeaux, Sauternes, port, Champagne. **1954** Madeira. **1953** Red Bordeaux, Tokaji, Champagne, sweet Germans, Côte Rôtie, Burgundy. **1952** Red Bordeaux, Madeira, Champagne, Barolo, Tokaji, Rhône, Burgundy. **1951** Terrible. **1950** Madeira.

1940–1949

1949 Bordeaux, Tokaji, sweet Germans, red Rhône, Burgundy. **1948** Port, Vega Sicilia. **1947** Bordeaux, Burgundy, port, Champagne, Tokaji, sweet Loire. **1946** Armagnac. **1945** Port, Bordeaux, Champagne, Chianti, sweet Germans, Alsace, red Rhônes and Burgundy. **1944** Madeira, port. **1943** Champagne, red Burgundy. **1942** Port, Rioja, Vega Sicilia. **1941** Madeira, Sauternes. **1940** Madeira.

ANNIVERSARY WINES

1902 Madeira. **1912** Port, Bordeaux. **1922** Madeira. **1932** Madeira.

Wine and Health

BETTER RED THAN DEAD?

"Wine is fit for man in a wonderful way, provided that it is taken with good sense by the sick as well as the healthy."

Hippocrates

"Drink a glass of wine after your soup. Steal a rouble from your doctor."

Russian proverb

SAVOIR VIVRE

Around 2200 BC a Sumerian produced the oldest known medical handbook, a pharmacopeia written on a clay tablet recommending wines for various ailments. In 1890, an Irish physician attributed the well-being of the inhabitants of France to their diet – in particular to the red wine they drank. A century later CBS television's 60 Minutes "French Paradox" programme revealed how much healthier Gallic wine drinkers were than Anglo-Saxon teetotallers.

BLOOD AND WINE

Numerous credible reasons have been given for the link between wine and health, including the simple fact that alcohol relieves stress that might otherwise cause disease. (This would help to explain why moderate consumption of other alcoholic drinks also appears to be beneficial.)

However, several of the leading scientists who gathered at the University Victor Segalen in Bordeaux in April 2001 believe that a complex mixture of 200 phenolic compounds to be found in red wine may be effective against a number of ailments, ranging from heart disease to cancer and Aids. Many of these come from the skins and seeds that are used in the making of red wine, but discarded when producing white. White wine has a tenth as many of these compounds as red.

WINE AND HEART DISEASE

According to research at the Université de Bourgogne, people who daily drink up to half a quart of red wine have higher levels of HDL (high density lipoproteins) – "good" cholesterol that escorts "bad" cholesterol away from the artery walls. Prof. Ludovic Drouet of the Hopital Lariboisière in Paris believes that wine may also act against the furring of arteries because polyphenols aid cell proliferation and hinder blood clotting. Heart attack victims are now advised to drink wine while convalescing.

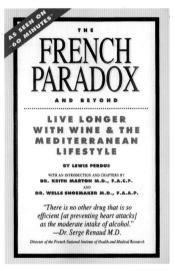

AS SEEN ON 60 MINUTES

THE

FRENCH PARADOX

AND BEYOND

....

LIVE LONGER WITH WINE & THE MEDITERRANEAN LIFESTYLE

BY LEWIS PERDUE

WITH AN INTRODUCTION AND CHAPTERS BY
DR. KEITH MARTON M.D., F.A.C.P.
AND
DR. WELLS SHOEMAKER M.D., F.A.A.P.

"There is no other drug that is so efficient [at preventing heart attacks] as the moderate intake of alcohol."
—*Dr. Serge Renaud M.D.*
Director of the French National Institute of Health and Medical Research

The book of the CBS 60 Minutes programme that sparked modern wine & health mania.

A recent study published in the British Journal of Pharmacology additionally associated the relaxation of blood vessels and reduced blood pressure to red wine consumption.

Resveratrol, an anti-fungal compound found in high concentration in grape skins has been shown to improve the lipid profile of volunteers drinking three glasses of red wine a day for two weeks. Resveratrol appears to be 20 times more powerful in its antioxidant affect than Vitamin E. Prof. Joseph Vercauteren of the University Victor Segalen suggests that the polyphenols mop up damaging chemicals in the body called free radicals more effectively than vitamins C and E because phenolic compounds found in red wine are fat soluble, while others can be dissolved in water.

WINE AND AIDS

Red wine may also be used to augment the treatment of Aids, according to Dr. Marvin Edeas of the Hôpital Antoine Béclère in Clamart, who is studying the way the polyphenols rejuvenate blood. It may also be effective against diseases such as sickle cell anaemia and thalassaemia.

WINE AND DIGESTION

Wine of both colours counters both constipation and diarrhoea, while white wine in particular stimulates the urinary functions. Wine also kills cholera bacteria and combats typhoid and trichinella, the poisonous compound in "bad" pork. Surprisingly, one researcher, Dr. Heinrich Kliewe, actually recommends that moderate amounts of wine can counteract some of the side effects of antibiotics.

WINE AND AGEING

Marie Antoinette apparently used to wash her face in red wine to protect the skin against wrinkles, and a Bordeaux health spa makes great use of extracts from grape seeds. Today, though, most researchers are more concerned with the way antioxidants in red wine appear to inhibit the effects of degenerative oxidation, such as strokes. Wine may also offer protection against Alzheimer's Disease; moderate wine drinkers in their 70s and 80s seem to remain more alert than their more abstemious contemporaries.

WINE AND VIRUSES

Apart from any beneficial effects of wine against the Aids virus, it may also combat other viruses. According to Dr. Jack Konowalchuk and Joan Speirs of the department of microbial hazards in Canada, the polyphenols in tannic red wine are effective against such viruses as those that cause cold sores, and may even act against genital Herpes 2.

WINE AND PREGNANCY

Despite the fears it arouses, the warning notices and the embarrassing scenes that have occurred in bars and restaurants between pregnant women and waiters, the risks associated with drinking wine while expecting a baby are actually very low. Fetal Alcohol Syndrome is rare outside the poorer inner cities of the US. In 1997, the UK Royal College of Obstetricians and Gynaecologists reported that up to 15 units of alcohol per week should do no harm to a foetus.

WINE AND CALORIES

There is no difference in calories between a Muscadet and a red Bordeaux (around 110 per glass). More alcoholic wines, such as California Zinfandels, Australian Shirazes, and some red Rhones, with strengths of 14 percent will have more calories, while sweeter, but less alcoholic German wines such as Liebfraumilch, that weigh in at 9 percent, have less than 80 calories. A Stanford University survey suggests the action of the wine on the metabolism somehow makes its calories less fattening.

WINE AND CANCER

Alcohol has been linked to rare occurrences of mouth and throat cancer – but only among smokers. Red wine is rich in gallic acid, an acknowledged anticarcinogenic, and wine's role in reducing stress has been controversially associated with a lower incidence of certain forms of cancer. Dr. Francis Raul of the University Louis Pasteur in Strasbourg believes that Resveratrol inhibits the proliferation of human intestinal cancerous cells and the formation of tumours in mice predisposed to intestinal tumours. Prof. Djavad Mossalayi of the Victor Segalen University has tested it on human cells, both normal and cancerous, and found it to be toxic to both. He thinks the action of wine on cancer cells may not be linked to its antioxidant properties but to the way it acts on the basic process of cell division. Keep watching.

HANGOVERS

All alcohol – especially vintage port – is hangover fare. The only way to be sure to avoid this fate is to drink plenty of water before going to bed. If you have failed to take this step, your best bet is to resort to healthy doses of vitamin B (Berocca tablets from Roche are useful, as is toast with Marmite or Vegemite yeast paste if these are available). Otherwise, go for protein and refreshing orange juice diluted with sparkling mineral water.

WINE AND MIGRAINE

Red wine, like chocolate, can inhibit a useful little enzyme called phenosulfotransferase-P, or PST-P, which detoxifies bacteria in the gut. An absence of PST-P is linked to migraine, which is why some people complain of headaches after drinking a glass or two of wine. Other people have found that red wine is also associated with episodic skin allergies. Sufferers from wine-related allergies (and this is probably a larger number than is commonly believed) may be encouraged to know that some of these conditions can come and go over time. Interestingly, there also seems to be differences in the effects of particular styles of wine. Makers of Chianti, for example, take pride in the fact that their wine seems to have lower amounts of histamines than reds from other regions. In other words, before assuming that you are permanently barred from drinking red or white, and while awaiting the results of further research into wine-related allergies, it may be worth sampling small doses of various kinds of wine.

WINE AND ASTHMA

One undeniable side effect of wines that are heavily dosed with sulphur dioxide (which is used to combat bacteria in most dried, bottled, and canned foods) is an incidence of asthma attacks among those who are susceptible to this condition. Red wines in general, and New World and organic wines in particular, have lower sulphur levels. The highest levels of sulphur will be in sweet white wines and wines with low alcohol levels.

Food and Wine

MATCHMAKING FOR BEGINNERS

One of the most daunting aspects of wine has always been the traditional obsession with serving precisely the right wine with any particular dish – of only ever drinking red with meat and white with fish or shellfish. It may be reassuring to learn that some of these time-honoured rules are just plain wrong. In Portugal, for example, fishermen love to wash down their sardines and salt cod with a glass or two of harsh red wine. In Burgundy they even poach fish in their local red.

On the other hand, the idea that a platter of cheese needs a bottle of red wine can be trashed in an instant. Just take a mouthful of red Bordeaux immediately after eating a little goat's cheese or Brie. The wine will taste metallic and unpleasant because the creaminess of the cheese reacts badly with the tannin – the toughness – in the wine. A dry white would be far more successful (its acidity would cut through the fat), while the Bordeaux would be shown at its best alongside a harder, stronger cheese. If you don't want to offer a range of wines, try sticking to one or two cheeses that really will complement the stuff in the glass.

Don't take anything for granted. Rare beef and red Bordeaux surprisingly fails the test of an objective tasting. The protein of the meat somehow makes all but the fruitiest wines taste tougher. If you're looking for a perfect partner for beef, uncork a Burgundy. If it's the Bordeaux that takes precedence, you'd be far better off with lamb.

The difference between an ideal and a passable food-and-wine combination can be very subtle. Most of us have after all happily quaffed red Bordeaux with our steak, but just as an avid cook will tinker with a recipe until it is just right, there's a lot to be said for making the occasional effort to find a pairing of dish and wine that really works. Like people who are happier as a couple than separately, some foods and wines simply seem to bring out the best in each other.

A Sense of Balance

There is no real mystery about the business of matching food and wine. Some flavours and textures are compatible, and some are not. Strawberry mousse is not really delicious with chicken casserole, but apple sauce can do wonders for roast pork.

The key to spotting which relationships are marriages made in heaven, and which have the fickleness of Hollywood romances, lies in identifying the dominant characteristics of the contents of both the plate and the glass. Then, learn by experience which are likely to complement each other, either through their similarities or through their differences.

Likely Combinations

It is not difficult to define particular types of food and wine, and to guess how they are likely to get along. A buttery sauce is happier with something tangily acidic, like a crisp Sauvignon Blanc, rather than a rich, buttery Chardonnay. A subtly poached fish won't appreciate a fruit-packed New World white, and you won't do pheasant pie any favours by pulling the cork on a delicate red.

What to Avoid

Some foods and their characteristics, though, make life difficult for almost any drink. Sweetness, for example, in a fruity sauce served with a savory dish seems to strip some of the fruitier flavours out of a wine. This may not matter if the stuff in your glass is a blackcurranty New World Cabernet Sauvignon, but it's bad news if it is a bone-dry white or a tough red with little fruit to spare.

Cream is tricky, too. Try fresh strawberries with Champagne – delicious; now add a little whipped cream to the equation and you'll spoil the flavour. Creamy and buttery sauces can have the same effect on a wine and call for a similarly creamy white – or a fresh, zippy one to cut through the fattiness.

Spices are very problematic for wine – largely due to the physical sensation of eating them rather than any particular flavour. A wine may not seem particularly nasty after a mouthful of chilli sauce; it will simply lose its fruity flavour and taste of nothing at all – which, in the case of a fine red seems to be a pity. The way a tannic red dries out the mouth will also accentuate the heat of the spice. The ideal wine for most Westerners to drink with any spicy dish would be a light, possibly slightly sweet, white or a light, juicy red. Chinese palates often react differently to these combinations, however. They like the burning effect of the chilli and see no point in trying to put out the fire with white wine.

Always Worth a Try

Some condiments actually bring out the best in wines. A little freshly ground pepper on your meat or pasta can accentuate the flavour of a wine, just as it can with a sauce.

Squeezing fresh lemon onto your fish will reduce the apparent acidity of a white wine – a useful tip if you have inadvertently bought a case of tooth-strippingly dry Muscadet. And, just as lemon can help to liven up a dull sauce, it will do the same for a dull white wine, such as a basic Burgundy or a Soave, by neutralizing the acidity and allowing other flavours to make themselves apparent. Mustard performs a similar miracle when it is eaten with beef, somehow nullifying the effect of the meat protein on the wine.

Marriage Guidance

In the following pages, I have suggested wines to go with a wide range of dishes and ingredients, taking the dominant flavour as the key point. Don't treat any of this advice as gospel – use it instead as a launchpad for your own food and wine experiments.

And, if no wine seems to taste just right, don't be too surprised. Heretical as it may seem, some dishes are actually more enjoyable with other drinks. The vinegar that is a fundamental part of a good relish, for example, will do no wine a favour. Even avid wine lovers might well find beer a far more pleasurable accompaniment.

Cooking with Wine

Finally, a word or two about how to make the best use of wine in the kitchen (apart from its role as refreshment following a vigorous session of egg-beating, and as a tranquilizer for the moments when sauces curdle and soufflés refuse to rise). The first (and most often forgotten) rule to remember is that wine that's not good enough to drink is probably not good enough to pour into the frying pan or casserole. At least, not unless you take a perverse pleasure in using and eating substandard ingredients. On the other hand, despite the advice of classic French recipes, your "coq au vin" won't be spoiled by your unwillingness to make it with a pricy bottle of Grand Cru Burgundy. A decent, humbler red will do perfectly well, though it is worth trying to use a similar style to the one suggested.

Second – and just as important – remember that, with the exception of a few dishes such as British sherry trifle or zabaglione, in which wine is enjoyed in its natural state, wine used as an ingredient needs to be cooked in order to remove the alcohol. So, add it early enough for the necessary evaporation to take place.

A

Almond Liqueur Muscats or Beaumes de Venise.
  Trout with Almonds Bianco di Custoza, Pinot Blanc.
Anchovies
  Fresh Anchovy (Boquerones) Albariño, Vinho Verde, Aligoté.
  Salade Niçoise Muscadet, Vinho Verde, or Beaujolais.
  Salted Anchovies Rioja red or white, Manzanilla or Fino sherry.
  Tapenade Dry sherry or Madeira.
Apple
  Apple Pie or Strudel Austrian off-dry white.
  Blackberry and Apple Pie Late harvest Riesling, Vouvray demi-sec.
  Roast Pork with Apple Sauce Off-dry Vouvray or Riesling.
  Waldorf Salad Dry Madeira.
Apricot Late harvest Sémillon or Riesling, Jurançon Moelleux.
Arroz con Pollo (Chicken and Rice) Côtes du Rhône, young Zinfandel,
  Navarra or Rioja "Joven."
Artichoke White Rhône.
  Artichoke Soup Dry Loire whites, Pinot Gris.
Arugula Pinot Grigio, young Viognier.
Asparagus
  Asparagus Crêpes au Gratin Muscadet, Vinho Verde, Cider.
  Asparagus Soup Fresh dry whites, Sauvignon Blanc.
Aubergine
  Stuffed Aubergines Beefy spicy reds like Bandol, Zinfandel, a good Southern
    Rhône or a full-bodied Italian.
Avocado
  Avocado with Prawns Champagne, Riesling Kabinett, Sauvignon Blanc,
    Pinot Gris, Australian Chardonnay.
  Avocado Vinaigrette Unoaked Chardonnay, Chablis.

B

Bacon Rich Pinot Gris or Alsace Riesling.
  Bacon with Marinated Scallops Fino sherry or mature Riesling,
    Shiraz-based Australians, Zinfandel from the US,
    or a heavy Cape red.
  Warm Bacon Salad New World Sauvignon Blanc,
    California Fumé Blanc, or a good Pouilly Fumé.
Banana
  Flambéed Banana with Rum Jurançon, Tokaji,
    Pedro Ximénez sherry, rum.
  Banoffee Pie Sweet Tokaji.
Barbecue Sauce Inexpensive off-dry white or a
  simple, fruity Cabernet.
  Spare Ribs with Barbecue Sauce Fruity Australian
    Shiraz, Grenache, or Zinfandel; spicy Côtes du
    Rhône from a ripe vintage; or an off-dry white.

Warm Bacon Salad

Basil Slightly sweet Chardonnay (i.e., California, commercial Australian).
  Pasta in Pesto Sauce New Zealand Sauvignon Blanc, Valpolicella.
Beans
  Bean Salad Spanish reds – Rioja and Rueda – or New Zealand Sauvignon Blanc.
  Baked Beans Light Zinfandel, Beaujolais, dry rosé, or beer.
  Cassoulet Serious white Rhône, Marsanne, or Roussanne; or reds including
    Grenache and Syrah from the Rhône, crunchy Italian reds, or Zinfandel.
Beef
  Beef with Green Peppers in Black Bean Sauce Off-dry German Riesling or
    characterful dry white, like white Rhône or Marsanne.
  Beef with Scallions and Ginger Off-dry German Riesling or one of the more
    serious Beaujolais Crus.
  Beef Stew Pomerol or St. Emilion, good Northern
    Rhône like Crozes Hermitage, Shiraz or Pinot
    Noir from the New World.
  Beef Stroganoff Tough, beefy reds like Amarone,
    Brunello di Montalcino, Barolo, Côte Rôtie, or
    really ripe Zinfandel.
  Beef Wellington Top Burgundy, Châteauneuf-
    du-Pape.
  Boeuf Bourguignon Australian Bordeaux-style,
    Barolo, or other robust reds with sweet fruit.
  Boiled Beef and Carrots Bordeaux Rouge,
    Valpolicella Classico, Australian Shiraz.

Beef Stroganoff

  Bresaola (Air-Dried Beef) Beaujolais,
    Barbera, and tasty reds from the Languedoc.
  Carpaccio of Beef Chardonnay, Champagne, Cabernet Franc, and Pomerol.
  Chilli con Carne Robust fruity reds, Beaujolais Crus, Barbera or Valpolicella,
    spicy reds like Zinfandel or Pinotage.
  Corned Beef Loire reds from Gamay or Cabernet Franc.
  Corned Beef Hash Characterful spicy reds from the Rhône or Southern France
  Creole-Style Beef Cheap Southern Rhône reds or Côtes du Rhône, Zinfandel.
  Hamburger Zinfandel or country reds from Italy or France, e.g., Corbières.
  Hungarian Goulash East European reds – Bulgarian Cabernet or Mavrud
    and Hungarian Kadarka – or Australian Shiraz.
  Meatballs Spicy rich Rhône reds, Zinfandel, Pinotage, and Portuguese reds.
  Panang Neuk (Beef in Peanut Curry) New World Chardonnay; New
    Zealand Sauvignon Blanc; or a spicy, aromatic white Rhône.
  Pastrami Zinfandel, good Bardolino, light Côtes du Rhône.
  Rare Chargrilled Beef Something sweetly ripe and flavoursome, but not too
    tannic. Try Chilean Merlot.
  Roast Beef Côte Rôtie, good Burgundy.
  Steak Pinot Noir and Merlot from the New World; Australian Shiraz;
    Châteauneuf-du-Pape; good, ripe Burgundy.
  Steak with Dijon Mustard Bordeaux, Cabernet Sauvignon from the
    New World, or Australian Shiraz.
  Steak and Kidney Pie/Pudding Bordeaux, Australian Cabernet Sauvignon,
    Southern Rhône reds, or Rioja.
  Steak au Poivre Cabernet Sauvignon, Chianti, Rhône reds, Shiraz, or Rioja.
  Steak Tartare Bourgogne Blanc; Beaujolais; Bardolino; or, traditionally, vodka.

Thai Beef Salad New Zealand or South African Sauvignon Blanc, Gewürztraminer, Pinot Blanc.

Beer (in a sauce)
Carbonnade à la Flamande Cheap Southern Rhône or Valpolicella.

Beetroot
Borscht Rich, dry Alsace Pinot Gris; Pinot Blanc; or Italian Pinot Grigio.

Black Bean Sauce
Beef with Green Peppers in Black Bean Sauce Off-dry German Riesling or characterful, dry white like white Rhône or Marsanne.

Blackberry
Blackberry and Apple Pie Late harvest Riesling, Vouvray demi-sec.

Black Cherry
Black Forest Gâteau Fortified Muscat, Schnapps, or Kirsch.

Blackcurrant
Blackcurrant Cheesecake Sweet, grapey dessert wines.
Blackcurrant Mousse Sweet sparkling wines.

Black Pudding Chablis, New Zealand Chardonnay, Zinfandel, or Barolo.

Blueberries
Blueberry Pie Tokaji (6 Puttonyos), late harvest Semillon or Sauvignon.

Brandy
Christmas Pudding Australian Liqueur Muscat, tawny port, rich (sweet) Champagne, Tokaji.
Crêpe Suzette Asti Spumante, Orange Muscat, Champagne cocktails.

Bream (freshwater) Chablis or other unoaked Chardonnay.

Bream (sea) White Rhône, Sancerre.

Brie Sancerre or New Zealand Sauvignon Blanc.

Broccoli
Broccoli and Cheese Soup Slightly sweet sherry – Amontillado or Oloroso.

Butter
Béarnaise Sauce Good dry Riesling.
Beurre Blanc Champagne Blanc de Blancs, dry Vinho Verde.

Butternut Squash
Butternut Soup Aromatic Alsace Gewürztraminer.

C

Cabbage
Stuffed Cabbage East European Cabernet.

Cajun Spices Beaujolais Crus.
Gumbo Zinfandel or maybe beer.

Camembert Dry Sauvignon Blanc or unoaked Chablis.

Capers Sauvignon Blanc.
Skate with Black Butter Crisply acidic whites like Muscadet or Chablis.
Tartare Sauce Crisply fresh whites like Sauvignon.

Caramel
Crème Caramel Muscat or Gewürztraminer Vendange Tardive.

Crème Caramel

Carp Franken Sylvaner, dry Jurançon, Hungarian Furmint.
Carrot
   Carrot and Coriander Soup Aromatic, dry Muscat; Argentinian Torrontes.
   Carrot and Orange Soup Madeira or perhaps an Amontillado sherry.
Cashew Nuts Pinot Blanc.
   Chicken with Cashew Nuts Rich aromatic white, Pinot Gris, or Muscat.
Cauliflower
   Cauliflower Cheese Fresh crisp Côtes de Gascogne white; Pinot Grigio;
     softly plummy Chilean Merlot; or young, unoaked Rioja.
Caviar Champagne or chilled vodka.
Celery
   Celery Soup Off-dry Riesling
Cheddar (mature) Good Bordeaux, South African Cabernet, port.
Cheese (general – also see individual entries)
   Cheeseburger Sweetly fruity oaky reds – Australian Shiraz, Rioja.
   Cheese Fondue Swiss white or Vin de Savoie.
   Cheese Platter Match wines to cheeses; don't put too tannic a red with too
     creamy a cheese, and offer white wines – which go well with all but the
     hardest cheese. Strong creamy cheeses demand fine Burgundy; blue cheese is made
     for late harvest wines; goat cheese is ideal with Sancerre, Pouilly Fumé, or other
     dry, unoaked Sauvignons. Munster is best paired with Alsace Gewurztraminer.
   Cheese Sauce (Mornay) Oaky Chardonnay.
   Cream Cheese, Crème Fraîche, Mozzarella, Mascarpone Fresh light dry whites
     – Frascati, Pinot Grigio.
   Raclette Swiss white or Vin de Savoie.
Cheesecake Australian botrytized Semillon.
Cherry Valpolicella, Recioto della Valpolicella, Dolcetto.
   Roast Duck with Cherry Sauce Barbera, Dolcetto, or Barolo.
Chestnut
   Roast Turkey with Chestnut Stuffing Côtes du Rhône, Merlot, or soft and
     mature Burgundy.
Chicken
   Barbecued Chicken Rich and tasty white, Chardonnay.
   Chicken Casserole Mid-weight Rhône, such as Crozes-Hermitage or Lirac.
   Chicken Chasseur Off-dry Riesling.
   Chicken Kiev Chablis, Aligoté, or Italian dry white.
   Chicken Pie White Bordeaux, simple Chardonnay, or else a light Italian white.
   Chicken Soup Soave, Orvieto, or Pinot Blanc.
   Chicken Vol-au-Vents White Bordeaux.
   Coq au Vin Shiraz-based New World reds, red Burgundy.
   Curry Chicken Gewürztraminer, dry white Loire, fresh Chinon.
   Devilled Chicken Australian Shiraz.
   Fricassée Unoaked Chardonnay.
   Lemon Chicken Muscadet, Chablis, or basic Bourgogne Blanc.
   Roast/Grilled Chicken Reds or whites, though nothing too heavy –
     Burgundy is good, as is Barbera, though Soave will do just as well.
   Roast/Grilled Chicken with Sage and Onion Stuffing Italian reds,
     especially Chianti; soft, plummy Merlots; and sweetly fruity Rioja.
   Roast/Grilled Chicken with Tarragon Dry Chenin (Vouvray or perhaps
     a good South African).

Saltimbocca (Cutlet with Mozzarella and Ham) Flavoursome, dry Italian whites
– Lugana, Bianco di Custoza, Orvieto.

Smoked Chicken Oaky Chardonnay, Australian Marsanne, or Fumé Blanc.

Southern Fried Chicken White Bordeaux, Muscadet, Barbera, light Zinfandel.

Tandoori Chicken White Bordeaux, New Zealand Sauvignon Blanc.

Chicken Liver (Sauté) Softly fruity, fairly light reds including Beaujolais,
Italian Cabernet or Merlot, or perhaps an Oregon Pinot Noir.

Chicken Liver Pâté Most of the above reds plus Vouvray Moelleux, Monbazillac,
or Amontillado sherry.

Chilli Cheap wine or cold beer.

Chilli Con Carne Robust fruity reds, Beaujolais
Crus, Barbera or Valpolicella, spicy reds like
Zinfandel or Pinotage.

Hot and Sour Soup Crisply aromatic English white,
Baden Dry.

Szechuan-Style Dry, aromatic whites; Alsace Pinot
Gris; Riesling; Grenache rosé; beer.

Thai Beef Salad New Zealand or South African
Sauvignon Blanc, Gewürztraminer, Pinot Blanc.

Chinese (general) Aromatic white –
Gewürztraminer, Pinot Gris, English.

Chives Sauvignon Blanc.

Chilli Con Carne

Chocolate Orange Muscat, Moscatel de Valencia.

Black Forest (Chocolate and Cherry) Gâteau
Fortified Muscat or Kirsch.

Chocolate Cake Beaumes de Venise, Bual or Malmsey Madeira, Orange Muscat,
sweet German, or fine Champagne.

Chocolate Profiteroles with Cream Muscat de Rivesaltes.

Dark Chocolate Mousse Sweet Black Muscat or other Muscat-based wines.

Milk Chocolate Mousse Moscato d'Asti.

Chorizo (Sausage) Red or white Rioja, Navarra, Manzanilla sherry, Beaujolais,
or Zinfandel.

Cinnamon Riesling Spätlese, Muscat.

Clams Chablis or Sauvignon Blanc.

Clam Chowder Dry white such as Côtes de Gascogne, Amontillado sherry,
or Madeira.

Spaghetti Vongole Pinot Bianco or Lugana.

Cockles Muscadet, Gros Plant, Aligoté, dry Vinho Verde.

Coconut (milk) California Chardonnay.

Green Curry Big-flavoured New World whites or Pinot Blanc from Alsace.

Cod Unoaked Chardonnay; good, white Burgundy; dry Loire Chenin.

Cod and Chips (French Fries) Any light, crisp, dry white, such as a Sauvignon
from Bordeaux or Touraine. Alternatively, try dry rosé or Champagne.
Remember, though, that English-style heavy-handedness with the vinegar will
do no favours for the wine. For vinegary fries, stick to beer.

Cod Roe (smoked) Well-oaked New World Chardonnay.

Lisbon-Style Cod Vinho Verde; Muscadet; light, dry Riesling.

Salt Cod (Bacalhão de Gomes) Classically Portuguese red or white – Vinho
Verde or Bairrada reds.

Smoked Cod Vinho Verde.

Coffee
  Coffeecake Asti Spumante.
  Coffee Mousse Asti Spumante, Liqueur Muscat.
  Tiramisu Sweet fortified Muscat, Vin Santo, Torcolato.
Coriander
  Carrot and Coriander Soup Aromatic, dry Muscat.
  Coriander Leaf Dry or off-dry English white.
  Coriander Seed Dry, herby Northern Italian whites.
Corn Rich and ripe whites – California Chardonnay.
  Corn on the Cob Light, fruity whites – German Riesling.
Courgette
  Courgette Gratin Good dry Chenin from Vouvray or South Africa.

Crab Chablis, Sauvignon Blanc, New World Chardonnay.
  Crab Cakes (Maryland-style) Rias Baixas Albariño.
  Crab Cioppino Sauvignon Blanc, Pinot Grigio.
  Crab Mousse Crisp dry whites – Baden Dry or Soave.
  Deviled Crab (spicy) New World Sauvignon, Albariño.
Cranberry
  Roast Turkey with Cranberry and Orange Stuffing Richly fruity reds like
    Shiraz from Australia, Zinfandel, or modern Rioja.
Crayfish
  Freshwater Crayfish South African Sauvignon, Meursault.
  Salad of Crayfish Tails with Dill Rich South African Chenin blends or
    crisp Sauvignon, white Rhône.
Cream When dominant not good with wine, particularly tannic reds.
Curry
  Beef in Peanut Curry New World Chardonnay; spicy, aromatic white Rhône.
  Coronation Chicken Gewürztraminer; dry, aromatic English wine; or a
    fresh Chinon.
  Curried Beef Beefy, spicy reds – Barolo, Châteauneuf-du-Pape, and
    Shiraz/Cabernet – or off-dry aromatic whites – Gewürztraminer, Pinot Gris.
    Or try some Indian sparkling wine or cold Indian beer.
  Curried Turkey New World Chardonnay.
  Tandoori Chicken White Bordeaux, New Zealand Sauvignon Blanc.
  Thai Green Chicken Curry Big New World whites or dry Pinot Blanc
    from Alsace.

D

Dill Sauvignon Blanc.
  Gravlax Ice cold vodka, Pinot Gris, or Akvavit.
Dover Sole Sancerre, good Chablis, unoaked Chardonnay.
Dried Fruit Sweet sherry, tawny port.
  Bread and Butter Pudding Barsac or Sauternes, Monbazillac, Jurançon.
    Muscat de Beaumes de Venise or Australian Orange Muscat.
  Mince Pie Rich, late harvest wine or botrytis-affected Sémillon.
Duck Pinot Noir from Burgundy, California, or Oregon, or off-dry German Riesling.

Cassoulet Serious white Rhônes, Marsanne, or Roussanne; or try reds including Grenache and Syrah from the Rhône, berryish Italian reds, or Zinfandel.

Confit de Canard Alsace Pinot Gris or a crisp red like Barbera.

Duck Pâté Chianti or other juicy herby red, Amontillado sherry.

Duck Pâté with Orange Riesling or Rioja.

Peking Duck Rice wine, Alsace Riesling, Pinot Gris.

Roast Duck Fruity reds like Australian Cabernet, a ripe Nebbiolo, or Zinfandel.

Roast Duck with Cherry Sauce Barbera, Dolcetto, or Barolo.

Roast Duck with Orange Sauce Loire red or a sweet white like Vouvray demi-sec.

Smoked Duck California Chardonnay or Fumé Blanc.

Duck Liver

Foie Gras de Canard Champagne, late harvest Gewürztraminer or Riesling, Sauternes.

E

Eel

Smoked Eel Pale, dry sherry; simple, fresh white Burgundy.

Egg

Crème Brûlée Jurançon Moelleux, Tokaji.

Eggs Benedict Unoaked Chardonnay, Blanc de Blancs, British Bucks Fizz, Bloody Mary.

Eggs Florentine Unoaked Chardonnay, Pinot Blanc, Aligoté, Sémillon.

Spanish Tortilla Young, juicy Spanish reds and fresher whites from La Mancha or Rueda.

F

Fennel Sauvignon Blanc.

Fig Liqueur Muscat.

Fish (general – also see individual entries)

Bouillabaisse Red or white Côtes du Rhône, dry rosé or peppery dry white from Provence, California Fumé Blanc, Marsanne, or Verdicchio.

Cumberland Fish Pie California Chardonnay, Alsace Pinot Gris, Sauvignon Blanc.

Fish Cakes White Bordeaux, Chilean Chardonnay.

Fish and Chips Most fairly simple, crisply acidic dry whites or maybe a rosé or Champagne (See Cod). Go easy with the vinegar.

Fish Soup Manzanilla, Chablis, Muscadet.

Kedgeree Aligoté, crisp Sauvignon.

Mediterranean Fish Soup Provençal reds and rosés, Tavel, Côtes du Rhône, Vin de Pays d'Oc.

Seafood Salad Soave, Pinot Grigio, Muscadet, or a lightly oaked Chardonnay.

Sushi Saké.

Frankfurter Côtes du Rhône or beer.

Fruit (general – also see individual entries)

> *Fresh Fruit Salad* Moscato d'Asti, Riesling Beerenauslese, or Vouvray Moelleux.
>
> *Fruit Flan* Vouvray Moelleux, Alsace Riesling Vendange Tardive.
>
> *Summer Pudding* Late harvest Riesling – German or Alsace.

G

Game (general – also see individual entries)

> *Cold Game* Fruity Northern Italian reds – Barbera or Dolcetto – good Beaujolais or light Burgundy.
>
> *Game Pie* Beefy reds, Southern French, Rhône, Australian Shiraz.
>
> *Roast Game* Big reds, Brunello di Montalcino, old Barolo, good Burgundy.
>
> *Well-hung Game* Old Barolo or Barbaresco, mature Hermitage, Côte Rôtie or Châteauneuf-du-Pape, fine Burgundy.

Garlic

> *Aïoli* A wide range of wines go well including white Rioja, Provence rosé, California Pinot Noir.
>
> *Garlic Sausage* Red Rioja, Bandol, Côtes du Rhône.
>
> *Gazpacho* Fino sherry, white Rioja.
>
> *Roast/Grilled Chicken with Garlic* Oaky Chardonnay or red Rioja.
>
> *Roast Lamb with Garlic and Rosemary* Earthy soft reds like California Petite Sirah, Rioja, or Zinfandel.
>
> *Snails with Garlic Butter* Aligoté and light white Burgundy or perhaps a red Gamay de Touraine.

Ginger Gewürztraminer or Riesling.

> *Beef with Onions and Ginger* Off-dry German Riesling, one of the more serious Beaujolais Crus.
>
> *Chicken with Ginger* White Rhône, Gewürztraminer.
>
> *Ginger Ice Cream* Asti Spumante or late harvest Sémillon.

Goat Cheese Sancerre, New World Sauvignon, Pinot Blanc.

> *Grilled Goat Cheese* Loire reds.

Goose A good Rhône red like Hermitage, Côte Rôtie, or a crisp Barbera; Pinot Noir from Burgundy, California or Oregon; or even off-dry German Riesling.

> *Confit d'Oie* Best Sauternes, Monbazillac.

Gooseberry

> *Gooseberry Pie* Sweet Madeira, Austrian Trockenbeerenauslese.

Goose Liver

> *Foie Gras* Best Sauternes, Monbazillac.

Grapefruit Sweet Madeira or sherry.

Grouse

> *Roast Grouse* Hermitage, Côte Rôtie, robust Burgundy, or good mature red Bordeaux.

Guinea Fowl Old Burgundy, Cornas, Gamay de Touraine, St. Emilion.

H

Haddock White Bordeaux, Chardonnay, Pinot Blanc, single-vineyard Soave, Australian unoaked Semillon.

Mousse of Smoked Haddock Top white Burgundy.

Smoked Haddock Fino sherry or oaky Chardonnay.

Hake Soave, Sauvignon Blanc.

Halibut White Bordeaux, Muscadet.

Smoked Halibut Oaky Spanish white Rioja, Australian Chardonnay, oaked white Bordeaux.

Ham

Boiled/Roasted/Grilled/Fried Ham Beaujolais-Villages, Gamay de Touraine, slightly sweet German white, Tuscan red, lightish Cabernet (e.g., Chilean), Alsace Pinot Gris, or Muscat.

Braised Ham with Lentils Light, fruity Beaujolais; Côtes du Rhône; Rioja or Navarra Crianza.

Honey-Roast Ham Riesling.

Oak-Smoked Ham Oaky Spanish reds.

Parma Ham (Prosciutto) Try a dry Lambrusco, Tempranillo Joven, or Gamay de Touraine.

Pea and Ham Soup Beaujolais.

Hare

Hare Casserole Good Beaujolais Crus or, for a stronger flavour, try an Australian red.

Jugged Hare Argentinian reds; tough Italians like Amarone, Barolo, and Barbaresco; inky reds from Bandol or the Rhône.

Hazelnut Vin Santo, Liqueur Muscat.

Warm Bacon, Hazelnut, and Sorrel Salad New World Sauvignon Blanc, California Fumé Blanc, or a good Pouilly Fumé.

Herbs (see individual entries)

Herring

Fresh Herrings Sauvignon Blanc, Muscadet, Frascati, or cider.

Roll-Mop Herring Savoie, dry Vinho Verde, Grüner Veltliner, Akvavit, cold lager.

Salt Herring White Portuguese.

Sprats Muscadet, Vinho Verde.

Honey Tokaji.

Baklava Moscatel de Setúbal.

Horseradish

Roast Beef with Horseradish California Pinot Noir or mature Burgundy.

Houmous French dry whites, Retsina, Vinho Verde.

I

Ice Cream (vanilla) Try Marsala, Australian Liqueur Muscat, Muscadelle, or Pedro Ximénez sherry.

Indian (general) Gewürztraminer (spicy dishes), New World Chardonnay (creamy/yogurt dishes), New Zealand Sauvignon Blanc (Tandoori).

J

Japanese Barbecue Sauce
  Teriyaki Spicy reds like Zinfandel or Portuguese reds.
John Dory Good, white Burgundy or Australian Chardonnay.

K

Kedgeree New World Sauvignon Blanc.
Kidney
  Lambs' Kidneys Rich, spicy reds – Barolo, Cabernet Sauvignon, Rioja.
  Steak and Kidney Pie/Pudding Bordeaux, Australian Cabernet Sauvignon,
    Southern Rhône reds or Rioja.
Kippered Herrings New World Chardonnay or a good fino sherry. Or, if
    you are having them for breakfast, Champagne, a cup of tea, or Dutch gin.

L

Lamb
  Casserole Rich and warm Cabernet-based reds from France, or California
    Zinfandel.
  Cassoulet Serious white Rhône, Marsanne, or Roussanne; or reds including
    Grenache and Syrah from the Rhône, berryish Italian reds, or Zinfandel.
  Cutlets or Chops Cru Bourgeois Bordeaux, Chilean Cabernet.
  Haggis Beaujolais, Côtes du Rhône, Côtes du Roussillon, Spanish reds,
    malt whisky.
  Irish Stew A good simple South American or Eastern European Cabernet
    works best.
  Kabobs Modern (fruity) Greek reds or sweetly ripe Australian
    Cabernet/Shiraz.
  Kleftiko (Lamb Shanks Baked with Thyme) Greek red from Nemea,
    Beaujolais, light Cabernet Sauvignon.
  Lancashire Hotpot Robust country red – Cahors, Fitou.
  Moussaka Brambly Northern Italian reds (Barbera, Dolcetto, etc), Beaujolais,
    Pinotage, Zinfandel, or try some good Greek wine from a modern producer.
  Roast Lamb Bordeaux, New Zealand Cabernet Sauvignon, Cahors, Rioja
    reserva, reds from Chile.
  Roast Lamb with Thyme Try a New Zealand Cabernet Sauvignon or Bourgeuil.
  Shepherd's Pie Barbera, Cabernet Sauvignon, Minervois, Zinfandel, Beaujolais,
    Southern French red.
Langoustine Muscadet, Soave, South African Sauvignon.
Leek
  Cock-a-Leekie Dry New World white, simple red Rhône.
  Leek in Cheese Sauce Dry white Bordeaux, Sancerre, or Australian Semillon.
  Leek and Potato Soup Dry whites, Côtes de Gascogne.
  Vichyssoise Dry whites, Chablis, Bordeaux Blanc.

Lemon
  Lemon Cheesecake Moscato d'Asti.
  Lemon Meringue Pie Malmsey Madeira.
  Lemon Sorbet Late harvest Sémillon or sweet Tokaji.
  Lemon Tart Sweet Austrian and German wines.
  Lemon Zest Sweet fortified Muscats.
Lemon Grass New Zealand Sauvignon, Sancerre, Viognier.
Lemon Sole Chardonnay.
Lentils Earthy country wines, Côtes du Rhône.
  Chicken Dhansak Sémillon or New Zealand Sauvignon.
  Dhal Soup Try Soave or Pinot Bianco.
Lime Australian Verdelho, Grüner Veltliner, Furmint.
  Kaffir Lime Leaves (in Thai Green Curry, etc.) Big-flavoured New World
    whites or Pinot Blanc from Alsace.
  Thai Beef Salad New Zealand or South African Sauvignon Blanc,
    Gewürztraminer, Pinot Blanc.
Liver
  Calves' Liver Good Italian Cabernet, Merlot, or mature Chianti.
  Fegato alla Veneziana Nebbiolo, Zinfandel, or Petite Sirah.
  Lambs' Liver Chianti, Australian Shiraz, or Merlot.
  Liver and Bacon Côtes du Rhône, Zinfandel, Pinotage.
Lobster Good white Burgundy.
  Lobster Bisque Grenache rosé, fresh German white, Chassagne-Montrachet,
    dry Amontillado sherry.
  Lobster in a Rich Sauce Champagne, Chablis, fine white Burgundy, good
    white Bordeaux.
  Lobster Salad Champagne, Chablis, German or Alsace Riesling.
  Lobster Thermidor Rich beefy Côtes du Rhône, oaky Chardonnay, or a
    good deep-coloured rosé from Southern France.

M

Mackerel Best with Vinho Verde, Albariño, Sancerre,
    and New Zealand Sauvignon.
  Smoked Mackerel Bourgogne Aligoté, Alsace
    Pinot Gris.
  Smoked Mackerel Pâté Sparkling Vouvray,
    Muscadet.
Mallard Côte Rôtie, Ribera del Duero, or Zinfandel.
Mango Best eaten in the bathtub with a friend and
    a bottle of Champagne! Otherwise, go for Asti
    Spumante or Moscato.
Marjoram Provençal reds.
Marsala
  Chops in Marsala Sauce Australian Marsanne.
Mascarpone
  Tiramisu Sweet fortified Muscat, Vin Santo, Torcolato.
Meat (general – also see individual entries)

Mackerel

Cold Meats Juicy, fruity reds, low in tannin, i.e., Beaujolais, Côtes du Rhône, etc.
Consommé Medium/Amontillado sherry.
Meat Pâté Beaujolais, Fumé Blanc, lesser white Burgundy.
Mixed Grill Versatile uncomplicated red – Australian Shiraz, Rioja.
Melon Despite its apparently innocent, juicy sweetness, melon can be very
   unfriendly to most wines. Try tawny port, sweet Madeira or sherry,
   Quarts de Chaume, late harvest Riesling.
Mincemeat
Mince Pie Rich, sweet, late harvest wine or botrytis-affected Sémillon.
Mint Beaujolais, young Pinot Noir, or try a New Zealand or Australian Riesling.
Thai Beef Salad New Zealand or South African Sauvignon Blanc,
   Gewürztraminer, Pinot Blanc.
Monkfish A light, fruity red such as Bardolino, Valpolicella, La Mancha Joven,
   or most Chardonnays.
Mushroom Merlot-based reds, good Northern Rhône,
   top Piedmontese reds.
Mushrooms à la Greque Sauvignon Blanc or
   fresh, modern Greek white.
Mushroom Soup Bordeaux Blanc, Côtes de
   Gasgogne.
Risotto with Fungi Porcini Top-notch Piedmontese
   reds – mature Barbera, Barbaresco, or earthy
   Southern French reds.
Stuffed Mushrooms Chenin Blanc, Sylvaner.
Wild Mushrooms Nebbiolo, red Bordeaux.
Mussels Sauvignon Blanc, light Chardonnay,
   Muscadet Sur Lie.
Moules Marinières Bordeaux Blanc or Muscadet
   Sur Lie.

Mushroom Soup

New Zealand Green-Lipped Mussels New Zealand Sauvignon Blanc.
Mustard Surprisingly, can help red Bordeaux and other tannic reds to go with beef.
Dijon Mustard Beaujolais.
French Mustard White Bordeaux.
Steak with Dijon Mustard New World Cabernet Sauvignon or Australian Shiraz.
Wholegrain Mustard Beaujolais, Valpolicella.

N

Nectarine Sweet German Riesling.
Nutmeg Rioja, Australian Shiraz, or, for sweet dishes, Australian late harvest.
Nuts Amontillado sherry, Vin Santo, and Tokaji.

O

Octopus Rueda white or a fresh, modern Greek white.
Olives Dry sherry, Muscadet, Retsina.

Salade Niçoise Muscadet, Vinho Verde, or Beaujolais.

Tapenade Dry sherry or Madeira.

Onion

Caramelized Onions Shiraz-based Australians, Zinfandel from the US, or a good Pinotage.

French Onion Soup Sancerre or dry, unoaked Sauvignon Blanc; Aligoté; white Bordeaux.

Onion/Leek Tart Alsace Gewürztraminer, New World Riesling, or a good unoaked Chablis.

Orange

Caramelised Oranges Asti Spumante, Sauternes, or Muscat de Beaumes de Venise.

Crêpe Suzette Sweet Champagne, Moscato d'Asti.

Orange Sorbet Moscato or sweet Tokaji.

Orange Zest Dry Muscat, Amontillado sherry.

Oregano Provençal reds, red Lambrusco, serious Chianti, or lightish Zinfandel.

Oxtail Australian Cabernet, good Bordeaux.

Oysters Champagne; Chablis; or other crisp, dry white.

Oyster Sauce

Beef and Snow Peas in Oyster Sauce Crisp, dry whites like Muscadet or a Northern Italian Lugana or Pinot Bianco, white Rhône, Gewürztraminer.

P

Paprika

Goulash Eastern European red like Bulgarian Cabernet or Mavrud, Hungarian Kadarka, or Australian Shiraz.

Parmesan Salice Salentino, Valpolicella.

Baked Chicken Parmesan with Basil Chenin Blanc, Riesling.

Parsley Dry, Italian whites – Bianco di Custoza, Nebbiolo, or Barbera.

Parsley Sauce Pinot Grigio, Hungarian Furmint, lightly oaked Chardonnay

Partridge

Roast Partridge Australian Shiraz, Gevrey-Chambertin, Pomerol, or St. Emilion.

Pasta

Lasagne Valpolicella, Barbera, Teroldego, Australian Verdelho or Sauvignon.

Pasta with Meat Sauce Chianti, Bordeaux Rouge.

Pasta with Pesto Sauce New Zealand Sauvignon Blanc, Valpolicella.

Pasta with Seafood Sauce Soave, Sancerre.

Ravioli with Spinach and Ricotta Pinot Bianco/Grigio, Cabernet d'Anjou.

Spaghetti with Tomato Sauce California Cabernet, Zinfandel, Chianti.

Spaghetti Vongole Pinot Bianco, Lugana.

Tagliatelle Carbonara Pinot Grigio or a fresh, red Bardolino or Beaujolais.

Peach Sweet German Riesling.

Peaches in Wine Riesling Auslese, Riesling Gewürztraminer Vendange Tardive, sweet Vouvray.

Peanuts

Beef in Peanut Curry New World Chardonnay; an aromatic, white Rhône.

Satay Gewürztraminer.

Pepper (corns)

    Steak au Poivre   Cabernet Sauvignon, Chianti, Barbera, Rhône reds, Shiraz, or Rioja.

Peppers (fresh green, red)   New Zealand Cabernet, Loire reds, crisp Sauvignon Blanc, Beaujolais, Tuscan red.

Peppers (yellow)   Fruity, Italian reds – Valpolicella, etc.

    Stuffed Peppers   Hungarian red – Bull's Blood; Zinfandel; Chianti; or spicy, Rhône reds.

Pheasant   Top-class, red Burgundy; good American Pinot Noir; mature Hermitage.

    Pheasant Casserole   Top class, red Burgundy; mature Hermitage.

    Pheasant Pâté   Côtes du Rhône, Alsace Pinot Blanc.

Pigeon   Good red Burgundy, rich Southern Rhône. Chianti also goes well.

    Warm Pigeon Breasts on Salad   Merlot-based Bordeaux or Cabernet Rosé.

Pike   Eastern European white.

Pine Nuts

    Pesto Sauce   New Zealand Sauvignon Blanc, Valpolicella.

Pizza

    Fiorentina   Pinot Bianco, Pinot Grigio, Vinho Verde, Sauvignon Blanc.

    Margherita   Pinot Grigio, light Zinfandel, dry Grenache rosé.

    Napoletana   Verdicchio, Vernaccia de San Gimignano, white Rhône.

    Quattro Formaggi   Pinot Grigio, Frascati, Bianco di Custoza.

    Quattro Stagioni   Valpolicella, Bardolino, light Chianti, good Soave.

Plaice   White Burgundy, South American Chardonnay, Sauvignon Blanc.

Plum

    Plum Pie   Trockenbeerenauslese, Côteaux du Layon.

Pork

    Cassoulet   Serious white Rhône, Marsanne, or Roussanne; or reds including Grenache and Syrah from the Rhône, berryish, Italian reds, or Zinfandel.

    Pork Casserole   Mid-weight, earthy reds like Minervois, Navarra, or Montepulciano d'Abruzzo.

    Pork Pie   Spicy reds, Shiraz, Grenache.

    Pork with Prunes   Cahors, mature Chinon, or other Loire red, or rich, southern French wine such as Corbières, Minervois, or Faugères.

    Pork Rillettes   Pinot Blanc d'Alsace, Menetou-Salon Rouge.

    Pork and Sage Sausages   Barbera, Côtes du Rhône.

    Pork Sausages   Spicy Rhône reds, Barbera.

    Pork Spare Ribs   Zinfandel, Australian Shiraz.

    Roast Pork   Rioja reserva, New World Pinot Noir, dry Vouvray.

    Roast Pork with Apple Sauce   Off-dry Vouvray or Riesling.

    Saucisson Sec   Barbera, Cabernet Franc, Alsace Pinot Blanc, or Beaujolais.

    Spare Ribs with Barbecue Sauce   Fruity Australian Shiraz, Grenache, or Zinfandel; spicy Côtes du Rhône from a ripe vintage or an off-dry white.

    Szechuan-Style Pork   Dry, aromatic whites; Alsace Pinot Gris; Riesling; Grenache rosé; beer.

Prawns   White Bordeaux; dry, Australian Riesling; Gavi.

    Prawn Cocktail   Light, fruity whites – German Riesling.

    Prawns in Garlic   Vinho Verde, Pinot Bianco.

    Prawn Vol-au-Vents   White Bordeaux, Muscadet.

    Thai Prawns   Gewürztraminer; dry, aromatic Riesling; or New Zealand Sauvignon Blanc.

Prunes Australian, late harvest Semillon.
  Pork with Prunes and Cream Sweet, Chenin-based wines or good
    Mosel Spätlese.
  Prune Ice Cream Muscat de Beaumes de Venise.

Q

Quail Light, red Burgundy; full-flavoured, white Spanish wines.
Quince Lugana.
  Braised Venison with Quince Jelly Rich and fruity Australian or Chilean reds;
    good, ripe Spanish Rioja; or a Southern French red.

R

Rabbit
  Rabbit Casserole Red Burgundy, New World Pinot Noir, or mature Châteauneuf-
    du-Pape.
  Rabbit in Cider Muscadet, demi-sec Vouvray, cider, or Calvados.
  Rabbit with Mustard Franken wine or Czech Pilsner beer.
  Rabbit in Red Wine with Prunes Good, mature Chinon or other Loire red.
  Roast Rabbit Tasty, simple, young Rhône – red, white, or rosé.
Raspberries New World, late harvest Riesling; Champagne; Beaujolais;
    demi-sec Champagne.
  Raspberry Fool Vouvray Moelleux.
Ratatouille Bulgarian red, Chianti, simple Rhône
    or Provence red, Portuguese reds, New Zealand
    Sauvignon Blanc.
Redcurrant (Cumberland sauce) Rioja,
    Australian Shiraz.
Red Mullet Dry rosé, California, Washington or
    Australian Chardonnay.
Rhubarb
  Rhubarb Pie Moscato d'Asti, Alsace, German or
    Austrian late harvest Riesling.
Rice
  Rice Pudding Monbazillac, sweet Muscat, Asti
    Spumante, or California Orange Muscat.

Ratatouille

Roast Lamb with Garlic and Rosemary Earthy
    soft reds like California Petite Sirah, Rioja, or Zinfandel.
Rocket Lugana, Pinot Blanc.
Roquefort The classic match is Sauternes or Barsac, but almost any full-flavoured,
    botrytized sweet wine will be a good partner for strong, creamy, blue cheese.
Rosemary Light red Burgundy or Pinot Noir.
Rum
  Flambéed Banana with Rum Jurançon, Tokaji, Pedro Ximénez sherry,
    and rum.

S

Saffron Dry whites especially Chardonnay.
  Bass in Saffron Sauce Riesling (German, Australian, or Austrian), Viognier.
  Paella with Seafood White Penedés, unoaked Rioja, Navarra, Provence rosé.
Sage Chianti, or country reds from the Languedoc. Otherwise Sauvignon
    Blancs are great, especially Chilean.
  Roast Chicken, Goose, or Turkey with Sage and Onion Stuffing Italian reds,
    especially Chianti; soft, plummy Merlots; fruity Rioja; and brambly Zinfandel.
Salami Good, beefy Mediterranean rosé; Sardinian red; Rhône red; Zinfandel;
    dry, aromatic Hungarian white.
Salmon
  Carpaccio of Salmon Cabernet Franc, Chardonnay, Australian reds, red
    Loire, Portuguese reds, Puligny-Montrachet.
  Grilled Salmon White Rhône (especially Viognier).
  Poached Salmon Chablis; good, white Burgundy; other Chardonnay;
    Alsace Muscat; white Bordeaux.
  Poached Salmon with Hollandaise Muscat, Riesling, good Chardonnay.
  Salmon Pâté Best white Burgundy.
  Salmon Trout Light Pinot Noir from the Loire, New Zealand; good, dry,
    unoaked Chardonnay, Chablis, etc.
Sardines Muscadet, Vinho Verde, light and fruity reds such as Loire,
    Gamay.
Scallops Chablis and other unoaked Chardonnay.
  Coquilles St. Jacques White Burgundy.
  Marinated Scallops with Bacon Fino sherry or mature Riesling.
  Scallops Mornay White Burgundy, Riesling Spätlese.
Sea Bass Good white Burgundy.
  Bass in Saffron Sauce Riesling (German, Austrian, or Australian), Viognier.
Seafood (general – also see individual entries)
  Platter of Seafood Sancerre, Muscadet.
  Seafood Salad Soave, Pinot Grigio, Muscadet, lightly oaked Chardonnay
Sesame Seeds Oaked Chardonnay.
Shrimps Albariño, Sancerre, New World Sauvignon, Arneis.
  Potted Shrimps New World Chardonnay, Marsanne.
Skate Bordeaux white, Côtes de Gascogne, Pinot Bianco.
Smoked Salmon Chablis, Alsace Pinot Gris, white
    Bordeaux.
  Avocado and Smoked Salmon Lightly oaked
    Chardonnay, Fumé Blanc, or Australian
    Semillon.
  Smoked Salmon Paté English oaked Fumé Blanc,
    New Zealand Chardonnay.
Smoked Trout
  Smoked Trout Paté Good, white Burgundy.
Snapper Australian or South African, dry white.
Sole Chablis, Muscadet.
Sorbet Like ice cream, these can be too cold/sweet
    for most wines. Try Australian fortified Muscats.
Sorrel Dry Loire Chenin or Sauvignon Blanc.

Sole

Soy Sauce Zinfandel or Australian Verdelho.
Spinach Pinot Grigio, Lugana.
  Eggs Florentine Chablis or unoaked Chardonnay, Pinot Blanc, Sémillion.
  Spinach/Pasta Bakes Soft, Italian reds (Bardolino, Valpolicella), rich whites.
Spring Rolls Pinot Gris, Gewürztraminer, or other aromatic whites.
Squab Good, red Burgundy; rich Southern Rhône; or Chianti.
  Warm Squab Breasts on Salad Merlot-based Bordeaux or Cabernet Rosé.
Squid Gamay de Touraine; Greek, Spanish, or Italian white.
  Squid in Batter Muscadet.
  Squid in Ink Nebbiolo or Barbera.
Stilton Tawny port.
Strawberries – No Cream Surprisingly, red Rioja, Burgundy
    (or other young Pinot Noir). More conventionally, sweet Muscats
    or fizzy Moscato.
  Strawberries and Cream Vouvray Moelleux, Monbazillac
  Strawberry Meringue Late harvest Riesling.
  Strawberry Mousse Sweet or fortified Muscat.
Sweetbreads Lightly oaked Chablis; Pouilly-Fuissé; or light, red Bordeaux.
  Sweetbreads in Mushroom, Butter, and Cream sauce Southern French
    whites, Vin de Pays Chardonnay.
Sweet and Sour Dishes (general) Gewürztraminer, Sauvignon Blanc
    (unoaked), or beer.

T

Taramasalata Oaked Chardonnay or Fumé Blanc.
Tarragon White Menetou-Salon or South African Sauvignon Blanc.
  Roast/Grilled Chicken with Tarragon Dry Chenin Blanc, Vouvray, dry Chenin.
Thyme Ripe and fruity Provençal reds, Rioja, Northern Italian whites.
  Roast Lamb with Thyme New Zealand Cabernet Sauvignon, Bourgeuil.
Toffee Moscatel de Setúbal, Eiswein.
  Banoffee Pie Sweet Tokaji.
Tomato
  Gazpacho Fino sherry, white Rioja.
  Pasta in a Tomato Sauce California Cabernet, Zinfandel, Chianti.
  Tomato Soup Sauvignon Blanc.
Tripe Earthy, French country red; Minervois; Cahors; Fitou.
Trout Pinot Blanc, Chablis.
  Smoked Trout Bourgogne Aligoté, Gewürztraminer, Pinot Gris.
  Trout with Almonds Bianco di Custoza, Pinot Blanc.
Truffles Red Burgundy, old Rioja, Barolo, or Hermitage.
Tuna
  Carpaccio of Tuna Australian Chardonnay, red Loire, Beaujolais.
  Fresh Tuna Alsace Pinot Gris, Australian Chardonnay, Beaujolais.
Turbot Best white Burgundy, top California or Australian Chardonnay.
Turkey
  Roast Turkey Beaujolais, light Burgundy, and rich or off-dry whites.
  Roast Turkey with Chestnut Stuffing Rhône, Merlot, or mature Burgundy.

V

Vanilla Liqueur Muscat.
  Crème Brûlée Jurançon Moelleux, Tokaji.
  Custard Monbazillac, sweet Vouvray.
Veal
  Blanquette de Veau Aromatic, spicy whites from Alsace or from the
    Northern Rhône.
  Roast Veal Light, Italian whites, or fairly light reds – Spanish or Loire;
    St. Emilion.
  Wienerschnitzel Austrian Grüner Veltliner or Alsace or Hungarian
    Pinot Blanc.
Vegetables
  Roasted and Grilled Light, juicy reds; Beaujolais; Sancerre; and Sauvignon
    Blanc. Unoaked or lightly oaked Chardonnay.
  Vegetable Soup Pinot Blanc, rustic reds such as Corbières, or southern
    Italian reds.
  Vegetable Terrine Good New World Chardonnay.
Venison Pinotage; rich red Rhône; mature Burgundy; earthy, Italian reds.
  Venison Casserole Australian Shiraz, American Zinfandel, South African red
    (Pinotage).
Vinegar
  Choucroute Garnie White Alsace (especially Riesling), Italian Pinot Grigio, or
    Beaujolais.
  Sauerkraut Pilsner beer.

W

Walnut Tawny port, sweet Madeira.
Watercress
  Watercress Soup Aromatic dry Riesling (Alsace or Australia).
Whitebait Fino sherry, Spanish red/white (Albariño, Garnacha, Tempranillo),
  Soave.

Y

Yams Depends on the sauce. When subtly prepared, try Pinot Blanc.
Yogurt Needs full-flavoured wines, such as Australian Semillon or
  New World Chardonnay.

Z

Zabaglione Rich sweet Marsala, Australian Liqueur Muscat, or a fortified
  French Muscat.

A–Z OF
WINE

HOW TO READ THE ENTRIES

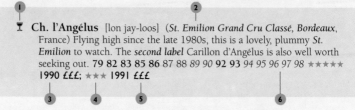

Ⓘ **Ch. l'Angélus** [lon jay-loos] (*St. Emilion Grand Cru Classé, Bordeaux, France*) Flying high since the late 1980s, this is a lovely, plummy *St. Emilion* to watch. The *second label* Carillon d'Angélus is also well worth seeking out. 79 **82 83 85 86** 87 88 *89 90* **92 93** *94 95 96 97 98* ★★★★★ **1990** £££; ★★★ *1991* £££

Ⓘ Names of wines are accompanied by a glass symbol: Ⓘ
Grape varieties are accompanied by a bunch of grapes: ❦
Wine regions appear in burgundy type.

② Words that have their own entry elsewhere in the A–Z appear in italic. Recommended wines may also be cross-referenced.

③ Throughout this section, examples are given of recommended vintages, producers, or wines which represent good examples of the region, style or maker.

④ Recommended wines are accompanied by stars:

　　★★★★★ *outstanding in their style.*
　　★★★★ *excellent in their style.*
　　★★★ *good in their style.*

⑤ Prices are indicated using the following symbols:

　　£ *under £7*　　**££** *£7–£15*　　**£££** *£15–£30*　　**££££** *over £30*

⑥ Poor vintages are not listed. Particularly good years that are ready to drink now are featured in bold; vintages that will improve with keeping are in italic.

PRONUNCIATION GUIDE

All but the most common words are followed by square brackets [ ], which enclose pronunciation guides. These use the "sounding-out" phonetic method, with the accented syllable (if there is one) indicated by capital letters. For example, **Spätlese** is pronounced as **SHPAYT-lay-zuh**. The basic sounds employed in this book's pronunciations are as follows:

a *as in* **can**	**ah** *as in* **father**	**ay** *as in* **day**	**ur** *as in* **turn**
ch *as in* **church**	**kh** *as in* **loch**	**y** *as in* **yes**	**zh** *as in* **vision**
ee *as in* **see**	**eh** *as in* **get**	**g** *as in* **game**	**i** *as in* **pie**
ih *as in* **if**	**j** *as in* **gin**	**k** *as in* **cat**	**o** *as in* **hot**
oh *as in* **soap**	**oo** *as in* **food**	**ow** *as in* **cow**	**uh** *as in* **up**

Foreign sounds To represent sounds not common in English, the following spellings are used in the pronunciation guide: **eu** is like a cross between **oo** and **a**; an italicized **n** or **m** is silent and the preceding vowel sounds nasal; an **ñ** is like an **n** followed by a **y** (as in **Bourgogne**); an italicized **r** sounds like a cross between **r** and **w**; **rr** sounds like a rolled **r**.

A

Abacus (*Napa*, California) An innovative (for California) concept by the long-established ZD winery of blending tiny quantities of different red vintages. (*Vega Sicilia* in Spain did it first). Quality is high but prices are astronomical.

Abadia Retuerta [ah-bah-dee-yah Reh-twehr-tah] (Spain) Close to *Ribera del Duero*, this large new venture benefits from the expertise of Pascal Delbeck of *Ch. Belair* in *St. Emilion*. Several equally recommendable cuvées, including Palomar, Pago Negralato, Valdebon, and Campanariol.

Abazzia Sant'Anastasia [ah-baht-zee-yah San-tan-nah-stah-zee-yah] (*Sicily* Italy) The hottest new star in Sicily, this estate makes a Cabernet – Litra – that can beat the *Super-Tuscans*, and some pretty fine *Chardonnay* – Baccante – as well as reds from the local Nero d'Avola.

Abboccato [ah-boh-kah-toh] (Italy) Semi-dry.

Abel-Lepitre [ah-bel luh-pee-tre] (*Champagne*, France) The wine to look for here is the Réserve Blanc de Blancs Cuvée C.

Abfüller/Abfüllung [ap-few-ler/ap-few-loong] (Germany) Bottler/bottled by.

Abocado [ah-boh-kah-doh] (Spain) Semi-dry.

Abreu Vineyards [Eh-broo] (*Napa*, California) Cult St. Helena winery with vineyards whose grapes go to such top *Napa* names as *Harlan Estate*. Don't bother to go looking in the stores, though; to lay your hands on a bottle, you'll have to be on the mailing list.

Abruzzi/zzo [ah-broot-zee/zoh] (Italy) Region on the east coast, with often dull *Trebbiano* whites and fast-improving *Montepulciano* reds. Castello di Salle; Dino Illuminati; Gianni Masciarelli; Eduardo Valentini.

AC (France) See *Appellation Contrôlée*.

Acacia [a-kay-shah] (*Carneros*, California) Long-established, but often underrated producer of *Chardonnay* and *Pinot Noir, Viognier* and *Zinfandel*. Under the same ownership as *Chalone, Edna Valley*, and *Carmenet*.
★★★★★ 1995 Reserve Pinot Noir £££££; ★★★★★ 1997 Chardonnay £££

Accordini [a-kor-DEE-nee] (*Veneto*, Italy) New *Valpolicella* star with fine vineyards. ★★★ 1994 Amarone Acinatico £££

Acetic acid [ah-see-tihk] This volatile acid (CH3COOH) features in small proportions in all wines. Careless winemaking can result in wine being turned into acetic acid, a substance most people know as vinegar.

Acidity Naturally occurring (*tartaric* and malic) acids in the grapes are vital to contributing freshness, and also help to preserve the wine while it ages. In reds and many cool region whites, the malic is often converted to lactic by a natural process known as *malolactic fermentation*, which gives the wines a buttery texture and flavour. In hotter countries (and sometimes cooler ones) the acid level may (not always legally) be adjusted by adding *tartaric* and citric acid.

Ackerman-Laurance [ah-kehr-man Loh-ronss] (*Loire*, France) One of the Loire's most reliable sparkling wine producers. Privilège is the top wine.

Aconcagua Valley [ah-kon-kar-gwah] (*Central Valley*, Chile) Region noted for blackcurranty *Cabernet Sauvignon*. The sub-region is *Casablanca*. Grapes from both are used by many Chilean producers. Concha y Toro, Errazuriz.

Tim Adams (*Clare Valley*, Australia) Highly successful producer of *Riesling*, rich peachy *Semillon*, and deep-flavoured Aberfeldy *Shiraz* and intense peppery Fergus *Grenache*. ★★★★★ 1998 The Fergus £££; ★★★★ 1999 Riesling ££

Adanti [ah-dan-ti] (*Umbria*, Italy) Star producer of spicy reds and herby Grechetto whites. ★★★★ 1997 Rosso dell Umbria Arquata £££

Adega [ah-day-gah] (Portugal) Winery – equivalent to Spanish *bodega*.

Adelaide Hills [ah-dur-layd] (*South Australia*) High-altitude region, long known for classy, lean *Riesling* and *Semillon*; now famous for *Sauvignon Blanc* and *Chardonnay* from *Ashton Hills*; for *Petaluma, Nepenthe*, and *Shaw & Smith*; for *Croser* sparkling wine; and the occasional *Pinot Noir*. See also the new sub-region of *Lenswood*. Ashton Hills; Chain of Ponds; Grosett; Heggies; Henschke; Mountadam; Nepenthe; Penfolds; Shaw & Smith; Geoff Weaver.

A

☒ **Weingut Graf Adelmann** [graf-ah-del-man] (*Württemberg,* Germany) One of the region's best estates, making good reds from grapes such as the *Trollinger,* Lemberger, and Urban. Look for Brüssele'r Spitze wines.

☒ **Adelsheim** [a-del-sime] (*Oregon,* USA) Classy, long-lived, but non-showy *Pinot Noir, Chardonnay,* and *Pinot Gris* from a producer with the look of an Old Testament prophet. ★★★★ 1998 Oregon Reserve Pinot Noir £££

☒ **Age** [ah-khay] (*Rioja,* Spain) Big, modern, highly commercial winery.

🍇 **Aglianico** [ah-lee-AH-nee-koh] (Italy) Thick-skinned grape grown by the Ancient Greeks. Now used to make *Taurasi* and *Aglianico del Vulture.*

☒ **Aglianico del Vulture** [ah-lee-AH-nee-koh del vool-TOO-reh] (*Basilicata,* Italy) Tannic liquoricey-chocolatey blockbusters made in Southern Italy on the hills of an extinct volcano. Older examples are labelled as Vecchio (3 years+) and Riserva (5 years+). Aarmando Martino; **D'Angelo; Basilium; Paternoster.**

☒ **La Agricola** (*Mendoza,* Argentina) One of this go-ahead country's most go-ahead wineries. The top wines are sold under the "Q" range. Picajuan Creek and Santa Julia are labels that are also worth looking out for.

Agricola vitivinicola (Italy) Wine estate.

Ahr [ahr] (Germany) Northernmost *Anbaugebiet,* making light-bodied reds.

Ajaccio [ah-JAK-see-yoh] (*Corsica,* France) Very mixed fare, but *Comte Peraldi* makes intense reds and whites. See also: **Gie Les Rameaux.**

☒ **Aigle** [eh-gl'] (*Vaud,* Switzerland) One of the few places in the world to find fresh, floral *Chasselas* (known here as *Dorin*). The *Pinot Noir* can be good too. **Baudoux, Testuz.**

🍇 **Airén** [i-REHN] (Spain) The world's most planted white variety. Dull and fortunately more or less restricted to the region of *La Mancha.*

☒ **Alban** (*Central Coast,* California) *Edna Valley* winery making waves with exciting *Rhône-*style reds (esp. *Grenache*) and whites. ★★★★ 1999 Estate Viognier £££

☒ **Albana di Romagna** [ahl-BAH-nah dee roh-MAN-yah] (*Emilia-Romagna,* Italy) Inexplicably, Italy's first white *DOCG.* Traditionally dull but improving white. Passita, sweeter whites are best. **Celli; Umberto Cesari; Conti; Ferrucci; Fattoria Paradiso; Madonia; Uccellina; Zerbina.**

🍇 **Albariño** [ahl-BAH-ree-nyoh] (*Galicia,* Spain) The Spanish name for the Portuguese *Alvarinho* and the peachy-spicy wine made from it in *Rias Baixas.* **Lagar de Cervera; Martin Codex;** *Pazo de Barrantes;* **Salnesu; Valdamor.**

☒ **Castello d'Albola** [KAS-teh-loh DAL-boh-la] (*Tuscany,* Italy) Top Tuscan Estate belonging to the increasingly dynamic firm of *Zonin.*

☒ **Alcamo** [ahl-Cah-moh] (Sicily) Distinctive, rich, dry white made from the local *Catarratto* grape. Rapitalà is the name to look for.

Alcohol This simple compound, technically known as ethanol, is formed by the action of yeast on sugar during fermentation.

🍇 **Aleatico** [ah-lay-AH-tee-koh] (Italy) Red grape producing sweet, *Muscat-*style, often fortified wines. Produces *DOCs* A. di Puglia and A. di Gradoli.

Alella [ah-LEH-yah] (*Catalonia,* Spain) *DO* district producing better whites (from grapes including the *Xarel-lo*) than reds. **Marfil; Marqués de Alella; Parxet.** ★★★★ 2000 Marqués de Alella Clasico £££

Alenquer [ah-lehn-kehr] (*Oeste,* Portugal) Coolish region producing good *Periquita* reds and *Muscat-*style *Fernão Pires* whites. Also making successful efforts from French varietals. **Quinta da Boavista; Quinta de Pancas.**

Alentejo [ah-lehn-TAY-joh] (Portugal) Province north of the Algarve whose elevation from its status as a source of bulk wine has recently been recognized by its division into five *DOCs:* Borba, Portalegre, Redondo, Reguengos, Vidigueira. This is the region where *JM da Fonseca* makes Morgado de Reguengo, *JP Vinhos* produces Tinta da Anfora and *Ch. Lafite* has its Quinta do Carmo. Cooperatives, such as the one at *Borba,* are improving too and this will increasingly be recognized as a place to find both quality and value. **Borba; Cartuxa; Cortes de Cima; Esporão; Herdade de Mouchao; Pera Manca;** *Quinta do Carmo;* Redondo, Jose de Sousa.

Alexander Valley (*Sonoma*, California) *Appellation* in which *Simi*, *Jordan*, *Murphy-Goode*, and *Geyser Peak* are based. *Turley* makes big *Zinfandels* here too. Red: **91 92 94 95** 96 97 98, 99, 00 White: 97 **98**, 99, 00 Alexander Valley Vineyards; Arrowood, Ch. St Jean; Clos du Bois; Geyser Peak; Godwin; Jordan; Marcassin; Murphy-Goode; Seghesio; Silver Oak; Simi; Stonestreet; Turley.

Algarve [ahl-garv] (Portugal) Huge, officially denominated region whose wines are – just about – worth drinking while in the region on holiday.

Ⓣ **Caves Aliança** [ah-lee-an-sah] (Portugal) Modern *Bairrada*, *Douro*, and better-than-average *Dão*. ★★★ 1997 Dão Reserva ££

Alicante (*Valencia*, Spain) Hot region producing generally dull stuff apart from the sweetly honeyed *Moscatels* that appreciate the heat.

🍇 **Alicante-Bouschet** [al-ee-KONT- boo-SHAY] Unusual dark-skinned and fleshed grapes traditionally used (usually illegally) for dyeing pallid reds made from nobler fare. *Rockford* in Australia uses it to make a good rosé.

🍇 **Aligoté** [Al-lee-goh-tay] (*Burgundy*, France) Lesser white grape at its best in the village of *Bouzeron*. G&J-H Goisot; Jayer-Gilles; A&P de Vilaine.

Ⓣ **Alion** [ah-lee-yon] (*Ribera del Duero*, Spain) New venture by the owners of *Vega Sicilia*, with fruitier, more modern wines. ★★★★★ 1995 Reserva £££

Ⓣ **Alkoomi** [al-koo-mee] (*Western Australia*) Young winery to watch, with some very recommendable *Sauvignon* and *Riesling*.

Ⓣ **All Saints** (*Rutherglen*, Australia) Good producer of *Liqueur Muscat* and *Tokay*.

Ⓣ **Allegrini** [ah-leh-GREE-nee] (*Veneto*, Italy) Top-class producer of single-vineyard *Valpolicella* and *Soave*. ★★★★ 1997 Palazzo della Torre £££

Ⓣ **Thierry Allemand** [al-mon] (*Rhône*, France) Producer of classic, concentrated, single-vineyard *Cornas* from a small 6-acre (2.5-hectare) estate. ★★★★★ 1998 Cornas Chaillot £££

Allier [a-lee-yay] (France) Spicy oak favoured by makers of white wine.

Ⓣ **Almaviva** [al-mah-vee-vah] (*Maipo*, Chile) New, pricy red co-production between *Mouton Rothschild* and *Concha y Toro*. ★★★★ 1997 £££

Almacenista [al-mah-theh-nee-stah] (*Jerez*, Spain) Fine unblended sherry from a single *solera* – the sherry equivalent of a single malt whisky. Lustau.

Ⓣ **Aloxe-Corton** [a-loss kawr-ton] (*Burgundy*, France) *Côte de Beaune commune* with tough, slow-maturing, sometimes uninspiring reds (including the *Grand Cru Corton*) and potentially sublime whites (including Corton-Charlemagne). Louis Latour's pricy whites can be fine. White: 85 86 88 89 90 92 95 96 97 98 Red: 85 86 87 88 89 90 95 96 97 98 99 Arnoux; Bonneau du Martray; Denis Bousse; Capitan-Gagnerot; Chandon de Briailles; Marius Delarche; Drouhin; Michel Gay; Antonin Guyon; Jadot; Patrick Javillier; Daniel Largeot; Leflaive; Prince de Mérode; André Nudant; Comte Senard; Tollot-Beaut; Michel Voarick.

Alsace [al-sas] (France) Northerly region whose warm microclimate enables producers to make riper-tasting wines than their counterparts across the Rhine. Wines are named after the grapes – *Pinot Noir, Gewürztraminer, Riesling, Pinot Gris, Pinot Blanc* (known as Pinot d'Alsace), *Sylvaner*, and (rarely) *Muscat*. In the right hands, the 50 or so *Grand Cru* vineyards yield better wines. *Late harvest* sweet wines are labelled *Vendange Tardive* and *Sélection des Grains Nobles*. White: 85 86 88 89 90 93 94 95 96 97 98 00 Albrecht; J Becker; Léon Beyer; Paul Blanck; Bott-Geyl; Albert Boxler; Ernest J & F Burn; Joseph Cattin; Marcel Deiss; Jean-Pierre Dirler; Dopff au Moulin; Faller; Hugel; Josmeyer; André Kientzler; Kreydenweiss; Kuentz-Bas; Albert Mann; Meyer-Fonné; Mittnacht-Klack; René Muré; Ostertag; Rolly Gassmann; Schlumberger; Schoffit; Bruno Sorg; Marc Tempé; Trimbach; Weinbach; Zind Humbrecht.

Ⓣ **Elio Altare** [Ehl-lee-yoh al-TAh-ray] (*Piedmont*, Italy) The genial, Svengali-like leader of the *Barolo* revolution and inspirer of *Clerico* and *Roberto Voerzio*. Tragically lost most of his 1998 harvest to mouldy corks. ★★★★★ 1997 Langhe Arborina; £££ ★★★★★ 1995 Barolo £££

Ⓣ **Altesino** [al-TEH-see-noh] (*Tuscany*, Italy) First-class producers of *Brunello di Montalcino, Cabernet* ("Palazzo"), and *Sangiovese* ("Altesi"). ★★★★ 1997 Alte d'Altesi £££

Alto Adige [ahl-toh AH-dee-jay] (Italy) Aka Italian Tyrol and Südtirol. *DOC* for a huge range of whites often from Germanic grape varieties; also light and fruity reds from the *Lagrein* and *Vernatsch* are particularly successful here. Cant. Prod. di Cortaccia; Cant. Prod. di Termeno; Cant. Vit. di Caldaro; Gaierhof; Giorgio Grai; Hofstätter; *Alois Lageder;* Maddalena; *Pojer & Sandri;* San Michele Appiano; Sta Maddalena; *Tiefenbrunner;* Viticoltori Alto-Adige.

🍇 **Alvarinho** [ahl-vah-reen-yoh] (Portugal) White grape aka *Albariño;* at its lemony best in *Vinho Verde* and in the *DO* Alvarinho de Monção.

Amabile [am-MAH-bee-lay] (Italy) Semi-sweet.

🍷 **Castello di Ama** [ah-mah] (*Tuscany,* Italy) Brilliant small *Chianti* estate. Great single vineyard Vigna l'Apparita wines and very fine *Chardonnay.*
★★★★★ 1996 Vigna l'Apparita £££

Amador County [am-uh-dor] (California) Intensely-flavoured, old-fashioned *Zinfandel.* Look for Amador Foothills Winery's old-vine *Zinfandels* and top-of-the-line stuff from *Sutter Home* and *Monteviña.*
Red: 86 87 **88** 89 **90 91** 92 94 95 96 97 99
White: **94** 95 96 97 99 *Quady,* Vino Noceto.

CHIANTI CLASSICO

1997
CASTELLO DI AMA

🍷 **Amarone** [ah-mah-ROH-neh] (*Veneto,* Italy) Literally "bitter"; used to describe *Recioto* wines fermented dry, especially *Amarone della Valpolicella.* Accordini; Ilegrini; Luigi Brunelli; Tommaso Bussola; Corte Sant' Alda; Masi; Angelo Nicolis; Quintarelli; Romano dal Forno; Tedeschi; Viviani; Zenato.

🍷 **Bodegas Amézola de la Mora** [ah-meh-THOH-lah deh lah MAW-rah] (*Rioja,* Spain) Eight-year-old estate producing unusually classy red *Rioja.*

🍇 **Amigne** [ah-meeñ] (*Valais,* Switzerland) Unusual white grape that makes traditional (non fruit-driven) wines in Vétroz. *J-R Germanier; Imesch.*

🍷 **Amity** [am-mi-tee] (*Oregon,* US) Maker of very high-quality berryish Pinot Noir, good dry *Gewürztraminer* and *late-harvest* whites. ★★★★ 1998 Pinot Noir £££

Amontillado [am-mon-tee-yah-doh] (*Jerez,* Spain) Literally "like Montilla." Often pretty basic medium-sweet *sherry,* but ideally fascinating dry, nutty wine. *Gonzalez Byass; Lustau; Sanchez Romate.*

🍷 **Ampelones Vassilou** [am-peh-loh-nehs vas-see-loo] (*Attica,* Greece) Producer of good new-wave Greek wines.

🍷 **Robert Ampeau** [om-poh] (*Burgundy,* France) Traditional Meursault producer whose Perrières is worth looking out for.

Amtliche Prüfungsnummer [am-tlish-eh proof-oong-znoomer] (Germany) Identification number on all *QbA/QmP* labels.

Anbaugebiet [ahn-bow-geh-beet] (Germany) Term for 13 large regions (e.g. *Rheingau*). *QbA* and *QmP* wines must include the name of their *Anbaugebiet* on their labels.

Anderson Valley (*Mendocino,* California) Small, cool area, good for white and sparkling wines including the excellent *Roederer.* Do not confuse with the less impressive Anderson Valley, New Mexico. Red: 89 **90 91 94 95** 96 97 99
White: 96 97 99 Edmeades; *Roederer; Steele;* Williams Selyem.

🍷 **Anderson Vineyard** (*Napa,* California) Stag's Leap producer of intense blackcurrant Cabernet and rich, full-flavoured Chardonnay.

🍷 **Andrew Will** (*Washington State*) Superstar producer of some of *Washington State's* – not to say North America's – best *Merlot, Cabernet Sauvignon,* and ("Sorella") Bordeaux blends. ★★★★★ 1998 Sorella £££

🍷 **Ch. Angélus** [on jay-loos] (*St. Emilion Premier Grand Cru Classé, Bordeaux,* France) Flying high since the late 1980s, this is a plummy, intensely oaky *St. Emilion.* The *second label* Carillon d'Angélus is worth seeking out. 79 81 **82 83** 85 86 87 88 89 90 **93 94** 95 96 97 98 99 00 ★★★★★ 1998 ££££

🍷 **Marquis d'Angerville** [don-jehr-veel] (*Burgundy,* France) Long-established *Volnay* estate with rich, long-lived traditional wines from here and from *Pommard.* ★★★★ 1998 Volnay Champans £££

A

- **Ch d'Angludet** [don gloo-day] (*Cru Bourgeois, Margaux, Bordeaux,* France) With a reputation built by the late Peter Sichel of *Chateau Palmer,* this is classy cassis-flavoured, if slightly earthy, wine that can generally be drunk young but is worth waiting for. 78 **82 83** 85 **86** 88 89 90 **91** 93 *94 95 96 97 98 99 00*
- **Angoves** [an-gohvs] (*Padthaway,* Australia) *Murray River* producer with reliable, inexpensive *Chardonnay* and *Cabernet* and great brandy. Wine quality is now being helped by a move into *Padthaway.*
- **Weingut Paul Anheuser** [an-hoy-zur] (*Nahe,* Germany) One of the most credible supporters of the Trocken movement, and a strong proponent of the *Riesling,* this excellent estate is also unusually successful with its *Ruländer* and *Pinot Noir.*
- **Finca la Anita** [feen-kah lah an-nee-tah] (*Mendoza,* Argentina) Organic, small-scale winery to watch. Innovative wines include a tasty *Syrah-Malbec* blend.
- **Anjou** [on-joo] (*Loire,* France) Dry and *Demi-Sec* whites, mostly from *Chenin Blanc,* with up to 20 per cent *Chardonnay* or *Sauvignon Blanc.* The rosé is almost always awful but there are good, light reds. Look for *Anjou-Villages,* in which *Gamay* is not permitted. Within Anjou, there are smaller, more specific ACs, most importantly *Savennières* and *Coteaux du Layon.* Red: 90 95 **96 97** 98 *99 00* White: **94** 95 96 97 98 *99 00* Sweet White: **85 88 89 90 94** 95 96 97 98 99 00. M. Angeli; Arnault et Fils; Baudoin; *Bouvet-Ladubay; Ch. du Breuil;* Dom. du Closel; Deslesvaux; Ch. de Fesles; Gaudard; Genaiserie; V. Lebreton; Ogereau; J. Pithon; Renou; *Richou;* Soucherie; Y. Soulez; Ch. la Varière.
- **Anjou-Coteaux de la Loire** [Koh-toh duh lah Lwarh] (*Loire,* France) Small, lesser-known appellation for varied styles of Chenin Blanc, including quite luscious late-harvest examples. Do not confuse with *Coteaux du Loir.* Ch. de Putille.
- **Anjou-Villages** [on-joo vee-larj] (*Loire,* France) Increasingly famous red wine appellation, thanks partly to Gérard Dépardieu's presence here as a (seriously committed) winemaker at Ch. de Tigné, and partly to the impressive quality of the juicy, potentially long-lived Cabernet-based red wines. Bablut; Closel; Ch. de Coulaine; C. Daviau; *Ch. de Fesles;* Ogereau; *Richou;* Rochelles; Pierre-Bise; J-Y. Lebreton; V. Lebreton; Ogereau; de Putille Montigilet; Richou; Dom. de Sablonettes; *Pierre Soulez;* Ch. de Tigné.
- *Annata* [ahn-nah-tah] (Italy) *Vintage.*
- **Roberto Anselmi** [an-sehl-mee] (*Veneto,* Italy) Source of classy dry *Soave* Classico wines as well as some extremely serious sweet examples. ★★★★ 1998 I Capitelli Recioto di Soave ££££
- **Antinori** [an-tee-NOR-ree] (*Tuscany,* Italy) Pioneer merchant-producer who has improved the quality of *Chianti,* with his Villa Antinori and Pèppoli, while spearheading the *Super-Tuscan* revolution with *Tignanello, Sassicaia,* and *Solaia,* and producing around 15,000,000 bottles of wine per year. There are also joint ventures in California (*Atlas Peak*), Washington State, and Hungary ★★★★★ 1997 Chianti Classico Badia a Passignano Riserva £££; ★★★★★ 1997 Solaia ££££; ★★★★ 1997 Tignanello ££££
- *AOC* (France) See *Appellation Contrôlée.*
- *AP* (Germany) See *Amtliche Prüfungsnummer.*
- *Appellation Contrôlée (AC/AOC)* [AH-pehl-lah-see-on kon troh-lay] (France) Official designation guaranteeing origin, grape varieties, and method of production and – in theory – quality, though tradition and vested interest combine to allow pretty appalling wines to receive the rubber stamp. Increasingly questioned by quality-conscious producers.
- **Aprémont** [ah-pray-mon] (Eastern France) Floral, slightly *petillant* white from skiing region. Marc Portaz; B&C Richel; Ch. de la Violette.
- *Apulia* [ah-pool-ee-yah] (Italy) See *Puglia.*
- **Aquileia** [ah-kwee-lay-ah] (*Friuli-Venezia Giulia,* Italy) *DOC* for easy-going, single-variety wines. The *Refosco* can be plummily refreshing. Tenuta Beltrame; Zonin.

A

Agricola Aquitania [ah-gree-koh-lah ah-kee-tah-nee-ya] (*Maipo*, Chile) Estate founded by Paul Pontallier (of Ch. Margaux) and Bruno Prats (formerly of Ch. Cos d'Fstournel) and overlooking the city of Santiago and close to premium housing land. Early vintages of the *Cabernet* were rather forbidding (and suffered from being unoaked). More recent efforts are richer, thanks partly to older vines and partly to a stay in cask. The top wine is Paul Bruno and the second wine, Uno Fuero.

Aragón [ah-rah-GONN] (Spain) Slowly up-and-coming region in which are situated Campo de Borja, Cariñena, Somontano.

Arbois [ahr-bwah] (Eastern France) AC region with light *Trousseau* and *Pinot Noir* reds and nutty dry Savignan (not to be confused with the Sauvignon) and *Chardonnay* whites. Also *sherry*-like *Vin Jaune*, sweet *Vin de Paille*, and sparkling wine. **Aviet; Ch d'Arlay; Bourdy; Dugois; Fruitière Viticole; Lornet; la Pinte; J Puffeney; Rolet; A&M Tissot; J Tissot.**

Ch. d' Arche [dahrsh] (*Sauternes 2ème Cru Classé, Bordeaux*, France) Greatly improved, but still slightly patchy. 83 **86 88 89** 90 93 94 95 97 98

Archery Summit (*Oregon*, USA) A recent venture in Yamhill County in Oregon by Gary Andrus of *Pine Ridge* in Napa. Both Pinot Noir and Pinot Gris are impressive – if pricy. ★★★★★ **1998 Pinot Noir Red Hills Estate £££**

Viña Ardanza [veen-yah ahr-dan-thah] (*Rioja*, Spain) Highly reliable, fairly full-bodied, long-lived, classic red Rioja made with a high proportion (40 per cent) of *Grenache*; good, oaky white, too. ★★★★ **1995 Tinto Reserva ££**

d'Arenberg [dar-ren-burg] (*McLaren Vale*, Australia) Excellent up-and-coming producer with memorably named, impressive sweet and dry table wines, and unusually dazzling fortifieds. ★★★★★ **1998 The Dead Arm £££; ★★★★★ 1998 The Ironstone Pressings £££.**

Argentina Fast up-and-coming nation with fine *Malbec*. It is also good for its *Cabernet* and *Merlot*, which have a touch more backbone than many efforts from Chile; and there are interesting wines made from Italian and French varieties. *Chardonnays* and grapey whites from the *Muscat*-like *Torrontes* are worthwhile too. **La Agricola; Finca la Anita; Leoncio Arizu; Balbi; Luigi Bosca; Canale; Catena; M Chandon** (Paul Galard; Terrazas); **Esmeralda; Etchart; Lurton; Morande; Navarro Correas; Norton; la Rural; San Telmo; Santa Ana; Torino; Trapiche; Weinert.**

Tenuta di Argiano [teh-noo-tah dee ahr-zhee-ahn-noh] (*Tuscany*, Italy) Instant success story, with top-class vineyards, and lovely juicy reds. ★★★★ **1995 Brunello di Montalcino ££££; ★★★★★ 1998 Solengo ££££**

Argyle (*Oregon*, US) Classy sparkling wine and still wines from Brian Croser (of *Petaluma*). ★★★★ **1997 Blanc de Blancs £££; ★★★★ 1998 Willamette Valley Reserve Chardonnay £££**

Arietta [ahr-ree-yeht-tah] (Napa, California) Maker of classy Bordeaux blends which, unusually, mimic Cheval Blanc by marrying *Merlot* with *Cabernet Franc*.

Ch. d'Arlay [dahr-lay] (*Jura*, France) Reliable producer of nutty *Vin Jaune* and light, earthy-raspberry Pinot Noir. ★★★★ **1998 Arbois Chardonnay £££**

Leoncio Arizu [Ah-ree-zoo] (*Mendoza*, Argentina) Variable, old-established producer. Also owns *Luigi Bosca*

Dom. de l'Arlot [dur-lahr-loh] (*Burgundy*, France) Brilliant, award-winning *Nuits-St.-Georges* estate under the same – insurance company – ownership as *Ch. Pichon-Longueville*. Delicate modern reds (including an increasingly impressive *Vosne-Romanée*) and a rare example of white *Nuits-St.-Georges*. ★★★★ **1998 Clos des Forêts £££**

Ch. d'Armailhac [darh-mi-yak] (*Pauillac 5ème Cru Classé, Bordeaux*, France). The wines from this château come from the same stable as *Mouton-Rothschild*, and show similar rich flavours, though never the same elegance. 82 83 85 **86 88 89** 90 92 93 94 95 96 97 98 99 00 ★★★★ **1998 ££££**

A

Ŧ Dom. du Comte Armand [komt-arh-mon] (*Burgundy*, France) The top wine from the Canadian-born winemaker here is the exceptional *Pommard Clos des Epeneaux*, but the *Auxey-Duresses* and *Volnay les Fremiets* are fine too. ★★★★ 1998 Pommard Clos des Epeneaux £££

❦ Arneis [ahr-nay-ees] (*Piedmont*, Italy) Spicy white; makes good, young, unoaked wine. **Deletto; Ceretto; Funtanin; Malvira; Serafino; Voerzio.**

Ŧ Ch. l' Arrosée, [lah-roh-say] (*St. Emilion Grand Cru Classé, Bordeaux,* France) Small, well-sited property with fruity intense wines. 79 81 **82** 83 **85 86** 88 **89** 90 **93** 94 95 96 97 98 99 00 ★★★★ 1995 ££££

Ŧ Arrowood (*Sonoma Valley,* California) Fine *Chardonnay, Merlot, Pinot Blanc, Viognier,* and *Cabernet* from former *Ch. St. Jean* winemaker. ★★★★ 1996 Sonoma Special Reserve Cabernet Sauvignon ££££

Ŧ Ismael Arroyo [uh-Roy-oh] (*Ribera del Duero*, Spain) A name to watch for flavoursome reds. ★★★★ 1997 Val Sotillo £££

Ŧ Artadi [ahr-tah-dee] (*Rioja*, Spain) Up-and-coming producer with particularly good *Crianza* and *Reserva* wines – and fast-rising prices. ★★★★ 1995 Rioja Pagos Viejos Reserva ££££

❦ Arvine [ah-veen] (Switzerland) Delicious, spicy white indigenous grape which has reminded some visiting Italians of their *Arneis.* **Bonvin; Chappaz; Provins; Rochaix**

Ŧ Bodegas Arzuaga [Ahr-thwah-gah] (*Ribera del Duero*, Spain) One of the growing number of new-wave estates in Ribera del Duero, with large acreage of vines and emphatically modern winemaking that is catching the attention of US critics. ★★★★★ 1996 Ribera del Duero Reserva Especial £££

Ŧ Matteo Ascheri [ash-sheh-ree] (*Piedmont*, Italy) Pioneering producer. Impressive single-vineyard, tobacco 'n berry wines, also *Nebbiolo, Syrah,* and *Viognier* and Freisa del Langhe. ★★★★ 1997 Montalupa Rosso ££££

Asciutto [ah-shoo-toh] (Italy) Dry.

Asenovgrad [ass-seh-nov-grad] (Bulgaria) Demarcated northern wine region with rich plummy *Cabernet Sauvignon, Merlot,* and *Mavrud.*

Ŧ Ashton Hills (*Adelaide Hills*, Australia) Small up-and-coming winery producing good Pinot Noir as well as subtle, increasingly creditable *Chardonnay* and *Riesling.* ★★★★ 1999 Pinot Noir £££

Assemblage [ah-sahm-blahj] (France) The art of blending wine from different grape varieties. Associated with *Bordeaux* and *Champagne.*

Assmanhausen [ass-mahn-how-zehn] (*Rheingau*, Germany) If you like sweet Pinot Noir, this is the place to come looking for it.

Ŧ Asti (*Piedmont*, Italy) Town famous for sparkling *Spumante*, lighter *Moscato d'Asti*, and red *Barbera d'Asti.* Red: 82 **85 88 89 90** 93 94 95 96 97 98 White: **Bera; Bersano; Contratto; Fontanafredda; Gancia; Martini.**

Astringent Mouth-puckering. Associated with young red wine. See *tannin.*

Aszu [ah-soo] (Hungary) The sweet syrup made from dried and "nobly rotten" grapes (see *botrytis*) used to sweeten *Tokaji.*

Ŧ Ata Rangi [ah-tah ran-gee] (*Martinborough*, New Zealand) Estate with high-quality *Pinot, Chardonnay,* and *Shiraz.* ★★★★ 1999 Craighall Chardonnay £££

Ŧ Atlas Peak (*Napa*, California) Antinori's US venture is proving more successful with Cabernet than with Sangiovese.

Ŧ Au Bon Climat [oh bon klee-Mat] (*Santa Barbara*, California) Top-quality producer of characterful and flavoursome *Pinot Noir* and particularly classy *Chardonnay.* ★★★★ 1997 Arroyo Grande Valley Talley Vineyard £££ ★★★★ 1997 Chardonnay Sandford & Benedict £££

Ŧ Dom. des Aubuisières [day Soh-bwee-see-yehr] (*Loire*, France) Bernard Fouquet produces impeccable wines ranging from richly dry to lusciously sweet. ★★★★ 1999 Vouvray Sec le Marigny £££

Auckland (New Zealand) All-embracing designation which once comprised a quarter of the country's vineyards. Often derided region, despite the fact that some vintages favour it over starrier areas such as *Marlborough. Collards; Coopers Creek; Goldwater Estate; Kumeu River; Matua Valley;* Sacred Hill; Stonyridge.

A

Aude [ohd] (Southwest France) Prolific *département* and traditional source of ordinary wine. Now *Corbières* and *Fitou* are improving as are the *Vins de Pays*, thanks to new grapes (such as the *Viognier*) and the efforts of firms like *Skalli Fortant de France, Val d'Orbieu,* and *Domaine Virginie.*

Ausbruch [ows-brookh] (Austria) Term for rich *botrytis* wine which is sweeter than *Beerenauslese* but less sweet than *Trockenbeerenauslese.*

Auslese [ows-lay-zuh] (Germany) Mostly sweet wine from selected ripe grapes, usually affected by *botrytis.* Third rung on the *QmP* ladder.

☨ **Ch. Ausone** [oh-zohn] (*St. Emilion Premier Grand Cru Classé, Bordeaux,* France) This producer is a pretender to the crown of top *St. Emilion.* The estate owes its name to the Roman occupation and can produce fine complex *claret.* Until the wine-making was taken over by *Michel Rolland* in 1995, the wine lacked the intensity demanded by critics. The 1998 is delicious, if less delicately perfumed than in the past, but the 2000 was my wine of the vintage. 79 81 **82 83 85 86** 88 **89 90** 92 93 94 *95 96 97 98 99 00* ★★★★★ **2000 ££££**

Austria Home of all sorts of whites, ranging from dry *Sauvignon Blancs,* greengagey *Grüner Veltliners,* and ripe *Rieslings* to especially luscious *late harvest* wines. Reds are increasingly successful too – particularly the *Pinot-Noir*-like *St. Laurents.* Bründlmayer; *Feiler-Artinger; Freie Weingärtner;* Holler; Juris; Knoll; *Alois Kracher;* Alois Lang; Münzenrieder; Nicolaihof; *Willi Opitz; Pichler;* Johan Tschida; *Prager; Ernst Triebaumer; Umathum.*

🍇 **Auxerrois** [oh-sehr-wah] (France) Named after the town in northern *Burgundy,* this is the Alsatians' term for a fairly dull local variety that may be related to the *Sylvaner, Melon de Bourgogne,* or *Chardonnay.* South Africa's winemakers learned about it when cuttings were smuggled into the *Cape* and planted there under the misapprehension that they were *Chardonnay.* In Luxembourg it is called the **Luxembourg Pinot Gris.**

☨ **Auxey-Duresses** [oh-say doo-ress] (*Burgundy,* France) *Côtes de Beaune* village best known for buttery whites, but producing rather more rustic, raspberryish, reds. A slow developer. **Robert Ampeau; Dom. d'Auvenay; Dom Chassorney;** *Coche-Dury; Comte Armand;* Jean-Pierre Diconne; *Louis Jadot; Olivier Leflaive; Michel Prunier;* Vincent Prunier; *Guy Roulot.*

AVA (US) Acronym for American Viticultural Areas, a recent attempt to develop an American *appellation* system. It makes sense in smaller, climatically coherent *appellations* like *Mount Veeder* and *Carneros*; much less so in larger, more heterogenous ones like *Napa.*

☨ **Quinta da Aveleda** (*Vinho Verde,* Portugal) Famous estate producing disappointing dry *Vinho Verde.*

Avelsbach [ahr-vel-sbarkh] (*Mosel,* Germany) Ruwer village producing delicate, light-bodied wines. Qba/Kab/Spät: **88 89 90 91 92 93 94 95 96** 97 98 99 00 Aus/Beeren/Tba: **83 85 88 89 90 91 92** 93 94 95 97 98 99 00

☨ **L'Avenir** [lah-veh-near] (*Stellenbosch,* South Africa) A new and fast-rising star in the *Cape,* thanks to a – for the region – historically unusual obsession with ripe fruit. The big fruit-salady *Chenin Blanc* is a star, as are the rich *Cabernet* and *Pinotage.* Some people will find the *Chardonnay* just a touch too hefty.

☨ **Avignonesi** [ahr-veen-yon-nay-see] (*Tuscany,* Italy) Ultra-classy producer of *Vino Nobile di Montepulciano, Super-Tuscans* such as Grifi, a pure *Merlot* described by an American critic as Italy's *Pétrus.* There are also serious *Chardonnay* and *Sauvignon* whites – plus an unusually good *Vin Santo.* ★★★★★ **1997 Avignonesi e Capannelle ££££**

☨ **Ayala** [ay-yah-lah] (*Champagne,* France) Underrated producer which takes its name from the village of Ay. ★★★ **Non Vintage £££**

Ayl [ihl] (*Mosel,* Germany) Distinguished *Saar* village producing steely wines. Qba/Kab/Spät: 86 88 **89** 90 91 92 *93 94* 95 96 97 98 99 00 Aus/Beeren/Tba: **83 85 88 89 90 91** 92 93 94 95 97 98 99 00

Azienda [ad-see-en-dah] (Italy) Estate.

B

B

☯ **Babcock** (*Santa Ynez*, California) Classy single-vineyard *Chardonnays* (*Mount Carmel*), *Pinot Noirs, Sangioveses, and Sauvignon Blancs*.

☯ **Babich** [ba-bitch] (*Henderson*, New Zealand) Family winery with wines from *Auckland, Marlborough*, and *Hawkes Bay*, source of the rich "Irongate" and Patriarch *Chardonnays*. The *Sauvignon Blanc* is good too. The reds improve with every vintage. ★★★★★ 1998 The Patriarch £££

☯ **Quinta da Bacalhôa** [dah ba-keh-yow] (*Setúbal*, Portugal) The innovative *Cabernet-Merlot* made by *Peter Bright* at *JP Vinhos*.

🍇 **Bacchus** [ba-kuhs] White grape. A *Müller-Thurgau-Riesling* cross, making light, flowery wine. **Denbies; Tenterden.**

☯ **Dom. Denis Bachelet** [dur-nee bash-lay] (*Burgundy*, France) Classy, small *Gevrey-Chambertin* estate with cherryish wines that are great young – and with five or six years of age. ★★★★★ 1996 Gevrey-Chambertin Les Corbeaux Vieilles Vignes £££

☯ **Backsberg Estate** [bax-burg] (*Paarl*, South Africa) *Chardonnay* pioneer, with good, quite Burgundian versions. ★★★ 1998 Klein Babylonstoren ££

Bad Dürkheim [baht duhr-kime] (*Pfalz*, Germany) Chief *Pfalz* town, producing some of the region's finest whites, plus some reds. Qba/Kab/Spät: 90 91 **92 93 94 95 96** 97 98 99 00 Aus/Beeren/Tba: **83 85 88 89 90** 91 92 **93 94 95** 96 97 98 99 00 *Kurt Darting;* Fitz-Ritter; Karl Schäfer.

Bad Kreuznach [baht kroyts-nahkh] (*Nahe*, Germany) The chief and finest wine town of the region, giving its name to the entire lower *Nahe*. 89 90 91 92 **93** 94 95 **96** 97 98 99 00 *Paul Anheuser;* von Plettenberg.

☯ **Baden** [bah-duhn] (Germany) Warm southern region of Germany, with ripe grapes to make dry (*Trocken*) wines. Some of these, such as "Baden Dry", are good, as are some of the *Pinot Noirs*. The huge *Winzerkeller* cooperative makes good wines, as do: Becker; Karl Heinz Johner; R Zimmerlin.

☯ **Baden Winzerkeller (ZBW)** [bah-den vin-zehr-keh-luhr] (*Baden*, Germany) Huge coop whose reliability has set *Baden* apart from the rest of Germany.

☯ **Badia a Coltibuono** [bah-dee-yah ah kohl-tee-bwoh-noh] (*Tuscany*, Italy) One of Italy's most reliable producers of *Chianti*, fairly-priced pure *Sangiovese*, and *Chardonnay*. Great mature releases. ★★★★ 1995 Chianti Classico Riserva £££; ★★★★ 1997 Sangioveto ££££

☯ **Badia di Morrona** [bah-dee-yah dee Moh-ROH-nah] (*Tuscany*, Italy) Up-and-coming estate with a notable *Super-Tuscan* in the shape of the N'Antia Cabernet-Sangiovese blend. ★★★★ 1997 Toscana N' Antia £££

🍇 **Baga** [bah-gah] (*Bairrada*, Portugal) The spicily fruity red variety of *Bairrada*.

☯ **Ch. Bahans-Haut-Brion** [bah-on oh-bree-on] (*Graves, Bordeaux*, France) The *second label* of Ch. *Haut-Brion*. Red: 82 83 85 **86** 87 88 **89** 90 92 93 94 95 96 97 98 99 00 ★★★★ 1998 ££££

☯ **Bailey's** (*Victoria*, Australia) Traditional, good Liqueur *Muscat* and hefty, old-fashioned *Shiraz*. Current wines are a little more subtle but still pack a punch. ★★★★ Founder Liqueur Muscat £££

☯ **Bairrada** [bi-rah-dah] (Portugal) *DO* region south of *Oporto*, traditionally making dull whites and tough reds. Revolutionary producers like *Sogrape, Luis Pato*, and *Aliança* are proving what can be done. Look for spicy blackberryish reds and creamy whites. Red: **87 88 90 91 92 94** 95 96 97 99

Baja California [bah-hah] (Mexico) The part of *Mexico* abutting the *California* border, best known for exporting illegal aliens and importing adventurous Californians and hippies. Baja California is also a successful, though little known, wine region, and is home to the Santo Tomas, Casa de Piedra, and *LA Cetto* wineries.

Balance Harmony of fruitiness, *acidity, alcohol*, and *tannin*. Balance can develop with age but should be evident (if sometimes hard to discern) in youth.

Balaton [bah-la-ton] (Hungary) Wine region frequented by *flying winemakers*, and producing fair-quality reds and whites.

B

Ⓨ Anton Balbach [an-ton bahl-barkh] (*Rheinhessen*, Germany) Potentially one of the best producers in the *Erden* region – especially for *late harvest* wines. ★★★★★ 1999 Riesling Eiswein Niersteiner Oelberg ££££

Ⓨ Bodegas Balbás [bal-bash] (*Ribera del Duero*, Spain) Small producer of juicy *Tempranillo* reds, *Bordeaux*-style *Cabernet* blends, and a lively rosé.

Ⓨ Balbi [bal-bee] (*Mendoza*, Argentina) Producer of good, inexpensive modern wines, including particularly appealing *Malbecs* and dry rosés.

Ⓨ Ch. Balestard-la-Tonnelle [bah-les-star lah ton-nell] (*St. Emilion Grand Cru Classé, Bordeaux*, France) Good, quite traditional *St. Emilion* built to last. 81 83 85 **86** 87 **88 89 90** 92 93 94 *95 96 97 98 99* 00

Ⓨ Balgownie Estate [bal-Gow-nee] (*Bendigo*, Australia) One of Victoria's most reliable producers of lovely, intense, blackcurranty *Cabernet* in *Bendigo*. *Chardonnays* are big and old-fashioned, and *Pinot Noirs* are improving. ★★★★★ 1998 Estate Shiraz £££

Ⓨ Bandol [bon-dohl] (*Provence*, France) *Mourvèdre*-influenced plummy, herby reds, and rich whites. Ch. de Pibarnon; *Dom. Tempier;* Dom. Tour de Bon; Ch. la Rouvière; Ch. Vannières.

Ⓨ Castello Banfi [veel-lah ban-fee] (*Tuscany*, Italy) US-owned producer with improving *Brunello* and *Vini da Tavola.* ★★★★★ 1997 Summus ££££

Ⓨ Bannockburn (*Geelong*, Australia) Gary Farr uses his experience at *Dom. Dujac* in *Burgundy* to produce concentrated *Pinot Noir* and *Shiraz* at home. The big *Chardonnay Bordeaux* blends are impressive too. ★★★★ 1997 Pinot Noir ££

Ⓨ Bannockburn by Farr (*Geelong*, Australia) Gary Farr's own label – also ✓ worth watching out for. ★★★★ 1999 Pinot Noir ££

Ⓨ Banyuls [bon-yools] (*Provence*, France) France's answer to *tawny port*. Fortified, *Grenache*-based, *Vin Doux Naturel*, ranging from off-dry to lusciously sweet. The *Rancio* style is more like *Madeira*. L'Etoile; Dom. Mas Amiel; Dom. du Mas Blanc; Clos de Paulilles; *Dom. de la Rectorie;* Dom. la Tour Vieille; Vial Magnères.

Ⓨ Barancourt [bah-ron-koor] (*Champagne*, France) Improving *Champagne* brand since its purchase by Vranken. Cuvée des Fondateurs is the top wine.

Ⓨ Antonio Barbadillo [bahr-bah-deel-yoh] (*Jerez*, Spain) Great producer of *Fino* and *Manzanilla.* ★★★★★ Obispo Gascon Palo Cortado ££

Ⓨ Barbaresco [bahr-bah-ress-koh] (*Piedmont*, Italy) DOCG *Nebbiolo* red, with spicy fruit, depth, and complexity. Approachable earlier (three to five years) than neighbouring *Barolo* but, in the right hands – and in the best vineyards – of almost as high a quality. 82 **85 88 89 90** 93 94 95 96 97 *98 Gaja;* Rino Varaldi; Castello di Neive; *Paitin; Pelissero; Alfredo Prunotto;* Albino Rocca.

Ⓨ Cascina la Barbatella [kah-shh-nah lah bahr-bah-teh-lah] (*Piedmont*, Italy) Rising star, focusing its attention firmly on the *Barbera* (as Barbera d'Asti and single-vineyard Vigna di Sonvico and Vigna dell'Angelo) as well as a good Cortese-*Sauvignon* blend called Noè after one of its makers.

🍇 Barbera [Bar-Beh-Rah] (*Piedmont*, Italy) Grape making fruity, spicy, characterful wine (e.g. B. d'Alba and B. d'Asti), with a flavour like cheesecake raisins. Now in *California, Mexico,* and *Australia* (at Brown Bros. and "I").

Ⓨ René Barbier [Ren-nay Bah-bee-yay] (*Penedès*, Spain) Dynamic producer of commercial wines and fine *Priorato.* ★★★★★ 1997 Priorato Clos Mogador ££

Ⓨ Barca Velha [bahr-kah vayl-yah] (*Douro*, Portugal) Portugal's most famous red, traditionally made from port varieties by *Ferreira*, now getting a quality boost. Also look out for Reserva Especial released in more difficult years.

Ⓨ Bardolino [bar-doh-lee-noh] (*Veneto*, Italy) Cherryish red. Can be dull – or a fruity alternative to *Beaujolais*. Also comes as Chiaretto Rosé. Best young unless from an exceptional producer. *Boscaini;* Fabiano Masi; Portalupi.

Ⓨ Gilles Barge [bahzh] (*Rhône*, France) Son of Pierre who won an international reputation for his fine, classic *Côte Rôtie*. Gilles, who now runs the estate, has also shown his skill with *St. Joseph*.

Ⓨ Guy de Barjac [gee dur bar-jak] (*Rhône*, France) A master of the *Syrah* grape, producing some of the best – and most stylish – *Cornas* around.

B

Ⓘ **Barolo** [bah-Roh-loh] (*Piedmont,* Italy) Noble *Nebbiolo* reds with extraordinary berryish, floral, and spicy flavours. Old-fashioned versions are dry and tannic when young but, from a good producer and year, can develop extraordinary complexity. Modern versions are oakier and more accessible. 82 **85 88** *89 90* **93** *95 96 97 Elio Altare; Batasiolo; Borgogno; Chiarlo; Clerico; Aldo Conterno;* Giacomo Conterno; *Conterno Fantino; Fontanafredda; Gaja; M Marengo; Bartolo Mascarello; Giuseppe Mascarello;* Pio Cesare; *Pira; F Principiano; Prunotto; Ratti; Sandrone; Scavino; Vajra;* Vietti; *Roberto Voerzio.*

Ⓘ **Baron de Ley** [bah-Rohn Duh lay] (*Rioja,* Spain) Small estate whose wines, French oak-aged, can be worth waiting for. ★★★★ 1995 Rioja Reserva ££

Barossa Valley [bah-ros suh] (Australia) Big, warm region north-east of Adelaide which is famous for traditional, old-vine *Shiraz* and *Grenache*, "*ports*", and *Rieslings* which age to oily richness. *Chardonnay* and *Cabernet* make subtler, classier wines along with *Riesling* in the higher altitude vineyards of the *Eden Valley* and *Adelaide Hills. Barossa Valley Estate; Basedow; Bethany;* Charles Cimicky; E&E; Elderton; Wolf Blass; Grant Burge; Hardy's; Henschke; Krondorf; Peter Lehmann; Melton; Orlando; Penfolds; Rockford; St. Hallett; Turkey Flat; Yalumba.

Ⓘ **Barossa Valley Estate** (*Barossa Valley*, Australia) Top end of BRL Hardy with good old-vine *Barossa* reds. ★★★★★ 1998 Moculta Shiraz £££

Ⓘ **Daniel Barraud** [Bah-roh] (*Burgundy*, France) Dynamic producer of single-*cuvée Pouilly-Fuissé*. ★★★★★ 1999 Pouilly Fuissé la Verchère £££

Barrique [ba-reek] (France) French barrel, particularly in *Bordeaux*, holding about 58 gallons (225 litres). Term used in Italy to denote (new) barrel ageing.

Ⓘ **Jim Barry** (*Clare Valley*, Australia) Producer of the dazzling, spicy, mulberryish *Armagh Shiraz* and great, floral Watervale Riesling.

Ⓘ **Barsac** [bahr-sak] (*Bordeaux*, France) AC neighbour of *Sauternes* with similar, though not quite so rich, *Sauvignon/Sémillon* dessert wines. 71 75 76 78 79 80 81 82 **83 85 86** 88 89 90 95 97 98 99 *Ch. Broustet; Ch. Climens; Ch. Coutet; Ch. Doisy-Dubroca; Ch. Doisy-Daëne; Ch. Nairac.*

Ⓘ **Ghislaine Barthod** [jee-lenn Bar-toh] (*Burgundy*, France) Top class Chambolle-Musigny estate. ★★★★★ 1998 Beaux Bruns £££

Ⓘ **De Bartoli** [day bahr-toh-lee] (*Sicily*, Italy) *Marsala* for drinking rather than cooking from a revolutionary producer who has voluntarily removed his Vecchio Samperi from the DSOC system. ★★★★ Vecchio Samperi ££

Ⓘ **Barton & Guestier** [bahr-ton ay geht-tee-yay] (*Bordeaux*, France) Highly commercial *Bordeaux* shipper. ★★★ 1998 Fondation 1725 ££

Ⓘ **Barwang** [bahr-wang] (*New South Wales*, Australia) *McWilliams* label for cool climate wines produced in newly-planted vineyards near Young in eastern *New South Wales.* ★★★★ 1998 Shiraz ££

Ⓘ **Basedow** [baz-zeh-doh] (South Australia) Producer of big, concentrated *Shiraz* and *Cabernet* and ultrarich *Semillon* and *Chardonnays.*

Basilicata [bah-see-lee-kah-tah] (Italy) Southern wine region chiefly known for *Aglianico del Vulture* and improving *IGT wines.* Basilium.

Basket Press Traditional winepress, favoured for quality reds by Australian producers such as *Chateau Reynella.*

Ⓘ **Bass Philip** (*Victoria*, Australia) Fanatical South *Gippsland* pioneer Philip Jones's fine *Burgundy*-like *Pinot.* ★★★★★ 1997 Premium Pinot Noir ££££

Ⓘ **Von Bassermann-Jordan** [fon bas-suhr-man johr-dun] (*Pfalz*, Germany) A traditional producer often using the fruit of its fabulous vineyards to produce fine *Trocken Rieslings.*

Ⓘ **Ch. Bastor-Lamontagne** [bas-tohr-lam-mon-tañ] (*Sauternes, Bordeaux,* France) Remarkably reliable classy *Sauternes*; inexpensive alternative to the big-names, often offering comparable levels of richness and complexity. Fine in 2000. 85 86 88 89 90 **94** 95 96 97 *98* 99 *00*.

B

☿ **Ch. Batailley** [bat-tih-yay] (*Pauillac 5ème Cru Classé, Bordeaux,* France) Approachable, quite modern tobacco-cassis-cedar *claret* from the same stable as Ch. Ducru-Beaucaillou. Shows more class than its price might lead one to expect. 70 78 79 **82 83 85 86** 87 **88 89 90** 94 95 *96 97 98 99 00*

☿ **Bâtard-Montrachet** [bat-tahr mon-rah-shay] (*Burgundy,* France) Wonderful, biscuity-rich white *Grand Cru* that straddles the border between the appellations of *Chassagne-* and *Puligny-Montrachet.* Often very fine; invariably expensive. *Cailot; Colin-Deleger; Joseph Drouhin; Jean-Noel Gagnard; Gagnard-Delagrange; Dom. Leflaive; Ch. de la Maltroye; Pierre Morey; Michel Niellon; Ramonet; Sauzet.*

☿ **Batasiolo** [bat-tah-see-oh-loh] (*Piedmont,* Italy) Producer of top-class *Barolo,* impressive cherryish *Dolcetto,* fresh *Moscato,* intense berryish *Brachetto,* and a subtle *Chardonnay.* ★★★★★ 1995 Barolo Bofani £££

☿ **Dom. des Baumard** [day boh-marh] (*Loire,* France) Superlative producer of great *Coteaux du Layon, Quarts de Chaume,* and *Savennières.* ★★★★★ 1999 Anjou Clos de la Folie ££££

☿ **Bava** [bah-vah] (*Piedmont,* Italy) Innovative producer making good *Moscato Barbera,* reviving indigenous grapes such as the rarely grown raspberryish *Ruche* as well as a rather wonderful traditional curious herb-infused *Barolo Chinato Cocchi.* Try it with one of Roberto Bava's other enthusiasms: dark chocolate. ★★★★ 1998 Stradivario ££

☿ **Béarn** [bay-ar'n] (*South West,* France) Highly traditional and often dull region. Lapeyre is the name to look out for.

☿ **Ch. Beau-Séjour (-Bécot)** [boh-say-zhoor bay-koh] (*St. Emilion Grand Cru Classé, Bordeaux,* France) Reinstated in 1996 after a decade of demotion. Now making fairly priced, greatly improved wine. **82** 83 85 **86** 88 89 90 92 93 94 95 96 97 98

☿ **Ch. Beau-Site** [boh-seet] (*St. Estèphe Cru Bourgeois, Bordeaux,* France) Benchmark *St. Estèphe* in the same stable as *Ch. Batailley.* 78 **82** 83 85 **86** **88** 89 90 92 93 94 95 *96 97 98 00*

☿ **Ch. de Beaucastel** [boh-kas-tel] (*Rhône,* France) The top *Châteauneuf-du-Pape* estate, using organic methods to produce richly gamey (for some, too gamey) long-lived, spicy reds, which reflect the presence in the blend of an unusually high proportion of Mourvèdre. There are also rare but fine creamy-spicy (*Roussanne-based*) whites. The Coudoulet Côtes du Rhône are a delight too. ★★★★★ 1998 Châteauneuf-du-Pape ££££

☿ **Beaujolais** [boh-zhuh-lay] (*Burgundy,* France) Light and fruity *Gamay* red. This wine is good chilled and for early drinking. *Beaujolais-Villages* is better, and the 10 *Crus* are better still. With age, these can taste like (fairly ordinary) *Burgundy* from the *Côte d'Or. Beaujolais Blanc,* which is made from *Chardonnay,* is now mostly sold as *St. Véran.* See Crus: *Morgon; Chénas; Brouilly; Côte de Brouilly; Juliénas; Fleurie; Regnié; St. Amour; Chiroubles; Moulin-à-Vent.*

☿ **Beaujolais-Villages** (*Burgundy,* France) From the north of the region, fuller-flavoured and more alcoholic than plain *Beaujolais,* though not necessarily from one of the named *Cru* villages. *Duboeuf; Dubost; Ch. es Jacques; Janin; Pivot; Large.*

☿ **Beaulieu Vineyard** [bohl-yoo] (*Napa Valley,* California) Historic winery getting back on its feet after years of neglect by its multi-national owners. The wines to look for are the Georges de Latour Private Reserve *Cabernets,* which have been consistently good (as a recent tasting of old vintages proved), and the new Signet ranger. Recent vintages of the Beau Tour *Cabernet Sauvignon* have been good too. Other wines are unexciting. ★★★★★ 1996 Georges de Latour Private Reserve ££££

B

Ⓧ *Beaumes de Venise* [bohm duh vuh-neez] (*Rhône*, France) *Côtes du Rhône* village producing spicy, dry reds and sweet, grapey, fortified *Vin Doux Naturel* from the *Muscat*. Dom. des Bernardins; *Chapoutier;* Dom. de Coyeux; Durban; de Fenouillet; *Paul Jaboulet Aîné;* la Soumade; *Vidal-Fleury.*

Ⓧ **Ch. Beaumont** [boh-mon] (*Haut-Médoc Cru Bourgeois, Bordeaux*, France) Impressive estate performing well again since 1998. 82 85 **86** 88 **89 90 93 95 96** 98 99 00

Ⓧ **Beaune** [bohn] (*Burgundy*, France) Large commune that gives its name to the *Côte de Beaune* and produces soft, raspberry-and-rose-petal *Pinot Noir*. As in *Nuits-St.-Georges*, there are plenty of *Premier Crus*, but no *Grands Crus*. The walled city is the site of the famous *Hospices* charity auction. Reds are best from *Michel Prunier, Louis Jadot, Bouchard Père et Fils* (since 1996), Ch. de Chorey, Albert Morot, and *Joseph Drouhin* – who also make a very successful example of the ultrarare white. Other good producers: Robert Ampeau; Arnoux Père et Fils; *Pascal Bouley;* Dubois; Génot-Boulanger; Germain (Ch. de Chorey); *Michel Lafarge;* Daniel Largeot; Laurent; *Jacques Prieur;* Rapet Père et Fils; Thomas-Moillard; *Tollot-Beaut.*

Ⓧ**Ch. Beauregard** [boh-ruh-gahr] (*Pomerol, Bordeaux*, France) Estate producing juicy oaky *Pomerol*. 82 85 **86** 88 *89 90* 93 95 96 97 98 99 00

Ⓧ **Ch. Beauséjour-Duffau-Lagarosse** [boh-say-zhoor doo-foh lag-gahr-ros] (*St. Emilion Premier Grand Cru Classé, Bordeaux*, France) Traditional tough, tannic *St. Emilion*. 82 83 85 86 88 89 90 93 94 95 96 98

Ⓧ **Beaux Frères** [boh frair] (*Oregon*) *Pinot Noir* winery launched by wine guru Robert Parker and his brother-in-law (hence the name).

Ⓧ **Graham Beck** (Robertson, South Africa) Associated with *Bellingham* and producer of some of South Africa's best sparkling wines. A Coastal Range of still wines are looking good too. ★★★★ Blanc de Blancs ££
Beerenauslese [behr-ren-ows-lay-zuh] (Austria/Germany) Sweet wines from selected, ripe grapes (Beeren), hopefully affected by *botrytis.*

Ⓧ **Ch. de Bel-Air** [bel-Ehr] (*Lalande-de-Pomerol, Bordeaux*, France) Impressive property making wines to make some *Pomerols* blush. 82 85 86 **88 89** 90 93 **94** 95 96 97 98 99

Ⓧ **Ch. Bel-Orme-Tronquoy-de-Lalande** [bel-orm-tron-kwah-duh-la-lond] (*Haut-Médoc Cru Bourgeois, Bordeaux*, France) Highly old-fashioned estate and wines. Under the same ownership (and philosophy) as *Rauzan Gassies*. Made a good 2000, but still has plenty of room for improvement.

Ⓧ **Ch. Belair** [bel-lehr] (*St. Emilion Premier Grand Cru Classé, Bordeaux*, France) Classy, delicate, long-lived *St. Emilion* with a very impressive 1998 and 1999. Compare and contrast with more "modern" neighbour *Ausone*, which used to be produced by Pascal Delbeck who still produces Belair. Don't confuse with the *Lalande-de-Pomerol Ch. de Bel-Air* (or any of the countless lesser Belairs scattered around *Bordeaux*). 78 **79 82 83 85 86** 88 89 90 93 95 96 97 98 99 00.

Ⓧ **Bellavista** (*Lombardy*, Italy) Commercial Franciacorta producers of classy sparkling and still wines. The Riserva Vittorio Moretti, which is only produced in top years, is the star of the show.

Ⓧ **Albert Belle** [bel] (*Rhône*, France) An estate that has recently begun to bottle its own excellent red and – oak – white Hermitage.

Ⓧ **Bellet** [bel-lay] (*Provence*, France) Tiny *AC* behind Nice producing fairly good red, white, and rosé from local grapes including the Rolle, the *Braquet*, and the *Folle Noir*. Pricey and rarely seen outside France. Ch. de Bellet.

Ⓧ **Bellingham** (South Africa) Highly commercial winery that has just been bought out by its management and is focusing increasingly on quality. *Cabernet Franc* is a particular success. Look for the Premium Range labels. ★★★★ 1998 Premium Cabernet Franc ££
Bendigo [ben-dig-goh] (*Victoria*, Australia) Warm region producing big-boned, long-lasting reds with intense berry fruit. *Balgownie;* Blackjack; Heathcote; *Jasper Hill; Mount Ida; Passing Clouds;* Water Wheel.

B

☟ **Benziger** [ben-zig-ger] (*Sonoma,* California) Classy wines from the family behind *Glen Ellen. Zinfandel* and *Chardonnay* are both stars. ★★★★
1997 Cabernet Sauvignon Sonoma County Reserve ££

☟ **Berberana** [behr-behr-rah nah] (*Rioja,* Spain) Increasingly dynamic producer of a range of fruitier young-drinking styles, as well as the improving Carta de Plata and Carta de Oro and Lagunilla *Riojas,* plus sparkling Marquès de Monistrol and the excellent Marquès de Griñon range. ★★★★ 1996 Viña Alarde Reserva £££; ★★★★ 1995 Rioja Reserva ££

☟ **Bercher** [behr-kehr] (*Baden,* Germany) Dynamic estate, producing impressive, modern, *Burgundy*-style reds and whites.
Bereich [beh-ri-kh] (Germany) Vineyard area, sub-division of an *Anbaugebiet.* On its own indicates *QbA* wine, e.g. *Niersteiner.* Finer wines are followed by the name of a (smaller) *Grosslage,* better ones by that of an individual vineyard.

☟ **Bergerac** [behr-jur-rak] (France) Traditionally *Bordeaux's* "lesser" neighbour but possibly soon to be assimilated into that regional *appellation.* The wines, though often pretty mediocre, can still be better value than basic red or white *Bordeaux,* while the *Monbazillac* can outclass basic *Sauternes.* Ch. Belingard; Court-les-Muts; des Eyssards; Grinou; la Jaubertie; de Raz; Tour des Gendres.

☟ **Bergkelder** [berg-kel-dur] (*Cape,* South Africa) Huge firm best known for its *Stellenryck* wines. Its cheaper *Fleur du Cap* range is likeable enough and the best of the *JC Le Roux* sparkling wines are first class. ★★★★ 1999 Stellenryck Chardonnay ££

☟ **Beringer Vineyards** [ber-rin-jer] (*Napa Valley,* California) Big Swiss-owned producer, increasingly notable for its single-vineyard *Cabernet Sauvignons* (Knights Valley, *Howell Mountain, Spring Mountain,* and Private Reserve), *Cabernet Francs,* and *Merlots; Burgundy*-like *Chardonnays;* and *late harvest* wines. ★★★★ 1995 Bancroft Ranch Merlot £££; ★★★★★ 1994 Chabot Cabernet £££
Bernkastel [berhrn-kah-stel] (*Mosel,* Germany) Town and area on the *Mittelmosel* and source of some of the finest *Riesling* (like the famous Bernkasteler Doktor), and a lake of poor-quality stuff. QbA/Kab/Spät: 90 91 92 93 94 95 96 97 98 99 00 Aus/Beeren/Tba: 83 85 88 89 90 91 92 93 94 95 96 97 98 99 00 Dr Loosen; JJ Prum; Von Kesselstadt; Wegeler Deinhard.

☟ **Bernardus** (*Monterey,* California) Producer of rich, unsubtle, fairly-priced, unashamedly New World-style *Sauvignon Blanc, Chardonnay,* and *Pinot Noir.* ★★★★ 1996 Chardonnay Monterey County ££

☟ **Berri Renmano** [ber-ree ren-mah-noh] (*Riverland,* Australia) The controlling force behind the giant *BRL Hardy,* with quality brands like *Thomas Hardy, Barossa Valley Estates, Chateau Reynella,* and *Houghton.* Under its own name, it is better known for inexpensive reds and whites.

☟ **Dom Bertagna** [behr-tan-ya] (*Vougeot,* France) Recently improved estate notable for offering the rare, (relatively) affordable *Premier Cru Vougeot* alongside its own version of the easier-to-find *Clos de Vougeot Grand Cru.* ★★★★ 1998 Vougeot les Petits Vougeots £££

☟ **Bertani** [behr-tah-nee] (*Veneto,* Italy) Producer of good *Valpolicella* and innovative wines such as the Le Lave Garganega-*Chardonnay* blend. ★★★★ 1997 Cabernet Sauvignon Villa Novare ££££

☟ **Best's Great Western** (*Victoria,* Australia) Under-appreciated winery in *Great Western* making delicious concentrated *Shiraz* from old vines, attractive *Cabernet, Dolcetto, Pinot Noir, Colombard,* and rich *Chardonnay* and *Riesling.* ★★★★★ 1998 Shiraz £££

☟ **Bethany** [beth-than-nee] (*Barossa Valley,* Australia) Impressive small producer of knockout *Shiraz.* ★★★★★ 1996 Reserve Shiraz £££

☟ **Bethel Heights** (*Oregon,* California) Long-established but now a rising star, with good Pinot Noir and particularly impressive Pinot Blanc and Chardonnay.

B

Ⅰ **Dom. Henri Beurdin** [bur-dan] (*Loire*, France) The estate at which you'll find benchmark white and rosé that demonstrates what can be achieved in *Reuilly*. ★★★★ 1999 Reuilly Blanc ££££

Ⅰ **Ch. Beychevelle** [bay-shur-vel] (*St. Julien 4ème Cru Classé, Bordeaux, France*) A fourth growth that achieves the typical cigar-box character of *St. Julien* but fails to excite. The *second label Amiral de Beychevelle* can be a worthwhile buy. Better than usual quality in 2000. 82 83 85 **86** 88 89 90 **94** 95 96 97 98 ★★★ 2000 ££££

Ⅰ **Léon Beyer** [bay-ur] (*Alsace*, France) Serious producer of lean long-lived wines. ★★★★ 1998 Riesling Ecaillers ££

Ⅰ **Beyerskloof** [bay-yurs-kloof] (*Stellenbosch*, South Africa) Newish venture, with Beyers Truter (of Kanonkop) on its way to producing South Africa's top *Cabernet* and *Stellenbosch Pinotage*. ★★★★ 1997 Stellenbosch ££

Ⅰ **Bianco di Custoza** [bee-yan-koh dee koos-toh-zah] (*Veneto*, Italy) Widely exported *DOC*. A reliable, crisp, light white from a blend of grapes. A better-value alternative to most basic *Soave*. **Gorgo; Portalupi; *Tedeschi*; le Vigne di San Pietro; *Zenato*.**

Ⅰ **Maison Albert Bichot** [bee-shoh] (*Burgundy*, France) Big *négociant* with excellent *Chablis* and *Vosne-Romanée*, plus adequate wines sold under a plethora of other labels. ★★★★ 1997 Charmes Chambertin £££

Ⅰ **Biddenden** [bid-den-den] (*Kent*, England) Producer showing impressive mastery of the peachy *Ortega*. ★★★ 1998 Ortega £

Bierzo [bee-yehrt-zoh] (*Castilla y Léon*, Spain) Up-and-coming region close to Galicia. Fresh whites made from the local Mencia grape are worth looking out for. Drink young. **Pérez Caramés**

Ⅰ **Bienvenue-Batard-Montrachet** [bee-yen-veh-noo bat-tahr mon ra-shay] (*Burgundy*, France) Fine white *Burgundy* vineyard with potentially gorgeous biscuit-like wines. **Carillon; Henri Clerc; Dom Leflaive; *Sauzet*.**

Ⅰ **Weingut Josef Biffar** [bif-fah] (*Pfalz*, Germany). *Deidesheim* estate that is on a roll at the moment with its richly spicy wines. ★★★★ 1997 Riesling Spätlese Pfalz Wachenheimer Altenburg ££

Ⅰ **Billecart-Salmon** [beel-kahr sal-mon] (*Champagne*, France) Producer of the stylish winners (the 1959 and 1961 vintages) of the Champagne of the Millennium competition held in Stockholm in 1999 at which I was a taster. Possibly the best all-arounder for quality and value, and certainly the *Champagne* house whose subtle but decidedly agable *non-vintage, vintage*, and rosé I buy without hesitation. Superlative. ★★★★★ 1995 Cuvée Nicolas François Billecart ££££

Ⅰ **Billiot** [bil-lee-yoh] (*Champagne*, France) Impressive small producer with classy rich sparkling wine. ★★★★ Cuvée de Reserve NV £££

Bingen [bing-urn] (*Rheinhessen*, Germany) Village giving its name to a *Rheinhessen Bereich* that includes a number of well-known *Grosslage*. QbA/Kab/Spät: 85 86 **88 89 90** 91 **92 93** 94 **95 96 97** 98 99 00 Aus/Beeren/Tba: **83 85 88 89 90** 91 **92 93 94** 95 96 97 98 99 00

Binissalem [bin-nee-sah-lem] (*Mallorca*, Spain) The holiday island is proud of its demarcated region, though why it's hard to say. José Ferrer's and Jaime Mesquida's wines are the best of the bunch.

Ⅰ **Biondi-Santi** [bee-yon-dee san-tee] (*Tuscany*, Italy) Big-name estate making absurdly expensive and sometimes disappointing *Brunello di Montalcino* that can be bought – after a period of vertical storage at room temperature – at the local trattoria. ★★★★ 1995 Brunello Di Montalcino ££££

Biscuity Flavour of savoury crackers often associated with the *Chardonnay* grape, particularly in *Champagne* and top-class mature *Burgundy*, or with the yeast that fermented the wine.

Ⅰ **Bitouzet-Prieur** [bee-too-zay pree-yur] (*Burgundy*, France) If you like classic *Meursault* and *Volnay* built to last rather than seduce instantly with ripe fruit and oak, try this estate's 1997 Volnay Caillerets and 1997 *Meursault Perrières*.

B

Dom. Simon Bize [beez] (*Burgundy,* France) Intense, long-lived, and good-value wines produced in *Savigny-lès-Beaune.* ★★★★ 1998 Savigny-lès-Beaune Guettes £££

Blaauwklippen [blow-klip-pen] (*Stellenbosch,* South Africa) Recently sold, large estate, veering between commercial and top quality. The *Cabernet* and *Zinfandel* are the strongest cards, but the *Chardonnay* is improving fast. ★★★ 1998 Cabernet Franc ££

Blagny [blan-yee] (*Burgundy,* France) Tiny source of unsubtle red (sold as Blagny) and potentially top-class white (sold as *Meursault, Puligny-Montrachet,* Blagny, Hameau de Blagny, or la Pièce sous le Bois). Red: 83 85 86 88 89 90 92 95 96 97 98 99 Ampeau; Chavy-Chouet; Jobard; Thierry Matrot.

Blain-Gagnard [blan gan-yahr] (*Burgundy,* France) Excellent creamy, modern *Chassagne-Montrachet.*

Blanc de Blancs [blon dur blon] A white wine, made from white grapes – hardly worth mentioning except in the case of *Champagne,* where *Pinot Noir,* a black grape, usually makes up 30–70 per cent of the blend. In this case, *Blanc de Blancs* is pure *Chardonnay.*

Blanc de Noirs [blon dur nwahrr] A white (or frequently very slightly pink-tinged wine) made from red grapes by taking off the free-run juice, before pressing to minimize the uptake of red pigments from the skin. Paul Bara; Duval-Leroy (Fleur de Champagne); Egly-Ouiriet.

Paul Blanck [blank] (*Alsace,* France) Top-class *Alsace* domaine, specializing in single *Cru* wines. ★★★★ 1997 Riesling Patergarten £££

Blandy's [blan-deez] (*Madeira,* Portugal) Brand owned by the Madeira Wine Company and named after the sailor who began the production of fortified wine here. Excellent old wines. Younger ones are less exciting. ★★★ 5 Year Old Malmsey ££; ★★★★ 1995 Harvest Colheita Malmsey ££

Blanquette de Limoux [blon ket dur lee-moo] (*Midi,* France) *Méthode Champenoise* sparkling wine, which, when good, is appley and clean. Best when made with a generous dose of *Chardonnay,* as the local *Mauzac* tends to give it an earthy flavour with age. ★★★★ Domaine de l'Aigle ££

Wolf Blass (*Barossa Valley,* Australia) Part of the huge Mildara-Blass operation (and thus owned by Fosters), this brand was founded by a German immigrant who prides himself on producing "sexy" (his term) reds and whites by blending wines from different regions of *South Australia* and allowing them plentiful contact with new oak. ★★★★ 2000 Gold Label Riesling £££

Blauburgunder [blow-boor-goon-durh] (Austria) The name the Austrians give their light, often sharp, *Pinot Noir.*

Blauer Portugieser [blow-urh por-too-gay-suhr] (Germany) Red grape used in Germany and Austria to make light, pale wine.

Blaufränkisch [blow-fren-kish] (Austria) Grape used to make refreshingly berryish wines that can – in the right hands – compete with the reds of the *Loire.*

Blockheadia Ringnosii (*Napa,* California) Despite the wacky name and label, this is a source of serious *Sauvignon* and *Zinfandel.*

Quinta da Boavista [keen-tah dah boh-wah-vees-tah] (*Alenquer,* Portugal) Starry estate producing a range of red and white wines, including Palha Canas, Quinta das Sete, and Espiga.

Boccagigabbia [Bbok-kah-ji-gah-bee-yah] (*Marche,* Italy) Top class estate, producing delicious *Pinot Noir* (Girone), *Cabernet* (Akronte), and *Chardonnay.*

Bocksbeutel [box-boy-tuhl] (*Franken,* Germany) The famous flask-shaped bottle of *Franken,* adopted by the makers of *Mateus* Rosé.

Bodega [bod-day-gah] (Spain) Winery or wine cellar; producer.

Bodegas y Bebidas [bod-day-gas ee beh-bee-das] (Spain) One of Spain's most dynamic wine companies, and maker of *Campo Viejo.*

B

Body Usually used as "full-bodied", meaning a wine with mouth-filling flavours and probably a fairly high alcohol content.

⏳ **Boekenhoutskloof** [ber-ken-hurt-skloof] (*Franschoek*, South Africa) Marc Kent's little winery is the source of the Cape's – and one of the worlds' – best Semillons. The Syrah and Cabernet are terrific too. Porcupine Ridge is the second label. ★★★★★ **1997 Semillon £££**

⏳ **Jean-Marc Boillot** [bwah-yoh] (*Burgundy*, France) Small *Pommard domaine* run by the son of the winemaker at *Olivier Leflaive*, and offering really good examples from neighbouring villages *Puligny-Montrachet* and *Volnay*. ★★★★★ **1998 Bourgogne £££**

⏳ **Jean-Claude Boisset** [bwah-say] (*Burgundy*, France) Dynamic *négociant* that now owns a long list of *Burgundy négociants*, including the excellent *Jaffelin* and the improved though still far from dazzling *Bouchard Aîné*. Boisset also makes passable wines in *Languedoc-Roussillon*.

⏳ **Boisson-Vadot** [bwah-son va-doh] (*Burgundy*, France) Classy, small *Meursault domaine*.

⏳ **Bolgheri** [bol-geh-ree] (*Tuscany*, Italy) Increasingly exciting and recently officially recognized region that was originally made famous by red superstars such as *Antinori's Sassicaia* and *Ornellaia*. Other impressive producers now include: *Belvedere, Grattamacco,* Tenuta dell'Ornellaia, Le Macchiole, and Satta, and there are some top-class whites made from the *Vermentino*.

⏳ **Bolla** [bol-lah] (*Veneto*, Italy) Producer of plentiful, adequate *Valpolicella* and *Soave,* and of smaller quantities of impressive single vineyard wines like Jago and Creso.

⏳ **Bollinger** [bol-an-jay] (*Champagne*, France) Great family-owned firm at *Ay*, whose full-flavoured wines need age. The luscious and rare *Vieilles Vignes* is made from pre-*phylloxera* vines, while the nutty *RD* was the first late-disgorged *Champagne* to hit the market. The 1988 RD is a current star. ★★★★ **1992 Grande Année ££££**

Bommes [bom] (*Bordeaux*, France) *Sauternes commune* and village containing several *Premiers Crus* such as *la Tour Blanche, Lafaurie-Peyrauguey, Rabaud-Promis,* and *Rayne Vigneau.* 70 **71 75** 76 **83** 85 86 88 89 90 95 96 97 98

⏳ **Ch. le Bon-Pasteur** [bon-pas-stuhr] (*Pomerol, Bordeaux*, France) The impressive private estate of *Michel Rolland*, who acts as consultant – and helps to make fruit-driven wines – for half his neighbours, as well as producers in almost every other wine-growing region in the universe.

⏳ **Domaine de la Bongran** [bon-grah] A good Macon from Jean Thévenet.

⏳ **Henri Bonneau** [bon-noh] (*Rhône*, France) *Châteauneuf-du-Pape* producer with two special *cuvées* – "Marie Beurrier" and "des Celestins" – and a cult following.

⏳ **Dom. Bonneau du Martray** [bon-noh doo mahr-tray] (*Burgundy*, France) Largest grower of *Corton-Charlemagne* and impressive producer thereof. Also makes a classy red *Grand Cru Corton.* ★★★★★ **1998 Corton ££££**

⏳ Bonnes Mares [bon-mahr] (*Burgundy*, France) Rich *Morey St. Denis Grand Cru.* Dom d'Auvenay; Bouchard Père; Clair Daü; Drouhin; Dujac; Fougeray de Beauclair; Groffier; Jadot; Laurent; Roumier; de Vogüé.

⏳ **Ch. Bonnet** [bon-nay] (*Bordeaux*, France) Top-quality *Entre-Deux-Mers château* whose wines are made by *Jacques Lurton.*

⏳ **F. Bonnet** [bon-nay] (*Champagne*, France) Reliable producer under its own and customers' names. Winemaker, Daniel Thibault also makes *Charles Heidsieck.* ★★★★ **Bonnet Rosé £££**

⏳ Bonnezeaux [bonn-zoh] (*Loire*, France) Within the *Coteaux du Layon*, this is one of the world's greatest sweet wine-producing areas, though the wines have often tended to be spoiled by heavy-handedness with sulphur dioxide. 76 83 **85** 86 **88 89** 90 93 *94* 95 96 97 99 *Ch. de Fesles*; Dom. Godineau; Les Grandes Vignes; René Renou; Sasonniere; Ch. la Varière.

B

Ⴤ **Bonny Doon Vineyard** (*Santa Cruz,* California) Randall Grahm, sorcerer's apprentice, and original "Rhône Ranger" also has an evident affection for unfashionable French and Italian varieties, which he uses for characterful red, dry, and *late harvest* whites. The sheep-like Californian wine industry needs more mavericks like Grahm. ★★★★★ 1996 Bonny Doon Carignan ££

Ⴤ **Bonvin Jean** [bon-van] (*Valais,* Switzerland) Top producer of traditional local varieties. ★★★★ 1996 Amigne du Valais

Ⴤ **Bonterra** *Fetzer's* recommendable organic brand.

Ⴤ **Tenuta Bonzara** [bont-zah-rah] (*Emilia Romagna,* Italy) *Cabernet Sauvignon* and *Merlot* specialists producing wines that compete with the starriest of *Super-Tuscans.*

Borba [Bohr-bah] (*Alentejo,* Portugal) See *Alentejo.*

Ⴤ **Bordeaux** [bor-doh] (France) Largest (supposedly) quality wine region in France, producing reds, rosés, and deep pink *Clairets* from *Cabernet Sauvignon, Cabernet Franc, Petit Verdot,* and *Merlot,* and dry and sweet whites from (principally) blends of *Sémillon* and *Sauvignon,* with a little *Muscadelle. Bordeaux Supérieur* denotes (relatively) riper grapes. The rare dry whites from regions like the *Médoc* and *Sauternes* are (curiously) sold as *Bordeaux Blanc,* so even the efforts by Châteaux d'Yquem and Margaux are sold under the same label as basic supermarket white. See *Graves, Médoc, Pomerol, St. Emilion, etc.*

Ⴤ **Borgo del Tiglio** [bor-goh dehl tee-lee-yoh] (*Friuli,* Italy) One of the classiest wineries in this region, hitting the target with a range of varieties that includes *Sauvignon Blanc, Chardonnay, Malvasia,* and Tocai Friulano.

Ⴤ **Giacomo Borgogno** [baw-gon-yoh] (*Piedmont,* Italy) Hitherto old-fashioned *Barolo* producer that is now embracing modern winemaking and producing fruitier, more immediately likeable wines. ★★★★ 1996 Barolo Classico ££££

Ⴤ **De Bortoli** [baw-tol-lee] (*Yarra* and *Riverina,* Australia) Fast-developing firm that startled the world by making a *botrytized,* peachy, honeyed "Noble One" *Sémillon* in the unfashionable *Riverina,* before shifting its focus to the very different climate of the *Yarra Valley.* Top wines here include trophy-winning *Pinot Noirs* and impressive *Shirazes.* Windy Peak is a second label. ★★★★ 1999 Noble One ££

Ⴤ **Bodega Luigi Bosca** [bos-kah] (*Mendoza,* Argentina) Good producer with good *Sauvignons* and *Cabernets.* ★★★★ 1996 Cabernet Sauvignon ££

Ⴤ **Boscaini** [bos-kah-yee-nee] (*Veneto,* Italy) Innovative producer linked to *Masi* and making better-than-average *Valpolicella* and *Soave.* Look out for individual-vineyard wines such as the starry Ca' de Loi Valpolicella. ★★★★ 1996 Amarone Della Valpolicella di Marano ££

Ⴤ **Boscarelli** [bos-kah-reh-lee] (*Tuscany,* Italy) The star producer of *Vino Nobile de Montepulciano* is also the place to find its own delicious Boscarelli *Super-Tuscan* and the exciting new De Ferrari blend of *Sangiovese* with the local Prugnolo Gentile. ★★★★ 1997 Boscarelli £££

Ⴤ **Boschendal Estate** [bosh-shen-dahl] (*Cape,* South Africa) Recent investment by its Anglo-American owners is helping to raise the game here. This is the place to find some of the *Cape's* best sparkling wine and one of its most European-style Shirazes. Watch out for the new *Pinot Noirs* too. ★★★★ 1998 Shiraz ££

Ⴤ **Ch. le Boscq** [bosk] (*St. Estèphe Cru Bourgeois, Bordeaux,* France) Improving property that excels in good vintages, but still tends to make tough wines in lesser ones. 82 83 85 86 87 88 **89** 90 92 **93 95 96 98 00**

Ⴤ **Le Bosquet des Papes** [bos-kay day pap] (*Rhône,* France) Serious *Châteauneuf-du-Pape* producer, making a range of styles that all last. The pure *Grenache* example is particularly impressive.

B

Botrytis [boh-tri-tiss] Botrytis cinerea, a fungal infection that attacks and shrivels grapes, evaporating their water and concentrating their sweetness. Vital to *Sauternes*, the finer German and Austrian sweet wines, and *Tokaji*. See *Sauternes, Trockenbeerenauslese, Tokaji.*

☵ **Bott-Geyl** [bott-gihl] (*Alsace,* France) Young producer, whose impressive *Grand Cru* wines suit those who like their *Alsace* big and rich. The oaked (*"barriques"*) *Pinot Gris* is quite unusual. ★★★★ 1998 Tokay Pinot Gris Appoline "Barriques" £££

Bottle-fermented Commonly found on the labels of US sparkling wines to indicate the *Méthode Champenoise*, and gaining wider currency. Beware, though – it can indicate inferior *"transfer method"* wines.

☵ **Pascal Bouchard** [boo-shahrr d] (*Burgundy,* France) One of the best small producers in *Chablis.* ★★★★ 1998 Chablis Vieilles Vignes ££

☵ **Bouchard Aîné** [boo-shahrr day-nay] (*Burgundy,* France) Once unimpressive merchant, now taken over by *Boisset* and improving under the winemaking control of the excellent Bernard Repolt.

☵ **Bouchard-Finlayson** [boo-shard] (*Walker Bay,* South Africa) Burgundy-style joint-venture between Peter Finlayson and Paul Bouchard, formerly of *Bouchard Aîné* in France. ★★★★ 1999 Galpin Peak Pinot Noir ££

☵ **Bouchard Père & Fils** [boo-shahrr pehr ay fees] (*Burgundy,* France) Traditional merchant with great vineyards. Bought in 1996 by the *Champagne* house of *Henriot*. The best wines are the *Beaunes,* as well as the La Romanée from *Vosne-Romanée*. Also doing wonders in *Chablis* at *William Fèvre*. ★★★★ 1998 Beaune Grèves de l'Enfant Jésus £££

☵ **Vin de Pays des Bouches du Rhône** (*Midi,* France) Dynamic region around *Aix* en *Provence*, focusing on *Rhône* and *Bordeaux* varieties. Top wines here include the great *Dom. de Trévallon*. Dom. des Gavelles.

☵ **Pascal Bouley** [boo-lay] (*Burgundy,* France) Producer of good, if not always refined, *Volnay*. ★★★★ 1998 Volnay Premier Cru £££

Bouquet Overall smell, often made up of several separate aromas. Used by Anglo-Saxon enthusiasts more often than by professionals.

☵ **Henri Bourgeois** [on-ree boor-jwah] (*Loire,* France) High-quality *Sancerre* and *Pouilly-Fumé* grower-négociant with a sense of humour (a top wine is called "la Bourgeoisie"). Also owns Laporte.

☵ **Ch. Bourgneuf-Vayron** [boor-nurf vay-roh] (*Pomerol, Bordeaux,* France) Fast-rising star with deliciously rich plummy *Merlot* fruit.

Bourgogne [boorr-goyn] (*Burgundy,* France) French for *Burgundy*.

☵ **Bourgueil** [boorr-goyy] (*Loire,* France) Red AC in the *Touraine,* producing crisp, grassy-blackcurranty, 100 per cent *Cabernet Franc* wines that can age well in good years like 1995. Amirault; Boucard; Caslot-Galbrun; Cognard; Delaunay; *Druet.*

☵ **Ch. Bouscassé** [boo-ska-say] (*Madiran,* France) See *Ch. Montus.*

☵ **Ch. Bouscaut** [boos-koh] (*Pessac-Léognan, Bordeaux,* France) Good, rather than great *Graves* property; better white than red.

☵ **J. Boutari** [boo-tah-ree] (*Greece*) One of the most reliable names in Greece, producing good, traditional red wines in Nemea and Naoussa.

☵ **Bouvet-Ladubay** [boo-vay lad-doo-bay] (*Loire,* France) Producer of good *Loire* sparkling wine and better *Saumur-Champigny* reds. A welcome new move has been the introduction of top-quality mini-cuvées, labelled as "les Non Pareils". ★★★★★ 1998 Chinon les Non Pareils £££

🍇 **Bouvier** [boo-vee-yay] (Austria) Characterless variety used to produce tasty but mostly simple *late harvest* wines.

Bouzeron [booz-rron] (*Burgundy,* France) *Côte Chalonnaise* village known for *Aligoté*. ★★★★★ 1999 Aligoté Aubert de Villaine ££

B

✗ **Bouzy Rouge** [boo-zee roozh] (*Champagne,* France) Sideline of a black grape village: an often thin-bodied, rare, and overpriced red wine, which can occasionally age well. Paul Bara; *Barancourt;* Brice; Ledru.

✗ **Bowen Estate** [boh-wen] (*Coonawarra,* Australia) An early *Coonawarra* pioneer proving that the region can be as good for *Shiraz* as for *Cabernet.*

✗ **Domaines Boyar** [boy-yahr] (*Bulgaria*) Privatized producers, especially in the *Suhindol* region, selling increasingly worthwhile "Reserve" reds under the Lovico label. Other wines are less reliably recommendable.

✗ **Ch. Boyd-Cantenac** [boyd-kon-teh-nak] (*Margaux 3ème Cru Classé, Bordeaux,* France) A third growth performing at the level of a fifth – or less.

🍇 **Brachetto d'Acqui** [brah-KET-toh dak-wee] (*Piedmont,* Italy) Eccentric *Muscatty* red grape. Often *frizzante.* Banfi; *Batasiolo;* Marenco.

✗ **Braida** [brih-dah] (*Piedmont,* Italy) A big producer whose range includes *Barberas* galore and some highly recommendable *Dolcetto* and *Chardonnay.*

✗ **Dom Brana** [brah-nah] (*Southwest,* France) One of the best producers of Irouleguy. ★★★★ 1998 Cuvée Harri Gorri ££

✗ **Ch. Branaire (-Ducru)** [brah-nehr doo-kroo] (*St.-Julien 4ème Cru Classé, Bordeaux,* France) New owners are doing wonders for this estate. Red: **82** 83 85 86 87 88 *89* 90 91 92 93 *95* 96 97 98 00 ★★★★ 1998 £££

✗ **Brand's Laira** [lay-rah] (*Coonawarra,* Australia) Traditional producer, much improved since its purchase by *McWilliams.* Delving into the world of *Pinot Noir* and sparkling *Grenache* rosé.

✗ **Ch. Brane-Cantenac** [brahn kon teh-nak] (*Margaux 2ème Cru Classé, Bordeaux,* France) Often underachieving *Margaux*; made a better wine than usual in 1999. The unprepossessingly named second label Ch. Notton can be a good buy. 78 79 82 83 85 **86** 87 88 89 90 95 96 98 ★★★★ 1999 £££

✗ **Branon** [brah-no'n] (*Graves, Bordeaux,* France) The first "Garage Wine" in the Graves, made in 2000 by Jean-Luc Thunevin and given an orgasmic response by critics who enjoy intensity and oak. Predictably pricy.

🍇 *Braquet* [brah-ket] (*Midi,* France) Grape variety used in *Bellet.*

Brauneberg [brow-nuh-behrg] (*Mosel,* Germany) Village best known for the *Juffer* vineyard. ★★★★★ 1997 Riesling Auslese Gold Cap Brauneberger; 1997 Juffer-Sonnenuhr Riesling Spätlese Fritz Haag ££££

Brazil Large quantities of light-bodied wine (including *Zinfandel* that is sold in the US under the Marcus James label) are produced in a rainy region close to Puerto Allegre. The Palomas vineyard on the *Uruguayan* border has a state-of-the-art winery and a good climate but has yet to make exciting wine.

✗ **Breaky Bottom** (Sussex, England) One of Britain's best, whose *Seyval Blanc* rivals dry wines made in the *Loire* from supposedly finer grapes.

✗ **Marc Bredif** [bray-deef] (*Loire,* France) Big, and quite variable *Loire* producer, with still and sparkling wine, including some good *Vouvray.*

✗ **Breganze** (*Veneto,* Italy) Little-known *DOC* for characterful reds and whites. Maculan is the star here.

✗ **Palacio de Brejoeira** [breh-sho-eh-rah] (*Vinho Verde,* Portugal) Top class pure *Alvarinho Vinho Verde.*

✗ **Bodegas Breton** [breh-tonn] (*Rioja,* Spain) Small, new-wave producer to watch for his Dominio de Conté single-vineyard wine.

✗ **Ch. du Breuil** [doo breuh-yee] (*Loire,* France) Source of good *Coteaux de Layon,* and relatively ordinary examples of other *appellations.* ★★★★ 1998 Coteaux de Layon, Vieilles Vignes, Beaulieu ££

✗ **Weingut Georg Breuer** [broy-yer] (*Rheingau,* Germany) Innovative producer with classy *Rieslings* and high-quality *Rülander.*

✗ **Bricco Manzoni** [bree-koh man-tzoh-nee] (*Piedmont,* Italy) Non-*DOC* oaky, red blend made by Rocche dei Manzoni from *Nebbiolo* and *Barbera* grapes grown in *Monforte* vineyards that could produce *Barolo.* ★★★★★ 1995 £££

✗ **Brick House** (*Oregon*) A small organic slice of *Burgundy* in Yamhill County founded by a former television reporter. The *Gamay* can be as good as the *Pinot* and the *Chardonnay.*

B

℥ **Bricout** [bree-koo] (*Champagne,* France) A cleverly marketed range of good-to-very-good wines including the Cuvée Spéciale Arthur Bricout.

℥ **Bridgehampton** (*Long Island*) Producer of first-class *Merlot* and *Chardonnay* good enough to worry a Californian.

℥ **Bridgewater Mill** (*Adelaide Hills,* Australia) More modest sister winery and brand to *Petaluma.* Recently bought by a US winery, so likely to be widely distributed in the US. Its fair prices should make it popular.

℥ **Peter Bright** Australian-born Peter Bright of the *JP Vinhos* winery produces top-class Portuguese wines, including Tinta da Anfora and Quinta da Bacalhoa. In addition he now produces a growing range in countries such as Spain, Italy, and Chile under the Bright Brothers label. ★★★★ 1998 Bright Bros. Palmela ££

℥ **Bristol Cream** (*Jerez,* Spain) See *Harvey's.*

℥ **Jean-Marc Brocard** [broh-kahrr] (*Burgundy,* France) Very classy *Chablis* producer with well-defined individual vineyard wines, also producing unusually good *Aligoté.* ★★★★★ 1999 Sauvignon de Saint-Bris £££

℥ **Brokenwood** (*Hunter Valley,* Australia) Long-established source of great *Sémillon, Shiraz,* and even (unusually for the *Hunter Valley*) *Cabernet.* Look for the "Cricket Pitch" bottlings. ★★★★ 1998 Cricket Pitch Shiraz ££

℥ **Brouilly** [broo-yee] (*Burgundy,* France) Largest of the 10 *Beaujolais Crus* producing pure, fruity *Gamay.* 94 95 96 97 98 Duboeuf; Cotton; Sylvain Fessy; Laurent Martray; Michaud; Piron; Roland; Ruet; Ch. des Tours.

℥ **Ch. Broustet** [broo-stay] (*Barsac 2ème Cru Classé, Bordeaux,* France) Rich, quite old-fashioned, well-oaked *Barsac* second growth. 70 **71 75** 76 **83 85 86 88 89 90** 95 96 97 98 99

℥ **Brown Brothers** (*Victoria,* Australia) Proudly family-owned and *Victoria*-focused winery with a penchant for new wine regions and grapes. The wines are reliably good, though for excitement you should look to the *Shiraz* and the *Liqueur Muscat.* The *Orange Muscat* and *Flora* remains a delicious mouthful of liquid marmalade, and the *Tarrango* is a good alternative to *Beaujolais.* The sparkling wine is a new success, and the Italian varietals are among the best in the New World. ★★★★★ 1996 Nebbiolo £££

℥ **David Bruce** (*Santa Cruz,* California) Long established *Zinfandel* specialist whose fairly-priced *Petite Sirah* and *Pinot Noir* are also worth seeking out.

℥ **Bruisyard Vineyard** [broos-syard] (*Suffolk,* England) High-quality vineyard. ★★★ 1998 Müller-Thurgau ££

℥ **Le Brun de Neuville** [bruhn duh nuh-veel] (*Champagne,* France) Good little-known producer with classy **vintage** and excellent rosé, non-vintage, and *Blanc de Blancs.* ★★★★ Cuvée Selection Brut ££

℥ **Willi Bründlmayer** [broondl-mi-yurh] (Austria) Oaked *Chardonnay* and *Pinots* of every kind, *Grüner Veltliner,* and even a fair shot at *Cabernet.* ★★★★ 1999 Grüner Veltliner Kamptal Alte Reben Qualitätswein Trocken £££

℥ **Lucien & André Brunel** [broo-nel] (*Rhône,* France) The Brunels' "Les Caillous" produces good, traditional, built-to-last *Châteauneuf-du-Pape.*

℥ **Brunello di Montalcino** [broo-nell-oh dee mon-tahl-chee-noh] (*Tuscany,* Italy) *DOCG* red from a *Sangiovese* clone. 78 79 81 **82 85 88 90 93** 94 95 96 97 Altesino; Argiano; Villa Banfi; Barbi; Tenuta Caparzo; Costanti; Lambardi; Col d'Orcia; Poggio Antico; Talenti; Val di Suga.

Brut [broot] Dry, particularly of *Champagne* and sparkling wines. Brut nature/sauvage/zéro are even drier, while *"Extra-Sec"* is perversely applied to (slightly) sweeter sparkling wine.

🍇 **Bual** [bwahl] (*Madeira*) Grape producing soft, nutty wine – wonderful with cheese. **Blandy's; Cossart Gordon; Henriques & Henriques.**

℥ **Buçaco Palace Hotel** [boo-sah-koh] (Portugal) Red and white wines made from grapes grown in *Bairrada* and *Dão.* They last forever but cannot be bought outside the Disneyesque hotel itself.

Bucelas [boo-sel-las] (Portugal) *DO* area near Lisbon, best known for its intensely coloured, aromatic, bone-dry white wines. *Caves Velhas.*

B

℧ **Buena Vista** [bway-nah vihs-tah] (*Carneros*, California) One of the biggest estates in *Carneros*, this is an improving producer of California *Chardonnay, Pinot Noir,* and *Cabernet*. Look out for Grand Reserve wines.

Bugey [boo-jay] (*Savoie*, France) *Savoie* district producing a variety of wines, including spicy white *Roussette de Bugey*, from the grape of that name.

℧ **Reichsrat von Buhl** [rike-srat fon bool] (*Pfalz*, Germany) This is one of the best estates in the Pfalz area, due in large part to the success of vineyards like the *Forster Jesuitengarten*. ★★★★ 1997 Forster Pechstein Riesling Kabinett £££

℧ **Buitenverwachting** [bite-turn-fur-vak-turng] (*Constantia*, South Africa) Enjoying a revival since the early 1980s, a showpiece organic *Constantia* winery making tasty organic whites.

Bulgaria Developing slowly since the advent of privatization and *flying winemakers*. Bulgaria's reputation still relies on its country wines and affordable *Cabernet Sauvignons* and *Merlots*. *Mavrud* is the traditional red variety and *Lovico, Rousse, Iambol, Suhindol,* and *Haskovo* the names to look out for.

℧ **Bull's Blood** (*Eger*, Hungary) The gutsy red wine, aka Egri Bikaver, which gave defenders the strength to fight off Turkish invaders, is mostly aenemic stuff now, but privatization has brought some improvement, especially thanks to winemaker *Tibor Gal*.

℧ **Bernard Burgaud** [boor-goh] (*Rhône*, France) Serious producer of *Côte Rôtie*. ★★★★ 1997 Côte Rôtie £££

℧ **Grant Burge** (*Barossa Valley*, Australia) Dynamic Shiraz specialist and – since 1993 – owner of *Basedows*. The Holy Trinity Rhône is fine but the oaky Meshach gets the attention. ★★★★★ 1995 Meshach £££

Burgenland [boor-gen-lund] (Austria) Wine region bordering *Hungary*, climatically ideal for fine sweet *Auslese* and *Beerenauslese*. Feiler-Artinger; Kollwentz-Römerhof; Helmut Lang; *Kracher; Opitz;* Wachter.

℧ **Weinkellerei Burgenland** [vine-kel-ler-ri boor-gen-lund] (*Neusiedlersee*, Austria) Cooperative with highly commercial *late harvest* wines.

℧ **Alain Burguet** [al-lan boor-gay] (*Burgundy*, France) One-man *domaine* proving how good plain *Gevrey-Chambertin* can be without heavy doses of new oak. ★★★★ 1997 Gevrey-Chambertin Vieilles Vignes £££

℧ **Burgundy** (France) Home to *Pinot Noir* and *Chardonnay*; wines range from banal to sublime, but are never cheap. See *Chablis, Côte de Nuits, Côte de Beaune, Mâconnais, Beaujolais,* and individual villages.

℧ **Leo Buring** [byoo-ring] (*South Australia*) One of the many labels used by the Southcorp (*Penfolds* etc.) group, specializing in ageable *Rieslings* and mature *Shiraz's*.

℧ **Weingut Dr. Bürklin-Wolf** [boor-klin-volf] (*Pfalz*, Germany) Impressive estate with great organic *Riesling* vineyards and fine, dry wines.

℧ **Ernest J&F Burn** [boorn] (*Alsace*, France) Classy estate with vines in the Goldert *Grand Cru*. Great traditional *Gewurztraminer, Riesling,* and *Muscat*. ★★★★ 1998 Gewurztraminer Goldert Clos St-Imer la Chapelle £££

Buttery Rich, fat smell often found in good *Chardonnay* (often as a result of *malolactic fermentation*) or in wine that has been left on its *lees*.

℧ **Buzet** [boo-zay] (*Southwest*, France) Eastern neighbour of *Bordeaux*, using the same grape varieties to make generally basic wines. Buzet; co-operative (Baron d' Ardeuil); Ch. de Gueyze; Tissot.

℧ **Byington** [bi-ing-ton] (*Santa Cruz*, California) Fine producer of *Chardonnay* (Spring Ridge Vineyard) and *Pinot Noir*, and a rare example of good California Semillon. ★★★★ 1995 Saint Charles Semillon £££

℧ **Byron Vineyard** [bi-ron] (*Santa Barbara*, California) Impressive *Santa Barbara* winery with investment from *Mondavi*, and a fine line in *Pinots* and (particularly good) subtly oaked *Chardonnays*. ★★★★ 1998 Santa Maria Chardonnay £££

C

Ca' del Bosco [kah-del-bos-koh] (*Lombardy*, Italy) Classic, if pricey, *barrique*-aged *Cabernet/Merlot* ("Maurizio Zanella") blends and fine *Chardonnay Pinot Noi* ("*Pinero*"), and *Pinot Bianco/Pinot Noir/Chardonnay Méthode Champenoise Franciacorta*. Look out also for the new Carmenero, made from the *Carmeniere*. ★★★★★ 1995 Franciacorta Cuvee Annamaria Clementi ££££

Luis Caballero [loo-is cab-i-yer-roh] (*Jerez*, Spain) Quality *sherry* producer responsible for the *Burdon* range; also owns *Lustau*.

Château La Cabanne [la ca-ban] (*Pomerol, Bordeaux,* France) Up-and-coming *Pomerol* property. 82 83 **85** 86 88 **89** 90 92 93 94 *95* 96 97 *98 99 00*

Cabardès [cab-bahr-des] (*Southwest,* France) Recent appellation north of Carcassonne using Southern and Bordeaux varieties to produce good, if mostly rustic, reds. Confusingly, some are Cabernet-Merlot dominated, while others lean toward the Rhône. Cabrol; Pennautier; Salitis; Ventenac.

Cabernet d'Anjou/de Saumur [cab-behr-nay don-joo / dur soh-moor] (*Loire,* France) Light, fresh, grassy, blackcurranty rosés, typical of their grape, the *Cabernet Franc.* 96 97 *98*

Cabernet Franc [ka-behr-nay fron] Kid brother of *Cabernet Sauvignon*; blackcurranty but more leafy. Best in the *Loire,* Italy, and increasingly in Australia, California, and Washington, of course, as a partner of the *Cabernet Sauvignon* and particularly *Merlot* in Bordeaux. See *Chinon* and *Trentino.*

Cabernet Sauvignon [ka-ber-nay soh-vin-yon] The great blackcurranty, cedary, green peppery grape of *Bordeaux*, where it is blended with *Merlot.* Despite increasing competition from the *Merlot*, this is still by far the most successful red varietal, grown in every reasonably warm winemaking country on the planet. See *Bordeaux, Coonawarra, Chile, Napa,* etc.

Marqués de Cáceres [mahr-kehs day cath-thay-res] (*Rioja,* Spain) Modern French-influenced *bodega* making fresh-tasting wines. A good, if anonymous, new-style white has been joined by a promising oak-fermented version and a recommendable rosé (*rosado*), plus a grapey *Muscat*-style white.

Ch. Cadet-Piola [ka-day pee-yoh-lah] (*St. Emilion Grand Cru Classé, Bordeaux,* France) Wines that are made to last, with fruit and *tannin* to spare. 79 **82 83 85** 86 88 89 **90** 92 **93** *94 95 96 97 98*

Cadillac [kad-dee-yak] (*Bordeaux,* France) Sweet but rarely luscious (non-*botrytis*) *Sémillon* and *Sauvignon* whites. Ch. Fayau is the star wine. Its *d'Yquem*-style label is pretty chic too. 88 89 90 94 95 96 97 98 Carsin; Cayla; Fayau; du Juge; Manos; Memoires; Reynon

Cahors [kah-orr] (*Southwest,* France) Often rustic wines produced from the local *Tannat* and the *Cot* (*Malbec*). Some are *Beaujolais*-like, while others are *tannic* and full-bodied, though far lighter than in the days when people spoke of "the black wines of Cahors". Ch. de Caix; la Caminade; du Cèdre; Clos la Coutale; *Clos de Gamot;* Gautoul; de Hauterivem; Haute-Serre; Lagrezette; Lamartine; Latuc; Prieuré de Cenac; Rochet-Lamother; Clos Triguedina.

Cain Cellars (*Napa,* California) Spectacular *Napa* hillside vineyards devoted to producing a classic *Bordeaux* blend of five varieties – hence the name of the wine. ★★★★★ 1997 Cain Five £££

Cairanne [keh-ran] (*Rhône,* France) Named *Côtes du Rhône* village known for good peppery reds. 85 88 89 **90** 92 93 **95** 96 97 98 99 00 Dom d'Ameilhaud; Aubert; Brusset; Oratoire St-Martin; Richaud; Tardieu-Laurent.

Cakebread (*Napa,* California) Long-established producer of rich reds, very good *Sauvignon Blanc, Chardonnay,* and improving *Pinot Noir.* ★★★★ 1997 Benchland Cabernet Sauvignon £££

Cairanne
Domaine de la Présidente
Côtes du Rhône
APPELLATION COTES-DU-RHONE-VILLAGES CONTROLEE
Mis en bouteille au Domaine
MAX AUBERT

C

Calabria [kah-lah-bree-ah] (Italy) The "toe" of the Italian boot, making Cirò from the local Gaglioppo reds and *Greco* whites. *Cabernet* and *Chardonnay* are promising, too, especially from *Librandi*. Watch out for new wave *Aglianico*.

☤ **Calem** [kah-lin] (*Douro,* Portugal) Quality-conscious, small *port* producer. The speciality *Colheita tawnies* are among the best of their kind.
★★★★ 1977 Vintage Port £££

☤ **Calera Wine Co.** [ka-lehr-uh] (*Santa Benito,* California) Maker of some of *California's* best, longest-lived *Pinot Noir* from individual vineyards such as Jensen, Mills, Reed, and Selleck. The *Chardonnay* and *Viognier* are pretty special too. ★★★★ 1997 Mount Harlan Viognier £££

California (US) Major wine-producing area of the US. See *Napa, Sonoma, Santa Barbara, Amador, Mendocino,* etc, plus individual wineries. Red: 84 85 86 87 **90 91** 92 **93** 95 96 97 98 White: **85** 90 91 92 **95** 96 97 98

☤ **Viña Caliterra** [kal-lee-tay-rah] (*Curico,* Chile) Sister company of *Errazuriz.* Now a 50-50 partner with *Mondavi* and co-producer of *Seña.* ★★★★ 1998 Cabernet Sauvignon £

☤ **Callaway** (*Temecula* California) An unfashionable part of California, and a deliciously unfashionable style of – unoaked – *Chardonnay.*

☤ **Ch. Calon-Ségur** [kal-lon say-goor] (*St. Estèphe 3ème Cru Classé, Bordeaux,* France) Traditional *St. Estèphe* now surpassing its status. Fine in 2000. 82 83 **85** 86 88 89 90 91 93 94 **95** 96 97 98 99 00 ★★★★★ 1998 ££££

☤ **Cambria** (*Santa Barbara,* California) Huge operation in the *Santa Maria Valley* belonging to the dynamic *Kendall Jackson* and producing fairly priced and good, if rarely complex, *Chardonnay, Pinot Noir, Syrah, Viognier,* and *Sangiovese.* ★★★★★ 1997 Late Harvest Viognier £££

☤ **Ch. Camensac** [kam-mon-sak] (*Haut-Médoc 5ème Cru Classé, Bordeaux,* France) Improving property following investment in 1994. **82** 85 **86** 88 89 90 91 92 93 **94 95** 96 97 98 00★★★★ 1998 £££

☤ **Cameron** (*Oregon,* US) John Paul makes terrific *Pinot Noir* in this Yamhill estate – plus some impressive *Pinot Blanc.*

Campania [kahm-pan-nyah] (Italy) Region surrounding Naples, known for *Taurasi, Lacryma Christi,* and *Greco di Tufo* and wines from *Mastroberadino.*

☤ **Campbells** (*Rutherglen,* Australia) Classic producer of fortified *Muscat* and rich, fortified reds under the Bobbie Burns label.
★★★★ 1998 Shiraz Durif Cabernet Sauvignon £££

☤ **Campillo** [kam-pee-yoh] (*Rioja,* Spain) A small estate producing *Rioja* made purely from *Tempranillo,* showing what this grape can do. The white is less impressive. ★★★★ 1995 Rioja Riserva ££

☤ **Bodegas Campo Viejo** [kam-poh vyay-hoh] (*Rioja,* Spain) A go-ahead, if underrated *bodega* whose *Reserva* and *Gran Reserva* are full of rich fruit. Albor, the unoaked red (pure *Tempranillo*) and white (*Viura*) are first-class examples of modern Spanish winemaking. ★★★★ 1997 Reserva ££

Canada Surprising friends and foes alike, British Columbia and, more specifically, *Ontario* are producing good *Chardonnay, Riesling,* improving *Pinot Noirs* and intense *Icewines,* usually from the *Vidal* grape. Cave Springs; Chateau des Charmes; Henry of Pelham; Hillebrand; Inniskillin; Jackson-Triggs; Konzelmann; Magnotta; Mission Hill; Pelee Island; Peller Estates; Pilliteri; Reif Estate; Stoney Ridge; Sumac Ridge; Vineland Estates.

☤ **Canard Duchêne** [kan-nah doo-shayn] (*Champagne,* France) Improving subsidiary of *Veuve Clicquot.* ★★★★ Grande Cuvée Charles VII £££

☤ **Canberra District** (*New South Wales,* Australia) Confounding the critics, a small group of producers led by *Doonkuna, Helm's,* and *Lark Hill* are making good *Rhône*-style reds and *Rieslings* in high-altitude vineyards here.

C

Ⴏ **Candido** [kan-dee doh] (*Apulia*, Italy) Top producer of deliciously chocolatey Salıce Salentino. ★★★★ 1997 Duca d'Aragona £££

Ⴏ **Canépa** [can-nay-pah] (Chile) Good rather than great winery, making progress with *Chardonnays* and *Rieslings* as well as reds that suffer from over-generous exposure to oak. ★★★★ 2000 Sauvignon Blanc ££

🍇 **Cannonau** [kan-non-now] (*Sardinia*, Italy) A red *clone* of the *Grenache*, producing a variety of wine styles from sweet to dry, mostly in *Sardinia*.

Ⴏ **Cannonau di Sardegna** [kan-non-now dee sahr-den-yah] (*Sardinia*, Italy) Heady, robust, dry-to-sweet, *DOC* red made from the *Cannonau*.

Ⴏ **Ch. Canon** [kan-non] (*St. Emilion Premier Grand Cru Classé, Bordeaux*, France) Back on track after a tricky patch in the 1990s. The keynote here is elegance rather than power. 82 83 **85 86** 87 **88 89 90** 93 95 96 **97** 98 00

Ⴏ **Ch. Canon de Brem** [kan-non dur brem] (*Canon-Fronsac, Bordeaux*, France) A very good *Moueix*-run *Fronsac* property. 81 **82** 83 85 86 88 **89** 90 92 93 **95** 96 **97** 98 00 ★★★★ 1998 ££

Ⴏ **Canon-Fronsac** [kah-non fron-sak] (*Bordeaux*, France) Small *appellation* bordering on *Pomerol*, with attractive plummy, *Merlot*-based reds from increasingly good value, if rustic, petits *châteaux*. 82 83 85 86 88 89 90 94 95 96 96 97 98 *Ch. Canon-Moueix;* Ch. Moulin Pey-Labrie.

Ⴏ **Ch. Canon-la-Gaffelière** [kan-non lah gaf-fel-yehr] (*St. Emilion Grand Cru Classé, Bordeaux*, France) High-flying estate run by an innovative, quality-conscious German who, in 1996, created the instant superstar *la Mondotte*. Rich, ultra-concentrated wine. 82 **85 86 88 89 90 93** 94 95 96 97 98 99 00

Ⴏ **Ch. Canon-Moueix** [kan-non mwex] (*Canon-Fronsac, Bordeaux*, France) A characteristically stylish addition to the *Moueix* empire in *Canon-Fronsac*. A wine to beat many a pricier *St. Emilion*.

Ⴏ **Ch. Cantemerle** [kont-mehrl] (*Haut-Médoc 5ème Cru Classé, Bordeaux*, France) A *Cru Classé* situated outside the main villages of the *Médoc*. Classy, perfumed wine with bags of blackcurrant fruit. 61 78 81 82 **83** 85 88 **89** 90 92 93 95 **96** 98 00 ★★★★ 1996 ££

Ⴏ **Ch. Cantenac-Brown** [kont-nak brown] (*Margaux 3ème Cru Classé, Bordeaux*, France) Now under the same ownership as Ch. Pichon Baron but at last showing the same class in 2000. 85 **86** 87 88 89 **90** 93 94 95 **97** 98 00

Canterbury (New Zealand) Following St. Helena's early success with Pinot Noir, Waipara in this region of the South Island has produced highly aromatic Riesling, Pinot Blanc, and Chablis-like Chardonnay. Giesen; Pegasus Bay; Melness; Mark Rattray; St. Helena; Sherwood Estate; Waipara Springs.

Cantina (Sociale) [kan-tee-nuh soh-chee-yah-lay] (Italy) Winery (cooperative).

Ⴏ **Capannelle** Good producer of rich *Super-Tuscan* wine near Gaiole.

Cap Corse [kap-korss] (*Corsica*, France) 17 villages in the north of the island produce great, floral Muscat as well as some attractive herby dry Vermentino. Antoine Arena; Dom de Catarelli; Clos Nicrosi.

Cap Classique [kap-klas-seek] (South Africa) Now that the term *"Méthode Champenoise"* has unreasonably been outlawed, this is the phrase developed by the South Africans to describe their Champagne-method sparkling wine.

Ⴏ **Ch. Cap-de-Mourlin** [kap-dur-mer-lan] (*St. Emilion Grand Cru Classé, Bordeaux*, France) Until 1983 when they were amalgamated, there were, confusingly, two different *châteaux* with this name. Good mid-range stuff. 79 81 **82 83** 85 86 88 89 90 93 94 95 96 98 00 ★★★★ 1995 ££

Ⴏ **Caparzo** [ka-pahrt-zoh] (*Tuscany*, Italy) Classy, *Brunello di Montalcino* estate producing wines that age brilliantly. ★★★★★ 1998 La Casa £££

Cape (South Africa) The area that includes all of South Africa's vineyards. See *Stellenbosch, Paarl, Franschhoek, Walker Bay, Robertson, Tulbagh, Worcester*, etc. Red: 89 **91 92** 93 94 **95** 96 **97** White: 94 **95** 96 **97 98** 99

Ⴏ **Cape Mentelle** [men-tel] (*Margaret River,* Western Australia) French-owned winery, founded, like *Cloudy Bay*, by David Hoehnen. Impressive *Semillon-Sauvignon, Shiraz, Cabernet* and a wild berryish *Zinfandel*, to shame many a Californian. ★★★★ 1998 Cabernet £££ ★★★★ 1996 Ironstone Zinfandel £££

C

☖ **Capel Vale** [kay-puhl vayl] (Southwest coast, Western Australia) Just to the north of the borders of *Margaret River*. Good *Riesling, Gewürztraminer*, and an improving Baudin blended red. ★★★★ 1998 Shiraz ££

☖ **Capezzana** [kap-pay-tzah-nah] (*Tuscany*, Italy) Conte Ugo Contini Bonacossi not only got *Carmignano* its *DOCG*, he also helped to promote the notion of *Cabernet* and *Sangiovese* as compatible bedfellows, helping to open the door for all those priceless – and pricy – *Super-Tuscans*. ★★★★★ 1998 Ghiaie della Furba £££.

Capsule The sheath covering the cork. Once lead, now plastic or tin. In the case of "flanged" bottles, though, it is noticeable by its transparency or absence.

☖ **Caramany** [kah-ram-man-nee] (*Midi*, France) New *AC* for an old section of the *Côtes du Roussillon*-Villages, near the *Pyréneés*. *Vignerons Catalans*.

Carbonic Maceration See *Macération Carbonique*.

☖ **Ch. Carbonnieux** [kar-bon-nyeuh] (*Graves Cru Classé, Bordeaux*, France) Since 1991, the whites have greatly improved and the raspberryish reds are among the most reliable in the region. Red: 82 85 **86** 88 **89 90** 91 92 94 95 96 97 **98 99** White: 93 **94 95 96** 97 **98 99** 00

☖ **Carcavelos** [kar-kah-veh-losh] (Portugal) *DO* region in the Lisbon suburbs producing usually disappointing fortified wines.

☖ **Cardinale** (California) *Kendall-Jackson's* top line, produced by a former star Mondavi winemaker from grapes grown on mostly hillside vines. The Royale white is impressively *Bordeaux*-like.

☖ **Ch. la Cardonne** [kar-don] (*Bordeaux*, France) *Cru Bourgeois* whose quality is improving since its sale by the Rothschilds of *Ch. Lafite*.

☖ **Carema** [kah-ray-mah] (*Piedmont*, Italy) Wonderful perfumed *Nebbiolo* produced in limited quantities largely by Cantina dei Produttori Nebbiolo.

🍇 **Carignan** [kah-ree-nyon] Prolific red grape making usually dull, coarse wine for blending, but classier fare in *Corbières, Minervois*, and *Fitou*. The key to good Carignan, as its Californian fan Randall Grahm of *Bonny Doon* says, lies in getting low yields from old vines. In Spain it is known as *Cariñena* and Mazuelo, while Italians call it Carignano.

☖ **Carignano del Sulcis** [ka-reen-yah-noh dehl sool-chees] (*Sardinia*, Italy) Dynamic *DOC* spearheaded by the Santadi cooperative.

☖ **Louis Carillon & Fils** [ka-ree-yon] (*Burgundy*, France) Great modern *Puligny* estate. ★★★★★ 1998 Puligny-Montrachet Champ Canet ££££

☖ **Cariñena** [kah-ree-nyeh-nah] (Spain) Important *DO* of Aragon for rustic reds, high in alcohol and, confusingly, made not from the *Cariñena* (or *Carignan*) grape, but mostly from the *Garnacha Tinta*. Also some whites.

🍇 **Cariñena** [kah-ree-nyeh-nah] (Spain) The Spanish name for *Carignan*.

☖ **Carmel** (Israel) Huge producer offering a wide range of pleasant but generally unremarkable wines.

☖ **Viña Carmen** [veen-yah kahr-men] (*Maipo*, Chile) Quietly developing a reputation as one of the best red wine producers in Chile. Increasingly organic. ★★★★ 1998 Nativa Chardonnay ££

🍇 **Carmenère** [kahr-meh-nehr] (Chile) Smoky-spicily distinctive grape that although almost extinct in Bordeaux is still a permitted variety for claret. Widely planted in Chile where it has traditionally been sold as Merlot. Look for examples like the Santa Inès Carmenère, *Carmen* Grand Vidure, or *Veramonte Merlot*. ★★★★ 1998 Carmen Grand Vidure ££

☖ **Carmenet Vineyard** [kahr-men-nay] (*Sonoma Valley*, California) Excellent and unusual winery tucked away in the hills and producing long-lived, very *Bordeaux*-like but approachable reds, fairly-priced *Chardonnay*, and also (even more unusually for California) good *Semillon-Sauvignon* and *Cabernet Franc*. ★★★★★ 1998 Dynamite Cabernet Sauvignon ££

C

Ⓧ Les Carmes-Haut-Brion [lay kahrm oh bree-yon] (*Bordeaux*, France) Small property neighbouring *Ch. Haut-Brion* in *Pessac-Léognan*. Good in 1999.

Ⓧ Carmignano [kahr-mee-nyah-noh] (*Tuscany*, Italy) Nearby alternative to *Chianti*, with the addition of more *Cabernet* grapes. See *Capezzana*.

Ⓧ Quinta do Carmo [Keen-tah doh Kar-moh] (*Alentejo*, Portugal) The Ch. Lafite Rothschilds' best foreign venture. Rich, tastily modern reds.

Carneros [kahr-neh-ros] (California) Small, fog-cooled, high-quality region shared between the *Napa* and *Sonoma Valleys* and used by just about everybody as a source for cool-climate grapes. Producing top-class *Chardonnay, Pinot Noir,* and now, *Merlot*. Some of the best examples are from from Hudson and Hyde vineyards. Red: 85 86 87 **90 91 92 93 95 96** 97. White: **95 96 97 98**. *Acacia; Carneros Creek; Cuvaison; Domaine Carneros; Domaine Chandon; Kistler;* Macrostie; *Marcassin; Mondavi; Mumm Cuvée Napa; Patz & Hall; Pine Ridge;* Ramey; *Saintsbury; Shafer; Swanson;* Truchard.

Ⓧ Domaine Carneros (*Napa Valley,* California) *Taittinger's* US sparkling wine – produced in a perfect and thus ludicrously incongruous replica of their French HQ. The wine, however, is one of the best New World efforts by the Champenois. ★★★★ **2000 Brut £££**

Ⓧ Carneros Creek (*Carneros*, California) Produces ambitious *Pinot Noir* under this name and somewhat better (and cheaper) berryish Fleur de Carneros.

Ⓧ Caronne-Ste-Gemme [kah-ronn-sant jem] (*Bordeaux*, France) Reliable Cru Bourgeois that delivers value – even in poorer vintages.

Ⓧ Carpineto [Kah-pi-neh-toh] (*Tuscany*, Italy) High-quality producer of *Chianti*, and *Chardonnay* and *Cabernet* that are sold under the Farnito label. ★★★★ **1997 Vino Nobile de Montepulciano £££**

Ⓧ Carr Taylor (*Sussex*, England) One of England's more business-like estates. Sparkling wines are the best buys.

Ⓧ Ch. Carras [kar-ras] (*Macedonia,* Greece) Greece's best-known estate, left behind by more modern producers. Now in new hands: we'll see.

Ⓧ Les Carruades de Lafite [kah-roo-ahd-dur la-feet] (*Pauillac, Bordeaux,* France) The second label of *Ch. Lafite*. Rarely (quite) as good as *les Forts de Latour*, nor *Ch. Margaux's Pavillon Rouge*.★★★★ **1998 £££**

Ⓧ Ch. Carsin [kahr-san] (*Bordeaux*, France) Finnish-owned, Aussie-style *Premières Côtes de Bordeaux* estate, proving that this *appellation* is capable of producing wines of class and complexity. Australian-born Mandy Jones makes particularly tasty whites using the Sauvignon Gris. 95 96 97 98 00 ★★★★ **2000 Cuvée Prestige Blanc ££**

Casa [kah-sah] (Italy, Spain, Portugal) Firm or company.

Casablanca [kas-sab-lan-ka] (*Aconcagua,* Chile) New region in *Aconcagua*; a magnet for quality-conscious winemakers and producing especially impressive *Sauvignons, Chardonnays,* and *Gewurztraminers. Caliterra;Viña Casablanca; Concha y Toro; Errazuriz; Santa Carolina; Santa Emiliana; Santa Rita; Veramonte;Villard.*

Ⓧ Viña Casablanca [veen-yah kas-sab-lan-ka] (*Casablanca*, Chile) Enterprising winery in the region of the same name. A showcase for the talents of winemaker *Ignacio Recabarren*.★★★★ **1997 Miraflores Cabernet Sauvignon ££**.★★★★ **1999 White Label Malbec ££**

Ⓧ Casanova di Neri [kah-sah-NOH-vah dee NAY-ree] (*Tuscany*, Italy) Fine producer of *Brunello* and *Rosso di Montalcino*. ★★★★ **1998 Rosso ££**

Ⓧ Casse Basse [kah-seh-bas-say] (*Tuscany*, Italy) Soldera's hard-to-find *Brunello di Montalcino* is developing a cult following in the US – and fetching crazily high prices.

Ⓧ Caslot-Galbrun [kah-loh gal-bruhn] (*Loire*, France) Top-class producer of serious, long-lived red *Loires*.

Ⓧ Cassegrain [kas-grayn] (*New South Wales*, Australia) Tucked away in the Hastings Valley on the east coast, but also drawing grapes from elsewhere. The wines can be variable, but are often impressive. ★★★★ **1996 Chambourcin ££**

C

Cassis [ka-sees] (*Provence,* France) Small coastal *appellation* producing (variable) red, (often dull) white and (good) rosé. **Clos Ste. Magdeleine**; **la Ferme Blanche.**

℥ **Castel del Monte** [Ka-stel del mon-tay] (*Puglia,* Italy) Interesting southern region where Rivera makes excellent Il Falcone reds and Bianca di Svevia whites. Grapes grown include the local Aglianico, Pampanuto, Bombino Bianco and Nero, and Nero di Troia.

℥ **Castelgiocondo** [kas-tel-jee-yah-kon-doh] (*Tuscany,* Italy) High-quality *Brunello* estate owned by *Frescobaldi.*

℥ **Castellare** [kas-teh-LAH-ray] (*Tuscany,* Italy) Innovative small *Chianti Classico* estate whose *Sangiovese-Malvasia* blend, Nera I Sodi di San Niccoló, *Vino da Tavola,* is worth seeking out.

℥ **Castellblanch** [kas-tel-blantch] (*Catalonia,* Spain) Producer of better-than-most *Cava* – but catch it young. ★★★ **Cava Brut Zero ££**

℥ **Casteller** [kas-teh-ler] (*Trentino-Alto Adige,* Italy) Pale red, creamy-fruity wines for early drinking, made from *Schiava.* See *Ca'Vit.*

℥ **Castello di Ama** [kas-tel-loh-dee-ah-mah] (*Tuscany,* Italy) Producer of great single-vineyard *Chianti Classico* (esp. the Bellavista Riserva) plus the stunning Vigna l'Apparita Merlot.

℥ **Castell'sches, Fürstlich Domänenamt** [kas-tel-shs foorst-likh Doh-mehn-en-ahmt] (*Franken,* Germany) Good Auslese Scheurebe and Rieslaner and dry Sylvaner. Dornfelder reds are interesting too.

℥ **Castillo de Monjardin** [kas-tee-yoh deh mon-har-deen] (*Navarra,* Spain). Navarra rising star with good *Chardonnay, Pinot Noir,* and *Merlot.*

Cat's pee Describes the tangy smell frequently found in typical *Müller-Thurgau* and unripe *Sauvignon Blanc.*

Catalonia [kat-tal-loh-nee-yah] (Spain) Semi-autonomous region that includes *Penedés, Priorato, Conca de Barberá, Terra Alta,* and *Costers del Segre.*

℥ **Catena Estate** [kat-tay-nah] (Argentina) Quality-focused part of the giant Catena-Esmeralda concern, helped by the expertise of ex-*Simi* Californian winemaker Paul Hobbs. ★★★★ **1999 Argento Malbec ££**

℥ **Cattier** [Kat-ee-yay] (*Champagne,* France) Up-and-coming producer with good non-vintage wines.

℥ **Dom. Cauhapé** [koh-ap-pay] (*Southwest,* France) Extraordinary *Jurançon* producer of excellent *Vendange Tardive* and dry wines from the *Manseng* grape. ★★★★ **1998 Jurançon Noblesse ££**

℥ **Cava** [kah-vah] (*Catalonia,* Spain) Sparkling wine produced in *Penedés* by the *Methode Champenoise,* but handicapped by innately dull local grapes and ageing, which deprives it of freshness. Avoid *vintage* versions and look instead for Anna de *Codorníu* and *Raimat* Cava – both made from *Chardonnay* – or such well-made exceptions to the earthy rule as *Juvé y Camps, Conde de Caralt, Cava Chandon,* and *Segura Viudas.*

Cava (Greece) Legal term for wood- and bottle-aged wine.

℥ **Cavalleri** [kah-vah-yah-ree] (*Lombardy,* Italy) One of the top sparkling wines in Italy. ★★★★ 1995 **Franciacorta Brut ££££**

Cave [kahv] (France) Cellar.

℥ **Cave Spring** (*Ontario,* Canada) One of Canada's most reliable producers, with especially good Chardonnay.

℥ **Caymus Vineyards** [kay-muhs] (*Napa Valley,* California) Traditional producer of concentrated Italianate reds (including a forceful *Zinfandel*) and a characterful *Cabernet Franc.* Liberty School is the *second label.* ★★★★★ **1997 Cabernet Sauvignon £££**

℥ **Dom. Cazes** [kahrs] (*Midi,* France) Maker of great *Muscat de Rivesaltes,* rich marmaladey stuff which makes most *Beaumes de Venise* seem dull.

℥ **Cellier le Brun** [sel-yay luh-bruhn] (*Marlborough,* New Zealand) Specialist producer of *Méthode Champenoise* sparkling wine originally founded by Daniel Le Brun, an expatriate Frenchman. ★★★ **Brut NV £££**

C

※ **Cencibel** [sen-thee-bel] (*Valdepeñas*, Spain) Alternative name for *Tempranillo*.

Central Coast (California) Increasingly interesting, geographically varied set of regions south of San Francisco, including *Santa Barbara, Monterey, Santa Cruz,* and *San Luis Obispo*. Hardly surprisingly, the wines made here vary widely too.

Ⅰ **Central Otago** [oh-tah-goh] (*South Island*, New Zealand) Exciting "new" region where *Pinot Noir, Gewurztraminer,* and *Riesling* flourish, despite a climate that was originally considered to be too cold for successful grape growing. Nowadays its success is increasingly attracting a similar cult following to *Marlborough*. Black Ridge; Chard Farm; *Felton Road*; Gibbston Valley; Rippon Vineyards.

Central Valley (California) Huge irrigated region controlled by giants which make three-quarters of the state's wines without, so far, matching the efforts of similar regions Down Under. New vineyards and a concentration on cooler parts of the region are paying off for the *Sauvignon Blanc* but I doubt the potential of the increasingly widely planted *Merlot*. Smaller-scale winemaking is beginning to help (this is wine-factory country), but good wines are still the exception to the rule. *Quady's* fortified and sweet wines are still by far the best wines here.

Central Valley (Chile) (Also referred to as the Central Valley Viticultural Region). This is the region in which most of *Chile's* wines are made. It includes *Maipo, Rapel, Maule,* and *Curico*, but not the new cool-climate region of *Casablanca*, which is in *Aconcagua*, further north.

Cépage [say-pahzh] (France) Grape variety.

Ⅰ **Cepparello** [chep-par-rel-loh] (*Tuscany*, Italy) Brilliant pure *Sangiovese IGT* made by Paolo de Marchi of *Isole e Olena*. Well worth laying down for a decade or more. ★★★★★ 1998 ££££

Ⅰ **Ceretto** [cher-ret-toh] (*Piedmont*, Italy) Producer of good modern *Barolos* and increasingly impressive single-vineyard examples, plus excellent La Bernardina varietals (Syrah, Pinot Noir, etc.) ★★★ 1999 Arneis Blange ££

Ⅰ **Ch. de Cérons** [say-ron] (*Bordeaux*, France) One of the best properties in little known *appellation* of *Cérons*. White: 83 86 88 89 90 ★★★★ 1990 Château de Cerons £££

Ⅰ **Ch. Certan de May** [sehr-ton dur may] (*Pomerol, Bordeaux,* France) Top-class *Pomerol* estate with subtly plummy wine. Made a great 2000. 70 75 78 79 81 82 83 85 86 87 88 89 90 94 95 96 98 00 ★★★★★ 1990 ££££

Ⅰ **Ch. Certan-Giraud** [sehr-ton zhee-roh] (*Pomerol, Bordeaux,* France) *Pomerol* estate recently bought by J.P. Moueix and now providing the grapes for his new Hosanna superstar wine. Buy pre-1998 vintages if you see them at auction.

※ **César** [say-zahr] (*Burgundy*, France) The forgotten plummy-raspberryish red grape of *Burgundy*, still vinified near *Chablis* by Simonnet-Fèvre.

Ⅰ **LA Cetto** [chet-toh] (*Baja California*, Mexico) With wines like LA Cetto's tasty *Cabernet* and spicy-soft *Petite Sirah*, not to mention the increasingly successful Italian varietals, it's hardly surprising that *Baja California* is now beginning to compete with the more northerly region across the US frontier. ★★★★ 1998 Petite Sirah ££

Chablais [shab-lay] (*Vaud*, Switzerland) A good place to find *Pinot Noir* rosé and young *Chasselas* (sold as *Dorin*).

Ⅰ **Chablis** [shab-lee] (*Burgundy*, France) When not overpriced, *Chablis* offers a steely European finesse that New World *Chardonnays* rarely capture. *Petits* and, more particularly *Grands Crus* should (but do not always) show extra complexity. A new Union, des Grands Crus de Chablis, founded in 2000, is intended to promote quality. We'll see. 85 86 88 89 90 92 94 95 96 97 98 JC Bessin; *Bichot; Billaud-Simon; Pascal Bouchard; J-M Brocard; La Chablisienne; D Dampt; René Dauvissat; D&E Defaix; J-P Droin; Joseph Drouhin; Durup; William Fèvre; Laroche; Louis Michel; Moreau-Naudin; S. Mosnier; Gilbert Picq; Raveneau; Servin; Tremblay; Verget; Vocoret.*

C

⚏ **La Chablisienne** [shab-lees-yen] (*Burgundy,*
France) Cooperative making wines from
Petit Chablis to *Grands Crus* under a host
of labels. Rivals the best estates in the
appellation. ★★★★ **1999 Chablis –**
Les Vignerons de Chablis £££

Chai [shay] (*France*) Cellar/winery.

⚏ **Chain of Ponds** (*South Australia*)
Enterprising Adelaide Hills winery with an
impressive *Chardonnay.* ★★★★ **1997 Chardonnay ££**

⚏ **Chalk Hill** (*Sonoma,* California) Producer of rich *Chardonnay,* stylish
Sauvignon Blanc, lovely berryish *Cabernet* and great *Sauternes*-style
whites. Chalk is ideal soil for Chardonnay. Here in California though,
the only chalk you would find is in the name of the winery. ★★★★
1996 Chardonnay £££

⚏ **Chalone** [shal-lohn] (*Monterey,* California) Under the same ownership as
Acacia, Edna Valley, and *Carmenet,* this 25-year old winery is one of the big
names for *Pinot Noir* and *Chardonnay.* Unusually *Burgundian,* long-lived.
★★★★ **1998 Chardonnay £££**

Chalonnais/Côte Chalonnaise [shal-lohn-nay] (*Burgundy,* France)
Source of lesser-known, less complex *Burgundies – Givry, Montagny, Rully,*
and *Mercurey.* Potentially (rather than always actually) good value, but the
Bourgogne Rouge is often a good buy.

⚏ **Chambers** (*Rutherglen,* Australia) Competes with *Morris* for the crown of
best *Liqueur Muscat* maker. The Rosewood is great.

⚏ **Ch. Chambert-Marbuzet** [shom-behr mahr-boo-zay] (*St. Estèphe Cru*
Bourgeois, Bordeaux, France) Characterful *Cabernet*-based *St. Estèphe.*

⚏ **Chambertin** [shom-behr-tan] (*Burgundy,* France) Ultra-cherryish, damsony
Grand Cru whose name was adopted by the village of Gevrey. Famous in the
14th century, and Napoleon's favourite. Chambertin Clos-de-Bèze, Charmes-
Chambertin, Griottes-Chambertin, Latricières-Chambertin, Mazis-
Chambertin, and Ruchottes-Chambertin are neighbouring *Grands Crus.*
76 78 79 83 85 87 88 89 90 92 93 94 95 96 97 Pierre Amiot; *Bachelet;*
Alain Burguet; Bruno Clair; Pierre Damoy; Drouhin; Dugat-Py; Dujac; Engel;
Faiveley; Groffier; Raymond Launay; *Leroy; Denis Mortet;* Bernard Meaume;
Jean Raphet; Roty; Henri Rebourseau; *Armand Rousseau;* Jean Trapet.

⚏ **Chambolle-Musigny** [shom-bol moo-see-nyee] (*Burgundy,* France) *Côte*
de Nuits village whose wines can be like perfumed examples from the *Côte*
de Beaune. Georges Roumier is the local star, and *Drouhin, Dujac,* and *Ponsot*
are all reliable, as are *Bertagna, Drouhin, Anne Gros, Ghislaine Barthod,*
Dominique Laurent Mugnier, de Vogüé, and *Leroy.*

⚏ **Champagne** [sham-payn] (*France*) Source of potentially the greatest
sparkling wines, from *Pinot Noir, Pinot Meunier,* and *Chardonnay* grapes.
See individual listings. 81 82 83 85 86 88 89 90 91 92 93

⚏ **Didier Champalou** [dee-dee-yay shom-pah-loo] (*Loire,* France) Estate
with serious sweet, dry, and sparkling *Vouvray.* ★★★★ **1999 Vouvray**
Fondraux ££

⚏ **Champy** [shom-pee] (*Burgundy,* France) Long-established, recently much-
improved *Beaune négociant.* ★★★★ **1997 Savigny-lès-Beaune £££**

⚏ **Clos la Chance** (*Napa,* California) Up-and-coming producer of good-value
Chardonnay.

⚏ **Dom. Chandon** [doh-mayn shahn-dahn] (*Napa Valley,* California) *Moët &*
Chandon's California winery has finally been allowed to compete with its
counterpart at *Dom. Chandon* in Australia.

⚏ **Dom. Chandon** [doh-mine shon-don] (*Yarra Valley,* Australia) Sold as
Green Point and proving that Australian grapes, grown in a variety of cool
climates, can compete with *Champagne.* Now joined by a creditable,
Chablis-like, still Colonades *Chardonnay.* ★★★★ **1997 Blanc de Blancs £££**

C

Dom. Chandon de Briailles [shon-dun dur bree-iy] (*Burgundy*, France) Good *Savigny-lès-Beaune* estate whose owner is related to the *Chandon* of *Champagne*. ★★★★ 1998 Corton ££££

Chanson [shon-son] (*Burgundy*, France) *Beaune* merchant hit by scandal in 2000 when its new owner Bollinger revealed that some wines were not what they should have been.

Ch. de Chantegrive [shont-greev] (*Graves, Bordeaux*, France) Large modern *Graves* estate with excellent modern reds and whites.

Chapel Down (*Kent*, England) David Cowdroy's impressive winery-only operation uses grapes sourced from vineyards throughout southern England.

Chapel Hill Winery (*McLaren Vale*, Australia) Pam Dunsford's impressively rich – some say too rich – reds and whites have recently been joined by a leaner, unoaked *Chardonnay*. ★★★★★ 1997 Shiraz £££

Chapelle-Chambertin [shap-pell shom-behr-ta'n] (*Burgundy*, France) See *Chambertin*.

Chappellet (*Napa*, California) Innovative winery with beautiful vineyards and the courage to make wines such as an oaked *Chenin Blanc*, Tocai Friulano, and "Moelleux" *late-harvest* wines rather than stick to mainstream *Chardonnay* and *Merlot*.

Chapoutier [shah-poo-tyay] (*Rhône*, France) Family-owned merchant rescued from its faded laurels by a new generation who are using more or less organic methods. Not all wines live up to their early promise but credit is deserved for the initiative of printing labels in braille. Now making wine in Australia. ★★★★ 1998 La Bernardine ££

Chaptalization [shap-tal-li-zay-shuhn] The legal (in some regions) addition of sugar during fermentation to boost a wine's *alcohol* content.

🍇 **Charbono** [shar-boh-noh] (California) Obscure grape variety grown in California but thought to come from France. Makes interesting, very spicy, full-bodied reds at *Inglenook, Duxoup*, and *Bonny Doon*.

🍇 *Chardonnay* [shar-don-nay] The great white grape of *Burgundy*, *Champagne*, and now just about everywhere else. Capable of fresh simple charm in *Bulgaria* and buttery hazelnutty richness in *Meursault* in the *Côte d'Or*. Given the right chalky soil, in regions like *Chablis*, it can also make wines with an instantly recognizable "mineral" character. In the New World, it tends to produce tropical flavours, partly thanks to warmer climates and partly thanks to the use of clones and cultured yeasts. Almost everywhere, its innate flavour is often married to (and for some traditionalists, often marred by) that of new oak. See regions and producers.

Vin de Pays du Charentais [shar-ron-tay] (*Southwest*, France) Competing with its brandy-producing neighbour Gasgogne, this region now makes pleasant light reds and whites. Blanchard.

Charmat [shar-mat] The inventor of the *Cuve Close* method of producing cheap sparkling wines. See *Cuve Close*.

Ch. des Charmes [day sharm] (*Ontario*, Canada) Good maker of *Pinot, Chardonnay*, and *Icewine*. ★★★★ 1997 Paul Bosc Estate Riesling Icewine £££

Charta [kahr-tah] (*Rheingau*, Germany) Syndicate formed in the *Rheingau* using an arch as a symbol to indicate (often searingly) dry (*Trocken*) styles designed to be suitable for ageing and drinking with food. Recently reborn with (thankfully) less rigorously dry aspirations, as part of the *VDP*.

Chartron & Trébuchet [shar-tron ay tray-boo-shay] (*Burgundy*, France) Good small merchant specialising in white *Burgundies*.

Chassagne-Montrachet [shah-san mon-rash-shay] (*Burgundy*, France) *Côte de Beaune* commune making grassy, *biscuity*, fresh yet rich whites and mid-weight, often rustic-tasting, wild fruit reds. Pricey but sometimes less so than neighbouring *Puligny* and as recommendable. White: 85 86 87 88 89 90 92 93 94 95 96 97 98 Red: 78 83 85 86 87 88 89 90 92 93 94 95 96 97 98 *Carillon; Marc Colin;* Colin-Déléger; *Jean-Noël Gagnard; Henri Germain; Ch. de Maltroye; M. Morey; Michel Niellon; J. Pillot; Roux; Ramonet.*

C

Ch. Chasse-Spleen [shas spleen] (*Moulis Cru Bourgeois, Bordeaux,* France) *Cru Bourgeois château* whose wines can, in good years, rival those of a *Cru Classé*. A slightly dull patch in the 1990s but is now back on track. 70 78 79 **81** 82 **83** 85 86 87 88 *89* 90 94 95 96 97 **98 99** ★★★★ **1998 £££**

Chasselas [shas-slah] Widely grown, prolific white grape making light often dull wine principally in Switzerland, eastern France, and Germany. Good examples are rare. *Pierre Sparr*.

Ch. du Chasseloir [shas-slwah] (*Loire,* France) Makers of good *domaine Muscadets*.

Château [sha-toh] (*Bordeaux,* France) Literally means "castle". Some châteaux are extremely grand, many are merely farmhouses. A building is not required; the term applies to a vineyard or wine estate. Château names cannot be invented, but there are plenty of defunct titles that are used unashamedly by large cooperative wineries to market their members' wines.

Château-Chalon [sha-toh sha-lo'n] (*Jura,* France) Like *Château Grillet,* this is, confusingly, the name of an appellation. Unlike *Château Grillet,* however, here there isn't even a vinous château. The name applies to top-flight *Vin Jaune,* the nutty, sherry-like wine which is aged for six years before hitting the market.

Chateau Ste. Michelle (*Washington State*) Very dynamic winery, making a success of highly commercial *Merlot, Syrah, Sauvignon,* and *Riesling*. Joint ventures with Dr. Loosen and Antinori are proving fruitful, and Columbia Crest is a good associated brand.

Chateau Woltner (*Napa,* California) Producer of a range of unusually Burgundian single-vineyard *Chardonnays,* whose style owes much to the winemaker's experience in France. Icewine. ★★★★★ **1996 Titus Vineyard Chardonnay £££**

Châteauneuf-du-Pape [shah-toh-nurf-doo-pap] (*Rhône,* France) Traditionally these are considered to be the best reds (rich and spicy) and whites (rich and floral) of the southern *Rhône*. There are thirteen varieties that can be used for the red, though purists favour *Grenache*. 78 81 83 85 88 89 90 93 94 *95* 96 Pierre André; *Ch. de Beaucastel;* Beaurenard; *Henri Bonneau; Bosquet des Papes; Lucien & André Brunel; Cabrières; Chapoutier; la Charbonnière; Clos des Mont-Olivet; Clos des Papes; Delas; Font de Michelle; Fortia la Gardine; Guigal; Jaboulet Aîné; la Mordorée; La Nerthe;* du Pegaü; *Rayas;* Réserve des Célestins; Tardieu-Laurent; Vieux Télégraphe.

Jean-Claude Chatelain [shat-lan] (*Loire,* France) Producer of classy individual *Pouilly-Fumés* and *Sancerre*.

Jean-Louis Chave [sharv] (*Rhône,* France) Gérard Chave and his son Jean-Louis run the best estate in *Hermitage*. These are great wines but they demand patience and are easily overlooked by those looking for richer, more instantly accessible fare. ★★★★★ **1997 Hermitage ££££**

Dom Gérard Chavy [shah-vee] (*Burgundy,* France) High-quality estate. ★★★★★ **1998 Puligny-Montrachet Les Perrières ££££**

Chehalem [sheh-hay-lem] (*Oregon*) Top class Yamhill producer of *Pinot Noir, Chardonnay,* and *Pinot Gris,* and benefitting from collaborating with the go-getting Patrice *Rion* from *Burgundy*.

Chenas [shay-nass] (*Burgundy,* France) Good but least well-known of the *Beaujolais Crus* – supposedly with a naturally woody flavour (Chêne = oak). Louis Champagnon; Daniel Robin, Hubert Lapierre, Bernard Santé, and *Duboeuf* make worthy examples.

Dom. du Chêne [doo-shehn] (*Rhône,* France) Small estate producing rich ripe *Condrieu* and top-class *St. Joseph*. The best *cuvée* is "Anais".

Chêne [shayn] (France) Oak, as in *Fûts de Chêne* (oak barrels).

🍇 **Chenin Blanc** [shur-nah-blo'n for France, shen nin blonk elsewhere] Honeyed white grape of the *Loire*. Wines vary from bone-dry to sweet and long-lived. High acidity makes it ideal for sparkling wine, while sweet versions benefit from *noble rot*. French examples are often marred by green unripe flavours and heavyhandedness with *sulphur dioxide*. Grown in South Africa (where it is known as *Steen*), in New Zealand (where it is lovingly – and successfully – grown by *Millton*), and Australia (where it is skilfully oaked by *Moondah Brook Steen*). It is generally disappointing in California (but see *Chappellet*). See *Vouvray, Quarts de Chaumes, Bonnezeaux, Saumur.*

Ch. de Chenonceau [sheh-non-soh] (*Loire*, France) Tourist attraction chateau that also produces high quality still and sparkling *Chenin Blanc.*

🍷 **Ch. Cheval Blanc** [shuh-vahl blon] (*St. Emilion Premier Grand Cru Classé, Bordeaux,* France) Supreme *St. Emilion* property, unusual in using more *Cabernet Franc* than *Merlot*. A truly great 2000. 75 76 78 79 80 **81 82 83 85 86** 87 88 89 **90** 92 93 **94 95 96 98 99 00** ★★★★ **1995 ££££**

🍷 **Dom. de Chevalier** [shuh-val-yay] (*Graves Cru Classé, Bordeaux,* France) Great *Pessac-Léognan* estate which proves itself in difficult years for both red and white. Very fine 1999s Red: **70 78** 79 **81 83** 85 **86** 87 **88 89 90** 92 93 **94** 95 96 **98 99** White: **83 85 87** 88 89 **90 92 93** 94 **95** 96 **98 99 00** ★★★★★ **1998 Blanc, Pessac-Léognan ££££**

Chevaliers de Tastevin [shuh-val-yay duh tast-van] (*Burgundy,* France) A brotherhood – *confrérie* – based in *Clos de Vougeot*. Wines approved at an annual tasting carry a special "tasteviné" label.

🍷 **Cheverny** [shuh-vehr-nee] (*Loire*, France) Light floral whites from *Sauvignon* and *Chenin Blanc* and now, under the new "Cour Cheverny" *appellation*, wines made from the limey local *Romarantin* grape. 97 **Caves Bellier; François Cazin; Ch de la Gaudronnière.**

🍷 **Robert Chevillon** [roh-behr shuh-vee-yon] (*Burgundy,* France) Produces long-lived wines. ★★★★★ **1997 Nuits-St.-Georges Les Chaignots £££**

🍷 **Chianti** [kee-an-tee] (*Tuscany*, Italy) (*Classico/Putto/Rufina*) *Sangiovese*-dominant, now often *Cabernet*-influenced, *DOCG*. Generally better than pre-1984, when it was usual to add wine from further south, and to put dull white grapes in with the black. Wines labelled with insignia of the *Classico, Putto,* or the *Rufina* areas are supposed to be better too, as are wines from *Colli Fiorentini* and *Colli Senesi*. Trusting good producers, however, is a far safer bet. 79 **82 85 88 90** 94 95 96 97 98 *Castello di Ama; Antinori; Frescobaldi; Castellare;* **Castell'**in Villa; *Isole e Olena; Fonterutoli Felsina; Ruffino;* Rocca di Castagnoli; *Selvapiana; Castello dei Rampolla; Castello di Volpaia.*

🍷 **Chiaretto di Bardolino** [kee-ahr-reh-toh dee bahr-doh-lee-noh] (*Lombardy*, Italy) Berryish, light reds and rosés from around Lake Garda. **Corte Gardoni; Guerrieri Rizzardi; Nicolis e Figli; Santi.**

🍷 **Michele Chiarlo** [mee-Kayleh Kee-ahr-loh] (*Piedmont*, Italy) Increasingly impressive modern producer of *single-vineyard Barolo, Monferrato, Barbaresco,* and *Barbera*. ★★★★★ **1996 Barolo Cerequio ££££**

🍷 **Chignin** [sheen-ya'n] (*Savoie*, France) Fresh red (made from the *Mondeuse*) and white wines that go especially well with cheese. **A&M Quénard.**

Chile Rising source of juicy, blackcurranty *Cabernet* and (potentially even better) *Merlot, Carmenère, Semillon, Chardonnay. Almaviva; Caliterra; Carmen; Concha y Toro; Errazuriz; Casa Lapostolle; Casablanca; Montes; Santa Rita; Undurraga; Veramonte* etc.

🍷 **Chimney Rock** (*Stag's Leap District*, California) Producer of serious, fairly priced *Cabernet*. ★★★★ **1997 Cabernet Sauvignon Reserve £££**

🍷 **Chinon** [shee-non] (*Loire*, France) An *AC* within *Touraine* for (mostly) red wines from the *Cabernet Franc* grape. Excellent and long-lived from good producers in ripe years; otherwise potentially thin and green. *Olga Raffault* makes one of the best, Otherwise: **Philippe Alliet; Bernard Baudry; Couly-Dutheil; Delauney; Ch. de la Grille; Charles Joguet; Logis de la Bouchardière.**

C

⏺ **Chiroubles** [shee-roo-bl] (*Burgundy*, France) Fragrant and early-maturing *Beaujolais Cru*, best expressed by the likes of Bernard Méziat. 85 87 **88 89** 90 **91** 93 94 95 97 98 **Emile Cheysson; Georges Duboeuf; Hubert Lapierre; Andrè Mètrat; Bernard Méziat; Alain Passot; Ch de Raousset.**

⏺ **Chivite** [shee-vee-tay] (*Navarra*, Spain) Innovative producer outclassing big name *Rioja bodegas*. ★★★ **1995 Gran Feudo Vinas Viejas Reserva ££**

⏺ **Chorey-lès-Beaune** [shaw-ray lay bohn] (*Burgundy*, France) Modest raspberry and damson reds once sold as *Côte de Beaune Villages* and now appreciated in their own right. 85 87 **88 89** 90 92 93 94 95 96 97 **Allexant; Arnoux; Ch. de Chorey;** *Drouhin;* **Gay; Maillard;** *Tollot-Beaut.*

⏺ **JJ Christoffel** [kris-tof-fell] (*Mosel*, Germany) Fine Riesling producer in Erden and Ürzig. ★★★★★ **1998 Ürziger Würzgarten Erdener Treppchen Auslese ££**

⏺ **Church Road** (*Hawkes Bay*, New Zealand) A Montana subsidiary that has established an identity for itself with a range of premium *Hawkes Bay* wines. Look out for the recently launched Tom red blend.

⏺ **Churchill** (*Douro*, Portugal) Dynamic young firm founded by Johnny Graham, whose family once owned a rather bigger *port* house. Good White Port. Red: 82 **85 91 92 95 96** 97 ★★★★★ **1998 Agua Alta Vintage Port £££**

⏺ **Chusclan** [shoos-klon] (*Rhône*, France) Named village of *Côtes du Rhône* with maybe the best *rosé* of the area. ★★★★ **1998 Caves de Chusclan ££**

⏺ **Cinque Terre** [chin-kweh-TEH-reh] (*Liguria*, Italy) Traditionally dull, dry, and sweet holiday whites. The regional cooperative is making good examples now, however.

🌱 **Cinsaut/Cinsault** [san-soh] Fruity-spicy red grape with high acidity, often blended with *Grenache*. One of 13 permitted varieties of *Châteauneuf-du-Pape*, and also in the blend of *Ch. Musar* in the *Lebanon*.

⏺ **Cirò** [chih-Roh] (*Calabria*, Italy) Thanks to the efforts of pioneering producer Librandi, these southern reds (made from Maglioppo) and whites (made from Greco) can be well worth buying.

⏺ **Ch. Cissac** [see-sak] (*Haut-Médoc Cru Bourgeois*, *Bordeaux*, France) Traditional *Cru Bourgeois*, close to *St. Estèphe*, making tough wines that last. Those who dislike *tannin* should stick to ripe vintages like 2000. **70 75 78** 81 **82** 83 **85 86** 88 89 **90 93 95** 96 97 98 **99 00** ★★★★ **1995 £££**

⏺ **Ch. Citran** [see-tron] (*Haut-Médoc Cru Bourgeois*, *Bordeaux*, France) Improving – though still not dazzling – *Cru Bourgeois*, thanks to major investment by the Japanese. 82 85 86 87 **88 89 90** 91 92 93 **94 95 96** 98 00

⏺ **Bruno Clair** [klehr] (*Burgundy*, France) *Marsannay* estate with good *Fixin*, *Gevrey-Chambertin*, *Morey-St.-Denis* (inc. a rare white), and *Savigny*. ★★★★ **1998 Marsannay Les Longeroies £££**

Clairet [klehr-ray] (*Bordeaux*, France) The word from which we derived *claret* – originally a very pale-coloured red from *Bordeaux*. Seldom used.

🌱 **Clairette** [klehr-ret] (*Midi*, France) Dull white grape of southern France.

⏺ **Clairette de Die** [klehr-rheht duh dee] (*Rhône*, France) The dry Crémant de Die is unexciting sparkling wine, but the "Méthode Dioise Traditionelle" (previously known as "Tradition") made with *Muscat* is invariably far better; grapey and fresh – like a top-class French *Asti Spumante*. **Cave Diose.**

⏺ **Auguste Clape** [klap] (*Rhône,* France) The supreme master of *Cornas*. Great, intense, long-lived traditional wines. ★★★★★ **1998 Cornas ££££**

⏺ **La Clape** [la klap] (*Languedoc-Roussillon*, France) Little-known *cru* within the *Coteaux de Languedoc* with tasty *Carignan* reds and soft, creamy whites. **Pech-Céleyran; Pech-Redon.**

Clare Valley [klehr] (South Australia) Slatey soil region enjoying a renaissance with quality *Rieslings* that age well, and deep-flavoured *Shiraz*, *Cabernet*, and *Malbec*. Also the region that took the matter of corked wine into its own hands – by bottling over half of its 2000 *Riesling* with *Stelvin* screwcaps. *Tim Adams; Jim Barry; Leo Buring; Grosset; Knappstein; Leasingham; Penfolds; Petaluma; Mitchells; Mount Horrocks; Pike; Sevenhill; Wendouree.*

C

Clarendon Hills (*Blewitt Springs*, South Australia) Now living up to the hype it prematurely received from US critics who were so wowed by the concentration of the wines here that they overlooked some evident faults. This is one of the most interesting and ambitious producers in Australia. Sidestep the overpriced Astralis and over-praised *Merlot*, and go for the old-vine *Grenache*. Whites are characterful too. ★★★★★ **1997 Grenache ££££**

Claret [klar-ret] English term for red *Bordeaux*.

Clarete [klah-reh-Tay] (Spain) Term for light red – frowned on by the EU.

Classed Growth (France) Literal translation of *Cru Classé*, commonly used when referring to the status of *Bordeaux châteaux*.

Classico [kla-sih-koh] (Italy) A defined area within a *DOC* identifying the supposedly best vineyards, e.g., *Chianti* Classico, *Valpolicella* Classico.

Henri Clerc et fils [klehr] (*Burgundy*, France) Top-class white *Burgundy* estate.

Ch. Clerc-Milon [klehr mee-lon] (*Pauillac 5ème Cru Classé, Bordeaux*, France) Juicy member of the *Mouton-Rothschild* stable. 78 81 **82** 83 85 **86** 87 88 **89 90** 92 93 94 **95 96** 98 99 ★★★★ **1995 £££**

Domenico Clerico [doh-meh-nee-koh Klay-ree-koh] (*Piedmont*, Italy) New-wave producers of a truly great *Barolo* and *Dolcetto*. Also of note is Arte, a delicious *Nebbiolo-Barbera* blend that could be described as a Piedmontese answer to all those hyped "*Super-Tuscans*". ★★★★★ **1996 Arte ££££**

Climat [klee-mah] (*Burgundy*, France) Individual named vineyard – not always a *Premier Cru*.

Ch. Climens [klee-mons] (*Barsac Premier Cru Classé, Bordeaux*, France) Gorgeous, but delicate, *Barsac* that easily outlasts many heftier *Sauternes*. 75 78 79 **80** 81 82 **83 85 86 88** 89 **90** 95 96 97 98 99

Cline (*Carneros*, California) A winery to watch for innovative Rhône-style wines, including a delicious *Roussanne* and a bizarrely wonderful sweet *late-harvest Mourvèdre*. California needs mavericks like this. ★★★★ **1997 Big Break Vineyard Late Harvest Mourvèdre £££**

Ch. Clinet [klee-nay] (*Pomerol, Bordeaux*, France) Starry property; lovely, complex, intense wines. 85 **86** 87 **88 89 90** 91 92 **93 95 96** 97 **98 99 00**

Clone [klohn] Specific strain of a given grape variety. For example, more than 300 clones of *Pinot Noir* have been identified.

Clos [kloh] (France) Literally, a walled vineyard.

Clos de Gamot [kloh duh gah-moh] (*Southwest*, France) One of the most reliable producers in *Cahors*.

Clos de la Roche [kloh duh lah rosh] (*Burgundy*, France) One of the most reliable *Côte d'Or Grands Crus*. 85 86 88 89 **90 95 97** *Drouhin; Dujac; Faivelay; Lecheneault; Leroy; Perrot-Minot; Ponsot; Jean Raphet; Louis Rémy; Rousseau.*

Clos de Mesnil [kloh duh may-neel] (*Champagne*, France) *Krug's* single vineyard *Champagne* made entirely from *Chardonnay* grown in the Clos de Mesnil vineyard. ★★★★★ **1989 ££££**

Clos de Tart [kloh duh tahr] (*Burgundy*, France) Fine *Grand Cru* vineyard in *Morey-St.-Denis*, exclusive to Mommessin. Wines repay keeping. ★★★★ **1998 ££££**

Clos de Vougeot [kloh duh voo-joh] (*Burgundy*, France) *Grand Cru* vineyard, once a single monastic estate, but now divided among more than 70 owners, some of whom are decidedly uncommitted to quality. *Amiot-Servelle; Robert Arnoux; Bertagna; Bouchard Père et Fils; Champy; Jean-Jacques Confuron; Joseph Drouhin; Engel; Jean Grivot; Anne Gros; Jean Gros; Faiveley; Leroy; Méo Camuzet; Mugneret-Gibourg; Jacques Prieur; Prieuré Roch; Jean Raphet; Henri Rebourseau; Dom. Rion; Ch. de la Tour.*

C

- **Ch. Clos des Jacobins** [kloh day zha-koh-Ban] (*St. Emilion Grand Cru Classé, Bordeaux,* France) Rich and ripe and long-lasting wine, if not always very complex.
- **Clos des Mont-Olivet** [kloh day mon-to-lee-vay] (*Rhône,* France) *Châteauneuf-du-Pape* estate with a rare mastery of white wine.
- **Clos des Papes** [kloh day pap] (*Rhône,* France) Producer of serious *Châteauneuf-du-Pape,* which – in top vintages – rewards cellaring.
- **Clos du Bois** [kloh doo bwah] (*Sonoma Valley,* California) Top-flight producer whose "Calcaire" *Chardonnay* and Marlstone *Cabernet Merlot* are particularly fine. ★★★★ **1996 Calcaire Chardonnay £££**
- **Clos du Clocher** [kloh doo klosh-shay] (*Pomerol, Bordeaux,* France) Reliably rich, plummy wine. 93 **94** 95 **96** 97 **98 99** ★★★★ **1998 £££**
- **Clos du Marquis** [kloh doo mahr-kee] (*St. Julien, Bordeaux,* France) The *second label* of *Léoville-Las-Cases.* 93 94 95 96 97 98 00
- **Clos du Roi** [kloh doo rwah] (*Burgundy,* France) *Beaune Premier Cru* that is also part of *Corton Grand Cru.*
- **Clos du Val** [kloh doo vahl] (*Napa Valley,* California) Bernard Portet, brother of Dominique who used to run *Taltarni* in Australia, makes stylish *Stag's Leap* reds – including *Cabernet* and *Merlot.* They develop with time. ★★★★ **1995 Reserve Stag's Leap Cabernet Sauvignon £££**
- **Clos l'Eglise** [klos lay-gleez] (*Pomerol, Bordeaux,* France) Spicy wines from a consistent small *Pomerol* estate. 83 85 86 88 89 **90 93 95 96** 97 *98 00*
- **Clos Floridène** [kloh floh-ree-dehn] (*Graves, Bordeaux,* France) Classy, oaked, white *Graves* made by superstar *Denis Dubourdieu.*
- **Clos Fourtet** [kloh-for-tay] (*Bordeaux,* France) Shifting from one branch of the Lurton family to another, this long-time under-performer is now part of André Lurton's portfolio. Watch this space.
- **Clos Mogador** [klohs-moh-gah-dor] (*Priorato,* Spain) *René Barbier's* rich, modern, juicy red from Priorato. A wine whose quality, fame – and price – have all helped to revolutionise the Spanish wine scene.
- **Clos Pegase** (*Napa,* California) The architectural masterpiece-cum-winery is worth a visit. The wines are less exciting.
- **Clos René** [kloh ruh-nay] (*Pomerol, Bordeaux,* France) Estate making increasingly concentrated though approachable wines.
- **Clos St. Denis** [kloh san dur-nee] (*Burgundy,* France) Top *Grand Cru* vineyard in *Morey St. Denis.* **Dujac; G Lignier; Ponsot.**
- **Clos St.-Landelin** [kloh San lon-duhr-lan] (*Alsace,* France) Long-lived wines; the sister label to *Muré.*
- **Clos Uroulat** [oo-roo-lah] (*Southwest,* France) A standard-bearer for the Jurançon appellation, with limited quantities of impeccably made dry and sweet examples.
- **Cloudy Bay** (*Marlborough,* New Zealand) Under the same French ownership as *Cape Mentelle,* this cult winery has a waiting list for every vintage of its *Sauvignon* (though the 1999 was less than dazzling). The *Chardonnay* is impressive, as are the rare *late-harvest* wines, and the Pinot Noir is a new success. The *Pelorus* sparkling wine, by an American winemaker, is less of a buttery mouthful than it used to be.
- **Clusel-Roch** [kloo-se rosh] (*Rhône,* France) Good, traditional *Côte Rôtie* and *Condrieu* producer. ★★★★ **1998 Côte Rôtie £££**
- **la Clusière** [kloo-see-yehr] (*Bordeaux,* France) Recent, tiny-production (250–300 case) *St. Emilion* microwine from the new owners of *Ch. Pavie.*
- **JF Coche-Dury** [kosh doo-ree] (*Burgundy,* France) A superstar *Meursault* producer whose basic reds and whites outclass his neighbours' supposedly finer fare. ★★★★★ **1998 Meursault Perrières £££**

C

Ÿ Cockburn Smithes [koh-burn] (*Douro*, Portugal) Unexceptional Special Reserve but producer of great *vintage* and superlative *tawny port*. 55 60 63 67 **70** 75 83 **85** 91 94 97 ★★★★ 10 Year Old Tawny £££

Ÿ Codorníu [kod-dor-nyoo] (*Catalonia*, Spain) Huge sparkling winemaker whose Anna de Codorníu is good *Chardonnay*-based *Cava*. The Raventos wines are recommendable too, as are the efforts of the *Raimat* subsidiary. The California offshoot Codorníu Napa's sparkling wine is *Cava*-ish and dull despite using *Champagne* varieties. The *Pinot Noirs* are more impressive.

Ÿ BR Cohn (*Sonoma*, California) A reliable source of Sonoma Valley *Cabernet Sauvignon*. ★★★★ 1997 Olive Hill Estate Vineyards Cabernet Sauvignon £££

Colchagua Valley [kohl-shah-gwah] (*Central Valley*, Chile) Up-and-coming sub-region. Bisquertt; *Casa Lapostolle*; *Undurraga*; *Los Vascos*.

Ÿ Coldstream Hills (*Yarra Valley*, Australia) Founded by lawyer-turned winemaker and wine writer *James Halliday*, now still run by him but in the same stable as *Penfolds*. Stunning *Pinot Noir*, *Chardonnay*, fine *Cabernets*, and *Merlots*. Proof that critics can make as well as break a wine! ★★★★ 1998 Reserve Pinot Noir £££. ★★★★ 1998 Briarston £££

Colheita [kol-yay-tah] (Portugal) Harvest or vintage – particularly used to describe *tawny port* of a specific year.

Ÿ Marc Colin [mahrk koh-lan] (*Burgundy*, France) Family estate with affordable wines from St. Aubin and a small chunk of (rather pricier) *Le Montrachet*. ★★★★ 1998 St.-Aubin Cheteniére £££

Ÿ Michel Colin-Deleger [koh-lah day-lay-jay] (*Burgundy*, France) Up-and-coming *Chassagne-Montrachet* estate. ★★★★★ 1996 Chassagne-Montrachet les Chamets ££££

Ÿ Collards [kol-lards] (*Auckland*, New Zealand) Small producer of lovely pineappley *Chardonnay* and appley *Chenin Blanc*.

Ÿ Collegiata [koh-lay-jee jah-tah] (*Toro*, Spain) Rich, red wine from the *Tempranillo* produced in a little-known region.

Colle/colli [kol-lay/kol-lee] (Italy) Hill/hills.

Ÿ Colli Berici [kol-lee bay-ree-chee] (*Veneto*, Italy) Red and white *DOC*.

Ÿ Colli Bolognesi [kol lee bol lon yeh see] (*Emilia-Romagna*, Italy) Up-and-coming region for *Merlot* and *Cabernet Sauvignon* reds and fresh white *Sauvignon Blanc* and the local *Pinot Bianco* and Pignoletto. Bonzara; Gaggioli.

Ÿ Colli Euganei [kol lee yoo-gah-nay] (*Veneto*, Italy) Hills near Padova where Vignalta produces its Gemola *Cabernet-Merlot*. Other wines are less impressive.

Ÿ Colli Orientali del Friuli [kol-lee oh-ree yehn-tah-lee del free-yoo-lee] (*Friuli-Venezia Giulia*, Italy) Lively, single-variety whites and reds from near the *Slovenian* border. Subtle, honeyed, and very pricey *Picolit*, too.

Ÿ Colli Piacentini [kol-lee pee-yah-chayn-tee-nee] (*Emiglia-Romagna*, Italy) A very varied *DOC*, covering characterful, off-dry Malvasia sparkling wine and the Bonarda-*Barbera*-based Guttiunio. la Stoppa; la Tosa; il Pociarello.

Ÿ Vin de Pays des Collines Rhodaniennes [kol-leen roh-dah nee-enn] (*Rhône*, France) The *Vin de Pays* region of the northern *Rhône*, using *Rhône* varieties, *Gamay* and *Merlot*. St. Désirat Cooperative; G Vernay.

Ÿ Collio [kol-lee-yoh] (*Friuli-Venezia Giulia*, Italy) High-altitude region with a basketful of white varieties, plus those of *Bordeaux* and red *Burgundy*. Refreshing and often restrained. Borgo Conventi; Borgo del Tiglio; L. Felluga; Gravner; Jermann; Puiatti; Schiopetto; Venica & Venica; Villa Russiz.

Ÿ Collioure [kol-yoor] (*Midi*, France) Intense *Rhône*-style *Languedoc-Roussillon* red, often marked by the presence of *Mourvèdre* in the blend. A good group of producers here are beginning to attract attention. Ch. de Jau; Dom du Mas Blanc; Clos de Paulilles; de la Rectorie; la Tour Vieille.

🌿 Colombard [kol-om-bahrd] White grape grown in *Southwest* France for making into Armagnac and good, light, modern whites by *Yves Grassa* and *Plaimont*. Also planted in Australia (*Primo Estate* and *Best's*) and the US, where it is known as French Colombard.

C

Jean-Luc Colombo [kol-lom-boh] (*Rhône*, France) Oenologist guru to an impressive number of *Rhône* estates – and producer of his own modern, oaky *Côtes du Rhône* and *Cornas*. ★★★★ 1998 Cornas Les Louvée £££

Columbia Crest (*Washington State*) Winery associated with *Ch. Ste. Michelle*. ★★★★ 1995 Reserve £££

Columbia Winery (*Washington State*) Producer of good, fairly priced, *Chablis*-style *Chardonnay* and *Graves*like *Semillon*, subtle single-vineyard *Cabernet*, especially good *Merlot*, *Syrah*, and *Burgundian Pinot Noir*. ★★★★ 1997 Otis Vineyard David Lake Signature Series Chardonnay ££

Commandaria [com-man-dah-ree-yah] (Cyprus) Rare raisiny dessert wine.

Commune [kom-moon] (France) Small demarcated plot of land named after its principal town or village. Equivalent to an English parish.

Vin de Pays des Comtés Rhodaniens [kom-tay roh-dah nee-yen] (*Rhône/Savoie*, France) Fresh, aromatic whites are the stars here (*Sauvignon*, *Viognier*) plus some juicy *Rhône* reds (*Grenache*, *Syrah*).

Vin de Pays des Comtés Tolosan [kom-tay toh-loh-so'n] (*Southwest*, France) Fast-improving blends of *Bordeaux* and indigenous grapes.

Conca de Barberá [kon-kah deh bahr-beh-rah] (*Catalonia*, Spain) Cool region where *Torres's* impressive Milmanda *Chardonnay* is made.

Viña Concha y Toro [veen-yah kon-chah ee tohr-roh] (*Maipo*, Chile) Steadily improving, thanks to winemaker *Ignacio Recabarren* and investment in *Casablanca*. Best wines are Don Melchior, Marques de Casa Concha, Trio, Casillero del Diablo, and *Almaviva*, its joint venture with *Mouton Rothschild*.

Condado de Haza [kon-dah-doh deh hah-thah] (*Ribera del Duero*, Spain) Impressive new venture from the owner of *Pesquera*.

Conde de Caralt [kon-day day kah-ralt] (*Catalonia*, Spain) One of the best names in *Cava*. Catch it young.

Condrieu [kon-dree-yuhh] (*Rhône*, France) One of the places where actor Gerard Dépardieu owns vines. Fabulous, pricey, pure *Viognier*: a cross between dry, white wine and perfume. Far better than the hyped and high-priced *Ch. Grillet* next door. 82 85 **88 89 90** 91 94 95 96 97 98 Ch. d'Ampuis; Patrick & Christophe Bonneford; Louis Chèze; Gilbert Chirat; *Yves Cuilleron;* Pierre Dumazet; *Philippe Faury; Pierre Gaillard; Michel Gerin; Etienne Guigal;* de Monteillet; *Antoine Montez; Robert Niero;* Alain Parent (& Gerard Dépardieu); *André Perret;* Phillipe & Christophe Pichon; *Hervé Richard; Georges Vernay;* Francois Villand; Gerard Villano.

Confréries [kon-fray-ree] (France) Promotional brotherhoods linked to a particular wine or area. Many, however, are nowadays more about pomp and pageantry, kudos and backslapping, than active promotion.

Jean-Jacques Confuron [con-foor-ron] (*Burgundy*, France) Innovative producer with good *Nuits-St.-Georges*, *Vosne-Romanée*, and *Clos Vougeot*. ★★★★★ 1996 Clos Vougeot £££

Cono Sur [kon-noh soor] (Chile) *Concha y Toro* subsidiary with a range of varietals, including a classy *Pinot Noir* from *Casablanca*. Back on form after the arrival of a new winemaker (in 1998). The Isla Negra wines are good too.

Ch. la Conseillante [lah kon-say-yont] (*Pomerol*, *Bordeaux*, France) Brilliant property with lovely, complex, perfumed wines. **70 75** 76 79 **81 82** 83 84 **85** 88 *89 90* 91 93 94 *95 96 97 98* 00

Consejo Regulador [kon-say-hoh ray-goo-lah-dohr] (Spain) Administrative body responsible for *DO* laws.

Consorzio [kon-sohr-zee-yoh] (Italy) Producers' syndicate.

Constantia [kon-stan-tee-yah] (South Africa) The first New World wine region. Until recently, the big name was *Groot Constantia*. Now *Constantia Uitsig*, *Klein Constantia*, *Buitenverwachting*, and *Steenberg* support the enduring reputation, but better wines are still often easier to find elsewhere in the Cape. *Klein Constantia's late-harvest* Vin de Constance is the region's flagship, recalling the days when Constantia wines were talked of in the same breath as port and *Bordeaux*.

C

❦ **Aldo Conterno** [al-doh kon-tehr-noh] (*Piedmont*, Italy) Great, traditional producer of single-vineyard *Barolo* (esp. Gran Bussia) and similarly top-class *Barbera*. Other varieties are well handled too, particularly Grignolino and Freisa. Nobody does it better.

❦ **Conterno Fantino** [kon-tehr-noh fan-tee-noh] (*Piedmont*, Italy) Another worthwhile Conterno. ★★★★★ 1996 Barolo Vigna del Gris ££££

❦ **Viñedos del Contino** [veen-yay-dos del con-tee-no] (*Rioja*, Spain) CVNE-owned *Rioja* Alavesa estate whose wines can have more fruit and structure than most. ★★★★ 1989 Rioja Reserva ££

Controliran (Bulgaria) Bulgarian version of *Appellation Contrôlée*

Coonawarra [koon-nah-wah-rah] (*South* Australia) Internationally acknowledged top-class mini-region, stuck in the middle of nowhere, with a cool(ish) climate, terra rossa (red) soil, and a long-brewed controversy over where precisely its boundaries ought to be drawn. (There are nearby "islands" of red soil whose wines have been excluded from the Coonawarra designation). The best Coonawarra reds are great, blackcurranty-minty *Cabernet Sauvignons* and underrated *Shirazes*. Whites are less impressive; big *Chardonnays* and full-bodied *Rieslings*. *Bowen Estate; Hardy's; Katnook; Lindemans; Mildara; Orlando; Petaluma; Parker Estate; Penfolds; Penley Estate; Ravenswood (Hollick); Rosemount; Rouge Homme; Yalumba; Wynns.*

❦ **Coopers Creek** (*Auckland*, New Zealand) Individualistic whites including a *Chenin-Semillon* blend, *Chardonnay*, *Sauvignon*, and *Riesling*.

❦ **Copertino** [kop-per-tee-noh] (*Apulia*, Italy) Fascinating berryish wine made from the "bitter-black" *Negroamaro*. ★★★★ 1997 Riserva Cantina Sociale ££

❦ **Corbans** (*Henderson*, New Zealand) Big producer (encompassing *Cooks*) making wines in several regions. Good, rich, *Merlot* reds (even, occasionally, from *Marlborough*). ★★★★ 1998 Cottage Block Cabernet Sauvignon - Cabernet Franc - Merlot ££

❦ **Corbières** [kawr-byayr] (*Languedoc-Roussillon*, France) Region where a growing number of small estates are now making tasty red wines. Ch. d'Aguilhar; Aiguilloux; Caraguilhes; des Chandelles; Etang des Colombes; Grand Caumont; Hélène; de Lastours; *Mont Tauch*; Pech-Latt; Vignerons de la Méditerranée; Meunier St. Louis; d'Ornaisons; les Palais du Révérend; St. Auriol; St. Estève; Celliers St. Martin; Salvagnac; Villemajou; *la Voulte Gasparets*.

❦ **Cordoba** (*Stellenbosch*, South Africa) Ambitious producer of wines high on the *Helderberg*, (so far) over-enthusiastically described as a local *"First Growth"*.

❦ **Cordon Negro** [kawr-don nay-groh] (*Catalonia*, Spain) Brand name for *Freixenet's* successful *Cava*. The matte-black bottle and generous marketing must account for sales. Not a sparkling wine I voluntarily drink.

❦ **Corino** [koh-ree-noh] (*Piedmont*, Italy) Up-and-coming winery, winning applause for the quality of its Barbera d'Alba. ★★★★ 1998 Pozzo £££

❦ **Coriole** [koh-ree-ohl] (*McLaren Vale*, Australia) *Shiraz* specialist that has diversified into *Sangiovese*. The *Semillons* and *Rieslings* are pretty good, too. ★★★★ 1997 Mary Kathleen Cabernet Blend 1997 £££

❦ **Corison** [kaw-ree-son] (*Napa*, California) Winery specializing in juicy *Cabernet*. ★★★★★ 1996 Cabernet Sauvignon Napa Valley £££

Corked Unpleasant, musty smell and flavour, caused by (usually invisible) mould in the cork. Affects at least 6% of bottles. Visit: www.corkwatch.com.

❦ **Cornas** [kaw-re-nas] (*Rhône*, France) Smoky, spicy *Syrah; tannic* when young, but worth keeping. 76 78 82 83 85 **88 89** 90 91 95 96 97 98 99 00 *Thierry Allemand; de Barjac; Chapoutier; Auguste Clape; Jean-Luc Colombo; Courbis; Eric & Joël Durand; Durvieu; Jaboulet Aîné; Juge; Jacques Lemercier; Jean Lionnet; Robert Michel; Michel Rochepertuis; de St. Pierre; Serette; Tain Cooperative; Tardieu-Laurent; Noël Verset; Alain Voge.*

C

⚱ **Fattoria Coroncino** [kawr-ron-chee-noh] (*Marche*, Italy) One of the best producers of *Verdicchio Castello dei Jesi Classico Superiore*.

Corsica (France) Mediterranean island making robust reds, whites, and rosés under a raft of *appellations* (doled out generously to assuage rebellious islanders). *Vins de Pays* (*de l'Ile de Beauté*) are often more interesting.

⚱ **Dom. Corsin** [kawr-san] (*Burgundy*, France) Reliable *Pouilly-Fuissé* and *St. Véran* estate. ★★★★ **1999 Pouilly Fuissé ££**

🍇 **Cortese** [kawr-tay-seh] (*Piedmont*, Italy) Herby grape used in *Piedmont* and to make *Gavi*. Drink young.

⚱ **Corton** [kawr-ton] (*Burgundy*, France) *Grand Cru* hill potentially making great, intense, long-lived reds and – as *Corton-Charlemagne* – whites. The supposedly uniformly great vineyards run a suspiciously long way around the hill. Reds can be very difficult to taste young; many never develop. White: 78 85 87 88 89 90 92 95 96 97 98 Red: 78 83 85 86 87 88 89 90 92 95 96 97 98 Bertrand Ambroise; *Bonneau du Martray; Chandon de Briailles; Dubreuil-Fontaine; Faiveley;* Laleur-Piot; *Louis Latour (white); Leroy;* Maillard; Nudant; *Jacques Prieur; Tollot-Beaut; Thomas Moillard.*

⚱ **Corzano & Paterno** [kawrt-zah-noh eh pah-tehr-noh] (*Tuscany*, Italy) Fine Chianti Colli Fiorentini and Vin Santo.

⚱ **Corvo** [kawr-voh] (*Sicily*, Italy) Brand used by Duca di Salaparuta for its recently repackaged pleasant reds and whites.

⚱ **Ch. Cos d'Estournel** [koss-des-tawr-nel] (*St. Estèphe 2ème Cru Classé Bordeaux*, France) Recently sold *estate* making top-class wines with *Pauillac* richness and fruit. Spice is the hallmark. 61 70 75 76 78 79 82 83 85 86 88 89 90 91 92 93 94 95 96 97 98 99 00

⚱ **Ch. Cos Labory** [koss la-baw-ree] (*St. Estèphe 5ème Cru Classé, Bordeaux,* France) Good, traditional, if tough, wines. 89 90 92 93 95 96 97 98 99 00

Cosecha [coh-seh-chah] (Spain) Harvest or *vintage*.

⚱ **Cosentino** (*Napa*, California) Producer of serious, long-lived reds.

⚱ **Cossart Gordon** (*Madeira*, Portugal) High-quality brand used by the *Madeira* Wine Co. ★★★★★ **10 year old Bual £££**

⚱ **Costanti** (*Tuscany*, Italy) Serious *Brunello di Montalcino* producer with classy, long-lived wines. ★★★★★ **1988 Brunello di Montalcino ££££**

Costers del Segre [kos-tehrs del say-greh] (*Catalonia*, Spain) DO created for the excellent *Raimat*, whose irrigated vineyards helped to persuade Spain's wine authorities to allow other producers to give thirsty vines a drink. ★★★★★ **1994 Raimat Cabernet Sauvignon Reserva £££**

Costers de Siurana [kos-tehrs deh see-yoo-rah-nah] (*Priorato*, Spain) One of the stars of *Priorato*. Grape varieties for the Clos de l'Obac include *Syrah, Cabernet, Merlot,* plus local *Garnacha, Cariñena,* and *Tempranillo.*

⚱ **Costières de Nîmes** [kos-tee-yehr duh neem] (*Midi*, France) An up-and-coming region whose *Syrah*-based reds can match the best of the Northern Rhône. Ch. de l'Amarine; de Campuget; Dom. des Cantarelles; Mas de Bressades; Ch. Mourges du Grès; de Nages; Tuilerie de Pazac; Valcombe.

⚱ **Costières du Gard** [kos-tee-yehr doo gahr] (*Southwest*, France) Fruity reds, rarer whites, and rosés.

🍇 **Cot** [koh] (France) The grape of *Cahors* and the *Loire* (aka *Malbec*).

⚱ **Cotat Frères** [koh-tah] (*Loire*, France) One of the few *Loire Sauvignon* producers to achieve superstar status in the US. The Cotats' *Sancerres* repay ageing and deserve their success. ·★★★★★ **1999 les Monts Damnés £££**

Côte d'Or [koht dor] (*Burgundy*, France) Geographical designation for the finest slopes, encompassing the *Côte de Nuits* and *Côte de Beaune*.

⚱ **Côte de Beaune (Villages)** [koht duh bohn] (*Burgundy*, France) The southern half of the *Côte d'Or*. With the suffix "*Villages*", indicates red wines from one or more of the specified *communes*. Confusingly, wine labelled simply "*Côte de Beaune*" comes from a small area around *Beaune* itself and often tastes like wines of that *appellation*. White: 86 87 88 89 90 92 95 96 97 98 99 Red: 78 85 88 89 90 91 92 95 96 97 98 99

C

℧ **Côte de Brouilly** [koht duh broo-yee] (*Burgundy*, France) *Beaujolais Cru*: distinct from *Brouilly* – often finer. Floral and ripely fruity; will keep for a few years. 88 89 90 **91** 94 95 **96** 97 98 99 00 *Duboeuf;* Pivot; Ch. Thivin.

℧ **Côte de Nuits (Villages)** [koht duh nwee] (*Burgundy*, France) Northern, and principally "red" end of the *Côte d'Or*. The suffix *"Villages"* indicates wine from one or more specified *communes*.

℧ **Côte Rôtie** [koh troh tee] (*Rhône*, France) Smoky yet refined *Syrah* (possibly with some white *Viognier*) from the northern *Rhône appellation* divided into "Brune" and "Blonde" hillsides. Most need at least six years. 76 78 80 82 83 85 86 88 89 90 91 95 96 98 99 00 Ch. d'Ampuis. *Barge;* Bonnefond; *Burgaud;* Champet; *Cuilleron; Clusel-Roch;* Gallet; *Gasse;* Gentaz-Dervieuz; *Gerin; Guigal; Jamet; Jasmin;* Ogier; *Rostaing;* Saugère; L. de Vallouit; *Vernay; Vidal Fleury; F. Villard.*

Côte(s), Coteaux [koht] (France) Hillsides.

℧ **Coteaux d'Aix-en-Provence** [koh-toh dayks on prov vons] (*Provence*, France) A recent *AC* region producing light floral whites, fruity reds, and dry rosés using *Bordeaux* and *Rhône* varieties. Château Calissanne; Ch. Revelette; Mas Ste.-Berthe; Ch. Vignelaure.

℧ **Coteaux d'Amazone** [koh-toh dah-mah-zohn] Despite huge investment piled into a spider's web of vineyards in the exciting Dottes-Commes region pionerred by Freya Hood between the Bay of Biscay and the Alta Vista hills, this area is proving a slow starter. Its net value has, if anything, dropped.

℧ **Coteaux d'Ancenis** [koh-toh don-suh-nee] (*Loire*, France) So far, only *VDQS* status for this region near Nantes, producing light reds and deep pinks from the *Cabernet Franc* and *Gamay*, and also *Muscadet*-style whites.

℧ **Coteaux d'Ardèche** [koh-toh dahr-desh] (*Rhône*, France) Light country wines, mainly from the *Syrah* and *Chardonnay*. A popular place with *Burgundians* to produce affordable alternatives to their own white wine.

℧ **Coteaux Champenois** [koh-toh shom-puh-nwah] (*Champagne*, France) Overpriced, mostly thin, acidic, still wine. *Laurent Perrier's* is about the best.

℧ **Coteaux du Languedoc** [koh-toh doo long-dok] (*Midi*, France) A big *appellation*, and a source of fast-improving rich reds such as *Pic St. Loup*.

℧ **Coteaux du Layon** [koh-toh doo lay-yon] (*Loire*, France) *Chenin Blancs*; some dry wines; sweet *Bonnezeaux* and *Quarts de Chaume*. Sweet White: 76 83 85 86 88 89 90 94 95 96 97 98 Perre Aguilas; Patrick Baudoin; Dom. des Baumard; Ch. Pierre Bise; Ch. du Breuil; Cady; Delesvaux, des Forges; Godineau; Guimoniere; Ch. la Plaisance; Ch. des Rochettes; de la Roulerie; des Sablonettes; Ch. Soucherie; la Varière.

℧ **Coteaux du Loir** [koh-toh doo lwahr] (*Loire*, France) Clean, vigorous whites from a *Loire* tributary. 96 97 98

℧ **Coteaux du Lyonnais** [koh-toh doo lee-ohn-nay] (*Rhône*, France) Just to the south of *Beaujolais*, making some very acceptable good-value wines from the same grapes. Descottes; *Duboeuf;* Fayolle; Sain Bel Co-operative.

℧ **Coteaux du Tricastin** [koh-toh doo tris-kass-tan] (*Rhône*, France) Southern *Rhône appellation*, emerging as a source of good-value, peppery-blackcurranty reds. Dom. de Grangeneuve; de Rozets; du Vieux Micoulier.

℧ **Coteaux Varois** [koh-toh vahr-rwah] (*Provence*, France) Inexpensive, fruity reds, whites, and rosés. Deffends.

℧ **Côtes de/Premières Côtes de Blaye** [koht duh/pruh-myerh koht duh blay] (*Bordeaux*, France) A ferryride across the river from *St. Julien*. Poor winemaking prevents many *estates* from living up to their potential. Premières are usually red; Côtes, white. 88 89 90 94 **95 96** 97 98 00 Ch. Bertinerie; Gigault; Haut-Sociondo; les Jonqueyres; Segonzac; des Tourtes.

C

 Côtes de Bourg [koht duh boor] (*Bordeaux*, France) Clay-soil region just across the water from the *Médoc* and an increasingly reliable source of good-value, *Merlot*-dominated, plummy reds. Red: 85 86 **88 89 90** 94 **95 96 97** 98 00 Brulesécaille; Falfas; Fougas; Guerry; les Jonquières; Maldoror; Repimplet; Robin; Roc-de-Cambes; Rousset; Tayac.

 Côtes de Castillon [koht duh kass-tee-yon] (*Bordeaux*, France) Region where the *Merlot* is often a lot more lovingly handled than in nearby *St. Emilion*. Ch. d'Aiguilhe; de Belcier; Cap de Faugères; Champ de Mars; Côte Montpezat; Grande Maye; Lapeyronie; de Parenchère; Pitray; Poupille; Robin.

 Côtes de Duras [koht duh doo-rahs] (*Bordeaux*, France) Inexpensive *Sauvignons*, often better value than basic *Bordeaux* Blanc. Amblard; Duras Cooperative; Moulin des Groyes.

 Côtes de Francs [koht duh fron] (*Bordeaux*, France) Up-and-coming region close to *St. Emilion*; increasingly good reds. Charmes-Godard; de Francs; la Claverie; la Prade; *Puygeraud*; Vieux Chateau Champs de Mars.

 Vin de Pays des Côtes de Gascogne [koht duh gas-koñ] (*Southwest*, France) Armagnac-producing region where dynamic producers *Yves Grassa* and the *Plaimont* cooperative used modern winemaking techniques on grapes that would in the past have been used for brandy. *Ugni Blanc* and *Colombard* are giving way to *Sauvignon Blanc*. *Grassa; Plaimont.*

 Côtes de Provence [koht dur prov-vonss] (*Provence*, France) Improving, good-value, fruity whites and ripe, spicy reds. The famous rosés, however, are often carelessly made and stored, but vacationers rarely notice that the so-called pink wine is a deep shade of bronze and decidedly unrefreshing. A region with as much appeal to organic winemakers as to fans of Mr Mayle's rural tales. Dom. la Bernarde; la Courtade; d'Esclans; Commanderie e Peyrassol; Gavoty; de Mireille; Ott; Rabiega; Richeaume; Vanniéres.

 Côtes de St. Mont [koht duh san-mon] (*Southwest*, France) Large *VDQS* area encompassing the whole of the Armagnac region. *Plaimont* is the largest and best-known producer.

 Vin de Pays des Côtes de Tarn [koht duh tarn] (*Southwest*, France) Fresh, fruity, simple reds and whites, mostly for drinking in-situ rather than outside France. Labastide-de-Levis Cooperative.

 Vin de Pays des Côtes de Thau [koht duh toh] (*Languedoc-Roussillon*, France) Fresh whites to drink with seafood in the canalside restaurants of *Sète*. Les Vignerons des Garrigues.

 Vin de Pays des Côtes de Thongue [koht duh tong] (*Languedoc-Roussillon*, France) Up-and-coming region between Béziers and Toulouse where the Domaines d'Arjolle, Condamine, l'Eveque, Teisserenc, and Deshenrys are making tasty modern wines.

 Côtes du Frontonnais [koht doo fron-ton-nay] (*Southwest*, France) Up-and-coming, inexpensive red (and some rosé); characterful wines. Ch. Baudare; Bellevue la Forêt; Cave de Fronton; le Roc; Viguerie de Beulaygue

 Côtes du Jura [koht duh joo-rah] (France) *Vin Jaune* and *Vin de Paille* are the styles to look for in this area close to Arbois, as well as sparkling wine and Poulsard and Trousseau reds. *Ch. d'Arlay;* Jean Bourdy; Couret; Delay.

 Côtes du Marmandais [koht doo mahr-mon-day] (*Southwest*, France) Uses the *Bordeaux* red grapes plus *Gamay*, *Syrah*, and others to make pleasant, fruity, inexpensive wines. Ch. de Beaulieu; Les Vignerons de Beaupuy; Cave de Cocument.

 Côtes du Rhône (Villages) [koht doo rohn] (*Rhône*, France) Spicy reds mostly from the southern *Rhône* Valley. The best supposedly come from a set of better *Villages* (and are sold as *CdR Villages*), though some single *domaine* "simple" *Côtes du Rhônes* outclass many *Villages* wines. *Grenache* is the key grape, though recent years have seen a growing use of the *Syrah*. Whites, which can include new-wave *Viogniers*, are improving. Red: 89 **90** 93 94 **95 96 97 98 99** Beaucastel (Coudoulet); Dom. de Beaurenard; Cabasse; les Goubert; *Grand Moulas; Guigal;* Richaud; la Soumade; Ste. Anne.

C

☕ **Côtes du Roussillon (Villages)** [koht doo roo-see-yon] (*Midi*, France) *Appellation* for red, white, and rosé of pretty variable quality. *Côtes du Roussillon Villages* is generally better. Brial; des Chênes; Fontanel; Força Réal; Gauby; de Jau; Vignerons Catalans.

☕ **Côtes du Ventoux** [koht doo von-too] (*Rhône*, France) Improving everyday country reds that are similar to *Côtes du Rhône*. 85 88 89 **90** 94 **95 96** 97 98 99 00 *Brusset; Jaboulet Aîné; Pascal; Perrin; la Vieille Ferme.*

☕ **Côtes du Vivarais** [koht doo vee-vah-ray] (*Provence*, France) Light southern *Rhône*-like reds, fruity rosés, and fragrant light whites.

Cotesti [kot tesh-tee] (Romania) Easterly vineyards growing varieties such as *Pinots Noir, Blanc, Gris,* and *Merlot*.

☕ **Cotnari** [kot nah-ree] (Romania) Traditional and now very rare white dessert wine. Has potential.

☕ **Bodegas el Coto** [el kot-toh] (*Rioja*, Spain) Small *estate* producing classy, medium-bodied El Coto and Coto de Imaz reds.

☕ **Cottin Frères** [cot-tah] (*Burgundy*, France) A new name that has been adopted by the Cottin Brothers who run the dynamic *Nuits-St.-Georges négociant* firm of *Labouré Roi*.

☕ **Quinta do Côtto** [keen tah doh kot-toh] (*Douro*, Portugal) Ports and intense, tannic, berryish red wines – labelled as Grande Escolha – produced in a more southerly part of the Douro River than most other vintage *ports*.

COTO DE IMAZ
RIOJA 1978
Denominación de Origen Controlada

☕ **Coulée de Serrant** [koo-lay duh seh-ron] (*Loire*, France) Great dry *Chenin* from a top property in *Savennières* run by *Nicolas Joly*, a leading champion of "biodynamique" winemaking. The Becherelle vineyard is fine too.

☕ **Paul Coulon et Fils** [Koo-lon] (*Rhône*, France) Serious *Rhône* producer.

Coulure [koo-loor] Climate-related winegrowing disorder. The condition causes reduced yields (and possibly higher quality) as grapes shrivel and fall off the vine.

☕ **Couly-Dutheil** [koo-lee doo-tay] (*Loire*, France) High-quality *Chinon* from vineyards just behind the *château* in which Henry II of England imprisoned his wife, Eleanor of Aquitaine. ★★★★ 1998 Clos de L'Echo £££

☕ **Viña Cousiño Macul** [koo-sin-yoh mah-kool] (*Maipo*, Chile) The most traditional producer in Chile. Reds are more successful than whites. ★★★ 1995 Finis Terrae ££

☕ **Pierre Coursodon** [koor-soh-don] (*Rhône*, France) Maker of superlative traditional *St. Josephs* that need time but develop layers of flavour and complexity that are lacking in many a pricier *Hermitage*.

☕ **Ch. Coutet** [koo-tay] (*Barsac Premier Cru Classé, Bordeaux*, France) Delicate neighbour to *Ch. Climens*, often making comparable wines: Cuvée Madame is top flight. 71 75 76 **81** 82 **83** 85 **86** 87 **88 89** 90 95 96 97 98 99

☕ **Ch. Couvent-des-Jacobins** [koo-von day zhah-koh-ban] (*St. Emilion Grand Cru Classé, Bordeaux*, France) Producer of juicy, plummy-spicy wines. **82** 83 85 86 88 **89 90 92 93** 94 95 96 98 99 00 ★★★ 1998 £££

Cowra [kow-rah] (*New South Wales*, Australia) Up-and-coming region, making a name for itself with *Chardonnay*, for which it will one day eclipse its better known but less viticulturally ideal neighbour, the *Hunter Valley*.

☕ **Dom. de Coyeux** [duh cwah-yuh] (*Rhône*, France) One of the best producers of *Côtes du Rhône* and *Muscat de Beaumes de Venise*.

☕ **Craggy Range** (*Hawkes Bay*, New Zealand) New kid on the block, with lots of US money behind it. Good *Sauvignon Blanc* and promising *Pinot Noir.*

☕ **Cranswick Estate** (*Riverina*, NSW, Australia) Successful producer making reliable, fairly-priced wines under its own and the Barramundi label and some great *late-harvest* whites. ★★★★ 1999 Vignette Botrytis Semillon ££

C

☨ **Quinta do Crasto** [kin-tah doh cras-toh] (*Douro*, Portugal) An up-and-coming small port producer with good red table wines too. ★★★★ 1998 Douro Reserva ££

☨ **Cream Sherry** (*Jerez*, Spain) Popular style (though not in Spain) produced by sweetening an *oloroso*. A visitor to *Harvey's* apparently preferred one of the company's *sherries* to the then popular "Bristol Milk". "If that's the milk," she joked, "this must be the cream."

Crémant [kray-mon] (France) Term previously used in *Champagne*, denoting a slightly sparkling style due to a lower pressure of gas in the bottle. Now used only elsewhere to indicate sparkling wine made by the traditional method, e.g., Crémant de *Bourgogne*, de *Loire*, and d'*Alsace*.

☨ **Crépy** [kray-pee] (*Savoie*, France) Crisp floral white from *Savoie*.

Criado y Embotellado (por) [kree-yah-doh ee em-bot-tay-yah-doh] (Spain) Grown and bottled (by).

Crianza [kree-yan-thah] (Spain) Literally keeping "con Crianza" means aged in wood – often preferable to the *Reservas* and *Gran Reservas*, which are highly prized by Spaniards but can taste dull and dried-out.

☨ **Crichton Hall** [kri-ton] (*Rutherford*, California) Small winery specializing in top-class *Chardonnay*.

☨ **Criots-Batard-Montrachet** [kree-yoh ba-tar mon rah-shay] (*Burgundy*, France) See *Montrachet*.

Crisp Fresh, with good *acidity*.

☨ **Lucien Crochet** [loo-see-yen kroh-shay] (*Loire*, France) Top maker of red and white *Sancerre*. The *Cuvée Prestige* wines in both colours are – unusually for this appellation – worth keeping. ★★★★★ 1997 Sancerre Prestige £££

☨ **Ch. le Crock** [lur krok] (*St. Estèphe Cru Bourgeois*, *Bordeaux*, France) Traditional property that, like *Léoville-Poyferré*, its stablemate, has shown great recent improvement. 82 83 85 86 88 **89 90** 92 93 **95** 96 **98** *99 00*

☨ **Croft** (Spain/Portugal) *Port* and *sherry* producer making highly commercial but rarely memorable wines. The *vintage port* is up to scratch. 55 60 **63** 66 67 **70** 75 77 82 **85** *94 97*

☨ **Ch. La Croix** [la crwah] (*Pomerol*, *Bordeaux*, France) Producer of long-lasting traditional wines.

☨ **Ch. la Croix-de-Gay** [la crwah duh gay] (*Pomerol*, *Bordeaux*, France) Classy *estate* whose complex wines have good, blackcurranty-plummy fruit. 81 **82 83** 85 86 **88 89 90** 91 92 93 *94 95 96 99 00*

☨ **Ch. Croizet-Bages** [krwah-zay bahzh] (*Pauillac 5ème Cru Classé*, *Bordeaux*, France) Underperformer showing some signs of improvement. **82** 83 85 86 87 88 **90** 92 93 94 *95 96 98 99 00*

☨ **Croser** [kroh-sur] (*Adelaide Hills*, Australia) Made by *Brian Croser* of *Petaluma* in the Piccadilly Valley, this is one of the New World's most *Champagne*-like sparkling wines. ★★★★ 1996 Brut £££

🍇 **Crouchen** [kroo-shen] (France) Obscure white grape known as Clare Riesling in Australia and Paarl Riesling in South Africa.

☨ **Crozes-Hermitage** [krohz ehr-mee-tahzh] (*Rhône*, France) Up-and-coming *appellation* in the hills behind supposedly greater *Hermitage*. Smoky, blackberryish reds are pure *Syrah*. Whites (made from *Marsanne* and *Roussanne*) are creamy but less impressive. And they rarely keep. Red: 83 85 88 89 90 91 **95 96 97 98 99** White: 89 90 91 94 95 96 **97** 98 00 *Dom Belle; Chapoutier; Colombier; Combier; Delas; Alain Graillot; Paul Jaboulet Aîné; Dom. du Pavilion-Mercure; Pochon; Sorrel; Tain l'Hermitage Cooperative.*

Cru Bourgeois [kroo boor-zhwah] (*Bordeaux*, France) Wines beneath the *Crus Classés*, supposedly satisfying certain requirements, which can be good value for money and, in certain cases, better than more prestigious *classed growths*. Since around half the wine in the *Médoc* comes from Crus Bourgeois (and a quarter from *Crus Classés*), don't expect the words to mean too much. A new plan to classify the Crus Bourgeois is being promoted with

C

the best of motives, but there seems to be every chance that any such classification will simply introduce more bureaucracy into a Gallic vinous world that is already suffering from a surfeit of legislation. In any case, the best Crus Bourgeois do not rely on membership of this club to attract customers. *d'Angludet; Beaumont; Chasse-Spleen; Citran; Haut-Marbuzet; Gloria; la Gurgue; Labégorce; Labégorce-Zédé; Marbuzet; Meyney; Monbrison; de Pez; Phélan-Ségur; Pibran; Potensac; Poujeaux; Siran; Sociando-Mallet; la Tour Haut-Caussin.*

Cru Classé [kroo klas-say] (*Bordeaux*, France) The best wines of the *Médoc* are crus classés, split into five categories from first (top) to fifth growth (or *Cru*) for the Great Exhibition in 1855. The *Graves*, *St. Emilion*, and *Sauternes* have their own classifications. Some chateaux make better or worse wine than others of the same classification.

☨ **Weingut Hans Crusius** [hans skroos-yuhs] (*Nahe*, Germany) Family-run *estate* prized for the quality of its highly traditional wines. Some of the best, ripest *Trocken* wines around.

Crusted Port (*Douro*, Portugal) An affordable alternative to *vintage* port – a blend of different years, bottled young, and allowed to throw a deposit. *Churchill's; Graham's; Dow's.*

☨ **Yves Cuilleron** [Kwee-yehr-ron] (*Rhône*, France) Rising star producing great (red and white) *St. Joseph* and *Condrieu*. If you want to experience great late-harvest *Viognier*, this is the place. ★★★★★ **1998 St. Joseph Serines £££**

☨ **Cullen** (*Margaret River*, Australia) Brilliant pioneering *estate* showing off the sensitive winemaking skills of Australian Winemaker of the Year (2000), Vanya Cullen. Source of stunning *Sauvignon-Semillon* blends, *claret*-like reds, a highly individual *Pinot Noir*, and a *Burgundian*-style *Chardonnay*. ★★★★★ **1999 Sauvignon Blanc Semillon £££**

Cultivar [kul-tee-vahr] (South Africa) South African for grape variety.

☨ **Ch. Curé-Bon-la-Madelaine** [koo-ray bon lah mad-layn] (*St. Emilion Grand Cru Classé, Bordeaux*, France) Very small *St. Emilion estate* next to *Ausone.* 78 81 **82** 83 **85 86** 88 **89 90 94 95 96** 97 98 99 00

Curico [koo-ree-koh] (Chile) Region in which *Torres, San Pedro,* and *Caliterra* have vineyards. Now being eclipsed by *Casablanca* as a source for cool-climate whites, but still one of Chile's best wine areas for red and white. *Caliterra; Echeverria; la Fortuna; Montes; Miguel Torres; Valdivieso.*

☨ **Cuvaison Winery** [koo-vay-san] (*Napa Valley*, California) Reliable Swiss-owned winery with high-quality *Carneros Chardonnay*, increasingly approachable *Merlot,* and now good *Pinot Noir.* Calistoga Vineyards is a *second label.*

Cuve close [koov klohs] The third-best way of making sparkling wine, in which the wine undergoes secondary fermentation in a tank and is then bottled. Also called the *Charmat* or *Tank method.*

Cuvée (de Prestige) [koo-vay] Most frequently a blend put together in a process called *assemblage.* Prestige *Cuvées* are (particularly in *Champagne*) supposed to be the best a producer has to offer. Bear in mind, however, that if a Champagne house can't offer a decent basic wine, there's no reason to put much trust in its smartly-packaged, highly-priced "prestige" wine.

☨ **Cuvée Napa** (*Napa*, California) The well-established California venture launched by *Mumm Champagne,* and still offering significantly better quality and value for money than the mothership back in France.

☨ **CVNE** [koo-nay] (*Rioja*, Spain) The Compania Vinicola del Norte de Espana (usually referred to as "koo-nay") is a large high-quality operation run by the owners of *Contino* and producing the excellent Viña Real in *Crianza, Reserva, Imperial,* or *Gran Reserva* forms in the best years, as well as a light *CVNE Tinto.* Some recent releases have been slightly less dazzling.

Cyprus Shifting its focus away from making ersatz "*sherry*". Even so, the best wine is still the fortified *Commandaria.*

D

Ⓣ Didier Dagueneau [dee-dee-yay dag guhn-noh] (*Loire*, France)
The iconoclastic producer of some of the best steely and oak-aged
Pouilly-Fumé, and even the occasional *late-harvest* effort that upsets
the authorities. Look out for the "Pur Sang" (made from rare,
ungrafted vines) and oak-fermented "Silex" bottlings. ★★★★★ 1998
Pur Sang £££

Ⓣ Romano dal Forno [roh-mah-noh dal for-noh] (*Veneto*, Italy)
Innovative estate for top-class Valpolicella (with some particularly
good *Amarones*).

Ⓣ Ch. Dalem [dah-lem] (*Fronsac, Bordeaux,* France) Maker of rich, full-
bodied *Fronsac* that easily matches many a *St. Emilion*. 82 83 **85** 86 88
89 90 91 93 **95** 96 97 98 99

Ⓣ Dalla Valle (*Napa*, California) One of the leading lights in the new
trend toward Italian flavours, this small winery makes a delicious
Super-Tuscan lookalike in the shape of the *Sangiovese-based* Pietre Rosso.

Ⓣ Dalwhinnie [dal-win-nee] (*Pyrenees, Victoria,* Australia) Quietly classy
producer close to *Taltarni*, whose reds and whites are made to last.
★★★★ 1998 Moonambel Shiraz £££

Ⓣ Dão [downg] (Portugal) Once Portugal's
best-known region – despite the
traditional dullness of its wines. Thanks
to pioneering producers like *Sogrape* and
Aliança, and the introduction of better
grape varieties such as the *Touriga
Nacional*, both reds and whites are
improving. Sogrape's Quinta dos
Carvalhais is particularly recommendable.
Red: **80 85 88 90 91 93** 94 95 96 97 98
Boas Quintas; Duque de Viseu; Porta dos
Cavaleiros; Quinta dos Roques; Casa de Santar.

Grão Vasco

Ⓣ Kurt Darting [koort dahr-ting] (*Pfalz*, Germany) New-wave producer
who cares more about ripe flavour than making the tooth-scouringly dry
wine favoured by some of his neighbours. *Rieslings* are terrific, but so are
examples of other varieties. Great *late-harvest* wines. ★★★★ 1998
Dürkheimer Hochbenn Riesling Kabinett £££

Ⓣ Ch. Dassault [das-soh] (*St. Emilion Grand Cru Classé, Bordeaux,* France)
Named after the producer of France's fighter planes, this is good, juicy
St. Emilion. 82 83 **85** 86 88 89 **90** 92 93 94 *95 96* 97 *98* 99 00

Ⓣ Ch. de la Dauphine [duh lah doh-feen] (*Fronsac, Bordeaux,* France)
Proof that *Fronsac* really did deserve its reputation in the days when it
was better-regarded than *St. Emilion*. **85** 86 87 88 **89 90** 92 93 94 *95
96* 97 *98* 99 00

Ⓣ Domaine d'Auvenay [Dohv-nay] (*Burgundy,* France) *Estate*
belonging to Lalou Bize Leroy, former co-owner of the *Dom. de la
Romanée-Conti*, and now at *Dom. Leroy*. Great, if pricy, long-lived,
examples of *Auxey-Duresses, Meursault, Puligny-Montrachet,* and
Grands Crus of the Côtes de Nuits. ★★★★★ 1997 Puligny-Montrachet
Les Folatières £££

Ⓣ René and Vincent Dauvissat [doh-vee-sah] (*Burgundy,* France)
One of the best *estates* in *Chablis*. Watch for other Dauvissats though,
the name is also used by the *La Chablisienne* cooperative.

Ⓣ Ch. Dauzac [doh-zak] (*Margaux 5ème Cru Classé, Bordeaux,* France)
Rejuvenated, following its purchase in 1993 by André Lurton of *Ch. la
Louvière*. **82** 83 **85** 86 **88 89 90** 93 94 95 96 97 **98** 99 00

Ⓣ Dealul Mare [day-al-ool mah-ray] (Romania) Carpathian region once
known for whites, now producing surprisingly good *Pinot Noir*.

D

☰ **Etienne & Daniel Defaix** [duh-fay] (*Burgundy*, France) Classy traditional *Chablis* producer, making long-lived wines with a steely bite. ★★★ 1997 Chablis Vieilles Vignes ££

Dégorgée (dégorgement) [day-gor-jay] The removal of the deposit of inert yeasts from *Champagne* after maturation.

☰ **Dehlinger** (*Sonoma*, California) *Russian River Pinot Noir* and *Chardonnay* specialist (with some great single-vineyard examples) that is proving highly successful with *Syrah* and *Cabernet Sauvignon*. ★★★★ 1997 Russian River Valley Late Bottled ReserveChardonnay ££

Deidesheim [di-dess-hime] (*Pfalz*, Germany) Distinguished wine town noted for flavoursome *Rieslings*. QbA/Kab/Spät: 85 86 88 89 90 91 92 93 94 95 96 97 98 Aus/Beeren/Tba: **83 85** 88 89 90 91 92 93 94 95 96 97 98 *Bassermann-Jordan; Josef Biffar; Reichsrat von Buhl; JL Wolf.*

☰ **Deinhard** [dine-hard] (*Mosel*, Germany) See *Wegeler Deinhard*.

☰ **Marcel Deiss** [dise] (*Alsace*, France) Small property producing some of the best wine in the region, including some unusually good *Pinot Noir*. ★★★★★ 1998 Riesling Altenberg de Bergheim ££££

☰ **Delaforce** [del-lah-forss] (*Douro*, Portugal) Small *port* house with lightish but good *vintage* and *tawny*. 58 60 **63 66** 70 74 75 **77 85 94 97** ★★★ 1995 Quinta da Corte Vintage Port £££

☰ **Delamotte** [del-lah-mot] (*Champagne*, France) Established among the *Chardonnay* vineyards of the Côte des Blancs in 1760, and now a subsidiary of *Laurent-Perrier* (and thus in the same group as *Salon*), this can be one of the best sources for *Blanc de Blancs Champagne*.

☰ **Delas Frères** [del-las] (*Rhône*, France) *Négociant* with great *Hermitage* vineyards and now promising much since its purchase by *Louis Roederer*. A name to watch. ★★★★★ 1997 Hermitage les Bessards ££££

☰ **Delatite** [del-la-tite] (*Victoria*, Australia) Producer of lean-structured, long-lived wines. The *Riesling* and, more particularly the *Gewurztraminer*, are the stars, but the Devil's River red is fine too. ★★★★ 1999 VS Limited Edition Riesling ££

☰ **Delbeck** [del-bek] (*Champagne*, France) Underrated little producer, whose wines are strongly *Pinot*-influenced.

☰ **Delegats** [del-leg-gats] (*Auckland,* New Zealand) Family firm that has hit its stride recently with impressively (for New Zealand) ripe reds, especially plummy *Merlots*. Look for the "Reserve" wines. The *second label* is "Oyster Bay". ★★★★ 1998 Reserve Hawkes Bay Merlot £££

☰ **Philippe Delesvaux** [Dels-voh] (*Loire*, France) Quality-conscious *Coteaux de Layon estate* with some good red too.

☰ **Delheim Wines** [del-hime] (*Stellenbosch*, South Africa) A commercial *estate* with lean, quite traditional reds and white.

☰ **DeLille Cellars** (*Washington State*) A small producer of very classy *Bordeaux*-style reds and whites under this and the Chaleur Estate labels.

☰ **André Delorme** [del-lorm] (*Burgundy*, France) Little-known *négociant* based in the Côte Chalonnaise and specializing in sparkling wines.

Demi-sec [duh-mee sek] (France) Medium-dry.

☰ **Demoiselle** [duh-mwah-zel] (*Champagne*, France). A new *Champagne* name to watch with attractive, light, creamy wines.

☰ **Denbies Wine Estate** [den-bees] (*Surrey*, England) Part tourist attraction, part winery, the largest wine *estate* England has so far produced. Sweet wines are the best of the batch so far. ★★★★ Special Late Harvest £££

Deutscher Tafelwein [doyt-shur tah-fuhl-vihn] (Germany) Table wine, guaranteed German as opposed to Germanic-style EC *Tafelwein*. Can be good value – and often no worse than *Qualitätswein*, the supposedly "quality" wine designation that includes every bottle of *Liebfraumilch*.

Deutsches Weinsiegel [doyt-shus vine-see-gel] (Germany) Seals of various colours – usually neck labels – awarded (over-generously) to supposedly higher quality wines. Treat with circumspection.

D

Ⓘ **Deutz** [duhtz] (*Champagne,* France, and also Spain, New Zealand, California) Reliable small but dynamic producer at home and abroad, now owned by *Roederer.* The *Montana Marlborough* Cuvée from New Zealand was created with the assistance of *Deutz,* as was the *Yalumba "D"* in Australia. Maison Deutz is a 150-acre cool-climate vineyard joint venture in California with Nestlé and *Deutz* where, unusually, a bit of *Pinot Blanc* goes into the – generally – excellent blend. The *Cuvée William Deutz* is the star wine. ★★★★★ 1995 Aqmor de Deutz ££££

Ⓘ **Devaux** [duh-voh] (*Champagne,* France) Small producer with a knack of producing fairly-priced wine and unusually good rosé and *Blanc de Noirs.*

Dézaley [days-lay] (*Vaud,* Switzerland) One of the few places in the world where the Chasselas (here called the *Dorin*) makes decent wine. **Pinget.**

Diabetiker Wein [dee-ah-beh-tih-ker vine] (Germany) Very dry wine with most of the sugar fermented out (as in a Diat lager); suitable for diabetics, but daunting for others.

Ⓘ **Diamond Creek** (*Napa Valley,* California) Big Name producer with a set of very good vineyards (Gravelly Meadow, Red Rock Terrace, and Volcanic Hill); toughly intense red wines which demand, and now – more than in the past – repay patience. ★★★★ 1995 Cabernet Sauvignon Volcanic Hill ££££

Ⓘ **Diamond Valley** (*Victoria,* Australia) Producer of one of Australia's – and the New World's best examples of *Pinot Noir.*

Schlossgut Diel [shloss-goot deel] (*Nahe,* Germany) Wine writer Armin Diel makes sublime dry and sweet *Rieslings* as well as some pioneering oaked *Rülander* and *Weissburgunder.*

Ⓘ **Dieu Donné Vineyards** [dyur don-nay] (*Franschhoek,* South Africa) Variable producer of quality varietals in the Franschhoek valley. The 1992 *Chardonnay* was legendary.

Ⓘ **Dom. Disznókó** [diss-noh-koh] (*Tokaji,* Hungary) Newly-constituted *estate* belonging to *AXA* and run by Jean-Michel Cazes of *Ch. Lynch-Bages.* Top-class modern sweet *Tokaji* and dry lemony *Furmint.* ★★★★★ 1995 Tokaji Aszu 5 Puttonyos £££

DLG (Deutsche Landwirtschaft Gesellschaft) (Germany) Body awarding medals for excellence to German wines – far too generously.

DO (Denominac/ion/ão de Origen) (Spain, Portugal) Demarcated quality area, guaranteeing origin, grape varieties, and production standards (everything, in other words except the quality of the stuff in the bottle).

Ⓘ **DOC (Denominación de Origem Controlada)** (Portugal) Replacing the old RD (Região Demarcada) as Portugal's equivalent of Italy's *DOCG.*

DOC (Denominacion de Origen Calificada) (Spain) Ludicrously, and confusingly, Spain's recently launched higher quality equivalent to Italy's *DOCG* shares the same initials as Italy's lower quality *DOC* wines. So far, restricted to *Rioja* – good, bad, and indifferent. In other words, this official designation should be treated – like Italy's *DOCs* and *DOCGs* and France's *Appellation Contrôlée* – with something less than total respect.

DOC(G) (Denominazione di Origine Controllata [e Garantita]) (Italy) Quality control designation based on grape variety and/or origin. "Garantita" is supposed to imply a higher quality level, but all too often it does no such thing and has more to do with regional politics than with tasty wines. It is worth noting, that the generally dull wines of *Albana di Romagna* received the first white *DOCG* (ahead of all sorts of more worthy candidates. However, the recently introduced IGT designation for quality wines previously sold as Vino da Tavola has helped to put DOC and DOCG into perspective as merely an indication of the region in which a wine was produced and its likely style.

Ⓘ **Ch. Doisy-Daëne** [dwah-zee dai-yen] (*Barsac 2ème Cru Classé, Bordeaux,* France) Fine *Barsac* property whose wines are typically more restrained than many a *Sauternes.* The 2000 is a star. The top wine is L'Extravagance. 76 78 79 81 82 83 85 86 **88 89 90** 91 94 95 96 **97 98 99 00**

D

☒ **Ch. Doisy-Dubroca** [dwah-zee doo-brohkah] (*Barsac 2ème Cru Classé, Bordeaux*, France) Underrated *estate* producing ultra-rich wines at often attractively low prices. 75 76 78 79 **81 83** 85 86 87 88 89 **90 95 96 97 98**

☒ **Ch. Doisy-Védrines** [dwah-zee vay-dreen] (*Barsac 2ème Cru Classé, Bordeaux*, France) Reliable *Barsac* property that made a stunningly concentrated 1989 (and a less impressive 1990). 70 **75 76** 78 79 81 **82 83** 85 86 **88** 89 90 92 93 95 96 **97 98 99**

🍇 **Dolcetto (d'Alba, di Ovada)** [dohl-cheh-toh] (*Piedmont*, Italy) Grape producing anything from soft everyday red to very robust and long-lasting examples. Generally worth catching quite young though. *Bests* use it to good effect in Australia. **Altare; Bava; Elvo Cogno;** *Aldo Conterno;* **Cortese;** *Vajra.*

Dôle [Dohl] (Switzerland) *Appellation* of *Valais* producing attractive reds from *Pinot Noir* and/or *Gamay* grapes. **Germanier.**

☒ **Dom Pérignon** [dom peh-reen-yon] (*Champagne*, France) *Moët et Chandon's Prestige Cuvée*, named after the cellarmaster who is erroneously said to have invented the *Champagne* method. Impeccable white and (rare) rosé. (*Moët* will disgorge older *vintages* to order). ★★★★ 1993 ££££

Domaine (Dom.) [doh-mayn] (France) Wine estate.

☒ **Domecq** [doh-mek] (*Jerez/Rioja*, Spain) Producer of (disappointing) *La Ina Fino* and the rare, wonderful *511A Amontillado* and Sibarita *Palo Cortado*.

☒ **Ch. la Dominique** [lah doh-mee-neek] (*St. Emilion Grand Cru Classé, Bordeaux*, France) High-flying property; one of the finest in *St. Emilion*. 70 **71** 78 79 81 **82** 83 **86 88 89 90** 93 94 **95** 96 97 **98 99 00**

☒ **Dominus** [dahm-ih-nuhs] (*Napa Valley*, California) *Christian Moueix* of *Ch. Petrus's* modestly named competitor to *Opus One* has now developed an accessibility that was lacking in early years. Even so, it is concentrated stuff that is built to last. ★★★★★ 1997 ££££

☒ **Donauland** [doh-now-lend] (Austria) Varied wine region associated with good *Grüner Veltliner* but without a specific style of its own.

☒ **Hermann Dönnhoff** (*Nahe*, Germany) Brilliant winemaker who crafts great *late-harvest* wine and *Eiswein* from his Hermannshöhle vineyard.

☒ **Doonkuna** [doon-koo-nah] (*New South Wales*, Australia) Small winery making decent red wine. ★★★★ 1997 Cabernet Merlot ££

☒ **Dopff "Au Moulin"** [dop-foh-moo-lan] (*Alsace*, France) *Négociant* with concentrated *Grand Crus*. ★★★★ 1997 Riesling Schoenenbourg £££

☒ **Dopff & Irion** [dop-fay-ee-ree-yon] (*Alsace*, France) Not to be confused with Dopff "Au Moulin" (now part of the Cave de Pfaffenheim), this is also a name to watch. ★★★ 1997 Riesling les Murailles £££

☒ **Vin de Pays de la Dordogne** [dor-doyn] (*Southwest*, France) To the east of *Bordeaux*, this improving region offers light *Bordeaux*-style wines.

☒ **Girolamo Dorigo** [Jee-roh-lah-moh doh-ree-goh] (*Friuli-Venezia Giulia*, Italy) Classy Collio Orientali del Friuli producer with good reds (made from grapes such as the local Pignolo and *Refosco*) and even more impressive whites including a *Chardonnay, Verduzzo*, and *Picolit*.

🍇 **Dorin** [doh-ran] (*Vaud*, Switzerland) Swiss name for *Chasselas* in the *Vaud*.

🍇 **Dornfelder** [dorn-fel-duh] (Germany) Sadly underrated early-ripening, juicy, berryish grape that is beginning to attract some interest among pioneering winemakers in the southern part of Germany.

Dosage [doh-sazh] The addition of sweetening syrup to naturally dry *Champagne* after *dégorgement* to replace the wine lost with the yeast, and to set the sugar to the desired level (even *Brut Champagne* requires up to four grams per liter of sugar to make it palatable).

Douro [doo-roh] (Portugal) The port region and river whose only famous table wine was the long-established *Barca Velha*. Now, however, thanks largely to port houses like Ramos Pinot and Niepoort, there's a growing range of other stars to choose from. **Barca Velha; Quinta do Cotto; do Crasto; Duas Quintas; do Fojo; da Gaivosa; Redoma; de las Rosa; Vale Dona Maria; Vale da Raposa; Vallado.**

D

Dourthe [doort] (*Bordeaux*, France) Highly dynamic *négociant* whose Dourthe No.1 offers unusually reliable red and – particularly white Bordeaux.

Doux [doo] (France) Sweet.

Ⅰ **Dow** [dow] (*Douro*, Portugal) One of the big two (with *Taylor's*) and under the same family ownership as *Warre*, *Smith Woodhouse*, and *Graham*. Great *vintage port* and similarly impressive *tawny*. The *single-quinta* Quinta do Bomfim wines offer a chance to taste the Dow's style affordably. 63 66 70 72 75 77 85 91 94 97

Ⅰ **Drappier** [drap-pee-yay] (*Champagne*, France) Small, reliably recommendable producer. ★★★★★ "Val des Demoiselles" Rosé £££

Ⅰ **Jean-Paul Droin** [drwan] (*Burgundy*, France) Good, small *Chablis* producer with approachable "modern" wines. ★★★★★ 1998 Chablis Grand Cru Valmur £££

Ⅰ **Dromana Estate** [droh-mah-nah] (*Mornington Peninsula,* Australia) Viticulturalist Gary Crittenden makes good, if light, *Chardonnay* and raspberryish *Pinot Noir*, as well as an impressive range of Italian varietals sold under the "I" label.

Ⅰ **Domaine Drouhin** [droo-an] (*Oregon*) Top *Burgundy* producer's highly expensive investment in the US that's increasingly producing world-class reds – thanks to Veronique Drouhin's skill and commitment and some of *Oregon's* best vineyards. ★★★★ Lauréne1997 Pinot Noir ££££

Ⅰ **Joseph Drouhin** [droo-an] (*Burgundy*, France) Probably *Burgundy's* best *négociant*, with first-class red and white wines that are unusually representative of their particular *appellations*. Also look out for the rare white *Beaune* from its own Clos des Mouches, top-class *Clos de Vougeot*, and unusually (for a *négociant*) high-quality *Chablis*. The Marquis de Laguiche *Montrachet* is sublime. ★★★★★ 1998 Beaune Clos des Mouches Rouge £££

Ⅰ **Pierre-Jacques Druet** [droo-ay] (*Loire*, France) Wonderfully reliable *Bourgueil* producer making characterful individual cuvées. ★★★★ 1996 Grand Mont £££

Dry Creek (*Sonoma*, California) A rare example of a California *AVA* region whose wines have an identifiable quality and style. Look out for *Sauvignon Blanc* and *Zinfandel*. Red: 84 85 86 87 90 91 92 93 95 96 97 98 White: 85 90 91 92 95 96 97 98. *Beaulieu Vineyard; Collier Falls; Dry Creek; Duxoup; Gallo Sonoma; Nalle; Pezzi-King; Quivira; Rabbit Ridge; Rafanell; Turley.*

Ⅰ **Dry Creek Vineyard** (*Sonoma*, California) Eponymous vineyard within the *Dry Creek AVA* making well-known *Fumé Blanc*, great *Chenin Blanc*, and impressive reds.

Ⅰ **Dry River** (*Martinborough*, New Zealand) Small *estate* with particularly impressive *Pinot Noir* and *Pinot Gris* and a delicious line in *late-harvest* wines.

Ⅰ **Duboeuf** [doo-burf] (*Burgundy*, France) The "King of *Beaujolais*", who introduced the world to the penny-candy flavour of young *Gamay*. Duboeuf offers good examples from individual growers, vineyards, and villages. These include reliable *nouveau*, good straightforward *Mâconnais* white, single *domaine Rhônes,* and now large amounts of commercial rather than fine Vin de Pays *Viognier*.

Ⅰ **Dubreuil-Fontaine** [doo-broy fon-tayn] (*Burgundy*, France) Quite traditional *estate*, producing full-flavoured red and white individual cuvées from the *Corton* hillsides.

Ⅰ **Duckhorn** (*Napa Valley*, California) Once the producer of dauntingly tough *Merlot*, Duckhorn is now making far more approachable examples of this and other varieties. Decoy, the second label, offers an affordable, earlier-drinking taste of the house style, while the unusual Paraduxx *Cabernet-Zinfandel* is a delicious and immediately likeable novelty.

DOW'S

1987
QUINTA DO BOMFIM
VINTAGE
PORT

E

Ɏ **Ch. Ducru-Beaucaillou** [doo-kroo hoh-ki-yoo] (*St. Julien 2ème Cru Classé, Bordeaux*, France) *"Super Second"* with a decidedly less obvious style than peers such as *Léoville-Las-Cases* and *Pichon-Lalande*. Especially good in 1996, 1997, and (brilliantly in) 1998 and 1999 after a disappointing patch in the late 1980s and early 1990s. The 2000 is fine too. Second wine is Croix-Beaucaillou. **70 75** 76 **78** 79 80 **81 82 83 85** 86 87 88 89 90 91 **93 95 96** 97 98 99 00

Ɏ **Dom. Bernard Dugat-Py** [doo-gah pee] (*Burgundy,* France) Superstar *Gevrey-Chambertin estate* with great vineyards, from which M. Dugat makes delicious and unusually fairly priced wines *Grand Cru* ★★★★★ 1998 Gevrey-Chambertin Premier Cru ££££

Ɏ **Ch. Duhart-Milon-Rothschild** [doo-ahr mee-lon rot-sheeld] (*Pauillac 4ème Cru Classé, Bordeaux*, France) Under the same management as *Lafite* and benefiting from heavy investment. 78 79 80 81 **82** 83 **85** 86 87 88 89 90 91 92 93 **95 96** 97 **98 99** 00

Ɏ **Dom. Dujac** [doo-zhak] (*Burgundy*, France) Cult *Burgundy* producer Jacques Seysses makes fine, long-lived, and quite modern wines from *Morey-St.-Denis* (including a particularly good *Clos de la Roche*), which are packed with intense *Pinot Noir* flavour. Now helped by Gary Farr of the excellent *Bannockburn* in Australia, and busily investing time and effort into vineyards in southern France. ★★★★★ 1998 Clos de la Roche ££££

Ɏ **Dulong** [doo-long] (*Bordeaux,* France) Reliable *negociant* that shocked some of its neighbours by producing *International Wine Challenge* medal-winning multiregional *Vin de Table* blends under the "Rebelle" label.

Dumb As in dumb nose, meaning without smell.

Ɏ **Dunn Vineyards** (*Napa Valley,* California) Randy Dunn makes tough, forbidding *Cabernets* from *Howell Mountain* for patient collectors. Give them time, though; eventually, they yield extraordinary spicy, berryish flavours. ★★★★★ 1997 Cabernet Sauvignon Howell Mountain ££££

Durbach [door-bahk] (*Baden,* Germany) Top vineyard area of this *Anbaugebiet*. Andreas Laible; Wolf-Metternich.

Ɏ **Ch. Durfort-Vivens** [door-for vee-va'ns] (*Margaux 2ème Cru Classé, Bordeaux,* France) Never really starry, but sometimes very classic, elegant wine from the owners of *Ch. Brane-Cantenac*. Recent vintages show decided improvement. 78 79 81 **82** 83 **85** 86 87 88 89 90 91 93 **95 96** 97 98 99

🍇 **Durif** [dyoor-if] See *Petite Sirah*.

Ɏ **Jean Durup** [doo-roop] (*Burgundy,* France) Modern *estate* whose owner believes in extending vineyards of *Chablis* into what some claim to be less distinguished soil, and not fermenting or maturing his wines in new oak. One, or both policies makes for wines that are good rather than great. The best wines are sold as Ch. de Maligny. ★★★ 1996 Chablis Vieilles Vignes ££

Ɏ **Duval-Leroy** [doo-val luh-rwah] (*Champagne,* France) Finally gaining a reputation outside France, Duval-Leroy was previously highly popular among retailers and restaurateurs to whom it supplied excellent own-label wines. Fleur de Champagne and Cuvée des Rois are worth looking out for.

Ɏ **Duxoup Wine Works** [duk-soop] (*Sonoma Valley*, California) Inspired winery-in-a-shed, producing fine *Syrah* from bought-in grapes.

E

Ɏ **E&E** (*Barossa,* South Australia) Top wine produced by *Barossa Valley Estate*.

Ɏ **Maurice Ecard** [Ay-car] (*Burgundy,* France) Very recommendable *Savigny-lès-Beaune* estate with good *Premier Cru* vineyards. ★★★★ 1997 Savigny-les-Beaune les Narbontons £££

Ɏ **Echeverria** [eh-che-veh-ree-yah] (*Maule,* Chile) Impressive Curico producer with good *Cabernets, Chardonnays,* and *Sauvignon Blancs*.

E

♟ **Echézeaux** [eh-shay-zoh] (*Burgundy*, France) *Grand Cru* between *Clos de Vougeot* and *Vosne-Romanée* and more or less an extension of the latter *commune*. *Flagey-Echézeaux*, a village on the relatively vineless side of the Route Nationale, takes its name from the "flagellation" used by the peasants to gather corn in the 6th century. Grands-Echézeaux should be finer.
Dujac; R Engel; Grivot; Henri Jayer; Jayer-Gilles; D. Laurent; Mongeard-Mugneret; Mugneret-Gibourg; de la Romanée-Conti; E. Rouget; F. Vigot.

♟ **L' Ecole No. 41** [ay-kohl] (*Washington State*) Superlative producer of classy *Chardonnay* and *Merlot*, as well as some lovely rich *Semillon*.
★★★★ 1998 Fries Vineyard Semillon ££££

Edelfäule [ay-del-foy-luh] (Germany) *Botrytis cinerea*, or "*noble rot*".

Edelzwicker [ay-del-zvick-kur] (*Alsace*, France) Generic name for a blend of grapes. The idea of blends is coming back – but not the name (see *Hugel*).

♟ **Edmunds St. John** (*Alameda*, California) Producer with his heart in the *Rhône* – and a taste for rich, spicy *Syrah* and *Zinfandel* reds. ★★★★★ 1995 Durell Vineyard Syrah ££££

♟ **Edna Valley Vineyard** (California) Long-standing maker of rich, buttery *Chardonnay* in the *AVA* of the same name. In the same stable as *Chalone*, *Carmenet* and *Acacia* and now in a joint Californian venture with *Penfolds*.

Eger [eg-gur] (Hungary) Region of Hungary where *Bull's Blood* is made.

♟ **Dom. de l'Eglise** [duh lay glees] (*Pomerol, Bordeaux*, France) Fairly priced, mid-line, wines. 79 82 83 85 86 88 89 **90** 95 96 97 98

♟ **Ch. l'Eglise-Clinet** [Lay gleez klee-nay] (*Pomerol, Bordeaux*, France) Terrific small estate that has gained – and earned – recent superstar status. 70 71 75 76 78 **79** 81 82 83 85 86 **88** 89 **90** 91 92 *93* **94** *95 96 97 98 99 00*
★★★★★ 1998 ££££

♟ **Egri Bikaver** [eh-grih bih-kah vehr] (*Eger*, Hungary) See *Bull's Blood*.

♟ **Cave Vinicole d'Eguisheim** [Eh-gees-hime] (*Alsace*, France) One of the most dynamic cooperatives in Alsace, with a range of grand cru vineyards (including Hengst and Speigel) and alternative brands: Wolfberger and Willm. Look for the Sigillé wines.

♟ **Eikendal Vineyards** [ehk-ken-dahl] (*Stellenbosch*, South Africa) Understated wines (esp. *Chardonnay*) from the *Helderberg*.

Eiswein/Eiswein [ice-vine] (Germany/Austria/Canada) Ultra-concentrated *late harvest* wine, made from grapes naturally frozen on the vine and often picked a long time after the rest of the crop. (Some German vintages are harvested in the January of the following year!). Hard to make (and consequently very pricy) in Germany but much easier and more affordable in *Canada* where "Icewine" is a huge success. Unlike other top-quality sweet wines, Eiswein does not rely on *noble rot*. In fact, this characteristic is normally absent because winemakers need frozen grapes in a perfect state.

Eitelsbach [ih-tel-sbahk] (*Mosel*, Germany) One of the top two *Ruwer* wine towns, and the site of the famed Karthäuserhofberg vineyard.

Elaborado y Anejado Por [ay-lah-boh-rah-doh ee anay-hahdo pohr] (Spain) "Made and aged for".

♟ **Elderton** (*Barossa Valley*, Australia) Highly commercial maker of big, rich, competition-winning wines, especially *Shiraz* and *Cabernet*.

Elever/éleveur [ay-lur-vay/ay-lur-vuhr] To mature or "nurture" wine, especially in the cellars of the *Burgundy négociants*, who act as éleveurs after traditionally buying in wine made by small estates.

Elgin [el-gin] (South Africa) Coolish – *Burgundy*-like – apple-growing country which is increasingly attracting the interest of big wine producers. Watch out for the Paul Cluver reds and whites from *Neil Ellis*. May eventually overshadow all but the best parts of *Stellenbosch* and *Paarl*.

I **Neil Ellis** (*Stellenbosch*, South Africa) New-wave Cape winemaker – and a pioneer of the new region of *Elgin*. ★★★ **2000 Sauvignon Blanc ££**

Eltville [elt-vil] (*Rheingau*, Germany) Town housing the *Rheingau* state cellars and the German Wine Academy, producing good *Riesling* with backbone. QbA/Kab/Spät: 85 86 **88 89 90** 91 **92 93 94 95 96 97** 98 Aus/Beeren/Tba: **83 85 88 89 90** 91 92 **93 94** 95 **96 97** 98

I **Elyse Wine Cellars** (*Napa*, California) *Zinfandel* specialist with *Howell Mountain Vineyards*. Look out too for the fine Cabernet and a Nero Misto spicy *Zinfandel-Petite Sirah* blend. ★★★★★ **1997 Napa Syrah £££**

Emilia-Romagna [eh-mee-lee-yah roh-ma-nya] (Italy) Region around Bologna best known for *Lambrusco*; also the source of *Albana*, *Sangiovese di Romagna*, and *Pagadebit*.

Enate [eh-nah-tay] (*Somontano*, Spain) Dynamic modern winery specializing in varietals, including particularly successful Chardonnays. ★★★ **Rosado ££**

En primeur [on pree-muh] New wine, usually *Bordeaux*. Producers and specialist merchants buy and offer wine *en primeur* before it has been released. In the US and Australia, where producers like *Mondavi* and *Petaluma* sell in this way, the process is known as buying "futures".

I **Ch. l'Enclos** [lon kloh] (*Pomerol*, *Bordeaux*, France) Gorgeously rich, fairly priced wines. 79 **82** 83 85 86 88 **89 90** 91 92 93 94 **95 96 97 98** *99* 00.

I **René Engel** [On-jel] (*Burgundy*, France) Producer of rich, long-lived wines in *Vosne-Romanée* and *Clos Vougeot*. ★★★★★ **1998 Vosne-Romanée ££££**

English wine Quality has improved in recent years as winemakers have moved from semi-sweet, mock-Germanic to dry mock-*Loire* and, increasingly, sparkling, aromatic-but-dry and *late harvest*. *Breaky Bottom; Thames Valley Vineyards; Nyetimber, Bruisyard; Three Choirs; Carr Taylor;* Chiltern Valley.

Enoteca [ee-noh-teh-kah] (Italy) Literally wine library or, now, wine shop.

I **Entre-Deux-Mers** [on-truh duh mehr] (*Bordeaux*, France) Once a region of appalling sweet wine from vineyards between the cities of *Bordeaux* and Libourne. Now a source of basic *Bordeaux* Blanc and principally dry *Sauvignon*. Reds are sold as *Bordeaux* Rouge. Both reds and whites suffer from the difficulty grapes have in ripening in cool years. **Ch. Bonnet; Fontenille; Sainte-Marie; Tour-de-Mirambeau; Turcaud.**

I **Erath Vineyards** [ee-rath] (*Oregon*, US) One of *Oregon's* pioneering *Pinot Noir* producers, now better than ever.

Erbach [ayr-bahkh] (*Rheingau*, Germany) Town noted for fine full *Riesling*, particularly from the Marcobrunn vineyard. QbA/Kab/Spät: 85 86 **88 89 90** 91 **92 93 94 95 96 97** 98 Aus/Beeren/Tba: **83 85 88 89 90** 91 **92 93 94** 95 96 97 98 *Schloss Reinhartshausen;* Schloss Schönborn.

Erbaluce [ehr-bah-loo-chay] (*Piedmont*, Italy) White grape responsible for the light dry wines of the *Caluso*, and the sweet sun-dried *Caluso Passito*.

I **Erbaluce di Caluso** [ehr-bah-loo-chay dee kah-loo-soh] (*Piedmont*, Italy) Dry, quite herby white made from the *Erbaluce* grape. Also used to make sparkling wine. ★★★★ **1998 Cieck, Calliope £££**

Erden [ehr-durn] (*Mosel-Saar-Ruwer*, Germany) In the *Bernkastel Bereich*, this northerly village produces some of the finest full, crisp, *Riesling* in the *Mosel*, and includes the famous Treppchen vineyard. QbA/Kab/Spät: 85 86 **88 89 90 92 93 94 95 96 97** 98 Aus/Beeren/Tba: **83 85 88 89 90** 91 **92 93 94** 95 97 *98 JJ Christoffel; Dr Loosen;* Mönchhof; Peter Nicolay.

Ermitage [ehr-mee-tahj] (Switzerland) The Swiss name for the *Marsanne*.

I **Errazuriz** [ehr-raz-zoo-riz] (*Aconcagua Valley*, Chile) One of Chile's big name producers and owner of *Caliterra*. Wines have been improved by input from *Mondavi*. Look out for the "Wild Ferment" *Chardonnay* and recently launched *Syrah*. The top wine, Don Maximiano is one of Chile's very best reds. ★★★★ **1998 El Descanso Estate Merlot ££**

Erzeugerabfüllung [ayr-tsoy-guhr-ap-few-loong] (Germany) Bottled by the grower/estate.

E

Y **Esk Valley** (*Hawkes Bay,* New Zealand) Under the same ownership as *Vidal* and *Villa Maria.* Successful with *Bordeaux*-style reds and juicy rosé. ★★★★★ 1997 Reserve Merlot/Malbec/Cabernet Sauvignon ££

Y **Esporão** [esp-per-row] (*Alentejo,* Portugal) Revolutionary wines (including some fascinating varietals) made with help from Australian-born, Portuguese-based *David Baverstock.*

Espum/oso/ante [es-poom-mo-soh/san-tay] (Spain/Portugal) Sparkling.

Y **Est! Est!! Est!!!** [ehst-ehst-ehst] (*Lazio,* Italy) Red named after the repeated exclamation of a bishop's servant when he found a good wine. Apart from the ones made by *Falesco,* today's examples rarely offer much to exclaim about.

Esters Chemical components in wine responsible for all those extraordinary odours of fruits, vegetables, hamster cages, and trainers.

Y **Estremadura** [ehst-reh-mah-doo-rah] (Portugal) Huge area producing mostly dull wine. Quintas da Pancas and Boavista show what can be done.

Estufa [esh-too-fah] (*Madeira,* Portugal) The vats in which *Madeira* is heated, speeding maturity and imparting its familiar "cooked" flavour.

Eszencia [es-sen-tsee-yah] (*Tokaji,* Hungary) Incredibly concentrated syrup made by piling around 220lb of *late harvested, botrytised* grapes into *puttonyos* and letting as little as three-quarters of a gallon of syrup dribble out of the bottom. This will only ferment up to about 4 per cent alcohol, over several weeks, before stopping completely. It is then stored and used to sweeten normal *Aszú* wines. The Czars of Russia discovered the joys of Eszencia, and it has been prized for its effects on the male libido. It is hard to find, even by those who can see the point in doing anything with the expensive syrup other than pouring it on ice cream. The easier-to-find *Aszú Essencia* (one step sweeter than *Aszú 6 puttonyos*) is far better value.

Y **Arnaldo Etchart** [et-shaht] (*Cafayate,* Argentina) Dynamic producer, benefiting from advice by *Michel Rolland* of *Pomerol* fame, and also investment by its French owners Pernod Ricard. The key wine here, though, is the grapey white *Torrontes.*

Y **l'Etoile** [eh-twah] (*Jura,* France) Theoretically the best *appellation* in the *Jura. Chardonnay* and *Savagnin* whites and sparkling wines can be good, and the *Vin Jaune* is of interest. Ch de l'Etoile; Michel Geneletti; Montbo

Y **Etude** [ay-tewd] (*Napa,* California) Thoughtful superstar consultant Tony Soter experiments by marrying specific sites and clones of *Pinot Noir.* Apart from these wines, there are good rich *Napa Cabernets* and *Carneros Chardonnays.* ★★★★★ 1996 Heirloom Carneros Pinot Noir £££

Y **Ch. l' Evangile** [lay-van-zheel] (*Pomerol, Bordeaux,* France) One of the top wines of 2000. A classy and increasingly sought-after property that can, in great *vintages* like 1988, 1989 and 1990, sometimes rival its neighbour *Pétrus,* but in a more *tannic* style. 75 78 79 **82 83 85 86** 87 88 89 90 92 93 95 96 97 98 99 00 ★★★★ 1998 ££££

Y **Evans Family/Evans Wine Co** (*Hunter Valley,* Australia) Len Evans's (founder, and ex-chairman of *Rothbury Vineyards*) own estate and company. Rich *Chardonnay* and *Semillon* as characterful and generous as their maker. See also *Tower Estates.*

Y **Evans & Tate** (*Margaret River,* Australia) Much improved producer with good *Chardonnay* and *Shiraz* (including an impressive *International Wine Challenge* trophy winner).

Y **Eventail de Vignerons Producteurs** [ay-van-tih] (*Burgundy,* France) Reliable source of *Beaujolais.*

Y **Eyrie Vineyards** [ai-ree] (*Oregon*) Pioneering *Pinot Noir* producer in the *Willamette Valley,* whose memorable success in a blind tasting of *Burgundies* helped to attract *Joseph Drouhin* to invest his francs in a vineyard here.

F

F **Fabre Montmayou** [fab-re mon-mey-yoo] (*Mendoza*, Argentina) Luján de Cuyo winery to watch for rich *Michel Rolland*-influenced reds.

F **Fairview Estate** (*Paarl*, South Africa) Progressive estate where Charles Back – both under his own name and under that of Fairview makes wines such as the wittily named and labelled "Goats do Roam". Also a good cheese producer. See also *Spice Route*.

F **Joseph Faiveley** [fay-vlay] (*Burgundy*, France) Impressive modern *négociant* with particular strength in vineyards in the *Côte de Nuits* and *Nuits-St.-Georges*. ★★★★ 1998 Nuits St Georges Clos de la Maréchale ££££

F **Falchini** [fal kee-noh] (*Tuscany*, Italy) One of the key producers of *Vernacchia di San Gimignano*.

F **Falerno del Massico** [fah-LEHR-noh del mah-see-koh] (*Campania*, Italy) Modern producers such as Villa Matilde are leading the renaissance of a region famous among Ancient Roman wine drinkers. Reds and whites from local varieties: *Falanghina (white) Piedirosso, Aglianico and Primitivo (red)*.

F **Falesco** [fah leh-skoh] (*Lazio*, Italy) Producer of fine – Montiano – *Merlot*, *Grechetto*, and *Est Est Est*.

F **Ch. Falfas** [fal-fas] (*Côtes de Bourg, Bordeaux,* France) One of the best estates in the *appellation* – and a fine example of biodynamic winemaking.

F **Bodegas Fariña** [fah ree-nah] (*Toro*, Spain) Top producer in Toro, making cask-aged (Gran Colegiata) and fruitier, non-cask-aged Colegiata.

F **Far Niente** [fah nee-yen-tay] (*Napa Valley*, California) Well regarded producer of sometimes over-showy *Chardonnay* and *Cabernet*.

F **Ch. de Fargues** [duh-fahrg] (*Sauternes, Bordeaux*, France) Elegant wines made by the winemaker at *Ch. d'Yquem* – and a good alternative. 70 71 75 76 78 79 80 83 85 86 88 89 90 95 96 97 98 99 ★★★★ 1997 ££££

F **Gary Farrell** (*Sonoma*, California) A Russian River *Pinot Noir* and *Merlot* maker to watch. ★★★★ 1997 Ladi's Vineyard Merlot ££££

Fat Has a silky texture which fills the mouth. More fleshy than meaty.

Fattoria [fah-tor-ree-ah] (Italy) *Estate*, particularly in *Tuscany*.

F **Faugères** [foh-zhehr] (*Midi*, France) With neighbouring *St. Chinian*, this gently hilly region is a major cut above the surrounding *Coteaux du Languedoc*, and potentially the source of really exciting red. For the moment, however, most still taste pretty rustic. Ch. des Adouzes; Gilbert Alquier; Ch. Chenaie; des Estanilles; Grézan; Cave Cooperative de Laurens; la Liquière; de Météore; Moulin Coudero; des Peyregran; du Rouge Gorge; St. Antonin.

F **Bernard Faurie** [fow-ree] (*Rhône*, France) Tournon-based producer who makes intense perfumed wines with great longevity.

F **Bodegas Faustino Martinez** [fows-tee-noh mahr-tee-nehth] (*Rioja*, Spain) Dependable *Rioja* producer with excellent (*Gran*) *Reservas*, fair whites, and a decent *cava*. ★★★ 1995 Reserva £££

🍇 **Favorita** [fahvoh-ree-tah] (*Piedmont*, Italy) Traditional variety from *Piedmont* transformed by modern winemaking into delicate floral whites. *Conterno; Villa Lanata; Bava.*

F **Weingut Feiler-Artinger** [fih-luh arh-ting-guh] (*Rust*, Austria) Superlative innovative producer of dry and, especially, *late-harvest* wines. ★★★★ 1999 Ruster Ausbruch Traminer £££

F **Fattoria di Felsina Berardenga** [fah-toh-ree-ah dee fehl-see-nah beh-rah-den-gah] (*Tuscany*, Italy) Very high-quality *Chianti* estate. ★★★★ 1997 Maestro Raro £££

F **Livio Felluga** [feh-LOO-gah] (*Friuli*, Italy) Estate with terrific range of pure varietals and blends (e.g. *Terre Alte: Sauvignon, Tocai and Pinot Bianco*).

F **Felton Road** (*Central Otago*, New Zealand) This is an instant superstar, producing what may be New Zealand's top *Pinot Noir* as well as some very stylish *Riesling*. ★★★★★ 1998 Block 3 Pinot Noir £££

F

🍇 **Fendant** [fon-don] (Switzerland) See *Chasselas*.

🍇 **Fer** [fehr] (*South-West*, France) Grape used to make *Marcillac*.
Fermentazione naturale [fehr-men-tat-zee-oh-nay] (Italy) "Naturally sparkling" but, in fact, indicates the *cuve close* method.

🍇 **Fernão Pires** [fehr-now pee-rehsh] (Portugal) *Muscat*ty grape, used to great effect by *Peter Bright* of the João Pires winery.

🍷 **Ch. Ferrand** [feh-ron] (*St. Emilion, Bordeaux*, France) Not to be confused with *Ferrand Lartigue,* this is a big estate, producing rather tough wines.

🍷 **Ch. Ferrand Lartique** [feh-ron lah-teek] (*St. Emilion Grand Cru*, *Bordeaux*, France) Small five-acre estate producing full-bodied rich wines.

🍷 **Luigi Ferrando** (*Piedmont* Italy) Producer in the Carema *DOC* of good *Nebbiolo*-based wines that are attractively light and elegant in style.

🍷 **Ferrari** [feh-rah-ree] (*Trentino*, Italy) A sexy name for some sexy *Champagne*-method sparkling wines. The Riserva del Fondatore is the star of the show.

🍷 **Ferrari-Carano** (*Sonoma*, California) Improving winery best known for its oaky, crowd-pleasing *Chardonnay, Cabernet Sauvignon, Zinfandel*, and rich *Merlot*. All these are good in their unsubtle way, but Siena, the Italianate *Sangiovese*-Cabernet blend, and the Syrah are both more interesting.

🍷 **AA Ferreira** [feh-ray-rah] (*Douro*, Portugal) Associated with *Sogrape*, this traditional Portuguese *port* producer is as famous for its excellent *tawnies* as for its *Barca Velha*, Portugal's best traditional unfortified red. ★★★★ Duque de Braganca 20 Year Old Tawny ££;

🍷 **Gloria Ferrer** (*Sonoma*, California) New World offshoot of *Freixenet* (the people behind *Cordon Negro*) making unmemorable sparkling wine and somewhat more interesting *Chardonnay* and *Pinot Noir* from its *Carneros* vineyards.

🍷 **Ch. Ferrière** [feh-ree-yehr] (*Margaux 3ème Cru Classé, Bordeaux*, France) Once small, now rather bigger, thanks to the convenience of belonging to the same owners as the *Margaux Cru Bourgeois, Ch. la Gurgue* – and the legal right to swap land between estates in the same appellation. 89 90 91 92 93 94 **95 96** 97 98 ★★★★ 1998 £££

🍷 **Ch. de Fesles** [dur fel] (*Loire*, France) Classic *Bonnezeaux* has now been joined by *Anjou* and *Savennières*. ★★★★★ 1998 Bonnezeaux ££££

🍷 **Sylvain Fessy** [seel-van fes-see] (*Burgundy*, France) Reliable small *Beaujolais* producer with wide range of *crus*.

🍷 **Henry Fessy** [on-ree fes-see] (*Burgundy*, France) Consistent *négociant*, vineyard owner and producer of *Beaujolais*.

🍷 **Fetzer** [fet-zuh] (*Mendocino*, California) Confusingly, this big producer offers quite different lines of wines in the UK and US – which helps to explain why the name is more respected in the US. Fortunately, the whole world can buy the excellent "Bonterra" line which is among the best examples of commercial organic wine in the world. ★★★★★ 1998 Bonterra Chardonnay ££; ★★★★★ 1998 Bonterra Zinfandel ££

🍷 **Nicolas Feuillatte** [fuh-yet] (*Champagne*, France) Quietly rising star with good-value wine. ★★★★ 1992 Palmes d'Or £££

🍷 **William Fèvre** [weel-yum feh-vr] (*Burgundy*, France) Quality *Chablis* producer that is now under the same (Henriot) ownership as *Bouchard Père & Fils*, and showing similar improvements in quality. Oak use, in particular, is more delicate. His efforts in Chile have got better with each vintage too. ★★★ 1998 Chablis Vaillons ££££

🍷 **Ch. Feytit-Clinet** [fay-tee klee-nay] (*Pomerol, Bordeaux*, France) A *Moueix* property with good, delicate wines. 79 81 **82** 83 **85** 86 87 **88** 89 90 94 95 96 97 98

🍷 **Fiano** [fee-yah-noh] (Italy) Herby white grape variety used to make Fiano di Avellino in the south.

🍷 **Les Fiefs-de-Lagrange** [fee-ef duh lag-ronzh] (*St. Julien, Bordeaux*, France) Recommendable *second label* of *Ch. Lagrange*.

F

✻ **Fiefs Vendéens** [fee-ef von-day-yi'n] (*Loire*, France) One of the few surviving VDQS regions, this area, which is close to Muscadet, offers a wide range of grape varieties – and fresh, light wines that are well worth buying in ripe vintages.

✻ **Ch. de Fieuzal** [duh fyuh-zahl] (*Pessac-Léognan Grand Cru* Classé, *Bordeaux*, France) *Pessac-Léognan* property returning to form and producing great whites and lovely raspberryish reds. Abeille de Fieuzal is *second label*. Red: 75 79 81 **82** 83 **85 86** 88 89 **90** 91 92 93 94 **95** 96 97 98 00 White: **85 88 89** 90 91 **92 93 96** 97 98 99 00

✻ **Ch. Figeac** [fee-zhak] (*St. Emilion Premier Grand Cru, Bordeaux*, France) Forever in the shadow of its neighbour, *Cheval Blanc*, and often unpredictable in its evolution, but still one of the most characterful *St. Emilions*. **64 70** 78 **82** 83 84 **85 86** 88 **89** 90 92 93 94 95 96 97 98 ★★★★★ **2000** ££££

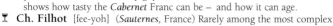

✻ **Granxa Fillaboa** [gran-shah fee-yah-boh-wah] (*Galicia*, Spain) one of the best *Albariño* producers in *Rias Baixas*.

✻ **Filliatreau** (*Loire*, France) Exemplary producer of Saumur Champigny which shows how tasty the *Cabernet* Franc can be – and how it can age.

✻ **Ch. Filhot** [fee-yoh] (*Sauternes*, France) Rarely among the most complex examples of Sauternes, this is nonetheless one of the most reliable sources of well-made, good value wine. ★★★★★ **1997** £££

Finger Lakes (*New York State*) Cold region whose producers struggle (sometimes effectively) to produce good *vinifera*, including *Pinot Noir* and *late-harvest Riesling*. *Hybrids* such as *Seyval Blanc* are more reliable. *Fox Run; Heron Hill; Lamaroux Landing; Wagner*.

Fining The clarifying of young wine before bottling to remove impurities, using a number of agents including *isinglass* and *bentonite*.

Finish What you can still taste after swallowing.

✻ **Fino** [fee-noh] (*Jerez*, Spain) Dry, delicate *sherry* which gains its distinctive flavour from the *flor* or yeast which grows on the surface of the wine during maturation. Drink chilled, with tapas, preferably within two weeks of opening. *Lustau; Barbadillo; Hidalgo; Gonzalez Byass*.

✻ **Firestone** (*Santa Ynez*, California) Good producer – particularly of good value *Chardonnay*, *Merlot* and *Sauvignon* and *late-harvest Riesling* – in southern California.

✻ **Fisher** (*Sonoma*, California) Top-class producer of limited-production, single-vineyard *Cabernets* and *Chardonnays* from hillside vineyards. ★★★★★ **1999** Whitney's Vineyard Chardonnay ££££

✻ **Fitou** [fee-too] (*Midi*, France) Long considered to be an upmarket *Corbières* but actually rather a basic southern *AC*, making reds largely from the *Carignan* grape. The wines here may have become more refined, with a woody warmth, but they never quite shake off their rustic air. **Ch. d'Espigne; Lepaumier; Lerys; de Nouvelles; Mont Tauch; de Rolland; Val d'Orbieu**.

✻ **Fixin** [fee-san] (*Burgundy*, France) Northerly village of *Côte de Nuits*, whose lean, tough, uncommercial reds can mature well. New-wave winemaking and later harvesting are thankfully introducing friendlier fare. **78** 79 **80** 82 83 **85** 86 87 **88 89 90** 92 95 96 97 98 Dom Bart; **Vincent Berthaut; Bruno Clair;** Michel Defrance; Derey Frères; Fougeray de Beauclair; Pierre Gelin; André Geoffroy; J-P Guyard; **Louis Jadot;** Philippe Joliet; Denis Philibert.

Flabby Lacking balancing acidity.

Flagey-Echézeaux [flah-jay eh-shay-zoh] (*Burgundy*, France) Village on the wrong (nonvine) side of the Route National 74 that lends its name to the *appellations* of *Echézeaux* and *Grands Echézeaux*.

F

☲ **Ch. La Fleur** [flur] (*St. Emilion, Bordeaux,* France) Small *St. Emilion* property producing softly fruity wines. **82** 83 85 86 88 **89 90 92 94 95 96** 97 **98 99 00**

☲ **Ch. la Fleur de Gay** [flur duh gay] (*Pomerol, Bordeaux,* France) *Ch. Croix de Gay's* best wine and thus heavily sought after. Showed improvement in 1998. Good in 2000. **82 86 88 89 90 94** 95 96 97 **98** *99* **00**

☲ **Ch. la Fleur-Pétrus** [flur pay-trooss] (*Pomerol, Bordeaux,* France) For those who find *Pétrus* a touch unaffordable, this next-door neighbour offers gorgeously accessible *Pomerol* flavour for (in *Pétrus* terms) a bargain price. 70 **75** 78 79 **81 82 83 85** 86 87 **88 89 90** 92 **93** *95 96 97* **98** *99* **00**

☲ **Fleurie** [fluh-ree] (*Burgundy,* France) One of the 10 *Beaujolais Crus,* ideally fresh and fragrant, as its name suggests. Best vineyards include La Madonne and Pointe du Jour. Dom. Bachelard and Guy Depardon are names to watch. 90 95 96 **97 98** J-M Aujoux; Berrod; P-M Chermette; M Chignard; Després; *Duboeuf;* Ch. Labourons; Dom de la Madone; A Métrat; André Vaisse.

Flor [flawr] Yeast which grows naturally on the surface of some maturing *sherries,* making them potential *finos.*

🌢 **Flora** [flor-rah] A cross between *Semillon* and *Gewürztraminer,* best known in *Brown Brothers Orange Muscat* and Flora.

☲ **Flora Springs** (*Napa Valley,* California) One good, unusual *Sauvignon Blanc* (Soliloquy) and classy *Merlot, Cabernet Sauvignon & Cabernet Franc* blend (Trilogy). ★★★★ **1996 Rutherford Hillside Reserve Cabernet £££**

☲ **Emile Florentin** [floh-ron-tan] (*Rhône,* France) Maker of ultra-traditional, ultra-*tannic,* chewy *St. Joseph.* ★★★★ **St. Joseph Clos de l'Arbalestrier £££**

Flying winemakers Young (usually) Australians and New Zealanders who have, since the 1980s, been despatched like vinous mercenaries to wineries worldwide to make better and more reliable wine than the home teams can manage. Often, as they have proved, all it has taken to improve the standards of a European cooperative has been a more scrupulous attitude towards picking ripe grapes (rather than impatiently harvesting unripe ones) and keeping tanks and pipes clean.

☲ **Ch. Fombrauge** [fom-brohzh] (*St. Emilion, Bordeaux,* France) *St. Emilion* that is improving since its purchase by the owners of *Malesan.* 82 83 85 **86 88 89 90** 92 93 **94 95** 96 97 98 99

☲ **Ch. Fonplégade** [fon-pleh-gahd] (*St. Emilion Grand Cru Classé, Bordeaux,* France) If you like your *St. Emilion* tough, this is for you. 78 **82** 83 85 86 87 88 89 **90** 94 95 96 97 98 ★★★ **1995 ££££**

☲ **Ch. Fonroque** [fon-rok] (*St. Emilion Grand Cru Classé, Bordeaux,* France) Property with concentrated wines, but not always one of *Moueix's* very finest. 70 **75** 78 **79 82 83 85** 86 88 **89 90** 92 93 94 95 96 97 98

☲ **Fonseca Guimaraens** [fon-say-ka gih-mah-rans] (*Douro,* Portugal) Now a subsidiary of *Taylor's* and hit by fire in 2000, but still independently making great *port.* In blind tastings the 1976 and 1978 and 1984 regularly beat supposedly classier houses' supposedly finer vintages. See also *Guimaraens.* Fonseca: 60 **63 66 70** 75 **77** 80 83 **84 85 95** Fonseca Guimaraens: 76 78 82 84 88 **92 94 98** ★★★★★ **1984 Fonseca Guimaraens Vintage Port £££**

☲ **JM da Fonseca Internacional** [fon-say-ka in-tuhr-nah-soh-nahl] (*Setúbal Peninsula,* Portugal) Highly commercial firm whose wines include Lancers, the *Mateus-*taste-alike sold in mock-crocks.

☲ **JM da Fonseca Successores** [fon-say-ka suk-ses-saw-rays] (*Estremadura,* Portugal) Unrelated to the *port* house of the same name and no longer connected to *JM da Fonseca Internacional.* Family-run firm, which with *Aliança* and *Sogrape* is one of Portugal's big three dynamic wine companies. Top reds include Pasmados, *Periquita* (from the grape of the same name), *Quinta da Camarate,* Terras Altas Dão, and the *Cabernet*-influenced "TE" *Garrafeiras.* Dry whites are less impressive, but the sweet old *Moscatel de Setúbals* are luscious classics. ★★★★ **1997 Moscatel de Setúbal, Terras do Sado ££££**

F

ℑ **Dom. Font de Michelle** [fon-duh-mee-shell] (*Rhône,* France) Reliable producer of medium-bodied red *Châteauneuf-du-Pape* and small quantities of excellent, almost unobtainable, white. ★★★★★ **1998 Etienne Gonnet £££**

ℑ **Fontana Candida** [fon-tah-nah kan-dee-dah] (*Lazio,* Italy) Good producer, especially for *Frascati*. The top wine is Colle Gaio, which is good enough to prove the disappointing nature of most other wines from this area.

ℑ **Fontanafredda** [fon-tah-nah-freh-dah] (*Piedmont,* Italy) Big producer with impressive *Asti Spumante* and very approachable (especially single-vineyard) *Barolo*. ★★★★ **1996 Barolo Serralunga ££££**

ℑ **Domaine de Font Sane** [fon-sen] (*Rhône,* France) Producer of fine *Gigondas* in a very underrated *AC*. Very traditional and full-bodied.

ℑ **Castello di Fonterutoli** (*Tuscany,* Italy) *Chianti* Classico producer of real class, which also produces great non-*DOC* blends: Concerto and Siepi. ★★★★★ **1997 Chianti Classico Riserva £££**

ℑ **Fontodi** [Fon-toh-dee] (*Tuscany,* Italy) Classy *Tuscan* producer with Flaccianello, a good *Vino da Tavola*. ★★★★ **1998 Chianti Classico £££**

ℑ **Foradori** [Foh-rah-doh-ree] (*Trentino,* Italy) Specialist producer of *Teroldego* (Granato is the reserve wine) plus an inventive *Chardonnay-Pinot Bianco-Sauvignon* white blend.

ℑ **Forman** (*Napa Valley,* California) Rick Forman makes good *Cabernet* and *Merlot* and refreshingly crisp *Chardonnay*.

Forst [fawrst] (*Pfalz,* Germany) Wine town producing great concentrated *Riesling*. Famous for the *Jesuitengarten* vineyard. QbA/Kab/Spät: **85 86 88** 91 92 93 94 95 96 97 98 Aus/Beeren/Tba: **83 85** 88 89 90 91 92 93 94 95 96 97 98 ★★★★ **1996 Forster Jesuitengarten, Dr V Basserman-Jordan £££**

ℑ **Fortant de France** [faw-tan duh frons] (*Languedoc-Roussillon,* France) Good-quality revolutionary brand owned by *Skalli* and specializing in varietal *Vin de Pays d'Oc*.

ℑ **Les Forts de Latour** [lay faw duh lah-toor] (*Pauillac, Bordeaux,* France) *Second label* of *Ch. Latour*. Not, as is often suggested, made exclusively from the fruit of young vines and wine which might otherwise have ended up in *Ch. Latour* – there are several vineyards whose grapes are grown specially for Les Forts – but, like the *second labels* of other top châteaux, this is still often better than lesser *classed growth châteaux'* top wines. Indeed in 1999, it was one of the best wines of the vintage. **82 83 85 86** 88 **90** 91 92 **93 94 95 96** 97 98 99 00

ℑ **Ch. Fourcas-Dupré** [foor-kah doo-pray] (*Listrac Cru Bourgeois, Bordeaux,* France) Tough, very traditional *Listrac*. 70 75 78 81 **82 83 85 86** 87 88 **89** 90 91 92 95 96 97 98 00

ℑ **Ch. Fourcas-Hosten** [foor-kah hos-ten] (*Listrac Cru Bourgeois, Bordeaux,* France) Firm, old-fashioned wine with plenty of "grip" for *tannin* fans. Better in 2000. 75 78 81 **82 83 85 86** 87 88 89 90 91 92 95 96 97 98

ℑ **Fox Run Vineyards** (*New York*) One of the most successful producers in the Finger Lakes, offering good sparkling wine, *Riesling*, and *Chardonnay*.

ℑ **Foxen** (*Santa Ynez,* California) Successful producer of single-vineyard *Pinot* and *Chardonnay*, now moving into *Syrah*. ★★★★ **1997 Syrah £££**

ℑ **Ch. Franc-Mayne** [fron-mayn] (*St. Emilion Grand Cru Classé, Bordeaux,* France) Dry, austere, traditional wines for those who like them that way. 85 86 87 88 **89 90** 94 95 96 ★★★ **1995 £££**

ℑ **Franciacorta** [fran-chee yah-kor-tah] (*Lombardy,* Italy) *DOC* for good, light, French-influenced reds but better noted for varied sparklers made to sell at the same price as – if not more than – *Champagne*. *Bellavista; Ca' Del Bosco; Cavalleri; Monte Rossa; Uberti*.

F

Franciscan Vineyards [fran-sis-kan] (*Napa Valley*, California) Now part of the huge Canandaigua company, reliable *Napa* winery whose Chilean boss Augustin Huneeus, has pioneered natural yeast wines with his *Burgundy*-like "Cuvée Sauvage" *Chardonnay* and has punctured the pretentious balloons of some of his neighbours. Now also making wine in Chile – at *Veramonte*. ★★★★ 1996 Magnificat £££

Ch. de Francs [duh fron] (*Côtes de Francs, Bordeaux*, France) Well-run estate which makes great-value crunchy, blackcurranty wine and, with *Ch. Puygeraud*, helps to prove the worth of this little-known region.

Franken [fran-ken] (Germany) *Anbaugebiet* making characterful, sometimes earthy, dry whites, traditionally presented in the squat flagon-shaped "*Bocksbeutel*" on which the *Mateus* bottle was modeled. One of the key varieties is the *Sylvaner* which explains the earthiness of many of the wines.

Franschhoek [fran-shook] (South Africa) Valley leading into the mountains away from Paarl (and thus cooler). The soil is a little suspect, however, and the best producers are mostly clustered at the top of the valley, around the picturesque eponymous town. **Boekenhoutskloof; Cabriere Estate; la Motte**

Frascati [fras-kah-tee] (*Latium,* Italy) Clichéd dry or semi-dry white from *Latium*. At its best it is soft and clean with a fascinating "sour cream" flavour. Drink within 12 months of *vintage*. **Fontana Candida; Costantini.**

Ca' dei Frati [kah day-yee frah-tee] (*Lombardy*, Italy) Fine producers, both of *Lugana* and *Chardonnay*-based sparkling wine.

Freemark Abbey (*Napa Valley*, California) Well-regarded (in the US) producer of good *Cabernet*. The Bosche examples are the ones to look for. ★★★★ 1995 Cabernet Sauvignon Bosche ££££

Freie Weingärtner Wachau [fri-eh vine-gehrt-nur vah-kow] (*Wachau,* Austria) Fine cooperative with great vineyards, dry and sweet versions of the *Grüner Veltliner* and gloriously concentrated *Rieslings* that outclass the efforts of many a big-name estate in Germany. ★★★★ 1998 Beerenauslese £££

Freisa [fray-ee-sah] (Italy) Characterful perfumed red wine grape with lovely cherryish, raspberryish flavours, popular with Hemingway and grown in *Piedmont* by producers like Gilli and *Vajra*. Drink young. **Bava; Aldo Conterno.**

Freixenet [fresh-net] (*Catalonia*, Spain) Giant in the *cava* field and proponent of traditional *Catalonian* grapes in sparkling wine. Its dull, off-dry big-selling *Cordon Negro* made from traditional grapes is a perfect justification for adding *Chardonnay* to the blend.

Marchesi de' Frescobaldi [mah-kay-see day fres-koh-bal-dee] (*Tuscany*, Italy) Family estate with classy wines: *Castelgiocondo*, Mormoreto (*Cabernet Sauvignon*-based wine), the rich white Pomino Il Benefizio *Chardonnay*, *Pomino Rosso* using *Merlot* and *Cabernet Sauvignon*, and Nippozano in *Chianti*. Now in joint venture to make *Luce* with *Mondavi*. ★★★★ 1997 Montesodi Chianti Rufina ££££ ★★★★★ 1997 Mormoreto ££££.

Freycinet [fres-sih-net] (*Tasmania*, Australia) Small East Coast winery with some of Australia's best *Pinot Noir* and great *Chardonnay*. Sadly, the giant Spanish sparkling-wine firm *Freixenet* has striven to prevent this label appearing outside Australia, despite the facts that *Freycinet* is an historic name in *Tasmania* and that this winery makes no sparkling wine. ★★★★ 1999 Pinot Noir £££

Friuli-Venezia Giulia [free-yoo-lee veh-neht-zee-yah zhee-yoo-lee-yah] (Italy) Northerly region containing a number of *DOCs*: Colli Orientali, *Collio*, Friuli Grave and Aquileia and *Isonzo*, which focus on single-variety wines like *Merlot, Cabernet Franc, Pinot Bianco, Pinot Grigio*, and *Tocai*. Quality varies enormously, ranging from dilute, over-cropped efforts to the complex masterpieces of producers like *Jermann;* Bidoli; *Puiatti; Zonin.*

J Fritz (*Sonoma*, California) Serious producer of *Dry Creek Sauvignon Blanc* that actually does repay ageing.

Frizzante [freet-zan-tay] (Italy) Semi-sparkling, especially *Lambrusco.*

G

Ⓣ **Frog's Leap** (*Napa Valley*, California) Winery whose owners combine organic winemaking skill with a fine sense of humour (their slogan is "Time's fun when you're having flies".). Tasty *Zinfandel*, "wild yeast" *Chardonnay*, and unusually good *Sauvignon Blanc*. ★★★ 1997 Rutherford £££

Ⓣ **Fronsac/Canon Fronsac** [fron-sak] (*Bordeaux*, France) *Pomerol* neighbours, who regularly produce rich, intense, affordable wines. They are rarely subtle. However, with some good winemaking from men like *Christian Moueix* of *Ch. Pétrus*, they can often represent some of the best buys in *Bordeaux*. Canon Fronsac is thought by some to be the better of the pair. 83 85 86 **88 89** 90 94 **95** 96 97 98 99 00.*Ch. Canon;* Cassagne; *Dalem;* Fontenil; Moulin Haut Laroque; Moulin Pey-Labrie;Vieille Cure.

Ⓣ **Ch. de Fuissé** [duh fwee-say] (*Burgundy*, France) Jean-Jacques Vincent makes wines comparable to some of the best of the *Côte d'Or*. The *Vieilles Vignes* can last as long as a good *Chassagne-Montrachet*; the other *cuvées* run in a close race. ★★★★★ 1998 Pouilly Fuissé Vieilles Vignes £££
Fumé Blanc [fyoo-may blahnk] Name originally adapted from *Pouilly Blanc Fumé* by *Robert Mondavi* to describe his California oaked *Sauvignon*. Now widely used – though not exclusively – in the New World for this style.

🍇 **Furmint** [foor-mint] (*Tokaji*, Hungary) Lemony white grape, used in Hungary for *Tokaji* and, given modern winemaking, good dry wines. See *Royal Tokaji Wine Co* and *Disznókö*.

Ⓣ **Rudolf Fürst** [foorst] (*Fraken*, Germany) One of Germany's best producers of ripe red Pinot Noir Spätburgunder, and some lovely floral *Riesling*.

Ⓣ **Fürstlich Castell'sches Domänenamt** [foorst-likh kas-tel-shes doh-mehnen-amt] (*Franken*, Germany) Prestigious producer of typically full-bodied dry whites from the German *Anbaugebiet* of *Franken*.
Fûts de Chêne (élévé en) [foo duh shayne] (France) Oak barrels (aged in).
Futures See *En Primeur.*

G

Ⓣ **Ch. la Gaffelière** [gaf-fuh-lyehr] (*St. Emilion Premier Grand Cru*, *Bordeaux*, France) Lightish-bodied but well-made wines. Not to be confused with *Ch. Canon la Gaffelière*. 82 83 85 **86 88 89** 90 **92 93** 94 95 96 97 98

Ⓣ **Dom. Jean-Noël Gagnard** [jon noh-wel gan-yahr] (*Burgundy*, France) A *domaine* with vineyards across *Chassagne-Montrachet*. There is also some *Santenay*. ★★★★ 1995 Chassagne-Montrachet Clos de la Maltroye ££££

Ⓣ **Jacques Gagnard-Delagrange** [gan-yahr duh lag-ronzh] (*Burgundy*, France) A top-class producer to follow for those traditionalists who like their white *Burgundies* delicately oaked.

Ⓣ **Gaia** [gai-ee-yahr] (*Nemea*, Greece) Up-and-coming modern estate.
Gaillac [gai-yak] (*South-West* France) Light, fresh, good-value reds and (sweet, dry, and slightly sparkling) whites, produced using *Gamay* and *Sauvignon* grapes, as well as the indigenous *Mauzac*. The reds can rival *Beaujolais*. Ch. Clement Ternes; Labastide de Levis; Robert Plageoles.

Ⓣ **Pierre Gaillard** [gai-yahr] (*Rhône*, France) A good producer of *Côte Rôtie*, *St. Joseph*, and *Condrieu*. ★★★★ 1998 St. Joseph ££££

Ⓣ **Gainey Vineyard** [gay-nee] (*Santa Barbara*, California) Classy *Merlot*, *Pinot* and *Chardonnay*. ★★★★ 1996 Limited Selection Merlot £££

Ⓣ **Gaja** [gai-yah] (*Piedmont*, Italy) In 1999, Angelo Gaja, the man who proved that wines from *Barbaresco* could sell for higher prices than top-class *clarets*, let alone the supposedly classier neighbours *Barolo*, announced that his highly prized – and priced – individual vineyard *Barbaresco* would henceforth be sold under the *Langhe* denomination. This would, he argued, focus attention on his excellent blended *Barolo* and *Barbaresco*. Whatever their legal handle, questioning the price of these wines is like querying the cost of a Ferrari.

G

Galestro [gah-less-troh] (*Tuscany*, Italy) The light white of the *Chianti* region. *Antinori; Frescobaldi.*

⊼ **E & J Gallo** [gal-loh] (*Central Valley*, California) The world's biggest wine producer; with around 60 per cent of the total California harvest. The top end *Cabernet* and (particularly impressive) *Chardonnay* from individual "ranch" vineyards and Gallo's own "Northern *Sonoma* Estate", a piece of land which was physically recontoured by their bulldozers. The new Turning Leaf wines are good too, at their level. The rest of the basic range, though much improved and very widely stocked, is still pretty ordinary.

★★★★★ 1997 Northern Sonoma Estate Cabernet £££

🍇 **Gamay** [ga-may] (*Beaujolais*, France) Light-skinned grape traditional to *Beaujolais* where it is used to make fresh and fruity reds for early drinking, usually by the *carbonic maceration* method, and more serious *cru* wines that resemble light *Burgundy*. Also successful in California (*J Lohr*), Australia (*Sorrenberg*), and South Africa (*Fairview*).

🍇 **Gamay** [ga-may] (California) Confusingly unrelated to the *Gamay*.

Gamey Smell or taste oddly reminiscent of hung game – associated with *Pinot Noir* and *Syrah*. Sometimes partly attributable to the combination of those grapes' natural characteristics with careless use of *sulphur dioxide*. Another explanation can be the presence of a vineyard infection called Brettanomyces, feared in California but often unnoticed in France where gamey wines are (sometimes approvingly) said to "renarder" – to smell of fox.

⊼ **Gancia** [gan-chee-yah] (*Piedmont*, Italy) Reliable producer of **Asti Spumante** and good dry *Pinot* di *Pinot*, as well as *Pinot Blanc* sparkling wine.

⊼ **Vin de Pays du Gard** [doo gahr'] (*Languedoc-Roussillon*, France) Fresh, undemanding red and rosé wines from the southern part of the *Rhône*. Drink young, and quite possibly chilled.

⊼ **Garganega** [gahr-gah-nay-gah] (Italy) White grape at its best – and worst – in *Soave* in the *Veneto*. In the right site and when not overcropped, it produces interesting almondy flavours. Otherwise the wines it makes are simply light and dull. Now being blended with *Chardonnay*.

🍇 **Garnacha** [gahr-na-cha] (Spain and France) See *Grenache*.

Garrafeira [gah-rah-fay-rah] (Portugal) Indicates a producer's *"reserve"* wine, which has been selected and given extra time in cask (minimum two years) and bottle (minimum one year).

⊼ **Vincent Gasse** [gass] (*Rhône*, France) Next to the La Landonne vineyard and producing superb, concentrated, inky black wines.

⊼ **Gattinara** [Gat-tee-nah-rah] (*Piedmont*, Italy) Red *DOC* from the *Nebbiolo* – varying in quality but generally full-flavoured and dry. 78 79 82 **85 88 89 90 93 94 95 96** 97 98 Travaglini.

⊼ **Domaine Gauby** [Goh-Bee] (*Côtes de Roussillon*, France) Serious *Roussillon* reds and (*Muscat*) whites. The Muntada *Syrah* is the top *cuvée*.

★★★★ 1999 Côtes de Roussillon Villages Muntada ££

⊼ **Gavi** [gah-vee] (*Piedmont*, Italy) Often unexceptional white wine from the *Cortese* grape. Compared by Italians to white *Burgundy*, with which it and the creamily pleasant Gavi di Gavi share a propensity for high prices.

★★★★★ 1998 Minaia, Martinetti ££££

⊼ **Ch. le Gay** [luh gay] (*Pomerol, Bordeaux*, France) Good *Moueix* property with intense complex wine. 70 **75 76** 78 79 **82 83 85** 86 88 **89 90** 94 **95 96** 97 98 ★★★★ 1998 £££

⊼ **Ch. Gazin** [Ga-zan] (*Pomerol, Bordeaux*, France) Increasingly polished since the mid-1980s. 85 86 **87** 88 **89 90** 92 93 **94 95** 96 97 98 ★★★★ 1995 ££££

G

Geelong [zhee-long] (*Victoria*, Australia) Cool region pioneered by Idyll Vineyards (makers of old-fashioned reds) and rapidly attracting notice with Clyde Park and with *Bannockburn's* and *Scotchman Hill's Pinot Noirs*.

Geisenheim [gi-zen-hime] (*Rheingau*, Germany) Home of the German Wine Institute wine school, once one of the best in the world, but now overtaken by more progressive seats of learning in France, California, and Australia. Qba/Kab/Spät: **85 86 88 89 90** 91 **92 93** 94 **95 96 97** Aus/Beeren/Tba: **83 85 88 89 90** 91 **92 93** 94 **95 96 97**

♀ **Ch. de la Genaiserie** [Jeh-nay-seh-Ree] (*Loire*, France) Classy, lusciously honeyed, single-vineyard wines from *Coteaux du Layon*. ★★★★★ **1995 Coteaux du Layon Chaume ££££**

Generoso [zheh-neh-roh-soh] (Spain) Fortified or dessert wine.

Genève [jer-nev] (Switzerland) Region best known for high quality, if often lightweight, *Gamay* and slightly sparkling "Perlan" *Chasselas*.

♀ **Gentilini** [zhen-tee-lee-nee] (*Cephalonia*, Greece) Nick Cosmetatos's impressive modern white wines, made using both classic Greek grapes and French varieties, should be an example to those of his countrymen who are still happily making and drinking stuff which tastes as fresh as an old election manifesto. ★★★ **1999 Gentilini Fumé ££££**

♀ **JM Gerin** [ger-an] (*Rhône*, France) A producer of good modern *Côte Rôtie* and *Condrieu*; uses new oak to make powerful, long-lived wines. ★★★★★ **1998 Côte Rôtie les Grandes Places ££££**

♀ **Gerovassilou** [jeh-roh-vah-see-loo] (*Cephalonia*, Greece) Producer of successful new-wave whites, including impressive *Viognier*.

♀ **Gevrey-Chambertin** [zheh-vray shom-behr-tan] (*Burgundy*, France) Best-known big red *Côte de Nuits commune*; very variable, but still capable of superb, plummy, cherryish wine. The top *Grand Cru* is *Le Chambertin* but, in the right hands, *Premiers Crus* like Les Cazetiers can beat this and the other *Grands Crus*. **78 83 85 88 89 90** 92 **95 96 97 98** *Denis Bachelet; Alain Burguet;* Bourrée (Vallet); *Champy,* Charlopin; *Bruno Clair;* P. Damoy; *Joseph Drouhin; Dugat-Py;* Dujac; *Leroy; Denis Mortet;* Henri Rebourseau; *Roty; Rossignol-Trapet;Armand Rousseau.*

🍇 **Gewürztraminer** [geh-voort-strah-mee-nehr] White (well, slightly pink) grape, making dry-to-sweet, full, oily-textured, spicy wine. Best in *Alsace* (where it is spelled Gewurztraminer, without the umlaut accent) but also grown in Australasia, Italy, the US, and Eastern Europe. Instantly recognisable by its parma-violets-and-lychees character. *Alsace; Casablanca.*

♀ **Geyser Peak** [Gih-Suhr] (*Alexander Valley,* California) Australian winemaker Darryl Groom revolutionized Californian thinking in this once Australian-owned winery with his *Semillon-Chardonnay* blend, and with reds which show an Australian attitude toward ripe *tannin*. A name to watch. Canyon Road is the good-value *second label.*

♀ **Ghemme** [gem-may] (*Piedmont,* Italy) Spicy *Nebbiolo* usually unfavourably compared to its neighbour Gatinara. Cantalupo is the star producer.

♀ **Ghiaie della Furba** see *Capezzana.*

♀ **Giaconda** [zhee-ya-kon-dah] (*Victoria,* Australia) Small winery hidden away high in the hills. Sells out of its impressive *Pinot Noir* and *Chardonnay en primeur*. The *Cabernet* is fine too. ★★★★★ **1998 Chardonnay £££**

♀ **Bruno Giacosa** [zhee-yah-koh-sah] (*Piedmont,* Italy) Stunning winemaker with a large range, including *Barolos* (Vigna Rionda in best years) and *Barbarescos* (Santo Stefano, again, in best years). Recent success with whites, including a *Spumante*. ★★★★ **1997 Barbaresco S.Stefano ££££**

♀ **Gie les Rameaux** [lay ram-moh] (*Corsica,* France) One of this island's top producers.

♀ **Giesen** [gee-sen] (*Canterbury,* New Zealand) Small estate, with particularly appley *Riesling* (plus a late harvest version) from *Canterbury*, and *Sauvignon* from *Marlborough*. ★★★★ **2000 Sauvignon Blanc ££**

G

℧ **Gigondas** [zhee gon-dass] (*Rhône*, France) *Côtes du Rhône commune*, with good-value, spicy/peppery, blackcurranty reds which show the *Grenache* at its best. A good competitor for nearby Châteauneuf. 78 79 **83 85 88** 89 90 93 94 **95 96** 98 Dom des Bosquets; Brusset; de Cabasse; du Cayron; *Delas;* Font-Sane; Entrefaux; des Espiers; les Goubert; *Guigal;* Pochon; *Sorrel;* de Thalabert; *Vidal-Fleury.*

℧ **Ch. Gilette** [zheel-lette] (*Sauternes, Bordeaux,* France) Eccentric, unclassified but of classed-growth quality *Sauternes* kept in tank (rather than cask) for 20 or 30 years. Rare, expensive, worth it. 49 53 59 **61 62 67 70 75 76 78**

Gimblett Road (*Hawkes Bay,* New Zealand). New appellation for New Zealand's – including the best land in Hawkes Bay.

Gippsland [gip-sland] (*Victoria,* Australia) Up-and-coming coastal region where *Bass Philip* and *Nicholson River* are producing fascinating and quite European-style wines. Watch out for some of Australia's finest *Pinot Noirs.*

℧ **Vincent Girardin** [van-son zhee-rahr-dan] (*Burgundy,* France) Reliable, dynamic *Santenay* producer and (since 1996) *négociant,* with vines in several other *communes.* ★★★★ **1998 Pommard les Chanlins £££**

Giropalette [zhee-roh-pal-let] Large machine which automatically and highly efficiently replaces the human beings who used to perform the task of *remuage.* Used by most *Champagne* houses which, needless to say, prefer to conceal them from visiting tourists.

℧ **Camille Giroud** [kah-mee zhee-roo] (*Burgundy,* France) Laudably old-fashioned family-owned *négociant* with no love of new oak and small stocks of great mature wine that go a long way to prove that good *Burgundy* really doesn't need it to taste good. ★★★★ **1998 Beaune les Cras £££**

Gisborne [giz-bawn] (New Zealand) North Island vine-growing area since the 1920s. Cool, wettish climate, giving New Zealand's best *Chardonnay.* An ideal partner for *Marlborough* in blends. White: **89 91** 94 **95 96 97** 98 99 00. *Corbans;* Matawhero; *Matua Valley;* Millton; *Montana;* Revington.

℧ **Ch. Giscours** [zhees-koor] (*Margaux 3ème Cru Classé, Bordeaux,* France) Recently-bought *Margaux* property which is only (since 1999) beginning to offer the quality associated with the vintages of the late 1970s. A good 2000. **71 75 76 78 79 81** 82 85 86 88 **89** 90 91 92 96 97 98 **00.**★★★ **2000 ££££**

℧ **Louis Gisselbrecht** [gees-sel-brekt] (*Alsace,* France) Recommendable grower and *negociant* which, like cousin Willy, has good vines in the Frankstein *Grand Cru.*

℧ **Givry** [zheev-ree] (*Burgundy,* France) *Côte Chalonnaise commune,* making typical and affordable, if rather jammily rustic, reds and creamy whites. French wine snobs recall that this was one of King Henri IV's favourite wines, forgetting the fact that a) he had many such favourites dotted all over France and b) his mistress – of whom he also probably had several – happened to live here. Red: **78 85 88 89 90** 92 93 **94 95 96 97** 98 Bourgeon; Derain; *Joblot;* Lumpp; Mouton; Ragot; Clos Salomon; Steinmaier; Thénard.

℧ **Glen Carlou** [kah-loo] (*Paarl,* South Africa) Small-scale winery with rich, oily, oaky *Chardonnay* and less convincing reds. ★★★ **1996 Chardonnay ££**

℧ **Glen Ellen** (*Sonoma Valley,* California) Dynamic firm producing large amounts of commercial tropical fruit juice-like *Chardonnay* under its "Proprietor's Reserve" label. Reds are better value.

Glenrowan [glen-roh-wan] (*Victoria,* Australia) Area near *Rutherglen* with a similar range of excellent *liqueur Muscats* and *Tokays.*

℧ **Ch. Gloria** [glaw-ree-yah] (*St. Julien Cru Bourgeois, Bordeaux,* France) One of the first of the super *Crus Bourgeois.* Now back on form.

℧ **Golan** [goh-lan] (Israel) One of the three principal labels used by the *Golan Heights Winery.*

℧ **Golan Heights Winery** [goh-lan] (Israel) California expertise is used to produce good *Kosher Cabernet* and *Muscat.* Labels include Gamla, Golan, and Yarden (used for the top wines).

G

✒ **Goldwater Estate** (*Auckland,* New Zealand) *Bordeaux*-like red wine specialist on *Waiheke Island* whose wines are expensive but every bit as good as many similarly-priced Californian offerings. The Sauvignon Blanc is fine too, if leaner than most New Zealand examples. ★★★★ **2000 Dog Point Sauvignon Blanc £££**

✒ **Gonzalez Byass** [gon-thah-leth bee-yass] (*Jerez,* Spain) If *sherry* is beginning to enjoy a long-awaited comeback, this is the company that should take much of the credit. Producer of the world's best-selling *fino, Tío Pepe* – and a supporting cast of the finest, most complex, traditional *sherries* available to mankind. ★★★★★ **Noë ££££**

✒ **Gordon Brothers** (*Washington State*) Grapegrowers-turned-winemakers, and now a name to look for when shopping for well-made *Washington State Merlot* and *Chardonnay* ★★★★ **1998 Chardonnay ££££**

✒ **Gosset** [gos-say] (*Champagne,* France) The oldest house in *Champagne* producing some marvellous and very long-lived *cuvées,* particularly the Celebris. ★★★★ **1995 Celebris ££££**

✒ **Henri Gouges** [Gooj] (*Burgundy,* France) Long-established estate, producing some truly classic long-lived wines. ★★★★★ **1998 Nuits-St.-Georges les Pruliers ££££**

✒ **Marquis de Goulaine** [goo-layn] (*Loire,* France) One of the best producers of *Muscadet* – and a butterfly museum to boot.
Goulburn Valley [gohl-boorn] (*Victoria,* Australia) Small, long-established region reigned over by the respectively ancient and modern *Ch. Tahbilk* and *Mitchelton,* both of whom make great *Marsanne,* though in very different styles. Also **Osicka; Plunkett; David Traeger.**

✒ **Gould Campbell** [goold] (*Douro,* Portugal) Underrated member of the same stable as *Dow's, Graham's* and *Warre's.* 60 63 66 70 75 77 80 83 85 91 94 97 ★★★ **1994 Late Bottled Vintage Port £££**

✒ **Goundrey** [gown-dree] (*Western* Australia) Winery in the up-and-coming region of *Mount Barker,* bought by an American millionaire who has continued the founder's policy of making fruity but not overstated *Chardonnay* and *Cabernet.* ★★★★ **1999 Goundrey Cabernet Merlot £££**
Graach [grahkh] (*Mosel-Saar-Ruwer,* Germany) *Mittelmosel* village producing fine wines. Best known for its *Himmelreich* vineyard. QbA/Kab/Spät: 85 86 **88 89 90 92 93 94 95 96 97** 98 Aus/Beeren/Tba: 83 85 **88 89 90 92 93 94 95 96 97** 98 *Deinhard; JJ Prüm; Max Ferd Richter; Von Kesselstadt.*

✒ **Grace Family Vineyards** (*Napa,* California) Small quantities – occasionally fewer than 100 – of *Cabernet* whose rarity makes for prices of £300-400 per bottle. (Remember, if potatoes were harder to grow, they'd cost more, too).

✒ **Graham** [gray-yam] (*Douro,* Portugal) Sweetly delicate wines that can outclass the same stable's supposedly finer but heftier *Dow's.* Malvedos is erroneously thought of as the Single *Quinta.* 55 60 **63 66** 70 75 **77** 85 91 94 97 ★★★★ **1997 Vintage Port £££**

✒ **Alain Graillot** [al-lan grai-yoh] (*Rhône,* France) Progressive-minded producer who should be applauded for shaking up the sleepy, largely undistinguished *appellation* of *Crozes-Hermitage,* using grapes from rented vineyards. All the reds are excellent, and La Guiraude is the wine from the top vineyard. ★★★★ **1998 Crozes Hermitage £££**
Grampians (*Victoria,* Australia) New name for *Great Western.*
Gran Reserva [gran rays-sehr-vah] (Spain) Quality wine aged for a designated number of years in wood and, in theory, only produced in the best *vintages.* However, Gran Reserva can on occasion be dried out and less worthwhile than *Crianza* or *Reserva.*

G

Grand Cru [gron kroo] (France) Prepare to be confused. Term referring to the finest vineyards and the – supposedly – equally fine wine made in them. It is an official designation in *Bordeaux, Burgundy, Champagne* and *Alsace*, but its use varies. In *Alsace* where there are 50 or so *Grand Cru* Vineyards, some are more convincingly grand than others. In *Burgundy Grand Cru* vineyards with their own *ACs*, e.g., *Montrachet*, do not need to carry the name of the village (e.g., *Chassagne-Montrachet*) on their label. Where these regions apply the designation to pieces of soil, in *Bordeaux* it applies to châteaux whose vineyards can be bought and sold. More confusingly, still *St. Emilion* can be described as either *Grand Cru*, *Grand Cru Classé* – or both – or *Premier Grand Cru Classé*. Just remember that in St. Emilion, the words *Grand Cru* by themselves provide absolutely no indication of quality at all.

✠ **Ch. Grand Mayne** [Gron-mayn] (*St. Emilion Grand Cru, Bordeaux,* France) Producer of rich, deeply flavoursome, modern *St. Emilion*. Not for traditionalists perhaps, but still due for promotion to *Premier Grand Cru* status. 82 83 85 86 87 88 **89 90 92 93** 94 95 96 97 98 99 00

✠ **Ch. du Grand Moulas** [gron moo-lahs] (*Rhône,* France) Very classy *Côtes du Rhône* property with unusually complex red wines.
Grand Vin [gron van] (*Bordeaux,* France) The first (quality) wine of an estate – as opposed to its *second label*.

✠ **Ch. Grand-Pontet** [gron pon-tay] (*St. Emilion Grand Cru Classé, Bordeaux,* France) Rising star with showy wines. 86 88 89 **90** 92 93 94 95 96 97 98.

✠ **Ch. Grand-Puy-Ducasse** [gron pwee doo-kass] (*Pauillac 5ème Cru Classé, Bordeaux,* France) Excellent wines from an over-performing fifth growth *Pauillac* property. 82 83 **85** 86 88 **89 90** 91 92 93 94 95 96 97 98 99 00.

✠ **Ch. Grand-Puy-Lacoste** [gron pwee lah-kost] (*Pauillac 5ème Cru Classé, Bordeaux,* France) Top-class fifth growth owned by the Borie family of *Ducru-Beaucaillou* and now right up there among the *Super Seconds*. 79 81 **82 83 85** 86 88 **89 90** 91 92 **93** 94 95 96 97 98 ★★★★★ **1998 £££**

✠ **Grande Rue** [grond-roo] (*Burgundy,* France) Recently promoted *Grand Cru* in Vosne-Romanée, across the way from Romanée-Conti (hence the promotion). Sadly, the Dom. Lamarche to which this *monopole* belongs is an improving but long-term underperformer.
Grandes Marques [grond mahrk] (*Champagne,* France) Once-official designation for "big name" *Champagne* houses, irrespective of the quality of their wines. Now, although the "Syndicat" of which they were members has been disbanded, the expression is still quite widely used.

✠ **Grands-Echézeaux** [grons EH-shay-zoh] (*Burgundy,* France) One of the best *Grand Crus* in *Burgundy*; and supposedly better than *Echézeaux*. The *Domaine de la Romanée-Conti* is a famous producer here.

✠ **Grange** [graynzh] (*South Australia*) *Penfolds'* and Australia's greatest wine – "The Southern Hemisphere's only first growth" – pioneered by Max Schubert in the early 1950s following a visit to Europe. From the outset, although Schubert was aiming to match top *Bordeaux*, he used *Shiraz* and American (rather than French) oak barrels and a blend of grapes from 70-year-old vines sited in several South Australian regions. Recently discovered in the US and thus a collector's item that sells out as soon as each *vintage* hits the streets. Tasty when young, it needs time for its true complexity to become apparent. 55 63 66 71 76 78 81 83 86 88 90 91 93 ★★★★★ 1993 **££££**

✠ **Dom de la Grange des Pères** [gronj day pehr] (*Languedoc,* France) A competitor for *Mas de Daumas Gassac*. Proves that a Vin de Pays de l'Hérault can produce wine that's better than many a bottle from a smart appellation.

G

Ⓣ **Grangehurst** [graynzh-huhrst] (*Stellenbosch*, South Africa) Concentrated modern reds from a small winery converted from the family squash court! Expanding. Good *Cabernet* and *Pinotage*. ★★★★ 1998 Pinotage ££

Ⓣ **Weingut Grans-Fassian** [grans-fass-yan] (*Mosel*, Germany) Improving estate with some really fine, classic wine – especially at a supposedly basic level. ★★★★ 1999 Trittenheimer Apotheke, Riesling Auslese Gold Cap ££

Ⓣ **Yves Grassa** [gras-sah] (*Southwest*, France). Pioneering producer of *Vin de Pays des Côtes de Gascogne* – moving from *Colombard* and *Ugni Blanc* into *Sauvignon* and *late-harvest* styles. ★★★ 1998 Chardonnay Tete de Cuvee £

Ⓣ **Elio Grasso** [eh-lee-yoh grah-so] (*Piedmont*, Italy) Producer of high quality, single-vineyard *Barolo* (Casa Maté and Chiniera), *Barbera*, *Dolcetto*, and *Chardonnay*.

Ⓣ **Alfred Gratien** [gras-see-yen] (*Champagne,* France) Good *Champagne* house, using traditional methods. Also owner of *Loire* sparkling winemaker Gratien et Meyer, based in *Saumur*. ★★★★★ 1985 £££

🍇 **Grauerburgunder** [grow-urh-buhr-goon-duhr] (Germany) Another name for *Pinot Gris*. *Müller-Catoir.*

Ⓣ **Dom. la Grave** [lah grahv] (*Graves*, *Bordeaux,* France) Small property in the *Graves* with a growing reputation for 100 per cent *Sémillon* whites.

Ⓣ **La Grave à Pomerol** [lah grahv ah pom-rohl] (*Pomerol*, *Bordeaux,* France) One of the excellent Christian *Mouiex's* characteristically stylish estates that shows off *Pomerol's* plummy-cherry fruit at its best.

Ⓣ **Grave del Friuli** [grah-veh del free-yoo-lee] (*Friuli-Venezia Giulia*, Italy) DOC for young-drinking reds and whites. *Cabernet*, *Merlot*, and *Chardonnay* are increasingly successful.

Ⓣ **Graves** [grahv] (*Bordeaux*, France) Large region producing vast quantities of red and white, ranging from good to indifferent. The best whites come from *Pessac-Léognan* in the northern part of the region and are sold under that *appellation*. Reds can have a lovely raspberryish character. Red: 70 78 79 81 82 83 85 **86 88 89** 90 **94 95** 96 97 98 00. White: 78 79 82 **83 85 86** 88 89 90 93 94 **95** 96 97 98 99 00. **Ch. d'Archambeau; de Chantegrive; Clos Floridène; Rahoul; du Seuil; Villa Bel Air.**

Ⓣ **Josko Gravner** [grahv-nehr] (*Friuli-Venezia Giulia*, Italy) Innovative producer with brilliant oaked *Chardonnay* and *Sauvignon Blanc* produced in *Collio* but not under the rules of that denomination. The blended white Breg, which includes no fewer than six varieties, is good too, as is Rujino, a mixture of *Merlot* and *Cabernet Sauvignon*.

Great Western (*Victoria*, Australia) Old name for region noted for *Seppelt's* sparkling wines including the astonishing "Sparkling *Burgundy*" *Shirazes*, for *Best's* and for the wines of *Mount Langi Ghiran*. Now renamed *Grampians*, though I suspect it will take time for enthusiasts to get used to the new name.

🍇 **Grechetto** [grek-keh-toh] (Italy) Subtly spicy white grape used to fine effect in *Umbria* by *Adanti, Falesco,* Goretti and Palazzone.

Ⓣ **Greco di Tufo** [greh-koh dee too-foh] (*Campania*, Italy) From *Campania*, best-known white from the ancient Greco grape; dry, characterfully herby southern wine. **Botromagno; Librandi; Mastroberardino; Feudi di San Gregoria.**

Greece This country is finally, if belatedly, beginning to modernize its very ancient wine industry. This means it is beginning to exploit the potential of a set of grapes grown nowhere else. Unfortunately, as Greece begins to rid itself of its taste for the stewed, oxidized styles of the past, the modern wines are so popular in the stylish restaurants in Athens that they tend to be both expensive and hard to find overseas. **Amethystos; Antonopoulos; Boutari; Ch. Carras; Gaia; Gentilini; Gerovassilou; Hatzimichalis; Ktima; Lazarides; Papantonis; Skouras; Strofilia.**

Ⓣ **Green Point** (*Yarra Valley*, Australia) See *Dom. Chandon*.

Ⓣ **Green & Red** (*Napa Valley*, California) Fast-rising star with impressive *Zinfandel*. ★★★★ 1997 Chiles Mills Zinfandel £££

G

🍇 **Grenache** [greh-nash] Red grape of the *Rhône* (aka *Garnacha* in Spain) making spicy, peppery, full-bodied wine, provided yields are kept low. Also used to make rosés across Southern France, Australia, and California.

🍇 **Grenache Blanc** [greh-nash blon] Widely grown throughout Southern France and Spain, where it is used to make mostly dull, slightly peppery, white wine. Treated with love and care, however, it can add welcome spice to a blend.

⊤ **Marchesi de Gresy** [mah-kay-see day greh-see] (*Piedmont,* Italy) Good producer of single-vineyard *Barbaresco*. ★★★★★ 1996 Martinenga £££

⊤ **Grgich Hills** [guhr-gich] (*Napa Valley,* California) Pioneering producer of *Cabernet Sauvignon*, *Chardonnay,* and *Fumé Blanc*. The name is a concatenation of the two founders – Mike Grgich and Austin Hills, rather than a topographical feature.

⊤ **Miljenko Grgich** [mell-yen-koh guhr-gich] (Croatia) The coast of Dalmatia gets the *Grgich Hills* treatment – and a Californian rediscovers his roots.

🍇 **Grignolino** [green-yoh-lee-noh] (*Piedmont,* Italy) Red grape and modest but refreshing cherryish wine, e.g. the *DOC* Grignolino d'Asti. Drink young.

⊤ **Ch. Grillet** [gree-yay] (*Rhône,* France) *Appellation* consisting of a single estate and producer of improving *Viognier* white. Neighbouring *Condrieu* is still better value. ★★★ 1996 Ch. Grillet ££££

⊤ **Marqués de Griñon** [green-yon] (*La Mancha, Rioja, Ribera del Duero,* Spain/Argentina) Dynamic exception to the dull *La Mancha* rule, making wines, with the help of *Michel Rolland*, which can outclass *Rioja*. The juicy *Cabernet Merlot* and fresh white *Rueda* have been joined by Durius, a blend from *Ribera del Duero*, an exceptional new *Syrah* and an extraordinary *Petit Verdot*. Look out too for new wines from Argentina. ★★★★ 1998 Dominio de Valdepusa Petit Verdot ££

⊤ **Griotte-Chambertin** [gree-yot] (*Burgundy,* France) see *Chambertin*.

⊤ **Bernard Gripa** [gree-pah] (*Rhône,* France) Maker of top-notch *St. Joseph* – ripe, thick, *tarry* wine that could age forever. ★★★★ 1997 St. Joseph £££

⊤ **Jean-Louis Grippat** [gree-pah] (*Rhône,* France) The domaine has been sold to Marcel Guigal, but Grippat was an unusually great white *Rhône* producer in *Hermitage* and *St. Joseph*. His reds in both appellations were less stunning, but worth buying in their subtler-than-most way. Look out for his Cuvée des Hospices. *St. Joseph* Rouge. ★★★★ 1998 Hermitage Blanc ££££

⊤ **Gristina** [gris-tee-nah] (*New York State*) Pioneering Long Island winery which has established a deserved local reputation for its *Merlot* and its *Chardonnay*. Both stand comparison with pricier California fare.

⊤ **Dom. Jean Grivot** [gree-voh] (*Burgundy,* France) Top-class *Vosne-Romanée* estate whose winemaker Etienne has one of the most sensitive touches in Burgundy. ★★★★ 1997 Vosne-Romanée Les Beaux Monts ££££

⊤ **Robert Groffier** [grof-fee-yay] (*Burgundy,* France) Up-and-coming estate with top-class wines from *Chambolle-Musigny*. ★★★★★ 1997 Clos de Vougeot ££££

⊤ **Groot Constantia** [khroot-kon-stan-tee-yah] (*Constantia,* South Africa) Government-run, 300-year-old wine estate and national monument that is finally making worthwhile - if not great - wines.

⊤ **Groote Post** [khroot-ter post] (*Darling,* South Africa) Blazing a trail in the "new" region of Darling in the West Coast a few miles from the Atlantic, this young estate is already producing one of the Cape's top *Sauvignon Blancs* and some very promising *Pinot Noir*.

⊤ **Dom. Anne Gros** [groh] (*Burgundy,* France) Unfortunately for one's wallet, the best wines from this *Vosne-Romanée domaine* are as expensive as they are delicious – but they are worth every cent. ★★★★★ 1998 Vosne Romanée Barreaux ££££

⊤ **Jean Gros** [groh] (*Burgundy,* France) Slightly less impressive *Vosne-Romanée* producer, but the *Clos Vougeots* are good. ★★★★ 1997 Clos du Vougeot ££££

G

☰ **Michel Gros** [groh] (*Burgundy*, France) Least recommendable of the Gros clan – unless you love toasty new oak as much as some US critics do.

🍇 **Gros Lot/Grolleau** [groh-loh] (*Loire*, France) The workhorse black grape of the *Loire*, particularly in *Anjou*, used to make white, rosé, and sparkling *Saumur*.

🍇 **Gros Plant (du Pays Nantais)** [groh-plon doo pay-yee non-tay] (*Loire*, France) Light, sharp white *VDQS* wine from the western *Loire*. In all but the best hands, serves to make even a poor *Muscadet* look good.

☰ **Grosset** [gros-set] (*Clare Valley*, South Australia) White (*Chardonnay*, *Semillon*, and especially *Riesling*) specialist now making great reds (the Gaia red *Bordeaux*-blend and lovely *Pinot Noir*). Give all wines time to develop. (Mrs. Grosset is responsible for the similarly brilliant *Mount Horrocks* wines). Both are in the (wine) news this year for leading the move to putting Clare Riesling into "*Stelvin*" screwcaps. ★★★★★ **2000 Polish Hill Riesling £££**

Grosslage [gross-lah-guh] (Germany) Wine district, the third subdivision after *Anbaugebiet* (e.g., *Rheingau*) and *Bereich* (e.g., *Nierstein*). For example, *Michelsberg* is a *Grosslage* of the *Bereich Piesport*.

☰ **Groth** [grahth] (*Napa Valley*, California) Serious producer of quality *Cabernet* and *Chardonnay*. ★★★★ **1997 Oakville Cabernet Reserve £££**

☰ **Grove Mill** (New Zealand) Young *Marlborough* winery with good *Sauvignon Blanc*, *Chardonnay* and *Riesling*. ★★★★ **1999 Sauvignon Blanc ££**

☰ **Ch. Gruaud-Larose** [groo-oh lah-rohz] (*St. Julien 2ème Cru Classé*, *Bordeaux*, France) Now under the same ownership as Chasse-Spleen, and right on form in 2000. The second wine is "Le Sarget".

🍇 **Grüner Veltliner** [groo-nuhr felt-lee-nuhr] Spicy white grape of Austria and Eastern Europe, producing light, fresh, aromatic wine – and for *Willi Opitz* an extraordinary *late harvest* version. *Knoll; Kracher;* Lang; Metternich-Sándor; *Opitz; Pichler; Prager;* Schuster; Steininger.

☰ **Bodegas Guelbenzu** [guhl-bent-zoo] (*Navarra*, Spain) Starry new-wave producer of rich red wines using local grapes and *Cabernet*. ★★★★ **1998 Garnacha ££**

☰ **Guerrieri-Rizzardi** [gwer-reh-ree rit-zar-dee] (*Veneto*, Italy) Solid organic producer, with good rather than great *Amarone* and single-vineyard *Soave Classico*.

☰ **Guffens-Heynen** [goof-fens ay-na(n)] (*Burgundy*, France) Rising star in *Pouilly-Fuissé* and the man behind the *Verget* empire.

☰ **E Guigal** [gee-gahl] (*Rhône*, France) Still the yardstick for *Rhône* reds, despite increased competition from *Chapoutier*. His extraordinarily pricey single-vineyard La Mouline, La Landonne and La Turque wines from *Côte Rôtie* and Château d'Ampuis wines are still ahead of the young turks and the "Brune et Blonde" blend of grapes from two hillsides remains a benchmark for this *appellation*. The basic red and white *Côtes du Rhône* are less exciting than they have been, however. ★★★★★ **1996 Côte-Rôtie Chateau d'Ampuis**

☰ **Guimaraens** [gee-mah-rens] (*Douro*, Portugal) Associated with *Fonseca*; underrated *port*-house making good wines. ★★★★★ **1984 Fonseca Guimaraens Vintage Port ££££**

☰ **Ch. Guiraud** [gee-roh] (*Sauternes Premier Cru Classé, Bordeaux*, France) *Sauternes* classed growth, recently restored to original quality. Good wines but rarely among the most complex sweet *Bordeaux*. 67 79 81 82 **83** 85 86 87 **88 89 90** 92 93 94 95 96 97 98 99 00.★★★★ **1997 ££££**

☰ **Weingut Gunderloch** [goon-duhr-lokh] (*Rheinhessen*, Germany) One of the few estates to make *Rheinhessen* wines of truly reliable quality. ★★★★ **1998 Nackenheim Rothenberg, Riesling Auslese Gold Cap £££**

☰ **Gundlach-Bundschu** [guhnd-lakh buhnd-shoo] (*Sonoma Valley*, California) Good, well-made, juicy *Merlot* and spicy *Zinfandel*.

☰ **Louis Guntrum** [goon-troom] (*Rheinhessen*, Germany) Family-run estate with a penchant for *Sylvaner*. ★★★★ **1997 Oppenheimer Herrenberg Silvaner Eiswein ££££**

G

Ⓨ Ch. la Gurgue [lah guhrg] (*Margaux Cru Bourgeois, Bordeaux*, France) *Cru Bourgeois* across the track from *Ch. Margaux*. Less impressive since the same owner's neighbouring *Ch. Ferrière* has both improved and increased its production, but the 1999 is a winner. 83 85 86 88 **89** 90 95 96 98 00

❦ Gutedel [goot-edel] (Germany) German name for the *Chasselas* grape.

Ⓨ Friedrich-Wilhelm Gymnasium [free-drikh vil-helm-gim-nahz-yuhm] (*Mosel*, Germany) Big-name estate that ought to be making better wine. ★★★★ 1998 Zeltinger Sonnenuhr Riesling Auslese Gold Cap £££

H

Ⓨ Weingut Fritz Haag [hahg] (*Mosel-Saar-Ruwer*, Germany) Superlative small estate with classic *Rieslings*. ★★★★ 1999 Brauneberger Juffer Sonnenuhr Riesling Kabinett ££££

Ⓨ Weingut Reinhold Haart [rine-hohld hahrt] (*Mosel*, Germany) *Piesport* star. ★★★★ 1998 Piesporter Goldtropfchen Riesling Auslese Gold Cap £££

Halbtrocken [hahlb-trok-en] (Germany) Off-dry. Usually a safer buy than *Trocken* in regions like the *Mosel, Rheingau* and *Rheinhessen*, but still often aggressively *acidic*. Look for *QbA* or *Auslese* versions.

Hallgarten [hal-gahr-ten] (*Rheingau*, Germany) Important town near *Hattenheim* producing robust wines including the (in Germany) well-regarded produce from *Schloss Vollrads*. QbA/Kab/Spät: 85 88 89 90 91 92 93 95 96 97 98 99 00. Aus/Beeren/Tba: 83 85 88 89 90 92 93 94 95 96 97 98 99 00

Ⓨ Hamilton Russell Vineyards (*Walker Bay*, South Africa) Pioneer of impressive *Pinot Noir* and *Chardonnay* at a winery in Hermanus at the southernmost tip of the *Cape*. Now expanded to include a *second label* – Southern Right – to produce a varietal *Pinotage*, and a *Chenin*-based white. Ashbourne, the top wine is pricy but recommendable.

Ⓨ Handley Cellars (*Mendocino*, California) Fine sparkling wine producer with a particularly good pure *Chardonnay Blanc de Blanc*. The still *Chardonnay* is pretty impressive, too.

Ⓨ Hanging Rock (*Victoria*, Australia) As in the movie, *Picnic at....*, this winery makes Australia's biggest, butteriest sparkling wine and some pretty good reds and whites. ★★★★ 2000 The Jim Jim Sauvignon Blanc £££

Ⓨ Hanzell (*Sonoma*, California) One of the great old names of California wine, and a pioneer producer of *Chardonnay* and *Pinot Noir*. The former grape is still a major success story – in its traditional California style.

Ⓨ BRL Hardy (*South* Australia) The second biggest wine producer in Australia, encompassing *Houghton* and *Moondah Brook* in *Western Australia, Leasingham* in the *Clare Valley, Redman* in *Coonawarra, E& E* in *Barossa*, Hardy's itself, and *Ch. Reynella*. *Hardy's* reliable range includes the commercial Nottage Hill, new Bankside, and Banrock Station, and multiregional blends, but the wines to look for are the top-of-the-line Eileen and Thomas Hardy. The *Ch. Reynella* wines from *McLaren Vale* fruit (and, in the case of the reds, using *basket presses*) are good, very lean examples of the region. Hardy's ventures in Italy (d'Istinto) and France (la Baume) are less impressive.

Ⓨ Hargrave Vineyard (*Long Island*, New York) Alex Hargrave's recently-sold, nearly 30-year-old winery put the North Fork of Long Island – not to say the island as a whole – on the wine map with its Chardonnay and Merlot. And it so impressed the owner of *Ch. Pichon-Lalande* when she visited that she apparently briefly considered making wine here.

Ⓨ Harlan Estate (*Napa Valley*, California) Fiercely pricey, small quantities of *Bordeaux*-style reds, made with input from *Michel Rolland*, and using grapes from hillside vineyards. Join the waiting list.

🍇 **Hárslevelü** [harsh-leh-veh-loo] (Hungary) White grape used in *Tokaji* and for light table wines.

Ⓨ **Hartenberg Estate** [gree-yay] (*Stellenbosch*, South Africa) A name to watch, for rich, ripe reds (including an unusually good Shiraz and the only example I've seen of Pontac, alias Teinturier du Cher, a seldom-grown red-fleshed French grape. Chardonnay and Riesling are fine, too.

Ⓨ **Harveys** (*Jerez*, Spain) Maker of the ubiquitous *Bristol Cream*. Other styles are unimpressive apart from the 1796 range and Club Classic.

Ⓨ **Haskovo** [hash-koh-voh] (Bulgaria) Along with the more frequently seen Stambolovo and Sakar, this is a name to look out for. All three are newly privatised cooperatives that can make good, rich, red wine.

Ⓨ **Hattenheim** [hat-ten-hime] (*Rheingau*, Germany) One of the finest villages in the *Rheingau*, with wines from producers such as *Balthasar Ress*, Von Simmern, *Schloss Rheinhartshausen*, and *Schloss Schönborn*.

Ⓨ **Hatzimichalis** [hat-zee-mikh-ahlis] (*Atalanti*, Greece) The face of future Greek winemaking? Hopefully. This self-taught producer's small estate makes variable but often top-notch *Cabernet Sauvignon*, *Merlot*, *Chardonnay*, and fresh dry Atalanti white. ★★★★ **1997 Merlot ££.**

Ⓨ **Ch. Haut-Bages-Averous** [oh-bahj-aveh-roo] (*Pauillac Cru Bourgeois, Bordeaux*, France) *Second label* of *Ch. Lynch-Bages*. Good-value blackcurranty *Pauillac*. 82 83 85 86 88 **89 90** 93 94 95 96 97 98 00

Ⓨ **Ch. Haut-Bages-Libéral** [oh-bahj-lib-ay-ral] (*Pauillac 5ème Cru Classé, Bordeaux*, France) Classy small property in the same stable as *Chasse-Spleen*. 75 78 **82** 83 85 **86** 87 88 89 **90** 91 93 94 95 96 97 98 00

Ⓨ **Ch. Haut-Bailly** [oh bai-yee] (*Pessac-Léognan Cru Classé, Bordeaux*, France) Recently sold: brilliant *Pessac-Léognan* property consistently making reliable, excellent-quality, long-lived red wines. A stunning 1998 and 2000. 61 64 **70** 78 **79** 81 83 **85** 86 87 **88 89 90** 92 **93 94** 95 96 97 98 99 00

Ⓨ **Ch. Haut-Batailley** [oh-ba-tai-yee] (*Pauillac 5ème Cru Classé, Bordeaux*, France) Subtly-styled wine from the same stable as *Ducru-Beaucaillou* and *Grand-Puy-Lacoste* 85 86 88 **89 90** 91 92 93 **95 96** 97 98 99 00

Ⓨ **Ch. Haut-Brion** [oh bree-yon] (*Pessac-Léognan Premier Cru Classé, Bordeaux*, France) Pepys' favourite wine and still the only non-*Médoc* first growth. Situated in the *Graves* on the outskirts of *Bordeaux* in the shadow of the gas company. Wines can be tough and hard to judge when young, but at their best they develop a rich, fruity, perfumed character which sets them apart from their peers. 1996, 1998, 1999, and 2000 were especially good, as – comparatively – were 1993, 1994, and 1995. Even so, competition is heating up from stablemate, la *Mission-Haut-Brion*. The white is rare and often sublime. Red: **61 70 71 75 78 79 82 85 86 88 89 90** 91 **92 93** 94 95 96 97 98 99 00. White: **85** 87 88 **89** 90 91 **92 93** 94 95 96 97 98 99

Ⓨ **Ch. Haut-Marbuzet** [oh-mahr-boo-zay] (*St. Estèphe Cru Bourgeois, Bordeaux*, France) *Cru bourgeois* which thinks it's a *cru classé*. Immediately imposing wine with bags of oak. Decidedly new-wave *St. Estèphe*.

Ⓨ *Haut-Médoc* [oh-may-dok] (*Bordeaux*, France) Large *appellation* which includes nearly all of the well-known *crus classés*. Basic *Haut-Médoc* should be better than plain *Médoc*. 82 83 **85** 86 88 **89 90** 94 95 96 97 98

Ⓨ *Haut-Montravel* [oh-mo'n rah-vel] (*South-West*, France) A potentially good alternative to *Monbazillac* and even *Sauternes*.

Ⓨ **Haut-Poitou** [oh-pwa-too] (*Loire*, France) A source of basic inexpensive *Sauvignon*.

Ⓨ **Hautes Côtes de Beaune** [oht-coht-duh-bohn] (*Burgundy*, France) Rustic wines from the hills above the big-name *communes*. Worth buying in good *vintages*; in poorer ones the grapes have problems ripening. The Cave des Hautes Côtes cooperative makes good examples.

Ⓨ **Hautes Côtes de Nuits** [oht-coht-duh-nwee] (*Burgundy*, France) This appellation produces mostly red wines that are slightly tougher than *Hautes Côtes de Beaune*.

H

Hawkes Bay (New Zealand) Major North Island vineyard area which is finally beginning to live up to the promise of producing top-class reds. Whites can be fine too, though rarely achieving the bite of *Marlborough*. *Babich;* Brookfields; Church Road; Cleview; *Craggy Range;* Delegats; Esk Valley; *Matua Valley,* Mills Reef; *Mission;* Montana; Morton Estate; Ngatarawa; CJ Pask; Sacred Hill; *Te Mata;* Trinity Hill; *Vidal;* Villa Maria; Unison.

Hedges (*Washington State*) Producer of good, rich, berryish reds from a number of the best vineyards in Washington State. ★★★★ 1998 Three Vineyards Red Mountain Reserve £££

Heemskerk [heems-kuhrk] (*Tasmania,* Australia) Generally underperforming winery until its purchase by its neighbour *Pipers Brook*. The *Jansz* sparkling wine label (originally launched as a joint venture with *Roederer*) now belongs to *Yalumba*, while Heemskerk's own (excellent) sparkling wine has been renamed *Pirie*, after the owner of *Pipers Brook*.

Dr. Heger [hay-gehr] (*Baden,* Germany) A brilliant exponent of the *Grauerburgunder* which ripens well in this warm region of Germany. Winkleberg Grauer Burgunder Spätlese Trocken £££

Heggies [heg-gees] (*South* Australia) Impressive *Adelaide Hills* label in the same camp as *Yalumba*. Lovely *Riesling, Viognier, Merlot, Pinot Noir,* and sweet wines. ★★★★ 1999 Heggies Viognier ££

Heida (hi-da] (Switzerland) Spicy Swiss grape variety, thought to be related to the *Gewürztraminer*. When carefully handled, produces wonderfully refreshing wines.

Charles Heidsieck [hide-seek] (*Champagne,* France) Innovative producer whose winemaker Daniel Thibaut (*Bonnet, Piper Heidsieck*) has recently introduced the clever notion of labelling non-*vintage* wine with a "mis en cave" bottling date. Wines are all recommendable. ★★★★★ Brut Réserve Mis en Cave 1997 £££; ★★★★★ 1995 Champagne Charlie ££££

Heidsieck Dry Monopole [hide-seek] (*Champagne,* France) A subsidiary of *Mumm* and thus until 1999 controlled by Seagrams. Wines with the same (low) quality aspirations as that brand. Even so, recent *vintages* have shown some improvement. ★★★ Diamont Bleu ££££

Heitz Cellars [hites] (*Napa Valley,* California) One of the great names of California and the source of stunning reds in the 1970s. More recent (pre-1992, when it had to be replanted following Californian *phylloxera*) releases of the flagship Martha's Vineyard *Cabernet* have tasted unacceptably musty, however, as have the traditionally almost-as-good Bella Oaks. At the winery and among some critics, such criticisms are apparently treated as lèse-majesté. Recent (post-1996) *vintages* of Martha's Vineyard wines are made from newly replanted (post-*phylloxera*) vines. Trailside Vineyard is a newish label for *Cabernet*.

Helderberg (*Stellenbosch,* South Africa) The mountain on which are situated some of the best vineyards in Stellenbosch, including *Vergelegen, Yonder Hill, Avontuur,* and *Cordoba*. Competes with *Simonsberg*.

Joseph Henriot [on-ree-yoh] (*Champagne,* France) Modern *Champagne* house producing soft, rich wines. Now also shaking things up and improving wines at its recently purchased *Bouchard Père et Fils négociant* and at the William Fèvre Chablis estate in *Burgundy*. ★★★★ Rosé £££

Henriques & Henriques [hen-reeks] (*Madeira,* Portugal) One of the few independent producers still active in *Madeira*. Top quality. ★★★★★ 15 Year Old Verdelho £££

Henry of Pelham (*Ontario,* Canada) One of Canada's better producers of Chardonnay – plus a rare recommendable example of the Baco Noir grape.

H

Ⓣ **Henschke** [hench-kee] (*Adelaide Hills*, Australia) One of the world's best. From the long-established Hill of Grace with its 130-year-old vines and (slightly less intense) Mount Edelstone *Shirazes* to the new Abbott's Prayer *Merlot-Cabernet* from *Lenswood*, the *Riesling*, and Tilly's Vineyard white blend, there's not a poor wine here; the reds last forever. ★★★★★ 1997 **Mount Edelstone £££**

Ⓣ **Vin de Pays de l'Hérault** [Eh-roh] (*Languedoc-Roussillon*, France) Large region made famous by the Aimé Guibert's *Mas de Daumas Gassac*. Other producers such as *Grange-des-Pères* and Domaine Limbardie are following in his footsteps.

Ⓣ **Hermitage** [ayr-mee-tazh] (*Rhône*, France) Supreme Northern *Rhône appellation* for long-lived pure *Syrah*. Whites are less reliable. Red: 76 78 82 83 85 88 89 90 91 95 96 97 98 White: 82 85 87 88 89 90 91 94 95 96 97 98 00 *Belle Père & Fils;* Michel Bernard; *Chapoutier;* Chave; Dom. Colombier; *Grippat; Guigal; Delas; Bernard Faurie; Jaboulet Aîné; Sorrel; Cave de Tain l'Hermitage;* Tardieu-Laurent.

Ⓣ **James Herrick** [heh-rick] (*Languedoc-Roussillon*, France) Dynamic Briton who brought an Australian philosophy to southern France, planting extensive *Chardonnay* vineyards and producing good-value varietal wine. Now part of Southcorp (*Penfolds* etc).

Ⓣ **The Hess Collection** (*Napa Valley*, California) High-class *Cabernet* producer high in the *Mount Veeder* hills named after the owner's art collection (see *Vinopolis*). The lower-priced Hess Select *Monterey* wines are worth buying, too.

    Hessische Bergstrasse [hess-ishuh behrg-strah-suh] (Germany) Smallest *Anbaugebiet* capable of fine *Eisweins* and dry *Sylvaners* which can surpass those of nearby *Franken*. QbA/Kab/Spät: 85 88 89 90 91 92 93 94 95 96 97 98 99 00 Aus/Beeren/Tba: 83 85 88 89 90 91 92 93 94 95 96 97 98 99 00

Ⓣ **Heuriger** [hoy-rig-gur] (Austria) Austria's equivalent of *Beaujolais* Nouveau – except that this newborn wine is white and sold by the carafe in cafés. Of interest if only as a taste of the way most wine used to be drunk.

Ⓣ **Heyl zu Herrnsheim** [highl zoo hehrn-sime] (*Rheinhessen*, Germany) Organic estate in *Nierstein* with good *Riesling* from the Plettenthal vineyard.

Ⓣ **Heymann-Löwenstein** [hay-mun lur-ven-shtine] (*Mosel-Saar-Ruwer*, Germany) A rising star with bone dry to lusciously sweet Rieslings.

Ⓣ **Vinicola Hidalgo y Cia** [hid-algoh ee-thia] (*Jerez*, Spain) Specialty producer of impeccable dry "La Gitana" *sherry* and a great many own-label offerings. ★★★★ **Manzanilla Pasada Pastrada Single Vineyard Sherry ££**

Ⓣ **Cavas Hill** [kah-vas heel] (*Penedés*, Spain) Best-known for its sparkling wine, but also producing rich, fruity *Tempranillo* reds. A name to watch as Spain's wine industry evolves.

Ⓣ **Hill-Smith** (South Australia) Dynamic but still very classy firm, under the same family ownership as *Pewsey Vale, Yalumba,* and *Heggies* Vineyard, and now active in Tasmania (Jansz sparkling wine), New Zealand (*Nautilus*), and California (where its *Voss* wines are made). Also produces the Australian wine sold by E&J Gallo under its own Garnet Point label. ★★★ **2000 Estate Sauvignon Blanc ££**

Hill-Smith Estate

Barossa Valley, Australia

CHARDONNAY 1986

S. SMITH & SON PTY. LTD. EDEN VALLEY ROAD ANGASTON SOUTH AUSTRALIA H.V. McALPINE PRESERVATIVE (220) ADDED

750ml PRODUCE OF AUSTRALIA

Ⓣ **Hillstowe** [hil-stoh] (*South Australia*) Up-and-coming producer in the *McLaren Vale*, using grapes from various parts of the region to produce stylish *Chardonnay, Sauvignon Blanc,* and *Cabernet-Merlot.* ★★★★ 1998 The Pinch Row Lenswood Merlot £££

Ⓣ **Hilltops** (*New South Wales*, Australia) Exciting new coolish-climate area previously known as Young. The pioneers are McWilliams, which established its Barwang estate and label here. Stand by for classy *Cabernet Sauvignon*, *Merlot*, and *Shiraz*. **Demondrille; Barwang.**

H

Himmelreich [him-mel-raikh] (*Mosel,* Germany) One of the finest
vineyards in *Graach.* See JJ Prum. QbA/Kab/Spät: **86 88 89** 90 **91 92 93 94
95 96 97** *98 99 00.*Aus/Beeren/Tba: **83 85 88 89 90 91 92 93 94** *95 96 97
98 99 00*

Franz Hitzberger [fruntz hits-ber-gur] (*Wachau,* Austria) A name to
remember for reliable dry *Grüner Veltliner* and *Riesling.*

☨ **Paul Hobbs** (*Sonoma,* California) Former winemaker at *Simi,* and currently
engaged as a consultant at *Catena* and *Valdivieso,* Paul Hobbs produces fine
Pinot Noir, lean *Cabernet,* and rich *Chardonnay* from the memorably-named
"Dinner Vineyard".

Hochfeinste [hokh-fine-stuh] (Germany) "Very finest".

Hochgewächs QbA [hokh-geh-fex] (Germany) Recent official designation
for *Rieslings* which are as ripe as a *QmP* but can still only call themselves
QbA. This from a nation supposedly dedicated to simplifying what are
acknowledged to be the most complicated labels in the world.

Hochheim [hokh-hihm] (*Rheingau,* Germany) Village whose fine *Rieslings*
gave the English the word *"Hock".* QbA/Kab/Spät: **85 86 88 89 90** 91 **92 93**
94 **95 96 97** *98 99 00.*Aus/Beeren/Tba: **83 85 88 89 90** 91 **92 93 94** *95 96
97 98 99 00.* Geh'rat Aschrott; Konigen Victoria Berg.

☨ **Reichsgraf zu Hoensbroech** [rike-sgrahf tzoo hoh-ern sbroh-urch]
(*Baden,* Germany) A large estate specializing in *Pinot Blanc*
(Weissburgunder) and *Gris* Grauburgunder.

☨ **Höffstatter** [Hurf-shtah-ter] (*Alto Adige,* Italy) Star, new wave producer
with unusually good *Pinot Noir* and *Gewurztraminer.*

☨ **Hogue Cellars** [hohg] (*Washington State*) Highly dynamic, family-owned
Yakima Valley producer of good *Chardonnay, Riesling, Merlot,* and *Cabernet.*
★★★★ 1996 Genesis Syrah £££

☨ **Hollick** (*Coonawarra,* Australia) A good, traditional producer; the
Ravenswood is particularly worth seeking out. ★★★★ 1998 Coonawarra
Cabernet-Merlot £££

☨ **Dom. de l'Hortus** [Or-Toos] (*Languedoc-Roussillon,* France) Exciting spicy
reds from *Pic St. Loup* in the *Coteaux de Languedoc* that easily outclass many
an effort from big-name producers in the *Rhône.* ★★★★ 1998 Grande
Cuvée £££

☨ **Hosanna** [Oh-zah-nah] (*Pomerol, Bordeaux,* France) Christian Moueix's
sleek new stablemate for *Petrus* – produced from the best part of the
Certan-Guiraud vineyard,

☨ **Hospices de Beaune** [os-peess duh bohn] (*Burgundy,* France) Hospital
whose wines (often *cuvées* or blends of different vineyards) are sold at an
annual charity auction, the prices of which are erroneously thought to set
the tone for the *Côte d'Or* year. In the early 1990s, wines were generally
substandard, improving instantly in 1994 with the welcome return of
winemaker André Porcheret who, before leaving once again, proved
controversial by (in 1997) making wines that struck some critics (not this
one) as too big and rich. In any case, be aware that although price lists often
merely indicate "Hospices de Beaune" as a producer, all of the wines bought
at the auction are matured and bottled by local merchants, some of whom
are a great deal more scrupulous than others.

☨ **Houghton** [haw-ton] (*Swan Valley,* Australia) Long-established subsidiary
of *Hardy's.* Best known in Australia for its *Chenin*-based rich white blend
traditionally sold down under as "White *Burgundy*" and in Europe as
"HWB". The Wildflower Ridge commercial wines are good, as are the
ones from *Moondah Brook.* Look out too for the more recently launched
Cabernet-Shiraz-Malbec "Jack Mann", named after one of *Western Australia's*
pioneering winemakers. (Incidentally, those who've followed the recent
evolution of the Australian wine industry may be interested to learn that
Mr. Mann was once quoted as saying that any wine that couldn't be enjoyed
after being diluted 50–50 with water was too light-bodied).

H

Weingut von Hovel [fon huh-vel] (*Mosel-Saar-Ruwer*, Germany) A 200-year-old estate with fine *Rieslings* from great vineyards. These repay the patience that they demand.

Howard Park (*Western Australia*) John Wade is one of the best winemakers in *Western Australia*. He is also one of the finest *Riesling* producers in the whole of Australia. Madfish Bay is the *second label*. ★★★★ 1998 **Cabernet Sauvignon Merlot £££**

Howell Mountain [how-wel] (*Napa Valley*, California) Increasingly well-respected hillside region in the north of the *Napa Valley*, capable of fine whites and reds that justify its *AVA*. Red: **85 86 87 90 91 92 93 95 96 97 98 99 00**. White: **85 90 91** 92 **95 96 97** 98 99 *00 Beringer; Duckhorn; Dunn; la Jota; Liparita; Turley.*

Huadong Winery (*Shandong Province*, China) Dynamic joint venture producing the basic commercial Tsing Tao brand of wines. Recent *vintages* have shown a marked improvement.

Alain Hudelot-Noëllat [ood-uh-loh noh-el-lah] (*Burgundy*, France) A great winemaker whose generosity with oak is matched, especially in his *Grand Cru Richebourg* and *Romanée St.Vivant*, by intense fruit flavours.

Huelva [wel-vah] (*Extremadura*, Spain) *DO* of the *Extremadura* region, producing rather heavy whites and fortified wines.

Gaston Huët [oo-wet] (*Loire*, France) Organic winemaker Noël Pinguet produces top-quality individual vineyard examples of *Sec, Demi-Sec*, and *Moëlleux* wines. The non-*vintage* sparkling wine, though only made occasionally, is top class too.

Hugel et Fils [oo-gel] (*Alsace*, France) Reliable *négociant*. Best are the *late harvest* and Jubilee wines. The wine "Gentil" revives the tradition of blending different grape varieties.

Hungary Country too long known for its infamous *Bull's Blood* and *Olasz Rizling*, rather than *Tokaji*. **Disznókö; Egervin; Megyer; Kym Milne; Nagyrede; Neszmély; Pajsos; Royal Tokay; Hugh Ryman.**

Hunter Valley (*New South Wales*, Australia) The best-known wine region in Australia is ironically one of the least suitable places to make wine. When the vines are not dying of heat and thirst they are drowning beneath the torrential rains which like to fall at harvest time. Even so, the *Shirazes* and *Semillons* – traditionally sold as "*Hermitage*", "*Claret*", "*Burgundy*," "*Chablis*," and "*Hunter Valley Riesling*" – develop remarkably. **Allandale; Allanmere; Brokenwood; Evans Family; Lake's Folly; Lindemans; McWilliams; Petersons; Reynolds; Rosemount; Rothbury Estate; Tyrrells; Wilderness Estate.**

Hunter's (*Marlborough*, New Zealand) One of *Marlborough's* most consistent producers of ripe fruity *Sauvignon Blancs* and now a quality sparkling wine. ★★★★ 1998 **Oak Aged Sauvignon Blanc £££**

Ch. de Hureau [oo-roh] (*Loire*, France) One of the few producers to excel in all styles of *Saumur*, from rich red to sparkling white.

Huxelrebe [huk-sel-ray-buh] Minor white grape, often grown in England but proving what it can do when harvested late in Germany. **Anselmann (Germany); Barkham Manor; Nutbourne Manor (England).**

Hybrid [high-brid] Crossbred grape *Vitis vinifera* (European) x *Vitis labrusca* (North American) – an example is *Seyval Blanc*.

Hydrogen sulphide Naturally occurring rotten egg-like gas produced by yeasts as a by-product of fermentation, or alternatively by *reductive* conditions. Before bottling, may be cured by *racking*. If left untreated, hydrogen sulphide will react with other components in the wine to form *mercaptans*. Stinky bottled wines may often be "cleaned up" by decanting or by the addition of a copper coin. Unfortunately, too many go unnoticed, especially in France where wines are still sometimes relaxedly described as smelling of foxes (*renarder*) and in Spain where there are lots of stinky examples of *Ribera del Duero*.

I

Iambol [yam-bohl] (*Southern Region*, Hungary) Large, former cooperative which now makes commercial *Merlot* and *Cabernet Sauvignon* reds, particularly for sale overseas under the Domaines Boyar label.

Icewine Increasingly popular Anglicization of the German term *Eiswein*, used particularly by Canadian producers making luscious, spicily exotic wines from grapes of varieties like *Vidal*, frozen on the vine.

IGT – Indicazione Geografiche Tipici (Italy) New designation designed to create a home for quality non-*DOC/DOCG* wines that were previously sold as *Vino da Tavola*. Originally derided by just about everyone, but now recognised as the masterstroke that allowed Italy's producers to play by Old and New World rules simultaneously.

Vin de Pays de l'Île de Beauté [eel-duh-bow-tay] (*Corsica*, France) Designation that includes varietal wines (including *Pinot Noir*, *Cabernet*, *Syrah*, and *Merlot* as well as local grapes). Often better than the island's *ACs*.

Imbottigliato nel'origine [im-bot-til-yah-toh neh-loh-ree-zhee-nay] (Italy) Estate-bottled.

Imperial(e) [am-pay-ray-ahl] (*Bordeaux*, France) Bottle containing almost six and a half litres of wine (eight and a half bottles). Cherished by collectors partly through rarity, partly through the longevity bottles give the contents.

India Source of generally execrable table wine and surprisingly reliable sparkling wine, labelled as Marquis de Pompadour or *Omar Khayam*.

Inferno [een-fehr-noh] (*Lombardy*, Italy) Lombardy DOC. *Nebbiolo* red that needs ageing for at least five years. ★★★ 1994 Nino Negri ££

Inglenook Vineyards [ing-gel-nook] (*Napa Valley*, California) Once-great winery which, like *Beaulieu*, fell into the hands of the giant Grand Metropolitan. The Gothic building and vineyards now belong appropriately to Francis Ford Coppola. The now far-from-dazzling brand has been sold to the giant Canandaigua which has also recently bought *Franciscan* and *Simi*.

Inniskillin (*Ontario*, Canada) Long-established, pioneering winery which produces some good *Icewines* (from the Vidal grape), highly successful *Chardonnay*, improving *Pinot Noir*, and a rare example of a good *Maréchal Foch*.

Institut National des Appellations d'Origine (INAO) (France) French official body which designates and (half-heartedly) polices quality, and outlaws a number of manifestly sensible techniques such as irrigation and the blending of *vintages*, which are permitted elsewhere. Which is why *Appellation contrôlée* wines are often inferior to – and sell at lower prices than – the newer *Vins de Pays*.

International Wine Challenge (England) Wine competition, held in London by WINE Magazine and in, Tokyo, China, Hong Kong, and Singapore. (The author is founder-chairman).

International Wine & Spirit Competition (England) Wine competition, held in London.

Iphofen (*Franken*, Germany) One of the finest places to sample wines made from the *Sylvaner*. Modern wine drinkers may, however, prefer the *Rieslings*, which are fruitier and less earthy in style.

IPR – Indicação de Proveniência Regulamentada (Portugal) Designation for wines that fall beneath the top – *DOC* – grade and above the basic Vinho Regional.

Irancy [ee-ron-see] (*Burgundy*, France) Little-known light reds and rosés made in an area near *Chablis* from a blend of grapes including the *Pinot Noir* and the little-known *César*. Curiously, Irancy has the dignity of *AC* status, whereas nearby *Sauvignon de St. Bris* is merely a VDQS region. *Brocard*; Simonnet-Fèbvre.

J

🍷 **Iron Horse Vineyards** (*Sonoma* Valley, California) One of the most
   consistent and best sparkling-wine producers in the New World. Reds and
   still whites are increasingly impressive too.

Irouléguy [ee-roo-lay-gee] (*Southwest*, France) Earthy, spicy reds and rosés,
   and improving whites from Basque country where names seem to include an
   abundance of the letter "x". *Dom. Brana;* Etxegaraya; Irouléguy Cooperative.

🍷 **Isbabel Estate** (*Marlborough*, New Zealand) Producer of reliably good,
   rather than great *Sauvignon*, but some rather more impressive Riesling, and
   a stunning late harvest wine. ★★★★★ 1999 Noble Sauvage ££££

Isinglass [Ih-sing-glahs] *Fining* agent derived from sturgeon bladders.

🍷 **Isole e Olena** [ee-soh-lay ay oh-lay-nah] (*Tuscany*, Italy) Brilliant
   pioneering small *Chianti* estate with a pure *Sangiovese Super-Tuscan*,
   Cepparello, and Italy's first (technically illegal) *Syrah*. ★★★★★ 1998
   Cepparello ££££

🍷 **Isonzo** [Ih-son-zoh] (*Friuli-Venezia Giulia*, Italy) One of the best *DOCs*
   in this region, offering a wide range of varietal wines from some very
   progressive producers. Lis Neris-Pecorari; Ronco del Gelso; *Vie di Romans.*

Israel Once the source of appalling stuff, but the new-style varietal wines are
   increasingly impressive. *Golan Heights; Carmel.*

🍷 **Ch. d'Issan** [dee-son] (*Margaux 3ème Cru Classé,*
   Bordeaux, France) Recently revived *Margaux* third
   growth with lovely, recognizable blackcurranty
   Cabernet Sauvignon intensity. Good in 2000.

🍇 **Italian Riesling/Riesling Italico** [ee-tah-lee-
   koh] Not the great *Rhine Riesling*, but another
   name for an unrelated variety, which also goes by
   the names *Welschriesling, Riesling Italico,* and
   Laski Rizling, and is widely grown in Northern and
   Eastern Europe. At its best in Austria.

Italy Tantalizing, seductive, infuriating. In many
   ways the most exciting wine nation in the world, though, as ever, in a state
   of change as it reorganizes its wine laws. See individual regions.

J

🍷 **J** (Sonoma, California) Reliable California sparkling wine, launched by *Jordan*
   and now independently produced by Judy *Jordan.*

🍷 **JP Vinhos** (*Portugal*) See *Peter Bright.*

🍷 **Paul Jaboulet Aîné** [zha-boo-lay ay-nay] (*Rhône,* France) The wine world
   was saddened to learn of the death last year from a heart attack of Gérard
   Jaboulet, the highly popular international face of this family *négociant*
   which owns the illustrious *Hermitage* La Chapelle vineyard. Despite being
   overshadowed nowadays by *Guigal*, this remains a reliable producer of a
   wide range of wines apart from the La Chapelle, including white *Hermitage,*
   chunky *St. Joseph,* good *Côtes du Rhône,* and *Châteauneuf-du-Pape.*
   ★★★★★ 1998 Hermitage la Chapelle £££

🍷 **Jackson Estate** (*Marlborough*, New Zealand) Neighbour of *Cloudy Bay* and
   producer of *Sauvignon*, which doesn't quite have that winery's luster at the
   moment. The sparkling wine is good though. ★★★★ 1997 Sparkling ££

🍷 **Jacob's Creek** (*South Australia*) Brilliantly commercial *South Australian*
   wines made by *Orlando* and taken up a major step by the recent
   introduction of a decent sparkling wine and classy trophy-winning "Limited
   Release" reds and whites.

🍷 **Jacquart** [zha-kahr] (*Champagne*, France) Large cooperative with some top-
   class wines.

🍇 **Jacquère** [zha-kehr] The slightly citrusy grape of *Savoie.*

J

♀ **Jacquesson et Fils** [jak-son] (*Champagne,* France) A small *Champagne* house that deserves to be better known, particularly for its delicately stylish *Blanc de Blancs.* ★★★★ 1995 Grand Cru Avize £££

♀ **Louis Jadot** [zha-doh] (*Burgundy,* France) Good, sometimes great, *Beaune négociant* with a growing number of its own top-class vineyards in *Beaune,* *Chassagne-,* and Puligny-Montrachet. Jadot has also been a pioneering producer of *Rully* in the *Côte Chalonnaise.* Whites are most impressive. ★★★★ 1998 Volnay Clos des Chênes £££

♀ **Jaffelin** [zhaf-lan] (*Burgundy,* France) Small *négociant,* particularly good at supposedly "lesser" *appellations* – *Rully Blanc* and *Monthelie* are particularly good – but winemaker Bernard Repolt (who is now also responsible for the improving wines at *Bouchard Aîné*) is now showing his skills across the board. ★★★★ 1998 Monthelie £££

♀ **Joseph Jamet** [zha-may] (*Rhône,* France) Top-class *Côte Rôtie* estate, making wines that are more stylish than many in this *appellation.* ★★★★ 1998 Côte Rôtie Côte Brune ££££

♀ **Jamieson's Run** (*Coonawarra,* Australia) *Mildara's* pair of prize-winning, good-value red and white wines. Just what commercial wines hould be. ★★★★ 1999 Jamieson's Run Merlot ££

♀ **Dom. de la Janasse** [ja-nass] (*Rhône,* France) High-quality *Châteauneuf-du-Pape* estate, producing three individual wines under this *appellation,* plus a good *Côtes du Rhône* les Garrigues. ★★★★ 1998 Côtes du Rhône les Villages £££

♀ **Jansz** [yantz] (*Tasmania,* Australia) See *Yalumba* and *Pirie.*

♀ **Vin de Pays du Jardin de la France** [jar-da'n duh lah fronss] (*Loire,* France) Large *Loire* region that can produce alternatives to the region's *appellations,* but tends to offer light, unripe whites.

♀ **Robert Jasmin** [zhas-man] (*Rhône,* France) Traditionalist *Côte Rotie* estate, producing great wine despite (or thanks to) his dislike of new oak. ★★★★★ 1995 Côte Rôtie ££££

Jasnières [zhan-yehr] (*Loire,* France) On rare occasions bone-dry and – even rarer – *Moelleux,* sweet *Chenin Blanc* wines from *Touraine.* Buy carefully. Poorly made, over-sulphured efforts offer a pricy chance to taste the *Chenin* at its worst. White: 86 88 89 90 94 95 96 97 99 00 Sweet White: 76 83 85 86 88 89 90 94 95 96 97 99 00

♀ **Jasper Hill** (*Bendigo,* Australia) Winery in Heathcote with a cult following for both reds and whites – especially those from the Georgia's Paddock vineyard. ★★★★ 1997 Emily's Paddock Shiraz Cabernet Franc ££

♀ **Jaume Serra** [how-may seh-rah] (*Penedès,* Spain) Privately owned company which recently relocated from *Alella* to *Penedès,* and is doing good things with *Xarel-lo.*

♀ **Patrick Javillier** [zha-vil-yay] (*Burgundy,* France) Reliable, small merchant making meticulous village *Meursault.* ★★★★ 1998 Meursault les Clous £££

♀ **Henri Jayer** [zha-yay] (*Burgundy,* France) Now retired cult winemaker who is still represented on labels referring to Georges et Henri. Also an influence on the wines of *Méo-Camuzet.*

♀ **Robert Jayer-Gilles** [zhah-yay-zheel] (*Burgundy,* France) *Henri Jayer's* cousin, whose top wines – including an *Echézeaux* – bear comparison with those of his more famous relative. (His whites – particularly the *Aligoté* – are good too). ★★★★★ 1998 Echézeaux ££££

Jerez (de la Frontera) [hay-reth] (*Spain*) Center of the *sherry* trade, giving its name to entire *DO* area. *Gonzalez Byass; Lustau; Hidalgo; Barbadillo.*

♀ **Jermann** [zhehr-man] (*Friuli-Venezia Giulia,* Italy) Brilliant winemaker who gets outrageous flavours – and prices – out of every white grape variety he touches. Look out for the *Vintage* Tunina blend of *Tocai, Picolit,* and *Malvasia,* and the "Dreams" white blend plus the Ribolla-based Vinnae and the single-vineyard Capo Martino. Also good at *Chardonnay, Pinot Gris, Pinot Blanc,* and the *Cabernets.* ★★★★ 1999 Pinot Grigio Special £££

Jeroboam [dzhe roh-bohm] Large bottle; in *Champagne* holding three litres (four bottles); in *Bordeaux,* four and a half (six bottles). Best to make sure before writing your cheque.

Jesuitengarten [yez-oo-witten-gahr-ten] (*Rheingau,* Germany) One of Germany's top vineyards – well handled by *Bassermann-Jordan.* QbA/Kab/Spät: 85 86 88 89 90 91 92 93 94 95 96 97 98 99 00.Aus/Beeren/Tba: 83 85 88 89 90 91 92 93 94 95 96 97 98 99 00

Jeunes Vignes [zhuhn veeñ] Denotes vines too young for their crop to be sold as an *Appellation Contrôlée* wine.

♀ **Dom. François Jobard** [fron-swah joh-bahr] (*Burgundy,* France) Great white wine estate in *Meursault.* ★★★★ 1997 Meursault Genevrières £££

♀ **Dom. Joblot** [zhob-loh] (*Burgundy,* France) One of the top *domaine*s in *Givry.* ★★★ 1998 Givry £££

♀ **Charles Joguet** [zho-gay] (*Loire,* France) Recently-retired producer of the single-vineyard *Chinon* wines that last. The good work continues, however, and this remains one of the essential names to remember in this region. ★★★★ 1999 Chinon, Clos de la Cure ££

Johannisberg [zho-han-is-buhrg.] (*Rheingau,* Germany) Village making superb *Riesling,* which has lent its name to a *Bereich* covering all the *Rheingau.* QbA/Kab/Spät: 85 86 88 89 90 91 92 93 94 95 96 97 98 Aus/Beeren/Tba: 83 85 88 89 90 91 92 93 94 95 96 97 98

🍷 **Johannisberg Riesling** [rees-ling] California name for *Rhine Riesling.*

♀ **Johannishof** [zhoh-hah-niss-hoff] (*Rheingau,* Germany) Family-owned estate with fine examples of wines from *Johannisberg* and *Rüdesheim.*

♀ **Weingut Karl-Heinz Johner** [karl-hihntz yoh-nuh] (*Baden,* Germany) Former winemaker at *Lamberhurst,* now making exceptional oaky *Pinot Noir* in southern Germany. Also makes wine in New Zealand.

♀ **Pascal Jolivet** [zhol-lee-vay] (*Loire,* France) Superstar producer of modern *Sancerre* and *Pouilly-Fumé.* ★★★★ 1999 Sancerre £££

♀ **Nicolas Joly** [Zhoh-lee] (*Loire,* France) The biodynamic owner-winemaker behind the *Coulée de Serrant* in *Savennières.*

♀ **Jordan** (*Stellenbosch,* South Africa) Young winery whose California-trained winemakers first hit the mark with *Sauvignon* and *Chardonnay,* and are now doing as well with *Cabernet* and *Merlot.* ★★★★ 1999 Jordan Estate Chardonnay £££

♀ **Jordan** (*Sonoma Valley,* California) *Sonoma* winery surrounded by the kind of hype more usually associated with *Napa.* Table wines – from the *Alexander Valley* – are mostly good rather than great, though *J* the sparkling wine is of *Champagne* quality. ★★★★★ "J," Sonoma County ££££

♀ **Joseph** (*South Australia*) *Primo Estate*'s label for its top wines and olive oils.

♀ **Josmeyer** [jos-mi-yur] (*Alsace,* France) Estate producing wines that are more delicate and restrained than those of some of its neighbours. ★★★★ 1998 Gewürztraminer les Folastries £££

♀ **Weingut Toni Jost** [toh-nee yohst] (*Mittelrhein,* Germany) A new-wave producer with (well-sited) vines in Bacharach, good reds, and a penchant for experimenting (often successfully) with new oak barrels. ★★★★★ 1998 Wallufer Walkenberg Riesling Eiswein £££

♀ **La Jota** [lah hoh-tah] (*Napa Valley,* California) Small *Howell Mountain* producer with stylish reds, including an unusually good *Cabernet Franc.* ★★★★ 1997 Howell Mountain Cabernet Franc £££

♀ **Judd's Hill** (*Napa Valley,* California) Young winery with dazzling *Cabernets.* ★★★★ 1997 Cabernet Sauvignon Napa Valley £££.

Juffer [yoof-fuh] (*Mosel,* Germany) Famous vineyard in the village of *Brauneberg.* QbA/Kab/Spät: 85 86 88 89 90 91 92 93 94 95 96 97 98 99 00 Aus/Beeren/Tba: 83 85 88 89 90 91 92 93 94 95 96 97 98 99 00.

Jug wine (California) American term for quaffable *Vin Ordinaire.*

♀ **Marcel Juge** [zhoozh] (*Rhône,* France) Producer of one of the subtlest, classiest examples of *Cornas.* ★★★★ 1995 Cornas £££

J

⚊ **Juliénas** [joo-lee-yay-nas] (*Burgundy,* France) One of the 10 *Beaujolais Crus,* producing classic, vigorous wine which often benefits from a few years in bottle. 85 87 **88 89** 90 **91** 93 94 95 96 97 98 E. Aujas; Jean Benon; Bernard Broyer; François Condemine; Georges Descombes; *Georges Duboeuf;* Eventail des Producteurs; Pierre Ferraud; Paul Granger; Ch. de Juliénas; Henri Lespinasse; Dom. Michel Tête; Raymond Trichard.

⚊ **Weingut Juliusspital** [yoo-lee-yoos-shpit-ahl] (*Franken,* Germany) Top-class estate whose profits benefit the poor and sick. A good source of *Riesling* and *Sylvaner.*

Jumilla [hoo-mee-yah] (Spain) *DO* region in northern Murcia, on the north side of the River Segura, traditionally known for heavy high-alcohol wines but increasingly making lighter *Beaujolais*-style ones.

⚊ **Jurançon** [zhoo-ron-son] (*Southwest,* France) Rich, dry, apricoty white wines and excellent sweet wines that are made from the *Gros* and *Petit Manseng* 83 85 86 **89 90** 92 93 *95* 96 98 99 Bellegarde; Dom. J-P Bousquet; *Brana;* Bru-Baché; Castera; *Cauhapé;* Clos Guirouilh; Clos Lapeyre; Cru Lamouiroux; Clos Uroulat.

⚊ **Justin** (*San Luis Obispo,* California) A winery to watch, with stunning reds, including a great *Cabernet Franc* and Isosceles, a *Bordeaux* blend. ★★★★★ 1997 Isosceles San Luis Obispo County Reserve.

⚊ **Juvé y Camps** [hoo-vay ee kamps] (*Catalonia,* Spain) The exception which proves the rule – by making and maturing decent cava from traditional grapes and excellent *vintage Brut.*

K

Kabinett (Germany) First step in German quality ladder, for wines which achieve a certain natural sweetness.

Kaiserstuhl-Tuniberg [ki-sehr shtool too-nee-behrg] (*Baden,* Germany) Supposedly the finest *Baden* Bereich (actually, it covers a third of *Baden's* vineyards) with top villages producing rich, spicy *Riesling* and *Sylvaner* from volcanic slopes. Top producers here include Dr. Heger, Bercher, and Karl-Heinz Johner. QbA/Kab/Spät: **90** 91 **92 93** 94 **95 96 97** 98 Aus/Beeren/Tba: **88 89** 90 91 **92 93** 94 95 96 97 98 *99 00*

Kallstadt [kahl-shtaht] (*Pfalz,* Germany) Village containing the best-known and finest vineyard of Annaberg, making luscious full *Riesling.* QbA/Kab/Spät: 85 86 **88 89** 90 91 **92 93 94** 95 96 97 *98 99 00* Aus/Beeren/Tba: **83 85 88 89 90** 91 **92 93 94** *95 96 97 98 99 00*

⚊ **Kalin** (Sonoma County, California) Producer of unusually long-lived *Pinot Noirs* and *Chardonnays.* Examples from the early 1990s seem younger than many of their peers. ★★★★ 1993 Pinot Noir, Cuvée DD ££££

⚊ **Kamptal** [kamp-tal] (*Niederösterreich,* Austria) Up-and-coming region for rich dry white *Grüner Veltliners* and *Rieslings,* thanks largely to the efforts of star producer *Bründlmayer.*

⚊ **Kanonkop Estate** [ka-non-kop] (*Stellenbosch,* South Africa) An estate with largely traditional equipment, but a modern approach to its unusually classy *Pinotage.* The light red blend, "Kadette," is good too, and *Bordeaux*-style "Paul Sauer" is one of the *Cape's* best. Rebuilding itself after the tragic devestation of the fires in 2000. ★★★★ 1997 Paul Sauer ££

⚊ **Kanzem** [kahnt-zem] (*Mosel-Saar-Ruwer,* Germany) Less well-known commune near Wiltingen.

⚊ **Karlsmühle** [kahl-smoo-lur] (*Mosel-Saar-Ruwer,* Germany) Very high-class estate producing good Riesling in the heart of the *Ruwer.*

⚊ **Karly** (Anmador County, California) A name to remember if you enjoy rich, dark *Zinfandels* with loads of character. Sadie Upton is the best of the single-vineyard examples. Try the *Syrah* and the Orange *Muscat* too.

K

☥ **Karthäuserhof** [kart-oy-ser-hof] (*Mosel-Saar-Ruwer,* Germany) This estate, which is located on the *Ruwer,* is not only the producer of great dry Rieslings in Eitelsbach, its bottles are also a very welcome exception to the generally uniform presentation of German labels. They are naked – apart from a stylish neck label. ★★★★★ 1997 Riesling Kabinett Eitelsbacher Karthäuserhofberg Karthäuserhof £££

☥ **Katnook Estate** (*Coonawarra,* Australia) Small estate making the highly commercial Deakin Estate wines as well as plenty of such innovative stuff as a *late harvest Coonawarra Chardonnay* and top-class *Coonawarra Merlot* and *Cabernet.* ★★★★ 1997 Prodigy Shiraz £££

☥ **Katsaros** [kaht-sah-rohs] (Greece) One of the classiest new-wave *Cabernet Sauvignon* producers in Greece.

☥ **Ch. Kefraya** [keh-frah-ya] (Lebanon) *Ch. Musar* is not the only Lebanese winery; this is the other one worth taking seriously.

🍇 **Kekfrankos** [kek-frenk-kosh] Another name for *Blaufränkisch.*

Kellerei/Kellerabfüllung [kel-luh-ri/kel-luh-rap few loong] (Germany) Cellar/producer/estate-bottled.

☥ **Kendall-Jackson** (*Clear Lake,* California) Extraordinarily dynamic, fast-growing producer at the centre of takeover rumours in 2001, making popular, consistent but somewhat off-dry "Vintner's Reserve" *Chardonnay* and *Sauvignon,* of which millions of cases are produced. Reds and "Grand Reserve" wines are better. Other associated brands include Cambria and (the more generally impressive) *Stonestreet.* ★★★★ 1997 Grand Reserve Cabernet Sauvignon ££

KENDALL-JACKSON

1988
The Proprietor's
CHARDONNAY
California

☥ **Kenwood Vineyards** (*Sonoma Valley,* California) Classy Sonoma winery with good single-vineyard *Chardonnays* and impressive *Cabernets* (including one made from the author Jack London's vineyard). The other stars are the brilliant *Zinfandel* and *Sauvignon.* ★★★★★ 1997 Valley of the Moon £££

🍇 **Kerner** [kehr-nuh] A white grape variety. A *Riesling*-cross that is grown in Germany and also widely in England. **Anselmann.**

☥ **Weingut Reichsgraf von Kesselstatt** [rikh-graf fon kes-sel-shtat] (*Mosel-Saar-Ruwer,* Germany) Large, impressive collection of four *Riesling* estates spread between the *Mosel, Saar,* and *Ruwer.* ★★★★ Ockfener Bockstein Riesling ££

Kiedrich [kee-drich] (*Rheingau,* Germany) Top village high in the hills whose vineyards can produce great intense *Rieslings.* QbA/Kab/Spät: 85 86 88 89 90 91 92 93 94 95 96 97 98 99 00 Aus/Beeren/Tba: 83 85 88 89 90 91 92 93 94 95 96 97 98 99 00

Kientzheim [keents-him] (*Alsace,* France) Village noted for its *Riesling.*

☥ **André Kientzler** [keent-zluh] (*Alsace,* France) Classy producer with better-than-average *Pinot Blanc.* ★★★★ 1998 Pinot Blanc d'Alsace ££

☥ **JF Kimich** [kih-mikh] (*Pfalz,* Germany) Fast-rising star making rich spicy wines typical of the *Pfalz. Gewürztraminers* are as good as *Rieslings.*

☥ **King Estate** (*Oregon*) Huge, glitzy new winery whose own vineyards are in part of the state that has yet to produce top-class wine. Releases so far include decent *Pinot Gris Reserve* and *Zinfandel.* The *Reserve Pinot Noir* is pleasant but so far unexceptional. ★★★ 1998 Pinot Noir £££

☥ **Kingston Estate** (*Murray Valley,* South Australia) Controversial commercial producer in the Riverland.

☥ **Kiona** [kih-yoh-nah] (*Washington State*) Small producer in the middle of nowhere with a penchant for berryish reds and intensely flavoured *late harvest* wines. ★★★★ 1997 Cabernet £££

Kir (*Burgundy,* France) A mixture of sweet fortified *Crème de Cassis* (regional speciality of *Burgundy*) with simple and often rather *acidic* local white wine (*Aligoté,* or basic *Bourgogne Blanc*) to produce a delicious summertime drink.

K

Ⓣ **Ch. Kirwan** [keer-wahn] (*Margaux 3ème Cru Classé, Bordeaux,* France) Belatedly coming out of prolonged doldrums. Still doesn't warrant its third growth status. 82 83 85 86 88 **89 90 93** 95 96 97 98 00

Ⓣ **Kistler** [kist-luh] (*Sonoma Valley,* California) Probably California's top *Chardonnay* producer, with a really dazzling range of uncompromising complex single-vineyard wines and fast-improving *Pinot Noirs. Burgundy* quality at *Burgundy* prices. ★★★★★ **1997 Kistler Vineyard Chardonnay £££**

Ⓣ **Klein Constantia** [kline kon-stan-tee-yah] (*Constantia,* South Africa) Small, dynamic estate on the site of the great 17th-century *Constantia* vineyard. After a slightly disappointing patch, wines seem to be right back on form and proving a credit to the *Constantia* region. The star wine is the sweet "Vin de Constance" which is sadly hard to find outside South Africa. ★★★★ **2000 Sauvignon Blanc ££**

Klüsserath [kloo-seh-raht] (*Mosel-Saar-Ruwer,* Germany) Small village best known for *Sonnenuhr* and Königsberg vineyards.

Ⓣ **Knappstein** [nap-steen] (*Clare Valley,* South Australia). Now part of the *Mildara-Blass* stable and no longer associated with founder Tim (see *Knappstein Lenswood*) but still producing good *Clare Valley* wines.

Ⓣ **Emerich Knoll** [knowl] (*Wachau,* Austria). Maker of stunning new-wave *Riesling* and *Grüner Veltliner* wines.

Koehler-Ruprecht [kurler-roop-recht] (*Pfalz,* Germany) Classy estate in Kallstadt, producing good *Riesling* and unusually fine *Spätburgunder.*

Ⓣ **Konnsgaard** [kons-gahd] (*Napa,* California) The former winemaker at *Newton,* and the unsung hero behind that winery's success, removes his light from under a bushel with his own top-class *Chardonnay.* ★★★★ **1997 £££**

Ⓣ **Konocti Cellars** [ko-nok-tih] (*Lake County,* California) Dynamic producer with good straightforward wines.

Kosher (Israel) Wine made under complex rules. Every seventh vintage is left unharvested and non-Jews are barred from the winemaking process.

Ⓣ **Korbel** [Kor-BEL] (*Sonoma,* California) Big producer of basic California sparkling wine. Better wines like Le Premier Reserve show what can be done.

Ⓣ **Kourtakis** [koor-tah-kis] (Greece) One of Greece's growing number of dynamic wine companies with unusually recommendable whites and the characterful native *Mavrodaphnes.* ★★★★ **1996 Kouros Nemea £££**

Ⓣ **Weinlaubenhof Weingut Alois Kracher** [Ah-loys krah-kuh] (*Neusiedlersee,* Austria) Frequent trophy winner at the *International Wine Challenge,* and source of world-class, (very) *late harvest* wines including an unusual effort which blends the *Chardonnay* with the *Welschriesling.* ★★★★★ **1997 Scheurebe Beerenauslese Nouvelle Vague No. 3 ££££**

Krems/Kremstal [krems] (*Wachau,* Austria) Town and *Wachau* vineyard area producing Austria's most stylish *Rieslings* from terraced vineyards.

Kreuznach [kroyt-znahkh] (*Nahe,* Germany) Northern *Bereich,* boasting fine vineyards situated around the town of *Bad Kreuznach.* QbA/Kab/Spät: 85 86 **88 89 90** 91 *92 93* 94 **95 96 97** 98 99 00 Aus/Beeren/Tba: **83 85 88 89 90** 91 *92 93 94* 95 96 97 98 99 00

Ⓣ **Dom. Kreydenweiss** [cry-den-vice] (*Alsace,* France) Top-class organic producer with particularly good *Muscat, Pinot Gris,* and *Riesling.* ★★★★ 1998 Riesling Kastelberg le Château £££

Ⓣ **Krondorf** [kron-dorf] (*Barossa Valley,* Australia) Fosters-owned winery specializing in traditional, big *Barossa* style wines. ★★★★ **1997 Krondorf Family Reserve Cabernet Sauvignon £££**

Ⓣ **Krug** [kroog] (*Champagne,* France) The *Ch. Latour of Champagne.* Great vintage wine, extraordinary rosé, and pure *Chardonnay* from the *Clos de Mesnil* vineyard. The *Grande Cuvée* is theoretically the ultimate non-vintage, thanks to the greater proportions of aged *Reserve* wine, but recent releases have been a little variable. Let's see what the effect the recent assimilation into the *Moët/Mercier/Veuve Clicquot/Pommery/Ruinart* stable will have.

L

Kruger-Rumpf [kroo-gur roompf] (*Nahe,* Germany) *Nahe* estate, demonstrating the potential of varieties like the *Scheurebe.* ★★★★★ 1998 Gold Cap Nahe Münsterer Pittersberg Riesling Auslese ££££

Kuentz-Bas [koontz bah] (*Alsace,* France) Reliable producer for *Pinot Gris* and *Gewurztraminer.* ★★★★ 1998 Pinot Gris Collection Rare £££

Kuhling-Gillot [koo-ling gil-lot] (*Rheinhessen,* Germany) Hitherto little-known producer who is now fast developing a reputation for rich and concentrated wines.

Kumeu River [koo-myoo] (*Auckland,* New Zealand) Michael Brajkovich is successful with a wide range of wines, including a very unusual dry *botrytis Sauvignon* which easily outclasses many a dry wine from *Sauternes.* ★★★★★ 1998 Mate's Vineyard Chardonnay £££

Kunde [koon-day] (*Sonoma,* California) Producer of good *Chardonnay* and *Zinfandel.* ★★★★ 1998 Sonoma Reserve Chardonnay £££

Weingut Franz Künstler [koonst-luh] (*Rheingau,* Germany) A new superstar producer with superlative *Riesling.* ★★★★ 1998 Hochheimer Hölle Riesling Auslese Gold Cap £££

KWV (*Cape,* South Africa) Huge cooperative formed by the South African government at a time when surplus wine seemed set to flood the industry and, for a long time, maintained by the National Party when it needed to keep members of the big wine cooperatives, well, cooperative. Winemaking has improved recently – especially the wines sold under the Cathedral Cellars label. Perold is the name of a new, pricy, "super-premium" red.

L

Ch. Labégorce [la-bay-gors] (*Bordeaux,* France) Good traditional *Margaux.* 75 79 81 **82 83 85** 86 88 **89 90** 94 95 96 97 98 00

Ch. Labégorce-Zédé [la-bay-gors zay-day] (*Margaux Cru Bourgeois, Bordeaux,* France). An estate that belongs to the same Thienpont family as *Vieux Château Certan* and *le Pin.* A name to remember for wine beyond its Bourgeois class. 81 82 **83 85 86** 88 **89 90** 92 94 95 96 97 98 99 00

Labouré-Roi [la-boo-ray rwah] (*Burgundy,* France) A highly successful and very commercial *négociant,* responsible for some quite impressive wines. See *Cottin Frères.* ★★★★ 1998 Vosne Romanée £££

Labrusca [la-broo-skah] *Vitis labrusca,* the North American species of vine, making wine which is often referred to as "foxy". All *vinifera* vine stocks are grafted on to *phylloxera*-resistant *labrusca* roots, though the vine itself is banned in Europe and its wines, thankfully, are almost unfindable.

Ch. Lacoste-Borie [la-cost-bo-ree] (*Pauillac, Bordeaux,* France) The reliable *second label* of *Grand-Puy-Lacoste.* ★★★★ 1998 £££

Lacryma Christi [la-kree-mah kris-tee] (*Campania,* Italy) Literally, "tears of Christ," the melancholy name for some amiable, light, rather rustic reds and whites. Those from Vesuvio are *DOC.* Grotta del Sole; Mastroberardino.

Ladoix [la-dwah] (*Burgundy,* France) Village (sometimes also referred to as Ladoix-Serrigny) including parts of *Corton* and *Corton-Charlemagne.* The village wines are not well-known and because of this some bargains are still to be found. White: 79 **85 86 88** 89 **90 92 95** 96 97 98 99 Red: 78 83 **85** 87 88 **89 90** 92 94 95 96 97 98 99 Capitain-Gagnerot; Chevalier Père et Fils; *Dubreuil-Fontaine;* Gay; Launay; Maréchale; André Nudant.

Patrick de Ladoucette [duh la-doo-set] (*Loire,* France) Intense *Pouilly-Fumé,* sold as "Baron de L". Other wines are greatly improved in recent years. ★★★★ 1998 Comte Lafond Blanc £££

Michel Lafarge [la-farzh] (*Burgundy,* France) One of the very best producers in *Volnay* – and indeed *Burgundy.* Fine, long-lived, modern wine. ★★★★ 1998 Volnay Clos des Chênes £££

L

℧ **Ch. Lafaurie-Peyraguey** [la-foh-ree pay-rah-gay] (*Sauternes Premier Cru Classé, Bordeaux*, France) Much-improved *Sauternes* estate that has produced creamy, long-lived wines in the 1980s and in the 1990s. 78 80 81 82 83 85 86 88 89 90 96 *95 97 98 00* ★★★★ 1990 ££££

℧ **Ch. Lafite-Rothschild** [la-feet roh-chihld] (*Pauillac Premier Cru Classé, Bordeaux*, France) Often almost impossible to taste young, this *Pauillac* first growth is still one of the monuments of the wine world – especially since the early 1980s. A brilliant 1998 and 2000. The *second wine, Carruades*, is worth looking out for, too. 61 78 **81 82** 83 84 85 **86** 87 **88 89 90** 91 92 93 *94 95 96 97 98 99 00* ★★★★ **2000 ££££**

℧ **Ch. Lafleur** [la-flur] (*Pomerol, Bordeaux*, France) *Christian Moueix's* pet *Pomerol*, often on a par with the wine *Moueix* makes at *Pétrus* – though in a more understated way. 61 62 66 70 75 78 79 **82** 83 85 86 88 89 90 92 93 94 *95 96 97 98 99 00*

℧ **Ch. Lafleur-Gazin** [la-flur-ga-zan] (*Pomerol, Bordeaux*, France) Another good *Moueix* wine. 82 83 **85** 86 **88** 89 **90** 92 93 94 95 96 97 98 99 00

℧ **Dom. des Comtes Lafon** [day comt la-fon] (*Burgundy*, France) The best domaine in *Meursault* (and one of the very best in the whole of Burgundy) with great vineyards in *Volnay*, a small slice of *Montrachet*, and a new venture with more affordable wines in the Mâconnais. The Côte d'Or wines last forever. Now biodynamic. ★★★★ **1998 Meursault Charmes ££££**

℧ **Ch. Lafon-Rochet** [la-fon-ro-shay] (*St. Estèphe 4ème Cru Classé, Bordeaux*, France) Very classy modern *St. Estèphe*. Impressive in 1998. 70 79 81 82 **83** 85 86 **88 89 90** 91 92 93 94 95 96 97 98 99 00

℧ **Alois Lageder** [la-gay-duh] (*Trentino-Alto Adige*, Italy) New-wave producer of the kind of wine the *Alto Adige* ought to make.
Lago di Caldaro [la-goh dih kahl-dah-roh] (*Trentino-Alto Adige*, Italy) Also known as the *Kalterersee*, using the local *Schiava* grape to make cool light reds with slightly unripe, though pleasant, fruit.

℧ **Ch. Lagrange** [la-gronzh] (*St. Julien 3ème Cru Classé, Bordeaux*, France) A once underperforming third growth rejuvenated by Japanese cash and local know-how (for a while from Michel Delon of *Léoville-las-Cases*). Look out for *Les Fiefs de Lagrange*, the impressive *second wine*.

℧ **Ch. Lagrange** [la-gronzh] (*Pomerol, Bordeaux*, France) Yet another *Moueix* property – and yet another good wine. 70 75 78 81 **82** 83 **85** 86 87 88 89 90 92 93 94 95 96 97 98 ★★★ 1998 £££

❀ **Lagrein** [la-grayn] (Italy) Cherryish red grape of northeast Italy.

℧ **Ch. la Lagune** [la-goon] (*Haut-Médoc 3ème Cru Classé, Bordeaux*, France) Lovely accessible wines which last well and are worth buying even in poorer years. A great 2000. 70 78 79 **82** 85 **86 88 89 90** 92 93 **94** 95 96 97 98 99 00.
Lake County (California) Vineyard district salvaged by improved irrigation techniques and now capable of some fine wines as well as *Kendall Jackson's* highly commercial efforts.

℧ **Lake's Folly** (*Hunter Valley*, Australia) Max Lake, surgeon-turned-winemaker/writer/researcher has great theories about the sexual effects of sniffing various kinds of wine. He is also a leading Australian pioneer of *Chardonnay*, with an unusually successful *Hunter Valley Cabernet Sauvignon*. Wines now made by Max's son, Stephen. ★★★★ 1998 Chardonnay £££

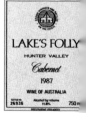

℧ **Lalande de Pomerol** [la-lond duh po-meh-rol] (*Bordeaux*, France) Bordering on *Pomerol* with similar, but less fine wines. Still generally better than similarly priced *St. Emilions*. Some good-value *Petits-Châteaux*. **Ch. Garraud; Grand Ormeau.**
Ch. Lalande-Borie [la-lond bo-ree] (*St. Julien, Bordeaux*, France) In the same stable as *Ch. Ducru-Beaucaillou*. Reliable wines. 82 85 86 88 89 **90** 91 92 93 94 95 96 97 98 99 00

℧ **Ch. Lamarque** [la-mahrk] (*Haut-Médoc Cru Bourgeois, Bordeaux*, France) Spectacular *château* with good, quite modern, wines.

L

Ⓣ **Lamborn Family** (*Napa Valley,* California) Small *Howell Mountain* producer, focusing on rich, concentrated, long-lived *Zinfandel*.

Ⓣ **Dom. des Lambrays** [lom-bray] (*Burgundy,* California) Under new ownership and promising further improvements in quality. Already very worthwhile, though. ★★★★ 1999 Clos des Lambrays £££

Ⓣ **Lambrusco** [lam-broos-koh] (*Emilia-Romagna,* Italy) Famous/infamous low-strength (7.5 per cent) sweet, sparkling UK and North American version of the sparkling, dry, red wine favoured in Italy. The real thing – which is less commercial, but far more fascinating with its dry, unripe cherry flavour – comes with a cork rather than a screw-cap. Barbolini; F Bellei; Cavicchioli; O Lini.

Ⓣ **Lamoureaux Landing** [lam-moh-roh] (*New York State*) Impressive young *Chardonnay* specialist in the *Finger Lakes.*

Ⓣ **Landmark** (*Sonoma,* California) Small *Chardonnay* specialist with rich, fruity, buttery wines from individual "Damaris" and "Overlook" vineyards, and blends of Chardonnay from Sonoma, Santa Barbara, and Monterey.

Landwein [land-vine] (Germany) The equivalent of a French *Vin de Pays* from one of 11 named regions. Often dry.

Ⓣ **Ch. Lanessan** [la-neh-son] (*Haut-Médoc Cru Bourgeois, Bordeaux,* France). Recommendable *Cru Bourgeois* now more influenced by new oak than it used to be, but still quite traditional fare.

Langelois [lung-ger-loyss] (*Kamptal,* Austria). One of the best wine communes in Austria – the place where you will find such producers as Hiedler and Bründlmayer.

Langhe [lang-gay] (*Piedmont,* Italy) A range of hills; when preceded by "*Nebbiolo* delle," indicates declassified *Barolo* and *Barbaresco.* Also, the denomination now used by Angelo *Gaja* for his single-vineyard wines.

Ⓣ **Ch. Langoa-Barton** [lon-goh-wah-bahr-ton] (*St. Julien 3ème Cru Classé, Bordeaux,* France) *Léoville-Barton's* (slightly) less complex kid brother. Often one of the best bargain classed growths in *Bordeaux.* Well made in poor years. 70 75 76 78 79 82 83 85 86 88 89 90 91 92 93 94 95 96 97 98 99 00 ★★★★★ 1998 ££££

Languedoc-Roussillon [long-dok roo-see-yon] (*Midi,* France) One of the world's largest wine regions (producing 10 per cent of the planet's wine) and, until recently, a major source of the wine lake. But a combination of government-sponsored uprooting and activity by *flying winemakers* and (a few) dynamic producers is beginning to turn this into a worrying competitor for the New World. The region includes appellations like *Fitou, Corbières and Minervois, Faugères, St. Chinian, Coteaux de Languedoc, Côtes de Roussillon,* and a torrent of *Vin de Pays d'Oc.* Sadly, many of the best, more ambitious, wines are hard to find outside France where they are developing a cult following among consumers who relish the value they often offer.

Ⓣ **Lanson** [lon-son] (*Champagne,* France) Much-improved *Champagne* house with decent non-vintage "Black Label", good *Demi-sec*, and fine *vintage champagne.* ★★★★ 1994 Blanc de Blancs ££££

Ⓣ **Casa Lapostolle** [la-pos-tol] (*Colchagua Valley,* Chile) Instant superstar. Belongs to the owners of Grand Marnier and benefits from the expertise of *Michel Rolland.* Cuvée Alexandre *Merlot* reds have been a classy instant success, though the whites need more work. The 1997 Clos Apalta *Merlot*-Carmenère blend is one of the (relatively) cheapest of Chile's new-wave flagship reds. It easily justifies its (£45) price tag. ★★★★★ 1997 Clos Apalta ££££

Ⓣ **Ch. Larcis-Ducasse** [lahr-see doo-kass] (*St. Emilion Grand Cru Classé, Bordeaux,* France) Lightish wines rarely live up to the potential of its hillside site. 66 78 79 81 82 83 85 86 88 89 90 94 95 96 97 98 00 ★★★ 1998 £££

Ⓣ **Ch. Larmande** [lahr-mond] (*St. Emilion Grand Cru Classé, Bordeaux,* France) A property to watch for well-made ripe-tasting wines. 85 86 88 89 90 92 93 94 95 96 97 98

L

Dom. Laroche [la-rosh] (*Burgundy*, France) Highly reliable *Chablis* négociant with some enviable vineyards of its own, including top-class *Premiers* and *Grands Crus*. At more affordable prices, there are also reliable southern French *Chardonnay Vin de Pays d'Oc* (including a tasty new super-premium red effort that is still – as we go to press – unnamed) and innovative wines from *Corsica*. ★★★★ **1998 Chablis Réserve de l'Obédiencerie £££**

Ch. Lascombes [las-komb] (*Margaux 2ème Cru Classé, Bordeaux*, France) Subtle second growth *Margaux* which can exemplify the perfumed character of this *appellation*, but has been underperforming until recently. A change of owners should improve matters, and the 2000 looks good. **70 75 82 83 85 86 88 89 90** *94 95 96 97 98 00* ★★★★ **1996 ££££**

Laski Riesling/Rizling [lash-kee riz-ling] (Former Yugoslavia) Yugoslav name for a white grape, unrelated to the *Rhine Riesling*, which is also known as the *Welsch, Olasz*, and *Italico* Riesling.

Ch. de Lastours [duh las-toor] (*Languedoc-Roussillon*, France) Combined winery and home for people with mental disabilities which frequently provides ample proof that *Corbières* can rival *Bordeaux*. Look out for the *cuvée* Simone Descamps. ★★★★ **1995 Corbières ££**

Late harvest Made from (riper) grapes picked after the main vintage. Should have at least some *botrytis*.

Late-bottled Vintage (Port) (LBV) (*Douro*, Portugal) Officially, bottled four or six years after a specific (usually nondeclared) *vintage*. Until the late 1970s, this made for a *vintage port*-style wine that matured early, was light and easy to drink, but needed to be decanted. Until recently, the only houses to persevere with this style were *Warre's* and *Smith Woodhouse*, labelling their efforts *"Traditional" LBV*. Almost every other LBV around was of the filtered, "modern" style pioneered by *Taylors*. These taste like upmarket *ruby* and *vintage character ports*, need no decanting, and bear little resemblance to real *vintage* or even *crusted port*. Belatedly, a growing number of producers are now confusingly offering "Traditional" as well as modern LBV. For the moment, buyers can tell one style from the other by reading the small print, but there are proposals from the port shippers to ban the use of the word "Traditional". If they do, the same name will be used for these two different styles of wine. As one very prominent retired *port* maker admitted, he and his competitors have always done well out of confusing their clients.

Latium/Lazio [lah-tee-yoom] (Italy) The vineyard area surrounding Rome, including *Frascati* and Marino. ***Fontana Candida;*** **Falesco**.

Louis Latour [loo-wee lah-toor] (*Burgundy*, France) Underperforming *négociant* who still pasteurizes his – to my mind, consequently muddy-tasting – reds, treating them in a way no quality-conscious New World producer would contemplate. Some whites, however, including *Corton-Charlemagne*, can be sublime, and Latour deserves credit for pioneering regions such as *Mâcon Lugny* and the *Ardèche*.

Ch. Latour [lah-toor] (*Pauillac Premier Cru Classé, Bordeaux*, France) Recently bought – from its British owners, Allied Domecq – by the same self-made French millionaire who recently bought Christie's. First growth *Pauillac* which can be very tricky to judge when young, but which develops majestically. *Les Forts de Latour* is the – often worthwhile – second label. The 1992 is a good example of a generally disappointing year and the 1999 and 2000 were both unquestionably among the very top wines of the vintage. **61** 62 64 **66** 67 **70** 73 **75** 76 **78** 79 80 81 **82** 83 **85 86 88 89 90 91 92 93** *94 95 96 97 98 99 00*

Ch. Latour-à-Pomerol [lah-toor ah po-meh-rol] (*Pomerol, Bordeaux*, France) A great-value, small (3,500-case) *Pomerol* estate under the same ownership as *Ch. Pétrus* and the same *Moueix* winemaking team. It is a little less concentrated than its big brother, but then it is around a quarter of the price, too. **82** 83 **85** 86 **88 89 90** 92 93 *94 95 96 98 00*★★★★ **1995 ££££**

L

℥ **Ch. Latour-Martillac** [la-toor mah-tee-yak] (*Graves Cru Classé, Bordeaux,* France) Good, sometimes overlooked reds and whites. Red: **88 89 90** *94 95 96 98 00* White: **89 90 93 94 96 97** *98 99 00*

Laudun [loh-duhn] (*Rhône,* France) Named village of *Côtes du Rhône,* with peppery reds and attractive rosés.

℥ **Laurel Glen** (*Sonoma Mountain,* California) Small hillside estate with *claret*-style reds that are respected by true Californian wine lovers. Terra Rosa is the accessible *second label.* ★★★★ 1998 Cabernet ££

℥ **Dominique Laurent** [Loh-ron] (*Burgundy,* France) A young *négociant* founded a few years ago by a former pastry chef who has rapidly shown his skills at buying and maturing top-class wines from several *appellation*s.

℥ **Laurent-Perrier** [law-ron pay-ree-yay] (*Champagne,* France) Historically one of the more reliable larger houses, though some recent bottlings have seemed variable. Grand Siècle is the most interesting wine.

℥ **Lavaux** [la-voh] (Switzerland) A major wine region to the north of Lake Geneva, broken down into several communal appellations such as Dezaleym Epesses and St.-Saphorin. This is a good place to taste varied examples of *Chasselas* (known here as "*Fendant*") and Pinot Noir.

℥ **Ch. Laville Haut-Brion** [la-veel oh-bree-yon] (*Graves Cru Classé, Bordeaux,* France) Exquisite white *Graves* that lasts for 20 years or more. 62 **66 75 82 83 85 86 88 89 90 93 94 95** *96 97 98 99 00*

℥ **Lawson's Dry Hills** (*Marlborough,* New Zealand) Producer of New Zealand's best 1999 *Sauvignon Blanc* and an unusually good *Gewürztraminer.*

℥ **Ch. Lazaridi** (Greece) One of Greece's best producers of red wines, making no use of the national appellation system.

℥ **Lazy Creek** (*Sonoma,* California) An Anderson Valley *Pinot Noir* producer to watch. ★★★★ 1998 Unfiltered Pinot Noir £££

℥ **Kostas Lazarides** (Greece) An up-and-coming producer of various styles of wine, including an unusually good rosé.

Lazio [lat-zee-yoh] (Italy) See *Latium.*

LBV (*Douro,* Portugal) See *Late-bottled Vintage.*

Lean Lacking body.

℥ **Leasingham** (*South Australia*) BRL *Hardy* subsidiary in the *Clare Valley* that makes top-flight reds and whites, including great *Shiraz, Cabernet,* and *Chardonnay.* ★★★★ 1998 Bin 61 Shiraz £££

Lebanon Best known for the remarkable *Ch. Musar* from the *Bekaa Valley.*

℥ **Leconfield** [leh-kon-feeld] (*South Australia*) Reliable producer of intense *Coonawarra* reds. (Ralph Fowler, the man behind the award-winning recent vintages, has his own wine now and works for *Chapoutier,* Australia).

Lees or lie(s) The sediment of dead yeasts that fall in the barrel or vat as a wine develops. *Muscadet* – like some other white wines – is aged *Sur Lie.* Producers of modern *Chardonnay* also leave their wine in its lees, stirring it occasionally to maximize richness – the rich flavour provided by the yeasts.

℥ **Leeuwin Estate** [loo-win] (*Margaret River,* Western Australia) Showcase winery (and concert venue) whose vineyards were originally picked out by *Robert Mondavi.* The genuinely world-class ("art label") *Chardonnay* is one of Australia's priciest and longest-lived. Other wines are less dazzling. ★★★★★ 1997 Art Series Chardonnay £££

℥ **Dom. Leflaive** [luh-flev] (*Burgundy,* France) Anne-Claude Leflaive has taken the domaine made famous by her father Vincent to new heights, possibly, she might argue, with the help of biodynamic methods. The various Montrachets (Chevalier, Batard etc.) are the stars here. All wines are hard to find, and well worth leaving for a few years in the cellar.

℥ **Olivier Leflaive** [luh-flev] (*Burgundy,* France) The négociant business launched by Vincent Leflaive's nephew in 1994. Mostly high-class white wines, with just the occasional red. (Wines can also be tasted in a bistro restaurant close to the cellars). ★★★★ 1998 Meursault Charmes £££

L

Ᵽ **Peter Lehmann** [lee-man] (*Barossa Valley*, Australia) The grand old man of the *Barossa*, Peter Lehmann and his son Doug make intense *Shiraz*, *Cabernet*, *Semillon*, and *Chardonnay* which make up in character (and value) what they lack in subtlety. Stonewell is the best red.
Length How long the taste lingers in the mouth.
Lenswood (*South Australia*) New region near *Adelaide*, proving its potential with *Sauvignon*, *Chardonnay*, *Pinot Noir*, and even (in the case of *Henschke's* Abbott's Prayer) *Merlot* and *Cabernet Sauvignon*. Pioneers include *Stafford Ridge*, *Shaw & Smith*, *Knappstein Lenswood*, and *Nepenthe*.

Ᵽ **Lenswood** [nap-steen] (*Lenswood*, South Australia) Tim and Annie Knappstein's brilliant *Sauvignon, Semillon, Chardonnay, Pinot Noir,* and *Cabernets*. ★★★★ 1998 Semillon £££

Ᵽ **Lenz Vineyards** [lentz] (*Long Island, New York*) One of the best wineries on Long Island, with particularly recommendable *Merlot* and *Chardonnay*.
León [lay-on] (Spain) Northwestern region producing acceptable dry, fruity reds and whites.

Ᵽ **Jean León** [zhon lay-ON] (*Catalonia*, Spain) American pioneer of Spanish *Chardonnay* and *Cabernet*, whose wines have greatly improved since its purchase by *Torres*. ★★★★ 1994 Cabernet Sauvignon £££

Ᵽ **Leone de Castris** [lay-oh-nay day kah-streess] (*Puglia*, Italy) A leading exponent of Salice Santino, Copertino, Salento Chardonnay, and pink Salento rosato. A name to watch as this region gathers prestige.

Ᵽ **Leonetti Cellars** [lee-oh-net-tee] (*Washington State*) One of the best red wine producers in the US. Now showing its skills with *Sangiovese* and an innovative "American" (Washington State/Dry Creek) *Merlot*.

Ᵽ **Ch. Léoville-Barton** [lay-oh-veel bahr-ton] (*St. Julien 2ème Cru Classé, Bordeaux*, France) Anthony Barton's daughter Liliane is now taking over here, and produces one of the most reliably classy wines in *Bordeaux,* without – unlike a great many of her neighbours – recourse to the machines that concentrate the juice to provide "bigger" flavours. Then, again, unlike them, she has the temerity to ask a reasonable rather than extortionate price for it. *Langoa Barton* is the sister property. Both made great 2000. **61 70 78 82 83 85 86 88 89 90 94** *95 96 97 98 99 00* ★★★★★ **2000 ££££**

Ᵽ **Ch. Léoville-las-Cases** [lay-oh-veel las-kahz] (*St. Julien 2ème Cru Classé, Bordeaux*, France) Impeccably made *St. Julien Super Second* whose quality now often matches its neighbour *Ch. Latour* – a fact that its owner Hubert Delon reflects in his prices. The *Clos du Marquis second label* is also good. **76 78 82 83 85 86 88 89 90 94** *95 96 97 98 99 00*

Ᵽ **Ch. Léoville-Poyferré** [lay-pwah-feh-ray] (*St. Julien 2ème Cru Classé, Bordeaux*, France) 1995, 1996 and 1997 showed the touch of *Michel Rolland* here. A rising star. The *second label* is Moulin Riche. **82 83 85 86 87 88 89 90 94** *95 96 97 98 99 00* ★★★★ **1998 ££££**

Ᵽ **Dom. Leroy** [luh-rwah] (*Burgundy*, France) Organic domaine in *Vosne-Romanée* founded by the former co-owner of the *Dom. de la Romanée-Conti* and making wines as good as those of that estate. Prices are stratospheric, but the humblest wines are better than other producers' *Grands Crus*.
★★★★★ **1998 Vosne Romanée Beaumonts ££££**

Ᵽ **Maison Leroy** [luh-rwah] (*Burgundy*) If you want to buy a really great old bottle of *Burgundy*, no matter the cost, this is the place to come.

⚘ **Lexia** [lex-ee-yah] See *Muscat d'Alexandrie*.

Ᵽ **Librandi** [lee-bran-dee] (*Calabria*, Italy) Another flagship winery from the fast-improving regions of Southern Italy. There are terrific examples of the Cirò grape, as well as Gravello, a great blend of the local Gaglioppo and the *Cabernet Sauvignon.*
Lie(s) See *Lees/Sur Lie*.
Liebfraumilch [leeb-frow-mihlch] (Germany) Seditious exploitation of the QbA system. Good examples are pleasant; most are alcoholic sugar-water bought on price alone.

L

� **Lievland** [leev-land] (*Stellenbosch*, South Africa) Estate which has a reputation in South Africa as a high-quality specialty producer of *Shiraz* and *late harvest* wines.

☙ **Hubert Lignier** [Lee-nee-yay] (*Burgundy*, France) Producer of classic long-lived *Morey-St.-Denis*. ★★★★★ 1998 Morey-St.-Denis £££

☙ **Limestone Ridge** (*South Australia*) *Lindemans'* often excellent *Coonawarra* red blend. ★★★★ 1996 Shiraz Cabernet £££

Limousin [lee-moo-zan] (France) Oak forest that provides barrels that are high in wood *tannin*. Better, therefore, for red wine than for white.

Limoux [lee-moo] (*Midi*, France) (Relatively) cool-climate, chalky soil *appellation* that was recently created for *Chardonnay* which was previously sold as *Vin de Pays d'Oc*. Stories of tankers of wine being driven north by night to *Burgundy* are hotly denied (in the latter region). See *Blanquette*.

☙ **Lindauer** [lin-dowr] (*Marlborough*, New Zealand) Good-value Montana sparkling wine. ★★★★ Special Reserve ££

☙ **Lindemans** (*South Australia*) Once *Penfolds'* greatest rival, now (like so many other once-independent Australian producers) its subsidiary. Noted for long-lived *Hunter Valley Semillon* and *Shiraz*, *Coonawarra* reds, and good-value multi-region blends, such as the internationally successful *Bin 65 Chardonnay*, *Bin 45 Cabernet*, and Cawarra wines.

☙ **Weingut Karl Lingenfelder** [lin-gen-fel-duh] (*Pfalz*, Germany) Great new-wave *Rheinpfalz* producer of a special *Riesling, Dornfelder, Scheurebe,* and an unusually successful *Pinot Noir*. ★★★★ 1998 Grosskarlbacher Osterberg Riesling Spätlese ££

☙ **Jean Lionnet** [lee-oh-nay] (*Rhône*, France) Classy *Cornas* producer whose Rochepertius is a worthwhile buy. The *St. Péray* is an unusually good example of its *appellation* too. ★★★★ 1997 Cornas £££

☙ **Ch. Liot** [lee-yoh] (*Barsac, Bordeaux*, France) Good light and elegant *Barsac*. 75 76 82 83 86 88 89 90 96 97 98 99 ★★★★ 1998 £££

Liqueur Muscat (*Rutherglen*, Australia) A wine style unique to Australia. Other countries make fortified *Muscats*, but none achieve the caramelized-marmalade and Christmas-pudding flavours that *Rutherglen* can achieve. Campbell's; Mick Morris; Seppelt; Yalumba.

Liqueur d'Expédition [lee-kuhr dex-pay-dees-see-yon] (*Champagne*, France) Sweetening syrup for *dosage*.

Liqueur de Tirage [lee-kuhr duh tee-rahzh] (*Champagne*, France) The yeast and sugar added to base wine to induce secondary fermentation (and hence the bubbles) in bottle.

Liquoreux [lee-koh-ruh] (France) Rich and sweet.

Liquoroso [lee-koh-roh-soh] (Italy) Rich and sweet.

☙ **Lirac** [lee-rak] (*Rhône*, France) Peppery, *Tavel*-like rosés, and increasingly impressive, deep berry-fruit reds. Red: 90 95 96 97 98 99 00 Ch. D'Aqueria; Bouchassy; Delorme; Ch. Mayne Lalande; André Méjan; Perrin.

☙ **Listel** [lees-tel] (*Languedoc-Roussillon*, France) Recently taken over, improving pioneer with vineyards on beaches close to Sète. Best wines: rosé ("Grain de Gris") and sparkling *Muscat* (Pétillant de Raisin).

Listrac-Médoc [lees-trak] (*Bordeaux*, France) Small *Haut-Médoc commune* near *Moulis*, though quite different in style. Clay makes this *Merlot* country, though this isn't always reflected in the vineyards. Wines tend to be toughly unripe and fun-free even in warm vintages. 82 83 85 86 88 89 90 94 95 96 97 98 99 Ch. Clarke; Fonréaud; Fourcas-Dupré; Fourcas-Hosten.

☙ **Littorai** (*Sonoma*, California) Classy *Chardonnay* from *Russian River Valley* (Mais Canyon Vineyard) and *Sonoma Coast* (Occidental Vineyard) where the Hirsch vineyard is also the source for some stylish *Pinot Noir*.

Livermore (Valley) [liv-uhr-mohr] (California) Warm-climate vineyard area with fertile soil producing full rounded whites, including increasingly fine *Chardonnay*. Red: 95 96 97 98 99 00 White: 96 97 98 99 00 *Bonny Doon;* Concannon; Livermore Cellars; *Wente.*

L

♟ **Los Llanos** [los yah-nos] (*Valdepeñas*, Spain) Commendable modern exception to the tradition of dull *Valdepeñas*, with quality mature reds.

♟ **De Loach** [duh lohch] (*Sonoma*, California) Look for the letters OFS – Our Finest Selection – on the *Chardonnay* and *Cabernet*. But even these rarely surpass the stunning individual vineyard *Zinfandels,* which are among the most characterful around.

♟ **J Lohr** [lohr] (*Santa Clara*, California) Often underrated winery worth knowing for its well-made affordable wines, particularly the Wildflower range, and now a selection of more classic noble styles. ★★★★ 1999 Cyprus Zinfandel ££; ★★★★ 1999 Hilltop Cabernet Sauvignon ££

Loire [lwahr] (France) An extraordinary variety of wines come from this picturesque area. There are inexpensive, traditional dry whites such as *Muscadet* and the classier *Savennières, Sancerre,* and *Pouilly-Fumé*; grassy summery reds (Chinon and Bourgueil); buckets of rosé – some good, most dreadful; glorious sweet whites (*Vouvray* etc.); and decent sparkling wines (also *Vouvray* plus *Crémant de Loire*). Stick to known growers and domaines. White: 90 94 95 97 98 99 00 Sweet White: 85 88 89 90 94 95 96 97 98 99 00 Red: 90 95 96 97 98 99 00

Lombardy [lom-bahr-dee] (Italy) Region (and vineyards) around Milan, known mostly for sparkling wine but also for increasingly interesting reds, such as Valcalepio and *Oltrepò Pavese*, and the whites of *Lugana*. Red: 90 94 95 96 97 98 99 00 ★★★★ 1998 Lugana Ca' dei Frati ££££

Long Island (*New York State*) A unique (usually ideal but occasionally hurricane-prone) microclimate where fields once full of potatoes are now yielding classy *Merlot* and *Chardonnay*. Local wines are sadly still less easy to find in Manhattan than many less impressive Californians, but a growing number of wine lovers are discovering them on vacation in the Hamptons. Bedell; Bridgehampton; Gristina; Hargrave; Lenz; Palmer; Peconic; Pindar.

♟ **Long Vineyards** (*Napa*, California) High-quality producer of long-lived *Cabernet Sauvignon*, *Chardonnay*, and *late-harvest Riesling*.

♟ **Longridge** (*Stellenbosch*, South Africa) Designer winery tailoring three lines (Longridge, Bay View, and Capelands) to export markets.

Lontue [lon-too-way] (Chile) Good Merlot region. *Lurton; San Pedro; Santa Carolina; Valdevieso.*

♟ **Weingut Dr. Loosen** [loh-sen] (*Mosel-Saar-Ruwer*, Germany) New-wave *Riesling* producer. One of the best and most reliable in the *Mosel*.

♟ **Lopez de Heredia** [loh-peth day hay-ray-dee-yah] (*Rioja*, Spain) Ultra-traditional winery with Viña Tondonia white and *Gran Reserva* reds. ★★★ 1993 Vina Tondonia Tinto Crianza ££

♟ **Louisvale** [loo-wis-vayl] (*Stellenbosch*, South Africa) Once avowed *Chardonnay* specialists, Louisvale's range has expanded to include some *Cabernet*-based reds. ★★★ 1997 Cabernet Merlot ££

♟ **Loupiac** [loo-peeyak] (*Bordeaux*, France) *Sauternes* styles, but lighter. *Clos-Jean; Ch. du Cros; Loupiac-Gaudiet; Mazarin; du Noble; de Ricaud.*

♟ **Ch. Loupiac-Gaudiet** [loo-pee-yak goh-dee-yay] (*Loupiac, Bordeaux*, France) A reliable producer of *Loupiac.*

Loureiro [loh-ray-roh] (Portugal) Good *Vinho Verde* grape.

♟ **Ch. la Louvière** [lah loo-vee-yehr] (*Graves, Bordeaux*, France) Reliable, rich, modern whites and reds. The second wine is called "L" de Louvière.

♟ **Fürst Löwenstein** [foorst ler-ven-shtine] (*Franken*, Germany) One of the very top producers of *Silvaner*.

♟ **Van Loveren** [van loh-veh-ren] (*Robertson*, South Africa) Family-owned estate producing good value-for-money wine. Concentrating primarily on classic fresh whites and soft reds. ★★★ 1998 Binnode Noir Muscadelle ££

Côtes du Lubéron [koht doo LOO-bay-ron] (*Rhône*, France) Light reds, pink and sparkling wines, and *Chardonnay*-influenced whites.

Ⴎ **Luce** [loo-chay] (Tuscany, Italy) Co-production between *Mondavi* and *Frescobaldi*, who have combined forces to produce a good, if pricey, red. The cheaper *second label*, Lucente, can be a good buy for earlier drinking.

Ⴎ **Lugana** [loo-gah-nah] (*Lombardy,* Italy) Potentially appley, almondy whites made from the *Trebbiano*.

Lugny [loo-ñee] (*Burgundy,* France) See *Mâcon*.

Ⴎ **Luna** (*Napa*, California) A name to remember for anyone looking for good Californian versions of Italian classics such as *Sangiovese*.

Ⴎ **Pierre Luneau** [loo-noh] (*Loire,* France) A rare beast: a top-class *Muscadet* producer. His experiments with new oak barrels have appealed to some US critics – I prefer the unwooded wines. Try the L d'Or.

Ⴎ **Cantine Lungarotti** [kan-tee-nah loon-gah-roh-tee] (*Umbria,* Italy) Highly innovative producer, and the man who single-handedly created the *Torgiano* denomination.

Ⴎ **Jacques & François Lurton** [loor-ton] Having succeeded at his father's *Ch. la Louvière* and *Ch. Bonnet*, Jacques makes wine worldwide. Look out for Hermanos Lurton labels from Spain and Bodega Lurton wines from Argentina.

Ⴎ **Ch. de Lussac** [loo-sak] (*Lussac St. Emilion, Bordeaux,* France) A name to watch out for in *Lussac St. Emilion*. 86 89 90 94 95 96 97 98 99 00

Ⴎ **Lussac St. Emilion** [loo-sak sant-ay-mee-yon] (*Bordeaux,* France) *St. Emilion* satellite with potential. 86 88 89 90 94 95 96 98 99 00

Ⴎ **Emilio Lustau** [loos-tow] (*Jerez,* Spain) Top-class *sherry* producer with great *almacanista* wines. ★★★★ Amontillado los Arcos ££

Lutomer [loo-toh-muh] (Slovenia) Area still known mostly for its (very basic) Lutomer *Laski Rizling*. It is currently, however, doing better things with *Chardonnay*.

Luxembourg [luk-sahm-burg] This small principality is the source of some pleasant, fresh, white wines from *Alsace*-like grape varieties, and generally dire sparkling wine.

Ⴎ **Ch. Lynch-Bages** [lansh bazh] (*Pauillac 5ème Cru Classé, Bordeaux,* France) Reliably overperforming fifth-growth *Pauillac*. Haut-Bages Averous is the *second label*. The (very rare) white is worth seeking out too. 82 83 85 86 88 89 90 95 96 97 98 99 00 ★★★★★ 2000 £££

Ⴎ **Ch. Lynch-Moussas** [lansh moo-sahs] (*Pauillac 5ème Cru Classé, Bordeaux,* France) Slowly improving. 86 88 89 90 94 95 96 97 98 99 00

M

Ⴎ *Macération carbonique* [ma-say-ra-see-yon kahr-bon-eek] Technique of *fermenting* uncrushed grapes under a blanket of carbon dioxide gas to produce fresh fruity wine. Used in *Beaujolais* and elsewhere.

Ⴎ **Machard de Gramont** [ma-shahr duh gra-mon] (*Burgundy*, France) Producer of fine *Nuits-St.-Georges*, *Vosne-Romanée*, and *Savigny-lès Beaune*.

Mâcon/Mâconnais [ma-kon/nay] (*Burgundy,* France) Look for the suffix *Villages, Superieur,* or Prissé, *Viré, Lugny*, or *Clessé*. The region contains *St.-Véran* and *Pouilly-Fuissé*. For straight Mâcon you could try *Jadot* or *Duboeuf*, but Jean Thévenet Dom. de la Bongran from Clessé is of *Côte d'Or* quality. Red: **95 96 97 98 99** White: **95 96 97 98 99 00** Barrault; Bonhomme; Deux Roches; Roger Lasserat; Manciat; Caves de Lugny; Cave de Prissé; Verget; J-J Vincent.

Ⴎ **Maculan** [mah-koo-lahn] (*Veneto*, Italy) A superstar producer of blackcurranty *Cabernet* Breganze, an oaked *Pinot Bianco-Pinot Grigio-Chardonnay* blend called Prato di Canzio, and the lusciously sweet *Torcolato*.

M

♈ **Madeira** [ma-deer-ruh] (Portugal) Atlantic island producing fortified wines, usually identified by style: *Bual, Sercial, Verdelho,* or Malmsey. Most is ordinary; some is finer fare of unique marmalady character. *Blandy; Cossart-Gordon; Barros e Souza; Henriques & Henriques.*

Maderization [mad-uhr-ih-zay-shon] Deliberate procedure in *Madeira,* produced by the warming of wine in *estufas.* Otherwise an undesired effect produced by high temperatures during transport and storage, resulting in a dull, flat flavour. A frequent problem in Asia – and unfortunately in the US, where wines are occasionally handled carelessly during the hot summer.

♈ **Madiran** [ma-dee-ron] (*South-West,* France) Robust reds made from *Tannat; tannic* when young, but worth ageing. *Aydie; Barréjat; Berthoumieu; Bouscassé; Dom. du Crampilh; Ch. Montus; Producteurs de Plaimont.*

♈ **Ch. Magdelaine** [Mag-duh-layn] (*St. Emilion Premier Grand Cru, Bordeaux,* France) Impeccable, perfumed wines. 61 70 71 75 78 79 81 82 83 85 86 88 89 90 94 *95 96 97 98 99 00* ★★★★ 1995 £££

♈ **Maglieri** [mag-lee-yeh-ree] (*McLaren Vale,* South Australia) Dynamic *Shiraz* specialist recently taken over by *Mildara-Blass.*

Magnum Large bottle containing the equivalent of two bottles of wine (one and a half litres in capacity). Wines age slower in big bottles, and fewer are produced. For both reasons, magnums tend to sell for more at auction.

♈ **Magrez-Fombrauge** [mah-grehz-fohm-broh'j] (*St Emilion, Bordeaux,* France) Successful – in 2000 – *garage wine* from the boss of *Malesan.*

Maipo [my-poh] (Chile) Historic region with many good producers. Reds are most successful, especially *Cabernet* and *Merlot,* and softer *Chardonnays* are also made. New varieties and enterprising organic vineyards are moving in, but vineyards close to Santiago, the capital, increasingly have to compete with the needs of housing developers. *Aquitania* (Paul Bruno); Canepa; *Carmen; Concha y Toro;* Cousino Macul; Peteroa; *Santa Carolina;* Santa Inés; *Santa Rita; Undurraga; Viña Carmen.*

Maître de Chai [may-tr duh chay] (France) Cellar master.

Malaga [ma-la-gah] (Spain) A semi-moribund Andalusian *DO* producing raisiny dessert wines of varying degrees of sweetness. Immensely popular in the 19th century; sadly very hard to find nowadays. **Lopez Hermanos.**

♈ **Ch. Malartic-Lagravière** [mah-lahr-teek lah-gra-vee-yehr] (*Pessac-Léognan Cru Classé, Bordeaux,* France) Previously slumbering estate, bought in 1994 by *Laurent Perrier.* Improving new-wave whites; reds need time. Red: **81 82 83 85 86 88 89 90 94** *95 96 97 98 99 00* White: **85 87 88 89 90 92 94 95** *96 97 98 99 00*

🍇 **Malbec** [mal-bek] Red grape, now rare in *Bordeaux* but widely planted in Argentina, the *Loire* (where it is known as the *Côt), Cahors,* and also in Australia. Producing rich, plummy, silky wines.

♈ **Malesan** [ma-les-son] (France) Dynamic brand (mostly) for *Bordeaux,* launched by the spirits group William Pitters. Can be good.

♈ **Ch. Malescasse** [ma-les-kas] (*Haut-Médoc Cru Bourgeois, Bordeaux,* France) Since 1993, wines have benefitted from being made by the former cellarmaster of *Pichon-Lalande.* **88 89 90 94** *95 96 97 98 99 00*

♈ **Ch. Malescot-St.-Exupéry** [ma-les-koh san tek-soo-peh-ree] (*Margaux 3ème Cru Classé, Bordeaux,* France) Understated but sometimes quite classy wines.

WEINERT

MALBEC

1 9 9 4

ESTATE BOTTLED
BODEGA Y CAVAS DE WEINERT S.A.

13.50 %Vol.   AGED IN OAK   mℓ 750

MENDOZA
PRODUCT OF ARGENTINA

♈ **Ch. de Malle** [duh mal] (*Sauternes 2ème Cru Classé, Bordeaux,* France) Good *Sauternes* property near Preignac, famous for its beautiful *château.* 83 85 86 88 89 90 *95 96 97 98 99* ★★★★ 1997 ££££

Malolactic fermentation [ma-loh-lak-tik] Secondary "fermentation" in which appley *malic acid* is converted into the "softer", creamier *lactic* acid by naturally present or added strains of bacteria. Almost all red wines undergo

M

a malolactic fermentation. For whites, it is common practice in *Burgundy*. Malolactic fermentation is used to a varying extent in New World countries, where natural acid levels are often low. An excess is recognizable as a buttermilky flavour.

♀ **Ch. de la Maltroye** [mal-trwah] (*Burgundy*, France) Classy modern *Chassagne*-based estate. All the wines are made by *Dom. Parent*. ★★★★
1997 Chassagne-Montrachet Clos du Château de la Maltroye £££

🍇 **Malvasia** [mal-vah-see-ah] *Muscatty* white grape vinified dry in Italy (as a component in *Frascati*), but far more successfully as good, sweet, traditional *Madeira*, in which country it is known as Malmsey. Not Malvoisie.

La Mancha [lah man-cha] (Spain) Huge region of inland Spain south of Madrid, known for mostly dull and old-fashioned wines. However, it is currently producing increasingly clean, modern examples. Also the place where the *Marquès de Griñon* is succeeding in his experiments with new techniques and grapes, especially *Syrah*.

♀ **Albert Mann** (*Alsace*, France) Top grower who always manages to express true varietal character without overblown flavours and excessive alcohol. ★★★★ **1998 Riesling Schlossberg £££**

🍇 **Manseng (Gros M. & Petit M.)** [man-seng] (*Southwest*, France) Two varieties of white grape grown in south-western France. Both are capable of extraordinary apricot-and-cream concentration, and the latter is used in the great *vendange tardive* wines of *Jurançon*. **Dom. Cauhapé; Grassa; Producteurs de Plaimont.**

♀ **Josef Mantler** [yoh-sef mant-lehr] (*Krems*, Austria) Reliable producer of both Grüner and Roter Veltliner as well as good *Riesling* and *Chardonnay*.

Manzanilla [man-zah-nee-yah] (*Jerez*, Spain) Dry tangy *sherry* – a *fino* style, widely (possibly mistakenly) thought to take on a salty tang from the coastal *bodegas* of Sanlucar de Barrameda. *Barbadillo; Don Zoilo; Hidalgo.*

♀ **Maranges** [mah-ronzh] (*Burgundy*, France) A hillside *appellation* promising potentially affordable, if a little rustic, *Côte d'Or* wines. White: **95 96 97 98 99 00** Red: **90 92 95 96 97 98 99 00** *Bachelet;* Pierre Bresson; Chevrot; *Drouhin;Vincent Girardin; Claude Nouveau.*

Marc [mahr] (France) Residue of seeds, stalks, and skins left after grapes are pressed. Often distilled into fiery brandy, e.g., Marc de Bourgogne.

♀ **Marcassin** (*Sonoma*, California) Helen Turley produces expressive – and, for some, sometimes a touch overblown – *Côte d'Or Grand Cru*-quality *Chardonnays* in tiny quantities from a trio of vineyards.

Marches/Le Marche [lay Mahr-kay] (Italy) Region on the Adriatic coast, below Venice. Best known for *Rosso Conero* and good, dry, fruity *Verdicchio* whites. **Boccadigabbia;** *Fattoria Coroncino;* Fazi Battaglia; *Garofoli; Gioacchino Garafolli; Umani Ronchi;* Vallerosa Bonci.

♀ **Marcillac** [mah-see-yak] (*Southwest*, France) Full-flavoured country reds, made principally from the *Fer*, possibly blended with some *Cabernet* and *Gamay*. Du Cros; Lacombe; Cave du Vallon-Valady.

🍇 **Maréchal Foch** [mah-ray-shahl fohsh] A *hybrid* vine producing red grapes in Canada and Eastern North America. *Inniskillin* makes a good example.

Margaret River (*Western* Australia) Cool(ish) vineyard area on the coast, almost at Australia's southwestern tip, now gaining notice for *Cabernet Sauvignon* and *Chardonnay*. Also one of Australia's only *Zinfandels*. White: **95 96 97 98 99 00** Red: **94 95 96 97 98 99 00** Brookland Valley; *Cape Mentelle; Cullen;* Devil's Lair; *Evans & Tate; Leeuwin; Moss Wood; Pierro;Vasse Felix;* Voyager Estate; *Ch. Xanadu.*

♀ **Margaux** [mahr-goh] (*Bordeaux*, France) Large, very varied *commune* with a concentration of *crus classés* including *Ch. Margaux, Palmer*, and *Lascombes*. Sadly, other wines that should be deliciously blackberryish are variable, partly thanks to the diverse nature of the soil, and partly through the producers' readiness to sacrifice quality for the sake of yields. Matters improved in 2000, however, which was a good vintage here.

M

🍷 **Ch. Margaux** [mahr-goh] (*Margaux Premier Cru Classé, Bordeaux,* France) Intense wines with cedary perfume and velvet softness when mature. The top *second label* is *Pavillon Rouge.* 82 83 84 85 86 87 88 89 90 94 *95 96 97 98 99 00* ★★★★★ **2000 £££££**

🍷 **Henry Marionet** [mah-ree-yoh-nay] (*Loire,* France) Top-class producer with great old-clone *Gamay* and distinctive whites made from the Romarantin.

🍷 **Markham** (*Napa Valley,* California) A producer to watch for fairly priced reds and whites.

Marlborough [morl-buh-ruh] (New Zealand) Cool-climate South Island region at the north-western tip of the island, opposite Wellington: excellent *Sauvignon, Chardonnay,* improving *Merlot* and *Pinot Noir,* good sparkling wines. White: 97 98 99 00 *Babich; Cellier le Brun; Cloudy Bay; Corbans Giesen; Grove Mill; Hunter's; Jackson Estate; Montana; Stoneleigh; Vavasour.*

🍷 **Marojallia** [mah-roh-jah-lee-yah] (*Bordeaux,* France) The first *garage wine* in *Margaux* – or the *Médoc* for that matter. Inevitably, from Jean-Luc Thunevin.

🍷 **Marne et Champagne** [mahr-nay-shom-pañ] (*Champagne,* France) Huge cooperative that owns the Besserat de Bellefon, *Lanson,* and Alfred Rothschild labels, and can provide good own-label wines.

🍷 **Ch. Marquis-de-Terme** [mahr-kee duh tehrm] (*Margaux 4ème Cru Classé, Bordeaux,* France) Traditional property with quite tough wines. 86 87 88 89 90 *95 96 98 99* ★★★ **1998 £££**

🍷 **Marsala** [mahr-sah-lah] (*Sicily,* Italy) Rich, fortified wine from *Sicily* for use in recipes such as Zabaglione. *De Bartoli; Cantine Florio; Pellegrino; Rallo.*

🍷 **Marsannay** [mahr-sah-nay] (*Burgundy,* France) Northernmost village of the *Côte de Nuits* with a range of largely undistinguished but, for *Burgundy,* affordable *Chardonnay,* and *Pinot Noir* (red and rosé). White: 95 96 97 98 99 00 Red: *95 96 97 98 99 Bruno Clair; Fougeray de Beauclair; Louis Jadot.*

🍇 **Marsanne** [mahr-san] (*Rhône,* France) Grape that is blended with *Roussanne* in northern *Rhône* whites. Also successful in the *Goulburn Valley* in *Victoria* for *Ch. Tahbilk* and *Mitchelton* and in California for *Bonny Doon.* Has a delicate, perfumed intensity when young, and fattens with age. Look for unoaked versions from Australia. *Bonny Doon; Guigal; Mitchelton; Tahbilk.*

Martinborough (New Zealand) Up-and-coming North Island region for *Pinot Noir* and *Chardonnay.* White: *97 98 99 00* Red: *95 96 97 98 99 00 Alana Estate; Ata Rangi; Dry River; Martinborough Vineyard; Palliser Estate.*

🍷 **Martinborough Vineyard** (*Martinborough,* New Zealand) Top Kiwi *Pinot Noir* and one of the best *Chardonnays.* ★★★★ **1999 Martinborough Vineyard Pinot Noir £££**

🍷 **Martinelli** (*Sonoma,* California) Century-old *Zinfandel* specialists, making rich intense reds from this variety and juicy *Pinot Noirs.*

🍷 **Bodegas Martinez Bujanda** [mahr-tee-neth boo-han-dah] (*Rioja,* Spain) New-wave producer of fruit-driven wines sold as *Conde de Valdemar.* Probably the most consistently recommendable producer in *Rioja.* ★★★★ **1994 Finca Valpiedra Reserva £££**

🍷 **Martini** (*Piedmont,* Italy) Good *Asti Spumante* from the producer of the vermouth house that invented "lifestyle" advertising – still, we're all guilty of something.

🍷 **Louis Martini** (*Napa Valley,* California) Grand old family-owned winery, right on form at the moment. Superlative long-lived *Cabernet* from the Monte Rosso vineyard. ★★★★ **1997 Monte Rosso Cabernet Reserve £££**

🍇 **Marzemino** [mahrt-zeh-mee-noh] (Italy) Grape that makes spicy-plummy wines.

🍷 **Mas Amiel** [mahs ah-mee-yel] (*Provence,* France) Wonderful rich *port*-like wine in the *appellation* of Maury. ★★★★ **1997 Maury Vintage £££**

M

℗ **Mas Brugière** [mas bro-gee-yehr] (*Languedoc-Roussillon*, France) Producer of top class, single-vineyard *Pic St. Loup.*

℗ **Mas de Daumas Gassac** [mas duh doh-mas gas-sac] (*Midi*, France) Groundbreaking *Vin de Pays* red from a blend including *Pinot Noir, Syrah, Mourvèdre*, and *Cabernet*. Good when young, but also lasts for ages. A white with *Viognier* is similarly impressive. ★★★★ **1998 Rouge £££**

℗ **Mas Jullien** [mas joo-lye'n] (*Languedoc-Roussillon*, France) The most stylish wines in the *Coteaux du Languedoc* (or elsewhere in southern France). Classic individual reds and whites from classic traditional grapes.

℗ **Mas Martinet** [mas mahr-tee-neht] (*Priorato*, Spain) One of a pair of dazzling *Priorato* wines. The *second label* is Martinet Bru.

℗ **Bartolo Mascarello** [mas-kah-reh-loh] (*Piedmont*, Italy) Great ultra-traditional *Barolo* specialist whose rose-petaly wine proves that the old ways can compete with the new. But they do call for patience.

℗ **Giuseppe Mascarello** [mas-kah-reh-loh] (*Piedmont*, Italy) Top-class *Barolo* estate (unconnected with that of *Bartolo Mascarello*), producing characterful wine from individual vineyards. Succeeds in tricky vintages. Great *Dolcetto*. ★★★★ **1995 Monprivato ££££**

℗ **Gianni Masciarelli** [mash-chee-yah-reh-lee] (*Abruzzo,* Italy) One of the starriest makers of Montepulciano d'Abruzzo.

℗ **Masi** [mah-see] (*Veneto,* Italy) Producer with reliable, affordable reds and whites and single-vineyard wines that serve as a justification for *Valpolicella's* denomination. ★★★★★ **1997 Serego Alighieri £££**

℗ **La Massa** [mah-sah] (*Tuscany,* Italy) Top class *Chianti* producer with a spectacularly good 1996 Chianti Classico.

℗ Massandra [mahsan-drah] (*Crimea,* Ukraine) Famous as the source of great, historic, dessert wines, now a place for okay *Cabernet Sauvignon.*

Master of Wine (MW) One of a small number of people (around 260) internationally who have passed a gruelling set of wine exams.

℗ **Mastroberadino** [maas-tro-be-rah-dino] (*Campania*, Italy) Top producer of rich *Taurasi* in Italy's south as well as fine Fiano di Avellino.

℗ **Matanzas Creek** [muh-tan-zuhs] (*Sonoma Valley,* California) Top-class complex *Chardonnay* (one of California's best), good *Sauvignon*, and high-quality accessible *Merlot*. ★★★★ **1997 Merlot ££££**

🍇 **Mataro** [muh-tah-roh] See *Mourvèdre.*

℗ **Mateus** [ma-tay-oos] (Portugal) Pink and white off-dry *frizzante* wine sold in bottles that are traditional in Franken, Germany, and with a label depicting a palace with which the wine has no connection. A 50-year-old marketing masterpiece. The name is now also used for more serious reds.

℗ **Thierry Matrot** [tee-yer-ree ma-troh] (*Burgundy*, France) Top-class white producer with great white and recommendable red *Blagny.*

℗ **Chateau Matsa** [maht-sah] (*Attica*, Greece) One of Greece's best new-wave producers.

℗ **Matteo Correggia** [mah-tey-yoh coh-rey-djee-yah] (*Piedmont*, Italy) One of Italy's best, excelling with Barbera d'Alba and Nebbiolo d'Alba.

℗ **Matthew Cellars** (*Washington State*) Up-and-coming maker of *Cabernet* and *Sémillon.*

℗ **Matua Valley** [ma-tyoo-wah] (*Auckland,* New Zealand) Reliable maker of great (*Marlborough*) *Sauvignon*, (Judd Estate) *Chardonnay*, and *Merlot*. Also producer of the even better *Ararimu* red and white. Shingle Peak is the *second label.* ★★★★ **1998 Ararimu Merlot-Cabernet £££**

℗ **Yvon Mau** [ee-von moh] (*Bordeaux & Southwest*, France) Highly commercial producer of *Bordeaux* and other, mostly white, wines from Southwest France. Occasionally good. ★★★ **1996 Premius ££**

℗ **Ch. Maucaillou** [mow-kai-yoo] (*Moulis Cru Bourgeois, Bordeaux,* France) *Cru Bourgeois* in the *commune* of Moulis regularly producing approachable wines to beat some *crus classés.* **90 94 95 96 97 98 99 00**

M

Maule [mow-lay] (Chile) Up-and-coming *Central Valley* region; especially for white wines but warm enough for red. **Santa Carolina; Carta Vieja.**

ℹ **Bernard Maume** [mohm] (*Burgundy*, France) Small *Gevrey-Chambertin* estate making long-lived wines. ★★★★ **1998 Gevrey-Chambertin £££**

ℹ **Bodegas Mauro** [mow-roh] (Spain) Just outside the *Ribera del Duero DO*, but making very similar rich red wines.

ℹ **Maury** [moh-ree] (*Languedoc-Roussillon*, France) Potentially rich sweet wine to compete with *Banyuls* and *port*. Sadly, too many examples are light and feeble. ★★★★ **1997 Mas Amiel Vintage £££**

🍇 **Mauzac** [moh-zak] (France) White grape used in southern France for *Vin de Pays* and *Gaillac*. Can be characterful and floral or dull and earthy.

🍇 **Mavrodaphne** [mav-roh-daf-nee] (Greece) Characterful indigenous Greek red grape, and the wine made from it. Dark and strong, needs ageing to be worth drinking. **Kourtakis.**

🍇 **Mavrud** [mah-vrood] (Bulgaria) Rustic, characterful red grape and wine.

ℹ **Maximin Grünhaus** [mak-siee-min groon-hows] (*Mosel-Saar-Ruwer*, Germany) Dr. Carl von Schubert's 1,000-year-old estate producing intense *Rieslings*. ★★★★★ **1999 Abtsberg Riesling Auslese ££££**

ℹ **Maxwell** (*McLaren Vale*, Australia) Reliable producer of *Shiraz, Merlot*, and *Sémillon*, and good mead.

ℹ **Mayacamas** [my-yah-kah-mas] (*Napa Valley*, California) Long-established winery on *Mount Veeder* with *tannic* but good old-fashioned *Cabernet*, and long-lived, rich *Chardonnay*. ★★★★ **1994 Cabernet Sauvignon ££££**

ℹ **Mazis-Chambertin** [mah-zee shom-behr-tan] (*Burgundy*, France) Grand Cru vineyard in which some of Gevrey-Chambertin's best producers have land.

ℹ **McGuigan Brothers** (*Hunter Valley*, Australia) Commercial and occasionally impressive stuff from the former owners of *Wyndham Estate*. Too often, however, wines are too oaky and/or too sweet.

McLaren Vale (*South Australia*) Region renowned for European-style wines, but possibly too varied in topography, soil, and climate to create its own identity. White: **97 98 99** Red: **95 96 97 98** 99 *D'Arenberg; Hardy's;* **Kays Amery, Maglieri; Geoff Merrill; Ch. Reynella; Wirra Wirra.**

ℹ **McWilliams** (*Hunter Valley*, Australia) Big, *Hunter Valley*-based, evidently non-republican firm with great traditional ("Elizabeth") *Sémillon* and ("Philip") *Shiraz*, which are now sold younger than previously and so may need time. Fortified wines can be good, too, as are the pioneering *Barwang* and improved *Brand's* wines. ★★★★ **1996 Elizabeth Semillon £££**

ℹ **Médoc** [may-dok] (*Bordeaux*, France) Area of *Bordeaux* immediately south of the *Gironde* and north of the town of *Bordeaux* in which the *Cru Classés* as well as far more ordinary fare are made. Should be better than basic *Bordeaux* and less good than *Haut-Médoc*. This is not always the case.

ℹ **Meerlust Estate** [meer-loost] (*Stellenbosch*, South Africa) Top *Cape* estate. Classy *Merlots* and a highly rated *Bordeaux*-blend called "Rubicon". ★★★★ **1998 Merlot £££**

ℹ **Gabriel Meffre** [mef-fr] (*Rhône*, France) Sound *Rhône* and, now, southern France producer under the Galet Vineyards and Wild Pig labels.

ℹ **Ch. Megyer** [meg-yer] (*Tokaji*, Hungary) French-owned pioneer of *Tokaji* and *Furmint*.

ℹ **Alphonse Mellot** [mel-loh] (*Loire*, France) Dynamic, quality-driven producer.

🍇 **Melnik** [mehl-neek] (Bulgaria) Both a grape variety and a commune where rich reds are produced.

🍇 **Melon de Bourgogne** [muh-lon duh boor-goyn] (France) Grape originally imported from *Burgundy* (where it is no longer grown) to the *Loire* by Dutch brandy distillers who liked its resistance to frost. Now grown for *Muscadet*.

ℹ **Charles Melton** (*Barossa Valley*, Australia) Lovely still and sparkling *Shiraz* and world-class rosé called "Rose of Virginia", as well as Nine Popes, a wine based on *Châteauneuf-du-Pape*. ★★★★ **1998 Nine Popes £££**

Mendocino [men-doh-see-noh] (California) Northern, coastal wine county known for unofficial marijuana farming and for its laid back winemakers who successfully exploit cool microclimates to make "European-style" wines. Red: **95 96 97 98 99** 00 White: **97 98 99 00** *Fetzer; Handley Cellars;* Hidden Cellars; Lazy Creek; *Parducci; Roederer; Scharffenberger.*

Mendoza [men-doh-zah] (Argentina) Source of good rich reds, traditional but bright-fruited, from firms including **La Agricola;** Bianchi; *Catena; Etchart;* Finca Flichman; *Lurton; Morande;* Norton; *la Rural;* San Telmo; *Trapiche;Weinert.*

Menetou-Salon [men-too sah-lon] (*Loire,* France) Bordering on *Sancerre,* making similar if earthier, less pricy *Sauvignon,* as well as some decent *Pinot Noir. Henri Pellé* makes the best. **De Beaurepaire;** R. Champault; Charet; Fournier; de Loye; *Pellé;* la Tour St Martin.

Dom. Méo-Camuzet [may-oh-ka-moo-zay] (*Burgundy,* France) Brilliant *Côte de Nuits* estate with top-class vineyards and intense, oaky wines, made, until his retirement, by the great *Henri Jayer.*

Mercaptans [mehr-kap-ton] See *Hydrogen sulphide.*

Mer Soleil [mehr soh-lay] (California) Producer of big, oaky, fruity, slightly old-fashioned Central Coast *Chardonnays.*

Melnik [mehl-neek] (Bulgaria) Both a grape variety and a commune where rich reds are produced.

Mercier [mehr-see-yay] (*Champagne,* France) Subsidiary, or is it sister company, of *Moët & Chandon,* and producer of improving but pretty commercial sparkling wine that, according to the advertisements, is the biggest seller in France.

Mercouri [mehr-koo-ree] (*Peloponnese,* Greece) Starry new-wave producer with good reds and very successful Roditis.

Mercurey [mehr-koo-ray] (*Burgundy,* France) *Côte Chalonnaise* village, where *Faiveley* makes high-quality wine. Red: **95 96 97 98 99** White: **96 97 98 99 00** Dom Brintet; Marguerite Carillon; Ch. de Chamirey; *Dom. Faiveley;* Genot-Boulanger; Michel Juillot; *Olivier Leflaive;* Meix-Foulot; *Pillot.*

Meridian (*San Luis Obispo,* California) Unusually good-value *Pinot Noir* from *Santa Barbara.* The *Merlot* and *Chardonnay* are impressive too.

Meritage (California) Term for red or white Bordeaux-style blends.

Merlot [mehr-loh] Red variety used to balance the more *tannic Cabernet Sauvignon* throughout the *Médoc,* where it is the most planted grape (as it is in *Pomerol* and *St. Emilion*). Increasingly, though not spectacularly, successful in the *Languedoc.* California's best include *Newton, Matanzas Creek,* and (recently) *Duckhorn.* Australia, South Africa, and New Zealand have had few real stars, but there are impressive efforts from *Washington State* and Chile. At best, appealing soft, honeyed, toffeeish wine.

Merricks Estate (*Mornington Peninsula,* Australia) Small estate specializing in *Shiraz.*

Geoff Merrill (*McLaren Vale,* Australia) The ebullient moustachioed winemaker who has nicknamed himself "The Wizard of Oz". Impressive if restrained *Semillon, Chardonnay,* and *Cabernet* in *McLaren Vale* under his own label, plus easier-going Mount Hurtle wines (especially the rosé).

Merryvale (*Napa Valley,* California) Starry winery with especially good Reserve and Silhouette *Chardonnay* and Profile *Cabernet.* ★★★★ 1997 Chardonnay Reserve £££

Louis Métaireau [meht-teh-roh] (*Loire,* France) The Cadillac of *Muscadet,* which comes here in the form of individual *cuvées.* Cuvée One is the star.

Méthode Champenoise [may-tohd shom-puh-nwahz] Term now outlawed by the EU from labels but still used to describe the way *Champagne* and all other quality sparkling wines are made. Labour intensive because bubbles are made by secondary fermentation in bottle, rather than in a vat or by the introduction of gas. Bottles are individually given the "*dégorgement* process", more champagne is added, and they are recorked.

Methuselah Same size bottle as an *Imperiale* (six litres). Used in *Champagne.*

M

Meursault [muhr-soh] (*Burgundy*, France)
Superb *Chardonnay* with nutty, buttery richness.
It has no *Grands Crus* but great *Premiers Crus*
like Charmes, Perrières, and Genevrières. There
is a little red, some sold as *Volnay-Santenots*.
White: 95 96 97 98 *99 00* **Ampeau; d'Auvenay;**
Coche-Dury; Drouhin; Henri Germain; Jobard;
Comtes Lafon; Michelot; Pierre Morey; Jacques Prieur;
Ch. de Puligny-Montrachet; Ropiteau; *Roulot; Roux*
Père et Fils; Verget.

Ch. de Meursault [muhr-soh] (*Burgundy*,
France) One of *Burgundy*'s few *châteaux* and worth a visit. The wines –
better than most produced by its owner, *Patriarche* – are good too. ★★★★★
1998 Clos du Château Blanc £££

Mexico See *Baja California*.

Ch. Meyney [may-nay] (*St. Estèphe Cru Bourgeois, Bordeaux*, France)
Improving *St. Estèphe* property, with wines that are richer in flavour than
some of its neighbours. **82 83 85 86 88 89 90 94** *95 96 97 98 99 00*

Miani [mee-yah-nee] (*Friuli-Venezia Giulia*, Italy) Enzo Pontoni's
scrupulous efforts to keep yields low make for brilliant examples of *Bordeaux*
red varieties, *Riesling*, and *Chardonnay*.

Peter Michael (*Sonoma*, California) UK-born Sir Peter Michael produces
stunning *Sonoma, Burgundy*-like *Chardonnay, Sauvignon*, and *Cabernet*.
★★★★★ **1997 Chardonnay Belle Cote £££**

Louis Michel et Fils [mee-shel] (*Burgundy*, France) Top-class *Chablis*
producer. ★★★★ **1998 Chablis Vaudésir ££££**

Robert Michel (*Rhône*, France) Produces softer *Cornas* than most from
this sometimes tough *appellation*: beautiful, strong yet silky wines.

Alain Michelot [mee-shloh] (*Burgundy*, France) Producer of perfumed,
elegant *Nuits-St.-Georges* that can be enjoyed young – but is worth keeping.

Dom. Michelot-Buisson [mee-shloh bwee-son] (*Burgundy*, France)
A great old *Meursault* property. Wines are rarely subtle, but they never lack
Meursault flavour. ★★★★ **1998 £££**

Micro-Wine/Micro-Vin Term used to describe limited-production wines
such as *le Pin* and *Screaming Eagle*.

Mildara Blass [mil-dah-rah] (*South Australia*) Dynamic, unashamedly
market-driven company whose portfolio includes *Rothbury, Yarra Ridge,*
Yellowglen, Wolf Blass, Balgownia, Mount Helen, *Stonyfell, Saltram*, and
Maglieri. Coonawarra wines, including the very commercial *Jamieson's Run*,
are best.

Millton Estate (*Gisborne*, New Zealand) James Millton is an obsessive, not
to say a masochist. He loves the hard-to-make *Chenin Blanc* and uses it to
make first-class organic wine in *Gisborne*. Sadly, it seems, most people
would rather buy his *Chardonnay*. ★★★★ **1999 Chenin £££**

Milmanda [mil-man-dah] (*Conca de Barbera*, Spain) *Torres*' top-label
Chardonnay. Classy by any standards.

Kym Milne Antipodean *flying winemaker* who has been quietly expanding
his empire with great success, particularly with Vinfruco in South Africa, at
Le Trulle in southern Italy, and at *Nagyrede* in Hungary.

Minervois [mee-nehr-vwah] (*Southwest*, France) Improving but varied reds.
Old-vine *Carignan* can be richly intense; *maceration-carbonique* wines from
younger *Carignan* can compete with *Beaujolais; Mourvèdre* can be
perfumed, and *Syrah*, spicy. Look for a newly-recognized sub-region called
la Livinière, where Jean-Christophe Piccinini is based. Elsewhere, an
enterprising Australian called Nerida Abbott is labelling a pure *Syrah* as
"*Shiraz*". Whites and rosés are considerably less interesting. **Abbott's**
Cumulus; Clos Centeilles; Gourgazaud; Ch. d'Oupia; Piccinini; Ste. Eulalie;
la Tour Boisée; Villerambert-Julien.

M

Mis en Bouteille au Ch./Dom. [mee zon boo-tay] (France) Estate-bottled.

✤ **Misket** (Bulgaria) Dullish, sometimes faintly herby white grape.

🍷 **Mission** (*Hawkes Bay*, New Zealand) Still run by monks nearly 150 years after its foundation, this estate is now one of the best in New Zealand.
★★★★ 1998 Reserve Cabernet £££

🍷 **Mission Hill** (*British Columbia*, Canada) Dynamic producer of various styles, ranging from *Riesling icewine* to *Merlot*.

🍷 **Ch. la Mission-Haut-Brion** [lah mee-see-yon oh-bree-yon] (*Pessac-Léognan Cru Classé, Bordeaux*, France) Tough but rich reds that rival and – possibly in 1999 – even overtake its supposedly classier neighbour *Haut-Brion*. 78 79 81 82 83 85 86 87 88 89 90 94 *95 96 97 98 99 00*

🍷 **Mitchell** (*Clare Valley*, Australia) Good producer of *Riesling* and of the Peppertree *Shiraz*, one of the *Clare Valley's* best reds. Also good for powerful *Grenache, Riesling, Sémillon*, and sparkling *Shiraz*.

🍷 **Mitchelton** (*Goulburn Valley*, Australia) A modern producer of *Marsanne* and *Sémillon. Late harvest Rieslings* are also good, as is a *Beaujolais*-style red, known as Cab Mac. The French-style Preece range – named after the former winemaker – is also worth seeking out.

Mittelhaardt [mit-tel-hahrt] (*Pfalz*, Germany) Central and best *Bereich* of the *Rheinpfalz*. QbA/Kab/Spät: **94 95 96 97** *98 99 00* Aus/Beeren/Tba: **90 91 92 93 94 95** *96 97 98 99 00*

Mittelmosel [mit-tel-moh-zul] (*Mosel-Saar-Ruwer*, Germany) Middle and best section of the *Mosel*, including the *Bernkastel Bereich*. QbA/Kab/Spät: **90 91 92 93 94 95 96 97** *98 99 00* Aus/Beeren/Tba: **90 91 92 93** *94 95 96 97 98 99 00*

Mittelrhein [mit-tel-rine] (Germany) Small, northern section of the *Rhine*. Good *Rieslings* that sadly are rarely seen outside Germany. QbA/Kab/Spät: **90 91 92 93 94 95 96 97** 98 99 00 Aus/Beeren/Tba: **90 91 92 93 94 95** *96 97 98 99 00 Toni Jost.*

🍷 **Mittnacht-Klack** [mit-nakt-clack] (*Alsace*, France) Seriously high-quality wines with particular accent on *"vendange tardive"* and *late harvest* wines.
★★★★ 1998 Riesling Schoenenbourg ££££

Moelleux [mwah-luh] (France) Sweet.

🍷 **Moët & Chandon** [moh-wet ay shon-don] (*Champagne*, France) The biggest producer in *Champagne. Dom Pérignon*, the top wine, and *vintage* Moët are reliably good, and new *cuvées* of "Brut Imperial NonVintage", though not always brilliant, show a welcome reaction to recent criticism. Watch out too for a good *Brut* rosé. ★★★★ 1995 Vintage Rosé £££

🍷 **Clos Mogador** [kloh MOH-gah-dor] (*Priorato*, Spain) Juicy, modern, and more importantly, stylish red wine from the once ultra-traditional and rustic region of *Priorato*. The shape of things to come. ★★★★ 1997 £££

🍷 **Moillard** [mwah-yar] (*Burgundy*, France) Middle-of-the-road *négociant* whose best wines are sold under the "Dom. Thomas Moillard" label.

🍷 **Monbazillac** [mon-ba-zee-yak] (*Southwest*, France) *Bergerac AC* using the grapes of sweet *Bordeaux* to make alternatives to *Sauternes*.

🍷 **Ch. Monbousquet** [mon-boo-skay] (*St. Emilion Grand Cru Classé, Bordeaux*, France) Rich, concentrated wines. The 1995 was notable.
90 93 94 *95 96 97 98 99 00*

🍷 **Ch. Monbrison** [mon-bree-son] (*Margaux, Bordeaux*, France) Reliable, constant overperformer. A great 1999. **85 86 88 89 90 94** *95 96 97 98 99 00*

🍷 **Mönchof** [mern-chof] (*Mosel*, Germany) Top *Mosel* producer in Ürzig.

🍷 **Ch. de Moncontour** [mon-con-toor] (*Loire*, France) Very recommendable and affordable source of *Vouvray*. ★★★ 1995 Vouvray Demi-Sec ££

🍷 **Robert Mondavi** [mawn-dah-vee] (*Napa Valley*, California) Pioneering producer of great Reserve *Cabernet* and *Pinot Noir*, and *Chardonnay*, and inventor of *oaky Fumé Blanc Sauvignon*. Co-owner of *Opus One* and now in a joint venture with *Caliterra* in Chile and *Frescobaldi* in *Tuscany*. ★★★★ 1997 Reserve Cabernet £££

M

ℤ **Mondeuse** [mon-durz] (*Tokaji*, Hungary) French-owned pioneer of *Tokaji* and *Furmint*.

ℤ **la Mondotte** [mon-dot] (*St. Emilion, Bordeaux*, France) Ultra-intense rich micro-wine produced by the owner of Canon la Gaffelière.

ℤ **Mongeard-Mugneret** [mon-zhahr moon-yeh-ray] (*Burgundy*, France) A reliable source of invariably excellent and sometimes stunningly exotic red *Burgundy*. ★★★★ 1998 Echézeaux £££

🍇 **Monica (di Cagliari/Sardegna)** [moh-nee-kah] (*Sardinia*, Italy) Red grape and wine of *Sardinia* producing drily tasty and fortified spicy wine.

ℤ **Marqués de Monistrol** [moh-nee-strol] (*Catalonia*, Spain) Single-estate *Cava*. Also successfully producing noble varietals. ★★★ 1996 Merlot $£

Monopole [mo-noh-pohl] (France) Literally, exclusive – in *Burgundy* denotes single ownership of an entire vineyard. Romanée-Conti and Château Grillet are good examples.

ℤ **Mont Gras** [mon gra] (*Colchagua*, Chile) Fast-improving winery. ★★★★★ 1999 Reserva Single Vineyard Carmenère £££

ℤ **Clos du Mont Olivet** [Mo(n)-toh-lee-vay] (*Rhône*, France) Good *Châteauneuf-du-Pape* producer. *Cuvée du Pape* is the top wine. ★★★★ 1998 Châteauneuf-du-Pape £££

ℤ **Les Producteurs du Mont Tauch** [mon-tohsh] (*Midi*, France) Southern cooperative with surprisingly good, top-of-the-line wines. ★★★★★ 1998 Reserve Baron de la Tour ££

ℤ **Montagne St. Emilion** [mon-tan-yuh san tay-mee-yon] (*Bordeaux*, France) A "satellite" of *St. Emilion*. Often very good-value *Merlot-dominant* reds which can outclass supposedly finer fare from *St. Emilion* itself. Drink young. 82 83 85 86 88 89 90 94 95 96 97 98 99 Ch. d'Arvouet; *Beauséjour*; Bonfort; Calon; Corbin; Faizeau; Fauconnière; Vieux Château Calon.

ℤ **Montagny** [mon-tan-yee] (*Burgundy*, France) Small hillside *Côte Chalonnaise commune* producing good, lean *Chardonnay* that can be a match for many *Pouilly-Fuissés*. Confusingly, unlike other parts of Burgundy *Premier Crus* here are not from better vineyards; they're just made from riper grapes. White: 90 92 93 95 96 97 98 Bertrand & Juillot; J-M Boillot; Cave de Buxy; Ch. de Davenay; Joseph Faiveley; Louis Latour; Olivier Leflaive; Bernard Michel; Moillard; Antonin Rodet; Ch. de la Saule; Jean Vachet.

ℤ **Montalcino** [mon-tal-chee-noh] (*Tuscany*, Italy) Village near Sienna known for *Brunello di Montalcino*, *Chianti's* big brother, whose reputation was largely created by *Biondi Santi*, whose wines no longer deserve the prices they command. *Rosso di Montalcino* is lighter. 78 79 82 85 88 90 94 95 96 97 98 Altesino; Banfi; Costanti; Frescobaldi; Poggio Antico.

ℤ **Montana** (*Marlborough*, New Zealand) Impressively consistent, huge firm with tremendous *Sauvignons*, improving *Chardonnays*, and good-value *Lindauer* and *Deutz Marlborough Cuvée* sparkling wine. Reds are improving but still tend to be on the green side. Look out for the Church Road wines and the smartly packaged single-estate wines such as the Brancott *Sauvignon*. ★★★★ 1998 Renwick Estate Chardonnay £££ ★★★★ 1999 Brancott Estate Sauvignon £££

ℤ **Monte Real** [mon-tay ray-al] (*Rioja*, Spain) Made by Bodegas Riojanos; generally decent, richly flavoured and *tannic Rioja*.

ℤ **Montecarlo** [mon-tay car-loh] (*Tuscany*, Italy) A wide variety of grapes are allowed here, including Rhône varieties such as the *Syrah* and *Roussanne* as well as the *Sangiovese* and the red and white *Bordeaux* varieties. Unsurprisingly, there are good *IGTs* too. Carmignani; Wandanna.

ℤ **Fattoria di Montechiari** [mon-tay-kee-yah-ree] (*Tuscany*, Italy) A fast-rising star in Montecarlo, producing rich, berryish, varietal reds under the Montechiari name using the *Cabernet Sauvignon*, *Sangiovese*, and *Pinot Noir*. The *Chardonnay* is worth looking out for too.

- Y **Bodegas Montecillo** [mon-tay-thee-yoh] (*Rioja*, Spain) Classy wines including the oddly named Vina Monty. The Cumbrero Blanco white is good, too. ★★★★ 1994 Gran Reserva £££
- Y **Montée de Tonnerre** [mon-tay duh ton-nehr] (*Burgundy*, France) Excellent *Chablis Premier Cru*.
- Y **Montefalco Sagrantino** [mon-teh-fal-koh sag-ran-tee-noh] (*Umbria*, Italy) Intense and very characterful, cherryish red made from the local Sagrantino grape.
- Y **Ch. Montelena** [mon-teh-lay-nah] (*Napa Valley*, California) Its two long-lived *Chardonnays* (from Napa and the rather better Alexander Valley) make this one of the more impressive producers in the state. The vanilla-and-blackcurranty *Cabernet* can be impenetrable. I prefer the *Zinfandel*.
- 🍇 **Montepulciano** [mon-tay-pool-chee-yah-noh] (Italy) Very confusingly, this is both a grape used to make rich red wines in central and south-eastern Italy (Montepulciano *d'Abruzzi*, etc) and the name of a wine-producing town in *Tuscany* (see *Vino Nobile di Montepulciano*) which (yes, you guessed) uses a different grape altogether.

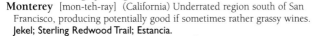

CHATEAU MONTELENA
ESTABLISHED 1882

NAPA VALLEY
Chardonnay
1985

PRODUCED & BOTTLED BY CHATEAU MONTELENA
WINERY · CALISTOGA, NAPA VALLEY CALIFORNIA · BW 4325
ALCOHOL 13.9% BY VOLUME

Monterey [mon-teh-ray] (California) Underrated region south of San Francisco, producing potentially good if sometimes rather grassy wines. Jekel; Sterling Redwood Trail; Estancia.

- Y **The Monterey Vineyard** (*Monterey*, California) Generally reliable inexpensive varietal wines now sold under the Redwood Trail label overseas. Go for the "Classic" range. Read the labels carefully though, especially if you might be expecting wines with these labels to reflect the vinous character of the *Monterey* region. In fact, as the small print reveals the contents may actually come from anywhere in California and have on occasion – when local stocks were low – been produced in the *Languedoc* region in France. This multinational approach is not uncommon these days – both E&J Gallo and Robert Mondavi have adopted it – and it certainly helps big brand-owners to maintain consistency. But it's a long way from wines that taste of the region in which they were made.
- Y **Monte Rossa** [mon-teh ros-sah] (*Lombardy*, Italy) A really top class Franciacorta producer with two key wines in the Satèn and Cabochon cuvées.
- Y **Viña Montes** [mon-tehs] (*Curico*, Chile) Leading Chilean oenologist, Aurelio Montes' go-getting winery with good reds, including the flagship Alpha M and improved *Sauvignon*. ★★★★★ 1998 Alpha M £££
- Y **Fattoria di Montevertine** [mon-teh-ver-TEE-neh] (*Tuscany*, Italy) Less famous outside Italy than *Antinori* and *Frescobaldi* perhaps, but just as instrumental in the evolution of modern *Tuscan* wine, and of the rediscovery of the *Sangiovese* grape. Le Pergole Torte is the long-lived top wine. Il Sodaccio is fine too, however.
- Y **Montevetrano** [mon-teh-veh-trah-noh] (*Campania*, Italy) A highly innovative producer proving that applying skilled winemaking to a novel blend of the local Aglianico and the *Cabernet Sauvignon* and *Merlot* can make for a world-class red wine.
- Y **Monteviña** [mon-tay-veen-yah] (*Amador County*, California) *Sutter Home* subsidiary, making exceptionally good *Zinfandel* from *Amador County* and reliable *Cabernet*, *Chardonnay*, and *Fumé Blanc*. ★★★ 1995 Zinfandel £££
- Y **Monthelie** [mon-tuh-lee] (*Burgundy*, France) Often overlooked *Côte de Beaune* village producing potentially stylish reds and whites. The appropriately named Dom. Monthelie-Douhairet is the most reliable estate. White: **85 86 88** 89 **90 92 95 96** 97 98 Red: **78** 80 83 **85 86 87 88 89** 90 92 **95 96** 97 98 99 *Coche-Dury; Jaffelin; Comtes Lafon; Olivier Leflaive; Leroy; Monthelie-Douhairet; Ch. de Puligny-Montrachet; Roulot.*

M

Montilla-Moriles [mon-tee-yah maw-ree-lehs] (Spain) *DO* region in which *sherry*-type wines are produced in *solera* systems. These are often so high in alcohol as to render fortification unnecessary. Good examples offer far better value than many sherries. Occasional successes achieve far more. **Pérez Barquero;** *Toro Albalá.*

☖ **Dom. de Montille** [duh mon-tee] (*Burgundy,* France) A lawyer-cum-winemaker whose *Volnays* and *Pommards*, if rather tough and astringent when young, are unusually fine and long-lived. Classy stuff.

☖ **Montlouis** [mon-lwee] (*Loire,* France) Neighbour of *Vouvray* making similar, lighter-bodied, dry, sweet, and sparkling wines. **Berger; Delétang; Levasseur; Moyer; la Taille aux Loups.**

☖ **Le Montrachet** [luh mon-ra-shay] (*Burgundy,* France) This appellation (also known as plain Montrachet) is shared between the villages of *Chassagne-* and *Puligny-Montrachet*, with its equally good neighbours *Bâtard-M.,* Chevalier-M., *Bienvenue-Bâtard-M*, and Criots-Bâtard-M. Potentially the greatest, biscuitiest white *Burgundy* – and thus dry white wine – in the world. *Marc Colin; Drouhin (Marquis de Laguiche); Comtes Lafon; Leflaive; Ramonet; Domaine de la Romanée-Conti; Sauzet.*

☖ **Montravel** [mon'-ravel] (Southwest France) Region with three separate *appellations*: Montravel itself, for dry *Sémillon/Sauvignon;* and *Côtes de Montravel* and Haut-Montravel, both of which produce semi-sweet, medium-sweet, and *late-harvest* whites. **Ch du Bloy; Pique-Serre; la Roche-Marot; Viticulteurs de Port Ste Foy.**

☖ **Ch. Montrose** [mon-rohz] (*St. Estèphe 2ème Cru Classé, Bordeaux,* France) Back-on-track *St. Estèphe* renowned for its longevity. More typical of the *appellation* than *Cos d'Estournel* but often less approachable in its youth. However, still maintains a rich, tarry, inky style. Especially good in 1994, though less so in 1995 and 1996. **61** 64 66 **70 75** 76 78 79 81 **82** 83 85 **86** 88 **89 90** 91 92 93 **94** 95 96 **97** 98 99

☖ **Ch. Montus** [mon-toos] (*Southwest,* France) Ambitious producer in *Madiran* with carefully oaked examples of *Tannat* and *Pacherenc de* Vic Bilh. *Bouscassé* is a cheaper, more approachable label.

☖ **Moondah Brook** (*Swan Valley,* Australia) An atypically (for the baking *Swan Valley*) cool vineyard belonging to *Houghtons* (and thus *Hardys*). The stars are the wonderful tangy *Verdelho* and richly oaky *Chenin Blanc*. The *Chardonnay* and reds are less impressive.

☖ **Moorilla Estate** [moo-rillah] (*Tasmania,* Australia) Long-established, recently reconstituted estate with particularly good *Riesling*.

☖ **Mór** [moh-uhr] (Hungary) Region gaining a name for its dry whites.

☖ **Moraga** (*Bel Air*, California) Multi-million dollar homes were demolished to create this steeply sloping seven-acre vineyard in the heart of Bel Air. So, the $50 price tag on its Bordeaux-like wine seems almost modest. The quality is good, too – thanks to the involvement of Tony Soter of *Etude*.

☖ **Morande** [moh-ran-day] (Argentina/Chile) Impressive winemaker, producing wine often from pioneering varieties that are grown on both sides of the Andes.

☖ **Moreau-Naudet** [moh-roh noh-day] (*Burgaundy,* France) Small, up-and-coming producer of *Chablis*. ★★★★ **1998 Chablis Caractère £££**

🍇 **Morellino di Scansano** [moh-ray-lee-noh dee skan-sah-noh] (*Tuscany,* Italy) Amazing cherry and raspberry, young-drinking red made from a clone of *Sangiovese*. **Cantina Cooperativa; Motta; le Pupile.**

☖ **Dom. Marc Morey** [maw-ray] (*Burgundy,* France) Estate producing stylish white *Burgundy*. ★★★★★ **1998 Chassagne-Montrachet Chevenottes £££**

☖ **Dom. Pierre Morey** [maw-ray] (*Burgundy,* France) Top-class *Meursault* producer known for concentrated wines in good vintages. ★★★★ **1998 Meursault Perrières £££**

☖ **Bernard Morey et Fils** [maw-ray] (*Burgundy,* France) Top-class producer in *Chassagne-Montrachet* with good vineyards here and in *St. Aubin*.

M

ℤ **Morey-St.-Denis** [maw-ray san duh-nee] (*Burgundy,* France) *Côtes de Nuits* village which produces deeply fruity, richly smooth reds, especially the *Grand Cru* "Clos de la Roche". Best producer is *Domaine Dujac,* which virtually makes this *appellation* its own. 76 **78** 79 **80** 82 83 **85** 86 87 **88 89** 90 92 **95 96** *Bruno Clair; Dujac; Faiveley; Georges Lignier; Hubert Lignier; Ponsot.*

ℤ **Morgon** [mohr-gon] (*Burgundy,* France) One of the 10 *Beaujolais Crus.* Worth maturing, as it can take on a delightful chocolate/cherry character. **89 90 91** 93 94 95 **96 97 98** Dom. Calon; *Georges Duboeuf (aka Marc Dudet);* Jean Descombes; *Sylvain Fessy;* Jean Foillard; Lapierre; Piron; Savoye.

🍇 **Morio Muskat** [maw-ree-yoh moos-kat] White grape grown in Germany and Eastern Europe and making simple, grapey wine.

Mornington Peninsula (*Victoria,* Australia) Some of Australia's newest and most southerly vineyards on a perpetual upward crescent. Close to Melbourne and under threat from housing developers. Good *Pinot Noir,* minty *Cabernet* and juicy *Chardonnay,* though the innovative T'Gallant is leading the way with other varieties. *Dromana; Paringa; Stonier; T'Gallant.*

ℤ **Morris of Rutherglen** (*Rutherglen,* Australia) Despite the takeover by *Orlando* and the retirement of local hero and champion winemaker Mick Morris, this is still an extraordinarily successful producer of delicious *Liqueur Muscat* and *Tokay* (seek out the Show Reserve). Also worth buying is a weird and wonderful *Shiraz-Durif* sparkling red. ★★★★ *Liqueur Muscat £££*

ℤ **Denis Mortet** [mor-tay] (*Burgundy,* France) Fast up-and-coming producer with intense, rich, dark, straight *Gevrey-Chambertin* that is every bit as good as some of his neighbours' *Grands Crus.* ★★★★ 1998 Gevrey-Chambertin Au Vellé *£££*

ℤ **Morton Estate** (*Waikato,* New Zealand) Producer of fine *Sauvignon, Chardonnay,* and *Bordeaux* styles. ★★★★ 1998 Black Label Merlot *££*

ℤ **Mosbacher** [moss-bahk-kur] (*Pfalz,* Germany) High-quality estate producing spicy *Rieslings* in Forst.

ℤ **Moscatel de Setúbal** [mos-kah-tel day say-too-bahl] (Portugal) See *Setúbal.*

🍇 **Moscato** [mos-kah-toh] (Italy) The Italian name for *Muscat,* widely used across Italy in all styles of white wine from *Moscato d'Asti,* through the more serious *Asti Spumante,* to dessert wines like *Moscato di Pantelleria.*

ℤ **Moscato d'Asti** [mos-kah-toh das-tee] (Italy) Delightfully grapey, sweet, and fizzy, low-alcohol wine from the *Muscat,* or *Moscato* grape. Far more flavoursome (and cheaper) than designer alcoholic lemonade. Drink young.

ℤ **Moscato Passito di Pantelleria** [pah-see-toh dee pan-teh-leh-ree-yah] (*Sicily,* Italy) Gloriously traditional sweet wine made on an island off *Sicily* from grapes that are dried out of doors until they have shrivelled into raisins.

ℤ **Mosel/Moselle** [moh-zuhl] (Germany) River and term loosely used for wines made around the Mosel and nearby Saar and Ruwer rivers. Equivalent to the "*Hock*" of the Rhine. (Moselblümchen is the equivalent of Liebfraumilch.) Not to be confused with France's uninspiring *Vins de Moselle.* The wines tend to have flavours of green fruits when young but develop a wonderful ripeness as they fill out with age. QbA/Kab/Spät: **89 90** 91 **92 93 94 95 96 97** 98 Aus/Beeren/Tba: 83 **85 88 89 90** 91 **92 93 94 95 96 97** 98 *Dr. Loosen;* JJ Christobel; Jakoby-Mathy; Freiherr von Heddersdorff; Willi Haag; Heribert Kerpen; Weingut Karlsmuhle; Karp-Schreiber; *Immich Batterieberg.*

ℤ **Lenz Moser** [lents moh-zur] (Austria) Big producer whose range includes crisp, dry whites and luscious dessert wines. Best efforts come from the Klosterkeller Siegendorf.

ℤ **Moss Wood** (*Margaret River,* Australia) Pioneer producer of *Pinot Noir, Cabernet,* and *Semillon.* The wines have long cellaring potential and have a very French feel to them. The *Semillon* is reliably good in both its oaked and unoaked form; the *Chardonnay* is big and forward and the *Pinot Noir* never quite living up to the promise of the early 1980s.

ℤ **La Motte Estate** [la mot] (*Franschhoek,* South Africa) Best known for top *Shiraz.* ★★★ 1997 Shiraz *£££*

M

☿ **Herdade de Mouchão** [Hehr-dah-day dey moo sha-'oh] (*Alentejo, Portugal*) Estate producing high-quality reds in this up-and-coming region.

☿ **J.P. Moueix** [mwex] (*Bordeaux*, France) Top-class *négociant*/producer, Christian *Moueix* specializes in stylishly traditional *Pomerol* and *St. Emilion* and is responsible for *Pétrus*, *La Fleur-Pétrus*, *Bel Air*, Richotey, and *Dominus* in California. (Do not confuse with any other Moueix's.)

☿ **Moulin Touchais** [moo-lan too-shay] (*Loire*, France) Producer of intensely honeyed, long-lasting, sweet white from *Coteaux du Layon*.

☿ **Moulin-à-Vent** [moo-lan-na-von] (*Burgundy*, France) One of the 10 *Beaujolais Crus* – big and rich at its best, like *Morgon*, it can benefit from ageing. 88 89 90 **91** 93 95 96 97 98. Charvet; Degrange; *Duboeuf*; Paul Janin; Janodet; Lapierre; *Ch. du Moulin-à-Vent*; la Tour du Bief.

☿ **Ch. Moulin-à-Vent** [moo-lan-na-von] (*Moulis Cru Bourgeois, Bordeaux*, France) Leading *Moulis* property. 82 83 85 86 89 90 94 96

☿ **Ch. du Moulin-à-Vent** [moo-lan-na-von] (*Burgundy*, France) Reliable producer of *Moulin-à-Vent*. 85 88 89 90 91 93 94 95 96 97 98

☿ **Moulis** [moo-lees] (*Bordeaux*, France) Red wine village of the *Haut-Médoc*; often paired with *Listrac*, but making far more approachable good-value *Crus Bourgeois*. 76 **78** 79 81 **82** 83 **85** 86 88 89 90 94 **95** 96 97 98 Ch. Anthonic; *Chasse-Spleen*; *Maucaillou*; Moulis; *Poujeaux*.

Mount Barker (Western Australia) Cooler-climate, southern region with great *Riesling*, *Verdelho*, impressive *Chardonnay*, and restrained *Shiraz*. White: 90 91 93 **94** 95 96 97 98 Red: 80 82 83 85 86 87 88 **90** 91 92 93 **94** 95 96 97 98 Frankland Estate; *Goundrey*; Howard Park; Plantagenet; Wignalls.

☿ **Mount Horrocks** (*Clare Valley*, Australia) Inventive *Shiraz* and *Riesling* producer that has made a speciality out of reviving an old method of winemaking called "Cordon Cut", which concentrates the flavour of the *Riesling* juice by cutting the canes some time before picking the grapes. ★★★★ 2000 Riesling £££

☿ **Mount Hurtle** (*McLaren Vale*, South Australia) See *Geoff Merrill*.

☿ **Mount Langi Ghiran** [lan-gee gee-ran] (*Victoria*, Australia) A maker of excellent cool-climate *Riesling*, peppery *Shiraz,* and very good *Cabernet*. ★★★★ 1998 Shiraz £££

☿ **Mount Mary** (*Yarra Valley*, Australia) Dr. Middleton makes *Pinot Noir* and *Chardonnay* that are astonishingly and unpredictably *Burgundy*-like in the best and worst sense of the term. The Quintet red and Triolet white versions of Bordeaux are more reliable. ★★★★★ 1998 Triolet £££

Mount Veeder (*Napa Valley*, California) Convincing hillside *appellation* producing impressive reds, especially from *Cabernet Sauvignon* and *Zinfandel*. Red: 84 85 86 87 **90** 91 92 **93** 95 96 97 98 White: 85 90 91 92 **95** 96 97 98 Hess Collection; Mayacamas; Mount Veeder Winery; Ch. Potelle.

☿ **Mountadam** (*High Eden Ridge*, Australia) Recently purchased by the giant LVMH which owns *Moët & Chandon, Krug,* and *Cloudy Bay*, this hilltop winery makes classy Burgundian *Chardonnay* and *Pinot Noir* (both still and sparkling) and an impressive blend called "The Red". Also worth seeking out are the *Eden Ridge* organic wines, the fruity *David Wynn* line and the "Samuel's Bay" *second label*. ★★★★ 1998 Chardonnay £££

🍇 **Mourvèdre** [mor-veh-dr] (*Rhône*, France) Floral-spicy *Rhône* grape usually found in blends. Increasingly popular in France and California where, as in Australia, it is called *Mataro*. Jade Mountain; Penfolds; *Ridge*.

Mousse [mooss] The bubbles in *Champagne* and sparkling wines.

Mousseux [moo-sur] (France) Sparkling wine – generally cheap and unremarkable.

☿ **Mouton-Cadet** [moo-ton ka-day] (*Bordeaux*, France) A brilliant commercial invention by Philippe de Rothschild who used it to profit handsomely from the name of *Mouton-Rothschild*, with which it has no discernible connection. The quality of – and more specifically the value for money offered by – these wines has traditionally been lamentable, but there have been heartening improvements recently. The "Réserve" is now better than the basic, and the recently launched white *Graves Réserve* creditable in its own right. Even so, there are generally better buys to be found on the shelves.

I **Ch. Mouton-Baronne-Philippe** [moo-ton ba-ron-fee-leep] (*Pauillac, 5ème Cru Classé, Bordeaux*, France) Known as Mouton d'Armailhac until 1933, then as Mouton-Baron-Philippe, then Mouton-Baronne-Philippe (in 1975) before becoming *Ch. d'Armailhac* in 1989.

I *Ch.* **Mouton-Rothschild** [moo-ton roth-child] (*Pauillac Premier Cru Classé, Bordeaux*, France) The only *château* to be elevated to a first growth from a second, Mouton can have gloriously rich, complex flavours of roast coffee and blackcurrant. Recent vintages were eclipsed by *Margaux, Lafite,* and *Latour,* but the 1998 and 1999 show a return to quality. 61 62 66 70 75 76 78 81 **82 83 85 86 88 89 90** 91 **93 94 95** 96 97 98 ★★★★ 1998 ££££

Mudgee [mud-zhee] (*New South Wales*, Australia) Australia's first *appellation* region, a coolish-climate area now being championed by *Rosemount* as well as by *Rothbury*. Botobolar; Huntington Estate.

I **Bodegas Muga** [moo-gah] (*Rioja*, Spain) Producer of good old-fashioned *Riojas*, of which Prado Enea is the best.

I **Jacques-Frederic Mugnier** [moo-nee-yay] (*Burgundy*, France) *Chambolle-Musigny* estate that makes long-lived wines from great vineyards, including Bonnes-Mares and *Musigny*. ★★★★ 1997 Chambolle-Musigny £££

I **Mulderbosch** [mool-duh-bosh] (*Stellenbosch,* South Africa) South Africa's answer to *Cloudy Bay*: exciting *Sauvignon* and *Meursault*-like *Chardonnay*, not to mention a red blend called Faithful Hound. ★★★★ 1998 Barrel-Fermented Chardonnay ££

I **Weingut Müller-Catoir** [moo-luh kah-twah] (*Pfalz,* Germany) Great new-wave producer using new-wave grapes as well as *Riesling*. Search out powerful Grauburgunder, Rieslaner, and *Scheurebe* wines. ★★★★★ 1998 Haardter Bürgergarten Riesling Spätlese £££

I **Egon Müller-Scharzhof** [moo-luh shahrtz-hof] (*Mosel-Saar-Ruwer,* Germany) Truly brilliant *Saar* producer. ★★★★★ 1998 Scharzhofberger Riesling Spätlese £££

🌿 **Müller-Thurgau** [moo-lur-toor-gow] (Germany) Workhorse white grape, which is a *Riesling* x *Sylvaner* cross. It is also known as *Rivaner*. Müller-Thurgau is used for making much unremarkable wine in Germany, but it also yields some gems for certain producers, such as *Müller-Catoir*. Very successful in England.

I **Mumm/Mumm Napa** [murm] (*Champagne,* France/California) Maker of slightly improved Cordon Rouge *Champagne* and far better *Cuvée Napa* from California. Newly (1999) sold by its owners, Seagram. Hopefully new owners will have greater ambitions. ★★★★ 1995 Cuvée Limitée £££

I **René Muré** [moo-ray] (*Alsace,* France) Producer of full-bodied wines, especially from the Clos St. Landelin vineyard. ★★★★ 1998 Riesling Vorbourg, Clos St. Landelin £££

Murfatlar [moor-fat-lah] (Romania) Major vineyard and research area that is currently having increasing success with *Chardonnay* (including some late-harvest sweet examples), and also with *Cabernet Sauvignon*.

I **Murphy-Goode** (*Alexander Valley,* California) Classy producer of white wines that are quite Burgundian in style and sell at – considering this is California – affordable prices. Murphy-Goode also makes a high quality Cabernet Sauvignon. ★★★★ 1997 Alexander Valley Brenda Block Reserve Cabernet £££

M

🍷 **Bodegas Marqués de Murrieta** [mar-kays day moo-ree-eh-tah] (*Rioja*, Spain) Probably Spain's best old-style *oaky* white (sold as Castillo Ygay), and a traditional version of *Rioja* that is increasingly hard to find nowadays. The red, at its best, is one of the most long-lived, elegant example of this region's wines. You should definitely look out for the old Castillo Ygays from the 1960s with their distinctive old-style labels.
★★★★ 1995 Blanco Reserva Especial £££

🍷 **Murrietta's Well** (*Livermore*, California) Wines made by blending *Zinfandel*, *Cabernet*, and *Merlot* are rare. That may be so, but the pioneering, berryish red wine from California that is sold by *Wente* under this name proves it an experiment many more producers should try.

🍷 **Ch. Musar** [moo-sahr] (*Ghazir*, Lebanon) Lebanon's leading winemaker *Serge Hochar* makes a different red every year, varying the blend of *Cabernet*, *Cinsault*, and *Syrah*. The style veers wildly between *Bordeaux*, the *Rhône*, and Italy, but certainly with Château Musar there's never a risk of becoming bored. Good vintages easily keep for a decade. The *Chardonnay*-based whites are less than dazzling, though, and the Rosé can be very old fashioned 86 88 89 91 93 95

🍇 **Muscadelle** [mus-kah-del] Spicy ingredient in white *Bordeaux*. Confusingly used in the region of *Rutherglen* in Australia to produce fortified wine known there as *Tokay*.

🍷 **Muscadet des Coteaux de la Loire/Côtes de Grand Lieu/de Sèvre et Maine** [moos-kah-day day koh-toh dur lah lwar/koht dur gron lyur/dur say-vr' eh mayn] (*Loire*, France) Emphatically non-aromatic wines that are made from the *Melon de Bourgogne* grape. Worthwhile examples of this wine are matured for a brief period before being bottled on their dead yeasts or *lees* (in French this is known as bottling "*sur lie*"). The Côtes de Grand Lieu is worth the trouble of looking for, as can be the rare Coteaux de la *Loire*. Sèvre et Maine, however, is less reliable. 98 **99** *Dom. de Chasseloir;* Bossard; Chéreau-Carré; Couillaud; Guindon; *de Goulaine; Pierre Luneau;* Metaireau; Marcel Sautejeau; Sauvion.

🍇 **Muscat** [mus-kat] Generic name for a species of white grape (aka *Moscato* in Italy) of which there are a number of different subspecies.

🍇 **Muscat à Petits Grains** [moos-kah ah puh-tee gran] Aka *Frontignan*, the best variety of Muscat and the grape responsible for *Muscat de Beaumes de Venise, Muscat de Rivesaltes, Asti Spumante, Muscat of Samos, Rutherglen* Muscats, and dry *Alsace* Muscats.

🍷 **Muscat de Cap Corse/Frontignan/Mireval/Rivesaltes/St. Jean de Minervois** (*Languedoc-Roussillon*, France) Potentially luscious fortified Muscats of which Rivesaltes is the most commonly encountered and St. Jean de Minervois is possibly the best.

🍇 **Muscat of Alexandria** [moos-kah] Grape responsible for *Moscatel de Setúbal, Moscatel de Valencia,* and sweet South Australians. Also known as *Lexia*. It is also grown in South Africa (where it is known by either of these names) and satisfies the sweet tooth of much of the Afrikaner population as Hanepoot.

🍇 **Muscat Ottonel** [moos-kah ot-oh-nel] *Muscat* variety grown in Middle and Eastern Europe.

🍷 **Musigny** [moo-zee-nyee] (*Burgundy*, France) Potentially wonderful *Grand Cru* from which *Chambolle-Musigny* takes its name. A tiny amount of white is produced here. 76 79 82 83 88 89 90 91 92 93 94 95 96 97 98 *De Vogüé; Groffier; Leroy; Mugnier; Prieur.*

Must Unfermented grape juice.

MW See *Master of Wine*.

N

Nackenheim [nahk-ehn-hime] (*Rheinhessen*, Germany) Village in the *Nierstein Bereich* that is unfortunately best known for its nowadays debased *Grosslage*, Gutes Domtal. QbA/Kab/Spät: **90 91 92 93 95 96 97** 98 99 Aus/Beeren/Tba: **90** 91 **92 93 94** 95 96 **97** 98 *Gunderloch;* Kurfürstenhof; Heinrich Seip.

Nahe [nah-huh] (Germany) *Anbaugebiet* producing wines which can in the right circumstances combine delicate flavour with full body. QbA/Kab/Spät: **88 89 90** 91 **92 93** 94 **95 96 97** 98 Aus/Beeren/Tba: **83 85 88 89 90** 91 **92 93 94** 95 **96 97** 98 *Crusius; Schlossgut Diel;* Hermann Donnhoff; Hehner Kiltz; *Kruger-Rumpf.*

☿ Ch. Nairac [nay-rak] (*Barsac 2ème Cru Classé, Bordeaux,* France) Delicious, lush, long-lasting wine sometimes lacking a little complexity but very fine in 1998.

☿ Nalle (*Sonoma,* California) Great *Dry Creek* producer of some of California's (and thus the world's) greatest *Zinfandel.*

Naoussa [nah-oosa] (Greece) Region producing dry red wines, often from the Xynomavro grape. *Boutari.*

Napa [na-pa] (California) Named after the Native American word for "plenty", this is a region with plentiful wines ranging from ordinary to sublime. Too many are commercially hyped; and none is cheap. Another problem is that the region as a whole is far too varied in altitude and winemaking conditions to make proper sense as a single *appellation*. On the other hand the 20 or so smaller *appellations* that are found within Napa, such as *Carneros, Stag's Leap, Howell Mountain,* and *Mt. Veeder* deserve greater prominence – as do nearby regions like *Sonoma.* Red: 86 87 **90 91** 92 **93 94 95 96 97** 98 White: 85 **90 91** 92 **95 96 97** 98 *Atlas Peak; Beaulieu; Beringer; Cain; Cakebread; Caymus; Chimney Rock; Clos du Val; Crichton Hall; Cuvaison; Diamond Creek; Dom. Chandon; Duckhorn; Dunn; Flora Springs; Franciscan; Frog's Leap; Heitz; Hess Collection; Ch. Montelena; Monteviña; Mumm; Newton; Niebaum-Coppola; Opus One; Ch. Potelle; Phelps; Schramsberg; Screaming Eagle; Shafer; Stag's Leap; Sterling; Turley.*

☿ Napa Ridge (California) Highly successful brand, most of whose pleasant, commercial wines are made with juice from grapes that have been grown outside *Napa.* (Exports from this producer are less confusingly labelled as "Coastal Ridge".)

☿ Nautilus Estate [naw-tih-luhs] (*Marlborough,* New Zealand) *Yalumba's* New Zealand offshoot. Sparkling wine and *Sauvignon.* ★★★ 1998 Marlborough Chardonnay ££

☿ Navajas [na-VA-khas] (*Rioja,* Spain) Small producer making impressive reds and *oaky* whites worth keeping.

☿ Navarra [na-VAH-rah] (Spain) Northern Spanish *DO,* located not far from Pamplona and the western Pyrenees, traditionally renowned for rosés and heavy reds but now producing wines to rival those from neighbouring *Rioja,* where prices are often higher. Look for innovative *Cabernet Sauvignon* and *Tempranillo* blends. 81 82 **83 85 87** 89 90 **91** 92 **94 95** 96 97 98 *Chivite; Guelbenzu;* Castillo de Monjardin; Vinicola Murchantina; Nekeas; *Ochoa;* Palacio de la Vega; Senorio de Sarria.

❦ Nebbiolo [neh-bee-oh-loh] (*Piedmont,* Italy) Grape of *Piedmont,* producing wines with tarry, cherryish, spicy flavours that are slow to mature but become richly complex – epitomized by *Barolo* and *Barbaresco.* Quality and style vary enormously depending on soil. Aka *Spanna.*

☿ Nederburg [neh-dur-burg] (*Paarl,* South Africa) Huge commercial producer. The Edelkeur *late harvest* wines are the gems of the cellar. Sadly, the best wines are only sold at the annual Nederburg Auction.

Négociant [nay-goh-see-yon] (France) Merchant who buys, matures, and bottles wine. See also *Eléveur.*

N

Négociant-manipulant (NM) [ma-nih-pyoo-lon] (*Champagne,* France)
Buyer and blender of wines for *Champagne,* identifiable by the NM number
which is mandatory on the label.

Ⓧ **Negroamaro** [nay-groh-ah-mah-roh] (*Puglia,* Italy) A Puglian grape whose
name means "bitter-black" and produces fascinating, spicy-gamey reds.
Found in *Salice Salentino* and *Copertino* and in a growing number of
increasingly impressive *IGT* wines.

Nelson (New Zealand) Small region, a glorious bus ride to the northwest
of *Marlborough. Neudorf* and *Seifried/Redwood Valley* are the stars.
White: 96 97 98 Red. **91 92 94** 95 **96 97** 98 99

Ⓧ **Nemea** [nur-may-yah] (Peloponnese, Greece) Improving cool(ish)
climate region for reds made from Agiorgitiko. *Boutari; Semeli;Tsantalis.*

Ⓧ **Nepenthe** [neh-pen-thi] (*Adelaide Hills,* South Australia) Instant star with
dazzling *Chardonnay, Semillon, Sauvignon, Pinot Noir, Cabernet-Merlot* and
Zinfandel. ★★★★ **1999 Pinot Gris £££**

Ⓧ **Ch. la Nerthe** [nehrt] (*Rhône,* France) One of the most exciting estates
in *Châteauneuf-du-Pape,* producing rich wines with seductive dark fruit.

Ⓧ **Ch. Nénin** [nay-nan] (*Pomerol, Bordeaux,* France) A château to watch
since its recent purchase by the extraordinary Michel Delon of *Ch.
Léoville-Las-Cases.*

Neuchâtel [nur-sha-tel] (Switzerland) Lakeside region. Together with Les
Trois Lacs, a source of good red and rosé, *Pinot Noir,* and *Chasselas* and
Chardonnay whites. **Ch. d'Auvernier; Porret.**

Ⓧ **Neudorf** [noy-dorf] (*Nelson,* New Zealand) Pioneering small-scale
producer of beautifully made *Chardonnay, Semillon, Sauvignon, Riesling,*
and *Pinot Noir.* ★★★★★ **1998 Moutere Hills Chardonnay £££**

Neusiedlersee [noy-zeed-lur-zay] (Austria) *Burgenland* region on the
Hungarian border. Great *late-harvest* and improving whites and reds.
Fieler-Artinger; Kracher; Lang;Willi Opitz; Tschida.

Nevers [nur-vehr] (France) Subtlest oak – from a forest in *Burgundy.*

New South Wales (Australia) Major wine-producing state, which is home
to the famous *Hunter Valley,* along with the increasingly impressive *Cowra,
Mudgee, Orange,* and *Murrumbidgee* regions. White: 85 86 87 88 90 **91**
94 **95 96** 97 98 Red: **82** 83 **85 86 87 88** 90 91 **93** 94 **95** 96 97 98

New Zealand Instant superstar with proven *Sauvignon Blanc* and
Chardonnay and – despite most expectations – increasingly successful
Merlots and more particularly *Pinot Noirs.* Syrah can work well too
occasionally, as can *Pinot Gris* and *Gewürztraminer. Cabernet Sauvignon,*
however, rarely ripens properly. Vintages vary, however (1998 was not a
great year for *Marlborough*). See *Marlborough, Martinborough, Hawkes Bay,
Nelson, Gisborne, Auckland.*

Ⓧ **Newton Vineyards** (*Napa Valley,* California) High-altitude vineyards with
top-class *Chardonnay, Merlot,* and *Cabernet,* now being made with help
from *Michel Rolland.*

Ⓧ **Neszmély** (Hungary) Progressive winery in Aszar-Neszmély producing good
commercial white wines.

Ⓧ **Ngatarawa** [na-TA-ra-wah] (*Hawkes Bay,* New Zealand) Small winery that
can make impressive reds and even better *Chardonnays* and *late harvest*
whites. ★★★★ **1998 Alwyn Reserve Cabernet £££**

Niagara (*Ontario,* Canada) Area close to the Falls of the same name, and to
the shores of Lakes Ontario and Erie, where the *Vidal* is used to make good
Icewine. Chardonnay, Riesling, and – though generally less successfully – red
varieties such as *Pinot Noir* and *Merlot* are now used too by some eager
producers. Watch this space.
Ch. des Charmes; Henry of Pelham; Inniskillin; Magnotta; Reif; Southbrook.

Ⓧ **Nicholson River** (*Gippsland,* Australia) The temperamental *Gippsland*
climate makes for a small production of stunning *Chardonnays,* some of
which are of a very Burgundian style.

N

� **Niebaum-Coppola** [nee-bowm coh-po-la] (*Napa Valley*, California) You've seen the movie. Now taste the wine. The *Dracula* and *Godfather* director's estate now includes the appropriately Gothic *Inglenook* winery, has some of the oldest vines about. Inglenook makes intensely concentrated *Cabernets* that will definitely suit the patient. ★★★★ 1997 Rutherford Rubicon ££££

☿ **Niederhausen Schlossböckelheim** [nee-dur-how sen shlos-berk-ehl-hime] (*Nahe*, Germany) State-owned estate producing highly concentrated *Riesling* from great vineyards.

☿ **Dom. Michel Niellon** [nee-el-lon] (*Burgundy*, France) Estate ranking consistently in the top five white *Burgundy* producers and making highly concentrated wines. ★★★★ 1997 Chassagne-Montrachet £££

☿ **Niepoort** [nee-poort] (*Douro*, Portugal) Small, independent *port* house making subtle vintage and particularly impressive *colheita tawnies*. A name to watch. ★★★★ 1997 Vintage Port £££

Nierstein [neer-shtine] (*Rheinhessen*, Germany) Village and (with *Piesport*) *Bereich* best known in the UK. Some fine wines, obscured by the notoriety of the reliably dull Niersteiner Gutes Domtal. QbA/Kab/Spät: 85 86 **88** 89 90 91 **92** 93 94 **95** 96 **97** 98 Aus/Beeren/Tba: 83 85 88 89 90 91 **92** 93 94 95 **96** 97 98 Balbach; *Gunderloch; Heyl zu Herrnsheim.*

☿ **Nieto & Senetiner** [nee-yeh-toh eh seh-neh-tee-nehr] (*Mendoza*, Argentina) Reliable wines sold under the Valle de Vistalba and Cadus labels.

☿ **Nigl** [nee-gel] (*Kremstal*, Austria) One of Austria's best producers of dry *Riesling* and *Grüner Veltliner.*

☿ **Weingut Nikolaihof** [nih-koh-li-hof] (*Niederösterreich*, Austria) One of the producers of some of the best *Grüner Veltliners* and *Rieslings* in Austria. ★★★★ 1999 Grüner Veltliner Smaragd Trocken £££

☿ **Nipozzano** [nip-ots-zano] (*Tuscany*, Italy) See *Frescobaldi.*

☿ **Nino Negri** [nee-noh neh-gree] (*Lombardy*, Italy) Casimiro Maule makes one of the best examples of Valtellina Sfursat.

☿ **Nobilo** [nob-ih-loh] (*Huapai*, New Zealand) Kiwi colony of the BRL Hardy empire making good *Chardonnay* from *Gisborne*, "*Icon*" wines from *Marlborough* including a pleasant, commercial off-dry *White Cloud* blend.

Noble rot Popular term for *botrytis cinerea.*

☿ **Vino Nocetto** (*Shendoah Valley, California*) Winery that has been unusually successful with Italian-style Sangiovese.

☿ **Normans** (*McLaren Vale*, Australia) Fast-improving *Cabernet* and *Shiraz* specialist. ★★★★ 1999 Lone Gum Merlot ££

☿ **Bodega Norton** [naw-ton] (*Argentina*) This is one of Argentina's most recommendable producers, producing a wide range of *varietal* wines. The "Privada" wines are the cream of the crop. ★★★★ 1999 Privada ££

Nouveau [noo-voh] New wine, most popularly used of *Beaujolais.*

☿ **Nova** [meg-yer] (*Tokaji*, Hungary) French-owned pioneer of wines including *Tokaji* and *Furmint.*

☿ **Quinta do Noval** (*Douro*, Portugal) Fine and potentially finer estate. The ultra-rare Nacional *vintage ports* are the jewel in the crown, made from ungrafted vines. Also of note are great *colheita tawny ports.*

☿ **Albet i Noya** [al-bet-ee-noy-ya] (*Spain*) Innovative producer with red and white traditional and imported varieties. A superstar in the making.

☿ **Nuits-St.-Georges** [noo-wee san zhawzh] (*Burgundy*, France) *Commune* producing the most *claret*-like of red *Burgundies*, properly tough and lean when young but glorious with age. Whites are good but ultra-rare. Red 78 79 **80** 82 83 **85** 86 87 **88** 89 90 91 92 93 **94** **95** 96 **97** 98 99 *Dom. de l'Arlot; Robert Chevillon; Jean-Jacques Confuron; Faiveley; Henri Gouges; Jean Grivot; Leroy; Alain Michelot; Patrice Rion; Henri & Gilles Remoriquet.*

☿ **Nuragus di Cagliari** [noo-rah-goos dee ka-lee-yah-ree] (*Sardinia*, Italy) Good-value, tangy, floral wine from the Nuragus grape.

NV Non-vintage, meaning a blend of wines from different years.

O

Ⓨ **Oakville Ranch** (*Napa Valley,* California) Potentially one of the *Napa's* most exciting red wine producers, but wines have so far been a little too tough.
Oaky Flavour imparted by oak casks which will vary depending on the source of the oak (American is more obviously sweet than French). Woody is usually less complimentary.

Ⓨ **Vin de Pays d'Oc** [pay-doc] (*Languedoc-Roussillon,* France) The world's biggest wine region, encompassing *appellations* such as *Corbières* and *Minervois* and several smaller *Vins de Pays* regions. Pioneers here include *Mas de Daumas Gassac* and *Skalli*.

Ⓨ **Bodegas Ochoa** [och-oh-wah] (*Navarra,* Spain) New-wave producer of creamy, fruitily fresh *Cabernet, Tempranillo,* and *Viura*.
Ockfen [ok-fehn] (*Mosel-Saar-Ruwer,* Germany) Village producing some of the best, steeliest wines of the *Saar-Ruwer Bereich*, especially *Rieslings* from the *Bockstein* vineyard. QbA/Kab/Spät: 85 86 **88 89 90** 91 **92 93 94 95** 96 97 98 Aus/Beeren/Tba: **83 85 88 89 90** 91 **92 93 94 95** 96 97 98 ★★★
1996 Ockfener Bockstein Riesling Reichsgraf von Kesselstatt ££
Oechsle [urk-slur] (Germany) Indication of the sugar level in grapes or wine.
Oeste [wes-teh] (Portugal) Western region in which a growing number of fresh, light, commercial wines are being made, of which the most successful has undoubtedly been Arruda. Red: 93 94 95 96 97 98
Oestrich [ur-strihckh] (*Rheingau,* Germany) Source of good *Riesling*. QbA/Kab/Spät: **85** 86 **88 89 90** 91 **92 93** 94 95 96 97 98 Aus/Beeren/ Tba: **89 90** 92 93 94 95 96 97 98 *Wegeler Deinhard; Balthazar Ress*.

Ⓨ **Michel Ogier** [ogee-yay] (*Rhône,* France) *Côte Rôtie* producer, making less muscular wines than most of his neighbours. ★★★★ **1998 Côte Rôtie £££**
Oïdium [oh-id-ee-yum] Fungal grape infection, shrivelling the berries and turning them grey.

Ⓨ **Ojai Vineyard** [oh-high] (*Santa Barbara,* California) The specialities here are a *Sauvignon-Semillon* blend and – more interestingly – a *Rhône*-like *Syrah*. ★★★★ **1995 Syrah Bien Nacido Vineyard £££**
Okanagan (*British Columbia,* Canada) This is the principal wine region in the west of Canada. Despite frosts, the *Pinot Noir* can produce good wine here. *Mission Hill.*

⚜ **Olasz Rizling** [oh-lash-riz-ling] (Hungary) Term for the *Welschriesling*.

Ⓨ **Ch. Olivier** [oh-liv-ee-yay] (*Pessac-Léognan Cru Classé, Bordeaux,* France) An underperformer which has yet to join the *Graves* revolution. Red: 82 83 85 86 88 89 90 91 92 93 94 95 96 98 White: 90 92 93 94 96 98
Oloroso [ol-oh-roh-soh] (*Jerez,* Spain) Style of full-bodied *sherry*, that is either dry or semi-sweet.

Ⓨ **Oltrepò Pavese** [ohl-tray-poh pa-vay-say] (*Lombardy,* Italy) Still and sparkling *DOC* made from local grapes including the characterfully spicy red Gutturnio and white Ortrugo. *Ca' di Frara; Tenuta il Bosco;* Cabanon; Fugazza; Mazzolina; Bruno Verdi.

Ⓨ **Omar Khayyam (Champagne India)** [oh-mah-ki-yam] (*Maharashtra,* India) *Champagne*-method wine which, when drunk young, has more than novelty value. The producer's cheeky name, "*Champagne* India", is a source of considerable annoyance to the Champenois, but they, in the shape of *Piper Heidsieck*, were happy enough to sell the Indians their expertise.

Ⓨ **Willi Opitz** [oh-pitz] (*Neusiedlersee,* Austria) Oddball pet food-manufacturer-turned-producer of a magical mystery tour of *late-harvest* and straw-dried wines (Schilfwein), including an extraordinary *botrytis* red labelled – to the discomfort of some Californians – "Opitz One". ★★★★★
1997 Opitz One Schilfwein £££
Oppenheim [op-en-hime] (*Rheinhessen,* Germany) Village in *Nierstein Bereich* best known – unfairly – for unexciting wines from the Krottenbrunnen. Elsewhere produces soft wines with concentrated flavour.

♈ Opus One (*Napa Valley*, California) Twenty-year-old co-production between *Mouton-Rothschild* and *Robert Mondavi*. Opus one is a classy, *claret*-like, blackcurranty wine that sells at an appropriately classy *claret*-like price. ★★★★★ 1998 ££££

Orange (*New South Wales*, Australia) Coolish region which, with *Cowra*, is likely to eclipse the nearby *Hunter Valley*. Try the Orange *Chardonnay* made by Philip Shaw of *Rosemount* from vineyards of which he is proud co-owner.

♖ Orange Muscat Another highly eccentric member of the *Muscat* family, best known for dessert wines in California by *Quady* and in Australia for the delicious *Brown Brothers Late Harvest Orange Muscat* and *Flora*.

Oregon Fashionable cool-climate state, whose winemakers make a speciality of growing *Pinot Noir*. The *Chardonnay*, *Riesling*, *Pinot Gris*, and sparkling wines show promise too. *Adelsheim; Amity; Argyle; Beaux Freres; Cameron; Chehalem; Dom Drouhin; Duck Pond; Erath; Eyrie; Henry Estate; King Estate; Ponzi; Rex Hill; Sokol Blosser.*

♈ Oriachovitza [oh-ree-ak-hoh-vit-sah] (Bulgaria) Major source of reliable *Cabernet Sauvignon* and *Merlot*.

♈ Orlando (South Australia) Huge, French-owned (Pernod-Ricard) producer of the world-class and surprisingly reliable *Jacob's Creek* wines. Look for "Reserve" and "Limited Release" efforts. The RF range is good but the harder-to-find Gramps and Flaxmans wines are more exciting. ★★★★★ 1998 Jacob's Creek Limited Release Shiraz Cabernet £££

Orléanais [aw-lay-yo-nay] (*Loire*, France) A vineyard area around Orléans in the Central Vineyards region of the *Loire*, specializing in unusual white blends of *Chardonnay* and *Pinot Gris*, and reds of *Pinot Noir* and *Cabernet Franc*. White: **95 96 97** 98 Red: **90 95** 96 97 98

♈ Ch. Olivier [oh-leev-ee-yay] (*Pessac-Léognan*, *Bordeaux*, France) Picturesque château that has been disappointing in some past years but seems to have improved in 1999.

♈ Ch. Les Ormes-de-Pez [awm dur-pay] (*St. Estèphe Cru Bourgeois*, *Bordeaux*, France) Often underrated stablemate of *Lynch-Bages* and made with similar skill. **82 83** 85 **86** 88 **89** 90 92 93 94 95 96 97 98 99

♈ Tenuta dell'Ornellaia [teh-noo-tah del-aw-nel-li-ya] (*Tuscany*, Italy) *Bordeaux*-blend *Bolgheri Super-Tuscan* from the brother of Piero Antinori. This is serious wine that is worth maturing. ★★★★ 1997 Ornellaia ££££

♖ Ortega [aw-tay-gah] This is a recently developed grape variety that is grown in Germany and England, though rarely to tasty advantage. *Biddenden* is an English producer that makes a good one, however; another is *Denbies*, which uses Ortega to produce *late-harvest* wine.

♈ Orvieto [ohr-vee-yet-toh] (*Umbria*, Italy) White Umbrian *DOC* responsible for a quantity of dull wine. Orvieto *Classico* is better. Look out for Secco if you like your white wine dry; *Amabile* if you have a sweet tooth. *Antinori; Bigi; La Carraia; Covio Cardetto; Palazzone.*

♈ Osbourne [os-sbaw-nay] (*Jerez*, Spain) Producer of a good range of *sherries* including a brilliant *Pedro Ximenez*.

♈ Dom. Ostertag [os-tur-tahg] (*Alsace*, France) Poet and philosopher André Ostertag's superb *Alsace domaine*. ★★★★ 1998 Riesling Muenchberg £££

Oxidation The effect (usually detrimental, occasionally – as in *sherry* – intentional) of oxygen on wine.

Oxidative The opposite to reductive. Certain wines – most reds, and whites like *Chardonnay* – benefit from limited exposure to oxygen during their fermentation and maturation, such as barrel ageing.

♈ Oyster Bay (*Marlborough*, New Zealand) See entry for *Delegats*. ★★★ 2000 Sauvignon Blanc ££

P

Paarl [pahl] (South Africa) Warm region in which *Backsberg* and *Boschendal* make a wide range of appealing wines. Hotter and drier than neighboring *Stellenbosch*. Red: **82 84** 86 **87** 89 **91 92** 93 94 95 96 97 98 White: **95** 97 98 *Charles Back/Fairview; KWV; Backsberg; Glen Carlou; Villiera; Plaisir de Merle.*

♈ **Pacherenc du Vic-Bilh** [pa-shur-renk doo veek beel] (*Southwest,* France) Rare, dry, or fairly sweet white wine made from the *Petit* and *Gros Manseng.* A speciality of *Madiran.* ★★★★★ 1998 Montus ££

♈ **Pacific Echo** New name for the highly recommendable sparkling wine producer, *Scharffenberger.*

Padthaway [pad-thah-way] (South Australia) Vineyard area just north of *Coonawarra* specializing in *Chardonnay* and *Sauvignon,* though reds work well here too. White: **94** 95 96 97 98 Red: **86 87** 88 **90 91** 94 95 96 97 98 *Angove's Hardys; Lindemans; Orlando; Penfolds.*

♈ **Pagadebit di Romagna** [pah-gah-deh-bit dee roh-man-ya] (*Emilia-Romagna,* Italy) Dry, sweet, and sparkling whites from the Pagadebit grape.

♈ **Pago de Carrovejas** [pah-goh deh kah-roh-vay-jash] (*Ribera del Duero,* Portugal) One of the best producers in Ribera del Duero.

♈ **Pahlmeyer** (*Napa Valley,* California) One of California's most interesting winemakers, producing *Burgundian Chardonnay* and a complex *Bordeaux-*blend red. ★★★★ 1997 Jayson £££

♈ **Paitin** [pie-teen] (*Piedmont,* Italy) The Sori Paitin vineyard in Barbaresco can offer Gaja quality at affordable prices.

♈ **Ch. Pajzos** [pah-zhohs] (*Tokaji,* Hungary) Serious, French-owned producer of new-wave *Tokay.* ★★★★ 1995 Tokay Aszú 5 Puttonyos £££

♈ **Bodegas Palacio** [pa-las-see-yoh] (*Rioja,* Spain) Underrated *bodega* with stylish, fruit-driven reds and distinctively oaky whites. Also helped by wine guru *Michel Rolland.*

♈ **Palacio de Fefiñanes** [pah-las-see-yoh day fay-feen-yah-nays] (*Galicia,* Spain) Fine producer of *Rias Baixas Albariño.*

♈ **Alvaro Palacios** [pah-las-see-yohs] (*Catalonia,* Spain) Superstar Priorato estate producing individual wines with rich, concentrated flavours. L'Ermita is the (very pricey) top wine. Finca Dofi and Les Terrasses are more affordable. ★★★★ 1996 Priorat les Terrasses ££

Palate Nebulous, not to say ambiguous, term describing the apparatus used for tasting (i.e., the tongue) as well as the skill of the taster (e.g., "he has a good palate").

♈ **Palette** [pa-let] (*Provence,* France) AC rosé and creamy white, well liked by holidayers in St. Tropez, who are so used to extortionate prices for cups of coffee that they don't notice paying more for a pink wine than for a serious red. The white, which can be very perfumed, is better value.

♈ **Palliser Estate** [pa-lih-sur] (*Martinborough,* New Zealand) Source of classy *Sauvignon Blanc, Chardonnay* and – increasingly – *Pinot Noir* from *Martinborough.* ★★★★ 2000 Sauvignon Blanc ££

♈ **Ch. Palmer** [pahl-mur] (*Margaux 3ème Cru Classé, Bordeaux,* France) The success story of the late Peter Sichel who died in 1998, this third-growth *Margaux* stands alongside the best of the *Médoc* and often outclasses its more highly ranked neighbours. Wonderfully perfumed. **61 66 70 71 75** 76 **78 79** 80 82 **83** 84 85 **86** 87 **88 89** 90 91 92 93 **94** 95 96 97 98 00

♈ **Palo Cortado** [pah-loh kaw-tah doh] (*Jerez,* Spain) Rare *sherry* pitched between *amontillado* and *oloroso. Gonzalez Byass; Hidalgo; Lustau;* Osborne; Pedro Romero; *Valdespino.*

🍇 **Palomino** [pa-loh-mee-noh] (*Jerez,* Spain) White grape responsible for virtually all fine *sherries* – and almost invariably dull white wine, when unfortified. Also widely grown in South Africa.

♈ **Panther Creek** (*Oregon*) Fine Pinot Noir producer in the Willamette Valley. The Shea Vineyard wines are worth cellaring for a while.

P

Ⅰ Ch. Pape-Clément [pap klay-mon] (*Pessac-Léognan Cru Classé, Bordeaux,* France) Great source of rich reds since the mid-1980s and, more recently, small quantities of delicious, peach-oaky white. Red: 70 **75** 82 83 85 **86** 88 89 90 92 **93** 94 95 96 97 98

Ⅰ Parducci [pah-doo-chee] (*Mendocino,* California) Steady producer whose *Petite Sirah* is a terrific bargain.

Ⅰ Dom. Alain Paret [pa-ray] (*Rhône,* France) Producer of a truly magnificent *St. Joseph* and *Condrieu*, in partnership with one of the world's best-known winemakers. (Though, to be fair, M Paret's associate, Gérard Départdieu does owe his fame to the movies rather than his efforts among the vines.) ★★★★ 1997 Condrieu, Lys de Volan ££££

Ⅰ Paringa Estate (*Mornington, Victoria,* Australia) With *T'Galant* and *Stoniers*, this is one of the stars of *Mornington Peninsula*. Fine *Shiraz*.

Ⅰ Parker Estate (*Coonawarra,* Australia) Small producer sharing its name with the US guru, and calling its (very pricey) red "First Growth". Should be awarded good marks for chutzpah. ★★★★ 1998 Terra Rossa Cabernet Sauvignon ££££

Ⅰ Parusso [pah-roo-soh] (*Piedmont,* Italy) Very fine single-vineyard Barolos (Munie and Rocche) and wines sold under the Langhe designation.

Pasado/Pasada [pa-sah-doh/dah] (Spain) Term applied to old or fine *fino* and *amontillado sherries*. Worth seeking out.

Ⅰ C.J. Pask [pask] (*Hawkes Bay,* New Zealand) *Cabernet* pioneer with excellent *Chardonnay* and *Sauvignon*. One of New Zealand's very best. ★★★★ 1998 Reserve Merlot £££

Paso Robles [pa-soh roh-blays] (*San Luis Obispo,* California) Warmish, long-established region, unaffected by coastal winds or marine fog, and good for *Zinfandel* (especially *Ridge*), *Rhône*, and Italian varieties. Plus increasingly successful *Chardonnays* and *Pinots*. Red: **85** 86 87 **90 91** 92 93 95 White: 85 90 91 92 **94** 95 96 97 98 99

Ⅰ Pasqua [pas-kwah] (*Veneto,* Italy) Producer of fairly priced, reliable wines. ★★★ 1999 Soave Superiore £

Passetoutgrains [pas-stoo-gran] (*Burgundy,* France) Wine supposedly made from two-thirds *Gamay*, one-third *Pinot Noir*, though few producers respect these proportions. Once the Burgundians' daily red – until they decided to sell it and drink cheaper wine from other regions.

Ⅰ Passing Clouds (*Bendigo,* Australia) "We get clouds, but it never rains ..." Despite a fairly hideous label, this is one of Australia's most serious red blends.

Passito [pa see-toh] (Italy) Raisiny wine made from sun-dried *Erbaluce* grapes in Italy. This technique is now used in Australia by *Primo Estate*.

Ⅰ Ch. Patache d'Aux [pa-tash-doh] (*Médoc Cru Bourgeois, Bordeaux,* France) Château producing traditional, toughish stuff. 83 85 88 **89 90** 93 95 96 97 98 ★★★ 1996 £££

Ⅰ Frederico Paternina [pa-tur-nee-na] (*Rioja,* Spain) Ernest Hemingway's favourite *bodega*.

Ⅰ Luis Pato [lweesh-pah-toh] (*Bairrada,* Portugal) One of Portugal's rare superstar winemakers, proving, among other things, that the *Baga* grape can make first-class spicy, berryish red wines. ★★★★ 1997 Quinta do Ribeirinho Primeira Escolha ££

Ⅰ Patriarche [pa-tree-arsh] (*Burgundy,* France) Huge merchant whose name is not a watchword for great *Burgundy*. The *Ch. de Meursault domaine*, however, is worthwhile.

Ⅰ Patrimonio [pah-tree-moh-nee-yoh] (*Corsica,* France) One of the best appellations in Corsica. Grenache reds and rosés and Vermentino whites. Dom. Aliso-Rossi; Arena; de Catarelli; Gentile; Leccia; Clos Marfisi; Orenga de Gaffory.

Ⅰ Patz & Hall (*Napa Valley,* California) The maker of delicious, unashamedly full-flavoured *Chardonnays*.

P

⟰ **Pauillac** [poh-yak] (*Bordeaux*, France) One of the four famous *"communes"* of the *Médoc*, Pauillac is the home of *Châteaux Latour, Lafite,* and *Mouton-Rothschild*, as well as the two *Pichons* and *Lynch-Bages*. The epitome of full-flavoured, blackcurranty *Bordeaux*; very classy (and pricey) wine. 70 75 76 **78** 79 **82** 83 **85 86** 88 89 90 94 95 96 97 98

⟰ **Clos de Paulilles** [poh-leey] (*Languedoc-Roussillon*, France) Top-class producer of *Banyuls* and of the little-known *appellation* of *Collioure*.

⟰ **Neil Paulett** [paw-let] (South Australia) Small, top-flight *Clare Valley Riesling* producer. ★★★★ 1999 Riesling ££

⟰ **Dr. Pauly-Bergweiler** [bur-gwi-lur] (*Mosel-Saar-Ruwer,* Germany) Ultra-modern winery with really stylish, modern, dry and late-harvest *Riesling*. ★★★★ 1999 Bernkasteler Badstube Riesling Spätlese ££

⟰ **Ch. Pavie** [pa-vee] (*St. Emilion Premier Grand Cru Classé, Bordeaux,* France) Recently purchased, impeccably made, plummily rich *St. Emilion* wines. 79 81 82 83 85 86 87 88 89 90 91 93 94 95 96 98

⟰ **Ch. Pavie-Decesse** [pa-vee dur-ses] (*St. Emilion Grand Cru Classé, Bordeaux,* France) Neighbour to *Ch. Pavie*, but a shade less impressive. 82 83 85 86 88 89 90 92 94 95 96 98

⟰ **Ch. Pavie-Macquin** [pa-vee ma-kan'] (*St. Emilion Grand Cru Classé, Bordeaux*) Returned to form since the late 1980s – and the producer of a startlingly good 1993.

⟰ **Le Pavillon Blanc de Ch. Margaux** [pa-vee-yon blon] (*Bordeaux,* France) The (rare) *Sauvignon*-dominated white wine of *Ch. Margaux* which still acts as the yardstick for the growing number of *Médoc* white wines. 85 86 89 **90 91** 92 95 96 97 99

⟰ **Pazo de Barrantes** [pa-thoh de bah-ran-tays] (*Galicia,* Spain) One of the newest names in *Rias Baixas*, producing lovely, spicy *Albariño*. Under the same ownership as *Marques de Murrieta,*

⟰ **Ca' del Pazzo** [kah-del-pat-soh] (*Tuscany,* Italy) Ultra-classy, *oaky Super-Tuscan* with loads of ripe fruit and oak.
Pécharmant [pay-shar-mon] (*Southwest,* France) In the *Bergerac* area, producing light, *Bordeaux*-like reds. Worth trying.

⟰ **Pedro Ximénez** (PX) [peh-droh khee-MEH-nes] (*Jerez,* Spain) White grape, dried in the sun to create a sweet, curranty wine, which is used in the blending of the sweeter *sherry* styles, and in its own right by *Osborne*, and by *Gonzalez Byass* for its brilliant Noe. Also produces a very unusual wine at *De Bortoli* in Australia. ★★★★ **Cream of Creams, Manuel de Argueso £££**

⟰ **Viña Pedrosa** [veen-ya pay-droh-sah] (*Ribera del Duero,* Spain) Modern blend of *Tempranillo* and classic *Bordelais* varieties. The Spanish equivalent of a *Super-Tuscan*.

⟰ **Clos Pegase** [kloh-pay-gas] (*Napa Valley,* California) Showcase winery with improving but historically generally overpraised wines. ★★★ 1996 Hommage £££

⟰ **Pelissero** [peh-lee-seh-roh] (*Piedmont,* Italy) Oaky Barberas, rich, dark Dolcetto, and lovely single-vineyard Barbaresco.

⟰ **Dom. Henry Pellé** [on-ree pel-lay] (*Loire,* France) Reliable producer of fruitier-than-usual *Menetou-Salon*. ★★★★ 1998 Menetou-Salon £££

⟰ **Pellegrini** (*Long Island,* New York) Producer of fine *Merlot* on the North Fork of Long Island.

⟰ **Pelorus** [pe-law-rus] (*Marlborough,* New Zealand) Showy, big, buttery, yeasty, almost Champagne-style New Zealand sparkling wine from *Cloudy Bay*.
Pemberton (Western Australia) Up-and-coming cooler climate region for more restrained styles of *Chardonnay* and *Pinot Noir*; *Picardy, Plantagenet,* and *Smithbrook* are the names to look out for.

P

✤ **Peñaflor** [pen-yah-flaw] (Argentina) Huge, dynamic firm producing increasingly good-value wines.

Penedés [peh-neh-dehs] (*Catalonia*, Spain) Largest *DOC* of *Catalonia* with varying altitudes, climates, and styles ranging from *cava* to still wines pioneered by *Torres* and others, though some not as successfully. The current trend toward increasing use of *varietals* such as *Cabernet Sauvignon*, *Merlot*, and *Chardonnay* allows more French-style winemaking without losing any of the intrinsic Spanish character. Belatedly living up to some of its early promise. White: 95 96 97 98 Red: 85 87 88 89 90 **91** 93 **94 95** 96 97 98 *Albet i Noya;* Can Feixes; Can Ráfols dels Caus; *Freixenet; Cavas Hill; Juvé y Camps;* Jean Leon; *Monistrol;* Puigi Roca; *Torres.*

✤ **Penfolds** (*South Australia*) Now associated with Rosemount. The world's biggest premium wine company with a high-quality line, from Bin 2 to *Grange*. Previously a red wine specialist but now rapidly becoming a skilful producer of still white wines such as the improving Yattarna (good but not yet living up to its supposed role as the "White *Grange*"). Under the same ownership as *Wynns, Seaview, Rouge Homme, Lindemans, Tullochs, Leo Buring, Seppelt,* and now James Halliday's *Coldstream Hills* and *Devil's Lair* in the *Margaret River.* ★★★★★ 1997 RWT £££

✤ **Penley Estate** (*Coonawarra*, Australia) High-quality *Coonawarra* estate with rich *Chardonnay* and very blackcurranty *Cabernet.* ★★★★ 1998 Coonawarra Cabernet Sauvignon £££

✤ **Peppoli** [peh-poh-lee] (*Tuscany*, France) One of *Antinori's* most reliable *Chianti Classicos.*

✤ **Comte Peraldi** [peh-ral-dee] (*Corsica*, France) High-class *Corsican* wine producer, now also making good wine in Romania. ★★★ 1998 Ajaccio CLos du Cardinal ££

✤ **Perez Pascuas** [peh-reth Pas-scoo-was] (*Ribera del Duero*, Spain) Producer of Viña Pedrosa, one of the top examples of *Ribera del Duero.*

✤ **Le Pergole Torte** [pur-goh-leh taw-teh] (*Tuscany,* Italy) Long-established pure *Sangiovese*, oaky *Super-Tuscan.* ★★★★★ 1997 Montevertine ££

🍇 **Periquita** [peh-ree-kee-tah] (Portugal) Spicy, tobaccoey grape – and the wine *J.M. da Fonseca* makes from it.

Perlé/Perlant [pehr-lay/lon] (France) Lightly sparkling.

Perlwein [pehrl-vine] (Germany) Sparkling wine.

Pernand-Vergelesses [pehr-non vehr-zhur-less] (*Burgundy,* France) *Commune* producing rather jammy reds but fine whites, including some *Côte d'Or* best buys. White: 85 86 87 **88** 89 **90** 92 *95 96 97 98* Red: 78 83 **85** 87 **88** 89 90 92 *95 96 97 98* Arnoux; Champy; *Chandon de Briailles; Dubreuil-Fontaine; Germain (Château de Chorcy);* Jadot; *Laleure-Piot; Pavelot; Rapet; Dom. Rollin.*

✤ **André Perret** (*Rhône,* France) Producer of notable *Condrieu* and some unusually good examples of *St. Joseph.* ★★★★ 1998 St. Joseph les Grisières £££

✤ **Joseph Perrier** [payh-ree-yay] (*Champagne,* France) Family-run producer whose long-lasting elegant *Champagnes* have a heavy *Pinot Noir* influence. ★★★★ 1995 Cuvée Royale Vintage ££££

✤ **Perrier-Jouët** [payh-ree-yay zhoo-way] (*Champagne,* France) Sadly underperforming *Champagne* house which, like *Mumm*, has now been sold by Canadian distillers, Seagram. Sidestep the non-vintage for the genuinely worthwhile – and brilliantly packaged – Belle Epoque prestige cuvée white and rosé sparkling wine. ★★★★ 1993 Belle Epoque ££££

✤ **Elio Perrone** [eh-lee-yoh peh-roh-nay] (*Piedmont,* Italy) There are good Barberas, Chardonnays and Dolcettos here, but the really distinctive wine is the Moscato.

✤ **Pesquera** [peh-SKEH-ra] (*Ribera del Duero*, Spain) Robert Parker dubbed this the *Ch. Pétrus* of Spain. Well, maybe. I'd say it's a top-class *Tempranillo* often equal to *Vega Sicilia* and the best of *Rioja.* ★★★★ 1995 Reserva ££

P

Pessac-Léognan [peh-sak lay-on-yon] (*Bordeaux*, France) *Graves commune* containing most of the finest *châteaux*. *Ch. Bouscaut; Carbonnieux; Fieuzal; Domaine de Chevalier; Haut-Bailly; Haut-Brion; Larrivet-Haut-Brion; Laville-Haut-Brion; La Louvière; Malartic-Lagravière; la Mission-Haut-Brion;* Smith-Haut-Laffite; *la Tour-Haut-Brion.*

☰ **Petaluma** [peh-ta-loo-ma] (*Adelaide Hills*, Australia) High-tech creation of *Brian Croser* and role model for other producers in the New World who are interested in combining innovative winemaking with the fruit of individually characterful vineyards. Classy *Chardonnays* from Piccadilly in the *Adelaide Hills, Clare Rieslings* (particularly good *late harvest*), and *Coonawarra* reds. Now owns *Smithbrook* and *Mitchelton*. ★★★★ 1998 Coonawarra £££

Pétillant [pay-tee-yon] Lightly sparkling.

☰ **Petit Chablis** [pur-tee shab-lee] (*Burgundy*, France) Theoretically, this is a less fine wine than plain *Chablis* – though plenty of vineyards that were previously designated as Petit Chablis are now allowed to produce wines sold as *Chablis*. Hardly surprisingly, the ones that are left as Petit Chablis are often poor value. 95 96 97 98 *La Chablisienne; Jean-Paul Droin; William Fèvre; Dom des Malandes.*

🌿 **Petit Verdot** [pur-tee vehr-doh] (*Bordeaux*, France) Highly trendy and excitingly spicy, if *tannic* variety traditionally used in small proportions in red *Bordeaux*, in California (rarely) and now (increasingly often) as a pure varietal in Australia (*Kingston Estate, Leconfield, Pirramimma*), Italy, and Spain (*Marqués de Griñon*).

☰ **Ch. Petit Village** [pur-tee vee-lahzh] (*Pomerol, Bordeaux*, France) Classy, intense, blackcurrantly-plummy *Pomerol* now under the same ownership as *Ch. Pichon-Longueville*. Worth keeping. 75 78 79 81 **82** 83 **85** 86 88 89 90 92 **93** 94 95 96 97 98 ★★★★ 1995 ££££

🌿 **Petite Sirah** [peh-teet sih-rah] Spicy red cousin of the *Syrah* grown in California and Mexico and as *Durif* in the *Midi* and Australia. *LA Cetto; Carmen; Fetzer; Morris; Parducci; Ridge; Turley.*

Petrolly A not unpleasant overtone often found in mature *Riesling*. Arrives faster in Australia than in Germany.

☰ **Ch. Pétrus** [pay-trooss] (*Pomerol, Bordeaux*, France) Until recently the priciest of all *clarets* (until *le Pin* came along). Voluptuous *Pomerol* hits the target especially well in the US, and is finding a growing market in the Far East. Beware of fakes (especially big bottles) which crop up increasingly often. **61** 62 **64** 66 **70 71 75** 76 78 **79** 81 82 83 85 86 88 89 90 92 93 94 95 96 97 98 99 ★★★★★ 1998 ££££

☰ **Pewsey Vale** [pyoo-zee vayl] (*Adelaide Hills*, Australia) Classy, cool-climate wines from winery under the same ownership as *Yalumba, Hill-Smith,* and *Heggies.*

☰ **Peyre Rose** [pehr rohz] (*Languedoc-Roussillon*, France) Truly stylish producer of *Coteaux du Languedoc Syrah* that competes with examples from the Northern *Rhône* – and sells at similar prices.

☰ **Ch. de Pez** [dur pez] (*St. Estèphe Cru Bourgeois, Bordeaux*, France) Fast-improving *St. Estèphe*, especially since its recent purchase by *Louis Roederer*. In good vintages, well worth ageing. 78 79 **82** 83 85 **86** 88 89 **90 93** 94 95 96 97 98

Pfalz [Pfaltz] (Germany) Formerly known as the *Rheinpfalz*, and before that as the *Palatinate*. Warm, southerly *Anbaugebiet* noted for riper, spicier *Riesling*. Currently competing with the *Mosel* for the prize of best of Germany's wine regions. QbA/Kab/Spät: **85** 86 **88 89 90** 91 92 93 94 95 96 97 98 Aus/Beeren/Tba: **83 85** 88 89 90 91 92 93 94 95 97 98 *Kurt Darting; Lingenfelder; Müller-Cattoir.*

P

℣ **Ch. Phélan-Ségur** [fay-lon say-goor] (*St. Estèphe Cru Bourgeois, Bordeaux,* France) A good-value property since the mid-1980s, with ripe, well-made wines. Could do better. 75 **82** 85 *88 89 90* 92 93 **94** *95* 96 97 98

℣ **Joseph Phelps** (*Napa Valley,* California) Pioneer *Napa* user of *Rhône* varieties (*Syrah* and *Viognier*), and a rare source of *late-harvest Riesling. Cabernet* is a strength. ★★★★ **1997 le Mistral £££**

℣ **Philipponnat** [fee-lee-poh-nah] (*Champagne,* France) Small producer famous for Clos des Goisses. Other wines are currently disappointing.

℣ **RH Phillips** (*California*) Producer whose great value California wines deserve to be better known.

Phylloxera vastatrix [fih-lok-seh-rah] Root-eating louse that wiped out Europe's vines in the 19th century. Foiled by grafting *vinifera* vines onto resistant American *labrusca* rootstock. Pockets of pre-phylloxera and/or ungrafted vines still exist in France (in a *Bollinger* vineyard and on the south coast – the louse hates sand), Portugal (in **Quinta do Noval's** "Nacional" vineyard), Australia, and Chile. Elsewhere, phylloxera recently devastated *Napa Valley* vines.

Piave [pee-yah-vay] (*Veneto,* Italy) DOC in *Veneto* region, including reds made from a *Bordeaux*-like mix of grapes.

℣ **Ch. Pibarnon** [pee-bah-non] (*Bandol,* France) Top-class producer of modern *Bandol*. 88 **89 90** 92 93 95 **96** 97 98 ★★★★★ **1998 £££**

℣ **Ch. Pibran** [pee-bron] (*Pauillac Cru Bourgeois, Bordeaux,* France) Small but high-quality and classically *Pauillac* property. 88 **89** *90* 95 96 98

℣ **Picardy** (*Pemberton,* Western Australia) Impressive new *Pinot Noir* and *Shiraz* specialist by the former winemaker of *Moss Wood.*

℣ **Pic St. Loup** [peek-sa'-loo] (*Languedoc-Roussillon,* France) Up-and-coming region within the *Coteaux du Languedoc* for *Syrah*-based, *Rhône*-style reds, and whites. *Dom. l'Hortus; Mas Bruguière.*

℣ **FX Pichler** [peek-lehr] (*Wachau Cru,* Austria) Arguably the best dry ("*Trocken*") winemaker in Austria – and certainly a great exponent of the *Grüner Veltliner* and *Riesling* at their richly dry best. ★★★★★ **1999 Grüner Veltliner Smaragd Trocken Wösendorfer Kollmütz ££££**

℣ **Ch. Pichon-Lalande** [pee-shon la-lond] (*Pauillac 2ème Cru Classé, Bordeaux,* France) The new name for Pichon-Longueville-Lalande. Famed **super second** and tremendous success story, thanks to top-class winemaking and the immediate appeal of its unusually high *Merlot* content. A great 1996, but surprisingly a slightly less exciting 1998. **61** 66 **70** 75 78 79 **82** 83 85 86 *88 89* **90** 91 *92* **93** 94 *95* 96 97 98 ★★★★ **1995 ££££**

℣ **Ch. Pichon-Longueville** [pee-shon long-veel] (*Pauillac 2ème Cru Classé, Bordeaux,* France) New name for Pichon-Longueville-Baron. An under-performing second growth *Pauillac* until its purchase by *AXA* in 1988. Now level with, and sometimes ahead of, *Ch. Pichon-Lalande,* once the other half of the estate. Wines are intense and complex. Les Tourelles, the *second label,* is a good-value alternative. **86** *88 89 90* 91 **92 93 94** *95 96* 97 98

🍇 **Picolit** [pee-koh-leet] (*Friuli,* Italy) Grape used to make both sweet and dry white wine. *Jermann* makes a good one.

℣ **Picpoul de Pinet** [peek-pool duh pee-nay] (South-West France) Underrated herby white that is particularly well made by Dom. St. Martin de la Garrigue.

Piedmont/Piemonte [pee-yed-mont/pee-yeh-mon-tay] (Italy) Ancient and modern north-western region producing old-fashioned, tough *Barolo* and *Barbaresco* and brilliant, modern, fruit-packed wines. Also makes *Oltrepò Pavese, Asti Spumante,* and *Dolcetto d'Alba.* See *Nebbiolo.*

℣ **Bodegas Piedmonte** [pee-yehd-mohn-teh] (*Navarra,* Spain) Confusingly named (see above), dynamic cooperative producing good reds from *Tempranillo, Cabernet,* and *Merlot.*

℣ **Pieropan** [pee-yehr-oh-pan] (*Veneto,* Italy) *Soave's* top producer, which more or less invented single-vineyard wines here and is still a great exception to the dull *Soave* rule. Lovely, almondy wine.

P

Ⴔ Pieroth [pee-roth] Huge company whose salesmen visit clients' homes offering wines that are rarely recommended by this or any other critic.

Ⴔ Pierro [pee-yehr-roh] (*Margaret River,* Australia) Small estate producing rich, buttery, *Meursault*-like *Chardonnay*. ★★★★ 1998 Chardonnay £££

Piesport [pees-sport] (*Mosel-Saar-Ruwer,* Germany) Produced in the *Grosslage Michelsberg*, a region infamous for dull German wine, and bought by people who think themselves above *Liebfraumilch*. Try a single-vineyard – Günterslay or Goldtröpchen – for something more memorable. QbA/Kab/Spät: 85 86 **88 89 90** 91 9? **93 94 95** 96 97 98 99 Aus/Beeren/ Tba: **83 85** 88 89 90 91 **92** 93 **94** 95 96 97 98 99

Ⴔ Pighin [pee-gheen] (*Friuli,* Italy) Good, rather than great Collio producer, with creditable examples of most of the styles produced here.

Ⴔ Pikes (*Clare Valley,* South Australia) Top-class estate with great *Riesling, Shiraz, Sangiovese,* and *Sauvignon*. ★★★★ 1998 Cabernet Sauvignon ££

Ⴔ Jean Pillot [pee-yoh] (*Burgundy,* France) There are three estates called Pillot in *Chassagne-Montrachet*. This one is the best – and produces by far the finest red.

Ⴔ Ch. le Pin [lur pan] (*Pomerol, Bordeaux,* France) Ultra-hyped, small, recently formed estate whose – admittedly delicious – wines sell at increasingly silly prices in the US and the Far East. The forerunner of a string of other similar honey-traps (see *Ch. Valandraud* and *la Mondotte*), and one of the wines that is helping to create a burgeoning trade in forged bottles. 81 82 83 85 86 87 88 89 90 92 93 94 95 96 97 98 99 ★★★★★ 1998 ££££

Ⴔ Pine Ridge (*Napa Valley,* California) Greatly improved *Stag's Leap* producer that is now also making good quality reds on *Howell Mountain*. The Oregon *Archery Summit* wines are also worth seeking out. ★★★★★ 199 Andrus Reserve ££££

Pineau de Charentes [pee-noh dur sha-ront] (*Southwest,* France) Fortified wine produced in the Cognac region.

Ⴔ Pingus [pin-goos] (*Ribeiro del Duero,* Spain) Probably the finest wine now being made in this region. Expect cleaner, richer, more modern wines than those from many of the neighbours. ★★★★★ 1996 Flor de Pingus ££££

Ⴔ Pinot Blanc/Bianco [pee-noh blon] Rather like *Chardonnay* without all that fruit, and rarely as classy or complex. Fresh, creamy, and adaptable. At its best in *Alsace* (Pinot d'Alsace), the Alto Adige in Italy (as *Pinot Bianco*), and in Germany and Austria (as *Weissburgunder*). In California, confusingly, a synonym for *Melon de Bourgogne*.

Ⴔ Pinot Chardonnay (Australia) Misleading name for *Chardonnay*, still used by *Tyrrells*. Don't confuse with *Pinot Noir/Chardonnay* sparkling wine blends such as the excellent *Seaview* and *Yalumba*.

Ⴔ Pinot Gris/Grigio [pee-noh gree] (*Alsace,* France) White grape of uncertain origins, making full, rather heady, spicy wine. Best in *Alsace* (also known as *Tokay d'Alsace*), Italy (as *Pinot Grigio*), and Germany (as *Ruländer* or *Grauburgunder*). Ernst Brun; Bott-Geyl; Dopff & Irion; Kreydenweiss; Ostertag; Piper's Brook; Schleret; Sorg; Cave de Turckheim; Weinbach (Faller); Zind–Humbrecht.

Ⴔ Pinot Meunier [pee-noh-mur-nee-yay] (*Champagne,* France) Dark, pink-skinned grape. Plays an unsung but major role in *Champagne*. Can also be used to produce a still varietal wine. Best's; Bonny Doon; William Wheeler.

Ⴔ Pinot Noir [pee-noh nwahr] Black grape responsible for all red *Burgundy* and in part for white *Champagne*. Also successfully grown in the New World with in sites whose climate is neither too warm nor too cold. Winemakers need the dedication which might otherwise have destined them for a career in nursing. Buying is like Russian roulette – once you've got a taste for that complex, raspberryish flavour, you'll go on pulling the expensive trigger. See *Oregon, Carneros, Yarra, Santa Barbara, Martinborough, Tasmania, Burgundy*.

P

🍇 **Pinotage** [pee-noh-tazh] (South Africa) *Pinot Noir* x *Cinsault* cross with a spicy, plummy character, used in South Africa and (now very rarely) New Zealand. Good old examples are brilliant but rare; most taste muddy and rubbery. New winemaking and international demand are making for more exciting wines. *Beyerskloof; Clos Malverne; Fairview; Grangehurst; Kanonkop; Saxenberg; Simonsig; Spice Route; Warwick.*

🍷 **Piper Heidsieck** [pi-pur hide-seek] (*Champagne,* France) Greatly improved *Champagne* made by Daniel Thibaut of *Charles Heidsieck.* The "Rare" is worth looking out for.

🍷 **Pipers Brook Vineyards** (*Tasmania,* Australia) Dr. Andrew Pirie, who recently bought *Heemskerk,* is a pioneering producer of fine *Burgundian Chardonnay, Pinot Noir,* and *Pinot Gris.* Ninth Island, the *second label,* includes an excellent unoaked *Chablis*-like *Chardonnay.* The new Pirie sparkling wine is good too. ★★★★ 1999 Riesling £££

🍷 **Pira** [pee-rah] (*Piedmont,* Italy) Chiara Boschis's impressive small *Barolo* estate makes long-lived wines from top-class vineyards.

🍷 **Producteurs Plaimont** [play-mon] (*Southwest,* France) Reliable cooperative in *Côtes de St. Mont* producing *Bordeaux*-lookalike reds and whites with some added interest derived from the use of local grapes. See also *Pacherenc du Vic-Bilh* and *Madiran.*

🍷 **Plaisir de Merle** [play-zeer dur mehrl] (*Paarl,* South Africa) Paul Pontallier of *Ch. Margaux* is helping to make ripe, soft reds and New World-style whites for *Stellenbosch Farmers' Winery* in this new showcase operation. ★★★★ 1997 Chardonnay ££

🍷 **Planeta** [plah-nay-tah] (Sicily, Italy) A name to watch among the growing number of starry producers in Sicily. Wines are well made and very fairly priced ★★★★ 1997 Merlot ££

🍷 **Plantagenet** (*Mount Barker,* Western Australia) This is a good producer of *Chardonnay, Riesling, Cabernet,* and lean *Shiraz* in this increasingly successful region in the southwest corner of Australia. ★★★★ 1998 Mount Barker Omrah Shiraz £££

🍷 **Plumpjack** (*Napa,* California) Small Cabernet specialist that hit the headlines by having the courage to bottle some of its Reserve *Cabernet* in screwtop bottles (to avoid cork taint). Bidders at the 2000 Napa Valley Charity Auction were undeterred and paid a record sum for the wine.

🍷 **Il Podere dell'Olivos** [eel poh-deh-reh del-oh-lee-vohs] (California) Pioneering producer of Italian varietals.

🍷 **Poggio Antico** [pod-zhee-yoh an-tee-koh] (*Tuscany,* Italy) Ultra-reliable *Brunello* producer. ★★★★ 1995 Altero ££££

🍷 **Pojer & Sandri** [poh-zhehr eh san-dree] (*Trentino,* Italy) Good red and white and, especially, sparkling wines.

🍷 **Pol Roger** [pol rod-zhay] (*Champagne,* France) Fine producer, with an unusually subtle non-vintage that improves with keeping. The Cuvée Winston Churchill (named in honour of a faithful fan) is spectacular, and the *Demi-sec* is a rare treat.

🍷 **Erich & Walter Polz** [poltz] (*Styria,* Austria) Producers of notable dry wines, including Pinot Blanc and Gris, and one of Austria's best examples of Sauvignon Blanc.

🍷 **Poliziano** [poh-leet-zee-yah-noh] (*Tuscany,* Italy) Apart from a pack-leading *Vino Nobile di Montepulciano,* this is the place to find the delicious Elegia and Le Stanze *Vini da Tavola.* ★★★★★ 1997 Asinone £££

🍷 **Pomerol** [pom-meh-rohl] (*Bordeaux,* France) With *St. Emilion,* the *Bordeaux* for lovers of the *Merlot,* which predominates in its rich, soft, plummy wines. *Ch. Pétrus* and *le Pin* are the big names but wines like *Petit Village* and *Clos René* abound. None are cheap because production is often limited to a few thousand cases (in the *Médoc,* 20,000–40,000 is more common). Quality is far more consistent than in *St. Emilion.* See *Pétrus, Moueix,* and individual châteaux. 79 81 **82 83 85** 86 **88 89** 90 **93** 94 *95* 96 97 *98* 99

P

☒ **Pomino** [poh-mee-noh] (*Tuscany,* Italy) Small *DOC* within *Chianti Rufina;* virtually a monopoly for *Frescobaldi* which makes a delicious, buttery, unwooded, white *Pinot Bianco/Chardonnay,* the oaky-rich Il Benefizio, and a tasty *Sangiovese/Cabernet.* ★★★ 1998 Pomino Bianco ££

☒ **Pommard** [pom-mahr] (*Burgundy,* France) Very variable quality *commune,* theoretically with a higher proportion of old vines, making slow-to-mature, then solid and complex reds. 78 85 86 87 **88 89 90 92 93 94 95 96 97** *98 99 Comte Armand; Jean-Marc Boillot; Girardin; Dominique Laurent; Leroy; Château de Meursault; de Montille; Mussy; Dom. de Pousse d'Or.*

☒ **Pommery** [pom-meh-ree] (*Champagne,* France) Back-on-track big-name with rich full-flavoured style. The top-label *Louise Pommery* white and rosé are tremendous. ★★★★★ 1990 Cuvée Louise ££££

☒ **Pongràcz** [pon-gratz] (South Africa) Brand name for the *Bergkelder's* (excellent) *Cap Classique* sparkling wine. ★★★★ Cap Classique ££

☒ **Dom. Ponsot** [pon-soh] (*Burgundy,* France) Top-class estate noted for *Clos de la Roche, Chambertin* and (rare) white *Morey-St.-Denis.* More affordable is the excellent *Gevrey.* ★★★★ 1998 Clos de la Roche £££

☒ **Ch. Pontet-Canet** [pon-tay ka-nay] (*Pauillac 5ème Cru Classé, Bordeaux,* France) Rich, concentrated, up-and-coming *Pauillac* benefitting since the early 1980s from the dedicated ambition of its owners who also have *Lafon-Rochet.* 82 83 85 86 88 89 90 91 93 94 *95 96 97 98 99 00*

☒ **Ponzi** [pon-zee] (*Oregon*) The ideal combination: a maker of good *Pinot Noir, Chardonnay,* and even better beer.

Port (*Douro,* Portugal) Fortified wine made in the upper *Douro* valley. Comes in several styles; see *Tawny, Ruby, LBV, Vintage, Crusted,* and *White port.*

☒ **Viña Porta** [veen-yah por-ta] (*Rapel,* Chile) Dynamic winery that specializes in juicy *Cabernet* and *Merlot.* The *Chardonnay* is good too.

☒ **Ch. Potelle** (*Napa Valley,* California) French-owned *Mount Veeder* winery that won fame when its stylish wines were served at the White House. Great Zinfandel. ★★★★ 1997 Mount Veeder Chardonnay £££

☒ **Ch. Potensac** [po-ton-sak] (*Médoc Cru Bourgeois, Bordeaux,* France) Under the same ownership as the great *Léoville-las-Cases,* and offering a more affordable taste of the winemaking that goes into that wine.

Pouilly-Fuissé [poo-yee fwee-say] (*Burgundy,* France) Variable white often sold at vastly inflated prices. Pouilly-Vinzelles, Pouilly-Loché, and other *Mâconnais* wines are often better value, though top-class Pouilly-Fuissé from producers like *Ch. Fuissé,* Dom. Noblet, or Dom. Ferret can compete with the best of the *Côte d'Or.* 95 96 97 98 99 00 *Barraud; Corsin;* Ferret; *Ch. Fuissé;* Lapierre; Noblet; Philibert; *Verget.*

☒ **Pouilly-Fumé** [poo-yee foo-may] (*Loire,* France) Potentially ultra-elegant *Sauvignon Blanc* with classic gooseberry fruit and "smoky" overtones derived from flint ("silex") subsoil. Like *Sancerre,* rarely repays cellaring. See *Ladoucette* and *Didier Dagueneau.* 95 96 97 99

☒ **Ch. Poujeaux** [poo-joh] (*Moulis Cru Bourgeois, Bordeaux,* France) Up-and-coming. reliable, plummy-blackcurrant wine. 79 82 83 85 86 88 89 90 91 92 93 94 95 96 97 *98 99 00* ★★★★ 1998 £££

Pourriture noble [poo-ree-toor nohbl] (France) See *Botrytis cinerea* or *noble rot.*

☒ **Dom. de la Pousse d'Or** [poos-daw] (*Burgundy,* France) One of the top estates in *Volnay.* (The *Pommard* and *Santenay* wines are good too.) ★★★★ 1997 Volnay Clos de la Bousse d'Or ££££

Prädikat [pray-dee-ket] (Germany) As in Qualitätswein mit Prädikat (*QmP*), the (supposedly) higher quality level for German and Austrian wines, indicating a greater degree of natural ripeness.

☒ **Franz Prager** [prah-gur] (*Wachau,* Austria) Top-class producer of a wide range of impressive *Grüner-Veltliners* and now *Rieslings.*

Precipitation The creation of a harmless deposit, usually of *tartrate* crystals, in white wine, which the Germans romantically call "diamonds."

P

Premier Cru [prur mee yay kroo] In *Burgundy*, indicates wines that fall between *village* and *Grand Cru* quality. Some major *communes* such as *Beaune* and *Nuits-St.-Georges* have no *Grand Cru*. Meursault Premier Cru, for example, is probably a blend from two or more vineyards.

☰ **Premières Côtes de Blaye** See *Côtes de Blaye*

☰ **Premières Côtes de Bordeaux** [prur-mee-yehr koht dur bohr-doh] (*Bordeaux*, France) Up-and-coming riverside *appellation* for reds and (often less interestingly) sweet whites. Whites: 90 95 96 97 *98 99 00* Carsin; Grand-Mouëys; Reynon.

Prestige Cuvée [koo-vay] (*Champagne,* France) The top wine of a *Champagne* house. Expensive and elaborately packaged. Some, like *Dom Pérignon*, are excellent; others less so. Other best-known examples include *Veuve Clicquot's* Grand Dame and *Roederer's* Cristal.

☰ **Preston Vineyards** (*Sonoma,* California) Winery making the most of *Dry Creek Zinfandel* and *Syrah*. A white Meritage blend is pretty good too, and there is an improving *Viognier*.

☰ **Pride Mountain** (*Napa,* California) Small Napa label whose Merlot is worth seeking out. ★★★★ 1997 Merlot £££

☰ **Dom. Jacques Prieur** [pree-yur] (*Burgundy*, France) Estate with fine vineyards. Increasingly impressive since takeover by *Antonin Rodet*.

☰ **Ch. Prieuré-Lichine** [pree-yur-ray lih-sheen] (*Margaux 4ème Cru Classé, Bordeaux,* France) Recently (1999) sold and – in 2000 – much improved *château* making good if rarely subtle blackcurranty wine that benefits from input by *Michel Rolland*. Thanks to its flamboyant previous owner, this is one of the very few *châteaux* with a gift shop and a helicopter landing pad on its roof. The 2001 vintage was controversial, striking some – including the editor of this guide – as too rich and dark for a Margaux. 82 83 85 86 88 89 90 93 94 *95 96 97 98 99 00*

Primeur [pree-mur] (France) New wine, e.g., *Beaujolais* Primeur (the same as *Beaujolais Nouveau*) or, as in *en primeur*, wine which is sold while still in barrel. Known in the US as futures.

☰ **Primitivo** [pree-mih-tee-voh] (*Puglia,* Italy) Italian name for the *Zinfandel*.

☰ **Primo Estate** [pree-moh] (South Australia) Extraordinarily imaginative venture among the fruit farms of the Adelaide Plains. Passion-fruity *Colombard*, sparkling *Shiraz*, and *Bordeaux* blends made *Amarone*-style, using grapes partially dried in the sun. The olive oil is good too. ★★★★ 1998 Joseph Cabernet Merlot £££

☰ **Principe de Viana** [preen-chee-pay de vee-yah-nah] (*Navarra,* Spain) Highly commercial winery producing large amounts of good value red and white wine. The Agramont label is particularly worthwhile.

☰ **Prinz zu Salm-Dalberg** [zoo sahlm dal-burg] (*Nahe,* Germany) Innovative producer with good red *Spätburgunder* and (especially) *Scheurebe*.

☰ **Priorato/Priorat** [pree-yaw-rah-toh/raht] (*Catalonia,* Spain) Highly prized/priced, sexy new-wave wines from a region once known for hefty alcoholic reds from *Cariñena* and *Garnacha* grapes. Rene Barbier (Clos Mogador); Costers del Siurana; Mas Martinet; Clos i Terrasses; J.M. Fuentes; Daphne Glorian; Alvaro Palacios; Pasanau Germans; Scala Dei; Vilella de la Cartoixa. ★★★★ 1998 Clos de L'Obac £££

Propriétaire (Récoltant) [pro-pree-yeh-tehr ray-kohl-ton] (France) Vineyard owner-manager.

☰ **Prosecco di Conegliano-Valdobbiàdene** [proh-sek-koh dee coh-nay-lee-anoh val-doh-bee-yah-day-nay] (*Veneto,* Italy) Soft, slightly earthy, dry and sweet sparkling wine made from the *Prosecco* grape. Less boisterous and fruity than *Asti Spumante*. Drink young. Bisol; Bortolin; Canevel; Produttori de Valdobbiadene; Ruggeri; Zardetto.

Provence [proh-vons] (France) Southern region producing fast-improving wine with a number of minor *ACs*. Rosé de Provence should be dry and fruity with a hint of peppery spice. See *Bandol, Coteaux d'Aix-en-Provence, Palette*.

P

I **Provins** [proh-vah'] (*Valais*, Switzerland) Dynamic cooperative, making the most of *Chasselas* and more interesting varieties such as the *Arvine*.

I **J.J. Prüm** [proom] (*Mosel-Saar-Ruwer*, Germany) *Riesling* producer with fine *Wehlener* vineyards. ★★★★ 1999 Graacher Himmelreich Riesling Kabinett £££

I **Dom. Michel Prunier** [proo-nee-yay] (*Burgundy*, France) Best estate in *Auxey-Duresses*. ★★★★ 1998 Auxey-Duresses Blanc £££

I **Alfredo Prunotto** [proo-not-toh] (*Piedmont*, Italy) Good *Barolo* producer recently bought by *Antinori*. ★★★★ 1996 Barolo Bussia £££

Puglia [poo-lee-yah] (Italy) Hot region, now making cool wines, thanks to *flying winemakers* like *Kym Milne*. Also see *Salice Salentino* and *Copertino*.

I **Puiatti** [pwee-yah-tee] (*Friuli-Venezia Giulia*, Italy) Producer of some of Italy's most stylish *Chardonnay, Pinot Bianco, Pinot Grigio*, and *Tocai Friulano*. The Archetipi wines are the cream of the crop.

I **Puisseguin St. Emilion** [pwees-gan san tay-mee-lee-yon] (*Bordeaux*, France) Satellite of *St. Emilion* making similar, *Merlot*-dominant wines which are often far better value. 82 83 85 86 88 89 90 94 *95 97 98 99 00*

I **Puligny-Montrachet** [poo-lee-nee mon-ra-shay] (*Burgundy*, France) Aristocratic white *Côte d'Or commune* that shares the *Montrachet* vineyard with *Chassagne*. Should be complex buttery *Chardonnay. Carillon, Sauzet, Ramonet, Drouhin*, and *Dom. Leflaive* are all worth their money. 85 86 88 89 90 92 95 *96 97 98 99 D'Auvenay; Carillon; Chavy; Drouhin; Leflaive (Olivier & Domaine); Marquis de Laguiche; Ch de Puligny-Montrachet; Ramonet; Sauzet.*

Vins de — Bourgogne

PULIGNY-MONTRACHET
1ᵉʳ CRU LES PERRIÈRES
APPELLATION PULIGNY-MONTRACHET 1ᵉʳ CRU CONTRÔLÉE
13.5% vol. 1994 750
Mis en bouteille au Domaine par Louis CARILLON et Fils Puligny-Montrachet Côte-d'Or - France
VITICULTEURS
PRODUCE OF FRANCE

Putto [poot-toh] (Italy) See *Chianti*.

Puttonyos [poot-toh-nyos] (*Tokaji*, Hungary) The measure of sweetness (from 1 to 6) of *Tokaji*. The number indicates the number of puttonyos (baskets) of sweet *aszú* paste added to the base wine.

I **Ch. Puygeraud** [Pwee-gay-roh] (*Bordeaux*, France) Perhaps the best property on the *Côtes de Francs*. 85 86 88 89 90 94 *95 96 97 98 99 00*

Pyrenees (*Victoria*, Australia) One of the classiest regions in *Victoria*, thanks to the efforts of *Taltarni* and *Dalwhinnie*. White: 92 94 *95 96 97 98 99 00* Red: 85 86 87 88 90 91 92 94 *95 96 97 98 99 00*

I **Pyrus** [pi-rus] (Australia) *Lindemans Coonawarra* wine that's right back on form. ★★★★★ 1997 Pyrus £££

Q

QbA Qualitätswein bestimmter Anbaugebiet: [kvah-lih-tayts-vine behr-shtihmt-tuhr ahn-bow-geh-beet] (Germany) Basic-quality German wine from one of the 13 *Anbaugebiete*, e.g. *Rheinhessen*.

QmP Qualitätswein mit Prädikat: [pray-dee-kaht] (Germany) *QbA* wine (supposedly) with "special qualities." The QmP blanket designation is broken into five sweetness rungs, from *Kabinett* to *Trockenbeerenauslese* plus *Eiswein*.

I **Quady** [kway-dee] (*Central Valley*, California) Makes "Starboard" (served in a decanter), *Orange Muscat* Essencia (great with chocolate), *Black Muscat* Elysium, low-alcohol Electra, and Vya Sweet Vermouth. ★★★★ Elysium £££

I **Quarles Harris** [kwahrls] (*Douro*, Portugal) Underrated *port* producer with a fine 1980 and 1983.

I **Quarts de Chaume** [kahr dur shohm] (*Loire*, France) Luscious but light sweet wines, uncloying, ageing beautifully, from the *Coteaux du Layon*. The *Dom. des Baumard* is exceptional. Sweet white: 76 83 85 86 88 89 90 *94 95 96 97 98 99 00 Dom des Baumard; Pierre Soulez.*

R

ϒ **Querciabella** [kehr-chee-yah-BEH-lah] (*Tuscany*, Italy) Top class *Chianti Classico* estate with a great *Sangiovese-Cabernet* blend called Camartina.

ϒ **Quilceda Creek** [kwil-see-dah] (*Washington State*) Producer of one of the best, most blackcurranty *Cabernets* in the American Northwest.

ϒ **Quincy** [kan-see] (*Loire*, France) Dry *Sauvignon*, lesser-known and sometimes good alternative to *Sancerre* or Pouilly-Fumé. Joseph Mellot.

ϒ **Quinault l'Enclos** [kee-noh lon-kloh] (*St. Emilion*, Bordeaux, France) Recently – 1997 – created, tiny-production wine from the same stable as la Croix de Gay and la Fleur de Gay, and produced from previously unvaunted land close to both *Pomerol* and the town of Libourne. Like most such wines, it's rich, dark, and concentrated.

Quinta [keen-ta] (Portugal) Vineyard or estate, particularly in the *Douro*, where "single Quinta" *vintage ports* are increasingly being taken as seriously as the big-name blends. See *Crasto, Vesuvio*, and *de la Rosa*.

ϒ **Quintessa** (*Napa*, Caifornia) Exciting venture from Agustin Huneeus, the man behind *Franciscan* and *Veramonte*

ϒ **Guiseppe Quintarelli** [keen-ta-reh-lee] (*Veneto*, Italy) Old-fashioned *Recioto*-maker producing some of the quirkiest, most sublime *Valpolicella*, recognizable by the apparently handwritten labels.Try the more affordable Molinara.

ϒ **Quintessa** (*Napa*, California) Napa label developing a cult following for its stylish blended red.

ϒ **Quivira** (*Sonoma*, California) Great *Dry Creek* producer of intense *Zinfandel* and *Syrah* and a deliciously clever *Rhône*-meets-California blend that includes both varieties.

ϒ **Qupé** [kyoo-pay] (*Central Coast*, California) Run by one of the founders of *Au Bon Climat*, this *Santa Barbara* winery produces brilliant *Syrah* and *Rhône*-style whites. ★★★★ 1997 Bien Nacido Chardonnay £££

R

ϒ **Ch. Rabaud-Promis** [rrah-boh prraw-mee] (*Sauternes Premier Cru Classé*, *Bordeaux*, France) Underperforming until 1986; now making top-class wines. 83 85 86 87 88 89 90 95 96 97 98 ★★★★ 1990 £££

ϒ **Rabbit Ridge** (*Sonoma*, California) Small producer with a fairly priced, very starry, Russian River Zinfandel ★★★★ 1996 Reserve Zinfandel Zinfandel £££

Racking The drawing off of wine from its *lees* into a clean cask or vat.

ϒ **Rafael Estate** [raf-fay-yel] (*Mendoza*, Argentina) Dynamic producer of great value *Malbec*-based reds with the assistance of *flying winemaker* Hugh Ryman.

ϒ **A Rafanelli** [ra-fur-nel-lee] (*Sonoma*, California) Great *Dry Creek* winery with great *Cabernet* Sauvignon. The *Zinfandel* is the jewel in the crown though. ★★★★ 1997 Dry Creek Zinfandel £££

ϒ **Olga Raffault** [ra-foh] (*Loire*, France) There are several Raffaults in *Chinon*; this is the best – and the best source of some of the longest-lived examples of this *appellation*.

ϒ **Le Ragose** [lay-rah-goh-say] (*Veneto*, Italy) A name to look out for in *Valpolicella* – for great *Amarone, Recioto*, and Valpolicella Classico (le Sassine).

ϒ **Raïmat** [ri-mat] (*Catalonia*, Spain) Innovative *Codorníu*-owned winery in the *Costers del Segre* region. *Merlot*, a *Cabernet/Merlot* blend called Abadia, and *Tempranillo* are interesting though less impressive than in the past, and *Chardonnay* – both still and sparkling – is good.

Rainwater (*Madeira*, Portugal) Light, dry style of *Madeira* popular in the US. ★★★ Berry Bros. & Rudd's Selected Rainwater ££

ϒ **Ch. Ramage-la-Batisse** [ra-mazh la ba-teess] (*Haut-Médoc Cru Bourgeois*, *Bordeaux*, France) Good-value wine from St. Laurent, close to *Pauillac*.

R

Ⓨ **Ramitello** [ra-mee-tel-loh] (*Molise,* Italy) Spicy-fruity reds and creamy citrus whites produced by di Majo Norante in Biferno on the Adriatic coast.

Ⓨ **Adriano Ramos Pinto** [rah-mosh pin-toh] (*Douro,* Portugal) Family-run winery that belongs to *Roederer. Colheita tawnies* are a delicious speciality, but the *vintage* wines and *single quintas* are good too.

Ⓨ **Dom. Ramonet** [ra-moh-nay] (*Burgundy,* France) Supreme *Chassagne-Montrachet* estate with top-flight *Montrachet, Bâtard,* and *Bienvenues-Bâtard-Montrachet* and fine complex *Premiers Crus.* Pure class; worth waiting for, too. ★★★★★ 1997 Chassagne-Montrachet Ruchottes £££

Ⓨ **João Portugal Ramos** [jwow por-too-gahl ramosh] (Portugal) One of this conservative country's best new-wave winemakers.

Ⓨ **Castello dei Rampolla** [kas-teh-loh day-ee ram-poh-la] (*Tuscany,* Italy) Good *Chianti*-producer whose wines need time to soften. The berryish Sammarco *Vino da Tavola* is also impressive.

Rancio [ran-see-yoh] Term for the peculiarly tangy, and yet highly prized, *oxidized* flavour of certain fortified wines, particularly in France (e.g., *Banyuls*) and Spain.

Ⓨ **Randersacker** [ran-dehr-sak-kur] (*Franken,* Germany) One of the most successful homes of the *Silvaner,* especially when made by Weingut *Juliusspital.*

Rapel [ra-pel] (Central Valley, Chile) Important sub-region of the *Central Valley,* especially for reds. Includes *Colchagua* and *Cachapoal.*

Ⓨ **Rapitalà** [ra-pih-tah-la] (*Sicily,* Italy) Estate producing a fresh, peary white wine from a blend of local grapes.

Ⓨ **Kent Rasmussen** (*Carneros,* California) One of California's too-small band of truly inventive winemakers, producing great *Burgundy*-like *Pinot Noir* and *Chardonnay* and Italianate *Sangiovese* and *Dolcetto.* Ramsey is a second label. ★★★★ 1998 Pinot Noir £££

Rasteau [ras-stoh] (*Rhône,* France) Southern village producing peppery reds with rich, berry fruit. The fortified *Muscat* can be good, too. Red: **88 89 90 95 96 97 98 99 00** Bressy-Masson; des Coteaux des Travers; Dom des Girasols; de la Grangeneuve; Marie-France Masson; Rabasse-Charavin; La Soumade; François Vache.

Ⓨ **Renato Ratti** [rah-tee] (*Piedmont,* Italy) One of the finest, oldest producers of *Barolo.*

Ⓨ **Rauenthal** [row-en-tahl] (*Rheingau,* Germany) *Georg Breur* is the most interesting producer in this beautiful village. Other names to look for include *Schloss Schönborn* and *Schloss Rheinhartshausen.*

Ⓨ **Ch. Rauzan-Gassies** [roh-zon ga-sees] (*Margaux 2ème Cru Classé, Bordeaux,* France) Compared to *Rauzan-Ségla* its neighbour, this property is still underperforming magnificently. Better in 2001.

Ⓨ **Ch. Rauzan-Ségla** [roh-zon say-glah] (*Margaux 2ème Cru Classé, Bordeaux,* France) For a long time this used to be an underperforming *Margaux.* Now, since its purchase by Chanel in 1994, it has become one of the best buys in *Bordeaux.* **70 82 83 85 86 88 89 90 91 92 93 94 95 96 97 98 99 00**

Ⓨ **Jean-Marie Raveneau** [rav-noh] (*Burgundy,* France) The long-established king of *Chablis,* with impeccably made *Grand* and *Premier Cru* wines that last wonderfully well. ★★★★★ 1997 Chablis Blanchot £££

Ⓨ **Ravenswood** (*Sonoma Valley,* California) Brilliant *Zinfandel*-maker whose individual-vineyard wines are wonderful examples of this variety. The *Merlots* and *Cabernet* are fine, too.

Ⓨ **Ravenswood** (South Australia) Label confusingly adopted by *Hollick* for its top *Coonawarra* reds (no relation to the above entry).

R

Ⓣ Raventos i Blanc [ra-vayn-tos ee blank] (*Catalonia*, Spain) Josep Raventos' ambition is to produce the best sparkling wine in Spain, adding *Chardonnay* to local varieties. ★★★★ **Cava Brut Reserva ££££**

Ⓣ Ch. Rayas [rye-yas] (*Rhône*, France) The only chance to taste *Châteauneuf-du-Pape* made solely from the *Grenache*. Pricey but good.

Ⓣ Raymond (*Napa Valley*, California) Maker of tasty, intense *Cabernets* and *Chardonnays*. ★★★★ 1998 **Cabernet Sauvignon Reserve £££**

Ⓣ Ch. Raymond-Lafon [ray-mon la-fon] (*Sauternes, Bordeaux*, France) Very good small producer whose wines deserve keeping. 75 80 82 83 85 86 89 90 95 96 97 98 99

Ⓣ Ch. de Rayne-Vigneau [rayn veen-yoh] (*Sauternes Premier Cru Classé, Bordeaux*, France) *Sauternes* estate, located at *Bommes*, producing a deliciously rich complex wine. 85 86 88 89 90 92 94 95 96 97 98 99 00 ★★★★ 1998 **££££**

RD (Récemment Dégorgée) (*Champagne*, France) A term invented by *Bollinger* for their delicious vintage *Champagne*, which has been allowed a longer-than-usual period (as much as 15 years) on its *lees*.

Ⓣ Real Companhia Vinicola do Norte de Portugal [ray-yahl com-pah-nee-yah vee-nee-koh-lah doh nor-tay day por-too-gahl] (*Douro*, Portugal) The full name of the firm that is better known as the *Royal Oporto Wine Co.* The best wines are the *tawny* ports; these are sold under the Quinta dos Carvalhas label. Other efforts – especially the *vintage ports* – are rarely worth buying

Ignacio Recabarren [ig-na-see-yoh reh-ka-ba-ren] (Chile) Superstar winemaker and Casablanca pioneer.

Recioto [ray-chee-yo-toh] (*Veneto*, Italy) Sweet or dry alcoholic wine made from semi-dried, ripe grapes. Usually associated with *Valpolicella* and *Soave*.

Récoltant-manipulant (RM) [ray-kohl-ton ma-nee-poo-lon] (*Champagne*, France) Term for an individual winegrower and blender, identified by what is known as the RM number on the label.

Récolte [ray-kohlt] (France) Vintage, literally "harvest."

Ⓣ Dom. de la Rectorie [rehc-toh-ree] (*Languedoc-Roussillon*, France) One of the two top names (with *Mas Blanc*) in *Banyuls*, and also an excellent producer of *Collioure*.

Ⓣ Redman (South Australia) Improved *Coonawarra* estate with intense reds. ★★★★ 1998 **Cabernet Sauvignon ££**

Ⓣ Redoma [ray-doh-mah] (*Douro*, Portugal) New-wave red and white table wines from the dynamic, yet reliable port producer Dirk *Nieport*.

Ⓣ Redwood Valley Estate See *Seifried*.

Ⓦ Refosco [re-fos-koh] (*Friuli-Venezia Giulia*, Italy) Red grape and its dry and full-bodied *DOC* wine. Benefits from ageing.

Ⓣ Regaleali [ray-ga-lay-ah-lee] (*Sicily*, Italy) Ambitious aristocratic estate, using local varieties to produce some of *Sicily's* most serious wines. ★★★★ 1995 **Rosso del Conti £££.**

Régisseur [rey-jee-sur] (*Bordeaux*, France) In *Bordeaux* (only), the cellar-master.

Ⓣ Régnié [ray-nyay] (*Burgundy*, France) Once sold as *Beaujolais Villages*, Régnié now has to compete with *Chiroubles*, *Chénas*, and the other *crus*. It is mostly like an amateur competing against professionals. Fortunately enough for Régnié, these particular professionals often aren't great. *Duboeuf* makes a typical example. 90 91 93 94 95 96 97 98 99 *Duboeuf; Dubost; Piron; Sapin; Trichard.*

Ⓣ Reguengos (*Alentejo*, Portugal) Richly flavoursome reds pioneered by Esporão and the Reguengos de Monsaraz cooperative.

Ⓦ Reichensteiner [rike-en-sti-ner] Recently developed white grape, popular in England (and Wales).

Ⓣ Reif Estate Winery [reef] (*Ontario*, Canada) Impressive *icewine* specialist. ★★★★ 1998 **Vidal Icewine ££££**

R

Ⓘ **Remelluri** [ray-may-yoo-ree] (*Rioja,* Spain) For most modernists, this is the nearest *Rioja* has got to a top-class, small-scale organic estate. Wines are more serious (and *tannic*) than most, but they're fuller in flavour, too, and they're built to last. ★★★★ 1996 La Granja Nuestra Senora de Remelluri ££

Remuage [reh-moo-wazh] (*Champagne,* France) Part of the *méthode champenoise,* the gradual turning and tilting of bottles so that the yeast deposit collects in the neck ready for *dégorgement.*

Reserva [ray-sehr-vah] (Spain) Wine aged for a period specified by the relevant *DO:* usually one year for reds and six months for whites and pinks.

Réserve [reh-surv] (France) Legally meaningless, as in "Réserve Personelle," but implying a wine selected and given more age.

Residual sugar Term for wines that have retained grape sugar not converted to *alcohol* by yeasts during fermentation. Bone-dry wines have less than 2 grams per litre of residual sugar. In the US, many so-called "dry" white wines contain as much as 10, and some supposedly dry red *Zinfandels* definitely have more than a trace of sweetness. New Zealand Sauvignons are rarely bone dry, but their *acidity* balances and conceals any residual sugar.

Ⓘ **Weingut Balthasar Ress** [bahl-ta-zah rress] (*Rheingau,* Germany) Good producer in *Hattenheim,* blending delicacy with concentration. ★★★★ 1999 Hattenheimer Nussbrunnen Riesling Auslese £££

Retsina [ret-see-nah] (Greece) Wine made the way the ancient Greeks used to make it – resinating it with pine to keep it from spoiling. Today, it's an acquired taste for non-holidaying, non-Greeks. Pick the freshest examples you can find (though this isn't easy when labels mention no vintage).

Reuilly [rur-yee] (*Loire,* France) (Mostly) white *AC* for dry *Sauvignons,* good-value, if sometimes rather earthy alternatives to nearby *Sancerre* and *Pouilly-Fumé* and spicy *Pinot* rosé. *Henri Beurdin; Bigonneau; Lafond.*

Ⓘ **Rex Hill Vineyards** (Oregon) Greatly improved *Pinot* specialist.

Ⓘ **Chateau Reynella** [ray-nel-la] (*McLaren Vale,* Australia) *BRL Hardy* subsidiary, mastering both reds and whites. ★★★★ Chateau Reynella Basket-Press Shiraz 1997 ££

Ⓘ **Ch. Reynon** [ray-non] (*Premier Côtes de Bordeaux,* France) Fine red and especially recommendable white wines from *Denis Dubourdieu.*

Rheingau [rine-gow] (Germany) Traditional home of the finest *Rieslings* of the 13 *Anbaugebiete;* now overshadowed by *Pfalz* and *Mosel.* QbA/Kab/Spät: 92 93 94 95 96 97 98 99 00 Aus/Beeren/Tba: 83 85 88 89 90 92 93 94 95 96 97 98 99 00 *Künstler; Balthasar Ress; Domdechant Werner'sches;* HH Eser.

Rheinhessen [rine-hehs-sen] (Germany) Largest of the 13 *Anbaugebiete,* now well known for *Liebfraumilch* and *Niersteiner.* Fewer than one vine in 20 is now *Riesling;* sadly, easier-to-grow varieties, and lazy cooperative wineries, generally prevail. There are a few stars, however. QbA/Kab/Spät: 90 91 92 93 94 95 96 97 98 99 00 Aus/Beeren/Tba: 83 85 88 89 90 91 92 93 94 95 96 97 98 99 00 *Balbach;* Keller; *Gunderloch.*

Ⓘ **Rhône** [rohn] (France) Fast-improving, exciting, packed with increasingly sexy *Grenache, Syrah,* and *Viognier* wines. See *St. Joseph, Crozes-Hermitage, Hermitage, Condrieu, Côtes du Rhône, Châteauneuf-du-Pape, Tavel, Lirac, Gigondas, Ch. Grillet, Beaumes de Venise.* White: 94 95 96 97 98 99 00 Northern Rhône Red: 76 78 82 83 85 88 89 90 91 95 96 97 98 99 00 Southern Rhône Red: 78 82 83 85 88 89 90 95 96 97 98 99 00

Ⓘ **Rias Baixas** [ree-yahs bi-shahs] (*Galicia,* Spain) The place to find spicy *Albariño.* Lagar de Cervera; *Pazo de Barrantes; Santiago Ruiz;* Valdamor.

Ⓘ **Ribatejo** [ree-bah-tay-joh] (Portugal) *DO* area north of Lisbon where *Peter Bright* and the cooperatives are beginning to make highly commercial white and red wine, but traditional *Garrafeiras* are worth watching out for, too.

R

Ribera del Duero [ree-bay-rah del doo-way-roh] (Spain) One of the regions to watch in Spain for good reds. Unfortunately, despite the established success of *Vega Sicilia* and of producers like *Pesquera, Pingus, Arroyo*, and *Alion*, there is still far too much poor winemaking. 82 **83 85 87 89 90** 91 92 94 *95 96 97 98 99* Arroyo; Pago de Carraovejas; Balbas; Pesquera; Pedrosa; Pingus; Hermanos Sastre; Valtravieso; *Vega Sicilia*.

Dom. Richeaume [ree-shohm] (*Provence*, France) Dynamic producer of good, earthy, long-lived, organic *Cabernet* and *Syrah*. Sadly, as with many other smaller organic wineries, quality can vary from bottle to bottle. Recommendable, nonetheless.

Richebourg [reesh-boor] (*Burgundy*, France) Top-class *Grand Cru* vineyard just outside *Vosne-Romanée* with a recognizable floral-plummy style. 76 **78** 79 80 82 83 85 86 87 88 89 90 92 93 94 *95 96 97 98 99* Grivot; Anne Gros; Leroy; Méo-Camuzet; D&D Mugneret; Noëllat; Romanée-Conti.

Richou [ree-shoo] (*Loire*, France) Fine *Anjou* producer with reliable reds and whites and fine, affordable, sweet whites from Coteaux de l'Aubance.

Weingut Max Ferd Richter [rikh-tur] (*Mosel-Saar-Ruwer*, Germany) Excellent producer of long-lived concentrated-yet-elegant *Mosel Rieslings* from high-quality vineyards. The *cuvée* Constantin is the unusually successful dry wine, while at the other end of the scale, the *Eisweins* are sublime. ★★★★★ 1998 Graacher Himmelreich Riesling Kabinet £££

John Riddoch (South Australia) Classic *Wynn's Coonawarra* red. One of Australia's best and longest-lasting wines. (Not to be confused with the wines that *Katnook Estate* sells under its own "Riddoch" label.)

Ridge Vineyards (*Santa Cruz*, California) Paul Draper, and Ridge's hilltop *Santa Cruz* and *Sonoma* vineyards, consistently produce some of California's very finest *Zinfandel, Cabernet, Mataro*, and *Chardonnay*. ★★★★★ 1997 Ridge Late-picked Paso Robles Zinfandel ££££

Riecine [ree-eh-chee-nay] (*Tuscany*, Italy) Modern estate with fine *Chianti* and an even more impressive la Gioia *Vino da Tavola*.

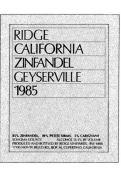

RIDGE CALIFORNIA ZINFANDEL GEYSERVILLE 1985

Riesling [reez-ling] The noble grape responsible for Germany's finest offerings, ranging from light, floral, everyday wines, to the delights of *botrytis*-affected sweet wines, which retain their freshness for decades. Reaching its zenith in the superbly balanced, racy wines of the *Mosel*, and the richer offerings from the *Rheingau*, it also performs well in *Alsace*, California, South Africa, and Australia. Watch out for the emergence of the *Wachau* region as a leader of the Austrian *Riesling* pack.

Riesling Italico See *Italian Riesling*, etc.

Ch. Rieussec [ree-yur-sek] (*Sauternes Premier Cru Classé, Bordeaux*, France) Fantastically rich and concentrated *Sauternes*, often deep in colour and generally at the head of the pack chasing *d'Yquem*. Owned by the Rothschilds of *Lafite*. R de Rieussec is the unexceptional dry white wine. 75 79 82 83 85 86 88 89 90 *95 96 97 98 99*

Rioja [ree-ok-hah] (Spain) Spain's best-known wine region, split into three parts. The Alta produces the best wines, followed by the Alavesa, while the Baja is the largest. Most Riojas are blends by large *bodegas*: small *Bordeaux*- and *Burgundy*-style estates are rare. New-wave Riojas are abjuring the tradition of long oak ageing and producing fruitier, modern wines, and "experimental" *Cabernet* is being planted alongside the traditional *Tempranillo* and lesser-quality *Garnacha*. Reds: 79 80 81 82 83 85 87 89 90 91 92 94 *95 96 98 99* Allende; *Amézola de la Mora; Ardanza; Artadi*; Baron de Ley; Berberana; Breton; *Campillo*; Campo Viejo; *Contino*; El Coto; Lopez de Heredia; *Marqués de Griñon*; Marqués de Murrieta; *Marqués de Riscal*; Marqués de Vargas; *Martinez Bujanda; Montecillo*; Ondarre; *Palacio; Remelluri; La Rioja Alta*; Riojanos.

R

La Rioja Alta [ree-ok-hah ahl-ta] (*Rioja,* Spain) Of all the big companies in *Rioja,* this is the most important name to remember. Its Viña Ardanza, Reserva 904, and (rarely produced) Reserva 890 are all among the most reliable and recommendable wines in the region. ★★★ 1995 Viña Ardanza Reserva £££

Dom. Daniel Rion [ree-yon] (*Burgundy,* France) Patrice Rion produces impeccably made modern Nuits-St.-Georges and Vosne-Romanées. ★★★★ 1998 Vosne-Romanee £££

Ripasso [ree-pas-soh] (*Veneto,* Italy) Winemaking method whereby newly made *Valpolicella* is partially refermented in vessels that have recently been vacated by *Recioto* and *Amarone.* Ripasso wines made in this way are richer, alcoholic, and raisiny. Increases the *alcohol* and *body* of the wine. *Tedeschi; Quintarelli; Masi.*

Marqués de Riscal [ris-kahl] (*Rioja,* Spain) Historic *Rioja* name now back on course thanks to more modern winemaking for both reds and whites. The Baron de Chirel is the recently launched top wine. ★★★★★ 1995 Baron de Chirel Reserva £££

Riserva [ree-zEHr-vah] (Italy) *DOC* wines aged for a specified number of years – often an unwelcome term on labels of wines like *Bardolino,* which are usually far better drunk young.

Ritchie Creek (*Napa,* California) Small producer with dazzling Cabernet from the region of Spring Mountain.

Rivaner [rih-vah-nur] (Germany) The name used for *Müller-Thurgau* (a cross between *Riesling* and *Silvaner*) in parts of Germany and *Luxembourg.*

Rivera [ree-vay-ra] (*Puglia,* Italy) One of the new wave of producers who are turning the southern region of *Puglia* into a source of interesting wines. The red Riserva il Falcone is the star wine here.

Riverina [rih-vur-ee-na] (*New South Wales,* Australia) Irrigated *New South Wales* region which produces basic-to-good wine, much of which ends up in *"Southeast Australian"* blends. Late-harvest *Semillons* can, however, be surprisingly spectacular. *Cranswick Estate, McWilliams.*

Rivesaltes [reev-zalt] (*Languedoc-Roussillon,* France) Fortified dessert wine of both colours. The white made from the *Muscat* is lighter and more lemony than *Beaumes de Venise,* while the *Grenache* red is like liquid Christmas pudding and ages wonderfully. *Cazes;* Ch. de Corneilla; Força Réal; Ch. de Jau; Sarda-Malet.

Giorgio Rivetti [ree-VAY-tee] (*Piedmont,* Italy) Superstar producer of wonderfully aromatic Moscato d'Asti, *Barbaresco,* and *Barbera.*

Riviera Ligure di Ponente [reev-ee-yeh-ra lee-goo-ray dee poh-nen-tay] (*Liguria,* Italy) Little-known northwestern region, close to Genoa, where local grapes like the *Vermentino* produce light aromatic reds and whites.

Robertson (South Africa) Warm area where *Chardonnays* and *Sauvignons* are taking over from the *Muscats* that used to be the region's pride. *Graham Beck; Springfield;* Robertson Winery; *Van Loveren;* Weltevrede.

Rocche dei Manzoni [rok-keh day-yee mant-zoh-nee] (*Piedmont,* Italy) The Nebbiolo-Barbera Bricco Manzoni is the top wine here, but the single-vineyard *Barolo* is good too and there's some lovely *Chardonnay.*

Rocca delle Macie [ro-ka del leh mah-chee-yay] (*Tuscany,* Italy) Reliable if unspectacular *Chianti* producer.

La Roche aux Moines [rosh oh mwahn] See *Nicolas Joly.*

Joe Rochioli [roh-kee-yoh-lee] (*Sonoma,* California) Brilliant *Russian River* Pinot Noir and *Chardonnay* producer whose name also appears on single-vineyard wines from *Williams Selyem.*

Rockford (*Barossa Valley,* Australia) Robert "Rocky" O'Callaghan makes a great intense *Barossa Shiraz* using 100-year-old vines and 50-year-old equipment. There's a mouthfilling *Semillon,* a wonderful Black *Shiraz* sparkling wine, and a magical *Alicante Bouschet* rosé, which is sadly only to be found at the winery. ★★★★ Black Shiraz £££

Antonin Rodet [on-toh-nan roh-day] (*Burgundy*, France) Very impressive *Mercurey*-based *négociant*, which has also improved the wines of the *Jacques Prieur domaine* in *Meursault*. **Ch. de Chamery; de Rully.**

Louis Roederer [roh-dur-rehr] (*Champagne*, France) This is still a family-owned *Champagne* house, and still one of the most reliable of these; its delicious non-vintage wine benefits from being cellared for a few years. Roederer's prestige Cristal remains a most deliciously "wine-like" *Champagne*. ★★★★★ **1993 Cristal ££££**

Roederer Estate [roh-dur-rehr] (*Mendocino*, California) No longer involved with the *Jansz* sparkling wine in *Tasmania* but making top-class wine in California, which is sold in the US as Roederer Estate and in the UK as Quartet. ★★★★ **Anderson Valley Brut £££**

Roero [roh-weh-roh] (*Piedmont*, Italy) *Nebbiolo* red and *Arneis* white (sold as Roero Arneis) which are now among Italy's most interesting wines. *Ceretto; Bruno Giacosa; Prunotto;* **Serafino; Vietti.**

Michel Rolland [roh-lon] Based in *Pomerol* and *St. Emilion*, Rolland is now an increasingly international guru-oenologist, whose taste for ripe fruit flavours is influencing wines from *Ch. Ausone* to Argentina and beyond.

Rolly-Gassmann [rroh-lee gas-sman] (*Alsace*, France) Fine producer of subtle, long-lasting wines which are sometimes slightly marred by an excess of *sulphur dioxide*.

Dom. de la Romanée-Conti [rroh-ma-nay kon-tee] (*Burgundy*, France) Aka "DRC". Small *Grand Cru* estate. The jewel in the crown is the Romanée-Conti vineyard itself, though *La Tâche* runs it a close second. Both can be extraordinary, ultraconcentrated spicy wine, as can the *Romanée-St.-Vivant*. The *Richebourg, Echézeaux*, and *Grands Echézeaux* and *Montrachet* are comparable to those produced by other estates – and sold by them for less kingly ransoms. ★★★★★ **1998 la Tâche ££££**

Romania Traditional source of sweet reds and whites, now developing drier styles from classic European varieties. Unreliability is a constant problem, though *flying winemakers* are helping, as is the owner of the *Comte Peraldi* estate in *Corsica*. Note that Romania's well-praised *Pinot Noirs* may be made from a different variety, mistaken for the *Pinot*.

Romarantin [roh-ma-ron-tan] (*Loire*, France) Interesting, limey grape found in obscure white blends in the *Loire*. See *Cheverny*.

Römerlay [rrur-mehr-lay] (*Mosel*, Germany) One of the *Grosslagen* in the *Ruwer* river valley. QbA/Kab/Spät: **85 86 88 89 90 91 92 93 94 95** *96 97 98 99 00* Aus/Beeren/Tba: **83 85 88 89 90 91 92 93 94** *95 96 97 98 99 00*

Ronchi di Manzano [ron-kee dee mant-zah-noh] (*Friuli-Venezia Giulia*, Italy) Famed in Italy for its *Merlot* (Ronc di Subule), this producer's most interesting wine may well be its rich white *Picolit*.

Ronco del Gnemiz [ron-koh del gneh-meez] (*Friuli-Venezia Giulia*, Italy) One of the world's few producers of great *Müller-Thurgau*, and some pretty good *Chardonnay* in the *Colli Orientali*.

Ronco delle Betulle [ron-koh deh-leh beh-too-leh] (*Friuli-Venezia Giulia*, Italy) Try the *Bordeaux*-blend Narciso here – or the *Tocai Friulano, Sauvignon, Pinot Bianco*, or *Grigio*. You won't be disappointed.

Rongopai [ron-goh-pi] (*Te Kauwhata*, New Zealand) Estate in a region of the North Island pioneered by *Cooks*, but which has fallen out of favour with that company and with other producers. The speciality here is *botrytis* wines, but the *Chardonnay* is good, too.

La Rosa (Chile) One of the fastest-growing wineries in Chile, with new vineyards and great winemaking from *Ignacio Recabarren*. Las Palmeras is a *second label*. ★★★★ **1999 Merlot £££**

Quinta de la Rosa (*Douro*, Portugal) Recently established estate producing excellent port and exemplary dry red wine, under guidance from David Baverstock, Australian-born former winemaker at *Dow's* and responsible for the wines of *Esporão*.

R

Rosato (Italy) Rosé.

Ⴧ **Rosé d'Anjou** [roh-zay don-joo] (*Loire*, France) Usually dull, semi-sweet pink from the *Malbec, Groslot* and (less usually) *Cabernet Franc.*

Ⴧ **Rosé de Loire** [roh-zay duh-lwahr] (*Loire*, France) The wine *Rosé d'Anjou* ought to be. Dry, fruity stuff. *Richou;* **Cave des Vignerons de Saumur.**

Ⴧ **Rosé de Riceys** [roh-zay dur ree-say] (*Champagne*, France) Rare and occasionally delicious still rosé from *Pinot Noir.* Pricey. **Alexandre Bonnet.**

Ⴧ **Rosemount Estate** (*Hunter Valley*, Australia) Ultra-dynamic company which, in 2000, merged with the giant Southcorp (*Penfolds, Lindemans* etc.); introduced the world to *oaky Hunter Chardonnay* with its Show Reserve and Roxburgh. Reliably good-value blends from other areas have followed, including impressive *Syrahs* and *Chardonnays* from the newly developed region of *Orange* and *Mountain Blue* from *Mudgee.* ★★★★ **1998 Balmoral Syrah £££; ★★★★★ 1998 Mountain Blue Shiraz Cabernet £££**

Ⴧ **Rosenblum** (*Alameda*, California) Terrific, characterful *Zinfandels* from a wide variety of individual vineyards in *Napa, Sonoma, Contra Costa,* and *Paso Robles.* There are also some great multi-regional Californian blends.

Ⴧ **Rossese di Dolceaqua** [ros-seh-seh di dohl-chay-ah-kwah] (*Liguria*, Italy) Attractive, generally early-drinking wines made from the Rossese. Single-vineyard examples like Terre Bianche's Bricco Arcagna are more serious.

Ⴧ **Dom. Rossignol-Trapet** [ros-seen-yol tra-pay] (*Burgundy*, France) Once old-fashioned, now more recommendable estate in *Gevrey-Chambertin.*

Ⴧ **Rosso Conero** [ros-soh kon-neh-roh] (*Marches*, Italy) Big, *Montepulciano* and *Sangiovese* red, with rich, herby flavour. Good-value, characterful stuff.

Ⴧ **Rosso di Montalcino** [ros-soh dee mon-tal-chee-noh] (*Tuscany*, Italy) *DO* for lighter, earlier-drinking versions of the more famous *Brunello di Montalcino.* Often better – and better value – than that wine. 85 88 90 91 93 94 95 96 97 *98* 99 *Altesino; Caparzo;* **Fattoria dei Barbi; Talenti.**

Ⴧ **Rosso Piceno** [ros-soh pee-chay-noh] (*Marches*, Italy) Traditionally rustic red made from a blend of the *Montepulciano* and *Sangiovese.*

Ⴧ **René Rostaing** [ros-tang] (*Rhône*, France) Producer of serious northern *Rhône* reds, including a (somewhat) more affordable alternative to *Guigal's* la Landonne. ★★★★ **1996 Côte Rôtie la Côte Blonde £££**

Ⴧ **Rothbury Estate** (*Hunter Valley*, Australia) Founded by Len Evans, Svengali of the Australian wine industry; the company is now – via *Mildara* – a subsidiary of Fosters. Rothbury is a great source of *Shiraz, Semillon,* and *Chardonnay* from the *Hunter Valley.* There are also wines from nearby *Cowra* and first-class *Sauvignon* from the bit of the estate that surfaces in *Marlborough*, New Zealand. ★★★★★ **1998 Hunter Valley Semillon £££; ★★★★★ 1999 Brokenback Shiraz £££**

Ⴧ **Joseph Roty** [roh-tee] (*Burgundy*, France) Superstar producer of a range of intensely concentrated but unsubtle wines in *Gevrey-Chambertin.* One of the first "new-wave" winemakers in Burgundy.

Ⴧ **Rouge Homme** (*Coonawarra*, Australia) Founded by the linguistically talented *Mr. Redman*, but now under the same ownership as *Penfolds* and *Lindemans.* This is increasingly one of the most reliable producers in *Coonawarra.* ★★★★ **1998 Shiraz-Cabernet £££**

Ⴧ **Dom. Guy Roulot** [roo-loh] (*Burgundy*, France) One of the greatest *domaines* in *Meursault.* ★★★★ **1997 Meursault Charmes £££**

Ⴧ **Georges Roumier** [roo-me-yay] (*Burgundy*, France) Blue-chip winery with great quality at every level, from village *Chambolle-Musigny* to the *Grand Cru*, Bonnes Mares, and (more rarely seen) white *Corton-Charlemagne.* ★★★★ **1998 Chambolle Musigny ££££**

Ⴧ **Round Hill** (*Napa*, California) A rare source of Californian bargains. Large-production, inexpensive *Merlots* and *Chardonnays* that outclass many a pricier offering from smart boutique wineries.

🍇 **Roussanne** [roos-sahn] (*Rhône*, France) With the *Marsanne*, one of the key white grapes of the northern *Rhône.*

R

Ȳ Armand Rousseau [roos-soh] (*Burgundy*, France) *Gevrey-Chambertin* top-class estate with a line of *Premiers* and *Grands Crus*. Well-made, long-lasting wines. ★★★★ 1998 Gevrey-Chambertin Clos St-Jacques ££££

Roussette de Savoie [roo-sette] (*Savoie*, France) The local name for the equally local Altesse grape. Fresh, easy-drinking fare.

Roussillon [roos-see-yon] (*Languedoc-Roussillon*, France) Vibrant up-and-coming region, redefining traditional varieties, especially *Muscat*.

Ȳ Ch. Routas [roo-tahs] (*Provence*, France) Impressive producer of intense reds and whites in the *Coteaux Varois*.

Ȳ Royal Oporto Wine Co. (*Douro*, Portugal) Large producer of occasionally (very occasionally) high-quality wines.

Ȳ The Royal Tokaji Wine Co. (*Tokaji*, Hungary) This is a recently-founded company which – with other foreign investors – helped to drag *Tokaji* into the late 20th (and early 21st) century with a succession of great single-vineyard wines. ★★★★★ 1996 Betsek 6 Puttonyos £££

Ȳ Rozendal Farm [rooh-zen-dahl] (*Stellenbosch*, South Africa) Impeccably made, organic, Bordeaux-style reds from a producer whose quality consciousness made him decide not to release the 1997 vintage.

Ȳ Rubesco di Torgiano [roo-bes-koh dee taw-jee-yah-noh] (*Umbria*, Italy) Modern red *DOCG*; more or less the exclusive creation of *Lungarotti*. ★★★ 1990 San Giorgio £££

Ȳ Rubino [roo-bee-noh] (*Umbria*, Italy) Rich "Super-Umbrian" red from the la Pazzola estate. Matches many a *Super-Tuscan*.

Ruby (*Douro*, Portugal) Cheapest, basic *port*; young, blended, sweetly fruity.

Ruby Cabernet [roo-bee ka-behr-nay] (California) A *Cabernet Sauvignon* and *Carignan* cross producing unsubtly fruity wines in California, Australia, and South Africa.

Ruche [roo-kay] (*Piedmont*, Italy) Raspberryish red grape from northern Italy producing early-drinking wines. Best from *Bava*.

Rüdesheim [rroo-des-hime] (*Rheingau*, Germany) Tourist town producing powerful *Rieslings*. QbA/Kab/Spät: 89 90 91 92 93 94 95 96 97 98 99 00 Aus/Beeren/Tba: 83 85 88 89 90 91 92 93 94 95 96 97 98 99 00 *Georg Breuer; August Kesseler; Josef Leitz; Schloss Schönborn; Staatsweingüter Kloster Eberbach.*

Ȳ Rueda [roo-way-dah] (Spain) *DO* in north-west Spain for clean, dry whites from the local *Verdejo*. Progress is being led most particularly by the *Lurtons*, *Marqués de Riscal*, and *Marqués de Griñon*.

Ȳ Ruffino [roof-fee-noh] (*Tuscany*, Italy) Big *Chianti* producer with impressive top-of-the-line wines, including the reliable *Cabreo Vino da Tavola*. 93 94 95 96 97 98 99 ★★★★ 1997 Toscana Romitorio di Santedame £££

Rufina [roo-fee-na] (*Tuscany*, Italy) A sub-region within *Chianti*, producing supposedly classier wine. 85 88 90 94 95 96 97 98 99

Ȳ Ruinart [roo-wee-nahr] (*Champagne*, France) High-quality sister to *Moët & Chandon*, with superlative *Blanc de Blancs*. ★★★★★ 1990 Blanc de Blancs £££

Ruländer [roo-len-dur] (Germany) German name for *Pinot Gris*.

Ȳ Rully [roo-yee] (*Burgundy*, France) *Côte chalonnaise commune* producing rich white and a red that's been called the "poor man"'s *Volnay*. See *Antonin Rodet*, *Jadot*, and *Olivier Leflaive*. Red: 86 87 88 89 90 92 95 96 97 98 99 White: 90 92 95 96 97 98 99 00 *Faiveley; Jacqueson; Jadot; Olivier Leflaive; Antonin Rodet.*

Ruppertsberg [roo-pehrt-sbehrg] (*Pfalz*, Germany) Top-ranking village with a number of excellent vineyards making vigorous fruity *Riesling*. QbA/Kab/Spät: 92 93 94 95 96 97 98 99 00 Aus/Beeren/Tba: 83 85 88 89 90 91 92 93 94 95 96 97 98 99 00 *Bürklin-Wolf; Kimich; Werlé.*

Ȳ la Rural [lah roo-rahl] (*Mendoza*, Argentina) Old-established producer, now making good, commercial wines. The Malbec is the strongest card.

Ȳ Rusden (*Barossa*, South Australia) Small, new estate gaining instant recognition in the US for its rich Barossa Cabernets and Grenaches.

R

Russe [rooss] (Bulgaria) Danube town best known in Britain for its reliable red blends but vaunted in *Bulgaria* as a source of modern whites.

Russian River Valley (California) Cult, cool-climate area to the north of *Sonoma* and west of *Napa*. Ideal for apples and good sparkling wine, as is proven by the excellent *Iron Horse*, which also makes impressive table wines. Great *Pinot Noir* country. Red: **95 96 97 98** *99* **00** White: **96 97 98 99 00** *Dehlinger; de Loach; Iron Horse; Kistler; Martinelli; Rochioli; Sonoma-Cutrer; Joseph Swann; Marimar Torres; Williams Selyem.*

Rust [roost] (*Burgenland,* Austria) Wine centre of *Burgenland,* famous for Ruster *Ausbruch* sweet white wine.

☫ **Rust-en-Vrede** (*Stellenbosch,* South Africa) Vastly improved estate, thanks to the efforts of a new generation. ★★★★ **1998 Estate Red ££**

☫ **Rustenberg** (*Stellenbosch,* South Africa) On a roll since 1996 with investment in the cellars (which put an end to musty flavours encountered in previous vintages), this is now a leading light in the Cape. The lower-priced Brampton efforts are quite good, too. ★★★★ **1999 Cabernet £££**

RUSTENBERG

Rutherford (California) *Napa* region in which some producers believe sufficiently to propose it – and its geological "bench" – as an *appellation.* Red: **85 86 87 90 91 92 93 95** 96 97 98 *99* 00 White: **94 95 96 97 98 99** 00

Rutherglen (*Victoria,* Australia) Hot area on the *Murray River* pioneered by gold miners. Today noted for rich *Muscat* and *Tokay* dessert and *port*-style wines. The reds are often tough and the *Chardonnays* are used by cool-region winemakers to demonstrate why *port* and light, dry whites are hard to make in the same climate. *All Saints; Campbells; Chambers; Morris; Pfeiffer; Seppelt; Stanton & Killeen.*

☫ **Rutz Cellars** (*Sonoma,* California) Competing with Kistler to produce superlative Russian River Chardonnay, Rutz offers the chance to taste a different Chardonnay from the Dutton Ranch vineyard.

Ruwer [roo-vur] (*Mosel-Saar-Ruwer,* Germany) *Mosel* tributary alongside which is to be found the *Römerlay Grosslage,* and includes Kasel, *Eitelsbach* and the great *Maximin Grünhaus* estate. QbA/Kab/Spät: **90 92 93 94 95 96 97** *98 99* 00 Aus/Beeren/Tba: 83 **85 88 89 90 92 93** *94 95 96 97 98 99* 00

Hugh Ryman [ri-man] *Flying winemaker* whose team turns grapes into wine under contract in *Bordeaux, Burgundy,* southern France, Spain, Germany, Moldova, Chile, California, South Africa, and Hungary. Wines tend to bear the initials HDR at the foot of the label – or one of Ryman's own brands: Santara, Kirkwood, Richemont, Rafael Estate.

☫ **Rymill** [ri-mil] (South Australia) One of several *Coonawarra* wineries to mention *Riddoch* on its label (in its Riddoch Run) and a rising star. Rymill at least has the legitimacy of a family link to *John Riddoch,* the region's founder. The *Shiraz* and *Cabernet* are first class, as are the whites and the sparkling wine. ★★★★ **1998 Merlot-Cabernet Franc-Cabernet Sauvignon £££**

S

Saale-Unstrut [zah-leh oon-shtruht] (Germany) Remember East Germany? Well, this is where poor wines used to be made there in the bad old days. Today, good ones are being produced, by producers like Lützkendorf.

Saar [zahr] (*Mosel-Saar-Ruwer,* Germany) The other *Mosel* tributary associated with lean, slatey *Riesling*. Villages include *Ayl, Ockfen,* Saarburg, Serrig, *Wiltingen.* QbA/Kab/Spät: **85 88 89 90 91 92 93** *94 95 96 97 98 99* 00 Aus/Beeren/Tba: **83 85 88 89 90 91 92** *93 94 95 96 97 98 99* 00

S

Sablet [sa-blay] (*Rhône*, France) Good *Côtes du Rhône* village. Red: 85 88 89 90 95 96 97 98 99 00

Ⱦ **Sachsen** [zak-zen] (Germany) Revived former East German region where Klaus Seifert is producing good *Riesling*.

Ⱦ **St. Amour** [san ta-moor] (*Burgundy*, France) One of the 10 *Beaujolais Crus* – usually light and fruity. 95 96 97 98 99 Billards; la Cave Lamartine; *Duboeuf;* Patissier; *Revillon.*

Ⱦ **St. Aubin** [san toh-ban] (*Burgundy*, France) Underrated *Côte d'Or* village for (jammily rustic) reds and rich, nutty, rather classier white; affordable alternatives to *Meursault*. White: 90 92 95 96 97 98 99 00 Red: 88 89 90 92 95 96 97 98 99 *Jean-Claude Bachelet; Champy; Marc Colin;* Hubert Lamy-Monnot; *Olivier Leflaive;* Henri Prudhon; *Ch de Puligny-Montrachet;* Roux Père et Fils; Gérard Thomas.

Ⱦ **St. Bris** [san bree] (*Burgundy*, France) Best known for its VDQS *Sauvignon de St. Bris*, this village close to *Chablis* can also make unusually good examples of the *Aligoté* grape. *Jean-Marc Brocard; la Chablisienne;* Joel et David Griffe; St Prix; Sorin Defrance.

Ⱦ **St. Chinian** [san shee-nee-yon] (*Southwest*, France) Neighbour of *Faugères* in the *Coteaux du Languedoc*, producing midweight wines from *Carignan* and other *Rhône* grapes. Ch. des Albières; de Astide Rousse; Babeau; Mas Champart; Clos Bagatelle; Canet-Valette; Cazel-Viel; Coujan; Cooperative de Roquebrun; Mas de la Tour; Maurel Fonsalade; Ch. Quartironi de Sars.

Ⱦ **St. Clement** (*Napa Valley*, California) Japanese-owned winery whose best wine is the Oroppas red blend. In case you were wondering, the name isn't a Native American word, but that of the owner spelled backward.

Ⱦ **St. Emilion** [san tay-mee-lee-yon] (*Bordeaux*, France) Large *commune* with varied soils and wines. At best, sublime *Merlot*-dominated *claret*; at worst dull, earthy and fruitless. Some 170 or so "*Grand cru*" St. Emilions are made in better-sited vineyards and have to undergo a tasting every vintage to be able to use these words on their labels, and too few fail. *Grand Cru Classé* refers to 68 *châteaux*, of which two – *Ausone* and *Cheval-Blanc* – are rated as "*Premier Grands Crus Classés*" and 11 are "*Premiers Grands Crus Classés* B." These ratings are reviewed every decade. Supposedly "lesser" satellite neighbours – *Lussac, Puisseguin, St. Georges*, etc. – often make better value wine than basic St. Emilion. 70 75 78 79 81 82 83 85 86 88 89 90 94 95 96 97 98 99 00 *Angélus; Ausone;* Beau-Séjour-Bécot; *Beauséjour; Belair; Canon; Canon la Gaffelière; Cheval Blanc; Clos des Jacobins; Clos Fourtet; Figeac; Franc Mayne; Grand Mayne; Larcis Ducasse; Magdelaine; la Mondotte; Pavie;* Tertre Rôteboeuf; *Troplong-Mondot;Trottevieille;Valandraud.*

Ⱦ **St. Estèphe** [san teh stef] (*Bordeaux*, France) Northernmost *Médoc commune* with clay soil and wines which can be a shade more rustic than those of neighbouring *Pauillac* and *St. Julien*, but which are often longer-lived and more structured than some of the juicy, easy-to-drink *St. Emilions* and *Pomerols* that tend to win approval from critics. 78 82 83 85 86 88 89 90 92 93 94 95 96 97 98 99 00 Calon-Ségur; *Cos d'Estournel; Haut-Marbuzet; Lafon-Rochet; Marbuzet; Montrose; de Pez; Ormes de Pez; Phélan-Ségur.*

Ⱦ **St. Francis** (*Sonoma*, California) Innovative winery with great *Zinfandels*, and Reserve *Chardonnays* and *Cabernets*. The first Californian to introduce artificial corks to protect wine drinkers from faulty bottles. ★★★★★ 1996 Cabernet Sauvignon £££; ★★★★★ 1997 Nunns Canyon Reserve Merlot £££

Ⱦ **St. Georges-St.Emilion** [san jorrzh san tay-mee-lee-yon] (*Bordeaux*, France) Satellite of *St. Emilion* with good *Merlot*-dominant reds, often better value than *St. Emilion* itself. Ch. Maquin St. Georges; St. Georges.

Ⱦ **St. Hallett** (*Barossa Valley*, Australia) Superstar *Barossa* winery specializing in wines from old ("old block") *Shiraz* vines. Whites (especially *Semillon* and *Riesling*) are good too. ★★★★ 1998 Blackwell Shiraz £££

Ⱦ **St. Hubert's** (*Victoria*, Australia) Pioneering *Yarra* winery with ultra-fruity *Cabernet* and mouth-filling *Roussanne* whites. ★★★★ 1998 Cabernet ££

S

⚯ **Chateau St. Jean** [jeen] (*Sonoma*, California) Named after the founder's wife; now Japanese-owned and a source of good single-vineyard *Chardonnays*, *late-harvest Rieslings* and *Bordeaux*-style reds. ★★★★ **1996 Cinq Cépages £££**

⚯ **St. Joseph** [san joh-sef] (*Rhône*, France) Potentially vigorous, fruity *Syrah* from the northern *Rhône*. Whites range from flabby to fragrant *Marsannes*. Red: **82 83 85 88 89 90 91 95** 96 97 98 99 00 *Chapoutier; Chave;* Courbis; *Coursodon; Cuilleron; Delas;* de Fauturie; *Gacho-Pascal; Gaillard; Graillot; Gripa; Grippat; Perret; Pichon;* St.-Désirat; *Trollo; Vernay.*

⚯ **St. Julien** [san-joo-lee-yen] (*Bordeaux*, France) Aristocratic *Medoc commune* producing classic rich wines, full of cedar and deep, ripe fruit. **70 75 76 78 79 81 82 83 85 86 88 89 90 94** 95 96 97 98 99 00 *Beychevelle; Branaire; Ducru-Beaucaillou; Gruaud-Larose; Lagrange; Langoa-Barton; Léoville-Barton; Léoville-Las-Cases; Léoville-Poyferré; Talbot.*

🍇 **St. Laurent** [sant loh-rent] (Austria) *Pinot Noir*-like berryish red grape, mastered, in particular, by *Umathum*.

⚯ **St. Nicolas de Bourgueil** [san nee-koh-lah duh boor-goy] (*Loire*, France) Lightly fruity *Cabernet Franc*; needs a warm year to ripen its raspberry fruit, but then can last for up to a decade. Can be lighter than Bourgueil. Yannick Amirault; *Caslot; Max Cognard;* Delauney; *Druet; Jamet;* Mabileau; Vallée.

⚯ **St. Péray** [san pay-reh] (*Rhône*, France) AC near *Lyon* for full-bodied, still white and *traditional method* sparkling wine, at risk from encroaching housing. J-F Chapoud; Auguste Clape; *Bernard Gripa; Marcel Juge; Jean Lionnet; Alain Voge.*

⚯ **Ch. St. Pierre** [san pee-yehr] (*St. Julien 4ème Cru Classé, Bordeaux*, France) Reliable *St. Julien* under the same ownership as *Ch. Gloria.*

⚯ **St. Romain** [san roh-man] (*Burgundy*, France) *Hautes Côtes de Beaune* village producing undervalued fine whites and rustic reds. Christophe Buisson; Chassorney; Germain et Fils; Iain Gras; *Jaffelin;* Thévenin-Monthelie.

⚯ **St. Véran** [san vay-ron] (*Burgundy*, France) Once sold as *Beaujolais Blanc*; affordable alternative to *Pouilly-Fuissé*; better than most *Mâconnais* whites. Ch. Fuissé is first class. White: 96 97 **98 99 00** *Barraud; Corsin;* Dom des Deux Roches; *Duboeuf; Ch. Fuissé;* Luquet; Pacquet.

⚯ **Ste. Croix-du-Mont** [sant crwah doo mon] (*Bordeaux*, France) Never as luscious, rich, and complex as the better efforts of its neighbour *Sauternes* – but often a far more worthwhile buy than wines unashamedly sold under that name. Sweet white: **90 92 93 94 95** 96 97 98

⚯ **Saintsbury** (*Carneros*, California) Superstar *Carneros* producer of unfiltered *Chardonnay* and – more specially – *Pinot Noir*. The slogan: "Beaune in the USA" refers to the winery's Burgundian aspirations. The Reserve *Pinot* is a world-beater, while the easy-going Garnet is the good *second label*. ★★★★ **1997 Brown Ranch Pinot Noir £££**

Sakar [sa-kah] (Bulgaria) Long-time source of much of the best *Cabernet Sauvignon* to come from *Bulgaria.*

⚯ **Castello della Sala** [kas-tel-loh del-la sah-lah] (*Umbria*, Italy) *Antinori's* overpriced but sound *Chardonnay, Sauvignon*. Also good *Sauvignon*/Procanico blend. ★★★★ **1996 Sauvignon della Sala ££**

⚯ **Ch de Sales** [duh sahl] (*Pomerol, Bordeaux*) Good but generally unexciting wine for relatively early drinking. Also worth looking out for is Stonyfell, which matches rich Shiraz flavours with an appealingly "retro" label.

⚯ **Salice Salentino** [sa-lee-chay sah-len-tee-noh] (*Puglia*, Italy) Spicy, intense red made from the characterful *Negroamaro*. Great value, especially when mature. *Candido; Leone de Castris;* Taurino; Vallone.

⚯ **Salomon-Undhof** [sah-loh-mon oond-hohf] (*Kremstal*, Austria) Top-class producer, with especially notable *Riesling.*

⚯ **Salon le Mesnil** [sah-lon lur may-neel] (*Champagne*, France) Small, traditional subsidiary of *Laurent-Perrier* with cult following for pure long-lived *Chardonnay Champagne*. Only sold as a single-vintage cuvée.

S

Ⓘ **Saltram** [sawl-tram] (South Australia) Fast-improving part of the *Mildara-Blass* empire. Rich, fairly priced *Barossa* reds and whites (also under the Mamre Brook label) and top-flight *"ports"*. ★★★★ **1998 Mamre Brook Shiraz £££**

Ⓘ **Samos** [sah-mos] (Greece) Aegean island producing sweet, fragrant, golden *Muscat* once called "the wine of the gods".

Ⓘ **Cellier des Samsons** [sel-yay day som-son] (*Burgundy,* France) Source of better-than-average *Beaujolais.*

San Luis Obispo [san loo-wis oh-bis-poh] (California) Californian region gaining a reputation for *Chardonnay* and *Pinot Noir*. Try *Edna Valley.* Red: 90 91 92 **93 95 96 97** 98 99 **00** White: **95 96** 97 98 99 00

Ⓘ **Viña San Pedro** [veen-ya san-pay-droh] (*Curico,* Chile) Huge *Curico* firm whose wines are quietly and steadily improving thanks to the efforts of consultant *Jacques Lurton*. ★★★★ **1997 Cabo de Hornos Cabernet Sauvignon £££**

Ⓘ **Sancerre** [son-sehr] (*Loire,* France) At its best, the epitome of elegant, steely dry *Sauvignon;* at its worst, oversulphured and fruitless. Reds and rosés, though well regarded and highly priced by French restaurants, are often little better than quaffable *Pinot Noir.* 95 96 97 **98 99 00** Bailly-Reverdy; Jean-Paul Balland; *Henri Bourgeois; Cotat;* Lucien Crochet; Vincent Delaporte; Pierre Dézat; Fouassier; de la Garenne; Gitton; les Grands Groux; *Pascal Jolivet; de Ladoucette;* Serge Laporte; Mellot; Thierry Merlin-Cherrier; Paul Millerioux; Natter; Vincent Pinard; Jean-Max Roger; *Vacheron;* André Vatan.

Ⓘ **Sanchez Romate** (*Jerez,* Spain) Top quality, old-established sherry producer with delicious NPU (Non Plus Ultra) Amontillado.

Ⓘ **Sandeman** (Spain/Portugal) North American-owned, generally under-performing, but occasionally dazzling *port* and *sherry* producer. Port: **55** 57 58 **60 62 63** 65 66 67 68 **70 72 75** 80 94 97 ★★★★★ **1997** Vintage Port £££

Ⓘ **Sanford Winery** (*Santa Barbara,* California) *Santa Barbara* superstar producer of *Chardonnay* and especially distinctive, slightly horseradishy *Pinot Noir.* ★★★★ **1997 Pinot Noir Sanford & Benedict Vineyard £££**

🌺 **Sangiovese** [san-jee-yoh vay-seh] (Italy) The tobaccoey, herby-flavoured red grape of *Chianti* and *Montepulciano,* now being used increasingly in *Vino da Tavola* and – though rarely impressively – in California. *Antinori; Atlas Peak; Bonny Doon; Isole e Olena.*

SANFORD

Chardonnay

SANTA BARBARA COUNTY

Ⓘ **Castello di San Polo in Rosso** [san-poh-loh in - ros-soh] (*Tuscany,* Italy) Reliable, quite traditional *Chianti Classico* estate.

Ⓘ **Luciano Sandrone** [loo-chee-yah-noh sahn-droh-nay] (*Piedmont,* Italy) With fellow revolutionaries *Clerico, Roberto Voerzio,* and *Altare,* Luciano Sandrone has spearheaded the move to modern *Barolo.* Great *Dolcetto* too.

Santa Barbara (California) Successful southern, cool-climate region for *Pinot Noir* and *Chardonnay. Au Bon Climat; Byron; Ojai; Qupé; Sanford.*

Ⓘ **Viña Santa Carolina** [ka-roh-lee-na] (Chile) Greatly improved producer, thanks to *Ignacio Recabarren* and vineyards in *Casablanca.* Good reds. ★★★★★ **1999 Santa Carolina Barrica Selection Chardonnay £££**

Santa Cruz Mountains [krooz] (California) Exciting region to the south of San Francisco. See *Ridge* and *Bonny Doon.* Red: 84 **85** 86 87 **90 91 92 93 95 96** 97 98 99 00 White: 95 96 **97 98 99 00**

Ⓘ **Santa Emiliana** (*Aconcagua,* Chile) Large producer with good Andes Peak offerings from *Casablanca,* and wines from the new southern region of Mulchen. ★★★★ **2000 Andes Peak Chardonnay ££**

Ⓘ **Santa Maddalena** [san-tah mah-dah-LAY-nah] (*Alto Adige,* Italy) Light, spicy-fruity red made from the Schiava. Rarely found outside the region, but well worth seeking out. **Cantina Produttori Sta. Maddalena; Gojer.**

S

♀ **Santa Rita** [ree-ta] (*Maipo,* Chile) Back on track after a slightly bumpy patch. The Casa Real is not only one of Chile's best and most fairly priced reds; it is also truly world class and the Carmenère, Cabernet "Triple C" a great value new arrival on the scene. ★★★★★ 1998 Casa Real £££; ★★★★★ 1998 Triple C £££

♀ **Santenay** [sont-nay] (*Burgundy,* France) Southern *Côte d'Or* village, producing pretty whites and good, though occasionally rather rustic, reds. Look for *Girardin* and *Pousse d'Or*. White: 90 92 95 **96 97 98 99** *00* Red: **90 92 95 96 97 98** *99 00* Roger Belland; *Fernand Chevrot; Marc Colin; Colin-Deléger; Girardin; Olivier Leflaive; Bernard Morey;* Lucien Muzet; Claude Nouveau; *Pousse d'Or;* Prieur Brunet.

♀ **Caves São João** [sow-jwow] (*Bairrada,* Portugal) Small company which produces high-quality *Bairrada*.

Sardinia (Italy) Traditionally the source of powerful reds (try *Santadi*) and whites, increasingly interesting *DOC* fortified wines, and new-wave modern reds to match the best *Super-Tuscans. Sella e Mosca*.

♀ **Paolo Saracco** [pow-loh sah-rak-koh] (*Piedmont,* Italy) Competing with *Vietti* for the role of top *Moscato*-maker. His *Chardonnay* Bianch del Luv is pretty impressive too.

♀ **Sarget de Gruaud-Larose** [sahr-jay dur groowoh lah-rohs] (*St. Julien, Bordeaux,* France) Reliable *second label* of *Ch. Gruaud-Larose*.

♀ **Sassicaia** [sas-see-kai-ya] (*Tuscany,* Italy) World-class *Cabernet*-based *Super-Tuscan* with more of an Italian than a *claret* taste. No longer a mere *Vino da Tavola* since the *DOC* Bolgheri was introduced in 1994.

♀ **Saumur** [soh-moor] (*Loire,* France) Heartland of variable *Chenin*-based sparkling and still wine, and potentially more interesting *Saumur-Champigny*. Red: **90 95 96 97 98** 99 00 White: 96 **97 98 99** *00* Sweet White: **89 90 94 95** *96 97 98 99 00 Ch. du Hureau;* Langlois-Château; Roches Neuves; Vatan; Cave des Vignerons de Saumur; Villeneuve.

♀ **Saumur-Champigny** [soh-moor shom-pee-nyee] (*Loire,* France) Crisp *Cabernet Franc* red; best served slightly chilled. Good examples are worth cellaring. **95 96 97 98** *99 00 Bouvet-Ladubay; Couly-Dutheil; Filliatreau;* Foucault; *Ch. du Hureau;* Langlois-Château; Targé; Vatan; de Villeneuve.

♀ **Saussignac** [soh-sin-yak] (*Southwest,* France) Historically in the shadow both of *Sauternes* and nearby Monbazillac, this sweet-wine region is enjoying a minor boom at the moment, thanks to a set of quality-conscious producers who are making wines to put many a Sauternes to shame. **Ch la Chabrier; des Eyssards; Ch Grinou; Dom. Léonce Cuisset; Dom de Richard, Ch. les Miaudoux, Tourmentine; le Payral; Clos d'Yvigne.** ★★★★ Saussignac AC Chateau Grinou £££

♀ **Sauternes** [soh-turn] (*Bordeaux,* France) Rich, potentially sublime, honeyed dessert wines from *Sauvignon* and *Sémillon* (and possibly *Muscadelle*) blends. Should be affected by *botrytis* but the climate does not always allow this. Quality has improved greatly, but there's still sometimes a tendency to be heavy-handed with *sulphur dioxide*. 78 79 80 81 82 **83 85 86 88 89 90 91 92** *95 97 98 99 00 Bastor-Lamontagne; Doisy-Daëne; Fargues; Filhot; Guiraud; Rieussec; Suduiraut; Yquem.*

♀ **Sauvignon Blanc** [soh-vin-yon-blon] "Grassy", "catty", "asparagussy", "gooseberryish" grape widely grown but rarely really loved, so often blended, oaked, or made sweet. In France, at home in the *Loire* and *Bordeaux*. New Zealand gets it right – especially in *Marlborough*. In Australia, *Knappstein, Cullens, Stafford Ridge,* and *Shaw & Smith* are right on target. *Mondavi's* oaked *Fumé Blanc* and *Kendall Jackson's* sweet versions are successful but *Monteviña, Quivira, Dry Creek, Simi,* and – in blends with the *Sémillon* – *Carmenet* are the stars. Chile makes better versions every year, despite starting out with a lesser variety. See *Caliterra, Casablanca, Canepa, Sta. Carolina,* and *Villard*. In South Africa, see *Thelema, Klein Constantia,* and *Neil Ellis*.

S

ȳ **Sauvignon de St. Bris** [soh-veen-yon-duh san bree] (*Burgundy,* France) *Burgundy*'s only *VDQS*. An affordable and often worthwhile alternative to *Sancerre*, produced in vineyards near *Chablis. Jean-Marc Brocard;* Moreau.

ȳ **Etienne Sauzet** [soh-zay] (*Burgundy,* France) First-rank estate whose white wines are almost unfindable outside collectors' cellars and Michelin-starred restaurants. ★★★★ 1998 Puligny-Montrachet les Combettes ££££

🍇 **Savagnin** [sa-van-yan] (*Jura,* France) No relation of the *Sauvignon;* a white *Jura* variety used for *Vin Jaune* and blended with *Chardonnay* for *Arbois*. Also, confusingly, the Swiss name for the *Gewürztraminer*.

ȳ **Savennières** [sa-ven-yehr] (*Loire,* France) Fine, if sometimes aggressively dry *Chenin Blanc* whites. Very long-lived. 86 88 89 90 94 95 96 97 98 99 00 *des Baumard;* Bise; du Closel; *Coulée de Serrant;* d'Epiré; *La Roche aux Moines;* de Plaisance; *Soulez.*

CLOS DE LA
Coulée de Serrant
APPELLATION SAVENNIÈRES · COULÉE DE SERRANT CONTRÔLÉE

Mᵐᵉ A. JOLY, Propriétaire-Viticulteur
au Château de la Roche-aux-Moines - 49170 SAVENNIÈRES
Mise en bouteille au Château

PRODUCT OF FRANCE   NET CONTENTS · 750 ML   ESTATE BOTTLED

ȳ **Savigny-lès-Beaune** [sa-veen-yee lay bohn] (*Burgundy,* France) Distinctive whites (sometimes made from *Pinot Blanc*) and raspberry reds. At their best can compare with *Beaune. Simon Bize; Chandon de Briailles; Ecard; Girard-Voillot; Girardin; Pavelot; Tollot-Beaut.*

Savoie [sav-wah] (Eastern France) Mountainous region near Geneva producing crisp, floral whites such as Abymes, *Apremont, Seyssel,* and *Crépy.*

ȳ **Saxenburg** (*Stellenbosch,* South Africa) Reliable producer of ripely flavoursome wines. Particularly good *Pinotage* and *Sauvignon Blanc.*

ȳ **Scavino** [ska-vee-noh] (*Piedmont,* Italy) Terrific new-wave, juicy reds, including single-vineyard *Barolos, Barberas* and *Dolcettos.* ★★★★ 1996 Barolo £££

ȳ **Willi Schaefer** [shay-fur] (*Mosel-Saar-Ruwer,* Germany) Grower in the Mosel vineyard of Himmelreich in the village of Graach (Grosslage Münzelay).

ȳ **Scharffenberger** [shah-fen-bur-gur] (*Mendocino,* California) Pommery-owned, independently-run producer of top-class, top-value sparkling wine. ★★★★ Scharffenberger Brut £££

ȳ **Scherrer** [sher-rer] (Tokaji, Hungary) French-owned pioneer of Tokaji and Furmint.

Scharzhofberg [sharts-hof-behrg] (*Mosel-Saar-Ruwer,* Germany) Top-class *Saar* vineyard, producing great *Riesling*. QbA/Kab/Spät: 85 86 88 89 90 91 92 93 94 95 96 97 9 99 00 Aus/Beeren/Tba: 83 85 88 89 90 91 92 93 94 95 96 97 98 Reichsgraf von Kesselstadt.

Schaumwein [showm-vine] (Germany) Low-priced sparkling wine.

🍇 **Scheurebe** [shoy-ray-bur] (Germany) *Riesling* x *Silvaner* cross, grown in Germany and in England. Tastes deliciously like pink grapefruit. In Austria, where it makes excellent sweet wines, they sometimes call it Samling 88. *Kurt Darting;* Hafner; Kadlec; *Alois Kracher; Lingenfelder.*

🍇 **Schiava** [skee yah-vah] (*Alto Adige,* Italy) Grape used in *Lago di Caldaro* and *Santa Maddalena* to make light reds.

Schilfwein [shilf-vine] (Austria) Luscious "reed wine" – Austrian *vin de paille* pioneered by *Willi Opitz.*

ȳ **Schiopetto** [skee yoh-peh-toh] (*Friuli-Venezia Giulia,* Italy) Gloriously intense, perfumed *Collio* white varietals to rival those of *Jermann.*

Schloss [shloss] (Germany) Literally "castle"; in practice, vineyard or estate.

Schist [shist] Type of slaty soil very suitable for growing vines.

ȳ **Schloss Böckelheim** [shloss ber-kell-hime] (*Nahe,* Germany) Varied southern part of the *Nahe.* Wines from the Kupfergrube vineyard and the State Wine Domaine are worth buying. QbA/Kab/Spät: 90 91 92 93 94 95 96 97 98 99 00 Aus/Beeren/Tba: 83 85 88 89 90 91 92 93 94 95 96 97 98 99 00.

ȳ **Schloss Lieser** [shloss lee-zuh] (*Mosel,* Germany) Excellent small estate related to *Fritz Haag.*

S

⟁ **Schloss Reinhartshausen** [shloss rine-harts-how-zehn] (*Rheingau,*
Germany) Innovative estate, successful with *Pinot Blanc* and *Chardonnay*
(the latter introduced following a suggestion by *Robert Mondavi*). The
Rieslings are good too. QbA/Kab/Spät: **90 91 92 93 94 95 96** 97 98 99 00
Aus/Beeren/Tba: **83 85 88 89 90 91 92 93 94** 95 96 97 98 99 00

⟁ **Schloss Saarstein** [shloss sahr-shtine] (*Mosel-Saar-Ruwer,* Germany)
High-quality *Riesling* specialist in *Serrig.* QbA/Kab/Spät: **90 91 92 93** 94
95 96 97 98 99 00 Aus/Beeren/Tba: **89 90 91 92** 93 94 95 96 97 98 99 00

⟁ **Schloss Schönborn** [shloss shern-born] (*Mosel-Saar-Ruwer,* Germany)
Unreliable but sometimes brilliant estate.

⟁ **Schloss Vollrads** [shloss fol-rahts] (*Rheingau,* Germany) Old-established
estate enjoying a renaissance under new ownership and management.

⟁ **Schloss Wallhausen** [shloss val-how-zen] (*Nahe,* Germany) Prinz zu
Salm-Dalberg's estate is one of the top best in the Nahe, producing fine dry
Riesling.
Schlossböckelheim [shloss berk-el-hime] (*Nahe,* Germany) Village
which gives its name to a large *Nahe Bereich,* producing elegant *Riesling.*
QbA/Kab/Spät: **90 91 92 93 94 95 96** 97 98 99 00 Aus/Beeren/Tba: **83
85 88 89 90 91 92 93 94** 95 96 97 98 99 00 Staatsweingut Niederhausen.

⟁ **Schlossgut Diel** [deel] (*Nahe,* Germany) Armin Diel is both wine writer
and winemaker. Co-author of the excellent *German Wine Guide,* his
Dorsheimer Goldloch wines are worth seeking out.

⟁ **Dom. Schlumberger** [shloom-behr-jay] (*Alsace,*
France) Great, sizeable estate whose subtle top-
level wines can often rival those of the somewhat
more showy *Zind-Humbrecht.* ★★★★ **1998**
Riesling Saering £££

⟁ **Schramsberg** [shram-sberg] (*Napa Valley,*
California) The winery that single-handedly put
California sparkling wine on the quality trail. Wines
used to be too big for their boots, possibly because
too many of the grapes were from warm vineyards
in *Napa.* The J. Schram is aimed at *Dom Pérignon*
and gets pretty close to the target. ★★★★ **1997 Blanc de Blancs ££££**

⟁ **Scotchman's Hill** (Victoria, Australia) *Pinot Noir* specialist in *Geelong.*
Sauvignons and *Chardonnays* have been less exciting.

⟁ **Screaming Eagle** (*Napa Valley,* California) Minuscule winery the size of
many people's living room, which has been producing around 200 bottles
of intense *Cabernet* per year since 1992 – and selling them at $100 a bottle.
The owners are avowedly trying to make California's greatest wine. Sadly,
most people will only ever read about it.

⟁ **Seaview** (South Australia) *Penfold's* brand for brilliantly reliable sparkling
wine and (less frequently) *McLaren Vale* red table wines. Look out for the
Edwards & Chaffey label, too. ★★★★ **1997 Chardonnay Blanc de Blancs £££**

⟁ **Sebastiani/Cecchetti Sebastiani** [seh-bas-tee-yan-nee] (*Sonoma Valley,*
California) Sebastiani makes unexceptional wine from *Central Valley* grapes.
The associated but separate Cecchetti Sebastiani, however, like the top end
of *Gallo,* makes really good stuff in *Sonoma.* The Pepperwood Grove wines
are good too.
Sec/secco/seco [se-koh] (France/Italy/Spain) Dry.
Second label (*Bordeaux,* France) Wine from a producer's (generally a
Bordeaux *château*) lesser vineyards, younger vines, and/or lesser *cuvées* of
wine. Especially worth buying in good vintages. See *Les Forts de Latour.*

⟁ **Segura Viudas** [say-goo-rah vee-yoo-dass] (*Catalonia,* Spain) The quality
end of the Freixenet Cava giant. ★★★ **Brut Reserva £££**

⟁ **Seifried Estate** [see-freed] (*Nelson,* New Zealand) Also known as *Redwood*
Valley Estate. Superb *Riesling,* especially *late-harvest* style, and very
creditable *Sauvignon* and *Chardonnay.*

S

Sekt [zekt] (Germany) Very basic sparkling wine – best won as a prize. Watch out for anything that does not state that it is made from *Riesling* – other grape varieties almost invariably make highly unpleasant wines. Only the prefix "Deutscher" guarantees German origin.

℥ **Selaks** [see-lax] (*Auckland*, New Zealand) Large company in Kumeu best known for the piercingly fruity *Sauvignon* originally made by a young man called Kevin Judd, who went on to produce *Cloudy Bay*. ★★★★ 2000 Sauvignon Blanc £££

℥ **Weingut Selbach-Oster** [zel-bahkh os-tehr] (*Mosel-Saar-Ruwer*, Germany) Archetypical *Mosel Riesling* of great finesse and balance. One of the region's best producers.

Sélection de Grains Nobles (SGN) [say-lek-see-yon duh gran nohbl] (Alsace, France) Equivalent to German *Beerenauslese*; rich, sweet *botrytized* wine from specially selected grapes. These wines are rare, expensive, and long-lived.

℥ **Sella e Mosca** [seh-la eh mos-kah] (*Sardinia*, Italy) Dynamic firm with a good *Cabernet* called Villamarina, the rich *Anghelu Ruju*, and traditional *Cannonau* which is also blended with *Cabernet* to produce the highly impressive *Tanca Farra*. ★★★★ Anghelu Ruju £££; ★★★★★ 1997 Tanca Farra £££

℥ **Fattoria Selvapiana** [fah-taw-ree-ya sel-va-pee-yah-nah] (*Tuscany*, Italy) Great *Chianti Rufina, vin santo,* and olive oil. ★★★★ 1996 Bucerchiale Riserva £££

℥ **Château Semeli** [seh-meh-lee] (*Attica*, Greece) Producer of classy Cabernet and Nemea reds.

🍇 **Sémillon** [in France: say-mee-yon; in Australia: seh-mil-lon and even seh-mih-lee-yon] Peachy grape generally blended with *Sauvignon* to make sweet and dry *Bordeaux*, and vinified separately in Australia, where it is also sometimes blended with *Chardonnay*. Rarely as successful in other New World countries, where many versions taste more like *Sauvignon*. Carmenet; Geyser Peak; McWilliams; Rothbury; Tyrrell; Xanadu.

℥ **Seña** [sen-ya] (Chile) A *Mondavi* and *Caliterra* co-production. A Mercedes of a wine: impeccably put together, and improving with every vintage, but, so far, still somehow a little less exciting than wines like *Santa Rita's* Triple C and *Casa Lapostolle's* Clos Apalta.

℥ **Sepp Moser** [sep moh-zur] (*Kremstal*, Austria) Serious producer of – especially – good *Grüner Veltliner* and late-harvest *Chardonnay* and *Riesling*.

℥ **Seppelt** (South Australia) *Penfolds* subsidiary and pioneer of the *Great Western* region where it makes rich still and sparkling *Shiraz* and Dorrien *Cabernet*. Other Seppelt sparkling wines are recommendable too, though the once-fine Salinger seems to have lost its way. ★★★★ 1998 Chalambar Shiraz £££; ★★★★★ 21 Year Old Para Tawny.

℥ **Serafini & Vidotto** [seh-rah-fee-noh eh vee-dot-toh] (*Veneto*, Italy) Francesco Serafini and Antonello Vidotto make great Pinot Nero.

℥ **Seresin** [seh-ra-sin] (*Marlborough*, New Zealand) New venture launched by a British movie cameraman. Impeccable vineyards and really impressive *Chardonnay*, *Sauvignon*, and a promising *Pinot Noir*.

Servir frais (France) Serve chilled.

℥ **Setúbal** [shtoo-bal] (Portugal) *DOC* on the *Setúbal Peninsula*.

Setúbal Peninsula (Portugal) Home of the *Setúbal DOC*, but now notable for the rise of two new wine regions, Arrabida and Palmela, where *JM Fonseca Succs* and *JP Vinhos* are making excellent wines from local and international grape varieties. The lusciously rich *Moscatel de Setúbal*, however, is still the star of the show.

℥ **Seyssel** [say-sehl] (*Savoie*, France) AC region near Geneva producing light white wines that are usually enjoyed in après-ski mood when no one is overly concerned about value for money. Maison Mollex; Varichon et Clerc.

S

🍇 **Seyval Blanc** [say-vahl blon] *Hybrid* grape – a cross between French and US vines – unpopular with EU authorities but successful in eastern US, Canada, and England, especially at *Breaky Bottom*.

🍷 **Shafer** [shay-fur] (*Napa Valley*, California) Top *Cabernet* producer in the *Stag's Leap* district, and maker of classy *Carneros Chardonnay* and *Merlot*. ★★★★ 1997 Red Shoulder Ranch Chardonnay £££

🍷 **Shaw & Smith** (*Adelaide Hills*, Australia) Recently founded winery producing one of Australia's best *Sauvignons* and a pair of increasingly *Burgundian Chardonnays* that demonstrate how good wines from this variety can taste with and without oak. ★★★★★ 1998 Reserve Chardonnay £££

🍷 **Sherry** (*Jerez*, Spain) The fortified wine made in the area surrounding *Jerez*. Wines made elsewhere – Australia, England, South Africa, etc. – may no longer use the name. See also *Almacenista; Fino; Amontillado; Manzanilla; Cream Sherry. Barbadillo; Gonzalez Byass; Hidalgo; Lustau.*

🍇 *Shiraz* [shee-raz] (Australia, South Africa) The *Syrah* grape in Australia and South Africa, named after its (erroneously) supposed birthplace in Iran. South African versions are lighter (and generally greener) than the Australians, while the Australians are usually riper and oakier than efforts from the *Rhône*. The move to cooler sites is broadening the range of Australian *Shiraz*, however. *Hardy's; Henschke; Maglieri; Lindemans; Rockford; Rothbury; Penfolds; Picardy; Plantagenet; St. Hallett; Saxenburg; Wolf Blass.*

🍷 **Shooting Star** (Lake County, California) One of California's avid proponents of Cabernet Franc. The Zinfandel and Cabernet Sauvignon are good too.

Sicily (Italy) Historically best known for *Marsala* and sturdy "southern" table wines. Now, however, there is an array of other unusual fortified wines and a fast-growing range of new-wave reds and whites, many made from grapes grown nowhere else. *De Bartoli; Corvo; Planeta; Regaleali; Terre di Ginestra.*

🍷 **Sieur d'Arques** [see-uhr dark] (*Languedoc-Roussillon*, France) High-tech cooperative in *Limoux* that ought to serve as a role model to its neighbours. Good *Blanquette de Limoux* sparkling wine and truly impressive *Chardonnays* sold under the Toques et Clochers label.

🍷 **Ch. Sigalas-Rabaud** [see-gah-lah rah-boh] (*Bordeaux*, France) Fine Sauternes estate, producing rich, but delicate, wines.

🍷 **Siglo** [seeg-loh] (*Rioja*, Spain) Good brand of modern red (traditionally sold in a burlap "sack") and old-fashioned whites.

🍷 **Signorello** (*Napa Valley*, California) Small winery making *Burgundian Chardonnay* with yeasty richness, *Bordeaux*-style *Semillon* and *Sauvignon* as well as *Cabernets* that are both blackcurrranty and stylish.

Silex [see-lex] (France) Term describing flinty soil, used by *Didier Dagueneau* for his oak-fermented *Pouilly-Fumé*.

🍇 **Silvaner** See *Sylvaner*.

🍷 **Silver Oak Cellars** (*Napa Valley*, California) Superb specialized *Cabernet* producers favouring fruitily accessible, but still classy, wines which benefit from long ageing in (American oak) barrels and bottled before release. Look out for older vintages of the single-vineyard Bonny's Vineyard wines, the last of which was made in 1991. ★★★★★ 1995 Napa Valley Cabernet £££

🍷 **Silverado** [sil-veh-rah-doh] (*Napa Valley*, California) Reliable *Cabernet*, *Chardonnay*, and now *Sangiovese* winery that belongs to Walt Disney's widow.

🍷 **Simi Winery** [see-mee] (*Sonoma Valley*, California) Recently sold (to the giant Canandaigua) and made famous by the thoughtful Zelma Long and her complex, long-lived Burgundian *Chardonnay*, archetypical *Sauvignon*, and lovely, blackcurrant *Alexander Valley Cabernet*. The current (excellent) Kiwi-born winemaker has so far remained in place, thank goodness. ★★★★ 1995 Cabernet £££

S

Bert Simon (*Mosel-Saar-Ruwer,* Germany) Newish estate in the *Saar* river valley with supersoft *Rieslings* and unusually elegant *Weissburgunder.*

Simonsberg (*Stellenbosch,* South Africa) The mountain on which *Thelema's* vineyards are situated.

Simonsig Estate [see-mon-sikh] (*Stellenbosch,* South Africa) Big estate with a very impressive commercial range, and the occasional gem – try the *Shiraz, Cabernet, Pinotage, Chardonnay* the Kaapse Vonkel sparkler. ★★★★ 1997 Reserve Merindol Shiraz ££

Sin Crianza [sin cree-an-tha] (Spain) Not aged in wood.

Sion [see-yo'n] (*Valais,* Switzerland) One of the proud homes of the grape the Swiss call the Fendant and outsiders know as *Chasselas.* Dull elsewhere, it can produce creditable (and even occasionally ageworthy) wines.

Ch. Siran [see-ron] (*Margaux Cru Bourgeois, Bordeaux,* France) Beautiful *château* outperforming its classification and producing increasingly impressive and generally fairly priced wines. 90 93 94 95 96 97 98 99 00

Skalli [skal-lee] (Languedoc-Roussillon France) Pioneering producer of quality *Vins de Pays* under the Fortant label.

Skillogalee [skil-log-gah-lee] (*Clare Valley,* Australia) Well-respected *Clare* producer, specializing in *Riesling,* but also showing his skill with reds. ★★★★ 1999 Gewurztraminer ££

Skin contact The longer the skins of black grapes are left in with the juice after the grapes have been crushed, the greater the *tannin* and the deeper the colour. Some non-aromatic white varieties (*Chardonnay* and *Semillon* in particular) can also benefit from extended skin contact (usually between six and 24 hours) to increase flavour.

Skouras (*Peloponnese,* Greece) Eager producer, making good Nemea reds and Viognier whites.

Sliven [slee-ven] Bulgarian region offering good-value, simple reds and better-than-average whites.

Slovakia Up-and-coming source of wines from grapes little seen elsewhere, such as the *Muscat*ty Irsay Oliver.

Slovenia Former Yugoslavian region in which *Laski Rizling* is king. Other grapes show greater promise.

Smith & Hook (*Mendocino,* California) Winery with a cult following for its zippy, blackcurrant *Cabernet Sauvignon.* These lack the ripe richness sought by most US critics, however.

Smith-Madrone (*Napa,* California) Long-established winery that bucks the trend by using the *Riesling* (which is being uprooted elsewhere) to make good wine. *Chardonnay* is good too.

Smith Woodhouse (*Douro,* Portugal) Part of the same empire as *Dow's, Graham's,* and *Warre's* but often overlooked. *Vintage ports* can be good, as is the house speciality *Traditional Late Bottled Vintage Port.* 60 63 66 70 75 77 85 94 97 ★★★★ 1997 Vintage Port £££

Ch. Smith-Haut-Lafitte [oh-lah-feet] (*Pessac-Léognan Cru Classé, Bordeaux,* France) Estate flying high under its new ownership. Increasingly classy reds and (specially) pure *Sauvignon* whites. Grape seeds from the estate are also used to make an anti-ageing skin cream called Caudalie. Red: 82 85 86 89 90 93 94 95 96 97 98 99 00 White: 92 93 94 95 96 97 98 99 00 ★★★★ 2000 White ££££

Smithbrook (Western Australia) *Pinot Noir* specialist in the southerly region of *Pemberton.* Now owned by *Petaluma.* ★★★★ 1999 Sauvignon Blanc £££

Soave [swah-veh] (*Veneto,* Italy) Mostly dull stuff, but *Soave Classico* is better; single-vineyard versions are best. Sweet *Recioto* di Soave is delicious. *Pieropan* is almost uniformly excellent. Anselmi; La Cappuccina; Inama; *Masi; Pieropan;* Pra; *Tedeschi;* Zenato.

Ch. Sociando-Mallet [soh-see-yon-doh ma-lay] (*Haut-Médoc Cru Bourgeois, Bordeaux,* France) A *Cru Bourgeois* whose oaked, fruity red wines are way above its status. 82 83 85 86 88 89 90 91 93 95 96 97 98 99 00

S

☙ **Sogrape** [soh-grap] (Portugal) Having invented *Mateus* Rosé half a century ago, this large firm is now modernizing the wines of *Dão* (with the new Quinta dos Carvalhais), *Douro* and *Bairrada*, and *Alentejo* (Vinha do Monte) bringing out flavours these once-dull wines never seemed to possess. *Sogrape* also owns the *port* house of *Ferreira* and is thus also responsible for *Barca Velha*, Portugal's top red table wine. The *Penfolds* of Portugal.

☙ **Sokol Blosser** (*Oregon*) Highly successful makers of rich *Chardonnay*. The *Pinot* is good too. ★★★★★ 1998 12 Row Block Pinot Noir £££

☙ **Solaia** [soh-lie-yah] (*Tuscany,* Italy) Yet another *Antinori Super-Tuscan*. A phenomenal blend of *Cabernet Sauvignon* and *Franc*, with a little *Sangiovese*. Italy's top red? ★★★★★ 1997 Solaia Antinori ££££

Solera [soh-leh-rah] (*Jerez*, Spain) Ageing system involving older wine being continually "refreshed" by slightly younger wine of the same style.

☙ **Bodegas Felix Solís** [fay-leex soh-lees] (*Valdepeñas*, Spain) By far the biggest, most progressive winery in *Valdepeñas*.

Somontano [soh-mon-tah-noh] (Spain) *DO* region in the foothills of the Pyrenees in Aragon, now experimenting with international grape varieties. COVISA; *Enate;* Pirineos; *Viñas del Vero.*

Sonnenuhr [soh-neh-noor] (*Mosel*, Germany) Vineyard site in the famous village of *Wehlen*. See *Dr Loosen*. QbA/Kab/Spät: 90 91 92 93 94 95 96 97 98 99 00 Aus/Beeren/Tba: 85 88 89 90 91 92 93 94 95 96 97 98 99 00

Sonoma Valley [so-noh-ma] (California) Despite the *Napa* hype, this lesser-known region not only contains some of the state's top wineries, it is also home to *E&J Gallo's* superpremium vineyard and *Dry Creek*, home of some of California's best *Zinfandels*. The region is subdivided into the *Sonoma, Alexander,* and *Russian River Valleys* and *Dry Creek*. Red: 95 96 97 98 99 00 White: 95 96 97 98 99 00 Adler Fels; *Arrowood; Carmenet; Ch. St Jean Clos du Bois; Dry Creek; Duxoup; E&J Gallo; Geyser Peak; Gundlach Bundschu; Cecchetti Sebastiani; Iron Horse; Jordan; Kenwood; Kistler; Laurel Glen; Matanzas Creek; Peter Michael; Quivira; Ravenswood; Ridge; St. Francis; Sonoma-Cutrer; Simi; Marimar Torres; Joseph Swan.*

☙ **Sonoma-Cutrer** [soh-noh-ma koo-trehr] (*Sonoma Valley*, California) Recently sold producer of world-class single-vineyard *Chardonnay* that can rival *Puligny-Montrachet*. The "Les Pierres" is the tops.

LES PIERRES VINEYARD

1986

SONOMA-CUTRER

CHARDONNAY
SONOMA VALLEY

ESTATE GROWN & BOTTLED BY SONOMA CUTRER VINEYARDS WINDSOR CA 95492

☙ **Marc Sorrel** [sor-rel] (*Rhône,* France) *Hermitage* producer who is – unusually – as successful in white as red. The "le Gréal" single-vineyard red is the wine to buy, though the "les Roccoules" white ages well.

☙ **Pierre Soulez** [soo-layz] (*Loire,* France) Producer of *Savennières*, especially Clos du Papillon and Roche-aux-Moines *late harvest* wines.

☙ **Ch. Soutard** [soo-tahr] (*St. Emilion, Bordeaux,* France) Traditional *St. Emilion* estate with long-lived wines that rely on far less oak than many.

South Africa Quality is patchy but improving, with riper, more characterful wine that apes neither France nor Australia. Below the top level, look for inexpensive, simple, dry and off-dry *Chenins*, lovely *late-harvest* and fortified wines, and surprisingly good *Pinotages*; otherwise very patchy. Red: 95 96 97 98 99 00 White: 95 96 97 98 99 Fairview; *Grangehurst; Klein Constantia; Jordan; Kanonkop; Mulderbosch; Plaisir de Merle; Saxenburg; Simonsig; Thelema;Vergelegen.*

South Australia Home of almost all the biggest wine companies, and still producing over half of Australia's wine. The *Barossa Valley* is one of the country's oldest wine regions, but like its neighbours *Clare* and *McLaren Vale*, faces competition from cooler areas like *Adelaide Hills*, *Padthaway*, and *Coonawarra*. Red: 90 91 94 95 96 97 98 99 00 White: 95 96 97 98 99 00

Southeast Australia A cleverly meaningless regional description. Technically, it covers around 85 per cent of Australia's vineyards.

Southwest France An unofficial umbrella term covering the areas between *Bordeaux* and the Pyrenees, *Bergerac, Madiran, Cahors, Jurançon*, and the *Vins de Pays* of the Côtes de Gascogne.

☙ Spanna [spah-nah] (*Piedmont*, Italy) The *Piedmontese* name for the *Nebbiolo* grape and the more humble wines made from it.

♈ Pierre Sparr (*Alsace*, France) Big producer offering a rare chance to taste traditional *Chasselas*.

♈ Spätburgunder [shpayt-bur-goon-dur](Germany) Alias of *Pinot Noir*.

Spätlese [shpayt-lay-zeh] (Germany) Second step in the *QmP* scale, *late-harvest*ed grapes making wine a notch drier than *Auslese*.

♈ Fratelli Speri [speh-ree] (*Veneto*, Italy) A fast-rising star with delicious . Monte Sant'Urbano Amarone della Valpolicella Classico.

♈ Spice Route (South Africa) Label showing the skills of Charles Back of Fairview. Good value, reliable wines from Malmesbury. Top wines are labelled "Flagship".

♈ Domaine Spiropoulos [spee-ro-poo-los] (*Peloponnese*, Greece) Fine producer of organic wine, including Porfyros, one of Greece's best modern reds.

♈ Spottswoode (*Napa Valley*, California) Excellent small producer of complex *Cabernet* and unusually good *Sauvignon Blanc*. Deserves greater recognition.
★★★★★ 1997 Cabernet Sauvignon £££

♈ Spring Mountain (*Napa Valley*, California) Revived old winery with great vineyards and classy, berryish *Cabernet*.

♈ Springfield Estate (*Robertson*, South Africa) Fast improving producer, with crisp dry *Sauvignons*, and a good "methode ancienne" Chardonnay.
★★★★ 2000 Special Cuvée Sauvignon Blanc £££

Spritz/ig [shpritz/ich] Slight sparkle/sparkling. Also *pétillant*.

Spumante [spoo-man-tay] (Italy) Sparkling.

♈ Squinzano [skeen-tzah-noh] (*Puglia*, Italy) Traditional, often rustic reds from the warm South. The *Santa Barbara* cooperative makes the best wines.

Staatsweingut [staht-svine-goot] (Germany) A state-owned wine estate such as Staatsweingüter *Eltville* (*Rheingau*), a major cellar in *Eltville*.

♈ Standing Stones (*New York State*) Recommendable Finger Lakes producer with an especially good Riesling.

♈ Stafford Ridge (*Adelaide Hills*, Australia) Fine *Chardonnay* and especially *Sauvignon* from *Lenswood* by Geoff Weaver, former winemaker of *Hardys*.

Stag's Leap District (*Napa Valley*, California) A long-established hillside region, specializing in blackcurranty *Cabernet Sauvignon*. Red: 84 85 86 87 90 91 92 93 95 *96 98 99 00* S. Anderson; *Clos du Val;* Cronin; Hartwell; *Pine Ridge; Shafer; Silverado Vineyards; Stag's Leap;* Steltzner.

♈ Stag's Leap Wine Cellars (*Napa Valley*, California) Pioneering supporter of the *Stag's Leap appellation*, and one of the finest wineries in California. The best wines are the Faye Vineyard, SLV, and Cask 23 *Cabernets*.
★★★★★ 1997 Cabernet Sauvignon £££

♈ Staglin (*Napa Valley*, California) Classy producer of stylish, Bordeaux-like *Cabernet* and pioneering *Sangiovese*. ★★★★★ 1997 Cabernet Sauvignon £££

Stalky or stemmy Flavour of the stem rather than of the juice.

♈ Stanton & Killeen (*Rutherglen*, Australia) Reliable producer of *Liqueur Muscat*. ★★★★ Rutherglen Liqueur Muscat ££

♈ Steele (*Lake County*, California) The former winemaker of *Kendall Jackson;* a master when it comes to producing fruitily crowd-pleasing *Chardonnays* from various regions and more complex *Zinfandel*.

Steely Refers to young wine with evident *acidity*. A compliment when paid to *Chablis* and dry *Sauvignons*.

☙ Steen [steen] (South Africa) Local name for (and possibly odd *clone* of) *Chenin Blanc*. Widely planted (over 30 per cent of the vineyard area). The best come from *Boschendal* and *Fairview*.

S

Steiermark/Styria (Austria) Sunny southern region where the *Chardonnay* is now being used (under the name of "Morillon") to produce rich, buttery, but often quite Burgundian wines.

Stellenbosch [stel-len-bosh] (South Africa) Centre of the *Cape* wine industry, and a climatically and topographically diverse region that, like the *Napa Valley*, is taken far too seriously as a regional *appellation*. Hillside sub-regions like Helderberg make more sense. Red: 91 92 **93 94 95 96 97 98** White: **95 96 97 98 99 00** *Bergkelder; Delheim; Neil Ellis; Grangehurst; Hartenburg; Jordan; Kanonkop; Meerlust; Mulderbosch; Rustenberg; Saxenburg; Stellenzicht; Thelema; Warwick.*

Stellenbosch Farmers' Winery (*Stellenbosch*, South Africa) South Africa's biggest producer, with Sable View, Libertas, *Nederburg*, *Plaisir de Merle*.

Stellenzicht Vineyards [stel-len-zikht] (*Stellenbosch*, South Africa) Sister estate of Neethlingshof, with a good *Sauvignon* and a *Shiraz* good enough to beat *Penfolds Grange* in a blind tasting. ★★★★ 1998 Syrah £££

Stelvin Brand of screwcap, specifically designed for wine bottled by its French manufacturer. Long respected by open-minded professionals, but disdained by consumers, Stelvins have had a new boost following the decision by a group of top Clare Valley Riesling producers to use them.

Sterling Vineyards (*Napa Valley*, California) Founded by Peter Newton (now at *Newton* vineyards) and once the plaything of Coca-Cola, this showcase estate now belongs to Canadian liquor giant Seagram. Among the current successes are the Reserve *Cabernet*, *Pinot Noir*, and fairly priced Redwood Trail wines. ★★★★ 1997 Reserve Cabernet Sauvignon ££

Weingut Georg Stiegelmar [stee-gel-mahr] (*Burgenland*, Austria) Producer of pricey, highly acclaimed, dry whites from *Chardonnay* and *Pinot Blanc*, *late-harvest* wines, and some particularly good reds from *Pinot Noir* and *St. Laurent*.

Stoneleigh (*Marlborough*, New Zealand) Reliable *Marlborough* label, now part of *Montana*. ★★★★ 1999 Riesling ££

Stonestreet (*Sonoma*, California) Highly commercial wines from the *Kendall-Jackson* stable. ★★★★ 1995 Alexander Valley Legacy £££

Stonier's [stoh-nee-yurs] (*Mornington Peninsula*, Australia) Small *Mornington* winery, successful with impressive *Pinot Noir*, *Chardonnay*, and *Merlot*. (Previously known as Stoniers-Merrick; and now a subsidiary of *Petaluma*.) ★★★★ 1998 Reserve Pinot Noir ££

Stony Hill (*Napa Valley*, California) Unfashionable old winery with the guts to produce long-lived, complex *Chardonnay* that tastes like unoaked *Grand Cru Chablis*, rather than follow the herd in aping buttery-rich *Meursault*. Individual wine for individualistic wine drinkers.

Stonyridge (*Auckland*, New Zealand) Rapidly rising star on fashionable Waiheke Island, making impressive, if pricey, *Bordeaux*-style reds.

Storybook Mountain (*Napa Valley*, California) Great individual-vineyard *Zinfandels* that taste good young but are built for the long haul. The *Howell Mountain* vines were replanted with *Cabernet Sauvignon*.

Structure The "structural" components of a wine include *tannin, acidity,* and *alcohol*. They provide the skeleton or backbone that supports the "flesh" of the fruit. A young wine with good structure should age well.

Ch. de Suduiraut [soo-dee-rroh] (*Sauternes Premier Cru Classé, Bordeaux*, France) Producing greater things since its purchase by French insurance giant, AXA. Top wines: "*Cuvée* Madame", "Crème de Tête". The 1999 was probably the Sauternes of the vintage.

Suhindol [soo-win-dol] (Bulgaria) One of *Bulgaria's* best-known regions, the source of widely available, fairly-priced *Cabernet Sauvignon*.

Sulphites US labelling requirement alerting those suffering from an (extremely rare) allergy to the presence of *sulphur dioxide*. Curiously, no such requirement is made of cans of baked beans and dried apricots, which contain twice as much of the chemical.

Sulphur dioxide/SO₂ Antiseptic routinely used by food packagers and winemakers to protect their produce from bacteria and *oxidation*.

🍷 **Super Second** (*Bordeaux*, France) *Médoc* second growths: *Pichon-Lalande, Pichon-Longueville, Léoville-las-Cases, Ducru-Beaucaillou, Cos d'Estournel*; whose wines are thought to rival – and cost nearly as much as – the first growths. Other overperformers include: *Rauzan-Ségla* and *Léoville-Barton, Lynch-Bages, Palmer, La Lagune, Montrose*.

Super-Tuscan (Italy) New-wave *Vino da Tavola/IGT* (usually red) wines, pioneered by producers like *Antinori*, which stood outside *DOC* rules, until those rules were changed. Generally *Bordeaux*-style blends or *Sangiovese* or a mixture of both.

Supérieur/Superiore [soo-pay-ree-ur/soo-pay-ree-ohr-ray] (France/Italy) Often relatively meaningless in terms of discernible quality. Denotes wine (well or badly) made from riper grapes.

Sur lie [soor-lee] (France) The ageing "on its *lees*" – or dead yeasts – most commonly associated with *Muscadet*, but now being used to make other fresher, richer, and sometimes slightly sparkling wines in southern France.

Süssreserve [soos-sreh-zurv] (Germany) Unfermented grape juice used to bolster sweetness and fruit in German and English wines.

🍷 **Sutter Home Winery** (*Napa Valley*, California) Home of robust red *Zinfandel* in the 1970s, and responsible for the invention of successful sweet "white" (or, as the non-colour-blind might say, pink) *Zinfandel. Amador County Zinfandels* are still good, but rarely exceptional. The M. Trinchero Founders Estate *Cabernet* and *Chardonnay* are worth looking out for.

🍷 **Joseph Swan** (*Sonoma*, California) Small Burgundian-scale winery whose enthusiastic winemaker, Rod Berglund, produces great single-vineyard, often attractively quirky, *Pinot Noir* and *Zinfandel*. ★★★★★ **1996 Russian River Valley Estate Pinot Noir £££**

Swan Valley (*Western Australia*) Hot old vineyard area; good for fortified wines and a source of fruit for *Houghton's* successful *HWB*. *Houghton* also produces cooler-climate wines in the microclimate of *Moondah Brook*.

🍷 **Swanson** [swon-son] (*Napa Valley*, California) Top flight, innovative producer of *Cabernet, Chardonnay, Sangiovese, Syrah*, and *late-harvest Semillon*.

Switzerland Produces increasingly enjoyable wines from grapes ranging from the *Chasselas, Marsanne, Syrah*, and *Pinot Noir* to the local *Cornallin* and *Petite Arvine*. See *Dôle, Fendant, Chablais*. Also the only country to use screw caps for much of its wine, thus facilitating recycling and avoiding the problems of faulty corks. Clever people, the Swiss.

🍇 **Sylvaner/Silvaner** [sill-vah-nur] Non-aromatic white grape, originally from Austria but found particularly in *Alsace* and *Franken*. Elsewhere, wines are often dry and earthy, though there are promising efforts in South Africa.

🍇 **Syrah** [see-rah] (*Rhône*, France) The red *Rhône* grape, an exotic mix of ripe fruit and spicy, smoky, gamey, leathery flavours. Skilfully adopted by Australia, where it is called *Shiraz* and in southern France for *Vin de Pays d'Oc*. Increasingly popular in California, thanks to "*Rhône* Rangers" like *Bonny Doon* and *Phelps*. See *Qupé, Marqués de Griñon* in Spain and *Isole e Olena* in Italy, plus *Côte Rôtie, Hermitage, Shiraz*.

T

TBA (Germany) Abbreviation for Trockenbeeren Auslese (qv).

🍷 **La Tâche** [la tash] (*Burgundy*, France) Wine from the La Tâche vineyard, exclusively owned by the *Dom. de la Romanée Conti*. Frequently as good as the rarer and more expensive "La Romanée Conti". ★★★★★ **1998 ££££**

Tafelwein [tah-fel-vine] (Germany) Table wine. Only the prefix "Deutscher" guarantees German origin.

T

Ch. Tahbilk [tah-bilk] (*Victoria,* Australia) Old-fashioned winemaking in the *Goulbourn Valley.* Great long-lived *Shiraz* from 130-year-old vines, surprisingly good *Chardonnay,* and lemony *Marsanne* which needs a decade. The second wine is Dalfarras. ★★★★ 1998 Shiraz ££; ★★★★ 1998 Cabernet Sauvignon ££

Cave de Tain L'Hermitage (*Rhône,* France) Reliable cooperative for *Crozes-Hermitage* and *Hermitage.* ★★★★ 1999 St. Joseph Nobles Rives £££

Taittinger [tat-tan-jehr] (*Champagne,* France) Producer of reliable non-vintage, and fine Comtes de *Champagne Blanc de Blancs* and Rosé.

Ch. Talbot [tal-boh] (*St. Julien 4ème Cru Classé, Bordeaux,* France) Reliable, if sometimes slightly jammy, wine. In the same stable as Ch. Gruaud Larose. Connétable Talbot is the *second label.* 2000 was a particular success. 75 78 79 81 82 83 84 85 86 88 89 90 92 93 94 95 96 97 98 99 00.

Talbott (*Monterey,* California) Serious small producer of elegant *Chardonnay* and *Pinot Noir* that lasts. ★★★★ 1997 Sleepy Hollow Chardonnay ££

Talley (*San Luis Obispo,* California) Serious small producer of elegant *Chardonnay* and *Pinot Noir* that lasts.

Taltarni [tal-tahr-nee] (*Victoria,* Australia) Until his recent departure, Dominique Portet made great European-style *Shiraz Cabernets* in this beautiful *Pyrenees* vineyard. ★★★★ 1998 Cabernet Sauvignon £££

Tannat [ta-na] (France) Rustic French grape variety, traditionally used in the blend of *Cahors* and in South America, principally in *Uruguay.*

Tannic See *Tannin.*

Tannin Astringent component of red wine that comes from the skins, seeds, and stalks, and helps the wine to age.

Tardy & Ange [tahr-dee ay onzh] (*Rhône,* France) Partnership producing classy *Crozes-Hermitage* at the Dom. de Entrefaux.

Tarragona [ta-ra-go-nah] (*Catalonia,* Spain) *DO* region south of *Penedés* and home to many cooperatives. Contains the better-quality *Terra Alta.*

Tarrawarra [ta-ra-wa-ra] (*Yarra Valley,* Australia) Increasingly successful *Pinot* pioneer in the cool-climate region of the *Yarra Valley. Second label* is Tunnel Hill. ★★★★ 1998 *Pinot Noir* £££

Tarry Red wines from hot countries often have an aroma and flavour reminiscent of tar. The *Syrah* and *Nebbiolo* exhibit this characteristic.

Tartaric Type of acid found in grapes. Also the form in which acid is added to wine in hot countries whose legislation allows this.

Tartrates [tar-trayts] Harmless white crystals often deposited by white wines in the bottle. In Germany, these are called "diamonds".

Tasmania (Australia) Cool-climate island, showing potential for sparkling wine, *Chardonnay, Riesling,* and *Pinot Noir.* White: 95 96 97 98 99 00 Red: 91 92 94 95 96 97 98 99 00 Freycinet; Heemskerk; Jansz; Moorilla; Piper's Brook; Pirie; Tamar Ridge.

Tastevin [tat-van] The silver *Burgundy* tasting cup used as an insignia by vinous brotherhoods (*confréries*), as a badge of office by sommeliers, and as an ashtray by the author. The *Chevaliers de Tastevin* organize annual tastings, awarding a mock-medieval Tastevinage label to the best wines. *Chevaliers de Tastevin* attend banquets, often wearing similarly mock-medieval clothes and ceremonial gowns.

Taurasi [tow-rah-see] (*Campania,* Italy) Big, old-fashioned *Aglianico.* Needs years to soften and develop a burned, cherry taste. *Mastroberardino.*

Cosimo Taurino [tow-ree-noh] (*Puglia,* Italy) The name to look for when buying Salice Salentino. The red Patrigliono and Notapanaro and the Chardonnay are worth looking for, too.

Tavel [ta-vehl] (*Rhône,* France) Dry rosé. Often very disappointing. Seek out young versions and avoid the bronze colour revered by traditionalists. Ch. d'Aquéria; Dom. de la Forcadière; de la Mordorée; du Prieuré; Ch. de Trinquevedel; de Valéry.

T

Tawny (*Douro*, Portugal) In theory, pale browny-red *port* that acquires its mature appearance and nutty flavour from long ageing in oak casks. *Port* houses, however, legally produce cheap "tawny" by mixing basic *ruby* with *white port* and skipping the tiresome business of barrel-ageing altogether. The real stuff comes with an indication of age, such as 10- or 20-year-old, but these figures are approximate. A 10-year-old *port* only has to "taste as though it is that old". *Colheita ports* are tawnies of a specific vintage. *Noval; Taylor's; Cockburn's; Dow's; Niepoort; Ramos Pinto; Calem.*

☂ **Taylor (Fladgate & Yeatman)** (*Douro*, Portugal) With *Dow's*, one of the "first growths" of the *Douro*. Outstanding *vintage port*, "modern" *Late Bottled Vintage*. Also owns *Fonseca* and *Guimaraens*, and produces the excellent *Quinta de Vargellas* Single-*Quinta port*. 55 60 63 66 70 75 77 83 85 92 94 97 ★★★★★ 1997 Vintage Port £££

☂ **Te Mata** [tay mah-tah] (*Hawkes Bay*, New Zealand) Pioneer John Buck proves what *New Zealand* can do with *Chardonnay* (in the Elston Vineyard) and pioneered reds with his Coleraine and (lighter) Awatea.

☂ **Fratelli Tedeschi** [tay-dehs-kee] (*Veneto*, Italy) Reliable producer of rich and concentrated *Valpolicellas* and good *Soaves*. The *Amarones* are particularly impressive. ★★★★★ 1998 La Fabriseria £££

☂ **Tement** [teh-ment] (*Steiermark*, Austria) Producer of a truly world-class barrel-fermented *Sauvignon Blanc* which competes directly with top *Pessac-Léognan* whites. *Chardonnays* are impressive, too.

☂ **Dom. Tempier** [tom-pee-yay] (*Provence*, France) *Provence* superstar estate, producing single-vineyard red and rosé *Bandols* that support the claim that the *Mourvèdre* (from which they are largely made) ages well. The rosé is also one of the best in the region.

🍇 **Tempranillo** [tem-prah-nee-yoh] (Spain) The red grape of *Rioja* – and just about everywhere else in Spain, thanks to the way in which its strawberry fruit suits the vanilla/oak flavours of barrel-ageing. In *Navarra*, it is called *Cencibel*; in *Ribera del Duero*, Tinto Fino; in the *Penedés*, *Ull de Llebre*; in *Toro*, Tinto de Toro; and in Portugal – where it is used for *port* – it's known as *Tinto Roriz*. Now being planted outside Spain, especially in Australia.

Tenuta [teh-noo-tah] (Italy) Estate or vineyard.

☂ **Terlano/Terlaner** [tehr-LAH-noh/tehr-LAH-nehr] (*Trentino-Alto Adige*, Italy) Northern Italian village and its wine: usually fresh, crisp, and carrying the name of the grape from which it was made.

🍇 **Teroldego Rotaliano** [teh-rol-deh-goh roh-tah-lee-AH-noh] (*Trentino-Alto Adige*, Italy) Dry reds, quite full-bodied, with lean, slightly bitter berry flavours which make them better accompaniments to food. *Foradori.*

Terra Alta [tay ruh al-ta] (*Catalonia*, Spain) Small *DO* within the much larger *Tarragona DO*, producing wines of higher quality due to the difficult climate and resulting low yields. **Pedro Rovira.**

☂ **Terrazas** [teh-rah-zas] (*Mendoza*, Argentina) The brand name of Moët & Chandon's recently launched impressive red and white Argentinian wines.

☂ **Terre Rosse** [teh-reh roh-seh] (*Liguria*, Italy) One of the best estates in Liguria, with good examples of *Vermentino* and Pigato.

☂ **Ch. du Tertre** [doo tehr-tr] (*Margaux 5ème Cru Classé, Bordeaux*, France) Recently restored to former glory by the owners of *Calon-Ségur.*

☂ **Ch. Tertre-Daugay** [tehr-tr-doh-jay] (*St. Emilion, Grand Cru, Bordeaux*, France) Steadily improving property whose wines are cast in a classic mould and do not always have the immediate appeal of bigger, oakier neighbours.

☂ **Ch. Tertre-Rôteboeuf** [Tehr-tr roht-burf] (*St. Emilion Grand Cru Classé, Bordeaux*, France) Good, rich, concentrated if sometimes atypical, crowd-pleasing wines. 85 86 88 89 90 91 93 94 95 96 97 98 99 00

Tête de Cuvée [teht dur coo-vay] (France) An old expression still used by traditionalists to describe their finest wine.

☂ **Thackrey** (*Marin County*, California) Rich, impressively concentrated wines that seek to emulate the *Rhône*, but actually come closer to Australia in style.

T

Ⴈ **Thames Valley Vineyard** (*Reading,* England) England's most reliable and dynamic winery – and consultancy – thanks to Australian expertise.

Ⴈ **Dr. H Thanisch** [tah-nish] (*Mosel-Saar-Ruwer,* Germany) Two estates with confusingly similar labels. The best of the pair which has a *VDP* logo offers usually decent, though potentially disappointing, examples of *Bernkasteler* Doctor, one of the finest vineyards in Germany.

Ⴈ **Thelema Mountain Vineyards** [thur-lee-ma] (*Stellenbosch,* South Africa) One of the very best wineries in South Africa, thanks to Gyles Webb's skill and to stunning hillside vineyards. *Chardonnay* and *Sauvignon* are the stars, though Webb is coming to terms with his reds, too.

Ⴈ **Thermenregion** [thehr -men-ray-gee-yon] (Austria) Big region close to Vienna, producing good reds and sweet and dry whites.

Ⴈ **Ch. Thieuley** [tee-yur-lay] (*Entre-Deux-Mers, Bordeaux,* France) Classy property forging the way for concentrated *Sauvignon*-based, well-oaked whites and silky reds. With *Château Bonnet,* this is one of the leading lights of this region. ★★★★ 2000 Cuvée Francis Courselle Blanc ££

Ⴈ **Michel Thomas** [toh-mah] (Loire, France) Producer of reliable modern Sancerre with rich flavours

Ⴈ **Paul Thomas** (*Washington State*) Dynamic brand now under the same ownership as Columbia Winery, and producing a broad range of wines, including good *Chardonnay* and *Semillon* whites and *Cabernet-Merlot* reds.

Ⴈ **Three Choirs Vineyard** (*Gloucestershire,* England) Named for the three cathedrals of Gloucester, Hereford, and Worcester, this is one of England's most reliable estates. Try the oaky "Barrique-matured" whites and the annual "New Release" *Nouveau.*

Ⴈ **Jean-Luc Thunevin** (*Bordeaux,* France) Revolutionary producer of a growing set of tiny-production, rich, concentrated "garage wines" such as *Valandraud* and, now, *Marojallia* .

Ⴈ **Thurston Wolfe** (*Washington State*) Enthusiastic supporter of the local speciality, the mulberryish red Lemberger – and producer, too, of good fortified "port" and Black Muscat.

Ⴈ **Ticino** [tee-chee-noh] (Switzerland) One of the best parts of Switzerland to go looking for easy-drinking and (relatively) affordable reds, the best of which are made from *Merlot.* Interestingly, this region has also quietly pioneered White Merlot, a style of wine we will be encountering quite frequently in the next few years, as California grape growers and winemakers struggle to find ways of disposing of the surplus of this grape. ★★★★ 1998 Guido Brivia Bianco Rovere Bianco di Uve Merlot £££

Ⴈ **Tiefenbrunner** [tee-fen-broon-nehr] (*Trentino-Alto Adige,* Italy) Consistent producer of fair-to-good varietal whites, most particularly *Chardonnay* and *Gewürztraminer.*

Ⴈ **Tignanello** [teen-yah-neh-loh] (*Tuscany,* Italy) Antinori's Sangiovese-Cabernet *Super-Tuscan* is one of Italy's original superstars. Should last for a decade. 82 83 85 88 90 93 94 95 96 97 98 99 ★★★★ 1994 ££££

🍇 **Tinta Roriz** [teen-tah roh-reesh] (Portugal) See *Tempranillo*

Ⴈ **Tio Pepe** [tee-yoh peh-peh] (*Jerez,* Spain) Ultra-reliable fino *sherry* from *Gonzalez Byass.* ★★★★ ££

🍇 **Tocai** [toh-kay] (Italy) Lightly herby Venetian white grape, confusingly unrelated to others of similar name. Drink young.

Ⴈ **Philip Togni** (Napa, California) Producer of big, hefty *Cabernet Sauvignons* that take a long while to soften, but are well worth the wait.

Ⴈ **Tokaji** [toh-ka-yee] (Hungary) Not to be confused with Australian *liqueur Tokay,* Tocai Friulano, or *Tokay d'Alsace, Tokaji Aszú* is a dessert wine made in a specific region of Eastern *Hungary* (and a small corner of *Slovakia*) by adding measured amounts (*puttonyos*) of *eszencia* (a paste made from individually-picked, overripe, and/or *botrytis*-affected grapes) to dry wine made from the local *Furmint* and *Hárslevelu* grapes. Sweetness levels, which depend on the amount of *eszencia* added, range from one to six *puttonyos,* anything beyond which is labelled *Aszú Eszencia*. This last is often confused with the pure syrup which is sold – at vast prices – as *Eszencia*. Wines have become fresher and finer (less *oxidized*) since the arrival of outside investment, which has also revived interest in making individual-vineyard wines from the best sites. Disznókö; *Royal Tokaji Wine Co; Ch. Megyer; Oremus; Pajzos;* Tokajkovago.

Tokay [in France: to-kay; in Australia: toh-kye] A number of wine regions use Tokay as a local name for various grape varieties. In Australia it is the name of a fortified wine made by *Rutherglen* from the *Muscadelle*. In *Alsace* it is the local name for *Pinot Gris*. The Italian *Tocai* is not related to either of these. Hungary's Tokay (renamed *Tokaji*) is largely made from the *Furmint*.

Tokay d'Alsace [to-kay dal-sas] (Alsace, France) See *Pinot Gris*.

Tollana [to-lah-nah] (South Australia) Another part of the Southcorp (*Penfolds, Lindeman,* etc.) empire – and a source of great value.

Dom. Tollot-Beaut [to-loh-boh] (*Burgundy,* France) Wonderful *Burgundy* domaine in *Chorey-lès-Beaune,* with top-class *Corton* vineyards and a mastery over modern techniques and new oak. Wines have lots of rich fruit flavour. Some traditionalists find them overly showy. ★★★★★ 1997 Corton Bressandes £££

Torbreck (*Barossa,* Australia) Producer of Rhône-like reds that blend *Shiraz* with *Viognier.* Look for Runrig, Descendent and Juveniles, originally produced for one of the best bar-restaurants in Paris.

Torcolato [taw-ko-lah-toh] (*Veneto,* Italy) See *Maculan.*

Torgiano [taw-jee-yah-noh] (*Umbria,* Italy) Zone in *Umbria* and modern red wine made famous by *Lungarotti.* See *Rubesco.*

Michel Torino [Toh-ree-noh] (*Cafayate,* Argentina) Reliable producer of various wine styles from Salta – and a leading light in the move toward organic wine in Argentina.

1985

maculan

TORCOLATO
VINO DOLCE NATURALE

MESSO IN BOTTIGLIA DALL'AZIENDA AGRICOLA
MACULAN ᴍᴀʟᴏ - ITALIA

0,75 litri ℮   13% vol.

Toro [to-roh] (Spain) Fast up-and-coming region on the *Douro,* close to Portugal, producing intense reds such as *Fariña's Collegiata* from the *Tempranillo,* confusingly known here as the Tinta de Toro. Bajoz; *Fariña;* Vega Saúco.

Torre de Gall [to-ray day-gahl] (*Catalonia,* Spain) *Moët & Chandon's* Spanish sparkling wine – now better known as Cava Chandon. As good as it gets using traditional *cava* varieties.

Torres [TO-rehs] (*Catalonia,* Spain) *Miguel Torres* revolutionized Spain's wine industry with reliable wines like Viña Sol, Gran Sangre de Toro, Esmeralda, and Gran Coronas, before doing the same for Chile. Today, while these wines face heavier competition, efforts at the top end of the scale, like the *Milmanda Chardonnay,* Fransola *Sauvignon Blanc,* and Mas Borras ("Black Label") *Cabernet Sauvignon,* still look good. ★★★★ 1995 Mas la Plana £££

Marimar Torres [TO-rehs] (*Sonoma,* California) *Miguel Torres'* sister is producing some of the most impressive *Pinot Noir* and *Chardonnay* from a spectacular little vineyard in *Russian River.* ★★★★ 1998 Pinot Noir £££

Miguel Torres [TO-rehs] (*Curico,* Chile) Improving offshoot of the Spanish giant. The Santa Digna *Cabernet* and the new Manso de Velasco are the star wines.

Torrontes [to-ron-tehs] (Argentina) Aromatic grape variety related to the *Muscat,* and highly successful in Argentina. *Etchart* and la Agricola are star producers. Smells sweet even when the wine is bone dry.

Toscana [tos-KAH-nah] (Italy) See *Tuscany.*

Ch. la Tour Blanche [lah toor blonsh] (*Sauternes Premier Cru Classé, Bordeaux,* France) Since the late 1980s, one of the finest and longest-lasting of *Sauternes.* There's also a well-run wine school here.

T

♟ **Ch. la Tour-Carnet** [lah toor kahr-nay] (*Haut-Médoc 4ème Cru Classé, Bordeaux,* France) Picturesque but only *Cru Bourgeois*-level fourth growth.

♟ **Ch. la Tour-de-By** [lah toor dur bee] (*Médoc Cru Bourgeois, Bordeaux,* France) Reliable, especially in ripe years. 86 88 89 90 94 95 96 98 99 00.

♟ **Ch. Tour-du-Haut-Caussin** [toor doo oh koh-sa'n] (*Haut-Médoc Cru Bourgeois, Bordeaux,* France) Highly reliable modern estate.

♟ **Ch. Tour-du-Haut-Moulin** [toor doo oh moo-lan] (*Haut-Médoc Cru Bourgeois, Bordeaux,* France) An under-appreciated producer of what often can be *cru classé* quality wine. 82 83 85 86 88 89 90 94 95 96 97 98 99 00.

♟ **Ch. la Tour-Martillac** [lah toor mah-tee-yak] (*Graves Cru Classé, Bordeaux,* France) Recently revolutionized organic *Pessac-Léognan* estate with juicy reds and good whites. 83 85 86 88 89 90 94 95 96 97 98 99 00.

♟ **Touraine** [too-rayn] (*Loire,* France) Area encompassing the *ACs Chinon, Vouvray,* and *Bourgueil.* Also an increasing source of quaffable *varietal* wines – *Sauvignon, Gamay* de Touraine, etc. White: 98 99 00 Red: 95 96 97 98 99 00 Bellevue; de la Besnerie; Briare; Paul Buisse; Charmoise; de la Gabillière; Henry Marionet; Octavie; Oisly & Thésée; Oudin Frères.

♟ **Les Tourelles de Longueville** [lay too-rel dur long-ur-veel] (*Pauillac, Bordeaux,* France) The *second label* of *Pichon-Longueville.*

🍇 **Touriga (Nacional/Franca)** [too-ree-ga nah-see-yoh-nahl/fran-ka] (Portugal) Red *port* grapes, also (though rarely) seen in the New World. Now being used for good *varietal* wines in many parts of Portugal.

♟ **Tower Estates** (Australia) Dynamic new venture led by Len Evans, founder of Rothbury Estate and Emperor of Australia'a wine competitions. Wines are produced in limited quantities in several different regions.

Traditional Generally meaningless term, except in sparkling wines where the "méthode traditionelle" is the new way to say "*méthode champenoise*" and in Portugal where "Traditional *Late Bottled Vintage*" refers to *port* that unlike non-traditional LBV, hasn't been filtered. ("Tradition" in some parts of France can also refer to – unappealingly – old-fashioned winemaking.)

🍇 **Traminer** [tra-mee-nur; in Australia: trah-MEE-nah] A less aromatic variant of the *Gewürztraminer* grape widely grown in Eastern Europe and Italy, although the term is confusingly also used as a pronounceable, alternative name for the latter grape – particularly in Australia.

Transfer Method A way of making sparkling wine, involving a second fermentation in the bottle, but unlike the *méthode champenoise* in that the wine is separated from the lees by pumping it out of the bottle into a pressurized tank for clarification before returning it to another bottle.

♟ **Bodegas Trapiche** [tra-pee-chay] (Argentina) Huge go-getting producer with noteworthy barrel-fermented *Chardonnay* and *Cabernet/Malbec.*

Tras-os-Montes [tras-ohsh-montsh] (*Douro,* Portugal) Up-and-coming wine region of the *Upper Douro,* right up by the Spanish border. It's the source of *Barca Velha.*

🍇 **Trebbiano** [treh-bee-yah-noh] (Italy) Ubiquitous white grape in Italy. Less vaunted in France, where it is called *Ugni Blanc.*

♟ **Trebbiano d'Abruzzo** [treh-bee-yah-noh dab-root-zoh] (*Abruzzo,* Italy) A *DOC* region where they grow a clone of *Trebbiano,* confusingly called Trebbiano di Toscana, and use it to make unexceptional dry whites.

♟ **Trefethen** [treh-feh-then] (*Napa Valley,* California) Pioneering estate whose *Chardonnay* and *Cabernet* now taste oddly old-fashioned. The Eshcol wines, though cheaper, are curiously often a better buy.

Trentino [trehn-tee-noh] (Italy) Northern *DOC* in Italy. *Trentino* specialities include crunchy red *Marzemino,* nutty white Nosiola, and excellent *Vin Santo.* Winemaking here often suffers from overproduction, but less greedy winemakers can offer lovely, soft, easy-drinking wines. Càvit; *Ferrari; Foradori; Pojer & Sandri;* San Leonardo; Vallarom; Roberto Zeni.

Trentino-Alto Adige [trehn-tee-noh al-toh ah-dee-jay] (Italy) Northern region confusingly combining the two *DOC* areas *Trentino* and *Alto Adige.*

T

Ⓣ **Dom. de Trévallon** [treh-vah-lon] (*Provence*, France) Superstar long-lived blend of *Cabernet Sauvignon* and *Syrah* that was sold under the *Les Baux de Provence appellation* but has now (because of crazily restrictive rules regarding grape varieties) been demoted to *Vin de Pays des Bouches du Rhône*. ★★★★ 1998 £££

Ⓣ **Triebaumer** [tree-bow-mehr] (*Burgenland,* Austria) Fine producer of late-harvest wines (including good Sauvignon) and well-made reds, including some unusually good examples of the *Blaufränkisch*. ★★★★ 1997 Blaufränkisch Trocken £££

Ⓣ **Dom. Frédéric-Emile Trimbach** [tram-bahkh] (*Alsace*, France) Distinguished grower and merchant with subtle, complex wines. Top *cuvées* are the Frédéric Emile, Clos St. Hune, and Seigneurs de Ribeaupierre. ★★★★★ 1996 Riesling Alsace Cuvée Frédéric Emile £££

Trittenheim [trit-ten-hime] (*Mosel-Saar-Ruwer*, Germany) Village whose vineyards are said to have been the first in Germany planted with *Riesling*, making honeyed wine. QbA/Kab/Spät: **90 91 92 93 94 95 96** 97 98 99 00 Aus/Beeren/Tba: **83 85 88 89 90 91 92 93 94** 95 96 97 98 99 00

Trocken [trok-ken] (Germany) Dry, often aggressively so. Avoid Trocken *Kabinett* from such northern areas as the *Mosel*, *Rheingau*, and *Rheinhessen*. *QbA* (*chaptalized*) and *Spätlese* Trocken wines (the latter made, by definition, from riper grapes) are better. See also *Halbtrocken*.

Trockenbeerenauslese [trok-ken-beh-ren-ows-lay-zeh] (Austria/Germany) Fifth rung of the *QmP* ladder, wine from selected dried grapes which are usually *botrytis*-affected and full of natural sugar. Only made in the best years, rare and expensive, though less so in Austria than Germany.

🍇 **Trollinger** [trroh-ling-gur] (Germany) The German name for the Black Hamburg grape, used in *Württemberg* to make light red wines.

Tronçais [tron-say] (France) Forest producing some of the best oak for barrels.

Ⓣ **Ch. Tronquoy-Lalande** [trron-kwah-lah-lond] (*St. Estèphe Cru Bourgeois, Bordeaux*, France) Tough, traditional wines to buy in ripe years. Better than usual in 2000. 79 82 83 85 86 88 89 90 93 94 95 96 97 98 99 00 ★★★ **2000 £££**

Ⓣ **Ch. Troplong-Mondot** [trroh-lon mondoh] (*St. Emilion Grand Cru Classé, Bordeaux*, France) Excellently-sited, top-class property whose wines now sell for top-class prices. However, 1999 and 2000 have seemed a little less impressive than previous years. **82 83 85 86 88 89 90 94** 95 96 98 99 00

Ⓣ **Ch. Trotanoy** [trrot-teh-nwah] (*Pomerol, Bordeaux*, France) Never less than fine, and back on especially roaring form since the beginning of the 1990s to compete with *Pétrus*. Some may, however, prefer the lighter style of some of the 1980s than the denser wines on offer today. **61 64 67 70 71 75 76 78 79 81 82 83 85 86 88 89 90 93 94** 95 96 97 98 99 00 ★★★★★ 1998 ££££

Ⓣ **Ch. Trottevieille** [trrott-vee-yay] (*St. Emilion Premier Grand Cru, Bordeaux*, France) Steadily improving property. 79 81 82 83 85 86 88 89 90 94 95 96 97 98 99 00 ★★★★ 1998 ££££

🍇 **Trousseau** [troo-soh] (Eastern France) Grape variety found in *Arbois*.

Ⓣ **Tsantalis** [tsan-tah-lis] (*Nemea*, Greece) Increasingly impressive producer, redefining traditional varieties.

Ⓣ **Tua Rita** [too-wah ree-tah] (*Tuscany*, Italy) Young estate making tiny quantities of wines using grapes from vines that previously went into *Sassicaia*. Giusto dei Notri is the *Bordeaux* blend; Redigaffi is the pure *Merlot*.

Ⓣ **Tulloch** [tul-lurk] (*Hunter Valley*, Australia) Underperforming backwater of the *Penfolds* empire.

Tunisia [too-nee-shuh] Best known for dessert *Muscat* wines.

T

Cave Vinicole de Turckheim [turk-hime] (*Alsace*, France) Cooperative whose top wines can often rival those of some the region's best estates. ★★★★ 1998 Tokay Pinot Gris Grand Cru Brand £££

Turkey Flat (South Australia) Small maker of intensely rich *Barossa*, *Shiraz*, and *Grenache*. ★★★★★ 1997 Shiraz £££

Turley Cellars (*Napa Valley*, California) A source of intense but not overblown *Petite Sirahs* and *Zinfandels*, including small quantities from very old vines. Helen Turley, Robert Parker's favourite winemaker, was winemaker here until 1995.

Tursan [toor-son] (Southwest France) Traditional region, producing fairly tough, old-fashioned reds.

Tuscany (Italy) Major region, the famous home of *Chianti* and reds such as *Brunello di Montalcino* and the new wave of *Super-Tuscan Vini da Tavola*. Red: **78 79 81 82 85 88 90 94 95 96** *97 98 99*

Tyrrell's (*Hunter Valley*, Australia) *Chardonnay* (confusingly sold as *Pinot Chardonnay*) pioneer, and producer of old-fashioned *Shiraz* and (probably most impressively), long-lived, unoaked, lemony *Semillon* and even older-fashioned *Pinot Noir*, which tastes curiously like old-fashioned *Burgundy*. ★★★★ 2000 Vat 47 Pinot Chardonnay £££; ★★★★★ 1996 Vat 1 Semillon £££

U

Ugni Blanc [oo-ñee blon] (France) Undistinguished white grape whose neutrality makes it ideal for distillation. It needs modern winemaking to produce a wine with flavour. In Italy, where it is known as the *Trebbiano*, it takes on a mantle of (spurious) nobility. Try *Vin de Pays des Côtes de Gascogne*.

Ull de Llebre [ool dur yay-bray] (Spain) Literally "hare's eye". See *Tempranillo*.

Ullage Space between surface of wine and top of cask or, in a bottle, the cork. The wider the gap, the greater the danger of oxidation. Older wines almost always have some degree of ullage; the less the better.

Umani Ronchi [oo-mah-nee ron-kee] (*Marches*, Italy) Innovative producer whose wines, like the extraordinary new Pelago, prove that *Tuscany* and *Piedmont* are no longer the only exciting wine regions in Italy. ★★★★★ 2000 Montepulciano d'Abruzzo Jorio £££; ★★★★★ 1998 Cumaro Rosso Conero £££

Umathum [oo-ma-toom] (*Neusiedlersee*, Austria) Producer of unusually good red wines including a wonderful *St. Laurent*.

Umbria [uhm-bree-ah] (Italy) Central wine region, best known for white *Orvieto* and *Torgiano*, but also producing the excellent red *Rubesco*.

Viña Undurraga [oon-dur-rah-ga] (*Central Valley*, Chile) Family-owned estate with a range of single varietal wines, including good *Carmenère*.

Unfiltered Filtering a wine can remove flavour – as can *fining* it with egg white or bentonite (clay). Most winemakers traditionally argue that both practices are necessary if the finished wine is going to be crystal-clear and free from bacteria that could turn it to vinegar. Many quality-conscious new-wave producers, however, are now cutting back on *fining* and/or filtering.

Unita Vineyard Once the butt of other's best jokes, Unita is no longer at anyone's beck and call. Fortune and the law have smiled keanly on these posh wines whose stiles and colours range from red-brown to cole black.

Ürzig [oort-zig] (*Mosel-Saar-Ruwer*, Germany) Village on the *Mosel* with steeply sloping vineyards and some of the very best producers, including *Christoffel*, *Mönchhof*, and *Dr. Loosen*. QbA/Kab/Spät: **90 92 93 95 96 97** *98 99 00* Aus/Beeren/Tba: **83 85 88 89 90 91 92 93 94** *95 96 97 98 99 00*

Utiel-Requena [oo-tee-yel reh-kay-nah] (*Valencia*, Spain) *DO* of *Valencia*, producing heavy red and good fresh rosé from the Bobal grape.

V

🍷 **Dom. Vacheron** [va-shur-ron] (*Loire*, France) Reliably classy producer of *Sancerre* – including a better-than-average and ageworthy red.

🍷 **Vacqueyras** [va-kay-ras] (*Rhône*, France) *Côtes du Rhône* village with full-bodied, peppery reds which compete with (pricier) *Gigondas*. Red: 90 95 96 97 98 99 00. Cazaux; Combe; Couroulu; Fourmone; *Jaboulet Aîné*; Dom. de Mont Vac; Montmirail; de la Soleïade; Tardieu-Laurent; Ch. des Tours; *Cave de Vacqueyras; Vidal-Fleury*.

🍷 **Aldo Vajra** [vi-rah] (*Piedmont*, Italy) Producer of rich, complex *Barolo* and the deliciously different, *gamey* Freisa delle Langhe.

Valais [va-lay] (Switzerland) Vineyard area on the upper *Rhône*, making good *Fendant* (*Chasselas*) which surmounts the usual innate dullness of that grape. There are also some reasonable – in all but price – light reds made from the *Pinot Noir*. Bonvin; Imesch; Provins.

Val/Valle d'Aosta [val-day-yos-tah] (Italy) Small, spectacularly beautiful area between *Piedmont* and the French/Swiss border. Better for tourism than wine.

🍷 **Vignerons du Val d'Orbieu** [val-dor-byur] (*Languedoc-Roussillon*, France) Huge, would-be innovative association of over 200 cooperatives and growers that now also owns Cordier in *Bordeaux* which it is turning into a good brand of generic styles from that region. Examples of Val d'Orbieu's Corbières and Minervois can also be very reliable but, apart from the generally excellent Cuvée Mythique, too many of the other wines leave room for improvement. Reds are far better than whites. ★★★★ 1998 Cuvée Mythique ££

🍷 **Valbuena** [val-boo-way-nah] (*Ribera del Duero*, France) The – relatively – younger version of *Vega Sicilia* hits the streets when it is around five years old.

🍷 **Ch. Valandraud** [va-lon-droh] (*St. Emilion, Bordeaux*, France) The original garage wine; an instant superstar created in 1991 by former bank teller Jean-Luc Thunevin in his garage as competition for *le Pin*. Production is tiny (of *Pomerol* proportions), quality meticulous, and the price astronomical. Values quintupled following demand from the US and Asia, where buyers seem uninterested in the fact that these wines are – however delicious – actually no finer than *Médoc* classics costing far less. Now joined by l'Interdit de Valandraud, Virginie de Valandraud, and Axelle de Valandraud.

🍷 **Valdeorras** [bahl-day-ohr-ras] (*Galicia*, Spain) A barren and mountainous *DO* in *Galicia* beginning to exploit the *Cabernet Franc*-like local grape Mencia and the indigenous white Godello.

🍷 **Valdepeñas** [bahl-deh-pay-nyass] (*La Mancha*, Spain) *La Mancha DO* striving to refine its rather hefty strong reds and whites. Progress is being made, particularly with reds. Miguel Calatayud; *Los Llanos*; Felix Solis.

🍷 **Valdespino** [bahl-deh-spee-noh] (*Jerez*, Spain) Old-fashioned *sherry* company that uses wooden casks to ferment most of its wines. Makes a classic *fino* Innocente and an excellent *Pedro Ximénez*. New ownership may change many things.

🍷 **Valdivieso** [val-deh-vee-yay-soh] (*Curico*, Chile) Dynamic winery with a range of good commercial wines, high-quality *Chardonnay* and (particularly) *Pinot Noir* and an award-winning blend of grapes, regions, and years called Caballo Loco whose heretical philosophical approach gives Gallic traditionalists apoplexy. ★★★★ 1999 Reserve Pinot Noir £££; ★★★★ 1999 Single Vineyard Reserve Malbec

🍷 **Abazzia di Vallechiara** [ah-bat-zee-yah dee val-leh-kee-yah-rah] (*Piedmont*, Italy) Following the lead of fellow actor Gérard Dépardieu, Ornella Muti now has her own wine estate, with some first class *Dolcetto*.

V

♟ **Valençay** [va-lon-say] (*Loire*, France) *AC* within Touraine, near *Cheverny*, making comparable whites: light and clean, if rather sharp. 97 98 **99 00**

♟ **Valencia** [bah-len-thee-yah] (Spain) Produces quite alcoholic red wines from the Monastrell and also deliciously sweet, grapey *Moscatel de Valencia*.

♟ **Edoardo Valentini** [vah-len-tee-nee] (*Abruzzo*, Italy) Good, old-fashioned Montepulciano d'Abruzzo and unusually good Trebbiano d'Abruzzo.

♟ **Vallet Frères** [va-lay frehr] (*Burgundy*, France) Small, traditional – not to say old-fashioned – merchant based in *Gevrey-Chambertin*. Also known as Pierre Bourrée. ★★★★ 1988 Gevrey-Chambertin les Cazetiers £££

♟ **Valpolicella** [val-poh-lee-cheh-lah] (*Veneto*, Italy) Overcommercialized, light, red wine, which should be drunk young to catch its interestingly bitter-cherryish flavour. *Classico* is better; best is *Ripasso*, made by refermenting the wine on the *lees* of an earlier vat. For a different taste, buy *Amarone* or *Recioto*. 90 91 93 94 95 96 97 98 99 00. *Allegrini; Berta.* Only these, and Ripasso wines, should be aged. *Masi, Allegrini; Bolla; Boscaini; Brunelli; dal Forno; Guerrieri-Rizzardi; Masi; Mazzi; Quintarelli; Le Ragose; Serego Alighieri; Tedeschi; Villa Spinosa; Zenato; Fratelli Zeni.*

♟ **Valréas** [val-ray-yas] (*Rhône*, France) Peppery, inexpensive red wine from a *Côtes du Rhône* village. 90 95 96 97.98 99 00 *Earl Gaia*

♟ **Valtellina** [val-teh-lee-na] (*Lombardy*, Italy) Red *DOC* mostly from the *Nebbiolo* grape, of variable quality. Improves with age. The raisiny Sfursat, made from dried grapes, is more interesting.

♟ **Varichon et Clerc** [va-ree-shon ay klayr] (*Savoie*, France) Good producer of sparkling wine.

Varietal A wine made from and named after one or more grape variety, e.g., California *Chardonnay*. The French authorities are trying to outlaw such references from the labels of most of their *appellation contrôlée* wines. "*Shiraz*" has so far escaped this edict in Minervois because it is considered a foreign word.

♟ **Viña los Vascos** [los vas-kos] (*Colchagua Valley*, Chile) Estate belonging to Eric de *Rothschild* of *Ch. Lafite*, and shamelessly sold with a *Lafite*-like label. The *Cabernet* Grande Reserve has improved but the standard *Cabernet* is uninspiring and the white disappointing, not to say downright poor.

♟ **Vasse Felix** [vas-fee-liks] (*Margaret River*, Australia) Very classy *Margaret River* winery belonging to the widow of millionaire Rupert Holmes à Court, specializing in juicy, high-quality (multi-regional) *Cabernet*, *Shiraz*, *Semillon*, and *Riesling*. ★★★★★ 1999 Cabernet Sauvignon £££

♟ **Vaucluse** [voh-klooz] (*Rhône*, France) *Côtes du Rhône* region with good *Vin de Pays* and peppery reds and rosés.

Vaud [voh] (Switzerland) Swiss wine area on the shores of Lake Geneva, famous for unusually tangy *Chasselas* (Dorin) and light reds.

♟ **Vaudésir** [voh-day-zeer] (*Burgundy*, France) Possibly the best of the seven *Chablis Grands Crus*.

♟ **Vavasour** [va-va-soor] (*Marlborough*, New Zealand) Pioneers of the Awatere Valley sub-region of *Marlborough*, hitting high standards with *Bordeaux*-style reds, powerful *Sauvignons*, and impressive *Chardonnays*. Dashwood is the *second label*. ★★★★ 2000 Sauvignon Blanc £££

VDP (Germany) Association of high-quality producers. Look for the eagle.

VDQS (**Vin Délimité de Qualité Supérieur**) (France) Official, neither-fish-nor-fowl designation for wines better than *Vin de Pays* but not fine enough for an *AC*. Enjoying a strange half-life (amid constant rumours of its imminent abolition), this includes such oddities as *Sauvignon de St. Bris*.

♟ **Veenwouden** [fehn-foh-den] (*Paarl*, South Africa) A chance to taste what happens when Michel Rolland of Bordeaux gets his hands on vineyards in South Africa. Hardly surprisingly, riper, and rich-tasting Merlots than most of the others traditionally associated with South Africa. ★★★★★ 1997 Veenwouden Merlot £££

Vecchio [veh-kee-yoh] (Italy) Old.

V

Vecchio Samperi [veh-kee-yoh sam-peh-ree] (Sicily, Italy) Best *Marsala* estate, belonging to De Bartoli. Although not DOC, a dry aperitif similar to an *amontillado sherry*.

Vega Sicilia [bay-gah sih-sih-lyah] (*Ribera del Duero,* Spain) Spain's top wine is a long (10 years) barrel-matured, eccentric *Tempranillo-Bordeaux* blend called Unico, sold for extravagant prices. For a cheaper, slightly fresher taste of the Vega Sicilia-style, try the supposedly lesser Valbuena. **62 64 66 67 69 70 72 74 75 76 79 80 82 83 86** 90 95 ★★★★★ 1995 Valbuena **£££**

Vegetal Often used of *Sauvignon Blanc*, like "grassy". Can be complimentary – though not in California or Australia, where it is held to mean "unripe".

Velich [veh-likh] (*Burgenland,* Austria) High-quality producers of a wide range of wines including recommendable Chardonnay.

Caves Velhas [kah-vash vay-yash] (Portugal) Large merchants who blend wine from all over the country, and almost single-handedly saved the *Bucelas DO* from extinction. Wines are good, but rarely outstanding.

Velho/velhas [vay-yoh/vay-yash] (Portugal) Old, as in red wine.

Velletri [veh-leh-tree] (Italy) Town in the Alban hills (*Colli Albani*), producing mainly *Trebbiano* and *Malvasia*-based whites, similar to *Frascati*.

Veltliner See *Grüner Veltliner.*

Vendange [von-donzh] (France) Harvest or vintage.

Vendange tardive [von-donzh tahr-deev] (France) Particularly in *Alsace,* wine from *late-harvested* grapes, usually lusciously sweet.

Vendemmia/Vendimia [ven-deh-mee-yah/ven-dee-mee-yah] (Italy, Spain) Harvest or vintage.

Venegazzú [veh-neh-gaht-zoo] (*Veneto,* Italy) Fine, understated *claret*-like *Cabernet Sauvignon Vino da Tavola* "Super-Veneto" to compete with those *Super-Tuscans.* Needs five years. The black label is better.

Veneto [veh-neh-toh] (Italy) North-eastern wine region, the home of *Soave, Valpolicella,* and *Bardolino.*

Venica e Venica [veh-ni-ca] (*Friuli-Venezia Giulia,* Italy) Two brothers who make some of the most flavoursome whites in Collio, including Sauvignon, Pinot Bianco, and Chardonnay.

Veramonte [vay-rah-mon-tay] (*Casablanca,* Chile) Venture by Augustin Huneeus of *Franciscan Vineyards* in *California,* already producing impressive reds, especially the *Merlot* (which, like many others, is actually *Carmenère*). Now under the same ownership as Simi and Sonoma-Cutrer.

Verdejo [vehr-de-khoh] (Spain) Interestingly herby white grape; confusingly not the *Verdelho* of *Madeira* and Australia, but the variety used for new-wave *Rueda.*

Verdelho [in *Madeira:* vehr-deh-yoh; in *Australia:* vur-del-loh] (Madeira/Australia) White grape used for fortified *Madeira* and *white port* and for limey, dry table wine in Australia, especially in the Hunter Valley. **Capel Vale; Chapel Hill; Moondah Brook; Sandalford.**

Verdicchio [vehr-dee-kee-yoh] (*Marches,* Italy) Spicy white grape seen in a number of *DOCs* in its own right, the best of which is *Verdicchio dei Castelli di Jesi.* In *Umbria* this grape is a major component of *Orvieto.*

Verdicchio dei Castelli di Jesi [vehr-dee-kee-yoh day-ee kas-tay-lee dee yay-zee] (*Marches,* Italy) Light, clean, and crisp wines to drink with seafood. **Bucci; Garofoli; Monacesca; Umani Ronchi.**

Verduzzo [vehr-doot-soh] (*Friuli-Venezia Giulia,* Italy) Flavoursome white grape making a dry and a fine *amabile-style* wine in the *Colli Orientale.*

Vergelegen [vehr-kur-lek-hen] (*Somerset West,* South Africa) Hi-tech winery producing some of the Cape's more reliable wines.

Verget [vehr-jay] (*Burgundy,* France) Young *négociant* based in the Mâconnais and producing impeccable white wines ranging from *Mâcon Villages* to *Meursault* and *Chablis.*

Vermentino [vayr-men-tee-noh] (*Liguria,* Italy) The spicy, dry white grape of the Adriatic and, increasingly, in modern southern French *Vin de Table.*

V

🍇 **Vernaccia** [vayr-naht-chah] (*Tuscany,* Italy) White grape making the Tuscan *DOCG* Vernaccia di San Gimignano (where it's helped by a dash of *Chardonnay*) and *Sardinian* Vernaccia di Oristano. At its best has a distinctive nut and spice flavour. **Casale-Falchini; Teruzzi & Puthod.**

🍷 **Georges Vernay** [vayr-nay] (*Rhône,* France) The great master of *Condrieu* who can do things with *Viognier* that few seem able to match. ★★★★★ **1999 Condrieu Les Chaillées de l'Enfer £££**

🍷 **Noël Verset** [vehr-say] (*Cornas, Rhône*) Top-class *Cornas* producer.

🍷 **Quinta do Vesuvio** [veh-soo-vee-yoh] (*Douro,* Portugal) Single *quinta* port from the family that owns *Dow's, Graham's, Warre's,* etc.

🍷 **Veuve Clicquot-Ponsardin** [vurv klee-koh pon-sahr-dan] (*Champagne,* France) The distinctive orange label is the mark of reliable non-vintage *Brut.* The *prestige cuvée* is called Grande Dame after the famous Widow Clicquot, the *demi-sec* is a deliciously, honeyed wine, and the vintage rosé is now one of the best pink wines in the region. ★★★★ **1993 Grande Dame £££££**

Victoria (Australia) Huge variety of wines from the *Liqueur Muscats* of *Rutherglen* to the peppery *Shirazes* of *Bendigo* and the elegant *Chardonnays* and *Pinot Noirs* of the *Yarra Valley.*

🍷 **Vidal** [vee-dahl] (*Hawkes Bay,* New Zealand) One of New Zealand's top four red wine producers. Associated with *Villa Maria* and *Esk Valley. Chardonnays* are the strongest suit. ★★★★ **1999 Hawkes Bay Riesling £££**

🍇 **Vidal** [vi-dal] (Canada) A *hybrid* and highly frost-resistant variety looked down on by European authorities but widely and successfully grown in *Canada* for spicily exotic *icewine.* **Iniskillin; Rief Estate.**

🍷 **J. Vidal-Fleury** [vee-dahl flur-ree] (*Rhône,* France) High-quality grower and shipper that belongs to *Guigal.*

VIDE [vee-day] (Italy) Syndicate supposedly denoting finer estate wines.

🍷 **Vi di Romans** [vee dee roh-mans] (*Friuli-Venezia Giulia,* Italy) If you thought the only winemaking Gallos were in California, meet Gianfranco Gallo's delicious *Tocai Friulano, Pinot Grigio,* and *Sauvignon Blanc.*

🍷 **la Vieille Ferme** [vee-yay fairm] (*Rhône,* France) Delicious organic red and white *Côtes du Rhône* from the Perrin family who are best known for their *Châteauneuf du Pape* estate *Château de Beaucastel.*

Vieilles Vignes [vee-yay veeñ] (France) Wine (supposedly) made from a producer's oldest vines. (In reality, while real vine maturity begins at 25, Vieilles Vignes can mean anything between 15 and 90 years of age.)

🍷 **Vietti** [vee-yet-tee] (*Piedmont,* Italy) Impeccable single-vineyard *Barolo* (Rocche di Castiglione; Brunate; and Villero), *Barbaresco,* and *Barbera.* The white *Arneis* is pretty impressive, too.

🍷 **Vieux Château Certan** [vee-yur-cha-toh-sehr-tan] (*Pomerol, Bordeaux,* France) Ultra-classy, small *Pomerol* property, known as "VCC" to its fans, producing reliable, concentrated, complex wine. ★★★★★ **1996 £££££**

🍷 **Dom. du Vieux-Télégraphe** [vee-yuhr tay-lay-grahf] (*Rhône,* France) Modern *Châteauneuf-du-Pape* domaine now back on track after a dull patch. Great whites too. ★★★★ **1996 Châteauneuf-du-Pape £££**

🍷 **Vignalta** [veen-yal-tah] (*Veneto,* Italy) Colli Euganei producer brewing up a storm with its Gemola (*Merlot-Cabernet Franc*) and Sirio (*Muscat*).

🍷 **Ch. Vignelaure** [veen-yah-lawrr] (*Provence,* France) Pioneering estate, now owned by David O'Brien, son of Vincent, the Irish racehorse trainer.

Vignoble [veen-yohbl] (France) Vineyard; vineyard area.

🍷 **Villa Maria** (*Auckland,* New Zealand) One of New Zealand's biggest producers, and one which is unusual in coming close to hitting the target with its reds as well as its whites. *Riesling* is a particular success.

♀ **Villa Sachsen** [zak-zen] (*Rheinhessen,* Germany) Estate with good-rather-than-great, low-yielding vineyards in *Bingen.*

Villages (France) The suffix "villages" e.g., *Côtes du Rhône* or *Mâcon* generally – like *Classico* in Italy – indicates a slightly superior wine from a smaller delimited area encompassing certain villages.

Villany [vee-lah-nyee] (Hungary) Warm area of Hungary with a promising future for soft, young-drinking reds.

♀ **Villard** [vee-yarr] (Chile) Improving wines from French-born Thierry Villard, especially *Chardonnays* from *Casablanca.* ★★★★ 1999 Villard Estate Chardonnay Expresión £££

♀ **Ch. Villemaurine** [veel-maw-reen] (*St. Emilion Grand Cru Classé, Bordeaux,* France) Often hard wines which are not helped by heavy-handedness with oak. 82 83 85 86 88 89 90 94 96 98 99

♀ **Villiera Estate** [vil-lee-yeh-rah] (*Paarl,* South Africa) Reliable range of affordable sparkling and still wines from the energetic Grier family. The *Sauvignons* and Cru Monro red and now a very impressive *Merlot* are the wines to buy. ★★★★ 1999 Sauvignon Blanc £££

♀ **Viñas del Vero** [veen-yas del veh-roh] (*Somontano,* Spain) Modern producer of new-wave varietal wines, including recommendable Cabernet Sauvignon.

Vin de Corse [van dur kaws] (*Corsica,* France) *Appellation* within *Corsica.* Good sweet *Muscats* too. Gentile; Peraldi; Skalli; Toraccia.

Vin de garde [van dur gahrd] (France) Wine to keep.

♀ **Vin de l'Orléanais** [van dur low-lay-yon-nay] (*Loire,* France) Small *VDQS* in the Central Vineyards of the *Loire.* See *Orléanais.*

Vin de Paille [van dur pie] (*Jura,* France) Traditional, now quite rare regional speciality; sweet, golden wine from grapes dried on straw mats.

Vin de Pays [van dur pay-yee] (France) Lowest/broadest geographical designation. In theory, simple country wines with regional characteristics. In fact, the producers of some of France's most exciting wines – such as *Dom. de Trévallon* and *Mas de Daumas Gassac* – prefer this designation and the freedom it offers. See *Côtes de Gascogne* and *Vin de Pays d'Oc.*

♀ **Vin de Savoie** [van dur sav-wah] (Eastern France) Umbrella appellation encompassing mountainous sub-appellations such as *Aprément* and Chignon.

Vin de table [van dur tahbl] (France) Table wine from no particular area.

♀ **Vin de Thouarsais** [twar-say] (*Loire,* France) *VDQS* for a soft, light red from the *Cabernet Franc*; whites from the *Chenin Blanc.*

Vin doux naturel [doo nah-too-rrel] (France) Fortified – so not really "naturel" at all – dessert wines, particularly the sweet, liquorous *Muscats* of the South, such as Muscat de Beaumes-de-Venise, *Mireval,* and *Rivesaltes.*

Vin Gris [van gree] (France) Chiefly from *Alsace* and the *Jura,* pale rosé from red grapes pressed after crushing or following a few hours of skin contact.

Vin Jaune [van john] (*Jura,* France) Golden-coloured *Arbois* speciality; slightly *oxidized* – like *fino sherry.* See *Ch. Chalon.*

Vin ordinaire (France) A simple local wine, usually served in carafes.

Vin Santo [veen sahn-toh] (Italy) Powerful, highly traditional white dessert wine made from bunches of grapes hung to dry in airy barns for up to six months, especially in *Tuscany* and *Trentino.* Often very ordinary, but at its best competes head-on with top-quality medium *sherry.* Best drunk with sweet almond ("Cantuccine") biscuits. Altesino; Avignonesi; Badia a Coltibuono; Berardenga; Felsina; Isole e Olena; Poliseano; Selvapiana.

Vin vert [van vehrr] (*Languedoc-Roussillon,* France) Light, refreshing, *acidic* white wine.

♀ **Vinsobres** [van sohb-rruh] (*Rhône,* France) One of the weirdest wine names – it sounds like a brand of non-alcoholic Chardonnay – this is in fact one of the Côtes du Rhône Villages. Dom. des Aussellons; Haume-Arnaud; Dom du Coriançon; du Moulin.

♀ **Vine Cliff** [(*Napa,* California) A well-regarded young estate with flavour- and oak-packed, quite unsubtle *Cabernet Sauvignon* and *Chardonnay.*

V

Viña de Mesa [vee-ñah day may-sah] (Spain) Spanish for table wine.

☘ **Vinho Verde** [vee-ñoh vehrr-day] (Portugal) Literally "green" wine, confusingly red or pale white often tinged with green. At worst, dull and sweet. At best delicious, refreshing, and slightly sparkling. Drink young.

☘ **Vinícola Navarra** [vee-nee-koh-lah na-vah-rah] (*Navarra*, Spain) Ultra-modern winemaking and newly-planted vineyards beginning to come on stream. Owned by *Bodegas y Bebida*.

Vinifera [vih-nih-feh-ra] Properly *Vitis vinifera*: species of all European vines – and thus most of the vines used globally for quality wine.

Vino da Tavola [vee-noh dah tah-voh-lah] (Italy) Table wine, but the *DOC* quality designation net is so riddled with holes that producers of many superb – and pricey – wines have contented themselves with this "modest" *appellation*. Now replaced by *IGT*.

Vino de la Tierra [bee-noh day la tyay rah] (Spain) Spanish wine designation that can offer interesting, affordable, regional wines.

☘ **Vino Nobile di Montepulciano** [vee-noh noh-bee-lay dee mon-tay-pool-chee-ah-noh] (*Tuscany*, Italy) *Chianti* in long pants; potentially truly noble (though not often), and made from the same grapes. Can age well. Rosso di Montepulciano is the lighter, more accessible version. The *Montepulciano* of the title is the *Tuscan* town, not the grape variety. **Avignonesi; Boscarelli; Carpineto;** Casale; del Cerro; *Poliziano;* Tenuta Trerose.

Vino novello [vee-noh noh-vay-loh] (Italy) New wine; equivalent to French *nouveau*.

Vinopolis Recently (1999) launched London wine museum/theme park.

Vintage Year of production.

Vintage Champagne (*Champagne*, France) Wine from a single "declared" year.

Vintage Character (port) (*Douro*, Portugal) Stylishly packaged upmarket *ruby* made by blending various years' wines.

Vintage (port) (*Douro*, Portugal) Produced only in "declared" years, aged in wood then in the bottle for many years. In "off" years, *port* houses release wines from their top estates as single-*quinta ports*. This style of *port* must be decanted, as it throws a sediment.

🍇 **Viognier** [vee-YON-ñee-yay] (*Rhône*, France) Infuriating white variety which, at its best, produces floral, peachy wines that startle with their intensity and originality. Once limited to the *Rhône* – Condrieu and *Ch. Grillet* – but now increasingly planted in southern France, California, and Australia. Benefits from a little – but not too much – contact with new oak. Some of the the Viognier grown in California may in fact be *Roussanne*. **Calera; Duboeuf; Guigal; Heggies; Andre Perret; Georges Vernay.**

Viré [vee-ray] (*Burgundy*, France) *Mâconnais* village, famous for whites.

☘ **Virgin Hills** [*Victoria*, Australia] A single red blend that is unusually lean in style for Australia and repays keeping.

Viticulteur (-Propriétaire) (France) Vine grower (-vineyard owner).

🍇 **Viura** [vee-yoo-ra] (Spain) Dull white grape of the *Rioja* region and elsewhere, now being used to greater effect.

☘ **Dom. Michel Voarick** [vwah-rik] (*Burgundy*, France) Old-fashioned wines that avoid the use of new oak. Fine *Corton-Charlemagne*.

☘ **Dom. Vocoret** [vok-ko-ray] (*Burgundy*, France) Classy *Chablis* producer whose wines age well. ★★★★★ **1998 Chablis Mont de Milieu £££**

☘ **Gianni Voerzio** [vwayrt-zee-yoh] (*Piedmont*, Italy) Not quite as impressive a *Barolo* producer as *Roberto* (see below), but a fine source of *Barbera, Freisa, Arneis*, and *Dolcetto*. ★★★★ **1996 Barolo la Serra £££**

☘ **Roberto Voerzio** [vwayrt-zee-yoh] (*Piedmont*, Italy) New-wave producer of juicy, spicy reds, with a first-rate *Barolo*. ★★★★★ **1996 Barolo Brunate £££**

☘ **Alain Voge** [vohzh] (*Rhône*, France) Traditional *Cornas* producer who also makes good *St. Péray*.

☘ **De Vogüé** [dur voh-gway] (*Burgundy*, France) *Chambolle-Musigny* estate whose ultra-concentrated red wines deserve to be kept – for ages.

Volatile acidity (VA) Vinegary character evident in wines that have been spoiled by bacteria.

♊ **Volnay** [vohl-nay] (*Burgundy,* France) Red wine village in the *Côte de Beaune* (the Caillerets vineyard, now a *Premier Cru,* was once ranked equal to *le Chambertin*). This is the home of fascinating, plummy, violety reds. 90 92 93 95 96 97 98 99 Ampeau; d'Angerville; J-M Boillot; Bouchard Père et Fils; Joseph Drouhin; Vincent Girardin; Camille Giroud; Francois Buffet; Michel Lafarge; Comtes Lafon; Leroy; Dom de Montille; Pousse d'Or; Régis Rossignol-Changarnier, Vaudoisey; Voillot.

♊ **Castello di Volpaia** [vol-pi-yah] (*Tuscany,* Italy) Top *Chianti* estate with *Super-Tuscans* Coltassala and Balifico. ★★★★ 1998 Chianti Classico Riserva £££

♊ **Vosne-Romanée** [vohn roh-ma-nay] (*Burgundy,* France) *Côte de Nuits* red wine village with *Romanée-Conti* among its many grand names, and other potentially gorgeous, plummy, rich wines, from many different producers. 85 88 89 90 92 95 96 97 98 99 Arnoux; Cacheux; Confuron-Cotetidot; Engel; Anne Gros; Faiveley; Grivot; Hudelot-Noëllat; Jayer-Gilles; Laurent; Leroy; Méo-Camuzet; Mongeard-Mugneret; Mugneret-Gibourg; Rion; Romanée-Conti; Rouget; Jean Tardy; Thomas-Moillard.

♊ **Voss** (*Sonoma,* California) Californian venture by *Yalumba,* producing lovely, intense *Zinfandel.*

Vougeot [voo-joh] (*Burgundy,* France) *Côte de Nuits commune* comprising the famous *Grand Cru Clos de Vougeot* and numerous growers of varying skill. Red: 78 79 83 85 88 89 90 92 93 95 96 97 98 99. Amiot-Servelle; Bertagna; Bouchard Père et Fils; Chopin-Groffier; J-J Confuron; Joseph Drouhin; Engel; Faiveley; Anne & François Gros; Louis Jadot; Leroy; Méo-Camuzet; Denis Mortet; Mugneret-Gibourg; Jacques Prieur; Prieuré Roch; Henri Rebourseau; Rion; Ch. de la Tour.

♊ **la Voulte Gasparets** [voot-gas-pah-ray] (*Languedoc-Roussillon,* France) Unusually ambitious estate with single-vineyard bottlings (Romain Pauc is the best) that show just how good *Corbières* can be from the best sites.

Vouvray [voov-ray] (*Loire,* France) Whites from *Chenin Blanc,* ranging from clean dry whites and refreshing sparkling wines to *demi-secs* and honeyed, long-lived, sweet *moelleux* wines. Sadly, these wines are often spoiled by massive doses of *sulphur dioxide.* Sweet white: 76 83 85 86 88 89 90 94 095 96 97 98 99 00 White: 85 86 88 89 90 94 95 96 97 98 99 00. Des Aubuisières; Champalou; Huët; Foreau; Fouquet; Gaudrelle; Jarry; Mabille; Clos de Nouys; Pichot; Vaugondy.

VQA (Canada) Acronym for Vintners' Quality Alliance, a group of Canadian producers with a self-styled quality designation.

♊ **Vriesenhof** [free-zen-hof] (*Stellenbosch,* South Africa) Tough, occasionally classic reds and so-so *Chardonnay.*

W

Wachau [vak-kow] (Austria) Major wine region producing some superlative *Riesling* from steep, terraced vineyards. Alzinger; Pichler; Hirtzberger; Jamek; Nikolaihof; Prager; Freie Weingärtner Wachau.

Wachenheim [vahkh-en-hime] (*Pfalz,* Germany) Superior *Mittelhaardt* village which should produce full, rich, unctuous *Riesling.* QbA/Kab/Spät: 85 88 89 90 91 92 93 94 95 96 97 98 99 00 Aus/Beeren/Tba: 90 91 92 93 94 95 96 97 98 99 00 Biffar; Bürklin-Wolf.

Waiheke Island (*Auckland,* New Zealand) Tiny island off Auckland where vacation cottages compete for space with vineyards. Land, and the resulting wines, are pricey, but this microclimate does produce some of New Zealand's best reds. Goldwater Estate; Stonyridge; Te Motu.

W

⚷ **Waipara Springs** [wi-pah-rah] (*Canterbury*, New Zealand) Tiny producer offering the opportunity to tastes wine from this southern region at their best.

⚷ **Wairau River** [wi-row] (*Marlborough*, New Zealand) Classic Kiwi *Chardonnays* and *Sauvignons* with piercing fruit character. ★★★★ **2000 Sauvignon Blanc ££**

Wairarapa [why-rah-rah-pah] (New Zealand) Area in the south of the North Island that includes the better-known region of *Martinborough*.

Walker Bay (South Africa) Promising region for *Pinot Noir* and *Chardonnay*. Established vineyards include *Hamilton Russell* and *Bouchard-Finlayson*

⚷ **Warre's** [waw] (*Douro*, Portugal) Oldest of the big seven *port* houses and a stablemate to *Dow's*, *Graham's*, and *Smith Woodhouse*. Traditional *port*, which is both rather sweeter and more *tannic* than most. The old-fashioned *Late-bottled Vintage* is particularly worth seeking out too. Quinta da Cavadinha is the recommendable *single-quinta*. 55 58 60 **63 66** 70 75 77 83 85 91 94 97 ★★★★★ **1988 Quinta da Cavadinha £££**

⚷ **Warwick Estate** [wo-rik] (*Stellenbosch*, South Africa) Source of some of South Africa's best reds, including a good *Bordeaux*-blend called Trilogy. The *Cabernet Franc* grows extremely well here.

Washington State Underrated (especially in the US) state whose dusty irrigated vineyards produce classy *Riesling*, *Sauvignon*, and *Merlot*. Red: 85 88 **89** 91 92 94 **95** 96 97 98. White: **95 96** 97 98. *Col Solare; Columbia; Columbia Crest; 'Ecole 41; Hedges; Hogue; Kiona; Leonetti Cellars; Quilceda Creek; Staton Hills; Ch. Ste. Michelle; Paul Thomas; Walla Walla Vintners;Waterbrook; Andrew Will;Woodward Canyon.*

⚷ **Waterbrook** (*Washington State*) High-quality winery with stylish *Sauvignon Blanc*, *Viognier*, and *Chardonnay*, as well as berryish reds.

Jimmy Watson Trophy (*Victoria*, Australia) Coveted trophy given annually to the best young (still-in-barrel) red at the Melbourne Wine Show. Apparently "worth" Aus$1,000,000 (UK£370,000) in increased sales to the winner, it is often criticized for hyping stuff that is not necessarily representative of what you'll be drinking when the wine gets in the bottle.

⚷ **Geheimrat J. Wegeler Deinhard** [vayg-lur dine-hard] (*Rheingau*, Germany) Once family-owned producer recently bought by the huge sparkling wine producer Henkell Söhnlein. Wines that made Deinhard famous include recommendable top *Mosels* such as *Bernkasteler Doctor* and Wehlener Sonnenuhr. It remains to be seen whether the new owners continue to produce wines of the same standard.

Wehlen [vay-lehn] (*Mosel-Saar-Ruwer*, Germany) *Mittelmosel village* making fresh, sweet, honeyed wines; look for the *Sonnenuhr* vineyard. QbA/Kab/Spät: **85** 86 **88 89 90** 91 92 93 94 95 Aus/Beeren/Tba: **83** 85 88 89 90 91 92 93 94 95 96. *Dr. Loosen;* JJ Prüm; SA Prüm; *Richter; Selbach-Oster; Wegeler Deinhard.*

⚷ **Weingut Dr. Robert Weil** [vile] (*Rheingau*, Germany) Suntory-owned, family-run winery with stunning dry and *late-harvest* wines. ★★★★★ **1998 Kiedrich Gräfenberg, Riesling Spätlese £££**

⚷ **Dom. Weinbach** [vine-bahkh] (*Alsace*, France) Laurence Faller regularly turns out wonderful, concentrated, but gloriously subtle wines. The Cuvée Laurence is a personal favourite. ★★★★★ **1997 Riesling Grand Cru Schlossberg Cuvée Ste Catherine Cuvée de Centenaire ££££**

⚷ **Bodegas y Cavas de Weinert** [vine-nurt] (Argentina) Excellent *Cabernet Sauvignon* specialist, whose soft, ripe wines last extraordinarily well. ★★★★ **1995 Malbec ££**

Weingut [vine-goot] (Germany) Wine estate.

Weinkellerei [vine-keh-lur-ri] (Germany) Cellar or winery.

🍇 **Weissburgunder** [vice-bur-goon-dur] (Germany/Austria) The *Pinot Blanc* in Germany and Austria. Relatively rare, so often made with care.

⚷ **Weissherbst** [vice-hairbst] (*Baden*, Germany) Spicy, berryish dry rosé made from various different grape varieties.

🌢 **Welschriesling** [velsh-reez-ling] Aka *Riesling Italico, Lutomer, Olasz, Laski Rizling*. Dull grape, unrelated to the *Rhine Riesling*, but with many synonyms. Comes into its own when affected by *botrytis*.

🍷 **Wendouree** (*Clare,* Australia) Small winery with a cult following for its often *Malbec*-influenced reds. Wines are very hard to find outside Australia but are well worth seeking out. ★★★★ 1996 Cabernet Malbec £££

🍷 **Wente Brothers** (*Livermore,* California) Gradually improving family company in the up-and-coming region of Livermore that, despite – or perhaps because of – such distracting enterprises as producing cigars and joint ventures in Mexico, Israel, and Eastern Europe, is still trailing in quality and value behind firms like *Fetzer*. The Canoe Ridge and Reliz Creek wines can be worthwhile, but *Murrieta's Well* is still the strongest card in the Wente pack. ★★★ 1997 Herman Wente Reserve Chardonnay ££

🍷 **Weingut Domdechant Werner'sches** [vine-goot dom-dekh-ahnt vayr-nehr-ches] (*Rheingau,* Germany) Excellent vineyard sites at *Hochheim* and *Riesling* grapes combine to produce a number of traditional wines that age beautifully.

Western Australia Very separate from the rest of the continent – some of the people here seriously dream of secession – this state has a very separate wine industry. Growing steadily southwards from their origins in the warm Swan Valley, close to Perth, the vineyards now include *Margaret River* – focus of Western Australian winemaking and fine for *Cabernet* and *Chardonnay*, Pemberton (a good area for *Pinot Noir*), and Great Southern.

🍷 **De Wetshof Estate** [vets-hof] (*Robertson,* South Africa) *Chardonnay* pioneer, Danie de Wet makes up to seven different styles of wine for different markets. The "Sur Lie" produced in the same way as *Muscadet* is probably the most interesting.

🍷 **William Wheeler Winery** (*Sonoma,* California) Inventive producer whose Quintet brings together such diverse grapes as the *Pinot Meunier*, the *Pinot Noir, Grenache,* and *Cabernet Sauvignon*.

🍷 **White Cloud** (New Zealand) Commercial white made by *Nobilo*.

White port (*Douro,* Portugal) Semi-dry aperitif, drunk by its makers with tonic water and ice, which shows what they think of it. *Churchill's* make a worthwhile version. ★★★★ Churchill's ££

🍷 **Whitehall Lane** (*Napa Valley,* California) Producer of an impressive range of *Merlots* and *Cabernets*.

🍷 **Wien** [veen] (Austria) Region close to the city of Vienna, producing ripe-tasting whites and reds. Mayer; Wieninger.

🍷 **Wild Horse** (*San Luis Obispo,* California) *Chardonnays, Pinot Blancs,* and *Pinot Noirs* are all good, but the perfumed *Malvasia Bianca* is the star.

Willamette Valley [wil-AM-et] (*Oregon*) The heart of Oregon's *Pinot Noir* vineyards, on slopes that drain into the Willamette River.

🍷 **Williams Selyem** [sel-yem] (*Sonoma,* California) Recently dissolved partnership producing fine *Burgundian*-style *Chardonnay* and *Pinot Noir*.

Wiltingen [vill-ting-gehn] (*Mosel-Saar-Ruwer,* Germany) Distinguished *Saar* village, making elegant, slatey wines. Well known for the *Scharzhofberg* vineyard. QbA/Kab/Spät: 85 86 **88 89 90** 91 **92 93 94** *95 96 97* 98 Aus/Beeren/Tba: **83 85 88 89** *90 91 92 93 94 95 96 97 98 99*

🍷 **Wing Canyon** (*Mount Veeder,* California) Small *Cabernet Sauvignon* specialist with vineyards high in the hills of *Mount Veeder*. Great, intense, blackcurranty wines.

Winkel [vin-kel] (*Rheingau,* Germany) Village with a reputation for complex delicious wine, housing *Schloss Vollrads* estate. QbA/Kab/Spät: 85 86 **88 89 90** 91 **92 93** 94 *95 96 97* 98 Aus/Beeren/Tba: **83 85 88 89** *90 91* **92 93** *94 95 96 97 98 99*

Wintrich [vin-trich] (*Mosel,* Germany) Less famous – but often more recommendable commune close to *Piesport*. Ohligsberg is the vineyard to look out for. *Rheinhold Haart.*

Winzerverein/Winzergenossenschaft [vint-zur-veh-rine/vint-zur-geh-noss-en-shaft] (Germany) Cooperative.

Wirra Wirra Vineyards (*McLaren Vale*, Australia) Reliable producer making first-class *Riesling* and *Cabernet* that, in best vintages, is sold as The Angelus.

Wither Hills (*Marlborough*, New Zealand) Instantly successful new venture from Brent Marris – former winemaker at *Delegat's*. ★★★★★ 2000 Sauvignon Blanc £££

WO (Wine of Origin) (South Africa) Official European-style certification system that is taken seriously in South Africa.

J.L. Wolf [volf] (*Pfalz*, Germany) Classy estate, recently reconstituted by *Dr. Loosen*. ★★★★★ 1999 J L Wolf Wachenheimer Goldbachel Spätlese Trocken £££

Wolfberger [volf-behr-gur] (*Alsace*, France) Brand used by the dynamic Eguisheim cooperative for highly commercial wines. ★★★ 1999 Gewurztraminer ££

Wolffer Estate (*New York*) Long Island winery gaining a local following for its *Merlot* and *Chardonnay*.

Wolff-Metternich [volf met-tur-nikh] (*Baden,* Germany) Good, rich *Riesling* from the granite slopes of *Baden*.

Woodward Canyon (*Washington State*) Small producer of characterful but subtle *Chardonnay* and *Bordeaux*-style reds that compete with some of the over-hyped efforts from California. *Semillons* are pretty impressive too. ★★★★ 1998 Columbia Valley Merlot £££

Württemberg [voor-thm-behrg] (Germany) *Anbaugebiet* surrounding the Neckar area, producing more red than any other German region.

Würzburg [foor-ts-burg] (*Franken*, Germany) Great *Sylvaner* country, though there are some fine *Rieslings* too. Bürgerspital; *Juliusspital.*

Wyken (*Suffolk*, UK) Producer of one of England's most successful red wines (everything's relative) and rather better *Bacchus* white.

Wyndham Estate (*Hunter Valley,* Australia) Ultracommercial *Hunter/Mudgee* producer that, like *Orlando*, now belongs to Pernod-Ricard. Wines are distinctly drier than they used to be, but they are still recognizably juicy in style. Quite what that firm's French customers would think of these often rather jammy blockbusters is anybody's guess. ★★★★ 1999 Bin 444 Cabernet Sauvignon ££

Wynns (*Coonawarra*, Australia) Subsidiary of *Penfolds*, based in *Coonawarra* and producer of the *John Riddoch Cabernet* and Michael *Shiraz*, both of which are only produced in good vintages and sell fast at high prices. There is also a big buttery *Chardonnay* and a commercial *Riesling*. ★★★★★ 1997 John Riddoch £££

X

Xanadu [za-na-doo] (*Margaret River*, Australia) The reputation here was built on *Semillon*, but the *Cabernet* and *Chardonnay* are both good, too. A recent takeover by venture capitalists who are eager to buy more wineries is helping to catapult Xanadu into the ranks of Australia's most dynamic producers. ★★★★ 2000 Chardonnay £££

 Xarel-lo [sha-rehl-loh] (*Catalonia*, Spain) Fairly basic grape exclusive to *Catalonia*. Used for *Cava*; best in the hands of *Jaume Serra*.

 Xynasteri [ksee-nahs-teh-ree] (Cyprus) Indigenous white grape.

Y

⌐ **"Y" d'Yquem** [ee-grek dee-kem] (*Bordeaux,* France) Hideously expensive dry wine of *Ch. d'Yquem,* which, like other such efforts by *Sauternes châteaux,* is of greater academic than hedonistic interest. (Under ludicrous Appellation Contrôlée rules, dry Sauternes has to be labelled as "Bordeaux" – like the region's very cheapest, nastiest dry white wine.)

Yakima Valley [yak-ih-mah] (*Washington State*) Principal winegrowing region of *Washington State.* Particularly good for *Merlot, Riesling,* and *Sauvignon.* Red: 85 88 **89** 91 92 94 *95 96* 97 98 White: **90 91 92 94 95** *96* 97 98. Blackwood Canyon; Chinook; Columbia Crest; Columbia Winery; Hogue; Kiona; Ch. Ste. Michelle; Staton Hills; Stewart; Tucker; Yakima River.

⌐ **Yalumba** [ya-lum-ba] (*Barossa Valley,* Australia) Associated with *Hill-Smith, Heggies, Pewsey-Vale,* and *Jansz* in Australia, *Nautilus* in New Zealand, and *Voss* in California. Producers of good-value reds and whites under the Oxford Landing label. Also produces more serious vineyard-designated reds, dry and sweet whites, and appealing sparkling wine, including *Angas Brut* and the excellent Cuvée One *Pinot Noir-Chardonnay.* ★★★★ 1995 The Signature £££

⌐ **Yarra Ridge** [ya-ra] (Australia) *Mildara-Blass* label that might lead buyers to imagine that its wines all come from vineyards in the *Yarra Valley.* In fact, like *Napa Ridge,* this is a brand that is used for wine from vineyards in other regions. European trade description laws, which are quite strict on this kind of thing, also apply to imported non-European wines, so bottles labelled "Yarra" and sold in the EU will be from Yarra.

Yarra Valley [ya-ra] (*Victoria,* Australia) Historic wine district whose "boutiques" make top-class *Burgundy*-like *Pinot Noir* and *Chardonnay* (*Coldstream Hills* and *Tarrawarra*), some stylish *Bordeaux*-style reds and, at *Yarra Yering,* a brilliant *Shiraz.* De Bortoli; Dom. Chandon (Green Point); Coldstream Hills; Diamond Valley; Long Gully; Mount Mary; Oakridge; St. Huberts; Seville Estate; Tarrawarra; Yarra Yering; Yering Station.

⌐ **Yarra Yering** [ya-ra yeh-ring] (*Yarra Valley,* Australia) Bailey Carrodus proves that the *Yarra Valley* is not just *Pinot Noir* country by producing a complex *Cabernet* blend, including a little *Petit Verdot* (Dry Red No.1) and a *Shiraz* (Dry Red No.2), in which he puts a bit of *Viognier.* Underhill is the *second label.* ★★★★ 1998 Dry Red Number One £££

⌐ **Yecla** [yeh-klah] (Spain) Generally uninspiring red wine region.

⌐ **Yellowglen** (South Australia) Producer of uninspiring basic sparkling wine and some really fine top-end fare, including the "Y", which looks oddly reminiscent of a sparkling wine called "J" from *Jordan* in California.

⌐ **Yering Station** (*Victoria,* Australia) High quality young *Yarra Valley* estate, with rich, but stylish, *Chardonnay* and *Pinot Noir.*

⌐ **Yeringberg** (*Victoria,* Australia) Imposing old *Yarra Valley* estate that used to produce disappointing wines. Now making *Rhône* style reds and whites that are worth looking out for.

⌐ **Yonder Hill** (*Stellenbosch,* South Africa) New winery making waves with well-oaked reds. ★★★★ 1998 Merlot ££

Yonne [yon] (*Burgundy,* France) Northern *Burgundy* département in which *Chablis* is to be found.

⌐ **Ch. d'Yquem** [dee-kem] (*Sauternes Premier Cru Supérieur, Bordeaux,* France) Sublime *Sauternes.* The grape pickers are sent out several times to select the best grapes. Not produced every year. Recently bought by the giant Louis-Vuitton Moët Hennessy group, which wants to sell wine through its duty-free shops in the Far East. Such is the wine world. ★★★★★ 1998 ££££

Z

Z

ℤ **Zaca Mesa** [za-ka may-sa] (*Santa Barbara*, California) Fast-improving winery with a focus on spicy *Rhône* varietals.

ℤ **Zandvliet** [zand-fleet] (*Robertson*, South Africa) Estate well-thought-of in South Africa for its *Merlot*.

ℤ **ZD** [zee-dee] (*Napa*, California) Long-established producer of very traditional, Californian, oaky, tropically fruity *Chardonnay* and plummy *Pinot Noir*. Also the producer of the highly acclaimed *Abacus*.

Zell [tzell] (*Mosel-Saar-Ruwer*, Germany) Bereich of lower *Mosel* and village, making pleasant, flowery *Riesling*. Famous for the *Schwarze Katz* (black cat) *Grosslage*. QbA/Kab/Spät: 85 88 89 90 91 *92 93 94 95 96 97 98*
Aus/Beeren/Tba: 83 85 88 89 *90 91 92 93 94 95 96 97 98*

Zema Etate [zee-mah] (*South Australia*) High-quality *Coonawarra* estate with characteristically rich, berryish reds.

ℤ **Zenato** [zay-NAH-toh] (*Veneto*, Italy) Successful producer of modern *Valpolicella* (particularly *Amarone*), *Soave*, and *Lugana*. ★★★★★ 1993 Amarone della Valpolicella Classico Riserva £££

Zentralkellerei [tzen-trahl-keh-lur-ri] (Germany) Massive central cellars for groups of cooperatives in six of the *Anbaugebiete* – the *Mosel-Saar-Ruwer* Zentralkellerei is Europe's largest cooperative.

ℤ **Fattoria Zerbina** [zehr-bee-nah] (*Emilia-Romagna*, Italy) The eye-catching wine here is the Marzeno di Marzeno *Sangiovese-Cabernet*, but this producer deserves credit for making one of the only examples of Albana di Romagna to warrant the region's *DOCG* status.

ℤ **Zevenwacht** [zeh-fen-fakht] (*Stellenbosch*, South Africa) One of South Africa's better producers of both *Shiraz* and *Pinotage*. Has also been successful with *Sauvignon Blanc* and *Pinot Noir*. ★★★★ 1999 Shiraz £££

ℤ **Zibibbo** [zee-BEE-boh] (*Sicily*, Italy) This is a good, light *Muscat* for easy summer drinking.

🍇 **Zierfandler** [zeer-fan-dlur] (Austria) Indigenous grape used in Thermenregion to make lightly spicy white wines.

ℤ **Zilliken** [tsi-li-ken] (*Saar*, Germany) Great *late-harvest Riesling* producer.

Zimbabwe An industry started by growing grapes in ex-tobacco fields is beginning to attain a level of international adequacy.

ℤ **Dom. Zind-Humbrecht** [zind-hoom-brekht] (*Alsace*, France) Extraordinarily consistent producer of ultraconcentrated, single-vineyard wines and good *varietals* that have won numerous awards from the *International Wine Challenge* and drawn *Alsace* to the attention of a new generation of wine drinkers. ★★★★ 1998 Riesling Rangen £££

🍇 **Zinfandel** [zin-fan-del] (California, Australia, South Africa) Versatile red grape, producing everything from dark, jammy, leathery reds in California, to (with a little help from sweet *Muscat*) pale pink "blush" wines, and even a little fortified wine that bears comparison with *port*. Also grown by *Cape Mentelle* and *Nepenthe* in Australia, and *Blauwklippen* in South Africa and, as *Primitivo*, by many producers in southern Italy. *Cline; Clos la Chance; De Loach; Edmeades; Elyse; Gary Farrell; Green & Red; Lamborn Family Vineyards; Ch. Potelle; Quivira; Rafanelli; Ravenswood; Ridge; Rocking Horse; Rosenblum; St. Francis; Steele; Storybook Mountain; Joseph Swan; Turley; Wellington.*

ℤ **Don Zoilo** [don zoy-loh] (*Jerez*, Spain) Classy *sherry* producer. ★★★★ Don Zoilo Oloroso ££

ℤ **Zonin** [zoh-neen] (*Veneto*, Italy) Dynamic company producing good wines in the *Veneto*, *Piedmont*, and *Tuscany*.

🍇 **Zweigelt** [tzvi-gelt] (Austria) Distinctive berryish red wine grape, more or less restricted to Austria and Hungary. *Angerer; Hafner; Kracher; Müller; Umathum.*

WINE
CHALLENGE
AWARDS
2001

International Wine Challenge

THE WORLD'S BIGGEST CONTEST

From tiny acorns... Way back in 1984, the wine writer and broadcaster Charles Metcalfe and I thought it might be interesting to compare a few English white wines with examples from other countries. The results would appear in a feature in *Wine*, the magazine we had launched a few months earlier. So, we collected together a representative collection of some 50 bottles, wrapped them in aluminium foil to hide their identities, set them out in the basement of a London restaurant, and invited a group of experts to taste and mark them out of 20. At the time, we naturally never imagined that our modest enterprise would develop into the world's biggest, most respected wine competition.

Two things helped to give the competition far more resonance than it might otherwise have had. First, there was the shameless journalistic hyperbole we employed in dubbing our tasting "The International Wine Challenge". And second, there was the fact that the home team surprised everyone by beating well-known bottles from Burgundy, the Loire, and Germany. The results – which, it has to be said, have never been repeated – caught the attention of the press throughout the world and of wine producers in other countries who quite reasonably demanded the chance to compete in a return match.

Suddenly, without intending to do so, we found ourselves running an annual event. The following year's Challenge attracted around 200 entries, while the third and fourth competitions saw numbers rise to 500 and 1,000 respectively. This annual doubling thankfully slowed down eventually, but by the end of the century we were within spitting distance of 10,000 entries, produced in countries ranging from France and Australia to Thailand and Uruguay. In May 2001 when the bottles were set out at the ExCel Centre in London for the latest competition, there were no fewer than 9,339 individual wines.

ORIGINS IN LONDON

It is no accident that the International Wine Challenge was born in London. For centuries, British wine drinkers have enjoyed the luxury of being able to enjoy wines from a wide variety of countries. Samuel Pepys may have been a fan of Château Haut-Brion from Bordeaux, but

plenty of other 18th-century sophisticates in London (and elsewhere in Britain) were just as excited about the sweet, late-harvest whites that were being produced at that time by early settlers in South Africa. More recently, over the last 50 years, as wine became steadily more popular, wines from California, Australia, New Zealand, and South America all found their way to these shores. Other arrivals were wines from regions like Languedoc-Roussillon in France and Southern Italy, that had often been overlooked. As the 21st century dawned, Britain's biggest supermarket chains boasted daunting ranges of 700–800

Every wine's identity is hidden within specially-produced bags.

different wines. A well-run competition provided an invaluable means of sorting the best and most interesting of these bottles from the rest.

The tasting panels

If the diversity of the wines on offer in London created a need for the International Wine Challenge, the calibre of Britain's wine experts provided the means with which to run the competition. The country that spawned the Institute of Masters of Wine – the trade body whose members have to pass the world's toughest wine exam – is also home to some of the most respected wine critics and merchants on the planet. These are the men and women – some 350 of them – who, along with winemakers and experts from overseas, make up the tasting panels for the Challenge.

Tasters used generously-proportioned Riedel glasses.

So, a set of wines might well have been judged by a group that included the director of a traditional city merchant, the buyer from a major supermarket, an Australian winemaker, a French sommelier, and a top wine critic from Portugal.

Two-round format

During the first of the two rounds of the competition, wines are assessed to decide whether they are worthy of an award – be it a medal or a seal of approval. At this stage, typicality is taken into account, and tasters are informed that they are dealing, for example, with Chablis, Chianti, or South African Chenin Blanc. Around 36 per cent of the wines are found wanting and these leave the competition with no award. A further 30 per cent receive Seals of Approval.

The medal-worthy entries, and the "seeded" entries that have already won recognition in the previous year's competition, then pass on to the second round. Now, the judges have to decide on the specific award each wine should receive – if any (they can still demote or throw wines out completely). At this stage, the wine's origins remain secret: there is no place for prejudices on behalf of or against a region or country.

Safety net

Before round one is completed, it is necessary to ensure that good wines are not overlooked: this can possibly be because of slight but all-too-frequent cork-taint, which is not always evident when the bottles are first poured. To this end, a team of "super-jurors" tastes the wines that have initially been marked down. Like all panelists, these are mostly professional buyers from leading merchants and retailers, and Masters of Wine. Their role is to undertake the daunting task of sniffing, sipping, and spitting the entries that have been rejected or thought worthy of a Seal of Approval rather than a medal.

Over 50,000 tasting notes were written over 10 days.

TROPHY WINNERS

Super-jurors also decide which Gold medal winners deserve the additional recognition of a Trophy. These supreme awards can be given – or withheld – for any style, region, or nationality of wine. The 2001 Trophy winners were as follows:

Sauvignon Blanc Villa Maria Private Bin Sauvignon Blanc 2000
Semillon Basedow Barossa Valley Semillon 2000
Chardonnay Stonier Reserve Chardonnay 1999
Riesling Ürziger Würzgarten Riesling Spätlese 1993
Late-harvest Loire Château la Varière Bonnezeaux 1997
Late-harvest German Escherndorfer Lump Riesling TBA 1999

Robert Joseph (far right), *International Wine Challenge chairman, is asked to adjudicate.*

Icewine Willow Heights Vidal Icewine 1998
Pinot Noir Gibbston Valley Reserve Pinot Noir 2000
Red Burgundy Volnay les Chevrets J Boillot 1999
Cabernet Sauvignon Jordan Cabernet Sauvignon 1998
Syrah/Shiraz Brokenwood Rayners Shiraz 1999
Italian Red Vino Nobile di Montepulciano, Vigna Asinone, Poliziano 1997
Barbera Seghesio Barbera 1999
Spanish Red Wine Guelbenzu Lautus 1998
Zinfandel St Francis Reserve Zinfandel 1998
Malbec Luigi Bosca Reserve Malbec 2000
Pinotage Spice Route Pinotage 1999
Champagne Charles Heidsieck Réserve Charlie Mis en Cave 1990
Champagne Blanc de Blancs Charles Heidsieck 1982 "Oenothèque"
Vintage Port Poças Vintage Port 1997
Tawny Port Warre's Twenty Year Old Tawny Port NV
Fino Sherry Fino Inocente NV
Amontillado Sherry Lustau Almacenista Jurado Amontillado
Pedro Ximenez Sherry Barbadillo la Cilla Pedro Ximenez
Madeira Henriques & Henriques 15 Year Old Verdelho

Top Trophy winners
Finest Red Brokenwood Rayners Shiraz 1999. **Finest White** Stonier Reserve Chardonnay 1999. **Finest Sparkling**   Charles Heidsieck Réserve Charlie Mis en Cave 1990/1982 "Oenotheque". **Finest Fortified** Henriques & Henriques 15-year-old Verdelho.

Details of all entries were recorded in the database.

Money no Object

One of the questions that is often asked about the International Wine Challenge concerns the account we take of the price of the wines we are tasting. Surely, some have argued, it is impossible to judge a £3.99 Bulgarian red by the same criteria that might be applied to a £39 Bordeaux. In fact, this was precisely the view we used to take in the early years of running the competition. Wines were assembled in "price bands", with one set of tasters being asked to turn their attention to £7–10 Chardonnay, while their neighbours were asked to assess wines made from the same grape and selling at under a fiver. When we analyzed the results, however, we discovered that the knowledge of how much each sample cost was often a hindrance to the tasters. Some were inclined to give higher marks to undeserving but pricier wines, while others proved to be more niggardly, refusing to reward glorious entries they thought expensive. There was another problem when medal-winning wines of different prices ended up on the same wine shelf. Why shouldn't browsers naturally imagine a gold medal winner to be intrinsically better than a costlier one with a silver?

There was also the possibility of a wholesaler or retailer raising or cutting a price after the competition. Would a Chardonnay that won a gold medal in the "Under a Fiver" category still deserve the award if its cost were to go up to, say £6.49? So, while we still endeavour to set wines out for tasting alongside bottles of a similar price, we give the judges no idea of their cost. Every award winner earned its spurs purely on the basis of its quality.

Great Value Awards

But that's not to say that we're not intested in value for money. Once the competition is over and the medals and Seals of Approval distributed, we carefully compare awards with prices. Entries that cost significantly less than the average for their level of medal get their own Great Value awards, over 750 of which are listed in the following pages, along with the Gold medal winners.

Following a separate blind-tasting by the super-jurors of the most highly-rated and widely-available Great Value wines, the very best buys of all are named Great Value Wines of the Year. Look out for these; they tend to fly out of the shops very quickly and, of course, once a vintage or cuvée has sold out, it can never be replaced.

THE GREAT VALUE WINES OF THE YEAR

Red
Cuvée Gabriel Vin de Pays d'Oc Merlot 2000
Penfolds Koonunga Hill Shiraz Cabernet 1999
Santa Ines Legado de Armida Cabernet Sauvignon Reserva 1999
Spice Route Pinotage 1999

White
Deakin Estate Colombard 2000
Villa Maria Private Bin Sauvignon Blanc 2000
Palo Alto Chardonnay 2000

Sparkling
Brown Brothers Pinot Noir Chardonnay NV
Seaview Blanc de Blancs 1998
Albert Etienne Champagne Brut.

OTHER WINE CHALLENGE COMPETITIONS

Having revolutionized the UK wine market, the International Wine Challenge began to spread to other parts of the globe. It now includes competitions in Hong Kong, Singapore, and Shanghai. In each case, as in London, the wines are judged by panels of local tasters and overseas experts. Despite all manner of possible variables, the same wines often triumph. The 1999 Evans & Tate Margaret River Shiraz, which was top red in the 2000 London International Wine Challenge, for example, also won the same accolade in 2001 in Hong Kong.

The wines, the tasters... and the team who make the Challenge happen.

HOW TO USE THE AWARDS LIST

Every wine in this list gained an award at the 2001 International WINE Challenge. The wines are listed by country and style, with up to six headings: red, white, sweet, rosé, sparkling, and fortified.

Under each heading the wines are listed in price order, from the least to the most expensive. Wines of the same price are listed in medal order: Gold, Silver, and Bronze.

All Silver and Bronze medal winners and Seal of Approval wines listed are entries that were also given Great Value awards, following comparison of their retail price and the average price for the award they received in the International Wine Challenge. Following consultation with leading off-licences, appropriate price limits were established for particular styles of wine. A Great Value sparkling wine or port, for example, might sell at a higher price than a red table wine with the same medal.

This list does not include the Silver and Bronze medal winners and Seals of Approval that did not win Great Value awards (for these, visit internationalwinechallenge.com). All of the 226 Gold medal winners and Trophy winners – the finest wines in the competition – do appear. For full details of the price limits that were used to allocate Great Value awards, turn to page 364.

Ⓖ	**LUIGI BOSCA RESERVE MALBEC 2000,** **LEONCIO ARIZU SA** Mendoza	Spicy rose which introduces the creamy, ripe, big berry palate full of vibrant, jammy concentrated fruit.	**£9.00**	Not available in the UK

The wine name, vintage, producer, and region | A tasting note provided by Challenge tasters | Average retail price

Codes for stockists (see page 365)

Symbols

Ⓖ *gold medal*
Ⓢ *silver medal*
Ⓑ *bronze medal*
✓ *seal of approval*
🍷 *wine of the year*
🏆 *trophy*

Gold medal winning wines are shaded this colour

Silver medal winning wines are shaded this colour

Bronze medal winning wines are shaded this colour

ARGENTINA

It seems unusual that we have not been drinking Argentinian wines for longer. Argentina is the fifth largest wine producer in the world. Furthermore, Argentina, in particular Mendoza, is acknowledged to have some of the very finest vineyards on the planet. The local climate, types of soil and the unusually high altitude combine to produce grapes of superb quality, with just the right combination of fruit, tannin, and sugar. The premium red wines made from Malbec, a variety originally from the South West of France, may turn out to be the next "Shiraz".

ARGENTINA • SPARKLING

(B)	**CHANDON ARGENTINA NV, CHANDON ESTATES** Mendoza	There is sunshine, ripe fruit, and hints of toast in this delicate and soft fizz.	**£8.20**	SGL MHU

ARGENTINA • WHITE

(B)	**CABALLO DE PLATA TORRONTES 2000, LA RIOJANA** La Rioja	Lemons and limes on the nose, with ripe-melon characteristics, and clean, aromatic, floral overtones.	**£3.50**	SAF SWS GHL WRW
✓	**CABALLO DE PLATA SHIRAZ MALBEC ROSADO 2000, LA RIOJANA** La Rioja	Excellent rosé. Refreshing with good acidity and ripe red fruit.	**£4.00**	SAF
(B)	**PARRA ALTA CHARDONNAY 2000, VINA PATAGONIA** Mendoza	An elegant and simple wine. Delicately infused tropical-fruit aromas with balancing acidity.	**£4.50**	WST ENO COM SOM
(B)	**CHANDON ARGENTINA NV, CHANDON ESTATES** Mendoza	There is sunshine, ripe fruit, and hints of toast in this delicate and soft fizz.	**£8.20**	SGL MHU
(G)	**Q FAMILIA ZUCCARDI CHARDONNAY 1999, LA AGRICOLA** Mendoza	Deep gold, concentrated, and rich; ripe fruit and caramelized oranges. Structural elements are in harmony with the fruit.	**£9.00**	TH

Pinpoint who sells the wine you wish to buy by turning to the stockist codes. If you know the name of the wine you want to buy, use the alphabetical index. If the price is your motivation, look out for the "Wine of the Year" symbol; the best red and white wines under £8, sparkling wines under £12, and champagne under £15. Happy hunting!

ARGENTINA • RED

✓	**CORCHO D'ORO MENDOZA RED NV,** **ZIMMERMAN GRAEFF** Mendoza	Delicate soft fruits on the nose and a gentle palate.	**£3.40**	WRT
✓	**CABALLO DE PLATA BONARDA BARBERA 2000,** **LA RIOJANA** Famatina Valley	Young, tangy, blackcurrant-scented wine, with a velvety palate.	**£3.50**	BGL NYW CTC
✓	**CORCHO D'ORO MALBEC 2000,** **ZIMMERMAN GRAEFF** Mendoza	Bramble and damson with a spicy finish.	**£3.60**	WRT
✓	**ARGENTINE MALBEC-BONARDA 2000,** **MARTINS** Mendoza	Citrusy, cherry nose with a jammy palate.	**£3.70**	CWS RAV WCR
Ⓑ	**ASDA SELECT BLEND ARGENTINIAN 2000,** **LA RIOJANA** Famatina Valley	Intense colour with ripe, smoky fruit, and well-balanced acidity and tannins. Full bodied, with a complex and lingering finish.	**£3.80**	ASD
✓	**ASDA ARGENTINIAN BONARDA 2000,** **LA AGRICOLA** Mendoza	Fruity red with a little spice on the finish.	**£3.80**	ASD
✓	**PICAJUAN PEAK MALBEC 2000,** **LA AGRICOLA** Mendoza	Lively red fruit, well-textured palate, and firm tannins.	**£3.80**	TOS
Ⓑ	**ARGENTINE TEMPRANILLO 2000,** **LA ARIGOLA** Mendoza	This forthcoming Argentinian red has a dusty nose and a bubblegum palate infused with a multitude of spices.	**£4.00**	SMF VGN
Ⓑ	**BODEGAS ROSARIO MALBEC 2000,** **JFL ARGENTINA SA** Mendoza	This lovely example of an Argentinian Malbec offers ripe, smoky, red berry and herb aromas.	**£4.00**	NTD
Ⓑ	**BODEGAS ROSARIO SHIRAZ 2000,** **JFL ARGENTINA SA** Mendoza	White pepper and spice aromas on the nose lead to complex and balanced fruit on the palate.	**£4.00**	NTD
Ⓑ	**CORAZON BONARDA 2000,** **LA RIOJCANA** Mendoza	Intense, jammy black fruits, and layers of raisins burst forth from this well-structured, powerful wine.	**£4.00**	WRC GCF

	Name	Description	Price	Code
B	**CORAZON BONARDA 2000, LA RIOJANA** Famatina Valley	Luscious spicy fruit laced with coffee and chocolate. Supple tannins contribute to the pleasure of this superb wine.	**£4.00**	BGL VGN
B	**SW ARGENTINIAN SYRAH 2000, LA RIOJANA** La Rioja	This Argentianian Syrah offers complex vanilla oak with hints of spicy fruits and a long finish.	**£4.00**	SAF
✓	**ANDES SUR TEMPRANILLO BONARDA 2000, ARRIERO** Mendoza	Bags of fruit, and good balance not masked with oak.	**£4.00**	HOH
✓	**ARGENTINIAN CABERNET SAUVIGNON 2000, LA RIOJANA** La Rioja	Pleasing balance with sweet fruit.	**£4.00**	SAF
✓	**ASDA ARGENTINIAN SANGIOVESE 2000, LA AGRICOLA SA** Mendoza	Vibrant red fruits and food-friendly acidity.	**£4.00**	ASD
✓	**ASDA ARGENTINIAN SHIRAZ 2000, LA RIOJANA** La Rioja	Baked fruits and firm tannins.	**£4.00**	ASD
✓	**BODEGAS ROSARIO 2000, JFL ARGENTINA SA** Mendoza	Black-cherry fruit with firm tannic structure.	**£4.00**	NTD
✓	**BRIGHT BROTHERS VISTALBA MALBEC 2000, PENAFLOR** Mendoza	Ripe peppery fruit with a moderate length.	**£4.00**	EHL
✓	**CO-OP ARGENTINE MALBEC 2000, LA RIOJANA** La Rioja	Pleasant bramble-leaf and sweet red fruits.	**£4.00**	CWS BBO WBR VIL
✓	**CO-OP ARGENTINE OLD VINES SANGIOVESE 2000, NORTON** Mendoza	Upfront style with fine red fruit.	**£4.00**	CWS
✓	**FOUR RIVERS MALBEC 2000, LUIS CORREAS** Mendoza	Bright brambly nose, with bright finish.	**£4.00**	PAT VGN
✓	**SW ARGENTINIAN BONARDA 2000, LA RIOJANA** La Rioja	Lifted, peppery sweet spices.	**£4.00**	SAF

(B)	**VILA BONARDA 1999, VINAS DE VILA** Mendoza	Ripe, blueberry fruit and raspberries blend harmoniously with firm but well-defined tannins.	**£4.30**	HAE SAF
(B)	**ETCHART RIO DE PLATA MALBEC 2000, BODEGAS ETCHART** Mendoza	This ruby-coloured wine offers youthful blackcurrants and toasty vanilla on the nose.	**£4.50**	CAX
(B)	**GRAFFIGNA SHIRAZ CABERNET SAUVIGNON 1999, BODEGAS GRAFFIGNA** San Juan	This easy-drinking wine has a luscious, fruit palate echoing with hints of leather and crushed pepper.	**£4.50**	CHN
✓	**ARGENTINIAN MALBEC NV, LES CAVES DE LANDIRAS** Mendoza	Ripe, baked fruit with a long sweet finish.	**£4.50**	GCF
(B)	**FINCA FLICHMAN SYRAH MENDOZA 1998, FINCA FLICHMAN** Mendoza	The slightly retiring fruit on the nose precedes a soft, melted chocolate palate with a subtle finish.	**£4.70**	DBY PBA BOO CNL
(B)	**CROTTA TEMPRANILLO 2000, VINOS CROTTA** Mendoza	An opulent figgy nose opens up into a berry-laden palate integrated with new oak and spice.	**£5.00**	YWL
(B)	**ETCHART RIO DE PLATA CABERNET SAUVIGNON 2000, BODEGAS ETCHART** Mendoza	Big fruits on the nose with hints of damson and blackberry, followed by a structured finish.	**£5.00**	ASD CAX
(B)	**FINCA EL RETIRO 2000, PACIFICO TITTARELLI SA** Mendoza	Rich cherries on the nose lead to a soft palate of warm fruits and gentle tannins.	**£5.00**	LIB
(B)	**FINCA LAS MARIAS MALBEC 2000, BODEGAS NIETO SENETINER** Mendoza	Lovely deep colour with spicy oak on the nose. The palate has mulberry fruits and hints of chocolate.	**£5.00**	CPR
(B)	**GRAFFIGNA MALBEC SELECCION ESPECIAL 1999, SA BODEGAS VIÑEDOS SANTIAGO** San Juan	This Malbec offers lovely ripe, black fruit and aromas of vanilla which follow through onto the palate.	**£5.00**	CHN
(B)	**SANTA JULIA BONARDA 2000, SANTA JULIA VINEYARDS** Mendoza	Sweet, cherry nose leads to a plummy palate with rounded tannins.	**£5.00**	THI
(B)	**SANTA JULIA MERLOT OAK AGED 2000, SANTA JULIA VINEYARDS** Mendoza	A full-throttle style with masses of fruit, although the nose will open out with some more age.	**£5.00**	THI

(B)	**SANTA JULIA TEMPRANILLO 2000,** **LA AGRICOLA** Mendoza	This very approachable and easy-drinking wine is full of strawberry and raspberry fruits sprinkled with spice.	**£5.00**	THI CAM UNS
(B)	**VILLA ATUEL SYRAH 1999,** **VILLA ATUEL** Mendoza	Strawberry fruits shine through on the nose; the palate has luscious, spiced-fruit flavours, and sturdy tannins.	**£5.30**	POR BEN WRC SOM
(S)	**COLECCION MALBEC 2000,** **MICHEL TORINO** Salta	Deep purpley-black in appearance with luscious black fruits and chewy tannins on the palate.	**£5.50**	HOH
(S)	**MENDOZA CABERNET SAUVIGNON 2000,** **FINCA EL RETIRO** Mendoza	Broad palate displaying cassis, with minty overtones and very firm tannins. Youthful with good length.	**£6.00**	POR GGW LIB
(S)	**MENDOZA SYRAH 2000,** **FINCA EL RETIRO** Mendoza	Classic Syrah characteristics on the palate. The zesty acidity works well with spicy fruit and gripping tannins.	**£6.00**	POR GGW LIB CTC VGN
(S)	**TERRAZAS ALTO MALBEC 2000, BODEGA TERRAZAS** Mendoza	Rich, dark cherry. Medium-bodied; integrated, oak undertones bind the tannins and fleshy fruit flavours together.	**£6.10**	CEB UNS NTD PRG
(S)	**TRIVENTO RESERVE SYRAH OAK BARREL AGED 1999,** **CONCHA Y TORO** Mendoza	Deep purple; sweet, jammy blackberry and coffee flavours laced with a touch of minty eucalyptus.	**£6.00**	CYT
(S)	**SANTA JULIA TEMPRANILLO SELECTION 1999,** **LA AGRICOLA** Mendoza	The nose is attractive with hints of raspberry and cherry. Opulent, spicy, silky tannins on the finish.	**£7.00**	ASD
(G)	**DON DAVID CABERNET SAUVIGNON 1999,** **MICHEL TORINO** Salta	Gives little away initially, then bursts forth with ripe, spicy fruit rounded out with warming alcohol and tannins.	**£7.00**	HOH BBO UNS ASH
(S)	**BALBI VINEYARD SHIRAZ RESERVA 1999,** **BODEGAS BALBI** Mendoza	This powerful wine is packed full of juicy, ripe fruit layered with chunky, blackberry fruit and light spice.	**£7.00**	ADD
(S)	**BRIGHT BROTHERS BARRICA SHIRAZ CABERNET 1999,** **PENAFLOR** San Juan	A silky blackberry and spicy palate integrates well with lively acidity, and finishes in persistent length.	**£7.00**	EHL
(S)	**CANDELA SYRAH 2000,** **BODEGAS ESCORIHUELA** Mendoza	Deep and concentrated in colour. On the nose, bramble fruits blend seductively with elegant, dark-coffee flavours.	**£7.00**	PLB TOS SOM

(S)	**CO-OP BIN 99 ARGENTINE CABERNET FRANC RESERVE 1999,** PENAFLOR, San Juan	Lush, deep purple in colour. Aromas of cedar integrate well with warm, sun-baked fruit.	**£7.00** CWS CHN
(S)	**DON DAVID CABERNET SAUVIGNON 2000, MICHEL TORINO** Salta	Spicy oak intermingles with strong, berry-fruit flavours, giving a pleasing complexity, well-supported with firm tannins.	**£7.00** HOH
(S)	**FANTELLI GRAN RESERVA 1999, FANTELLI** Mendoza	Deep purple colour; lovely, balanced oak-fruit on the palate. The finish is long, complex, and spicy.	**£7.00** BGL
(S)	**SANTA JULIA PINOT NOIR RESERVA 1999, SANTA JULIA VINEYARDS** Mendoza	Deep garnet colour already. Plummy, chocolatey aromas notify the senses of a sweet, jammy palate.	**£7.00** THI
(S)	**SANTA JULIA TEMPRANILLO RESERVA 1999, LA AGRICOLA** Mendoza	Medium-bodied wine with lovely, soft, strawberry flavours underlying a spicy finish with soft tannins.	**£7.00** UNS THI
(S)	**CABALLERO DE LA CEPA RESERVE MALBEC 1999, FINCA FLICHMAN** Mendoza	Ripe, baked, jammy fruits precede a green-fruit palate, with a hint of linseed oil on the finish.	**£7.30** SGL
(S)	**CABALLERO DE LA CEPA RESERVE SYRAH 1998, FINCA FLICHMAN** Mendoza	Medium-weight body, with juicy, black fruits, and a herby, smoky finish. Great, lingering length.	**£7.30** SGL
(G)	**LUIGI BOSCA RESERVE MALBEC 2000, LEONCIO ARIZU SA** Mendoza	Spicy nose which introduces the creamy, ripe, big-berry palate, full of vibrant, jammy, concentrated fruit.	**£9.00** Not available in the UK
(G)	**MALBEC RESERVA ALTOS LAS HORMIGAS 1999, ALTOS LAS HORMIGAS** Mendoza	Inky, ripe Malbec showing great fruit-depth, powerful concentration, and great elegance on the finish.	**£14.20** J&B

Pinpoint who sells the wine you wish to buy by turning to the stockist codes. If you know the name of the wine you want to buy, use the alphabetical index. If the price is your motivation, look out for the 'Wine of the Year symbol; the best red and white wines under £8, sparkling wines under £12 and champagne under £15. Happy hunting!

AUSTRALIA

Another great year for the darling of the UK wine consumer. Over five pounds, Australia is the UK's best-selling wine country, overtaking France last year. The British wine drinker seems more comfortable with the honest marketing approach and up-front ripe flavours from down under than the ever more complex message coming from over the Channel. Furthermore, Aussie wines are become more sophisticated yearly. These styles are providing a wonderful new direction away from the big bold styles with which Australia has made its name.

AUSTRALIA · SPARKLING

SACRED HILL BRUT CUVÉE NV, (B) **DE BORTOLI** South-East Australia	Gentle mousse, with light, bready characters behind toasty fruit and a lively, refreshing finish.	**£5.50**	BOR
STAMP OF AUSTRALIA SPARKLING CHARDONNAY (B) **PINOT NOIR NV, BRL HARDY** South-East Australia	Has a pink tinge, with light apple and cherry notes on the nose, and a lively mousse.	**£6.10**	BGN NTD HBR TPE
SEAVIEW BRUT NV, SOUTHCORP WINES EUROPE (S) **LTD** South-East Australia	Soft-fruit characters and crisp acidity, balanced by a refreshing, dry finish in the classic Brut style.	**£6.80**	POR UNS PEF
JACOB'S CREEK SPARKLING CHARDONNAY-PINOT NOIR (B) **NV, ORLANDO WYNDHAM** South-East Australia	Lively, fine mousse with bright, pale appearance. Ripe-melon and tropical-fruit palate. A rich, honeyed finish.	**£7.00**	BGN NTD ASD UNS
SOMERFIELD AUSTRALIAN SPARKLING CHARDONNAY (B) **1995, SOUTHCORP** South-East Australia	Pale, golden-straw colour, with hints of rose petals. Dry, refreshing melon and mandarins, with an understated finish.	**£7.00**	SMF PEF NRW NYW
HARDYS NOTTAGE HILL SPARKLING CHARDONNAY ✓ **1999, BRL HARDY** South-East Australia	Rich, toasty nose with hints of tropical fruit, delicate mousse, and balanced, crisp acidity.	**£7.00**	NTD HBR AMW
SEAVIEW CHARDONNAY BLANC DE BLANCS 1998, (S) **SOUTHCORP WINES PTY LTD** South-East Australia	Nutty, Chardonnay-fruit characteristics, integrated yeast flavours, and creamy richness with great length and clean finish.	**£9.00**	PEF
SEAVIEW PINOT CHARDONNAY 1998, (B) **SOUTHCORP WINES PTY LTD** South-East Australia	Ripe melon and pineapple on the nose and the palate, with a fresh, dry, clean finish.	**£9.00**	UNS PEF

(S) **BROWN BROTHERS PINOT NOIR CHARDONNAY NV, BROWN BROTHERS WINES** Victoria	A full, ripe-melon nose, with hints of peach and pineapple, and toasty overtones on a lengthy finish.	**£9.80**	CPW BRB SMF
(S) **SEPPELT SALINGER 1995, SOUTHCORP WINES PTY LTD** Victoria	A rich, creamy nose, with ripe fruit flavours, a soft mousse, and a pleasant finish.	**£10.00**	PEF

AUSTRALIA • WHITE

✓ **SOMERFIELD AUSTRALIAN DRY WHITE 2000, SOMERFIELD** South-East Australia	Light, tropical, and fruit-filled wine, with good acidity in an easy-drinking style.	**£3.00**	SMF
✓ **SW AUSTRALIAN OAKED COLOMBARD 2000, BRL HARDY** South-East Australia	Spicy lemons and peachy hints over an acidic backbone and persistence on the palate.	**£3.50**	SAF
(B) **BLEND Z DRY WHITE, PARSONS BROOK** South-East Australia	Heady, white flowers on the nose; ripe fruit and crisp acidity round out the palate.	**£3.50**	MCT
(B) **BANROCK STATION COLOMBARD CHARDONNAY 2000, BRL HARDY** South Australia	Ripe key limes and vibrant, fresh, green apples. Good length and complexity.	**£4.10**	NTD UNS NTD HBR
✓ **CO-OP AUSTRALIAN CHARDONNAY 2000, ANGOVE'S PTY LIMITED** South Australia	This wine shows good balance and harmony with a light citrus approach.	**£4.00**	CWS
✓ **DIAMOND RIDGE CHARDONNAY 2000, WESTERN WINES LTD** South-East Australia	Full-bodied and vanilla-scented, this clean wine has loads of appeal and in a style for everyone.	**£4.00**	WST
✓ **KALGOORIE CHARDONNAY 1999, SOUTHCORP** South-East Australia	Crisp and attractive lemon and lime fruit. A refreshing change from many over-oaked wines.	**£4.00**	NTD
✓ **SOMERFIELD AUSTRALIAN SEMILLON CHARDONNAY 2000, SOUTHCORP** South-East Australia	Soft, buttery palate with an abundance of tropical fruits.	**£4.00**	SMF
✓ **SPRINGTOWN CHARDONNAY 2000, HG BROWN** South-East Australia	Restrained fruit and a subtle use of oak gives a great palate and nuances of Burgundy.	**£4.00**	MAC

✓	**STONERIDGE COLOMBARD/ CHARDONNAY NV, ANGOVES** South-East Australia	Refreshing, with attractive butternut qualities, and a balanced, well-heeled finish.	**£4.00**	WRT
✓	**TORTOISESHELL BAY SAUVIGNON SEMILLON 2000, CASELLA WINES** New South Wales	Deep amber shades boast tropical melons and butterscotch on the palate. Good intensity and body.	**£4.00**	SWS JNW CST
Ⓢ	**ANDREW PEACE CHARDONNAY 2000, ANDREW PEACE WINES** Victoria	Fantastic, juicy fruit blended with hints of vanilla spice and baked bananas. Well-integrated oak lingers on the finish.	**£4.20**	ASD BGL JSS CNL VGN
Ⓑ	**BANROCK STATION CHARDONNAY 2000, BRL HARDY WINE COMPANY** South Australia	Fair dinkum Ozzie Chardonnay with baked apple and melon fruit, and a good mineral streak.	**£4.60**	BGN NTD UNS NTD
Ⓢ	**DEAKIN ESTATE CHARDONNAY 2000, WINGARA GROUP** Victoria	Concentrated nose with a hint of spice. Intergrated caramel and toasty oak are married to the honeyed fruit.	**£5.10**	GGW WST
Ⓢ	**OXFORD LANDING CHARDONNAY 2000, YALUMBA** South-East Australia	Clean, rich, tropical fruit and buttery aromas are followed by zesty peach and lime acidity.	**£5.30**	BGN NTD SGL ASD
Ⓑ	**HARDYS NOTTAGE HILL CHARDONNAY 2000, BRL HARDY WINE COMPANY** South-East Australia	Ripe, citrus peel on the nose balanced by buttery almonds on the palate.	**£5.40**	BGN NTD UNS NTD
Ⓑ	**JACOB'S CREEK CHARDONNAY 2000, ORLANDO WYNDHAM** South-East Australia	This ever-popular wine can always be relied upon, whatever the occasion. Ripe fruit and well-judged use of oak.	**£5.00**	BGN NTD ASD UNS
Ⓑ	**JINDALEE CHARDONNAY 2000, JINDALEE ESTATES** Victoria	Limes and melons on the nose. Layers of fruit and oak meld into a complex wine with good depth.	**£5.00**	WTS UNS EHL
Ⓢ	**JACOB'S CREEK RIESLING 2000, ORLANO WYNDHAM** Australia	Fragrant lime, white peach, and citrus aromas give way to a rich, mouthwatering palate of tingling limes and apples.	**£5.00**	Widely Available
Ⓑ	**THOMAS MITCHELL CHARDONNAY 2000, MITCHELTON** Victoria	Upfront, citrus fruit with cutting acidity and pronounced fruit, nicely infused with toasty oak flavours.	**£5.00**	JEF
Ⓖ	**BASEDOW BAROSSA VALLEY SEMILLON 2000, BASEDOW WINES** South Australia	Intense, spicy wine with concentrated tropical fruit, given balance and depth by clever use of sweet oak.	**£7.00**	HFI

(S) **LENNARD'S CROSSING CHARDONNAY 2000, McGUIGAN WINES** South-East Australia	Last year it won bronze; this year, its rich, buttery qualities have nosed it into silver position.	**£6.50**	VNO
(G) **MARIENBERG COTTAGE CLASSIC CHARDONNAY 2000, MARIENBERG WINE CO PTY LTD,** South Australia	Lemony character with tropical-fruit aromas. A creamy, buttery texture with toffee oak. Supple and crisp.	**£6.80**	HFI BNK VGN
(S) **KINGSTON ESTATE CHARDONNAY 1999, KINGSTON ESTATE** South Australia	Lemony acidity marries splendidly with the toasty oak, leaving a lingering finish in the mouth.	**£7.00**	KOM
(S) **YALUMBA BAROSSA CHARDONNAY 2000, YALUMBA** South Australia	A generous, well-structured wine, which expresses clean, mineral flavours layered with soft, golden fruit.	**£7.00**	NEG RNS JSS TRO
(S) **SANDALFORD ELEMENT CHARDONNAY 2000, SANDALFORD WINES** West Australia	This wine exhibits depth and complexity, with underlying tones of subtle, vanilla oak and ripe, tropical fruit.	**£7.00**	HBJ
(G) **WILLOW BRIDGE SAUVIGNON BLANC SEMILLON 2000, WILLOW BRIDGE ESTATE** West Australia	A very smooth, civilized wine of great length and thought-provoking depth, with a beguiling, smoky edge.	**£7.20**	GGW AUS
(G) **GAPSTED CHARDONNAY 1999, VICTORIAN ALPS WINE CO** Victoria	Mineral edge and ripe, tropical-fruit flavours; toasty, biscuity oak. A boost of alcohol on the long finish.	**£8.50**	Not available in the U.K.
(G) **HILLSTOWE SAUVIGNON BLANC 2000, HILLSTOWE** South Australia	This is an aromatic-style Sauvignon with plenty of fresh nettles, and a touch of rich honey.	**£8.90**	ENO
(G) **XANADU CHARDONNAY 2000, XANADU** West Australia	French oak-influenced nose with toast, cinnamon, and orange peel. Soft, rich, and spicy with style and verve.	**£9.00**	PLB
(G) **STONIER RESERVE CHARDONNAY 1999, STONIER** Victoria	Citrus and peach aromas with buttery cashews. Stone-fruit flavours with a grapefruit zing. Structural, rich, and stunning.	**£11.00**	MZC
(G) **TARRAWARRA CHARDONNAY 1998, TARRAWARRA** Victoria	Rich, toasty oak and vanilla spice from nose to finish beautifully matches the ripe, tropical fruit.	**£16.00**	CRI PEF

Pinpoint who sells the wine you wish to buy by turning to the stockist codes. If you know the name of the wine you want to buy, use the alphabetical index. If the price is your motivation, look out for the 'Wine of the Year' symbol; the best red and white wines under £8, sparkling wines under £12 and champagne under £15. Happy hunting!

AUSTRALIA • RED

✓	**ASDA KARALTA RED NV BRL HARDY** Southeast Australia	Gamey and spicy, complex nose, light bodied with a good clean finish.	**£3.00**	ASD
✓	**BADGERS CREEK SHIRAZ CABERNET 2000, LES GRANDS CHAIS DE FRANCE** Southeast Australia	Juicy red colour, spicy tones with plum flavours and soft tannins.	**£3.00**	GCF OWC
✓	**TESCO AUSTRALIAN SHIRAZ NV, SIMEON WINES** Southeast Australia	Juicy cherries and chocolate on the palate, with firm tannins.	**£3.30**	TOS BDR
✓	**KALGOORIE OAKED RED 1999, SOUTHCORP** Southeast Australia	Elegant red fruit with good balance and spicy finish.	**£3.50**	NTD
✓	**SOMERFIELD AUSTRALIAN DRY RED 2000, SOUTHCORP** Southeast Australia	Quaffing style with soft, jammy fruits and a decent alcoholic kick to finish.	**£3.50**	SMF
Ⓢ	**MIGHTY MURRAY MASTERPEACE RED 2000, ANDREW PEACE WINES** Victoria	Bright ruby red colour, sweet jammy fruits on the nose with light hints of black pepper.	**£4.00**	ASD BGL VGN
Ⓑ	**CO-OP JACARANDA HILL SHIRAZ 2000, ANGOVE'S** South Australia	A classic: layers of mint and ripe blackberry jam, with lively acidity lifting the fruit-laden palate.	**£4.00**	CWS
Ⓑ	**SEPPELT MOYSTON SHIRAZ CABERNET 2000, SEPPELT SONS LTD.** Southeast Australia	Upfront mint and bramble fruits on the nose and the palate. Dark chocolate and oak define the finish.	**£4.00**	MCT
Ⓑ	**TORTOISESHELL BAY MOURVEDRE SHIRAZ 2000, CASELLA WINES** New South Wales	This medium-bodied wine oozes with jammy black fruits on the nose and palate, which has a zesty acidity.	**£4.00**	SWS SMF
✓	**CARRAMAR ESTATE MERLOT 2000, CASELLA WINES** New South Wales	Brambles and redcurrants with a lovely textured finish with good length.	**£4.00**	SWS DBY AUC WSO
Ⓖ	**PARSONS BROOK SHIRAZ MALBEC 2000, PARSONS BROOK** Southeast Australia	The full, toasty oak balances the richness of the fruit and leads into a long, warm, friendly finish.	**£4.50**	UNS MCT

(S)	**OPAL RIDGE SHIRAZ CABERNET 2000, MIRANDA WINES** Southeast Australia	Warm, powerful yet elegant fruit nose. Fabulous flavours of plump spicy fruit layered with distinct wood characteristics.	**£4.50**	HOH SAF SMF
(B)	**SACRED HILL SHIRAZ CABERNET 2000, DE BORTOLI** Southeast Australia	This deeply coloured wine has herbaceous green peppers on its framework and a palate laced with opulent fruit.	**£4.70**	GGW SGL BOR
(B)	**HARDYS STAMP OF AUSTRALIA CABERNET SAUVIGNON MERLOT 2000, BRL HARDY** Southeast Australia	Rich, fruity palate and balanced tannins on the palate and giving to a long finish.	**£4.90**	NTD HBR
(S)	**SOMERFIELD AUSTRALIAN CABERNET SAUVIGNON 1999, SOUTHCORP** Southeast Australia	Bright red colour with a fresh nose of summer red fruits. Medium bodied with a soft finish.	**£5.00**	SMF PEF WCR
(S)	**WILDLIFE MATARO SHIRAZ 1999, KINGSTON ESTATE** South Australia	Deep red colour, the nose displays complex aromas of spices, baked jammy red fruits, and hints of eucalyptus.	**£5.00**	KOM
(B)	**BANROCK STATION SHIRAZ 2000, BRL HARDY WINE COMPANY** South Australia	Subtle blueberries with vanilla overtones and a hint of mint.	**£5.00**	NTD ASD UNS
(B)	**GOSLING CREEK SHIRAZ 1999, D'AQUINO'S** New South Wales	Vanilla and chocolate dominate the underlying cloves and mandarins, which develop gradually in the mouth.	**£5.00**	CHN EHL
(B)	**JINDALEE SHIRAZ 2000, RIVERINA WINES** South Australia	Figs and plums, with an underlying suggestion of greengage fruits. Surprisingly light-bodied and accessible.	**£5.00**	UNS WTS DBY WSO
(B)	**KELLY'S PROMISE SHIRAZ 2000, ANDREW GARRETT VINEYARD ESTATES** Southeast Australia	Great colour extraction and lush ripe aromas denote a palate of spicy fruit with balanced acidity.	**£5.00**	THI
(B)	**WOOLPUNDA CABERNET SAUVIGNON 1999, THOMSON VINTNERS** South Australia	Red fruit and tobacco nose, with a blackberry palate and a touch of spice on the finish.	**£5.00**	AHW
(B)	**YELLOW TAIL SHIRAZ 2000, CASELLA WINES** New South Wales	This big, juicy Shiraz reflects its Australian climate with warm jammy fruit filling the full-bodied palate.	**£5.00**	SWS SAF

Pinpoint who sells the wine you wish to buy by turning to the stockist codes. If you know the name of the wine you want to buy, use the alphabetical index. If the price is your motivation, look out for the "Wine of the Year" symbol; the best red and white wines under £8, sparkling wines under £12, and champagne under £15. Happy hunting!

(B) **BAROSSA VALLEY GRENACHE 2000,** **PETER LEHMANN** South Australia	This garnet-coloured offering opens into an explosion of ripe red berry fruits laced with vanilla oak.	**£5.20**	UNS PLE
(S) **WINE CELLARS SHIRAZ CABERNET SAUVIGNON 2000,** **GARNET POINT VINEYARDS** Southeast Australia	Dark spice and pepper nose; big sweet fruit on the palate balanced by spirited acidity and subtle tannins.	**£5.30**	NTD ASD E&J
(S) **BLACK LABEL 2000,** **McGUIGAN WINES** Southeast Australia	Concentrated cassis nose, rounded oak, and a touch of mint. Full, rich palate with integrated tannins.	**£5.50**	VNO
(S) **SHIRAZ ANDREW PEACE 2000,** **ANDREW PEACE WINES** Victoria	The palate is rich with hints of liquorice, chocolate, and jammy red fruits, followed by a powerful finish.	**£5.50**	ASD BGL VGN
(G) **PIRRAMIMMA PETIT VERDOT 1998,** **A.C. JOHNSTON PTY LTD.** South Australia	Powerful wine with exceptional fruit concentration and extravagent oak. Beautifully integrated, yielding great finesse.	**£5.90**	PRG BBO
(G) **XANADU SECESSION SHIRAZ CABERNET 2000,** **XANADU** Western Australia	Peppery damson fruit and black cherry nose with herbal, leathery fruit. Soft, full oak and rounded tannins.	**£6.00**	ASD PLB
(S) **LITTLE BOOMEY CABERNET MERLOT 2000,** **CABONNE VINTNERS** New South Wales	Cedarwood and cigar box aromas on the nose, with sweet blackberry and morello cherry palate.	**£6.00**	D&D
(S) **LITTLE BOOMEY MERLOT 2000, CABONNE VINTNERS** New South Wales	Minty nose with ripe blackcurrant on the palate and just a hint of cinnamon. Intense finish.	**£6.00**	D&D
(S) **SIMON GILBERT CARD SERIES MUDGEE SHIRAZ 1999,** **SIMON GILBERT** New South Wales	From one of the most underrated wine areas in Australia. A late harvest allows for rich ripe fruit.	**£6.00**	POR BEA PBA AMW
(S) **W2 SHIRAZ CABERNET 2000,** **WIRRA WIRRA** Southeast Australia	Lovely mulberry and herbal Cabernet notes combine fantastically with elegant spice from the Shiraz grape.	**£6.00**	WST
(S) **WAKEFIELD ESTATE PROMISED LAND SHIRAZ CABERNET 2000, WAKEFIELD ESTATE** South Australia	Spicy and peppery on the palate with baked red fruit characters. The finish is long and complex.	**£6.00**	SWS
(S) **WIRREGA SHIRAZ 1999,** **WIRREGA VINEYARD** South Australia	Black fruits on the nose with hints of pepper and spices, well balanced and a savoury finish.	**£6.00**	VVI DBY

(G) **D'ARRY'S ORIGINAL 1999, D'ARENBERG** South Australia	Medium to full red-purple colour with sweet aromas of blueberry and cherry, together with a hint of mint.	**£6.30**	GGW PEF GRO
(S) **DEEN DE BORTOLI VAT 9 CABERNET SAUVIGNON 1999, DE BORTOLI** Southeast Australia	Youthful nose with full red berry fruit, mint, and a touch of sweetness. Firm tannins on the finish.	**£6.30**	GGW SGL BOR
(S) **HERITAGE ROAD SHIRAZ 1999, HERITAGE ROAD WINERY** South Australia	Powerful chunky black fruit and minty palate lined with complex vanilla oak underscores and a silky creamy finish.	**£6.50**	VNO
(S) **MCGUIGAN BIN 4000 2000, MCGUIGAN WINES** Southeast Australia	Blackcurrant and eucalyptus on the nose. Good acidity, balance, and silky, ripe fruit. Full-bodied with fabulous length.	**£6.50**	VNO
(G) **DEEN DE BORTOLI VAT 1 DURIF 1999, DE BORTOLI** Southeast Australia	Firm structure supported by dry tannin, biscuity oak and plenty of soft fruit character.	**£6.80**	GGW BDR SGL BOR
(G) **PENFOLDS KOONUNGA HILL SHIRAZ CABERNET 1999, SOUTHCORP WINES PTY LTD** South Australia	The Cabernet provides rich minty flavours to complement the brambly, plummy fruit of the Shiraz.	**£7.00**	POR BGN NTD UNS
(S) **COCOPARRA SHIRAZ 1998, CRANSWICK ESTATE** New South Wales	Medium bodied with rich spicy flavours and hints of vanilla oak, and a long finish.	**£7.00**	AUS CHN
(S) **PADTHAWAY CABERNET SAUVIGNON 1999, TATACHILLA** South Australia	Intense ruby colour with rich fruity aromas. Lovely deep, bramble fruits and good length.	**£7.00**	D&D WFB
(S) **SHIRAZ RESERVE ANDREW PEACE 2000, ANDREW PEACE WINES** Victoria	Intense red in colour, the nose is rich with excellent balanced fruit and oak flavours.	**£7.00**	ASD BGL TAN
(S) **TEMPLE BRUER SHIRAZ MALBEC 1998, TEMPLE BRUER** South Australia	Deep concentrated purple hue. This huge wine possesses layer upon layer of spicy blackberry fruit and toasty oak.	**£7.00**	ASD PLB
(S) **WOLF BLASS SHIRAZ 2000, WOLF BLASS WINES** South Australia	Subtle bouquet of spiced character with hints of dark chocolate and wood leading to enormous depth and richness.	**£7.00**	NTD ASD UNS
(S) **WYNDHAM ESTATE BIN 444 CABERNET SAUVIGNON 1999, ORLANDO WYNDHAM** Southeast Australia	Medium purple in colour with a fine structured palate of bramble fruits and cedar wood.	**£7.00**	NTD ASD CAX

	Wine	Description	Price	Codes
(S)	**JJ McWilliams Merlot 1998,** **McWilliams** New South Wales	Complex blackcurrant fruit on the nose with hints of vanilla oak. The finish is complex and persistent	**£7.20**	UNS CRI
(S)	**Wakefield Estate Cabernet Sauvignon 1999,** **Wakefield Estate** South Australia	Sweet fruit and vanilla essence on the nose with real depth of fruit and a complex finish.	**£7.20**	UNS SWS AUC
✓	**Voyager Estate Cabernet Sauvignon Merlot 1996,** **Voyager Estate** Western Australia	Elegant and fragrant, with an intensely fruity, plummy palate.	**£8.20**	J&B
(G)	**Blue Pyrenees Cabernet Sauvignon 1999,** **Blue Pyrenees Estate** Victoria	A minerally edge, with intense, ripe fruit and chocolate. Huge concentration and weight culminate in a powerful finish.	**£9.00**	MKV
(G)	**Jacob's Creek Limited Release Shiraz Cabernet 1995, Orlando Wyndham** Southeast Australia	Powerful, intense, and muscular, with a rich, berried spiciness and gripping tannins to finish.	**£10.00**	CAX
(G)	**Leasingham Clare Valley Bin 61 Shiraz 1998,** **BRL Hardy Wine Company** South Australia	Succulent herbal character reminiscent of tarragon and liquorice. Sweet vanilla oak, ripe fruit, and supple tannins.	**£10.00**	ASD UNS ASD HBR
(G)	**St Andrews Estate Shiraz 2000,** **Wakefield Estate** South Australia	The Shiraz fruit character of brambles and aromatic, herbal rosemary notes is wonderfully counteracted by the toasty oak.	**£10.00**	ECA
(G)	**Willows Vineyard Shiraz 1998,** **Willows Vineyard** South Australia	Ripe fruit and soft tannins, complemented by the caramel and chocolate notes from the oak.	**£10.00**	AWA NRW FQU POR
(G)	**Mount Ida Shiraz 1999,** **Beringer Blass** Victoria	Violets, cocoa, and blackcurrant flavours integrated well with balanced new oak and soft, rounded tannins.	**£11.00**	WFB
(G)	**Gapsted Durif 1998,** **Victorian Alps Wine Co** Victoria	Rich wine displaying heady plum and truffle aromas supported by grippy tannins. Excellent depth and persistence.	**£11.90**	Not available in the UK
(G)	**Penley Estate Reserve Shiraz Cabernet 1997,** **Penley Estate** South Australia	Leathery, peppery blackcurrant fruit with clean, mellow, coconut oak flavours; rich complexity with ripe tannins.	**£11.90**	L&W WTR
(B)	**Stowells of Chelsea Mataro Shiraz NV,** **Matthew Clark** Southeast Australia	Brick-red colour enhances a fruit-driven palate with aromas of medicinal eucalyptus and freshly brewed coffee.	**£12.00**	NTD ASD MCT

(G) **FAMILY RESERVE OLD VINE BAROSSA SHIRAZ 1998, MIRANDA WINES** South Australia	A well-made, beautifully structured wine with glorious, rich oak. Well integrated with ripe minty fruit.	**£12.40**	POR HOH
(G) **VASSE FELIX CABERNET SAUVIGNON 1999, VASSE FELIX** Western Australia	Packed with cassis and eucalyptus, plums and red fruit; stylish, understated oak. The fruit has a lingering finish.	**£13.60**	CPW BEN NEG
(G) **NEPENTHE PINOT NOIR 1999, NEPENTHE VINEYARDS** South Australia	Chocolate-tinged Pinot with plenty of ripe strawberry and cherry fruit. A velvety finish.	**£14.20**	CEB SWS TOS
(G) **WIRRA WIRRA THE ANGELUS CABERNET SAUVIGNON 1998, WIRRA WIRRA** South Australia	Still youthful, with big, leathery fruit. Spicy; dry, substantial tannin; a powerful, concentrated showstopper of a wine.	**£14.50**	WTS JEF GHL RAV TMW
(G) **ANNIE'S LANE COPPER TRAIL SHIRAZ 1998, BERINGER BLASS** South Australia	Toasty oak balances the concentrated, smoky, tarry black berry fruit and hefty broad tannins.	**£15.00**	WFB DBY QRW FWM
(G) **BAROSSA VALLEY ESTATES EBENEZER SHIRAZ 1998, BRL HARDY WINE COMPANY** South Australia	Deep colour and immense fruit on the nose leads into a rich concentrated palate with integrated oak.	**£15.00**	UNS HBR
(G) **COLDSTREAM HILLS RESERVE CABERNET SAUVIGNON 1998, SOUTHCORP WINES PTY LTD** Victoria	A cool-mint nose; an edge of acidity to the rich palate. A monster of a wine lurks within.	**£15.00**	PEF
(G) **HOLLICK WILGHA SHIRAZ 1998, HOLLICK** South Australia	The rich coconut, oaky nose gives way to a fresh minty palate, finishing on a silky smooth note.	**£15.00**	SCK
(G) **VASSE FELIX SHIRAZ 1999, VASSE FELIX** Western Australia	Dark, concentrated cassis with cherry, liquorice, and blackberry flavours integrating well with spicy new oak.	**£15.10**	CPW BEN NEG
(G) **GRANT BURGE THE HOLY TRINITY 1997, GRANT BURGE** South Australia	Maturity is becoming apparent as the primary fruit shows some spicy, fruitcake elements and oak integration.	**£15.40**	GGW FSA
(S) **WIRRA WIRRA RSW SHIRAZ 1998, WIRRA WIRRA** South Australia	Aromas of damson and spice. The palate is rich with ripe berry fruits and hints of black pepper.	**£15.50**	NTD WST
(G) **KNAPPSTEIN LENSWOOD VINEYARDS PINOT NOIR 1999, LENSWOOD VINEYARDS** South Australia	Powerful, ripe strawberry flavours dominate this delicate wine of exceptional finesse.	**£17.00**	BWC

(G) **REDBANK SALLYS PADDOCK 1999,** **REDBANK WINERY** Victoria	Smoky leather; dark fruit and tar aromas. Superb balance, with complex fruit and a chewy finish.	**£17.00**	NEG
(G) **TIM ADAMS THE ABERFELDY 1999,** **TIM ADAMS WINES** South Australia	Excellent harmony of brambly liquorice fruit and integrated wood followed by a long, punchy fruit finish.	**£17.00**	AWA SWS WRW BOO
(G) **YERING STATION RESERVE PINOT NOIR 2000,** **YERING STATION** Victoria	Intense, rich raspberry fruit mingles with the coffee and toast flavours from the nicely integrated oak.	**£17.50**	SCK
(G) **MERRICKS PINOT NOIR 1999,** **STONIER** Victoria	Powerful wine bursting with red fruit aromas and a long and warming finish.	**£18.00**	MZC
(G) **TARRAWARRA PINOT NOIR 1998,** **TARRAWARRA** Victoria	Well-balanced, luxurious Pinot Noir with intense, ripe red fruits, silky tannins, and great length.	**£18.00**	CRI
(G) **BROKENWOOD RAYNERS SHIRAZ 1999,** **BROKENWOOD** New South Wales	Full, rich, and ripe with minty, black pastille fruit and a very long dry finish.	**£18.50**	H&H
(G) **ELDERTON CABERNET SHIRAZ MERLOT 1997,** **ELDERTON** South Australia	The minty, eucalyptus nose with its caramel-oak undercarriage continues through to a ripe, jammy palate.	**£19.90**	POR BDR FWM
(G) **ROSEMOUNT GSM 1999,** **ROSEMOUNT** South Australia	Lovely fresh, big Shiraz with no rough edges. Shows splendid extracted colour with masses of charm.	**£19.90**	ASD ROS PEF WBR
(G) **GLAETZER MALBEC CABERNET SAUVIGNON 1996,** **GLAETZER VINEYARDS** South Australia	Inviting nose with complex chocolate, tobacco, and mint on the palate. The finish is long and compelling.	**£21.20**	GRT
(G) **STONEWELL SHIRAZ 1995,** **PETER LEHMANN** South Australia	Rich, smooth palate with intense, powerful, firm structure is surrounded by ripe, savoury, black berry and peppery fruit.	**£23.70**	BDR PLE WTS DBY
(G) **ROSEMOUNT SHOW RESERVE SHIRAZ 1998,** **ROSEMOUNT** South Australia	Menthol, herbal, black berry fruits appear within this massive structure, supported by wonderfully toned tannins.	**£25.00**	ROS CTC DBY VDV
(G) **DIAMOND VALLEY ESTATE PINOT NOIR 1999,** **DIAMOND VALLEY** Victoria	Delicious fruit intertwines with farmyard notes and a touch of chocolate, yielding a fine and complex wine.	**£25.50**	HOT

(G)	**ELDERTON COMMAND SHIRAZ 1997,** **ELDERTON** South Australia	Warm, ripe nose leads into an explosive palate with a warming background of alcohol and huge ripe fruit.	**£26.50**	POR BDR FWM
(G)	**ROSEMOUNT ORANGE VINEYARDS CABERNET SHIRAZ 1998, ROSEMOUNT** New South Wales	Big, forward, ripe black fruit of excellent concentration; generous but soft, with tannic grip to hold it together.	**£35.00**	ROS
(G)	**ROSEMOUNT ORANGE VINEYARDS SHIRAZ 1999,** **ROSEMOUNT** New South Wales	This wine is dripping with ripe jammy fruit, smoky oak, and just a lick of tar.	**£35.00**	ROS
(G)	**WYNNS MICHAEL SHIRAZ 1998,** **SOUTHCORP WINES PTY LTD** South Australia	Full-bodied with a marvellous intensity of black pastille and cherry fruit, and sweet oak layers on the finish.	**£40.00**	POR BDR PEF
(G)	**MESHACH SHIRAZ 1996,** **GRANT BURGE** South Australia	Full of blackcurrant and pepper flavours, supported with smooth mocha and vanilla notes from perfectly integrated oak.	**£42.40**	GGW UNS FSA

AUSTRALIA • SWEET

(S)	**BIMBADGEN ESTATE BOTRYTIS SEMILLON 1999,** **BIMBADGEN ESTATE** New South Wales	A pronounced botrytis nose, scented with orange zest. The palate is rich and complex with good length.	**£10.00**	HBJ

AUSTRALIA • FORTIFIED

(B)	**STANTON & KILLEEN RUTHERGLEN MUSCADELLE NV, STANTON & KILLEEN** Victoria	Pale greenish amber with mocha and mint on the nose; mango and caramelized oranges on the palate.	**£6.50**	WSG
(B)	**STANTON & KILLEEN RUTHERGLEN MUSCAT NV,** **STANTON & KILLEEN** Victoria	Rich raisin aromas, with toffee and caramel characters and impressive length.	**£6.50**	GGW UNS WSG
(B)	**CARLYLE MUSCAT NV,** **CARLYLE WINES** Victoria	An elegant, amber glassful of round, savoury fruit; there is vanilla on the waxy finish.	**£7.00**	REN
(B)	**SEPPELT DP63 SHOW MUSCAT NV,** **SOUTHCORP WINES PTY LTD** Victoria	Big, bold style, laden with toasty plum, orange peel, and toffee complexity, backed by an intense, sticky finish.	**£7.50**	PEF

(S)	**Show Liqueur Muscat NV, De Bortoli** Victoria	Tawny in colour with a tightly-coiled nose of caramel, nuts, mocha, and roast coffee beans.	**£8.00**	BOR
(G)	**Brown Brothers Liqueur Muscat NV, Brown Brothers Wines** Victoria	Lovely nutty and fruitcake-laden wine with intense nutmeg aromas, woven into a warm, spirity finish.	**£11.70**	POR CPW

AUSTRIA

Austrian wine has never totally recovered from the government wine scandal in the early 1980s. This really is a great shame because, while they could never be accused of being cheap, Austrian wines offer almost peerless consistency, and some of the finest dry and sweet white wines made in Europe today. The dessert wines from such luminaries as Alois Kracher and Willi Opitz have catapulted them deservedly into the wine superleague, while the fine, dry Rieslings from such regions as Wachau and Steiermark offer a purer, even more regal expression of the grape than all but the very best German and Alsatian examples.

AUSTRIA • WHITE

(G)	**Sauvignon Classique Walter Skoff 2000, Walter Skoff** Südsteiermark	Light and delicate with a gooseberry, citrous nose and honeyed pineapple and apple flavours. Racy acidity.	**£12.00**	Not available in the UK

AUSTRIA • SWEET

(G)	**Ruster Ausbruch 1998, Weingut Friedrich Seiler** Burgenland	A sweet, intense concentrate of marmalade and honeyed fruit; a tight-rope balance with stunning length.	**£7.50**	Not available in the UK
(G)	**Bouvier Trockenbeerenauslese 1998, Weingut Hans Gangl** Burgenland	Sweet marmalade botrytis fruit over a viscous body with a clean strip of acidity. An elegant orange-peel finish.	**£8.90**	Not available in the UK
(G)	**Scheiblhofer Traminer Trockenbeerenauslese 1998, Scheiblhofer** Neusiedlersee-Hügelland	Zippy acidity and lusciousness define this mature, rich wine with a floral nose and a honeyed palate.	**£11.60**	Not available in the UK

(G) **SAMLING 88 1999,** **HANS TSCHIDA** Neusiedlersee-Hügelland	A floral nose with elements of botrytis. Creamy texture with peaches, spice, and mangoes; a keen, dry finish.	**£14.30**	Not available in the UK
(G) **SCHILFWEIN 1999,** **HANS TSCHIDA** Neusiedlersee-Hügelland	Highly complex bouquet of honey, pineapple, and flowers. Glorious botrytis; toffee and orange peel in the mouth.	**£16.60**	Not available in the UK
(G) **FINK NEUBURGER** **TROCKENBEERENAUSLESE** **1999, FINK HERMANN** Burgenland	Deep burnt gold with a concentrated botrytis nose; masses of spicy mango fruit. Harmonious, ripe, and long.	**£21.60**	Not available in the UK
(G) **CHARDONNAY** **WELSCHRIESLING TBA NO. 7** **NOUVELLE VAGUE 1998,** **ALOIS KRACHER,** Burgenland	Clean, pure citrus peel; apple and pear sweetness kept in shape by a high balancing acidity. Luscious.	**£22.00**	NYW
(G) **EISWEIN SCHAUREBE 1999,** **WILLI OPITZ** Neusiedlersee-Hügelland	Pure honeyed pear nose; clear, rich peach flavours of amazing integrity and concentration are sharpened by refreshing acidity.	**£29.80**	T&W
(G) **TROCKENBEERENAUSLESE** **1988,** **WEINGUT HAUS MARIENBURG** Burgenland	Spices, toffee, honey, raisins, and bitter orange with botrytis overtones. Great concentration and a long, luscious finish.	**£56.30**	Not available in the UK

BULGARIA

Modern-day drinkers might be surprised to learn that the wine-making heritage of this country goes back to around 3,000 years ago, to a time when parts of the country were important wine-growing regions of Ancient Greece. The huge commercial success of "cheap and cheerful" Bulgarian wines during the mid-1980s made them a reliable household shopping item for anyone who had to buy wine on a tight budget. Disappointingly, Bulgarian wines have failed to evolve to a higher level over the last 15 years. The wines currently on offer can, however, provide acceptable, everyday drinking at supermarket prices.

BULGARIA • WHITE

✓ **SOMERFIELD COUNTRY WHITE** **2000,** **LOVICO SUHINDOL** Danube Plain	Buttery nose with fresh lemony aromas and well-balanced fruit and acidity.	**£3.00**	LUV

✓ MHV **BULGARIAN CHARDONNAY SAUVIGNON BLANC NV, VINEX PRESLAV** Eastern Region	Delicate, pleasant, nice soft fruits.	**£3.20**	MHV
✓ **KHAN KRUM CHARDONNAY 2000, VINEX PRESLAV** Eastern Region	Clean subtle nose with delicate melon and peach fruits; well-balanced acidity and medium length.	**£3.50**	LUV
Ⓑ **TUK TAM SAUVIGNON BLANC 2000, LUK VINPROM TARGOUISH** Sub-Balkan Region	Cleanly made, with citrus and light gooseberry fruits. Great on its own.	**£4.00**	NTD G2W
✓ **BLUERIDGE CHARDONNAY 2000, BLUERIDGE** Sub-Balkan Region	Tropical melons and zingy citrus.	**£4.00**	DBO
✓ **PRESLAV BARREL FERMENTED CHARDONNAY 2000, VINEX PRESLAV** Eastern Region	Refreshing grapefruit bouquet with nice peach character.	**£4.00**	LUV SAF

BULGARIA • RED

✓ **BULGARIAN MERLOT NV, LUK VINIPROM HASKOVO** Southern Region	Blackcurrants and blackberry fruits with dry finish.	**£3.40**	MHV VGN
✓ **TUK TAM BULGARIAN MERLOT 2000, LUK VINPROM HASKOVO** Sub Balkan Region	Easy drinking with juicy blackcurrants.	**£3.70**	NTD G2W
✓ **BLUERIDGE AMERICAN BARREL MERLOT 1999, DOMAINE BOYAR** Sub-Balkan Region	Sweet, mixed berry compote style.	**£4.00**	DBO
✓ **BLUERIDGE MERLOT BARRIQUE 1999, DOMAINE BOYAR** Sub-Balkan Region	Good fruit with oaky backbone.	**£4.00**	BGN DBO
✓ **DOMAINE BOYAR PREMIUM RESERVE MERLOT 1998, DOMAINE BOYAR IAMBOL** Iambol	Firm tannins and good fruit concentration.	**£4.00**	DBO
✓ **STOWELLS OF CHELSEA CABERNET SAUVIGNON 2000, MATTHEW CLARK** Lyaskovets	Soft, balanced fruit flavours.	**£4.00**	ASD MCT SAF

CHILE

An enormous diversity of wine styles are now available from this country. Chile can produce elegant, aromatic Sauvignon Blancs from Casablanca Valley and rich Australian-styled Syrahs from Maipo. This is partly due to the remarkable length of the country and the huge range of latitudes and climates that it covers. However, the wines that have forced the wine world to take notice are the world-class Bordeaux-style reds. At their best, they effortlessly blend the rich pure fruit of the New World with the supreme balance and elegance of Bordeaux itself.

CHILE • WHITE

(B)	**LES GRANDS CHAIS DE FRANCE SAUVIGNON BLANC CHARDONNAY 1999,** Central Valley	Toasty oak aromas with some spicy flavours and plenty of ripe fruit character.	**£3.00**	GCF
✓	**CASA DE CAMPO SAUVIGNON BLANC 2000, VIÑA BELLAVISTA** Central Valley	Refined nose with mineral qualities and fruity textured palate.	**£3.50**	GCF VGN
✓	**CASA T CHILEAN WHITE 2000, VIÑA SAN PEDRO** Lontue	Elegant yet focused. Shows good acidic balance with a ripe grapefruit finish.	**£3.50**	NTD
✓	**VIÑA SAN PEDRO CHILEAN SAUVIGNON BLANC 2000, VIÑA SAN PEDRO** Curicó	Harmonious and herbaceous fruit characters with good acidic backbone. Great for the BBQ.	**£3.50**	ASD
✓	**SAN ANDRES CHILEAN VINO BLANCO, VICAR SA** Central Valley	Gentle aromas of tropical fruit and ripe melon. Tight palate with good follow-through.	**£3.60**	MHV
✓	**CO-OP LONG SLIM CHARDONNAY-SEMILLON 2000, R&R WINES** Curicó	Honey and melon aromas infused with sweet toasty oak. Well-textured palate with a strong finish.	**£3.80**	CWS MAD VGN
✓	**LOS CAMACHOS SAUVIGNON BLANC 2000, VSP LONTUÉ** Central Valley	Striking asparagus nose with balanced acidity. Harmonious and long fruit concentration finish.	**£3.80**	WRT
✓	**CANEPA SEMILLON 2000, VIÑA CANEPA** Rapel	Pungent aromas of asparagus and cut grass. Tight yet yielding on the finish.	**£4.00**	WTS UNS THI

✓	**CASA TECOPILLA CHARDONNAY 2000, VIÑA SAN PEDRO** Lontue	Elegant hints of vanilla pods and pineapple in this ripe and well-balanced Chardonnay.	**£4.00**	NTD
✓	**SAINSBURY'S CHILEAN SAUVIGNON BLANC 2001, VIÑA SAN PEDRO** Curicó	Subtle, flinty, lime aromas with an essence of ripe fruit and a round but crisp palate.	**£4.00**	JSM
✓	**SOMERFIELD CHILEAN SEMILLON CHARDONNAY 2000, MORNADE** Central Valley	Soft melon fruit with an acidic backbone and broad finish.	**£4.00**	SMF
Ⓑ	**VIÑA SAN PEDRO 35 SOUTH CHARDONNAY 2000, VIÑA SAN PEDRO** Curicó	Rich, round, and beautifully made. Opulent, creamy flavours are balanced by a crisp, lively acidity.	**£4.80**	BUC
Ⓖ	**PALO ALTO CHARDONNAY 2000, AGUIRRE** Pisco	Tropical fruits and aromatics with hints of oak. Steely, powerful structure. Sensual and round with a singing finish.	**£5.00**	HOH WTS FEN
Ⓑ	**ISLA NEGRA CHARDONNAY 2000, VINA CONO SUR SA** Rapel	Tropical, melon-tinged fruit, with creamy, well-balanced oak flavours.	**£5.00**	WST
Ⓑ	**LA PALMERIA CHARDONNAY 2000, VIÑA LA ROSA** Rapel	Soft, warm, lime fruit flavours with hints of orange and a gently creamy tail.	**£5.00**	UNS HWL
Ⓑ	**PORTA CHARDONNAY 1999, CORPORA** Central Valley	Well-made wine showing ripe, tropical fruit aromas and a clean mineral tang.	**£5.00**	SEA BDR
Ⓑ	**PORTA CHARDONNAY 2000, CORPORA** Central Valley	Full-bodied and ripe wine showing good fruit depth and balance.	**£5.00**	SEA
Ⓢ	**VILLARD ESTATE CHARDONNAY EXPRESIÓN 1999, VILLARD FINE WINES** Casablanca	Sweet pineapple and baked biscuit aromas precede a clean, fresh, and ripe fruit palate.	**£7.00**	CPR

CHILE • RED

Ⓑ	**CASA ALVARES CHILEAN CABERNET SAUVIGNON NV, LOURDES SA** Central Valley	Rounded, blackcurrant bouquet with hints of vanilla oak and a soft finish.	**£3.00**	GDF JCP VGN

✓	**Co-Op Long Slim Cabernet-Merlot 2000,** Curicó	Cassis nose with concentrated length and slightly confected fruit on the palate.	**£3.80**	CWS
Ⓑ	**U. Founders Collection Cab. Sauvignon 1997, Undurraga** Chile	Easy-drinking, juicy wine with well-balanced tannins and good length.	**£4.00**	PLB
✓	**Asda Chilean Merlot 2000, Viña Cono Sur SA** Central Valley	Lightly vegetal nose with some interesting complexity. Showing a bright fruity finish.	**£4.00**	ASD
✓	**Casa Tecopilla Cabernet Sauvignon 2000, Viña San Pedro** Lontue	Easy drinking, good claret style, with nuances of oak and a restrained but chewy finish.	**£4.00**	NTD
✓	**Casa Tecopilla Merlot 2000, Viña San Pedro** Lontue	Pleasant soft fruits, easy drinking with a warm alcoholic finish that persists.	**£4.00**	NTD
✓	**Co-Op Chilean Cabernet Sauvignon 2000, Viña San Pedro** Curicó	Soft, fruity, well-balanced wine showing spicy tones on the nose and a light yet persistent finish.	**£4.00**	CWS
✓	**Co-Op Chilean Old Vines Carignan 1999, Viña Segu** Curicó	Perfumed nose with chocolatey brambly fruits and toothsome tannins.	**£4.00**	CWS
✓	**Gato Negro Cabernet Sauvignon 2000, Viña San Pedro** Curicó	Easy drinking, soft and fruity, with a plump finish showing chocolatey flavours.	**£4.00**	BUC
✓	**MHV San Andres Chilean Cabernet Sauvignon 2000, Viña Carta Vieja** Central Valley	Solid fruit with oaky backbone and warm drying finish.	**£4.00**	MHV
✓	**Safeway Chilean Cabernet Merlot 2000, Viña Cono Sur SA** Central Valley	Full, herbally scented red with soft dense red fruit flavours and clean finish.	**£4.00**	SAF
✓	**Sainsbury's Chilean Cabernet Sauvignon 2000, Viña La Rosa** Rapel	Earthy, mushroomy nose with blackcurrant palate and a good finish.	**£4.00**	JSM
✓	**San Andres Chilean Merlot 2000, Viña Carta Vieja** Maule	Plummy palate showing good texture with good length and subtle finish.	**£4.00**	MHV

✓	**SCORPIUS SYRAH 2000,** **VIÑA SIEGEL** Rapel	Plums and damsons on the nose, giving an nice easy drinking wine with a spicy finish.	**£4.00** THW
(B)	**CARTA VIEJA CABERNET SAUVIGNON 2000,** **CARTA VIEJA** Maule	Cassis-driven aromas give way to a wonderful purity of fruit. A soft, pure wine.	**£4.20** WBU VGN
(G)	**TERRANOBLE RESERVA CARMENÉRE 2000,** **VIÑEDOS TERRANOBLE S.A.** Maule	Mouthfilling wine with a dense savoury nose, concentrated fruit, and ripe tannic structure.	**£4.20** Not available in the UK
(S)	**SANTA CAROLINA ANTARES MERLOT 2000,** **VIÑA SANTA CAROLINA SA** Maule	Deep crimson-red colour. A medley of ripe fruits on the nose and palate, with firm tannins.	**£4.50** PFC
(S)	**TIERRA ARENA CABERNET SAUVIGNON 2000,** **AGUIRRE** Pisco	Dense, rich, fruity nose with lots of spice. Very well balanced with a soft velvety finish.	**£4.50** HOH
(B)	**LOS TORUNOS CABERNET SAUVIGNON 1999,** **LA RONCIERE** Rapel	Big bouquet of deep ripe blackberry fruit on the palate, with a fresh, creamy finish.	**£4.50** HAE
(B)	**SOUTHERN STAR CHILEAN MERLOT 2000,** **KINGSLAND WINES** Rapel	Tobacco aromas with a creamy, fruity palate, firm tannins, and a juicy finish.	**£4.50** KWS
(B)	**VIÑA MORANDE MERLOT 2000,** **VIÑA MORANDE** Central Valley	A deep purple colour and masses of full, ripe fruit on the palate. A clean finish.	**£4.50** SAF
(B)	**VIÑA MORANDE SYRAH 2000,** **VIÑA MORANDE** Central Valley	Earthy and spicy characters with a deep red colour. The finish is long and peppery.	**£4.50** SAF CWA VIL
(S)	**TERRA NOBLE CABERNET SAUVIGNON 2000,** **TERRA NOBLE** Maule	Deep colour with an intensely fruity nose. Well balanced with good integration of vanilla oak.	**£4.60** MCT
(S)	**LA PALMERIA MERLOT 2000,** **VIÑA LA ROSA** Rapel	Dark ruby with sour cherry aromas on the nose. Soft, fruit-driven style with soft tannins.	**£4.70** HWL
(B)	**VIÑA SAN PEDRO 35 SOUTH MERLOT 2000,** **VIÑA SAN PEDRO** Curicó	Big on aroma with clean, sweet fruit on the palate and bags of oaky tannin to finish.	**£4.80** NTD BUC NRW

(B)	**ANDES PEAKS CABERNET SAUVIGNON 2000, SANTA EMILIANA** Rapel	A beautiful balance of ripe creamy fruit and rich new oak with a clean mineral edge.	**£4.90**	POR CPR
(B)	**ANDES PEAKS MERLOT 2000, SANTA EMILIANA** Rapel	Good, fresh, red fruits on the nose. Fruity, peppery, spicy palate, with medium length and good balance.	**£4.70**	POR CPR
(G)	**ISLA NEGRA CABERNET SAUVIGNON 2000, VIÑA CONO SUR SA** Rapel	Some green pepper complexity and savoury secondary characters. A fruit-dominated powerhouse with warm alcohol.	**£5.00**	WST
(S)	**CASILLERO DEL DIABLO CABERNET SAUVIGNON 2000, CONCHA Y TORO** Maipo	An inviting blueberry nose with a whiff of ice cream vanilla. Lovely length developing into complex finish.	**£5.00**	CYT NYW CTC
(S)	**MORANDÉ PIONERO MERLOT 2000, VIÑA MORANDE** Central Valley	Full-bodied, oaky wine with a perfumed nose, balanced acidity, and good tannins. A great food wine.	**£5.00**	THI
(S)	**TERRA ANDINA CABERNET SAUVIGNON 2000, TERRA ANDINA** Central Valley	Fresh berry fruits on the nose. A ripe palate with real freshness and balance on the finish.	**£5.00**	BGN CAX
(S)	**TERRA ANDINA MERLOT 2000, TERRA ANDINA** Central Valley	Clean fruity nose with lots of plum and spice on the palate and a elegant fruity finish.	**£5.00**	CAX ECA BGN CNL
(S)	**TERRAMATER CABERNET SAUVIGNON 2000, TERRAMATER** Maipo	Dark core with a lovely ripe, dark berry nose. Firm tannins on a good fruity palate.	**£5.00**	ASD ASD BGL
(S)	**VIÑA ALAMOSA CABERNET SAUVIGNON 2000, VIÑA DE LAROSA** Central Valley	Inky black colour with a huge amount of ripe fruit flavours, spicy tannins, and a complex finish.	**£5.00**	GRT
(B)	**ANTU MAPU CARMENERE 2000, LOMAS DE CAUQUENES** Maule	A great example of the juicy Chilean Carmenere grape, producing a deliciously soft, textured wine.	**£5.00**	G2W
(B)	**CALIBORO CARIGNAN RESERVA 2000, VIÑA SEGU** Maule	This huge wine has ripe, juicy fruits wrapped in good tannin and acidity. Powerful and extremely flamboyant.	**£5.00**	HWL
(B)	**CASILLERO DEL DIABLO MERLOT 2000, CONCHA Y TORO** Rapel	Full, juicy wine with cassis, mint, oodles of fruit, and a long jammy finish.	**£5.00**	CYT MHV

(B) CONDE DE ACONCAGUA MERLOT 1998, BODEGAS CONDE DE ACONCAGUA SA Central Valley	Oaky nose with a slightly confected fruit palate. Well balanced and good length.	**£5.00**	FDB
(B) CONO SUR PINOT NOIR 2000, VIÑA CONO SUR SA Rapel	Forward fruits on the nose lead to a silky palate of mouth-watering ripe strawberries; long, seductive finish.	**£5.00**	ASD UNS WST
(B) ISLA NEGRA SYRAH 2000, VIÑA CONO SUR SA Rapel	Attractive oaky aromas on the nose with a bramble-packed palate of fruit and long-lasting tannins.	**£5.00**	WST GYW
(B) PALMERAS ESTATE OAK AGED MERLOT 1999, SANTA EMILIANA Maipo	Almost black intensity; ripe fruits and minty overtones with nice integrated tannins.	**£5.00**	CPR D&D CAM VIL
(B) PALO ALTO MERLOT 2000, AGUIRRE Pisco	Very intense fruit on nose and palate, with green pepper and coconut oak giving sweetness on the finish.	**£5.00**	HOH L&T SAF
(B) TERRAMATER CABERNET CARMENERE 2000, TERRAMATER Maipo	The light, juicy fruit style has notes of red berries rounded out with a soft, velvety finish.	**£5.00**	ASD BGL
(B) TERRAMATER MALBEC 2000, TERRAMATER Curicó	Inky black, with a very attractive herbaceous nose and warm ripe black fruit on the palate.	**£5.00**	BGL
(B) TERRAMATER ZINFANDEL SHIRAZ 2000, TERRAMATER Maipo	Sweet cassis fruits and mulberries fuse with earthy notes. Chewy tannins complete this well-rounded wine.	**£5.00**	BGN ASD BGL
(B) TESCO FINEST CHILEAN CABERNET SAUVIGNON RESERVE 2000, VALDIVIESO Central Valley	Black cherry, chocolate, and blackcurrant aromas, with good balance and a rounded finish.	**£5.00**	TOS
(B) TESCO FINEST CHILEAN MERLOT RESERVE 2000, VALDIVIESO Central Valley	Heady blackcurrant bouquet, minty flavours, and a long finish.	**£5.00**	TOS
(S) CABERNET SAUVIGNON TERRA VEGA 1999, LUIS FELIPE EDWARDS Rapel	Rich cassis and tobacco on the nose. Ripe blackcurrant fruit on the palate and a complex finish.	**£5.50**	MWW
(S) CARMEN MERLOT 2000, VIÑA CARMEN Central Valley	Full-bodied, slightly herbaceous and minty style. Good structure and length.	**£5.80**	SGL

(S)	**SANTA CAROLINA RESERVADO CABERNET 1999,** **SANTA CAROLINA** Central Valley	Deep plum colour. Strawberry fruit on the nose and a distinctive, oak backbone. Lovely finish.	**£5.80**	PFC
(S)	**SANTA CAROLINA RESERVADO MERLOT 1998,** **VIÑA SANTA CAROLINA SA** Central Valley	Soft, ripe fruits with supple tannins on the palate and good length. A delightful wine.	**£5.80**	PFC
(S)	**MERLOT 2000 DE GRAS,** **MONT GRAS** Rapel	Rich, warm, plummy fruits on the nose. A lovely, firm structure holds together a dark, fruity core.	**£6.00**	ENO
(G)	**SANTA INES LEGADO DE ARMIDA CABERNET SAUVIGNON RESERVA 1999,** **SANTA INES,** Maipo	A tarry, cedary mass of intense cassis evolves beautifully with spicy notes. Profound; superb balance and length.	**£6.00**	IWS
(S)	**BARREL SELECTION CABERNET SAUVIGNON 1999,** **VALDIVIESO** Central Valley	Deep purple with a fruity nose and spicy palate. Medium length and good depth.	**£6.00**	GGW BWL
(S)	**CASABLANCA CABERNET SAUVIGNON 1999,** **VIÑA CASABLANCA** Rapel	Summer fruits and lovely red berries on the nose. Lovely oaky tannins lead to a balanced finish.	**£6.50**	POR MOR
(S)	**LA PALMERIA MERLOT RESERVE 2000,** **VIÑA LA ROSA** Rapel	Lovely fruit and smoky nose, with loads of soft, dark fruits, and an intensely chewy finish.	**£6.00**	HWL
(S)	**LAS CASAS DEL TOQUI CABERNET SAUVIGNON 2000,** **LAS CASAS DEL TOQUI** Cachapoal	Green pepper and blackcurrant on the nose. The palate is rich in cassis, mint, and coffee.	**£6.00**	CPR CVR TPE
(S)	**MORANDÉ TERRARUM MERLOT 1999,** **VIÑA MORANDÉ SA** Maipo	Ripe, bramble fruit on the nose with a wonderful fruity palate and soft tannins. Excellent finish.	**£6.00**	UNS THI
(S)	**TARAPACÁ RESERVA SYRAH 2000,** **TARAPACÁ** Maipo	Full of juicy fruit, with warm, plum-pudding flavours on the palate. Round body with spicy undertones.	**£6.00**	EHL
(S)	**TERRAMATER RESERVA MERLOT 2000,** **TERRAMATER** Maule	Sweet, vanilla oak and rhubarb on the nose. Full-palate spice and bramble fruits, and a sour finish.	**£6.00**	BGL
(S)	**TRIO CABERNET SAUVIGNON 1999,** **CONCHA Y TORO** Maipo	Warm red fruit with a touch of leafy character. Rich, ripe palate with an open, plummy finish.	**£6.00**	CYT CTC

Ⓢ **ERRAZURIZ CABERNET SAUVIGNON 1999,** **ERRAZURIZ** Aconcagua	Dark youthful colour with a lovely warm nose. A huge, dense palate of chocolate and cassis. Fantastic finish.	**£6.50**	HMA SKW WTS CTC
Ⓢ **LAS LOMAS MERLOT 1999,** **LOMAS DE CAUQUENES** Maule	Soft, ripe, cherry fruit on the nose, with a touch of green pepper on the palate.	**£6.50**	G2W
Ⓢ **VIÑA ALAMOSA CABERNET SAUVIGNON RESERVE 1999,** **VIÑA DE LAROSA** Central Valley	Intensely fruity nose with cedar and cigar box on the palate. Shows good length and elegance.	**£6.50**	GRT
Ⓢ **CASABLANCA MERLOT 1999,** **VIÑA CASABLANCA** Aconcagua	Deep colour with intense plummy fruits and ripe oak on the palate. Soft tannins and good length.	**£7.00**	POR MOR BLS ASH
Ⓢ **CONO SUR MERLOT RESERVE 2000,** **VIÑA CONO SUR SA** Rapel	Vibrant, dark ruby colour, intense, rich-fruit flavours, with well-balanced tannins and a long length. Consistent quality.	**£7.00**	UNS WST
Ⓢ **CONO SUR PINOT NOIR RESERVE 1999,** **VIÑA CONO SUR SA** Rapel	Medium-bodied with well-structured tannins that complement the gentle acidity of this well-rounded wine.	**£7.00**	UNS WST
Ⓢ **PRIVATE RESERVE CABERNET SAUVIGNON 1998,** **VIÑA CANEPA** Curicó	Jammy, cassis fruits with a lingering intensity. Firm tannins, well-structured, with integrated oak and good length.	**£7.00**	UNS THI WCR VGN
Ⓢ **RESERVE CABERNET SAUVIGNON 1999,** **VALDIVIESO** Central Valley	Intense plummy fruit, soft and well-rounded. Light tannins, good balance, and a long finish.	**£7.40**	GGW BWL
Ⓢ **RESERVE PINOT NOIR 1999,** **VALDIVIESO** Central Valley	Medium-bodied, with vanilla-oak undertones complementing the well-balanced acidity and light tannins. Lingering finish.	**£7.40**	GGW BWL
Ⓢ **VERAMONTE MERLOT 1999,** **VERAMONTE VINYARDS** Maipo	Intense blackcurrant fruit, a smoky style, and youthful tannins. Coffee- and chocolate-oak flavours, with roundness.	**£7.50**	GGW SKW
Ⓢ **MARQUES DE CASA CONCHA MERLOT 1999,** **CONCHA Y TORO** Rapel	Ripe blackberry and rich plummy fruits on both the nose and the palate, with a hint of savoury.	**£7.50**	CYT
Ⓖ **LUIS FELIPE EDWARDS C S DOÑA BERNARDA 1999,** **LUIS FELIPE EDWARDS** Rapel	Huge, fat, super-ripe fruit expertly integrated with caramel, coconut oak. Plenty of tannins and complex fruit character.	**£13.00**	D&D

FRANCE

Like it or loathe it, more fine wine is made in France, than in any other country in the world. Demand is such that the best wines fetch almost incomprehensible prices. The balance of power is slowly shifting, however, which is evident in the top prices paid for Californian, Australian, and even Chilean wines. What French wines have over the young pretenders are centuries of evolution in a gastronomic heritage that makes them faultless when matched with classic cuisine. Also, when Bordeaux, Burgundy, or Champagne is good, it is still peerless.

FRANCE • SPARKLING

✓ **MHV Christian Saccard Blanc De Blancs Vin Mousseux Brut NV,** C.F.G.V., Loire	A clean, crisp nose with dry, well-rounded fruit and a dry finish.	**£4.40**	MHV
Ⓑ **Pierre Larousse Blanc de Blancs Brut NV, Wissembourg** Alsace	Nice mousse, bright in appearance with hints of melon and peach. Lively yet balanced acidity.	**£5.00**	THI
✓ **Sparkling Saumur Brut NV, C.F.G.V.** Loire	Light and lemony, with a delicate bouquet and well-judged dosage.	**£6.50**	MHV HVW
Ⓑ **Sparkling Vouvray Cuvée Hélène Dorléans 1997, Frederic Bourillon** Loire	Elegant nose of toasty bread and honey. The palate is rich with complexity and structure.	**£7.00**	THI
Ⓑ **Cuvée Flamme NV, Gratien & Meyer** Loire	Gentle mousse with a touch of honey and lemon. The wine is complex with a good length.	**£9.00**	VIC ODD
Ⓖ **Pannier Brut Selection NV, Champagne Pannier** Champagne	Elegant, with a rich, aged character, and ripe, zingy fruit finishing in a yeasty complexity.	**£11.90**	Not available in the U.K.
Ⓢ **Safeway Albert Etienne Brut NV, Marne et Champagne Diffus,** Champagne	Burnt-caramel aromas blend seductively with elegant fruit flavours, leading to a dry, crisp finish.	**£14.00**	SAF
Ⓢ **Davy's Célébration Champagne NV, Gardet** Champagne	Lively mousse with a pale gold colour, toasty and buttery hints with an attractive fruit finish.	**£14.50**	DVY

	Wine	Tasting Notes	Price	Stockists
(S)	**JEAN MOUTARDIER BRUT SELECTION NV,** **DOMAINE JEAN MOUTARDIER** Champagne	Yeasty and toasty nose combined with lemon and apple flavours. Lively but well-balanced acidity on the finish.	**£15.00**	GRT WRT BFD FEN
(G)	**HEIDSIECK MONOPOLE & CO EXTRA DRY NV,** **HEIDSIECK MONOPOLE & CO** Champagne	A very attractive, big-bodied, biscuity style of champagne with yeasty notes and a good lining of fruit.	**£18.00**	SEA
(G)	**CHAMPAGNE H BLIN ET CIE 1995,** **H BLIN ET CIE** Champagne	Biscuity yeast-driven wine has the freshness of lemon sherbet and melon and citrus fruit.	**£19.00**	JBF
(G)	**FLEUR DE CHAMPAGNE ROSE DE SAIGNEE NV,** **CHAMPAGNE DUVAL-LEROY** Champagne	A rich, full-flavoured style of Rose Champagne with toasty, bready notes, fresh-fruit flavours and solid length.	**£20.20**	DUL VGN
(G)	**BEAUMONT DES CRAYÈRES FLEUR DE PRESTIGE 1995,** Champagne	Attractive flavours of citrus and green apple with hints of biscuit. Refreshing, delightful finish with a long length.	**£21.50**	HOH JAR
(G)	**FLEUR DE CHAMPAGNE VINTAGE 1995,** **CHAMPAGNE DUVAL-LEROY** Champagne	Forward, big fruit and intense biscuit flavours explode on the palate with a forthright mousse.	**£23.40**	DUL SMF
(G)	**CHAMPAGNE JACQUART VINTAGE BRUT MOSAIQUE 1992, CHAMPAGNE JACQUART** Champagne	Pale, golden hue and rounded creamy style, indicates good bottle age and gives it a level of complexity.	**£24.00**	PAT
(G)	**CHAMPAGNE JOSEPH PERRIER CUVÉE ROYALE VINTAGE 1995,** **CHAMPAGNE JOSEPH PERRIER** Champagne	Complex aromas of burnt caramel vie with hints of vanilla and creamy ripe fruits for attention.	**£23.80**	SGL CHN
(G)	**R DE RUINART VINTAGE CHAMPAGNE 1995,** **RUINART** Champagne	Powerful and intense on the nose, showing the depth and balance of an aged wine.	**£29.00**	RUK HBJ
(G)	**GRAND ROSE NV,** **CHAMPAGNE GOSSET** Champagne	Perfumed nose, stylish fruit structure, and fine mousse. Quintessential Champagne with complexity and firmness.	**£33.00**	MKV THS
(G)	**MOËT AND CHANDON BRUT IMPÉRIAL VINTAGE LD 1992,** **MOËT AND CHANDON** Champagne	Rich, bready, yeast flavours are balanced beautifully with ripe fruit against a firm middle palate.	**£32.00**	WTS GGW MHU
(G)	**VEUVE CLICQUOT ROSÉ RESERVE 1995, VEUVE CLICQUOT PONSARDIN** Champagne	An elegant, soft, creamy style, attractive with a delicate nose of strawberries and raspberries for a summery wine.	**£39.00**	UNS PRG

(G)	**BLANC DE CHARDONNAY 1993,** **POL ROGER** Champagne	Honeyed, nutty development on the nose with a weighty, tropical palate reminiscent of lemon rind.	**£44.20**	BEN POL
(G)	**RESERVE CHARLIE MIS EN CAVE 1990,** **CHAMPAGNE P&C HEIDSIECK** Champagne	Aromas dominated by Pinot Noir fruit, with underlying bready, yeasty flavours and a broad, firm, tannic structure.	**£50.00**	MAX
(G)	**POMMERY LOUISE BLANC 1989,** **POMMERY** Champagne	Delicate and elegant, with a fine mousse. Excellent mouthfeel of creamy caramel and biscuits; a long, complex finish.	**£55.00**	PFC
(G)	**CUVÉE WILLIAM DEUTZ 1995,** **CHAMPAGNE DEUTZ** Champagne	Hints of roses and strawberries give way to elegant smooth richness of good depth and complexity.	**£60.00**	BWC
(G)	**DOM RUINART BLANC DE BLANCS 1993,** **RUINART** Champagne	Honeyed fruit with crisp acidity makes this refreshing to drink and provides a backbone for further cellaring.	**£60.00**	RUK
(G)	**DOM PÉRIGNON 1993,** **MOËT & CHANDON** Champagne	A zingy, grassy, clean Champagne with a sound structure and pleasant fruit-flavour with yeasty undertones.	**£66.70**	POR CPW SGL ASD
(G)	**CHAMPAGNE CHARLIE 1985,** **CHAMPAGNES P&C HEIDSIECK** Champagne	Complex, toasty, biscuity honeyed flavours which are beautifully complimented with fine bubbles and crisp acidity.	**£76.00**	MAX
(G)	**CUVÉE SIR WINSTON CHURCHILL 1993,** **POL ROGER** Champagne	A yeasty, biscuity, bready style of wine, backed up with weighty fruit offering great complexity and depth.	**£70.70**	POR POL DBY FQU
(G)	**TAITTINGER COMTES DE CHAMPAGNE BLANC DE BLANC BRUT 1995,** **TAITTINGER,** Champagne	This is a big-style Champagne with a just off-dry flavour and layers of flavour from savoury to honey.	**£77.90**	SGL HMA
(G)	**TAITTINGER COMTES DE CHAMPAGNE ROSE BRUT 1995,** **TAITTINGER** Champagne	Appley acidity combines with ripe, ultra-pure fruit and a broad structure underlying a soft, elegant mousse.	**£80.00**	HMA
(G)	**CHARLES HEIDSIECK BLANC DE BLANCS OENOTHEQUE 1982,** **DANIEL THIBAULT** Champagne	Stunning. Nuts and orange peel with indescribably complex fruit. Perfectly mature with incredible power and finesse.	**£89.00**	WTS
(G)	**DOM PÉRIGNON ROSÉ 1990,** **MOËT & CHANDON** Champagne	The nose offers rich, ripe bread and butter aromas, followed by attractive summer fruits on the palate.	**£165**	UNS MHU

FRANCE • WHITE

(B)	**Château De La Colline Blanc 2000,** Château De La Colline South West	Pleasant, green-apple nose with well-balanced acidity and a fresh, crisp finish.	**£2.10**	H
✓	**Touraine Sauvignon Ackerman Laurance 2000,** Ackerman Laurance Loire	Refined gooseberry and citrus flavours with simple but crisp, balanced fruit	**£2.50**	IWS SAF
(B)	**Calista De La Colline 1998,** Château De La Colline South West	Gentle touches of cinnamon on the nose; light, toasty, buttery flavours; and well-balanced fruit finish.	**£2.50**	HBV
✓	**Cave de Masse Sweet White NV,** Cave de Masse South West	Rich honeysuckle laced with grapefruit aromas.	**£2.90**	MCT FWM BBR
✓	**Baron d'Arignac Sweet 1999, Les Grands Chais de France** South West	Sweet citrus and peach fruit balanced by good acidity.	**£3.00**	GCF
✓	**Blason De Maucaillou 2000,** Dourthe Bordeaux	Fragrant, green-apple fruit with some creaminess, and ripe fruit flavours on the palate.	**£3.00**	THA
✓	**Safeway Vin de Pays de l'Ardeche Medium Dry 2000, Uvica** Rhône	Broad pear and baked-apple fruit flavours with an off-dry palate.	**£3.00**	SAF
✓	**Safeway Vin de Pays de Vaucluse 2000,** Vignobles du Peloux Vaucluse	Soft, apple-fool fruit flavours, with surprising body, and a clean, fresh, unoaked finish.	**£3.00**	SAF
✓	**Sainsbury's Chardonnay Vin de Pays d'Oc 2000,** Promocom Vin De Pays	Round and creamy, with a delicate bouquet of peach and melon.	**£3.00**	JSM
✓	**Grenache Blanc Vin de Pays d'Oc 1999,** Fancalieu Languedoc-Roussillon	Delicate, pear-drenched drink, with a rounded, soft finish	**£3.10**	MCT
✓	**Henri Vallon Muscadet Sevre et Maine 2000,** Jean Beauquin Loire	Tongue-tingling; fruit overlain with delicate perfume.	**£3.20**	WRT SAF

✓	**RENARDS HILL COLOMBARD SAUVIGNON 2000,** **LES CAVES DE LANDIRAS** Languedoc-Roussillon	Fresh greengage and lime-fruit aromas with a clean, crisp finish.	**£3.30**	GCF
✓	**MHV MUSCADET AC 2000,** **DOMINIQUE BAUD** Loire	Young delicate Cox's apple fruit with light body and a thirst-quenching freshness.	**£3.40**	MHV
Ⓑ	**SAINSBURY'S MUSCAT DE ST JEAN DE MINERVOIS NV, CAVE DE ST JEAN DE MINERVOIS** Languedoc-Roussillon	Gentle floral notes to the aromatic nose. Luscious, grapey palate with a fresh yet warming quality.	**£3.50**	JSM
✓	**MEDITERRANEAN WHITE 2000,** **CHATEAU L'ERMITAGE** Languedoc-Roussillon	Soft, gluggable pear and peach fruit with a soft palate.	**£3.50**	FEE
✓	**VIN DE PAYS DES COTEAUX DE L'ARDÉCHE 2000, LES VIGNERONS ARDECHOIS** Languedoc-Roussillon	Attractive, baked-apple fruit notes with lingering, minerally palate.	**£3.50**	SMF
✓	**FORTANT DE FRANCE CHARDONNAY BLANC 2001,** **FORTANT DE FRANCE** Vin de Pays	Light melon and citrus aroma, with soft, luscious, fruit flavours and a touch of toasty oak.	**£3.60**	MCT
✓	**FORTANT DE FRANCE SAUVIGNON BLANC 2000,** **FORTANT DE FRANCE** Vin de Pays	Remarkably broad greengage and elderflower fruit with a touch of honey. Adequate acidity holds the palate together.	**£3.60**	MCT
Ⓑ	**SOMERFIELD MUSCADET 2000,** **JEAN BEAUQUIN** Loire	Well-defined, crisp, and clean fruit, with a lively finish.	**£3.60**	SMF
✓	**BORDENEUVE VINS DE PAYS CÔTES DE GASCOGNE 2000,** **BORDENEUVE** Languedoc-Roussillon	Green apple and citrus aromas with a cleansing, refreshing crispness on the palate.	**£3.60**	SMF
✓	**LA CAMPAGNE MARSANNE CHARDONNAY 2001,** **LA CAMPAGNE** Languedoc-Roussillon	Subtle, tropical-fruit nose with a hint of ripe peach, good weight, and an elegant finish.	**£3.70**	MCT
✓	**SAUVIGNON BLANC LA CAMPAGNE 2000,** **ALAIN CIRIGNAN** Vin De Pays	Reliable, good, sturdy character, with fresh cut-grass and subtle tropical fruit.	**£3.70**	MCT
✓	**BERRYS' HOUSE WHITE,** **JEAN-LUC TERRIER** France	Pale gold colour, with a light lemon and buttery nose, and balanced acidity with soft citrus characters.	**£4.00**	BBR

✓	**MUSCADET DE SEVRE ET MAINE SUR LIE, CHATEAU DE LA MALONNIÉRE** Loire	Gently perfumed fruit and textured palate with finesse.	**£4.00**	MCT
Ⓢ	**BORDEAUX SAUVIGNON CALVET 2000, CALVET** Bordeaux	Pleasant nose with herbaceous hints, followed by a crisp palate packed with green and citrus fruits.	**£4.00**	WTS GYW SAF
Ⓑ	**ASDA TRAMONTANE SAUVIGNON BLANC 2000, FONCALIEU** Vin De Pays	Fresh, lively gooseberry on a dry, minerally palate. A good match for white fish.	**£4.00**	ASD
Ⓑ	**DONJON DE LA TOUR WHITE NV, DEVEREUX** Languedoc-Roussillon	Aromatic, with fresh hints of peach and pear on a vibrant palate.	**£4.00**	ADE
Ⓑ	**FONCALIEU LA CITÉ CHARDONNAY 2000, FONCALIEU** Languedoc-Roussillon	Soft apricot on the nose, with delicate aromas of melon and peach. Well-balanced, with fresh acidity.	**£4.00**	WTS
Ⓑ	**KIWI CUVEE CHARDONNAY VIN DE PAYS DU JARDIN 2000, LACHETEAU** Loire	Surprisingly rich, aromatic approach, with tropical-fruit flavours on an evenly balanced palate.	**£4.00**	BGN WST
Ⓑ	**LES TERRASSES D'AZUR CHARDONNAY VIN DE PAYS D'OC 2000, CASTEL FRÉRES** Languedoc-Roussillon	Well-integrated nose, with delicate aromas of white fruits and peaches, is well-supported by a crisp finish.	**£4.00**	L&T
Ⓑ	**MAUREGARD BORDEAUX BLANC YVON MAU 2000, YVON MAU** Bordeaux	Light and cleanly presented, with a subtly herbaceous character.	**£4.00**	UNS YVM
✓	**CHARDONNAY FRÉDÉRIC ROGER VDP 2000, FRÉDÉRIC ROGER SDVA** Languedoc-Roussillon	Bright colour with light almond aromas, a touch of mineral, and good length.	**£4.00**	BGL
✓	**CHARDONNAY VINS DE PAYS JARDIN DE LA FRANCE 2000, DOMAINE BAUD** Loire	Subtle, fresh lime-fruit aromas with a citrus palate	**£4.00**	SMF JCP
✓	**DESTINÉA SAUVIGNON BLANC JOSEPH MELLOT 1999, JOSEPH MELLOT** Loire	Fresh, zesty cut-grass and minerals, yet with earthy undertones.	**£4.00**	MCT
✓	**FRENCH CONNECTION CIRENACHE SAUVIGNON BLANC VDP 2000,** Rhône	Svelte and stylish with good length.	**£4.00**	BGN BGL SAF

✓	**GRENACHE VIOGNIER LES PORTES DE MEDITERRANÉE 2000, CAVES SAINT PIERRE** Rhône	Heady alcoholic number with perfume overtones showing an overtly warm finish.	**£4.00**	THI
✓	**L'ESCHENAUER CHARDONNAY 2000, LES CAVES DE LANDIRAS** Languedoc-Roussillon	Subtle citrus-fruit characters, with a pleasant, mouth-filling finish.	**£4.00**	GCF
✓	**LE BREUILLAC NV, LES CAVES DE LANDIRAS** South West	Fat, juicy, and ripe. Floral and refreshing fruit characters on the palate.	**£4.00**	GCF
✓	**MHV MUSCADET SEVRE & MAINE SUR LIE 2000, JEAN BEUQUIN** Loire	This fresh wine is bright and attractive, showing a well-textured finish.	**£4.00**	MHV
✓	**SAFEWAY CHARDONNAY, VIN DE PAYS DE L'HERAULT 2000, LES DOMAINES VIRGINIE** Vin de Pays de l'Herault	Light touch of dairy product, well-integrated with delicate, ripe fruits.	**£4.00**	SAF
✓	**SAUVIGNON CUVÉE RÉSERVE VDP D'OC 2000, VIGNERONS DES TROIS TERROIRS** Vin de Pays d'Oc	Green gooseberry and herbaceous flavours, with a tight finish.	**£4.00**	SAF
✓	**STOWELLS OF CHELSEA CHARDONNAY MARSANNE VDP 2000, MATTHEW CLARK** Vin De Pays	Elegant, straightforward fruit, with a dry, minerally finish.	**£4.00**	MCT
✓	**TOURAINE SAUVIGNON LE CHALUTIER 2000, LE CHALUTIER** Loire	Freshly squeezed lemon and limes with a similar styled palate.	**£4.00**	JSM MWW SGL DBY
Ⓑ	**JACQUES VERITIER BLANC VDP DES CÔTES DE GASCOGNE 2000, RIGAL** South West	Fresh citrus and light mineral characters. A good all-purpose white.	**£4.00**	ENO J&B
✓	**LA DIVA SAUVIGNON 1999, DONATIEN BAHUAUD** Loire	Interesting, ripe, tropical-fruit notes, with soft-styled palate and clean finish.	**£4.00**	MCT
Ⓑ	**CHARDONNAY ROBERT SKALLI 2000, LES VINS SKALLI LTD** Vin De Pays	Soft, gentle fruit with subtle melon intensity and traces of creaminess.	**£4.40**	MCT
Ⓑ	**COTE SAUVAGE CHARDONNAY 2000, LES DOMAINES DE FONTCAUDE** Languedoc-Roussillon	Tropical fruits balanced by a light, buttery character. Refreshing, with an elegant finish.	**£4.50**	WST

(B)	**LYRIQUE CHARDONNAY VINS DE PAYS 2000, TERROIRS CLUB** Languedoc-Roussillon	Apple on the nose, with tropical fruits and peaches. Fresh, crisp palate with good length.	**£4.50**	BGL
✓	**DOM BRIAL MUSCAT DE RIVESALTES AC 2000, CAVE DE VIGNERONS DE BAIXAS** Languedoc-Roussillon	A golden, grapey, aromatic wonder from this esteemed southern region.	**£4.50**	BGL CAX BGN SAF
(G)	**MUSCAT DE BEAUMES DE VENISE NV, LES VIGNERONS DES BEAUMES DE VENISE** Rhône	Drink this wine young and chilled, and appreciate its perfumed bouquet and luscious honeyed fruit on the palate.	**£5.00**	WTS
(B)	**JAMES HERRICK CHARDONNAY 2000, SOUTHCORP WINES PTY LTD** Languedoc-Roussillon	Soft apple and citrus flavours. Fresh, crisp acidity is well-balanced by the tropical-fruit characters.	**£5.00**	NTD UNS NTD SAF
(B)	**WINTER HILL CHARDONNAY 2000, FONCALIEU** Vin De Pays	Crisp, green fruit with wisps of oak coming over the well-textured palate.	**£5.00**	PLB
✓	**MUSCAT DE BEAUMES DE VENISE 1999, VIGNERONS DE BEAUMES DE VENISE** Rhône	Supple orange and peach aromas rise from a powerful palate.	**£5.00**	THI
(G)	**CHÂTEAU HAUT REYGNAC 2000, DIRECT WINES LTD** Bordeaux	Light gooseberry and asparagus fruit is bolstered with crisp acidity, and spicy, floral flavours on the palate.	**£5.50**	BDR VDO
(S)	**MICHEL LAROCHE SOUTH OF FRANCE CHARDONNAY 2000, LAROCHE** Languedoc-Roussillon	A subtle, tropical fruit with an elegant and complex finish, and a finely balanced acidity.	**£6.00**	BWL
(S)	**COTEAUX DU LAYON ROCHEFORT FUT DE CHÊNE 1999, DOMAINE DE LA MOTTE** Loire	Subtle honey and peaches on the nose, sweet on the palate, with layers of complexity and balanced acidity.	**£9.00**	3DW
(G)	**ROSENBERG PINOT BLANC 1999, DOMAINE BARMÉS BUECHER** Alsace	Deep golden colour, aromatic nose and crisp, zingy attack on the palate of lemon sherbet flavours.	**£9.90**	GON
(G)	**CRU BARREJAT 1995, BARREJAT** Bordeaux	Rich raisins, marmalade, and burnt sugar. Honeyed liquid gold with flavours of dried apricots and crisp acidity.	**£39.30**	J&B
(G)	**CORTON CHARLEMAGNE 1997, DOMAINE BONNEAU DU MARTRAY** Burgundy	Opulent, complex white Burgundy, still with a long life ahead. Multi-layered fruit, breadth, intensity, and elegance	**£50.00**	J&B

FRANCE • ROSÉ

✓	**SAFEWAY VIN DE PAYS DE L'ARDECHE ROSE 2000, UVICA** Ardeche	Juicy fruit and mouthwatering acidity makes for perfect summer glugging.	**£3.20**	SAF
✓	**CO-OP VIN DE PAYS D'OC SYRAH ROSE NV, DELTA DOMAINES** Languedoc-Roussillon	Nice, elegant, fruity style with good, refreshing acidity.	**£3.50**	CWS
(B)	**BIG FRANKS DEEP PINK 2000, BIG FRANK** Languedoc-Roussillon	Lovely strawberry colour with good vibrant fruit on the nose, and intense berry flavours on the palate.	**£4.00**	GYW
✓	**LE MIDI LANGUEDOC ROSÉ 2000, VIGNERONS LES TROIS TERROIRS** Vin De Pays	Soft, bright, inviting style with lovely, refreshing acidity.	**£4.00**	JSM
✓	**T CÔTES-DU-RHÔNE ROSE 2000, VIGNOBLES DU PELOUX** Rhône	Good, crisp rosé with fine fruit and balance.	**£4.00**	TOS

FRANCE • RED

✓	**CARMINÉ DE LA COLLINE 1998, CHATEAU DE LA COLLINE** South West	Straightforward and fruity, this wine shows spice and a light finish.	**£2.50**	HBV
✓	**LE FAVORI GRENACHE SYRAH 1999, LES CAVES DE LANDIRAS** Languedoc-Roussillon	Good red fruits with well-integrated oak and a backbone of warm alcohol.	**£2.70**	GCF
✓	**LE HAVRE 2000, LES CAVES DE LANDIRAS** Languedoc-Roussillon	Light juicy fruits, touches of lavender, and a good, clean finish.	**£2.70**	GCF
✓	**MHV VIN DE TABLE ROUGE MEDIUM NV, DOMINIQUE BAUD**	Ripe, spicy palate, with firm intergrated tannins, and a clean finish.	**£2.90**	MHV
✓	**LES FRERES VINS DE PAYS GARD ROUGE NV, LES FRERES** Alsace	Chewy fruits on the palate, with oaky backbone coming through.	**£3.00**	MCT

(B)	**CORBIERES ROUGE 1999, LES VIGNERONS VAL D'ORBIEU** Languedoc-Roussillon	Pronounced spicy cinnamon nose leads to simple, red fruit, enhanced by balancing acidity and firm tannins.	**£3.00**	SMF BLU
(B)	**DEVEREUX PORTAN & CARIGNAN 2000, DEVEREUX** Languedoc-Roussillon	Possessing a lively youthfulness, this easy-drinking wine is laced with enticing flavours of leafy redcurrants.	**£3.00**	ADE
✓	**ALEXIS LICHINE NV, LES CAVES DE LANDIRAS** Languedoc-Roussillon	Rich fruits with nuances of spice and nuts, and nice, oaky tannins.	**£3.00**	GCF
✓	**SAINSBURY'S CORBIERES 2000, LES VIGNERNONS DE LA MEDITERRANEE** Languedoc-Roussillon	Balanced red fruits with a rich, chewy palate, and a clean, slightly acidic finish	**£3.00**	JSM
✓	**SAFEWAY CORBIERES 2000, GRANDS VINS SELECTION** Corbieres	Jammy, red-fruit characters with fresh, fruity length on the palate.	**£3.00**	SAF
✓	**SAFEWAY MINERVOIS 2000, CASTEL & FRERES** Minervois	Ripe, fruity aromas with nuances of spice and good depth of palate.	**£3.00**	SAF
✓	**SAFEWAY VIN DE PAYS DE VAUCLUSE RED 2000, VIGNOBLES DU PELOUX** Vaucluse	Soft, ripe fruit and well-integrated balance.	**£3.00**	SAF
✓	**VIN ROUGE VDP 2000, VIGNOBLES DU PELOUX** Rhône	A generous wine, with a fresh-fruit palate and firm tannins.	**£3.00**	BGL
(B)	**CÔTES DU RHÔNE AC 2000, VIGNOBLES DU PELOUX/BOTTLE GREEN** Rhône	A bombardment of berry fruits with hints of sweetshop. Interesting concentration is supported by rounded tannins.	**£3.20**	BGN BGL
✓	**LE CAPRICE MALBEC VDP 1999, LE CAPRICE**	Clean, red fruits and hints of ripe cherries, and firm tannins on the finish.	**£3.20**	MCT HDS VGN
✓	**CORBIERES CAVE FONCALIEU 2000, CAVE FONCALIEU**	Earthy blackcurrants and mushrooms, with nice, fruity length.	**£3.20**	MCT
✓	**RENARDS HILL GRENACHE MERLOT 2000, LES CAVES DE LANDIRAS** Languedoc-Roussillon	Floral, bright fruits and nuts, and showing medium length and good texture.	**£3.30**	GCF

✓	**SOMERFIELD CÔTE DU RHÔNE 2000,** **CELLIERS ENCLAVE DES PAPES** Rhône	Great fruit concentration, with a drying palate and moderate finish.	**£3.30**	SMF
Ⓢ	**CO-OP VIN DE PAYS D'OC MERLOT NV,** **VAL D'ORBIEU** Languedoc Roussillon	The mature cherry and liquorice nose becomes a rich, blackcurrant palate that lingers well on the finish.	**£3.50**	CWS SAF
✓	**CHEVAL D'OR CABERNET SAUVIGNON 2000,** **VIGNERONS DE CATALIN** Languedoc-Roussillon	Rustic cassis and plum fruit and showing some spice characters with dry structure.	**£3.50**	WRT
✓	**CÔTES DU LUBERON AC 2000,** **VIGNOBLES DU PELOUX** Rhône	Summer fruits with herbs on the nose, and a backbone of firm tannins.	**£3.50**	BGL WSG BNK BOO
✓	**FONCALIEU SOMERFIELD MINERVOIS AOC 1999,** **FONCALIEU** Languedoc-Roussillon	Bright, fruity characters with a refreshing palate and good follow through.	**£3.50**	SMF
✓	**JEAN ST HONORE CÔTES DU ROUSSILLON 2000,** **BESSIERE SA** Languedoc-Roussillon	Ripe fruits and pepper on the nose, with peppery characters following on the palate.	**£3.50**	NTD
✓	**MHV CORBIERES NV,** **TRESCH** Languedoc-Roussillon	Fruit concentration on the nose continues on the palate, with a drying finish.	**£3.50**	MHV
✓	**BERGERAC ROUGE 2000,** **CAVES LEONARD** South West	Red fruit and a tinge of cedarwood aromas culminate in a well-rounded palate.	**£3.70**	MHV
✓	**JEAN ST HONORE VIN DE PAYS D'OC CABERNET SAUVIGNON 2000, VINIVAL** Languedoc-Roussillon	Soft, fruity nose showing promise with firm tannic grip on the palate.	**£3.70**	NTD
✓	**LA VIEILLE ROCHE CLARET NV,** **GRANDS VINS DE GIRONDE** Bordeaux	Raspberry and blackcurrant aromas, with a wisp of herbs and spice on the palate.	**£3.70**	NTD
✓	**MHV MINERVOIS NV,** **CHARLES DE ROCHE** Languedoc-Roussillon	Young, fruity, juicy red with a backbone of spice and an earthy finish.	**£3.70**	MHV
✓	**VIN DE PAYS D'OC MERLOT,** **PRODIS** Languedoc-Roussillon	Sweet fruit upfront, with forest nuances, and finishing with good balance.	**£3.80**	MHV

(G) **Cuvée Gabriel Merlot 2000,** **Domaine de Brau** Languedoc-Roussillon	Developing farm aromas mingle with ripe cherry and raspberry fruit.	**£4.00**	WTS VRT
(S) **Les Terrasses d'Azur Cabernet Sauvignon Vin De Pays d'Oc 2000, Castel** Languedoc-Roussillon	Blackberry and sweet, red fruits on the nose, with a balanced array of spices and good length.	**£4.00**	L&T
(B) **Chateau Gaubert A.C Corbières 2000,** **Caroline de Beaulieu** Languedoc-Roussillon	Deep purple, with mild pepper spice on the nose, and round, mature, berry character on the palate.	**£4.00**	JBF
(B) **Foncalieu Reserve St Marc Shiraz 2000,** **Foncalieu** Vin De Pays	This lightly-coloured, delicately scented wine offers soft, mixed fruits supported by a backbone of firm tannins.	**£4.00**	JSM BDR
(B) **Old Git Red, Cotes du Ventoux 2000,** **Ets Paul Boutinot Sarl** Rhône	The name might suggest this wine is as tough as old boots. Fortunately, it's quite the opposite.	**£4.00**	ASD PBA
(G) **Gallerie Tempranillo Syrah 2000,** **Domaine Virginie** Languedoc-Roussillon	Inky purple colour, with complex mulberry, summer, and hedgerow fruits, beautifully balanced with sweet oak.	**£4.00**	WTS..
(B) **Somerfield Fitou NV,** **Mont Tauch** Languedoc-Roussillon	Intense tobacco and tar nose leads to pepper and liquorice on the palate. An accessible Fitou.	**£4.00**	SMF TOS
(B) **Stowells of Chelsea Merlot NV,** **Matthew Clark** Languedoc-Roussillon	Intense inky colour. Ripe berry palate and fresh bouquet. Easy-drinking, food-friendly acidity and tannins.	**£4.00**	BGN NTD ASD
(B) **T Finest Corbieres 2000,** **Mont Tauch** Languedoc-Roussillon	Deep plummy aromas with layers of warm, attractive spices. Balanced acidity and firm tannins complete the package.	**£4.00**	TOS WCR
✓ **Côtes du Rhône Louis Mousset 2000,** **Louis Mousset** Rhône	Cherry aromas and a medium body, with a spicy medium-bodied palate.	**£4.00**	STG SEA VGN
✓ **Dark Horse Cahors Malbec Barrique Aged AC 2000,** **Vins Du Grand Sud Ouest** South West	Excellent colour and nose giving red fruits, and a palate with a youthful finish.	**£4.00**	BGL
✓ **Domaine de Diserto 2000,** **Les Grands Chais de France** Corsica	Creamy palate of warm red and slightly tropical fruits, finishing round and approachable.	**£4.00**	GCF

✓	**DOMAINE DE LA PERRIÈRE CORBIÈRES 2000, MONT TAUCH** Languedoc-Roussillon	Cherry and plums abound from the nose, with a well-balanced finish.	**£4.00**	THI
✓	**DONJON DE LA TOUR RED NV, DEVEREUX** Languedoc-Roussillon	Hints of violet and spices come through primarily, and finishing with good tannin and a tight structure.	**£4.00**	ADE
✓	**FITOU NV, TRESCH** Languedoc-Roussillon	Balanced fruit-weight and heady alcohol come together with a plum finish.	**£4.00**	MHV SAF
✓	**FOLENVIE CABERNET MERLOT 2000, YVON MAU** Bordeaux	Brambles and stewed fruits on the nose coming together with a dry finish.	**£4.00**	YVM DBY NRW WES
✓	**GAILLAC AC 2000, COMPAGNIE DES VINS DU GRAND SUD OUEST** South West	Warm earthy fruits and mushrooms on the nose, red-fruit palate, and a clean finish.	**£4.00**	BGL ODD
✓	**LAZY LIZARD SYRAH 2000,**	Rich, ripe, fruity aromas with spices and a touch of meatiness on the palate.	**£4.00**	PBA
✓	**LE FAISAN 2000, RHODANIENNE** Rhône	Leather and vegetal fruit characters on the nose, backed with good structure and finish.	**£4.00**	IWS WTS HVW CTC
✓	**LE FAUVE ROSE DE SYRAH VDP 2000, TERROIR CLUB** Languedoc-Roussillon	Raspberries and ripe berries abound with spice and a silky finish.	**£4.00**	BGL FRW
✓	**LE MIDI CABERNET SAUVIGNON 2000, VIGNERONS LES TROIS TERROIRS,** Vin De Pays	Restrained fruit and a rustic character dominate, finishing quite dry.	**£4.00**	SGL JSM
✓	**LES TERRASSES D'AZUR MERLOT VIN DE PAYS D'OC 2000, CASTEL FRÉRES** Languedoc-Roussillon	Cassis on the nose, with hints of plummy fruits, and a slightly gamey mid-palate.	**£4.00**	L&T
✓	**LES TOURELLES AC 2000, COMPAGNIE DES VINS DU GRAND SUD OUEST** South West	Subdued fruit showing a barn-yard character, finishing with stylish length.	**£4.00**	BGL SAF
✓	**OAKED CÔTES DU RHÔNE AC 2000, VIGNOBLES DU PELOUX** Rhône	Cherry and raspberry aromas are complimented with medium concentration, and an attractive drying palate.	**£4.00**	BGN BGL blu NYW CTC

✓	**ORGANIC ROUGE VIN DE PAYS DES CÔTES DE THONGUES 2000, DOMAINE BASSAL** Languedoc-Roussillon	Fresh and fruity style, with clean tannins and integrated oak.	**£4.00**	VRT WTS CWS SAF ESL
✓	**SPAR SALAISON SHIRAZ CABERNET 1998, MAUREL VEDEAU** Languedoc-Roussillon	Cedar, cherry, and a touch of cigar box on the nose with nuances of leather on the finish.	**£4.00**	THI
✓	**SYRAH MALBEC FRÉDÉRIC ROGER VDP 2000, FRÉDÉRIC ROGER SDVA** Languedoc-Roussillon	Spicy nose and blackcurrant palate, with a pleasant length to round the wine out.	**£4.00**	BGL SAF
✓	**VIN D'UNE NUIT 2000, SCA LES COTEAUX DU PIC** Languedoc-Roussillon	Young, jammy, red fruits and a confected palate giving a supple, quaffing wine.	**£4.00**	MIS
✓	**VIVA CORSICA 2000, LES GRANDS CHAIS DE FRANCE** Corsica	Appealing, crunchy fruits and a real rustic character on the finish.	**£4.00**	GCF
✓	**LA LANDE ROUGE VDP DES L'HERAULT 2000, LGI** South West	Plummy, sappy, foreground fruit with a confected character on the palate, and a jammy finish.	**£4.00**	ENO
Ⓢ	**CABERNET SAUVIGNON ROBERT SKALLI 1999, ROBERT SKALLI** Languedoc-Roussillon	Cigar-box and cherry nose. Soft, sweet fruit on the palate, and a lovely, full finish.	**£4.40**	MCT
Ⓑ	**MERLOT ROBERT SKALLI 1999, ROBERT SKALLI** Languedoc-Roussillon	Warm, tarry fruit and gentle oak cover a big structure that provides pleasant length.	**£4.40**	MCT
Ⓑ	**CHATEAU DE L'ABBAYE FLEURIE 2000, QUINSON** Beaujolais	Mature appearance, with soft fruit on the nose and the palate. Sound, chewy tannins on the moderate length.	**£4.50**	GCF
Ⓑ	**FITOU RÉSERVE PARTICULIÈRE 1999, MONT TAUCH** Languedoc-Roussillon	Vegetal notes accent the warm, sweet fruit on the palate. Crushed pepper and redcurrants on the finish.	**£4.50**	THI
Ⓑ	**LES MARIONNETTES MERLOT VDP 1999, TERROIR CLUB** Languedoc-Roussillon	Fresh, upfront red fruits with a deep palate and good length.	**£4.50**	BGL
✓	**WILD PIG SYRAH 2000, DOMAINES DU SOLEIL** Languedoc-Roussillon	Young and fruity, showing a lot of style. A concentrated finish brings this wine together.	**£4.50**	UNS GYW

(B)	**GRAND RHONE 1999, SOCIETE NOUVELLE MANGUIN** Rhône	Delicate nose, with excellent raspberry concentration on the palate. Zippy acidity and structured tannins.	**£4.60**	ABY
(S)	**ABBOTTS AMMONITE 2000, ABBOTTS** Languedoc Roussillon	A distinctive nose of savoury, grilled meats is counteracted by brooding, dark-forest fruits on the palate.	**£5.00**	GYW SMF
(S)	**CHATEAU THEZANNES CORBIERES 1998, CAVES ROCBERES** Languedoc-Roussillon	Opulent, spicy fruit on the nose, followed by a rich, creamy palate, with hints of raspberries and vanilla.	**£5.00**	CWS
(S)	**CUVÉE SELECTION 2000, SCA LES COLEAUX DU PIC** Languedoc-Roussillon	Elegantly perfumed, with good structure and complex aromas of herbs and violets, followed by a clean finish.	**£5.00**	MIS
(S)	**MHV CLARET OAK AGED 1999, YVON MAU** Bordeaux	Very aromatic, cedar nose. Soft, spicy fruit, with an even layer of tannins and a fruity finish.	**£5.00**	MHV
(S)	**PLAN MACASSAN 2000, CVBG** Rhône	Bright, red colour with a peppery nose, hints of blackberry, and a light touch of liquorice.	**£5.00**	DOU
(S)	**TESCO FINEST VDP D'OC CAB SAUV 1998, MAUREL VEDEAU** Languedoc-Roussillon	Fresh blackcurrant on the nose with integrated, creamy oak, spicy cherry fruit, and good length.	**£5.00**	TOS
(B)	**BEAUJOLAIS VILLAGES 2000, VAUCHER PÈRE ET FILS** Burgundy	Youthful colour, with attractively fruity nose. Darker fruits on the palate, with soft tannins on the finish.	**£5.00**	TOS AVB NRW CEB
(B)	**COTES DU RHONE VILLAGES AC 2000, DOMAINE DE CANTEMERLE** Rhône	Light, youthful appearance offers bramble fruits spiced up with white pepper fresh from the grinder.	**£5.00**	WST
(B)	**ELIANE'S SINGLE VINEYARD MINERVOIS 2000, PROMOCOM** Languedoc-Roussillon	Very appealing, with summer fruits on the palate, and underlying tannins which support the structure.	**£5.00**	JSM
(B)	**LA BAUME CABERNET SAUVIGNON 1999, BRL HARDY WINE COMPANY** Languedoc-Roussillon	Good ripe fruit on the nose. Meaty structure, with a delicious chocolate character. Very smooth and well balanced.	**£5.00**	HBR
(B)	**MAGELLAN 'LES COLLINES' 2000, DOMAINE MAGELLAN** South West	Deep red colour with a spicy nose. Hints of raspberry and strawberry with a soft finish.	**£5.00**	POL

(B) MAISON SICHEL MEDOC NV, MAISON SICHEL Bordeaux	Very attractive tobacco-scented nose. Lovely fruity palate with a hint of cedar. Very upfront with medium length.	**£5.00**	SMF
(B) MERLOT VINS DE PAYS D'OC 2000, BARON PHILLIPE DE ROTHSCHILD Vins de Pays d'Oc	Vibrant colour with a berry nose. Young, but well-integrated creamy tannins. Will benefit from a little more ageing.	**£5.00**	NTD PRG
(B) SAINSBURY'S CUVÉE PRESTIGE CLARET 2000, VINTEX SOVICOP Bordeaux	Youthful wine with bags of deep plum and blackcurrant fruit, and a dry finish.	**£5.00**	JSM
(B) SARACEN, COTEAUX DU LANGUEDOC 2000, DOMAINE DES COURTILLES Languedoc-Roussillon	This crowd-pleasing wine is a definite all-rounder, with opulent yet elegant fruit and a substantial finish.	**£5.00**	WST
(B) SINGLE VINEYARD CORBIÉRES GRUISSAN 2000, PROMOCOM Languedoc-Roussillon	Pronounced vegetal aromas on the nose leading to toasty oak and subtle fruit. Moderate length.	**£5.00**	JSM
(B) SOMERFIELD OAK AGED CLARET NV, MAISON SICHEL Bordeaux	Ruby red with nose showing some development. Soft cherry fruit on the palate. Well-balanced acidity and tannins.	**£5.00**	SMF
(B) TERRES D'AUTAN NEGRETTE CABERNET FRANC 2000, CAVE DE FRONTON South West	Intense bramble fruits with a touch of spice. Medium-bodied, with spirited acidity, and supple tannins.	**£5.00**	BDR WCR VGN
(S) ABBOTTS CIRRUS 1999, ABBOTTS Languedoc-Roussillon	A stoutly-built wine, with ripe, sweet fruits on the nose, and moderate tannins, finishing long and complex.	**£6.00**	GYW
(S) MANSENOBLE VIN DE PAYS DE COTEAUX DE MIRAMONT 1999, CHATEAU MANSENOBLE Languedoc-Roussillon	Deep ruby with an intensely plummy nose. Very forward fruit, with some depth on the finish.	**£6.00**	COO
(S) MORGON LES CHARMES 1998, GERARD BRISSON Beaujolais	Pungent aromas of freshly-picked red fruits rise from the nose of this graceful and complex wine.	**£6.00**	CWS GSJ
(S) SOLSTICE 1999, DOMAINES DU SOLEIL Languedoc-Roussillon	Deep red in colour, with a very attractive nose of herbs, spices, and red fruits.	**£6.00**	GYW
(S) JEAN ST HONORE VIN DE PAYS D'OC SYRAH 2000, VINIVAL Languedoc-Roussillon	Aromas of damson and spice, the palate is rich with ripe, berry fruits, and hints of black pepper.	**£6.50**	NTD WST

(S)	**CHÂTEAU ROUSSELLE CÔTES DE BOURG 1999, VINCENT & NATHALIE LEMAITRE** Bordeaux	Subtle nose, but with rich, chewy, soft fruits, and a medium body. Good structure and firm tannins.	**£6.80**	3DW
(S)	**COTES DU RHONE 2000, DOMAINE BRUSSET** Rhône	Medium-bodied with a combination of tannins and ripe red fruits; hints of white pepper on the finish.	**£6.70**	ENO JNW J&B
(S)	**CHATEAU DE LA TOUR, RESERVE DE CHATEAU 1998, DOURTHE** Bordeaux	Classy damson and cherry fruit. Neatly integrated, stylish oak, and a firm structure of silky tannins.	**£7.00**	THA BDR
(S)	**MORGON FLOWER LABEL 2000, GEORGES DUBOEUF** Burgundy	Refined nose of dark fruits. The weighty palate possesses masses of fruit underpinned by silky tannins.	**£7.00**	BWC AVB GHL N&P
(S)	**CHÂTEAU HAUT VIGNEAU PREMIÈRES CÔTES DE BLAYE 1999, VINCENT LEMAITRE** Bordeaux	A light, plummy nose with a slightly restrained fruity palate, with a good, grippy character.	**£7.40**	3DW
(G)	**CHÂTEAU PLAISANCE 1997, GINESTET** Bordeaux	Plummy, spicy, cherry nose. Ripe fruit overlays the fine structure; a harmonious, elegant wine of balance.	**£7.50**	SMF SAF
(S)	**VINUS DU CHATEAU PAUL MAS COTEAUX DU LANGUEDOC 2000, MAS-APLIN** Languedoc-Roussillon	Very bright, dark colour gives way to aromas of stewed red fruits and chocolate flavours.	**£7.50**	SWS
(G)	**MERCUREY 1ER CRU LES BYOTS 1999, DOMAINE L MENAND PÈRE ET FILS** Burgundy	This wine shows incredible balance; ripe fruit, silky tannins, and fine acidity in perfect harmony.	**£9.40**	3DW
(G)	**CROZES HERMITAGE ROUGE 1999, OLIVIER DUMAINE** Rhône	This wine offers a huge peppery, minty, smoky nose with savoury notes and perfumed, red berry flavours.	**£10.00**	LIB
(G)	**DOMAINE PARIZE GIVRY 1ER CRU GRANDES VIGNES 1998, DOMAINE PARIZE** Burgundy	Classic Givry with rich fruit and violet notes balanced by fine tannins.	**£10.50**	GRT
(G)	**LAURUS GIGONDAS 1999, GABRIEL MEFFRE** Rhone	In this Southern Rhône red, berry fruit and sweet, vanilla oak intermingle on the palate.	**£13.00**	GYW
(G)	**BEAUNE PREMIER CRU LES EPENOTTES 1998, DOMAINE PARENT** Burgundy	Stylish wine with enticing wild strawberry aroma, and elegant and harmonious structure.	**£15.00**	CHN SAF NYW

(G)	**VOSNE ROMANEE IER CRU AUX BRÛLÉES 1999, DOMAINE MICHEL GROS** Burgundy	This wine exhibits splendid concentration, sweet oak, and excellent structure. Will age well.	**£18.30**	XXGRO
(G)	**VOLNAY 1998, DOMAINE DUBREUIL FONTAINE** Burgundy	An elegant wine with good, ripe-fruit concentration, and a light but persistent finish.	**£18.40**	ABY
(G)	**GEVREY CHAMBERTIN VIEILLES VIGNES 1999, DOMAINE HERESZTYN** Burgundy	Perfumed wine with good red fruit intensity, fine structure, and tremendous finesse.	**£20.00**	WTS
(G)	**PETITE L'EGLISE 1995, PETITE L'EGLISE** Bordeaux	Outstanding Pomerol at a relatively reasonable price. Smooth, silky fruit, with a broad, creamy, vanilla-oak veneer.	**£20.00**	J&B
(G)	**GEVREY-CHAMBERTIN 1997, DENIS MORTET** Burgundy	Impressive, come-hither, cherryish red from a new star. Intense fruit, firmish tannins, and sweet oak. Delicious.	**£22.00**	J&B
(G)	**CHATEAU HAUT BATAILLEY PAUILLAC 1995, CHATEAU HAUT BATAILLEY** Bordeaux	Textbook Pauillac from the Ducru-Beaucaillou stable. Seductive generosity from a ripe vintage Drink now or keep.	**£25.00**	J&B
(G)	**CLOS VOUGEOT 1999, DOMAINE MICHEL GROS** Burgundy	Restrained wine of considerable concentration and elegance displaying ripe, red fruits and a deft touch of oak.	**£25.50**	Not available in the UK
(G)	**VOLNAY LES CHEVRETS 1999 J BOILLOT 1999, JEAN BOILLOT** Burgundy	Wonderful, deep wine with a delicious sweet-savoury quality on the palate, and a long and harmonious finish.	**£29.00**	WTS
(G)	**CLOS DE TART 1998, MOMMESSIN** Burgundy	Beautifully perfumed, if slightly developed, nose leads to a toasty palate of mature red fruit. Drink up.	**£33.10**	Not available in the UK
(G)	**PAVILION ROUGE DE CHATEAU MARGAUX 1996, CHATEAU MARGAUX** Bordeaux	Second wine from a first growth. Classed growth quality. Supple, elegant, and beautifully perfumed with black fruits.	**£36.00**	J&B
(G)	**CHATEAU LA DOMINIQUE 1995, CHATEAU LA DOMINIQUE** Bordeaux	Generous, opulent St Emilion from a great vintage. Toasty oak seamlessly blended with rich, berry fruits. Well worth keeping.	**£40.00**	POR J&B
(G)	**CHATEAU LA MISSION HAUT BRION 1995, CHATEAU LA MISSION HAUT BRION** Bordeaux	Top-class Bordeaux, combining earthy richness with plummy fruit and dense tannins. Superb, but best after five more years.	**£90.00**	J&B

FRANCE • SWEET

(G)	**CHÂTEAU LA VARIÉRE 1997, JACQUES BEAUJEAU** Loire	Wonderfully complex, honeyed peaches. The intense palate is creamy and ripe, with pineapple chunks, apricots. Concentrated.	**£19.70**	Not available in UK
(G)	**CHATEAU CLIMENS BARSAC 1997, CHATEAU CLIMENS** Bordeaux	Temptingly drinkable, opulent, powerful wine with honey, dried apricots, and caramel cream. Still a baby; keep if you can!	**£48.00**	J&B

FRANCE • FORTIFIED

(G)	**NOILLY PRAT (DRY) NV, NOILLY PRAT SA** Languedoc-Roussillon	Herbs on the nose; dry and bitter yet refreshing, it cleanses the palate with limes and almonds.	**£6.60**	POR FDB

GERMANY

Wine consumers still have a perception of German wines that is tarnished by the lakes of indifferent Hock and Liebraumilch consumed in the UK over the past 30 years. The reality is that German wines from every wine-growing region in the country have been ludicrously overlooked. From totally dry to exceptionally sweet, these wines provide a purity, delicacy, and balance rarely found elsewhere. Go on – try one!

GERMANY • WHITE

✓	**SOMERFIELD HOCK NV, PETER MERTES** Rhein	Simply fresh and pleasantly aromatic, with herbs and somewhat spicy undertones.	**£2.00**	SMF
✓	**BEREICH BERNKASTEL 2000, J BRADER** Mosel-Saar-Ruwer	Slightly refined nose, with an English-apple, floral palate. Zippy acidity on the finish.	**£2.70**	MCT
✓	**SOMERFIELD NIERSTEINER GUTES DOMTAL QBA NV, RHEINBERG KELLEREI** Rheinhessen	Unctuous, aromatic, floral blossoms with simple, straight-up acidity.	**£3.00**	SMF

✓	**SOMERFIELD RÜDESHEIMER ROSENGARTEN QBA, RUDOLF MULLER** Nahe	Delicate, floral, spicy hints interspersed with elderflower-blossom tones on the finish.	**£3.00**	SMF
✓	**MORIO MUSKAT 2000, ST URSULA** Pfalz	Tangy, bright acidity balances the over-ripe fruit in this wine.	**£3.10**	SMF
Ⓑ	**SOMERFIELD NIERSTEINER SPIEGELBERG KABINETT 1999, RUDOLF MULLER** Rheinhessen	Classically fresh and light-hearted, off-dry German Riesling.	**£3.30**	SMF
✓	**CO-OP BEREICH BERNKASTEL RIVANER 1999, ZIMMERMANN-GRAEFF** Mosel-Saar-Ruwer	Lemon-sherbet zip with minerals and a keen, zippy palate.	**£3.30**	D&D
✓	**BLACK TOWER DRY RIESLING KENDERMANN 2000, REH KENDERMANN GMBH** Rheinhessen	Packed with ripe peaches galore. Quite dry on the finish, with lingering flavours.	**£4.20**	RHC SAF
Ⓑ	**BOCKENHEIMER GRAFENSTUCK BA 1998, ZIMMERMANN-GRAEFF & MULLER,** Pfalz	Rich, aromatic nose of honey and thick-cut marmalade, followed by a long, sweet, complex finish.	**£4.00**	D&D
Ⓖ	**URZIGER WURZGARTEN RIESLING SPATLESE 1993, CHRISTOFFEL-BERRES** Mosel-Saar-Ruwer	Floral, off-dry fruit, with white peach and lemony flavours. Fresh acidity brings it together on a long finish.	**£5.00**	MWW
Ⓑ	**DEINHARD LILA NV, DEINHARD** Mosel-Saar-Ruwer	Persistent, lively mousse with a light, petrolly, and lemony nose followed by a refreshing acidity.	**£6.00**	HOH
Ⓖ	**BASSERMAN JORDAN RIESLING 2000, BASSERMAN JORDAN** Pfalz	Classic Pfalz riesling with a floral nose, intensely sweet palate, balanced by piercing acidity.	**£6.50**	WTS
Ⓖ	**MONTAUIA GRAUBUGUNDER SPÄTLESE TROCKEN BARRIQUE 1999, WEINGUT AM STEIN** Franken	Concentrated nose and luscious palate, with harmonious grip of fruit, oak, and acidity.	**£10.50**	Not available in the UK
Ⓖ	**HOCHEIMER DOMDECHANEY RIESLING SPÄTLESE 1997, FRANZ KÜNSTLER** Rhein	Rich, concentrated Riesling with honeyed sweetness beautifully counterbalanced by lively acidity.	**£20.10**	J&B
Ⓖ	**MSR TROCKENBEERENAUSLESE 1992, SCHMITT SOHNE** Mosel-Saar-Ruwer	Deep amber colour and intense honeyed, caramelized nose; powerful botrytis flavours are perfectly cut with zesty acidity.	**£35.00**	Not available in the U.K.

(G)	**ESCHERNDORFER LUMP RIESLING TBA 1999, WEINGUT HORST SAUER** Franken	Lemon and smoky-petrol aromas. Grapefruit and baked apples; zingy citric acidity. Very full-bodied and moreish.	**£49.00** NYW
(G)	**ESCHENDORFER LUMP RIESLING EISWEIN 1999, WEINGUT HORST SAUER** Franken	Developing, petrolly nose; pure floral and pineapple flavours. The unctuous sweetness has crisp acidity for balance.	**£53.00** NYW

HUNGARY

Of all the East European wine-producing countries, Hungary seems to show the most promise. It boasts a cornucopia of indigenous grape varieties, offering delicious drinking for under £4.00. Noble European varietals such as Sauvignon Blanc, Pinot Gris, and Chardonnay are also doing very well. Don't forget the sublime, intensely sweet wines of Tokaji, which still lay claim to being the world's most underrated dessert wines.

HUNGARY • SPARKLING

(B)	**CHAPEL HILL SPARKLING CHARDONNAY NV, BALATONBOGLAR** Balatonboglar	Biscuit, bread, and light nuts flavour on the nose, with a soft mousse and medium finish.	**£5.00** MYL WTS

HUNGARY • WHITE

(B)	**THE UNPRONOUNCABLE GRAPE CSERSZEGI FUSZERES 2000, HILLTOP NESZMELY** North Transdanubia	Vibrant and aromatic, in a fresh, clean, easy-drinking style.	**£3.00** BGL
✓	**WOODCUTTER'S WHITE 2000, HILLTOP NESZMELY** North Transdanubia	Herbs, blossoms; inviting, fresh flavours, with a crisp, grapey palate.	**£3.30** SAF
✓	**HILLTOP HÁRSLEVELÜ 1999, HILLTOP NESZMELY** Tokaj-Hegyalja	Perfumed-lime aromas, with decent mouthfeel, and a zippy finish.	**£3.50** BGL
✓	**NAGYRÉDE ESTATE CHARDONNAY 2000, NAGYREDE** Nagyrede	Delicate floral and citrus nose, with a creamy texture.	**£3.50** MYL NYW CTC

✓	**SafeWay Hungarian Chardonnay, Buda 2000, Hilltop Neszmely** North Transdanubia	Creamy, floral nose with hints of butterscotch, and well-balanced fruit acidity with a crisp finish.	**£3.50**	SAF
✓	**MHV Hungarian Chardonnay 2000, The Hanwood Group** Sopron	Floral, appley fruit, with fresh acidity, and a clean finish.	**£3.60**	MHV
✓	**Csárdás 2000 Csardas Bor** Eteyeki	Sherbet-lemon fruit, with fresh, balancing acidity.	**£3.80**	MYL
✓	**Matra Mountain Sauvignon Blanc 2000, Hilltop Neszmely** North Transdanubia	Classic Sauvignon Blanc. Crunchy, kiwi-fruit aromas with a grassy, pungent palate and cleansing acidity.	**£3.80**	SAF
✓	**ZZ Zenit/Zefir 2000, Hungarovin** Eteyeki	Aromatic, ripe-green aromas, with a fresh, neutral flavour.	**£3.80**	MYL
ⒷB	**Emerald Sauvignon Blanc 2000, Hilltop Neszmely** North Transdanubia	Grassy and herbaceous hints, with well-balanced acidity and complex aromas of ripe fruits.	**£4.00**	TOS
ⒷB	**Spice Trail White 2000, Szolskert Co-op** Nagyrede	Intriguingly aomatic nose and fresh fruit-salad palate.	**£4.00**	MYL SAF VGN
✓	**Pazmand Chardonnay Unoaked 2000, Hungarovin** Pazmand	Intense, crisp, well-made wine, with clean hints of lemon and lime, and mouth-watering acidity	**£4.00**	MYL
✓	**Szölö Chardonnay Leányka 2000, Egervin Co. Limited** Northern Massif	Floral and green-apple hints with fresh peach and lime on the palate.	**£4.00**	D&D
✓	**Szölö Pinot Gris Leányka 2000, Egervin Co. Limited** Northern Massif	Spicy, slightly honeyed flavours, with a crisp lift of citrus fruit, and good mouthfeel.	**£4.00**	D&D MHV

HUNGARY • RED

✓	**Chapel Hill Merlot 2000, Balatonboglar** Balatonboglar	Fresh, red-cherry fruit aromas, with bright, flavoursome palate and soft tannins.	**£3.50**	MYL

✓	**HILLTOP MERLOT 2000,** **HILLTOP NESZMÉLY** South Transdanubia	Subtle, red-berry fruit aromas with medium-weight, Bordelais flavours.	**£3.50**	BGL
✓	**MHV HUNGARIAN COUNTRY RED NV,** **THE HANWOOD GROUP** South Dunantul	Easy-drinking, fresh, fruity red with simple, rustic fruit.	**£3.60**	MHV
✓	**HUNGARIAN CABERNET SAUVIGNON 2000,** **THE HANWOOD GROUP** Szekszard	Simple, curranty, fruit aromas, with a balanced, fresh palate.	**£3.80**	MHV TOS
✓	**HILLTOP RIVERVIEW KEKFRANKOS MERLOT 2000,** **HILLTOP NESZMELY** North Transdanubia	Light, easy-drinking, with a fragrant finish.	**£4.00**	BGN ASD BGL SAF
✓	**SPICE TRAIL RED 2000,** **HUNGAROVIN**	Pungent blueberry nose, with a long, sweet palate.	**£4.00**	MYL SAF
✓	**SZÖLÖ KÉKFRAKOS 2000,** **EGERVIN CO. LIMITED** Northern Massif	Plummy, damson fruit, in a clean, simple, tight style, with bright acidity.	**£4.00**	D&D
✓	**SZÖLÖ KÉKFRAKOS CABERNET 2000,** **EGERVIN CO. LIMITED** Northern Massif	Vibrant red fruits, with typical, structured tannins.	**£4.00**	D&D

HUNGARY • SWEET

Ⓖ	**DISZNÒKÖ TOKAJI ASZÙ 5 PUTTONYOS 1996,** **DOMAINE DISZNÒKÖ** Tokaj-Hegyalja	Gold colour, with an intense honeyed and citrus nose. The palate is sweet, elegant, and complex.	**£7.80**	Not available in the UK
Ⓢ	**TOKAJI ASZU 1990,** **HILLTOP NESZMELY** Tokaji	A fragrant, honeyed, peach nose. Attractive peachy fruit and good botrytis character with well-balanced acidity.	**£9.70**	SAF CPW AMW SOM
Ⓖ	**ST STEPHANS CROWN TOKAJI 5 PUTTONYOS ASZU 1994,** **KOVAGO ESTATE** Tokaj-Hegyalja	The nose is all caramel, burnt toffee, and marmalade. Spicy, honeyed fruit; will only get better.	**£11.00**	MYL
Ⓖ	**TOKAJI ASZU 6 PUTTONYOS 1994,** **CROWN ESTATES** Tokaj-Hegyalja	Deep gold, with an attractive tangerine and burnt-toffee nose. A layered palate; soft, sweet peaches, and beeswax.	**£30.00**	POL

ITALY

Italy produces more wine than any other country in the world, making in excess of 6 millon tonnes a year. The labelling system is ludicrously complicated, and with dozens of unpronounceable varieties that most consumers have never heard of, Italy has always had difficulty getting its quality message across. In truth, there has never been a better time to buy Italian wine. Recent vintages have been brilliant, particularly 1997, which has been a success the length and breadth of the country. The budget-conscious should look to Southern Italy and Sicily.

ITALY • WHITE

✓	**CASTELBELLO MEDIUM WHITE ASOI, COSSANO BELBO** Italy	Pleasantly perfumed, with ripe-apple flavours, and a crisp finish.	**£2.80**	MCT
✓	**SENTIERO BIANCO, VINO DA TAVOLA NV, TERRE CORTESI** Marche	Fresh, zesty wine, with a good spicy character, underlined by clean acidity.	**£3.00**	SAF
✓	**SLVE 2000, GRUPPO ITALIANO VINI** Veneto	Restrained almonds and attractive yellow fruits come together with good balance.	**£3.60**	M&M VGN
✓	**SICILIAN WHITE 2000, FIRRIATO** Sicily	Tangy wine displaying ripe fruit and a clean, crisp finish.	**£3.90**	UNS MHV
Ⓢ	**TESCO CATTARRATTO CHARDONNAY 2000, FIRRIATO** Sicily	Fresh aromas of ripe peaches and pear, with lively, crisp acidity on the finish.	**£4.00**	TOS
Ⓑ	**D'ISTINTO CATARRATTO CHARDONNAY 1999, BRL HARDY WINE COMPANY** Sicily	Light gold colour, with rich buttery aromas. Smooth and fruity with well-balanced acidity.	**£4.00**	NTD HBR
Ⓑ	**SAINSBURY'S SICILIAN GRECANICO 2000, SETTESOLI** Sicily	Lean and dry, citrus-style fruit, with a crisp finish, and showing a zesty aftertaste.	**£4.00**	JSM
✓	**CATARRATTO CHARDONNAY 2000, FIRRIATO** Sicily	Lime and citrus aromas with a clean, crisp palate, and a long finish.	**£4.00**	WTS IWS

✓	**MEZZOMONDO CHARDONNAY VALLAGARINA IGT 2000, MGM MONDO DEL VINO** Trentino-Alto Adige	Full and rich, with a delicate prickle on the finish, and complex aromas of butter and melon.	**£4.00**	WST
Ⓢ	**TREBBIANO D'ABRUZZO 2000, FARNESE** Marche	Honeyed citrus aromas, with nutty characters coming through, and a clean finish.	**£4.00**	BDR
✓	**CARDETO ORVIETO CLASSICO DOC 2000, COVIO** Umbria	Generously rounded green fruits, with characteristic, grippy finish.	**£4.50**	WTS UNS WST
Ⓑ	**TRULLI CHARDONNAY 2000, CANTELE** Apulia	Restrained, elegant nose of tropical fruits. Bananas and pineapples on the palate. Good concentration and length.	**£4.60**	BGN UNS IWS SAF
Ⓑ	**MARC XERO CHARDONNAY 2000, CANTELE** Apulia	Clean tropical fruits, good crisp acidity, and a decent length of finish.	**£5.00**	NTD ASD IWS SAF

ITALY · RED

✓	**DONELLI LANCELLOTTA DELL'EMILIA NV, DONELLI VINI** Italy	Soft, sweet fruits and firm tannins giving good balance for this style.	**£2.30**	M&M
Ⓑ	**SAN CIRIACO VALPOLICELLA 1999, BOSCAINI PAOLO & FIGLI SPA** Veneto	Well-made, easy-drinking wine offers rich, blackcurrant crumble and good, firm structure to the length.	**£2.70**	EHL
✓	**CASTELBELLO SOFT RED TABLE WINE NV, BELBO** Italy	Ripe, cherry fruits and integrated oak show well, giving a textured palate.	**£2.80**	MCT
✓	**COLLEZIONE MARCHESINI 1998, CASTELLI ROMANI** Latium	Soft and light tannins coming through this mature blend.	**£3.00**	MCT
✓	**COLLEZIONE MARCHESINI 2000, CASTELLI ROMANI** Latium	Juicy, lively, easy-drinking red that shows a freshness that jumps from the glass.	**£3.00**	MCT
✓	**ALDI MONTEPULCIANO 1999, CA.GI.SPA** Abruzzi	Intense colour with ripe-cherry fruit, and a firm finish.	**£3.00**	VEX JSS TRO PIM

	Wine	Description	Price	
✓	**CABERNET LINEA CORTE VIGNA 1999,** **ENOITALIA CALMASINO** Veneto	Simple, well-made wine, with clean fruit and palate to match.	**£3.00**	MCT MAD BLS WCR
✓	**MERLOT DEL VENETO LINEA CORTE VIGNA 2000,** **LINEA CORTE VIGNA** Veneto	Simple wine with good varietal characters, and soft palate.	**£3.00**	MCT HMA MAD WCR
✓	**MONTEPULCIANO D'ABRUZZO 1999,** **COLLEZIONE MARCHESINI** Abruzzi	Balanced fruit and oak, with a raspberry finish.	**£3.30**	MCT
✓	**MONTEPULCIANO D'ABRUZZO 2000,** **COLLEZIONE MARCHESINI** Abruzzi	Good fruit-intensity with firm tannins and a bitey finish.	**£3.30**	MCT UNS WRK VGN
✓	**ROSSO VERONESE 1999,** **FABIANO** Verona	Fresh, clean, red fruit with an acidic kick, and delicious finish	**£3.30**	SAF
✓	**CABERNET SAUVINGON MARCHESINI 1999,** **MARCHESINI** Veneto	Light, easy-drinking, with some nice, cherry fruit.	**£3.40**	MCT
ⓢ	**CANONICO SALENTO NEGROAMARO 1999,** **CO-OP AGRICOLA DUE PLAME** Apulia	Lively characters of Negroamaro shine through. The pronounced oak is well integrated and the palate balanced and silky.	**£3.50**	CTL
✓	**MERLOT DEL PIAVE 2000,** **LA MARCA** Veneto	Warm, red fruits on the nose, and cherry palate, with soft tannins	**£3.50**	IWS
✓	**SOMERFIELD BARDOLINO DOC NV,** **PASQUA** Veneto	Tangy fruit and middle-weighted palate, with a good, dry finish.	**£3.50**	SMF
✓	**MHV BARDOLINO,** **SARTORI** Veneto	Spicy red fruits, with some good cherry fruit, and a drying finish.	**£3.70**	MHV VGN
✓	**DOLCETTO D'ALBA SAN ORSOLA 1999,** **SAN ORSOLA** Piedmonte	Spice and herbs with a complex fruity palate and a dry finish.	**£3.90**	MCT
✓	**DOLCETTO D'ALBA SAN ORSOLA 2000,** **SAN ORSOLA** Piedmonte	Soft and fruity, mouthfilling wine, with a jammy finish.	**£3.90**	MCT

(S)	**MEZZOMONDO MONTEPULCIANO D'ABRUZZO DOC 2000, MONDO DEL VINO** Abruzzi	An elegant, restrained nose of plums and dates belies a well-ripened warmth. Good depth and lengthy finish.	**£4.00**	WST
(S)	**TESCO FINEST ITALIAN MERLOT 2000, CONCILIO** Trentino	Almost black, opaque core. Great viscosity, rich, crunchy blackcurrant fruit, with a deep complexity and soft tannins.	**£4.00**	TOS
(B)	**NOLITA MONTEPULCIANO D'ABRUZZO DOC 2000, MGM MONDO DEL VINO** Abruzzi	The Montepulciano grape is known for producing some excellent, jam-packed wines, and this one is no exception.	**£4.00**	WST
(B)	**SERINA PRIMITIVO TARANTINO, PUGLIA 2000, CALATRASI** Apulia	Mixed spices on the nose, with rich, ripe, baked-damson fruit flavours.	**£4.00**	SAF
✓	**ALTANA DI VICO MERLOT REFOSCO 2000, BOTTER** Veneto	Red-berry fruits and soft tannins finish with a great texture.	**£4.00**	FTH
✓	**CO-OP BARRELAIA 2000, PICCINI** Tuscany	Rounded and delicious, with reasonable length and puckering finish.	**£4.00**	CWS
✓	**DOMANI MONTEPULCIANO D'ABRUZZO 1999, CASA GIRELLI** Abruzzo	This wine displays good earthy fruit, and good mouthfeel with its firm tannins.	**£4.00**	NTD
✓	**IL PADRINO SANGIOVESE IGT 2000, MGM MONDO DEL VINO** Sicily	Palate shows good blackberry and stewed-plum fruit, with a rich finish.	**£4.00**	WST
✓	**MEZZOMONDO NEGROAMARO IGT 2000, MGM MONDO DEL VINO** Apulia	Sweet, soft, red fruits showing a full palate but finishing with a supple, tannic structure.	**£4.00**	WST TOS
✓	**MHV CHIANTI 2000, PICCINI** Tuscany	Light, simple, spicy cherry and plum fruit with herbaceous overtones	**£4.00**	MHV
✓	**MHV TUSCAN RED 2000, CECCHI** Tuscany	Classic style with fruity complexity, and a bit of a kick on the finish.	**£4.00**	MHV
✓	**MHV VALPOLICELLA OAK AGED NV, SARTORI** Veneto	Gentle balance of fruit and oak in a traditional North East Italian style.	**£4.00**	MHV VGN

✓	**SAINSBURY'S SICILIAN SANGIOVESE 2000, SETTESOLI** Sicily	Light, juicy, fruit flavours on the nose, with these delicious characters following to the palate	**£4.00**	JSM BEN CTC VGN
✓	**SANGIOVESE 1999, BARBI** Orvieto	Pleasant, cherry aromas in this well-balanced wine.	**£4.00**	PLB VGN
✓	**SAFEWAY YOUNG VATTED VALPOLICELLA 2000, SARTORI** Valpolicella	Light, fruity palate with a gentle finish. Perfect chilled for summer drinking.	**£4.00**	SAF
✓	**TERRA VIVA ROSSO VDT 2000, PERLAGE/BOTTLE GREEN** Italy	Clean, raspberry and cherry fruit make up this straightforward wine.	**£4.00**	BGL DBY SOM
✓	**TERRALE CATTARATO 2000, CALATRASI** Sicily	Rich nose and soft-fruit palate makes for very easy drinking.	**£4.00**	PLB SMF BWL VGN
✓	**TERRE MONTALBANO 2000, MONTALBANO** Friuli-Venezia Giulia	Ripe, cherry-fruit flavours, and a lovely, soft finish.	**£4.00**	VRT AVB
✓	**TESCO TUSCAN RED 2000, CECCHI** Tuscany	Light and fruity, with a rounded palate.	**£4.00**	TOS
✓	**VINIMAR ROSSO PICENO 2000, JOHN WORONTSCHAK** The Marches	Rounded fruit palate and light finish.	**£4.00**	EHL
Ⓑ	**CABERNET FRIULVINI 1999, FRIULVINI** Friuli-Venezia Giulia	Light, juicy wine with tinned-berry aromas. Easy drinking, summer quaffer.	**£4.10**	MCT
Ⓑ	**IL PAPAVERO ROSSO VINODATAVOLA 2000, MGM MONDO DEL VINO** Abruzzi	Lovely, perfumed nose precedes a palate of apple compote and blackcurrants. The sweetness carries through on the finish.	**£4.20**	WST
Ⓑ	**LA NATURE ORGANIC MONTEPULCIANO D'ABRUZZO DO 2000, CARLO VOLPI** Abruzzi	The nose is initially reluctant, but opens up with time. The black, chunky fruit is supported by solid tannins.	**£4.50**	BGL
Ⓑ	**MONTE DABRO MONTEPULCIANO D'ABRUZZO DOC 2000, MONDO DEL VINO** Abruzzi	A touch of tar on the nose yields to a palate composed of black and red-berry fruits.	**£4.50**	WST CAM DBY RHV

(B)	**SOMERFIELD CABERNET SAUVIGNON NV, GRUPPO ITALIANO VINI** Veneto	Hints of spice and cedar on the nose. Lovely, sweet, fruit palate, fresh acidity, and structure.	**£4.50**	M&M JAG VGN
(B)	**TRULLI PRIMITIVO 1999, CANTELE** Apulia	Rich, purple-red with luscious, round fruit on the palate; hints of spice on the length.	**£4.50**	BGN ASD ASD IWS
(B)	**MODELLO DELLE VENEZIE 1999, MASI** Veneto	Juicy, fruit aromas on the nose are followed by toasty oak and a peppery finish.	**£4.50**	BWC HOH AVB CTC
(B)	**PRIMITIVO DEL SALENTO CALEO 1999, BOTTER** Apulia	Very attractive, bold, red fruits dominate the palate. Subtle oak and structural tannins bind the elements tightly together.	**£4.80**	FTH
(G)	**CASALE VECCHIO MONTEPULCIANO 2000, FARNESE VINI SRL** Abruzzi	Sweet oak and fruit explode on the palate with pepper, chocolate, cedar, and plum. A great modern style.	**£5.00**	Not available in the UK
✓	**CHIANTI 2000, CECCHI** Tuscany	Bittersweet fruit overlays a spicy structure.	**£5.00**	UNS IWS SAF
(G)	**TRE UVE VINO DA TAVOLA 1999, MGM MONDO DEL VINO** Abruzzi	Jammy, ripe fruit with a pure nose, and juicy, spicy, mid-palate flavours. Well-balanced oak and crisp acidity.	**£5.00**	WST
(S)	**CAMALETTO WMC MONTEPULCIANO D'ABRUZZO DOC 1999, CASA GIRELLI** Trentino-Alto Adige	Bitter cherry and berry-fruit flavours give a clean, easy style, some firm tannins, and an interesting complexity.	**£5.00**	VEX
(S)	**CAMALETTO WMC NERO D'AVOLA MERLOT IGT 2000, CASA GIRELLI** Trentino-Alto Adige	Subtle fruity nose and a rich palate of blackberries and strawberries. Softening tannins and an excellent finish.	**£5.00**	BGN VEX SAF G&M
(S)	**NATURAL STATE MONTEPULCIANO D'ABRUZZO DOC 2000, MONDO DEL VINO,** Abruzzi	Sweet-fruited nose yields to a mouthful of red fruits. Balanced tannin, good extraction and length characterize this stunner.	**£5.00**	WST JBF
(S)	**PROMESSA ROSSO SALENTO 2000, PROMESSA** Apulia	This succulent offering has soft tannins while retaining the robustness for which Salento is justifiably famous.	**£5.00**	POR GGW BEN LIB
(B)	**CALISSANO BARBERA 1999, CALISSANO** Piedmont	Youthful style, with a scent of cassis and herbs. Round, weighty body adds another dimension to this wine.	**£5.00**	BWL ENO CAM JNW

(B) **L'ARCO CABERNET FRANC 1999, JOHN WORONTSCHAK** Friuli-Venezia Giulia	Deep ruby, showing incredibly elegant fruit, with a hint of perfume on the nose. Well-structured, good depth.	**£5.00**	EHL
(B) **LA BROCCA PRIMITIVO 1999, BASILIUM** Apulia	Rich, ripe, black fruit lingers in the mouth, with oak and pepper flavours coming through on the finish.	**£5.00**	HOH
(B) **LARCO CABERNET FRANC 2000, CABERT** Friuli-Venezia Giulia	This wine displays good bramble fruit, light smoky oak, and chewy tannins.	**£5.00**	EHL
(B) **PROMESSA NEGROAMARO 2000, PROMESSA** Apulia	Soft tannins are well-balanced and restrained. A little aeration will bring this wine out of its shell.	**£5.00**	POR GGW BEN UNS LIB
(B) **ROSSO PICENA SUPERIORE ROCCA DI AQUAVIVA 1998, TERRE CORTESI MONCARO** Marche	Attractive summer fruits mingle with blackcurrant notes, creating a complex and compelling wine.	**£5.00**	EUW
(B) **ROSSO PICENO ROCCA DI AQUAVIVA 2000, TERRE CORTESI MONCARO** Marche	This youthful, medium-bodied wine offers vibrant, red-berry fruits and supple tannins.	**£5.00**	EUW
(S) **NERO D'AVOLA 2000, VILLA TONINO** Sicily	A basketful of sweet, black, sun-ripened Morello cherries fill the palate of this attractive wine.	**£5.10**	GGW BEN LIB
✓ **DUE PALME SALICE SALENTINO ROSSO 1999, CO-OP AGRICOLA DUE PLAME** Apulia	Full-bodied with some herb and spice on the finish.	**£5.20**	BDR CTL
(S) **SOLFERINO NEGROAMARO IGT 1999, MGM MONDO DEL VINO** Apulia	Developing red fruits appear on the nose, and an abundance of dried fruit on the palate.	**£5.20**	BDR WST
(S) **FARNESE SANGIOVESE 2000, FARNESE VINI** Abruzzi	Inky wine with masses of red fruit, and incredible concentration and depth. Needs time to really shine.	**£5.20**	BDR UNS BDR VGN
(B) **PRIMITIVO DI PUGLIA 2000, PROMESSA** Apulia	Warm, baked fruits on the palate mingle with linseed and plum nuances on the finish.	**£5.30**	POR GGW BEN LIB
(S) **MONRUBIO ROSSO DELL UMBRIA 1999, CANTINA MONRUBIO** Umbria	Ruby red, with unctuous, stone fruits on the nose, and juicy cherries on the palate.	**£5.50**	MER

(S)	**ACCADEMIA DEL SOLE SANGIOVESE/NEGROAMARO 2000,** **CALATRASI,** Puglia	Dark ruby colour with intense red-fruit characters. Soft berries on the palate with a good length.	**£5.70**	GGW BWL SAF NYW
(S)	**NERO D'AVOLA RISERVA 2000, VILLA TONINO** Sicily	Good, fleshy fruit is well-distributed over a firm structure of balanced tannins. The finish is long and elegant.	**£5.90**	GGW LIB
(G)	**TRE UVE ULTIMA VdT 1999, MGM MONDO DEL VINO** Abruzzi	Hints of spice, a mouthful of sweet, ripe fruit with firm tannins and a long finish.	**£6.00**	WST
(S)	**BOTTE CABERNET FRANC 1999, CABERT** Friuli-Venezia Giulia	This deeply coloured wine has a rich blackcurrant nose and an almost savoury palate of mouthwatering red fruit .	**£7.00**	EHL
(S)	**FALESCO VITIANO 2000, FALESCO** Umbria	Blueberries and old wood rise from the nose. Slightly baked red fruit wrestles with astringent tannin.	**£7.20**	GGW CES
(S)	**VALPOLICELLA CLASSICO SUPERIORE 1997, VIGNETO ETORE RIGHETTI** Veneto	Ripe red cherries and mouthwatering acidity abound in this rich and complex, but eminently drinkable wine.	**£7.50**	MWW
(B)	**RIPASSO RITOCCO 1998, VALPANTENATOC** Veneto	Upfront juicy forest fruits underscored by dark chocolate and plums. Suble tannins on the lengthy finish.	**£8.00**	ENO
(G)	**CAMELOT 1999, FIRRIATO** Sicily	Immense berry and plum fruits integrate with vanilla oak; fairly grippy tannins support this big, juicy wine.	**£10.00**	IWS
(G)	**TANCA FARRA 1997, TENUTE SELLA & MOSCA** Sardinia	Smoky red fruit and tobacco. Good, creamy length. Sardinia has a great future and a long track record.	**£10.70**	ALI VGN
(G)	**PRIMA MANO PRIMITIVO DI PUGLIA 1999, A MANO** Apulia	Complex and multi-layered, this offers an oaky nose with minty, brambly fruit, fresh acidity, and powerful tannins.	**£11.00**	POR GGW LIB
(G)	**SANT ANGIOLO CHIANTI CLASSICO 1997, CASTELLI DEL GREVEPESA** Tuscany	Classic textbook Chianti Classico. Cigar-box and red-cherry flavours integrate well with firm tannins.	**£11.00**	VIN
(G)	**VILLA ARCENO MERLOT 1998, KENDALL JACKSON** Tuscany	Soft, strawberry flavour with minty, red-berry notes; good, grippy tannins and an open-textured palate.	**£11.30**	Not available in the UK

MERLOT 1999, BORGO CONVENTI (G) Friuli-Venezia Giulia	Fresh, peppery, creamy blackcurrant on a juicy, fleshy palate; soft fruit integrates well with restrained oak.	**£12.00**	ALI ODD DEL SAF
LA FABRISERIA 1998, TEDESCHI (G) Veneto	Classic liquorice, herbal, minty flavours on the nose are mirrored on the palate which has a smooth texture.	**£13.50**	HOH AVB CTC VGN
AMARONE, VIA NOVA 1998, VALPANTENAIA ✓ Veneto	Fruity aromas and a fresh palate.	**£14.00**	ENO
CUMARO ROSSO CONERO 1998, UMANI RONCHI (G) The Marches	Berry fruit on the nose gives way to a juicy mouthful with marked mint finesse and integrated oak.	**£15.50**	ENO
POLICALPO MONFERRATO ROSSO 1998, CASCINA CASTLE'T (G) Piedmont	Immense Christmas cake and amazing ripe fruit in a mouthful of sweet plums and blackberries with good structure.	**£17.00**	ALI
NERO D'AVOLA SANTA CECILIA 1998, PLANETA (G) Sicily	The big Nero d'Avola grape gives this wine its black pepper, leafy, earthy aromas and fruit-filled palate.	**£18.00**	ENO
COLONNA ALESSANDRA BARBERA DEL MONFERRATO 1998, COLONNA (G) Piedmont	Sweet chocolate depth and complexity. Plenty of primary fruit with fat texture enhanced by the beautifully integrated oak.	**£20.00**	RSS
VINO NOBILE DI MONTEPULCIANO VIGNA ASINONE 1997, POLIZIANO, Tuscany (G)	Crisp acid and firm tannins complement the ripe fruit and provide the basis for a long, dry finish.	**£23.30**	ENO FQU SOM SKW
CHIANTI CLASSICO RISERVA 1997, CASTELLO DI FONTERUTOLI (G) Tuscany	Mature, evolved nose with concentration of blackberry fruit, oak, and vanilla. Firm tannins and good fruit extract.	**£24.00**	WTS UNS
AMARONE DELLA VALPOLICELLA CLASSICO 1997, ALLEGRINI (G) Veneto	Super-ripe morello cherry, blackberry flavours combine with vanilla-flavoured new oak to give a complex, deep wine.	**£28.70**	POR GGW BEN LIB

ITALY • FORTIFIED

TERRE ARSE MARSALA VERGINE NV, FLORIO (G) Sicily	Lusciously sweet, concentrated marsala with woody notes running through a range of wild, secondary, maturing characters.	**£11.40**	ENO

ITALY • SWEET

(G)	**VIN SANTO DE CAPEZZANA RISERVA 1995, TENUTA DI CAPEZZANA** Tuscany	Complex, oxidative maturation in the oloroso-style finish. Burnt, nutty flavours and candied fruit.	**£15.00**	GGW BEN LIB
(G)	**VERDICCHIO DEI CASTELLI DI JESI PASSITO TORDIRUTA 1998, TERRE CORTESI MONCARO** Marche	Rich, honeyed and marmalade-coated palate integrates well with the naturally high, zesty acidity of the grape.	**£21.00**	EUW

ITALY • VERMOUTH

(B)	**TINDELLA ROSSO NV, CAVES DE COMMANDERIE** Sicily	Deep tawny colour with orange hues; the alluring, sweet nose has a complex, nutty character.	**£2.00**	DWI
✓	**TINDELLA BIANCO NV, CAVES DE COMMANDERIE** Sicily	Aromatic, floral, and herby nose.	**£2.00**	DWI
(S)	**VINELLI BIANCO NV, CAVES DE COMMANDERIE** Sicily	A herby and spicy vermouth made to a traditional recipe. Mix with lemonade or soda.	**£2.30**	DWI
(S)	**SOMERFIELD VERMOUTH ROSSO, BARBERO** Piedmont	Sweet, herbal nose with hints of spiced hazelnut and strawberry fruits.	**£3.00**	SMF
✓	**SOMERFIELD VERMOUTH BIANCO, BARBERO** Piedmont	Fresh, aromatic, and sweet palate.	**£3.00**	SMF
✓	**MHV BARONA BIANCO VERMOUTH NV, WINE SERVICES EUROPE** Italy	Sweet, floral, and herby nose.	**£3.20**	MHV

ITALY • LOW ALCOHOL

✓	**SOMERFIELD LAMBRUSCO ROSATO 5.5% NV, DONELLI VINI** Italy	Light, fruity, easy-drinking.	**£2.40**	M&M

NEW ZEALAND

New Zealand wines have the highest average price of any country in the world. There are many reasons for this, not least the huge demand and relatively small supply of the wonderfully pungent Sauvignon Blancs of the Marlborough district. But what the Kiwis have to offer doesn't end there. Pinot Gris and Riesling are showing great promise, and the best Chardonnays are world-class. The biggest improvements, however, have been in the red wines. Recent warm vintages have produced impressive Cabs, and South Island Pinot Noir is the next big thing.

NEW ZEALAND • SPARKLING

(B)	**LINDAUER SPECIAL RESERVE NV,** **MONTANA WINES LTD** Marlborough	Pale salmon with aromas of strawberry fruit. The palate is crisp and complex, with Pinot Noir lending full flavour.	**£9.00**	MTW
✓	**PELORUS 1996, CLOUDY BAY** Marlborough	Broad and rich, with a fine mousse Mild vanilla with youthful, green, herbal fruit.	**£14.50**	POR CEB BDR PRG

NEW ZEALAND • WHITE

✓	**TIKI RIDGE DRY WHITE 2000,** **MONTANA**	Well-balanced, delivering clean fruit and intense floral character.	**£4.00**	WTS
(B)	**AZURE BAY CHARDONNAY SEMILLON 2000,** **MONTANA WINES** North Island	Good fruit salad and floral aromas with a gently minerally undercurrent.	**£5.00**	MTW
(S)	**SANCTUARY CHARDONNAY 1999,** **GROVE MILL** Marlborough	New Zealand's climate is cooler than you may imagine which imparts an elegancy and subtlety into the wines.	**£5.50**	JSM
(G)	**HOUSE OF NOBILO SAUVIGNON BLANC 2000,** **BRL HARDY WINE COMPANY** North Island	Herbs, figs, and gooseberries. Complex layers of asparagus, grass, and spice with a lovely dose of tropical fruit.	**£6.50**	HBR
✓	**HOUSE OF NOBILO SAUVIGNON BLANC 2000,** **NOBILO VINTNERS LTD.** Marlborough	Ripe fruit lies behind clean, floral, soda-like minerals. Limey acidity gives the wine character and depth.	**£6.50**	HBR MAD PIM TPE

(G)	**VILLA MARIA PRIVATE BIN SAUVIGNON BLANC 2000, VILLA MARIA** Marlborough	Wonderfully balanced wine with tropical fruits galore underscored by gooseberry hints and a zingy, fresh acidity.	**£7.00**	ASD UNS SAF

NEW ZEALAND • RED

(B)	**NEW ZEALAND RED WINE, LINDEN ESTATE** Hawke's Bay	Fruity red showing good balance and medium body, with clean acidity and medium length.	**£4.30**	MHV WTS WRK COM
(S)	**TERRACE VIEW CABERNET MERLOT 1999, KEMBLEFIELD ESTATE** Hawke's Bay	Sweet mint and soft-fruit palate. A well-made, medium-weight wine with a warm, jammy finish.	**£5.00**	CWS
(S)	**STONELEIGH VINEYARDS PINOT NOIR 1999, STONELEIGH VINEYARDS LTD.** Marlborough	Juicy cherries blend with toasted oak. Ripe tannins and subtle acidity complete the complexity of this wine.	**£6.00**	MTW
(S)	**MONTANA EAST COAST PINOTAGE 2000, MONTANA WINES** East Coast	Inviting juicy fruit on the nose. Fleshy, overripe plums and raspberry flavours integrate well with oak underscores.	**£7.00**	MTW
(S)	**GROVE MILL PINOT NOIR 1999, GROVE MILL** Marlborough	LIght pinot fruit on the nose leading to a palate layered with delicate strawberries with dominant oak flavours.	**£7.50**	CRI
(G)	**MATARIKI PINOT NOIR 1999, MATARIKI WINES LTD** Hawke's Bay	Lovely, red-fruit Pinot character married to layers of sweet oak, affording great balance and complexity.	**£12.00**	AHW
(G)	**MATUA VALLEY ARARIMU MERLOT CABERNET SAUVIGNON 2000, MATUA VALLEY,** Hawke's Bay	Toasty oak enhances a herbal, redcurrant palate with rich complexity. Grippy tannins enhance the long, smooth finish.	**£12.50**	Not available in the U.K.
(G)	**GIBBSTON VALLEY RESERVE PINOT NOIR 1999, GIBBSTON VALLEY WINES** Central Otago	Modern style Pinot with pronounced red-berry fruit and undertones of creamy vanilla.	**£17.30**	Not available in the U.K.
(G)	**GIBBSTON VALLEY RESERVE PINOT NOIR 2000, GIBBSTON VALLEY WINES** Central Otago	This is a wine of compelling depth, balance, and complexity, showing good fruit richness and sweet oak.	**£17.30**	Not available in the U.K.
(S)	**CRAB FARM JARDINE CABERNET SAUVIGNON 1998, CRAB FARM** Hawke's Bay	Aromas of spice, black fruits laced with mint. The palate offers hints of chocolate and toasty oak.	**£18.00**	NWG

ⓖ **THE AVIATIOR 1998, ALPHA DOMUS** Hawke's Bay	Blackcurrants and liquorice laced with eucalyptus, chocolate, and masses of vanilla oak.	**£20.00**	MKV

PORTUGAL

Portugal needs absolutely no introduction for its sublime fortified red wines from the Douro Valley. Vintage Port is at last beginning to fetch the prices it deserves, because of a new-found demand for this style. Value hunters should keep a look-out for Traditional LBV or vintage Tawny, also known as Colheita, which both offer tremendous complexity for the money. The table wines of Portugal can no longer be ignored, with Douro, and Alentejo producing reds with easily enough concentration and class to give the Spaniards and Italians a fright. Slowly but surely, the whites are getting there too.

PORTUGAL • WHITE

✓ **ALTA MESA 2000, DFJ VINHOS** Estremadura	Perfumed blossoms pervade this light-bodied wine with wisps of citrus.	**£3.30**	PFT BGN D&F
Ⓑ **RAMADA 2000, DFJ VINHOS** Estremadura	Floral fruit characters with light hints of citrus and a green-apple finish.	**£3.50**	PFT D&F SAF
Ⓑ **LORIDOS BRANCO DE BRANCAS 1996, JP VINHOS** Estremadura	Pale gold; buttery nose with hints of toast and bread. Burnt caramel and lemon characters; long and complex.	**£3.90**	EHL
✓ **FIUZA SAUVIGNON BLANC 2000, FIUZA & BRIGHT** Ribatejo	Hints of fresh gooseberry and freshly cut grass with a crisp acidity.	**£4.00**	EHL

PORTUGAL • RED

✓ **ALTA MESA 2000, DFJ VINHOS** Estremadura	Abundant, soft and sweet fruit on the palate, with a well-rounded finish.	**£3.30**	PFT BGN D&F ESL

✓	**TESCO PORTUGESE RED NV,** **JP VINHOS** Portugal	Pleasant, fruity wine that gives loads of acidic buzz.	**£3.00**	EHL
✓	**MÁ PARTILHA 1998,** **JP VINHOS** Terras do Sado	An abundance of sweet prune flavours over a great, fleshy backbone.	**£3.80**	EHL
✓	**SAFEWAY BAIRRADA 1998,** **SOGRAP** Bairrada	Light, fruity, easy-drinking wine with a touch of white pepper and acidic backbone finish.	**£3.90**	SAF
✓	**TINTO DA ANFORA 1999,** **JP VINHOS** Alentejo	Soft tannins and a hint of oak, with lovely fruit and spice palate.	**£4.00**	EHL SAF
✓	**JP GARRAFEIRA 1995,** **JP VINHOS** Terras do Sado	Rounded, fruity wine with sweet, bright, fruit palate and cedar characters.	**£4.20**	BDR EHL
Ⓢ	**CO-OP BIG BAGA 1999,** **DFJ VINHOS** Beiras	Red cherry in colour. Intense raspberries and smoky red-berry fruits follow through onto the palate.	**£4.50**	D&F DBY NYW G&M
Ⓑ	**MONTE VELHO 2000,** **ESPORÃO** Alentejo	This perky Portuguese number is rich red in colour, boasting opulent peppery characters and oozing fresh juice.	**£4.50**	JEF SAF
Ⓑ	**BRIGHT BROS. DOURA** **TORCULAR 1999,** **BRIGHT BROTHERS** Douro	Yet another competent wine from this producer; intense fruits sewn up with a slight stalky edge.	**£5.00**	EHL
Ⓑ	**DUQUE DE VISEU TINTO 1998,** **VINHOS SOGRAPE** Dao	Elegance and style: soft strawberry aromas and a simple yet pleasing palate beckon to be drunk now.	**£5.00**	SGL
Ⓑ	**MEIA ENCOSTA 1999,** **SOC. VINHOS BORGES** Dao	This stunner epitomizes the soft, fruit-driven style with its delicate scented palate and unassuming tannins.	**£5.00**	SGL
Ⓢ	**FIUZA CABERNET SAUVIGNON** **1998,** **FIUZA & BRIGHT** Ribatejo	Bright red colour with cassis and black fruits. Good structure with soft tannins and an earthy, spicy finish.	**£5.00**	EHL
Ⓢ	**FIUZA MERLOT 1998,** **FIUZA & BRIGHT** Ribatejo	Delicate perfumed nose with aromas of velvety ripe damsons and plums that follow through onto the palate.	**£5.00**	EHL

BELA FONTE BAGA 1999, **DFJ VINHOS** Beiras Ⓑ	Bright brick-red in colour with upfront red berries. The palate finishes on a soft, rounded note.	**£5.20**	PFT D&F
BELA FONTE JAEN 1999, **DFJ VINHOS** Beiras Ⓑ	The slightly restrained nose hides the lusciously sweet cherry fruits that lie hidden just beneath the surface.	**£5.20**	PFT D&F SAF
MONTE DAS ANFORAS 1999, **JP VINHOS** Alentejo ✓	Chocolate and spicy hints on the nose with a gripping tannic palate showing good weight.	**£5.49**	EHL
VINHA GRANDE 1997, **FERREIRA** Douro Ⓢ	Subtle flavours of oak underline a middle palate of spice and layers of upfront tannins.	**£7.50**	BWC
GRAND ARTE TOURIGA FRANCA 2000, **DFJ VINHOS** Estremadura Ⓢ	The palate is packed with luscious cherries and violets with underscores of rich damson fruit.	**£7.50**	D&F REY DBY HST JSS
INCÓGNITO 1999, **HANS KRISTIAN JORGENSEN** Alentejo Ⓖ	Strawberries and cream character with elegant structure and freshness of fruit overlaid with a touch of vanilla oak.	**£7.80**	Not Available in the U.K.
GRAND ARTE TOURIGA FRANCA, **DFJ VINHOS** Estremadura Ⓢ	Intense purple colour with complex, baked-berry fruit flavours. The finish is long, with balanced, sweet tannins.	**£8.90**	PFT D&F VGN

PORTUGAL • FORTIFIED

QUINTA DO SAGRADO FINE TAWNY NV, **AA CALEM & FILHO SA** Douro Ⓑ	Intense dried figs and caramel on the nose; vanilla and melted toffee on the palate.	**£4.20**	LAU
QUINTA DO SAGRADO RUBY NV, **AA CALEM** Douro Ⓑ	Rich and velvety with straightforward fruit flavours. Good weight of sweet raisins on the finish.	**£4.20**	LAU
SW FINE RUBY PORT NV, **SMITH WOODHOUSE CA** Douro ✓	Bright, fresh maraschino and plum fruit in this youthful spirity style.	**£5.00**	SAF CWS WCR CST
POÇAS LATE BOTTLED VINTAGE PORT 1996, **MANOEL D POÇAS JUNIOR VINHOS SA,** Douro Ⓖ	This wine is big and masculine on the palate with firm tannins underlying the concentrated fruit.	**£5.00**	Not available in the UK

✓	**Quinta Do Sagrado Vintage Character NV, AA Calem** Douro	Bright red colour with a sweet nose of red-backed fruits. Upfront flavours with a warming finish.	**£5.00**	LAU
Ⓑ	**Co-Op Ruby Port NV, Symington Family** Douro	Ripe, warm nose with sweet red fruits and a seductive, spicy, velvety mouthfeel; good finish.	**£5.20**	CWS MWW ODD BRF
Ⓑ	**Old Master Ruby Port NV,** Douro	Warm, jammy fruits; complex aromas of ripe, juicy raisins and earth; a satisfyingly long-lasting finish.	**£5.50**	MCT JMC
Ⓖ	**Justino's Madeira Colheita 1995, Vinhos Justino Henriques** Madeira	The nutty, burnt-caramel aromas and rich spiciness on the palate balances well with crisp acidity.	**£5.60**	Not available in the U.K.
Ⓑ	**Tawny Port NV, Syminton Family** Douro	Pale brown colour, a light nutty nose, subtle caramel flavours, and a properly balanced finish.	**£5.90**	CWS
✓	**Co-Op Vintage Character Port NV, Symington Family** Douro	Shows sign of maturity with almond, nuts, and dried fruits.	**£6.90**	CWS JSS G&M
Ⓑ	**Asda Finest Reserve Port NV, Symington Port Companies** Douro Valley	Sweet, dark-red fruits nose with a touch of ripe, dried-summer fruits and figs.	**£7.00**	ASD
Ⓑ	**Dow's Fine Ruby Port NV, Silva & Cosens** Douro	Warm bramble fruits fill the palate with good texture; rounded flavours last and last on the rich finish.	**£7.00**	JEF
✓	**Safeway Vintage Character NV, Smith Woodhouse CA** Douro	Bright red colour, a delicate style with good fruit flavours and a warm, spicy finish.	**£7.00**	SAF
Ⓑ	**Quinta Do Sagrado 10 Year Old NV, AA Calem** Douro	Subtle caramel and light nutty characters on the nose, with a well-balanced mouthful of sweetness and acidity.	**£7.20**	LAU GHC
Ⓑ	**MHV Regimental Special Reserve Port NV, Silva & Cosens** Douro	Straightforward in style, with a long, rich, and spicy mouthfeel complimented by a complex finish.	**£7.40**	MHV
Ⓑ	**Delaforce Special White Port, CD Vintners SOC Vitivinicola SA,** Douro	Luscious nose of walnuts and honey. Soft, round palate with balanced acidity and a good finish.	**£7.50**	PFC

	Wine	Notes	Price	Stockists
✓	**CROFT TRIPLE CROWN,** **CROFT** Douro	Subtle fruit and good texture.	**£7.50**	PFC SMF
Ⓑ	**CO-OP LATE BOTTLED** **VINTAGE PORT 1995,** **SYMINGTON FAMILY** Douro	Spicy, raisin-fruit flavours with hints of sweet, candied peaches lead to a satisfyingly long finish.	**£7.60**	CWS
Ⓑ	**SMITH-WOODHOUSE LBV** **1995,** **SMITH WOODHOUSE CA** Douro	Full and complex, with plenty of fruits and dried-raisin flavours which merge well on the elegant finish.	**£7.60**	SAF
Ⓢ	**FONSECA BIN 27,** **FONSECA** Douro	Mature and sophisticated, rich with plenty of concentration, well-made with good structure and a lingering finish.	**£8.00**	MZC
Ⓖ	**QUINTA DO NOVAL FINE RUBY,** **QUINTA DO NOVAL** Douro	Rich fruitcake and berry flavours run over a firm palate giving an elegant blend of fruit and tannins.	**£8.10**	PRG JMC
Ⓑ	**T FINEST MADEIRA NV,** **MADEIRA WINE COMPANY** Madeira	Orange peel, figs, spices, and walnuts on the complex, aromatic nose; a sweet but well-balanced palate.	**£8.30**	TOS SAF
Ⓑ	**OSBORNE LATE BOTTLED** **VINTAGE 1996,** **OSBORNE** Douro	Good level of richness, with sweet figs, plums, and hints of black cherry on the palate.	**£9.00**	HBJ
Ⓖ	**WARRE'S OTIMA TEN YEAR** **OLD TAWNY PORT NV, WARRE** **& CA SA OPORTO** Douro	Nutty and spicy overtones, finely structured, full flavoured, with a zingy edge to compliment its complexity of flavour.	**£9.10**	WTS SAF DBY JNW
Ⓑ	**DOW'S LATE BOTTLED** **VINTAGE 1995,** **SILVA & COSENS** Douro	Elegant style with mature red-fruit aromas; the palate is complex, developed, and nicely balanced.	**£9.50**	ASD JEF
Ⓢ	**FERREIRA L.B.V.** **1996,** **FERREIRA** Douro	Wonderfully soft, rich fruit with a dark colour. A round and structured palate with good length.	**£10.00**	BWC
Ⓑ	**PORTAL CELLAR RESERVE PORT** **NV,** **QUINTA DO PORTAL** Douro	Sweet, dried-fruit characters with an elegant touch of vanilla and a long, spicy finish.	**£10.00**	CHN HST GRO M&V
Ⓢ	**ROZÈS LATE BOTTLE VINTAGE** **RESERVE EDITION 1994,** **ROZÈS** Douro	Intense dark colour with hints of violets, this concentrated wine is full of flavours with a complex finish.	**£11.00**	VRA

(S)	**SAINSBURY'S TEN YEAR OLD TAWNY PORT NV, TAYLORS** Douro	Orange-tawny colour, complex nutty aromas on the nose with hints of burnt toffee and walnuts.	**£11.00**	JSM
(B)	**CHURCHILL'S LATE BOTTLED VINTAGE PORT 1996, CHURCHILL GRAHAM, LDA** Douro	A rich, big bodied Port that shows some evolution of its sweet, Christmas pudding fruit.	**£11.40**	POR PFT CPW CGL
(S)	**QUINTA NOVA DE NOSSA SENHORA DO CARMO LATE BOTTLED VINTAGE PORT 1996, J.W. BURMESTER,** Douro	Intense aromas of dried fruits with concentration and complexity. Well structured with a long, punchy finish.	**£12.00**	HBJ SAF
(S)	**BLANDY'S FIVE YEAR OLD VERDELHO MADEIRA NV, MADEIRA WINE COMPANY SA** Madeira	Fine, delicate, citrus aromas on the nose with a gentle touch of honey and plenty of flavour.	**£12.70**	BEN JEF
(S)	**DOW'S CRUSTED PORT BOTTLED 1997 NV, SILVA & COSENS** Douro	Amazing depth and concentration of red fruits aromas. Rich, juicy, and exuberant on the finish.	**£13.40**	CPW JEF
(G)	**POÇAS VINTAGE PORT 1996, MANOEL D POÇAS JUNIOR VINHOS SA** Douro	Spicy, leathery aromas with fragrant, toffeed fruit and lively acidity work harmoniously with the grippy tannins.	**£14.90**	BWL VGN
(G)	**WARRES TRADITIONAL LATE BOTTLED VINATGE PORT 1992, SYMINGTON** Douro	Elegant structure with ripe, diverse fruit. Warm, raisiny flavours show through the layers of chocolate and coffee.	**£15.60**	WTS SGL
(G)	**POÇAS VINTAGE PORT 1997, MANOEL D POÇAS JUNIOR VINHOS SA** Douro	Plenty of firm tannins, but has a core of sweetness that lifts it through to the finish.	**£16.90**	Not available in the U.K.
(G)	**QUINTA DO CASTELINHO VINTAGE PORT 1997, CASTELINHO VINHOS** Douro	Rich, spicy fruit aromas leading into a soft, rounded palate which is packed with complex fruit.	**£18.00**	NID
(G)	**PORTO POÇAS COLHEITA TAWNY PORT 1970, MANOEL D POÇAS JUNIOR VINHOS SA,** Douro	Complex floral, treacly, walnut flavours and nutty, classically rancio aromas indicate the maturity of this Port.	**£19.70**	Not available in the U.K.
(G)	**VAU VINTAGE 1999 VINTAGE PORTO 1999, SANDEMAN & CA SA** Douro	Full-bodied with luscious fruit, intense sweetness and rounded, balanced framework that holds and integrates the alcohol.	**£20.00**	ODD HAS NYW CTH
(G)	**PORTO KOPKE COLHEITA 1977, C.N. KOPKE & CO LTD.** Douro	Almond, nutty, and caramelized nose with layers of fruit flavours and more developed smoky notes.	**£20.00**	HST

	Wine	Description	Price	Stockists
G	**QUINTA INFANTADO VINTAGE PORT 1997,** **QUINTA INFANTADO** Douro	Concentrated berry aromas with warm, but not overpowering, alcohol and grippy tannins. A wine with a great future.	**£21.00**	Not available in the UK
G	**QUINTA DA ERVAMOIRA,** **RAMOS PINTO** Douro	Rich orangey fruit with flavours of caramel and toffee layer the palate with crisp acidity and supple tannins.	**£21.30**	BEN MMD
G	**GRAHAM'S MALVEDOS VINTAGE PORT 1995, W & J GRAHAM** Douro	It is powerful and rich with a spicy nose and sweet mouth-filling fruit on the palate.	**£22.20**	POR JEF
G	**DOW'S TWENTY YEAR OLD TAWNY PORT NV, SILVA & COSENS** Douro	Tarry, burnt-toffee aromas jostle with spicy, raisiny fruit and lead into an impressive orange-peel finish.	**£23.80**	JEF SAF
G	**15 YEAR OLD BUAL NV, HENRIQUES & HENRIQUES** Madeira	Nutty, fruitcake-scented wine which shows great balance, length, and complexity.	**£24.50**	HWL
G	**15 YEAR OLD VERDELHO NV, HENRIQUES & HENRIQUES** Madeira	The nose is deep and inviting with wonderful walnut, coffee, and spice notes steeped in orange and caramel.	**£24.50**	HWL
G	**BURMESTER VINTAGE PORT 1997,** **J.W. BURMESTER** Douro	Deep and concentrated with rich, sweet fruit in perfect balance with its firm structure and rounded tannins.	**£25.00**	HBJ CTC VGN
G	**WARRE'S TWENTY YEAR OLD TAWNY PORT NV,** **WARRE & CA SA** Douro	Ripe, round, and sweet, with pleasant oaky notes and nuttiness on the palate that is firm and long.	**£26.00**	JEF DBY FEN
G	**QUINTA DO CRASTO VINTAGE PORT 1995,** **QUINTA DO CRASTO** Douro	Showy, elegant style with a spicy, plummy nose and rich damson and fruitcake palate, and a long finish.	**£28.00**	ENO SMF
G	**DOW'S QUINTA DA SENHORA DA RIBEIRA 1999,** **SILVA & COSENS** Douro	It is showing super-concentrated, rich, mulberry fruit on the nose and a luscious, smooth, rounded palate.	**£30.00**	JEF
G	**MARTINEZ VINTAGE PORT 1985, MARTINEZ GASSIOT** Douro	Immense peppery fruit and spicy palate set within a clear framework of fine tannin and balanced acidity.	**£42.00**	WSG

Pinpoint who sells the wine you wish to buy by turning to the stockist codes. If you know the name of the wine you want to buy, use the alphabetical index. If the price is your motivation, look out for the "Wine of the Year" symbol; the best red and white wines under £8, sparkling wines under £12, and champagne under £15. Happy hunting!

SOUTH AFRICA

The strides being made by the more keenly priced brands and mid-priced producers is startling. Pinotage, South Africa's own grape, is finding new levels of sophistication even at the lower price levels, and the Chardonnays between £7 and £10 could make a very good case for being the best-value examples in the world. At the top end of the market, Cabernets with uncannily Bordelais flavours, maybe with a touch more ripeness and grip, are competing with world-class examples from the New and Old World alike.

SOUTH AFRICA • SPARKLING

(B)	**GRAHAM BECK BRUT NV, GRAHAM BECK WINES** Robertson	Very pleasant nutty characters that leap from a fruity nose; a balanced and long finish.	**£7.90**	GGW BWL SAF
(S)	**PONGRACZ NV, DISTELL,** Stellenbosch	Delightful, mature toasty aroma, and balanced.	**£7.99**	PFC

SOUTH AFRICA • WHITE

✓	**SOMERFIELD SOUTH AFRICAN DRY WHITE 2000, SONOP** Western Cape	Bursting with kiwi and melon; perfect for a summer's day.	**£3.00**	SMF
✓	**SONOP CAPE WINERY MEDIUM WHITE 2001, SONOP** Western Cape	Full-flavoured citrus fruit and fresh grassiness with a lime finish.	**£3.00**	SAF
✓	**TABLE PEAK COLOMBARD NV, TABLE PEAK** Western Cape	Clean and floral, with fresh, bracing acidity and good length.	**£3.40**	MCT
✓	**KATHENBERG WESTERN CAPE WHITE NV, WINECORP** Western Cape	Simple, delicate wine with apricot and apple fruits balanced by crisp acidity.	**£3.50**	WRT
✓	**PIETERS DRIFT COLOMBARD CHARDONNAY NV, HIPPO CREEK WINES LTD** Western Cape	Pineapple and melon bouquet and good refreshing acidity.	**£3.50**	DWL

✓	**SOUTH AFRICAN CHENIN BLANC 2001, SWARTLAND WINERY** Swartland	Prominent fruit-salad aromas layered with citrus and crispness from the acidity.	**£3.50**	JSM VGN
✓	**LAMBERTS BAY COLOMBARD CHENIN BLANC 2000/1, LAMBERTS BAY** Western Cape	Warm, ripe, plump tropical fruit and floral bouquet giving to a fresh finish.	**£3.70**	WAV NRW SOM
✓	**VALE OF PEACE COLOMBARD 2000, VREDENDAAL** Olifantsriver	Unctuous, round honeydew melon flavours with a tightness on the palate.	**£3.80**	SAF
✓	**ROBERTSON SILVER SANDS CHARDONNAY 2000, ROBERTSON WINERY** Robertson	Fresh citrus aromas with lively acidity finishing with good length.	**£3.80**	ABY
✓	**CULLINAN VIEW SAUVIGNON BLANC 2001, CULLINAN VIEW** Breede River Valley	Bursting with nettles and peppers, this cheeky white has good balance of acidity.	**£3.90**	MCT
Ⓑ	**DOUGLAS GREEN COLOMBARD CHARDONNAY 2000, DGB PTY LTD** Western Cape	Zingy, fresh white with clean lemon-zest character. Good all-purpose drinker.	**£4.00**	EHL
Ⓑ	**KUMALA CHENIN BLANC 2001, WESTERN WINES LTD** Western Cape	Grassy notes with clean, refreshing melon and light citrus flavours.	**£4.00**	WST
Ⓑ	**SPRINGFIELD ESTATE FIREFINCH SAUVIGNON BLANC 2000, SPRINGFIELD ESTATE** Robertson	Light floral nose with herbal hints on a lively, grassy palate.	**£4.00**	TOS
Ⓑ	**STOWELLS OF CHELSEA CHENIN BLANC NV, MATTHEW CLARK** Coastal	Ripe, fruity bouquet and easy pear and banana flavours.	**£4.00**	BGN NTD MCT
✓	**CAPE CHENIN BLANC OAK-AGED 2000, STELLENBOSCH VINEYARDS** Stellenbosch	Lovely balanced wine with a honeyed nose and ample palate with a hint of spiciness.	**£4.00**	CWS VGN
✓	**DANIE DE WET CHARDONNAY SUR LIE UNWOODED 2001, DANIE DE WET** Robertson	Appealing nose with a crisp, green fruit, a well-balanced palate, and a refreshing finish.	**£4.00**	NTD ASD RSS SAF
✓	**HAZY VIEW CHENIN BLANC 2000, HALLGARTEN** Paarl	Laced with grapefruit and lime fruits, this wine shows great drinkablity.	**£4.00**	HOH

✓	**KUMALA CHARDONNAY 2000, WESTERN WINES LTD** Western Cape	Classic tropical-fruit flavours and maybe a whisp of creaminess gives great texture.	**£4.00**	WST
✓	**KUMALA CHARDONNAY 2001, WESTERN WINES LTD** Western Cape	Clean and fresh tropical fruit supported by defined and bracing acidity.	**£4.00**	WST
✓	**LONG MOUNTAIN CHENIN BLANC 2000, LONG MOUNTAIN WINE COMPANY** Western Cape	Apples, pears, and sherbet on the nose move to lemons on the finish.	**£4.00**	CAX
✓	**LUTZVILLE CHENIN BLANC 2000, LUTZVILLE VINEYARDS** Lutzville Valley	Shy to begin with, this wine opens to be a floral number with an acidic backbone.	**£4.00**	SWS
✓	**VINFRUCO OAK VILLAGE CHENIN BLANC 2000, VINFRUCO** Coastal	Honey and mushroom nose, the oak is in the background, giving to the fruit on the fore-palate.	**£4.00**	VNF
✓	**RYLANDS GROVE BARREL FERMENTED CHENIN 2000, STELLENBOSCH VINEYARDS** Stellenbosch	This wine exhibits good fruit and sweet, well-integrated oak.	**£4.00**	TOS
✓	**SOMERFIELD SOUTH AFRICAN CHARDONNAY 2000, VINFRUCO** Robertson	Apple pie and spice make all things, including this South African Chardonnay from Somerfields nice!	**£4.00**	SMF
✓	**TWO TRIBES WHITE 2000, WESTERN WINES LTD**	Some good peachy fruit overlies a slight vegetal character.	**£4.00**	NTD WST
Ⓢ	**VAN LOVEREN SAUVIGNON BLANC 2001, VAN LOVEREN** Robertson	Pale colour with intense tropical-fruits nose. Refreshing palate with a touch of asparagus on the finish.	**£4.70**	SGL RSS
✓	**GOLD MUSCAT 2000, WELTEVREDE**	Intense perfumed sweetness and fruit, coming together with a texturous palate.	**£5.00**	HOH
Ⓢ	**NIEL JOUBERT CHARDONNAY 2000, NIEL JOUBERT** Paarl	Butterscotch and tart marmalade characteristics on the palate with an undercurrent of soft vanilla oak which infuses throughout.	**£5.00**	VNO
Ⓢ	**HOOPENBURG CHARDONNAY WINE MAKERS SELECTION 2000, HOOPENBURG** Stellenbosch	Intense citrus aromas overlay toasty oak nuances that are echoed on its deliciously creamy palate.	**£6.10**	ABY HST BEL

G	**PLAISIR DE MERLE CHARDONNAY 1999, DISTELL** Paarl	Old World style; New World purity. Lemony, honeyed fruit with balanced oak; a classy wine, fine-grained, and focused.	**£9.10**	Not available in the U.K.

SOUTH AFRICA • RED

✓	**ASDA SOUTH AFRICAN CABERNET SAUVIGNON 2000, WINECORP** Western Cape	Juicy berries and a hint of spice giving to a toasty oak finish.	**£3.60**	ASD WTS CWS FQU
✓	**CO-OP ELEPHANT TRAIL CINSAULT-MERLOT 2000, ASHWOOD** Western Cape	Soft and feminine and refreshingly long. Perfect for a crisp start to an outdoor meal.	**£3.80**	CWS ODD MWW DBY
✓	**ASDA CAPE MERLOT 2000, WINECORP** Western Cape	Sour plum fruit and dark cherries, good body, and a restrained drying finish.	**£4.00**	ASD VGN
✓	**CO-OP CAPE RUBY CABERNET OAK-AGED 2000, VINFRUCO** Robertson	Soft fruity palate with a hint of pepper and dark plums. Well palated with soft finish to boot.	**£4.00**	CWS SAF
✓	**MALAN ROUGE DU CAP, MALAN VINTNERS** Western Cape	Soft juicy nose with a round palate and well-structured finish.	**£4.00**	HAE
✓	**SW SOUTH AFRICAN CINSAUT 2000, STELLENBOSCH VINEYARDS** Stellenbosch	Loads of berry fruit and wisps of dry spice and showing a balanced finish.	**£4.00**	SAF
B	**DOUGLAS GREEN PINOTAGE 1999, DGB PTY LTD** Western Cape	Subtle smoky aromas precede a lush palate laden with red fruit and freshly ground white pepper.	**£4.50**	EHL
B	**KUMALA CINSAULT PINOTAGE 2000, WESTERN WINES LTD** Western Cape	The elegant, scented nose gives way to crushed cranberries and raspberries; perfect for early drinking.	**£4.70**	BGN NTD WST SAF
S	**GOATS DO ROAM 2000, WINES OF CHARLES BACK** Coastal	On the palate, stewed, jammy plums are apparent with an underlying layer of green fruits.	**£5.00**	WTS CHN
S	**NATURAL STATE CAPE SOLEIL PINOTAGE 2000, SONOP WINE FARM** Western Cape	Robust and powerful with great concentration, this wine has an open palate with a euclyptus finish.	**£5.00**	WST CWS

(S)	**WESTERN CAPE SHIRAZ CABERNET 2000, BELLINGHAM** Western Cape	Bright-red, ruby colour, plummy nose with ripe fruit flavours and warm spicy hints.	**£5.00**	EHL
(B)	**NATURAL STATE SHIRAZ 2000, SONOP WINE FARM** Western Cape	Vibrant purple colour; hot sun-baked fruit on the nose, and a cornucopia of spices on the palate.	**£5.00**	WST BBR DBY
(B)	**ROCKBRIDGE CABERNET SAUVIGNON 1999, VIN FRUCO** Coastal	Sweet cassis, leather, and mint on the nose. Fleshy fruit, good balance, and medium length.	**£5.00**	VNF
(B)	**TESCO FINEST BEYERS TRUTER PINOTAGE 2000, BEYERSKLOOF** Coastal	This deep purple wine is packed with warm blackcurrant aromas followed by silky vanilla and spiced raspberry palate.	**£5.00**	TOS
(S)	**LYNGROVE RESERVE CABERNET SAUVIGNON MERLOT 2000, LYNGROVE WINERIES** Western Cape	Dark brick with an intense nose. Delicious chocolate notes with firm tannins and a long finish.	**£5.70**	FEE SAF VGN
(S)	**APOSTLES FALLS CABERNET SAUVIGNON 1999, STELLENBOSCH VINEYARDS** Stellenbosch	Chunky cassis and summer fruits on the palate with firm tannins and great structure.	**£6.00**	SAF
(S)	**FAIRVIEW PINOTAGE 2000, WINES OF CHARLES BACK** Coastal	Intense smoky aromas blending with freshly ground coffee flowing to a creamy soft palate packed with caramalized plums.	**£6.00**	CHN
(S)	**LA BRI CABERNET SAUVIGNON RESERVE 1999, LA BRI** Paarl	Intense palate with great body and structure. Resembles good Claret, but with an American-oak backbone.	**£6.00**	BXT
(G)	**VERGELEGEN MERLOT 1998, VERGELEGEN** Stellenbosch	Red berry fruits, leather, mulberries, and spice with a rounded structure are underpinned by smooth tannins.	**£6.10**	ODD JSM
(S)	**CABERNET SAUVIGNON WINE MAKERS SELECTION 1998, HOOPENBURG** Stellenbosch	Sweet fruit followed by a lovely, toasty oak character, firm spicy fruit, and a long, dark chocolatey finish.	**£7.00**	ABY
(S)	**BEAUMONT PINOTAGE 1999, BEAUMONT** Walker Bay	Abundant bramble fruit with a hint of smoke on the palate leads to fine-tuned tannin structure.	**£7.00**	FTH
(S)	**BUSHMANS CREEK MERLOT 1998, BUSHMAN'S CREEK** Western Cape	Loads of sweet fruit and eucalyptus on the nose with a touch of tobacco on the palate.	**£7.00**	ALL

(S) **SENTINEL CABERNET SAUVIGNON 1999, COPPOOLSE & FINLAYSON** Coastal	Lovely vibrant berry fruits and a very inviting nose. Fully concentrated palate with complexity and good length.	**£7.00**	SEA BEL CNL
(G) **SPICE ROUTE PINOTAGE 1999, CHARLES BACK WINES** Swartland	Ripe raspberries and cherries shine through on the nose and the palate of this well-structured wine.	**£8.00**	UNS ENO
(G) **FAIRVIEW PRIMO PINOTAGE 2000, WINES OF CHARLES BACK** Coastal	Cherry and blackcurrant aromas give way to a creamy, intense raspberry palate; massive structure on velvety tannins.	**£9.00**	CHN
(G) **VERGELEGEN CABERNET SAUVIGNON 1998, VERGELEGEN** Stellenbosch	Blackcurrant and eucalyptus flavours abound; sweet vanilla oak and a rich chocolate finish. Good depth and complexity.	**£9.60**	ODD JSM
(G) **JORDAN CABERNET SAUVIGNON 1998, JORDAN ESTATE** Stellenbosch	Sweet, ripe fruit with chocolate and earthy leather. Seductive flavours and some complexity drive an elegant finish.	**£9.90**	GGW CPW UNS AUS
(G) **KAAPZICHT STEYTLER PINOTAGE 1999, KAAPZICHT** Stellenbosch	Intense rich nose of ripe raspberry and blackcurrant gives way to a stylish, ripe, plummy palate.	**£15.00**	SCK UNS DBY PFT

SPAIN

If one wine-producing country could be said to have an embarrassment of riches, it would be Spain. Cava is by far the best selling fizz in the world. Sherry is arguably the world's most interesting, complex, and well-priced fortified wine. The reds aren't too bad either, with well-known and well-loved classics such as Rioja and Navarra, and interesting, up-and-coming regions, which include Somontano and Priorat. New, exciting varieties of white grapes such as Albarino and Verdejo from the cooler regions of the North West complete a veritable tuck-shop of interest and individuality.

SPAIN • SPARKLING

✓ **ASDA CAVA NV, CORDORNIU** Catalonia	Refreshing, aromatic, and well-made.	**£4.50**	ASD

(B)	**CAVA BRUT NV, SANT SADURNI D'ANOIA** Catalonia	Lively mousse with hints of apples and peaches. Crisp and refreshing, with a delicate touch of biscuity aromas.	**£5.00**	MHV
✓	**SOMERFIELD CAVA BRUT 1998, CASTELL DE VILARNAU** Catalonia	Good mousse with light fruity nose, fine aftertaste, and firm acidity.	**£5.00**	SMF
(B)	**CAVA BRUT NV, MARQUES DE MONISTRL** Catalonia	Clean, attractive nose, appealing ripe fruits and fresh, toasty aromas. Lively but well-balanced acidity level.	**£5.40**	NTD SGL NTD CWS
✓	**DUC DE FOIX 1998, COVIDES SCCL** Catalonia	Mature on the nose, with a touch of biscuit. Attractive flavours with a dry finish.	**£5.50**	STB
✓	**CUVÉE 21 NV, PARXET** Catalonia	Lively mousse and fine, waxy lime flavours.	**£6.20**	POR MOR VGN
✓	**CAVA TORREBLANCA BRUT NV, VIÑA TORREBLANCA SL** Catalonia	Persistent mousse, pale straw colour, attractive grassy aromas with good weight. Will improve.	**£6.30**	CRE
✓	**RAVENTOS I BLANC CAVA L'HEREU NV, JOSEP MARIA RAVENTOS I BLANC**	Typically waxy lemon aromas and broad palate. Acidty is fresh but well rounded.	**£7.00**	WAW
✓	**VINTAGE CAVA 1997, MARQUES DE MONISTROL** Penedes	Ripe fruit and attractive yeasty flavours with evident bottle-age characters.	**£7.00**	TOS
✓	**CHANDON SPAIN CAVA NV, CHANDON ESTATES** Penedes	Nicely balanced fruit flavours with a fine mousse and a classic nose of yeast autolysis.	**£7.50**	SGL MHU
✓	**FREIXENET CORDON NEGRO BRUT NV, FREIXENET** Catalonia	Refreshing lemon hints with a fine mousse and light toasty biscuit aromas.	**£7.40**	Widely Available
(B)	**CODORNIU CUVÉE RAVENTÓS BRUT NV, CODORNIU** Catalonia	Toasty aromas followed by intense ripe fruit flavours; a delicate palate with a long finish.	**£8.00**	CON
(B)	**RAIMAT CHARDONNAY CAVA BRUT NV, RAIMAT** Catalonia	A youthful wine showing ripe tropical flavours, light touch of toast, and hints of vanilla and white fruits.	**£9.00**	CON

SPAIN • WHITE

✓	**ASDA MOSCATEL DE VALENCIA NV, GANDIA** Valencia	Surprisingly delicate for this style of wine, possessing good floral character and rich honeyed fruit.	**£3.30**	ASD FQU
✓	**PENEDES MEDIUM DRY WHITE 2000, COVIDES** Catalonia	Penedès is an important wine region in Catalonia, home to this gluggable wine.	**£3.50**	MHV
(S)	**CRUZ DE PIEDRA MACABEO 2000, VIRGEN DE LA SIERRA** Aragón	Fresh varietal character uncluttered by oak. Floral, sherbet fruit, clean acidity, well-bodied palate.	**£4.00**	VVI SAF
✓	**SW MOSCATEL DE VALENCIA 2000, GANDIA** Valencia	Orange blossom and honey combine to give a delightful wine.	**£4.00**	BGN SAF
✓	**DE MULLER MOSCATEL AÑEJO NV, DE MULLER SA REUS**	Vivid ripe oranges, with honeyed lime overtones.	**£4.30**	L&S
(G)	**CAPELLANIA 1996, MARQUES DE MURRIETA** Rioja	Classic white Rioja with creamy complexity, American oak, and a bright lemony acidity with an immense length.	**£9.00**	MMD SAF

SPAIN • RED

✓	**TOTUM TEMPRANILLO, VI & VINOS I SAU**	Rich fruit and coffee with medium length.	**£2.90**	LNA
✓	**ALLOZO TEMPRANILLO 2000, BODEGAS CENTRO ESPAÑOLAS** La Mancha	Strawberries and cream with lovely ripe finish.	**£3.40**	BOE
(S)	**TEMPRANILLO GARNACHA GRAN LOPEZ CDB 2000, SANTO CRISTO**	Deep, juicy black in colour, with a subtle nose of ripe, jammy fruits. Great structural tannins.	**£3.50**	IWS
✓	**CO-OP TEMPRANILLO OAK-AGED NV, FELIX SOLIS** Castilla-La Mancha	Sweet plummy fruit and vanilla nuances showing medium length.	**£3.50**	CWS

✓	**VIÑA ALBALI TEMPRANILLO 2000, FELIX SOLIS** Castilla-La Mancha	Sweet and jammy, with bright and red-fruit palate and a good drying finish.	**£3.50**	FEE
✓	**GRANDUC HILLSIDE VINEYARD TEMPRANILLO LA MANCHA 2000, BODEGAS SAN ISIDRO** La Mancha	Sumptuous fruit, good structure, and medium-weighted palate.	**£3.60**	SAF JSS WRW
✓	**GRANDUC TEMPRANILLO 2000, GRANDUC WINERY** La Mancha	Warm nose with a vibrant fruit palate and simple juicy finish.	**£3.60**	MYL SAF TMW SAB
✓	**FOUR WINDS TINTO NAVARRA 2000, BODEGAS MARCO REAL** Navarra	Light fruits on the nose with a touch of age coming through on the palate.	**£3.80**	SAF
✓	**YOUNG VATTED TEMPRANILLO 2000, BODEGAS CENTRO ESPAGNOLAS,** La Mancha	Stewed fruit with bright finish. Well-weighted for the style with a drying red-fruit finish.	**£3.80**	SAF
✓	**RIOJA VEGA 2000, BODEGAS MUERZA** Rioja	Dark ruby showing leathery tones with a complementary palate.	**£3.80**	BOE
Ⓑ	**ED'S RED DO 2000, BODEGAS CENTRO ESPANOLAS** La Mancha	Deep in colour with youthful cherries on the nose and attractive, fresh fruit-salad flavours on the palate.	**£4.00**	WST
Ⓑ	**VENTUROSO TEMPRANILLO GARNACHA 2000, COVINCA** Zaragoza	Lifted black cherry aromas follow through onto the palate where lively acidity and structured tannins rule.	**£4.00**	IWS BDR
Ⓑ	**VINA ARMANTES 2000, SAN GREGORIO** Calatayde	Light layers of sweet raspberry fruit, elegantly held together with gentle tannins.	**£4.00**	IWS
Ⓑ	**VINA FUERTE GARNACHA 2000, SAN GREGORIO** Calatayde	Youthful, green fruits with soft raspberry and pepper sauce hints on the palate.	**£4.00**	IWS WTS
✓	**ASDA OAKED TEMPRANILLO NV, ALASTAIR MALING** Somontano	Good, spicy fruit backbone with a black pepper and plum finish.	**£4.00**	ASD
✓	**CAMPOBARRO OAKED TEMPRONILLO 2000, SAN MARCOS** Extremadura	Subtle, juicy fruit nose, showing through well-balanced oak and dark-red fruit on the mid-palate.	**£4.00**	MYL

✓ **CLEARLY ORGANIC TEMPRANILLO 2000, GRANDUC** La Mancha	Youthful black fruits backed with easy tannins and a "funky" Old World finish.	**£4.00**	MYL SAF
✓ **CO-OP TIERRA SANA TEMPRANILLO ORGANIC 1999, PARRA JIMENEZ** Castilla-La Mancha	Fruity nose with soft tannins on the palate backed with subtle nuances of cigar.	**£4.00**	CWS TOS
✓ **CRUZ DE PIEDRA GARNACHA 2000, VIRGEN DE LA SIERRA** Aragón	Ripe red fruits jump from the glass with great concentration on the finish.	**£4.00**	VVI SAF
✓ **EL LEON 2000, BODEGAS CASTRO VENTOSA** Castilla y León	Blueberries and touches of stone fruit with a spicy finish.	**£4.00**	EHL SAF
✓ **LA VIDA MONESTRAL GARNACHA 2000, MASIA LES COMES**	Blackcurrant palate with easy drinking length and a tight style of finish.	**£4.00**	D&D
✓ **MARQUES DE NOMBREVILLA RED DO 2000, SOCIEDAD COOPERATIVA SAN ALEJANDRO,** Aragón	Young, bright black fruits, with fruity depth on the palate and showing weight on the finish.	**£4.00**	BGL
✓ **PERGOLA TEMPRANILLO 2000, COOP DEL CAMPO DULCE NOMBRE DE JESUS** Castilla-La Mancha	Young fruits on the nose and firm fruit.	**£4.00**	EHL
✓ **POEMA GARNACHA 2000, BODEGAS JALON** Aragón	Aromas of spice and pepper, clean palate with a bright texturous finish.	**£4.00**	POR MOR VGN
✓ **VIÑA ALBALI VALDEPEÑAS CRIANZA 1996, VIÑA ALBALI** Castilla-La Mancha	Sweet and fruity nose with great balance and a drying tannic and plum-driven palate.	**£4.00**	FEE VGN
✓ **VINA SARDANA 2000, SAN GREGORIO** Calatayde	Vibrant red-fruit style with good depth and a lovely plum finish.	**£4.00**	IWS
Ⓑ **MHV NAVARRA MERLOT CABERNET 1999, BODEGAS PIEDMONTE** Navarra	Deep purple. Cassis fruit and a slightly green, leafy quality. Cherries and soft tannins fill the mouth.	**£4.40**	MHV
Ⓑ **FUENTE DEL RITMO DO 1999, BODEGAS CENTRO ESPAÑOLAS** Castilla-La Mancha	Ripe fruits of the forest integrating well with soft oak and gentle tannins.	**£4.50**	WST

(B) **PRINCIPE DE VIANA TEMPRANILLO 1999, BODEGAS PRINCIPE DE VIANA** Navarre	Slightly earthy aromas; hints of mushroom lead to a fruit-driven palate with distinctive underlying oak flavours.	**£4.80**	BOE
(S) **LUBERRI TINTO 2000, LUBERRI** Rioja	Textbook, ripe primary fruit with lots of extracted flavour building to a full, weighty palate.	**£5.00**	AWS
(G) **CASTILLO DE MONTBLANC CABERNET SAUVIGNON MERLOT 1999, CONCAVINS** Conca de Barbera	Blackberries, mushrooms, and briar aromas rise from the glass. The complex palate has floral and earthy ripe-plum flavours.	**£5.00**	HWL
(G) **RIOJA PRIMI 2000, LUIS GURPEGUI MUGA** Rioja	Ripe black cherry on the nose with big fruit, grippy tannins, firm American oak, and balancing acidity.	**£5.00**	BWL SAF
(S) **LA VIDA CABERNET/ TEMPRANILLO 2000, MASIA LES COMES**	Delightful match of the blackcurrant weight of the Cabernet Sauvignon with redcurrant Tempranillo.	**£5.00**	D&D MWW HWL VGN
(S) **MARQUES DE MONISTROL CABERNET SAUVIGNON 1998, MARQUES DE MONISTROL** Catalonia	Dark ruby colour with a soft, fruity palate. A very substantial wine with a lovely perfumed nose.	**£5.00**	ABU
(S) **SIGLO 1881 TINTO 1999, BODEGAS AGE** Rioja	Smoky damson fruit, softening tannins, and a structure blending effortlessly with the fruit.	**£5.00**	MER SAF
(B) **CARMESI BARRIQUE GARNACHA TEMPRANILLO 1999, SAN GREGORIO** Calatayde	Aromatic dried herbs dominate the nose; blackcurrant-driven fruit and oak take control of the palate.	**£5.00**	IWS
(B) **DURIUS TINTO 1998, MARQUES DE GRIÑON** Alto Duero	Upfront cherries are supported by an elegant framework of tannins; the palate ends in a long, slinky finish.	**£5.00**	ABU
(B) **ONE BUNCH GARNACHA 2000, GRANDES VINOS Y VINEDOS** Carinena	This wine has the flavour of crushed raspberries, the texture of silk, and a long, lingering finish.	**£5.00**	PLB SMF
(B) **OROBIO TEMPRANILLO 1999, ARTADI** Rioja	A sweet seductive aroma followed by well-balanced acidity and tannins leading to a long finish.	**£5.00**	VTS CWS
(B) **TESCO HUGE JUICY RED 2000, SAN GREGORIO** Somontano	Vibrant red in colour; youthful nose with generous juicy strawberries and spice on the palate.	**£5.00**	TOS

(B) **ZORRO CABERNET MONASTRELL DO 2000, FINCA LUZON** Murcia	Inky purple intensity with a raspberry nose. Blackcurrant palate with a hint of smokiness and firm tannic finish.	**£5.00**	WST
(S) **CONDE DE VALDEMAR 1998, BODEGAS MARTINEZ BUJANDA** Rioja	An elegant style with juicy black fruit and hints of oak, well-integrated tannins, and a good spicy length.	**£7.00**	BMB
(G) **MAS IGRENS FA206 1999, ANPI WINES** Priorat	Rich, ripe, spicy fruit and a smoky character are underlined by chocolate-flavoured oak and a firm texture.	**£9.50**	VRT
(G) **VIÑAS DEL VERO BLECUA 1998, VIÑAS DEL VERO** Somontano	Black fruit aromas are enhanced by rich, spicy oak to give this brooding wine massive structure.	**£24.50**	FXT
(G) **GUELBENZU LAUTUS 1998,** Navarra	Masses of ripe-berry fruit and toasty, chocolate, new-oak flavours with perfect balance and weight. Very long finish.	**£29.00**	POR MOR

SPAIN • FORTIFIED

(B) **TESCO SUPERIOR MANZANILLA, SANCHEZ ROMATE** Andalucia	Light, elegant, hazelnut-scented delight with a dry, nutty palate; good finish.	**£3.50**	EHL
(B) **TESCO SUPERIOR OLOROSO SECO, SANCHEZ ROMATE** Andalucia	Dry figgy fruit is made complex and interesting by the rancio oxidative character. Concentrated, off-dry style.	**£3.50**	EHL
✓ **ASDA MANZANILLA, REAL TESORO** Andalucia	Attractive, tangy nose; clean broad palate.	**£3.90**	PLB FRW BOO CNL JEF
(B) **SAINSBURY'S FINO, CROFT** Andalucia	A traditional nose of almonds and flowers complements a classic, well-structured palate. Pungent yet delicate.	**£4.00**	JSM
(B) **SOMERFIELD AMONTILLADO SHERRY, ESPINOSA DE LOS MONTEROS** Andalucia	A rich, refined toffee nose and a full, slightly savoury, palate of some age and elegance.	**£4.00**	SMF
(B) **SOMERFIELD CREAM SHERRY, ESPINOSA DE LOS MONTEROS** Andalucia	Richly sweet, the orange peel and almond fruit nicely balanced by a well-cut acidity.	**£4.00**	SMF VRT VGN

(B)	**TESCO SUPERIOR PALO CORTADO, SANCHEZ ROMATE** Andalucia	Caramelized fruit character integrates wonderfully with a lean, nutty complexity which drifts into a lovely, long finish.	**£4.00**	EHL
✓	**SOMERFIELD FINO SHERRY, ESPINOSA DE LOS MONTEROS** Andalucia	Aromas of fresh straw and almonds.	**£4.00**	SMF
(B)	**REGENCY AMONTILLADO SHERRY,** Andalucia	Caramel and dried fruit on the elegant, savoury yet slightly sweet palate, full of rich hazelnuts.	**£4.10**	MCT OWC VIL WCS
✓	**REGENCY FINO SHERRY, LACAVE Y CIA** Andalucia	An unusual yet attractive yeasty twist on the traditional style.	**£4.10**	MCT CDL
✓	**CO-OP CREAM SHERRY, LUIS CABELLERO** Andalucia	A luscious blend of nuts and raisins with aged mocha notes.	**£4.20**	CWS
(B)	**FINO, LUIS CABALLERO S.A.** Andalucia	Pale straw-coloured. Almonds and refreshing, mouthwatering fruit. A classic example of the genre.	**£4.40**	SAF
✓	**GRAN CAPATAZ FINO SHERRY, ANTONIO BARBADILLO** Andalucia	An atypically intense, almond-scented Fino.	**£4.40**	MHV CNL
✓	**SAFEWAY AMONTILLADO, LUIS CABALLERO S.A.** Andalucia	Medium-dry, with orange peel on the palate.	**£4.40**	SAF
✓	**SAFEWAY CREAM, LUIS CABALLERO S.A.** Andalucia	Dry and sweet meet in this intense yet balanced cream sherry.	**£4.40**	SAF GHL NYW BEN
✓	**CABRERA FULL RICH CREAM, GONZALEZ BYASS** Andalucia	Intense, textural dried fruits; well balanced.	**£4.40**	WRT POR WRT VGN
✓	**CABRERA PALE DRY FINO, GONZALEZ BYASS** Andalucia	Pungent, delicate nose; classic light fruit in the mouth.	**£4.50**	WRT WRT DBY HST
(S)	**TESCO FINEST AMONTILLADO, SANCHEZ ROMATE** Andalucia	Caramel, orange peel, and nutty nose with a smooth, rich palate and a lingering aftertaste.	**£5.00**	EHL

✓	**SAINSBURY'S MEDIUM DRY AMONTILLADO, MARGAU BROS** Andalucia	Pale gold, feminine style, with a long finish.	**£5.00**	JSM
✓	**TESCO FINEST SOLERA RICH CREAM, SANCHEZ ROMATE** Andalucia	Velvety, concentrated, and complex mouthful of raisins.	**£5.00**	EHL
✓	**WAITROSE FINO, CABALLERO EMILIO LUSTAU** Andalucia	Forward, fresh, earthy floral notes give way to a refreshingly austere palate.	**£5.00**	WTS
Ⓖ	**CANASTA SUPERIOR CREAM, BODEGAS WILLIAMS & HUMBERT SL** Andalucia	It has a concentrated nose and intense, full, sweet-caramel palate with hints of figs, coffee, and chocolate.	**£5.50**	EHL
Ⓢ	**DRY SACK FINO, BODEGAS WILLIAMS & HUMBERT SL** Andalucia	Restrained tangy seaside tones and an aromatic nutty quality. Finesse and good fruit on the finish.	**£5.50**	EHL
Ⓑ	**WAITROSE SOLERA JEREZANA MANZANILLA, EMILIO LUSTAU** Andalucia	Pale gold with walnut notes, it has nutty, complex fruit with a lovely, elegant, fine finish.	**£5.80**	WTS
Ⓑ	**BERRYS' FINE DRY OLOROSO, ANTONIO BARBADILLO** Andalucia	A powerful, off-dry, concentrated plate of dark caramelized fruits with a long, warming, nutty finish.	**£6.80**	BBR
Ⓖ	**TÍO PEPE, GONZÁLEZ BYASS SA** Andalucia	A refreshing saltiness with underlying flavours of almonds and orange peel with a creamy bone dry palate.	**£7.90**	WTS POR ASD UNS
Ⓖ	**FINO INOCENTE, VALDESPINO** Sherry	The lovely nutty character on the nose is reflected on the palate with a touch of salty tanginess.	**£8.00**	PLB
Ⓖ	**ALMACENISTA JURADO MANZANILLA AMONTILLADO, EMILIO LUSTAU** Andalucia	Luminescent amber hue and a clean, focused nose with a complex nutty character, spicy flavour, and delicate aromas.	**£8.60**	BEN BDR M&V
Ⓖ	**ALMACENISTA ZAMORANO, OLOROSO, EMILIO LUSTAU** Sherry	Treacle-brown colour offers caramel, nuts, and fruitcake aromas showing maturity, along with toffee and tobacco flavours.	**£8.70**	BEN BDR M&V
Ⓢ	**MANZANILLA PAPIRUSA, EMILIO LUSTAU** Andalucia	Medium-bodied with fresh and zingy white grapefruit softened with a smooth, slightly savoury essence of Madagascar vanilla.	**£8.50**	BEN M&V

(S)	**PEDRO XIMENEZ EL CANDADO, VALDESPINO** Andalucia	Dark, rich chocolate brown in colour. Unctuous seductive mouthfeel; treacle and raisins; a sheer delight.	**£9.00**	PLB DBY GHL BTH BEN
(S)	**OLD EAST INDIA, EMILIO LUSTAU** Andalucia	Tanned leather and roasted walnuts on the nose lead to a medium-sweet palate of raisins and caramel.	**£10.30**	BEN UNS M&V
(G)	**DON PEDRO XIMENEZ DULCE GRAN RESERVA 1972, BODEGAS TORO ALBALÁ** Andalucia	A great warmth here, with burnt caramel, nuts, molasses, and orange flavours that reflect on the finish.	**£12.00**	MOR
(G)	**BARBADILLO LA CILLA PEDRO XIMENEZ, ANTONIO BARBADILLO SA** Andalucia	Deep rich colour, intense nose and massive flavours ranging from sweet Greek coffee to raisins and liquorice.	**£16.50**	SGL JEF
(G)	**NOÉ, GONZÁLEZ BYASS SA** Andalucia	Rich Dundee cake and raisiny flavours run through the intense sweetness to sensuously glide across the palate.	**£22.00**	FDB

USA

Most wine drinkers think that all American fine wine comes from California, but this is a misperception. There are superb wines made in Oregon and Washington, but that is basically that, with the exception of a few notable vineyards in New York State, Texas, and Virginia. California has now evolved to the point where every style and grape variety has been tried and tested, but production is concentrated on Bordeaux-style reds and whites, some sublime Chardonnays, and wonderfully rich, fruity reds made from the Zinfandel grape. Good Rhone and Italian styled wines are appearing.

USA • WHITE

(S)	**WINES OF THE WORLD COASTAL CHENIN BLANC, CALIFORNIA DIRECT LIMITED** California	Pineapple and apricot on the nose with a well-balanced acidity and a fresh crisp finish.	**£3.00**	CDL
(S)	**STOWELLS OF CHELSEA CHARDONNAY COLOMBARD NV, MATTHEW CLARK** California	Fine, elegant Chardonnay-based wine with an aromatic hint from the Colombard grape.	**£4.00**	MCT

(B)	**MONTHAVEN CHARDONNAY 2000, GRANDS CHAIS DE FRANCE** California	This attractive wine possesses juicy, ripe tropical fruits oozing with flavour and fresh, lively acidity.	**£5.00**	GCF
(S)	**CANYON ROAD CALIFORNIA CHARDONNAY 1999, CANYON ROAD** California	This Californian wine is bursting with sweet mangos and hints of spicy oak on the palate.	**£7.00**	MAX
(G)	**BONTERRA VINEYARDS ROUSSANNE 2000, BONTERRA VINEYARDS** California	Its rounded texture has a tropical, peach blossom nose and a nutty creaminess on the palate.	**£10.00**	BRF
(G)	**E& J GALLO STEFANI RANCH VINEYARD CHARDONNAY 1997, E&J GALLO** California	Yeasty, toasted aromas and integrated wood on the rich-fruit palate, which builds up to an intense finale.	**£11.00**	E&J

USA • RED

✓	**CALIFORNIA MOUNTAIN VINEYARDS ZINFANDEL SHIRAZ 1999, CALIFORNIA MOUNTAIN VINEYARDS,** California	Lovely black cherry and red-fruit palate.	**£4.00**	GCF TOS SMF
(B)	**BLOSSOM HILL WINERY CABERNET SAUVIGNON 1999, BLOSSOM HILL WINERY** California	Inky intense colour, with red fruit on the nose. Smoky blackcurrants and assertive tannins on the palate.	**£5.00**	BGN NTD ASD PFC
(S)	**PEPPERWOOD GROVE 1999, CECCHETTI SEBASTIANI CELLAR** California	Gentle cassis fruit and tobacco on the nose with a smooth and sweet palate and an easy finish.	**£6.50**	VNO
(S)	**FETZER VINEYARDS VALLEY OAKS SYRAH 1998, FETZER VINEYARDS** California	White pepper and berry aromas precede a complex spiciness and dark cherries, finishing with soft tannins.	**£7.00**	UNS WTS
(B)	**MONTERRA SYRAH 1998, DELICATO MONTERRA** California	This impressively ripe wine is rampant with smoky, tarry fruit; it possesses rounded structure and zesty acidity.	**£8.49**	EHL
(G)	**CYPRESS ZINFANDEL 1999, J. LOHR** California	Rich chocolate nose with hints of coffee followed by spicy, plummy fruit rounded off with a lingering finish.	**£9.50**	ENO
(G)	**KENT RASMUSSEN WINERY CARNEROS PINOT NOIR 1998, KENT RASMUSSEN** California	Huge ripe, spicy fruit with overtones of blackberries and nicely judged oak, with grippy tannins and a spicy finish.	**£15.50**	GGW FWM

(G) **SEGHESIO BARBERA 1999, SEGHESIO FAMILY VINEYARDS** California	A big, balanced wine with ripe, chunky fruit and herbal notes demonstrating fantastic complexity.	**£18.00**	LIB
(G) **ST FRANCIS RESERVE CABERNET SAUVIGNON 1996, ST FRANCIS** California	Mint over deep brambles and soft oak. Good savoury flavours with grippy tannins, balanced acid, and caramel warmth.	**£18.50**	POR HMA
(G) **ST FRANCIS RESERVE MERLOT 1996, ST FRANCIS** California	Elegant and mature; liquorice, dried fruit, coffee and cedar. Soft, spicy tannins and integrated oak	**£19.00**	POR HMA
(G) **ST FRANCIS RESERVE ZINFANDEL 1998, ST FRANCIS** California	Immense concentration with endless plums and minty fruit interspersed with rich spicy notes and American oak.	**£19.00**	POR HMA DBY MAD
(G) **ST FRANCIS NUNN'S CANYON VINEYARD RESERVE MERLOT 1997, ST FRANCIS WINERY,** California	Rich oak; flavours of coffee and cedar enhance the blackcurrant fruit. Warm, deep flavours with spice and ripeness.	**£20.00**	HMA
(G) **HILLTOP CABERNET SAUVIGNON 1997, J. LOHR** California	The classic minty blackcurrant nose is just what New World cabernet style should be all about.	**£23.40**	ENO**G**

Pinpoint who sells the wine you wish to buy by turning to the stockist codes. If you know the name of the wine you want to buy, use the alphabetical index. If the price is your motivation, look out for the "Wine of the Year" symbol; the best red and white wines under £8, sparkling wines under £12, and champagne under £15. Happy hunting!

OTHER COUNTRIES

Good wines are available from countries that would never have been given a moment's consideration even as recently as ten years ago. Canada is making tiny quantities of dessert wine that can more than compete with Europe's finest. Mediterranean wines from countries such as Morocco, Malta, and Greece are fast improving, and may eventually become forces to be reckoned with in the not-too-distant future. Uruguay and even Brazil are showing considerable potential, while our very own English wines are now being taken seriously by the European Community. Who knows where wine will be produced next?

CANADA

CANADA • WHITE

(G)	**SOUTHBROOK TRIOMPHE CHARDONNAY 1998, SOUTHBROOK WINERY** Ontario	Intense, ripe fruit packed with toasty oak and a buttery texture. This weight is counterbalanced with zippy acidity.	**£12.00**	VNO

CANADA • SWEET

(G)	**WILLOW HEIGHTS VIDAL ICEWINE 1998, WILLOW HEIGHTS ESTATE,** Ontario	Unctuous, pungent nose which reflects a spicy apricot palate. Luscious, but with clear acidity and superb length.	**£19.40**	Not available in the UK	♔
(G)	**MISSION HILL FAMILY ESTATE VIDAL ICEWINE 1998, MISSION HILL FAMILY ESTATE** British Columbia	Wonderful grass and candied orange-peel aromas contribute to the complex aroma Moderate acidity, yet far from cloying.	**£19.80**	CEB	
(G)	**GRAND RESERVE RIESLING ICEWINE 1998, JACKSON TRIGGS** British Columbia	Seductive citrus peel and honeyed nose elegantly flowing into an unctuous, bitter-oranage palate with superb acidity.	**£32.80**	HOH	

CYPRUS

CYPRUS • RED

✓	**CO-OP ISLAND VINES CYPRUS RED 2000, SODAP**	Mediterranean, stewed-berry fruit flavours, and balanced tannins.	**£3.50**	CWS SAF

Pinpoint who sells the wine you wish to buy by turning to the stockist codes. If you know the name of the wine you want to buy, use the alphabetical index. If the price is your motivation, look out for the "Wine of the Year" symbol; the best red and white wines under £8, sparkling wines under £12, and champagne under £15. Happy hunting!

CYPRUS • WHITE

✓	**CYPRUS WHITE 2000, SODAP/BOTTLE GREEN**	Soft, spicy, summer party wine with both breadth and freshness.	**£3.50**	BGL
✓	**CO-OP ISLAND VINES WHITE 2000, SODAP**	Pleasant, aromatic, summer thirst-quencher.	**£3.50**	CWS
✓	**CO-OP MOUNTAIN VINES SEMILLON 1999, SODAP** Troodos South	Pleasantly soft, typically broad Semillon flavours. Ripe with a clean finish.	**£4.00**	CWS

ENGLAND

ENGLAND • SPARKLING

✓	**CHAPEL DOWN BRUT NV, ENGLISH WINES PLC** Kent	Fresh, floral flavours with good, gentle, toasty backbone, a firm acidity, and good depth.	**£7.00**	TVD
ⓑ	**CHAPEL DOWN VINTAGE BRUT 1995, ENGLISH WINES PLC** Kent	Delicate fruit flavours with a well-balanced acidity, structure, and finesse.	**£10.00**	TVD

ENGLAND • WHITE

✓	**ASTLEY VINEYARDS PREMIUM MEDIUM DRY NV, ASTLEY VINEYARDS** Worcestershire	Simple, refreshing, and laden with floral fruit notes.	**£4.00**	AST

Pinpoint who sells the wine you wish to buy by turning to the stockist codes. If you know the name of the wine you want to buy, use the alphabetical index. If the price is your motivation, look out for the "Wine of the Year" symbol; the best red and white wines under £8, sparkling wines under £12, and champagne under £15. Happy hunting!

GEORGIA

GEORGIA • RED

✓	**MATRASSA CAUCASUS VALLEY 2000, GEORGIAN WINES SPIRITS** Kakheti	Powerful rustic red with savoury fruit flavours and firm tannins.	**£4.00**	EGE SAF

GREECE

GREECE • FORTIFIED

✓	**SAMOS VIN DOUX GREEK MUSCAT AOC NV, UNION DE CO-OP DE SAMOS** Samos	Lush, honeyed, and strong, from the homeland of this varietal.	**£3.10**	SMF MCT

MEXICO

MEXICO • WHITE

Ⓢ	**CASA GRANDE CHARDONNAY 1999, CASA MADERO**	Fresh and bright, with hints of pineapple and melon. The finish is well-balanced with complex aromas.	**£7.00**	EHL

Pinpoint who sells the wine you wish to buy by turning to the stockist codes. If you know the name of the wine you want to buy, use the alphabetical index. If the price is your motivation, look out for the "Wine of the Year" symbol; the best red and white wines under £8, sparkling wines under £12, and champagne under £15. Happy hunting!

MEXICO • RED

(B)	**L.A. Cetto Petit Sirah 1998,** **L.A. Cetto** Baja-California	This wine offers a palate of intense baked fruits lightly spiced with warming cinnamon. Well-balanced.	**£5.40**	WTS CEB

MOROCCO

MOROCCO • RED

✓	**Atlas Vineyards Merlot 2000, Castel Fréres** Meknès-Fès	Leafy aroma supported by firm chocolate fruit.	**£4.00**	L&T
✓	**Atlas Vineyards Cabernet Sauvignon 2000, Castel Fréres** Meknès-Fès	Jammy fruit and dry balanced tannins.	**£4.00**	L&T
(B)	**Atlas Vineyards Syrah 2000, Castel Fréres** Meknès-Fès	This wine has a purple inky depth infused with rich berries and hints of sweetness on the finish.	**£4.00**	L&T

ROMANIA

ROMANIA • WHITE

✓	**River Route Limited Edition Chardonnay 2000, Carl Reh Winery srl** Vanju-Mare-Orevita	Light, creamy wine with good citrus character.	**£4.00**	RHC

ROMANIA • RED

✓	**RIVER ROUTE MERLOT 1999, CARL REH WINERY SRL** Recas	Youthful, racy cherry fruit with decent texture and balance.	**£2.99**	RHC
✓	**ROMANIAN PRAIRIE MERLOT 2000, CARL REH WINERY SRL** DeaLul Mare	Cherry and raspberry fruit with a firm earthy grip and balanced acidity.	**£3.00**	RHC
✓	**PINOT NOIR 2000, S.E.R.V.E. SA** Dealul Mare	Red fruits of the forest on the nose allied to a young vibrant palate.	**£3.50**	NTD EHL
✓	**PRAMOVA VALLEY CABERNET SAUVIGNON 1999, PRAMOVA WINECELLARS SA** Dealul Mare	Light-bodied with a touch of sweet oak characters and a touch of strawberry. and cassis.	**£3.60**	BGN HAE
✓	**PRAMOVA VALLEY PINOT NOIR 1999, PRAMOVA WINECELLARS SA** Dealul Mare	Red cherry and strawberry flavours with a soft, rounded palate.	**£3.60**	BGN HAE SAF VGN
✓	**ROMANIAN MERLOT 1998, THE HANWOOD GROUP** Tohani	Young and fruity with good raspberry character.	**£3.80**	MHV CTC BWL VGN
✓	**RIVER ROUTE LE MERLOT 1999, CARL REH WINERY SRL** Vanju-Mare-Orevita	Classic juicy Merlot. Flavours of plum and cherry with supple tannins and a bright fresh finish.	**£4.00**	RHC DBY CNL AUS
✓	**EAGLE VALLEY RESERVE 2000, S.E.R.V.E. SA** Dealul Mare	Sweet plummy palate with firm tannins.	**£4.00**	NTD EHL

URUGUAY

URUGUAY • RED

✓	**BRIGHT BROTHERS MERLOT TANNAT 2000, ESTABECIMIENTO JUANICO** Juanico	Fresh fruit with a gamey, rustic edge and a bit of grip.	**£4.00**	EHL

GREAT VALUE WINES

All of the wines listed in the previous pages won awards at the 2001 International Wine Challenge. The Silver and Bronze medals and the Seal of Approval wines are the entries which were also given Great Value awards, following comparison of their retail price and the average price for the award they received in the International Wine Challenge. Following consultation with leading off-licences, appropriate price points were established for particular styles of wine. A Great Value sparkling wine or port, for example, might sell at a higher price than a red table wine with the same medal.

While we have excluded from these pages the Silver and Bronze medal winners and Seals of Approval that did not win Great Value awards (for these, you will have to go to internationalwinechallenge.com), all of the 226 Gold medal winners and Trophy winners – the finest wines in the competition – do appear. For full details of the price limits that were used to allocate Great Value awards, see below:

CATEGORY		STILL REDS AND WHITES	SPARKLING, PORT, AND MADEIRA	SWEET, FORTIFIED, MUSCAT, AND SHERRY
Gold medal	Ⓖ	Less than **£12.51**	Less than **£20.01**	Less than **£15.01**
Silver medal	Ⓢ	Less than **£7.51**	Less than **£15.01**	Less than **£10.01**
Bronze medal	Ⓑ	Less than **£5.01**	Less than **£10.01**	Less than **£7.51**
Seal of Approval	✓	Less than **£4.01**	Less than **£7.51**	Less than **£5.01**

STOCKIST CODE INDEX

		Tel	Fax
ABU	**Bodegas Unidas Ltd** bu@bodegas.freeserve.co.uk	01494 676 263	01494 676 441
ABY	**Anthony Byrne Wine Agencies** claude@abfw.co.uk	01487 814 555	01487 710 831
ADD	**Allied Domecq** lynne.garratt@adswell.com	0140 322 2703	0140 322 2794
ADE	**Adel (UK) Ltd** wines@adel-wine.com	0208 994 3960	0208 747 1122
AHW	**AH Wines Ltd** frances@ahwines.co.uk	01935 850 116	01935 851 264
ALI	**Alivini Company Ltd** mirellas@alivini.com	0208 880 2526	0208 442 8215
ALL	**Alliance Wine Company Ltd** lizdonnelly@alliancewine.co.uk	01505 506 060	01505 506 066
ASD	**Asda Stores Ltd** gjrober@asda.co.uk	0113 241 9172	0113 241 7766
AST	**Astley Vineyards**	01299 822 907	01299 822 907
AUS	**Australian Wineries (UK) Ltd** km@australianwineries.co.uk	01780 755 810	01780 482 721
AWA	**Australian Wine Agencies** csmith@austwine.co.uk	01753 544 546	01753 572 5200
AWS	**Albion Wine Shippers** albion@lambsconduitst.compuserv.co.uk	0207 242 0873	0207 831 8225
BBR	**Berry Bros & Rudd** orders@bbr.com	0870 900 4300	0870 900 4301
BDR	**Laithwaites** duncanhurley@directwines.co.uk	0118 903 0903	0118 903 1073
BEN	**Bennetts** enquiries@bennettsfinewines.com	01386 840 392	01386 840 974
BGL	**Bottle Green Ltd** joanna-wilson@bottlegreen.com	0113 205 4500	0113 205 4501
BGN	**Budgens Stores Limited** christine.sandys@budgens.co.uk	0208 864 2800	0208 422 1596
BMB	**Bodegas Martinez Bujanda** bujanda@bujanda.com	+34 9 41 12 21 88	+34 9 41 12 21 11
BOE	**Bodegas UK**	+020 7627 1414	+020 7498 7851
BOR	**de Bortoli Wines UK Ltd** debortoli@talk21.com	01725 516 467	01725 516 403
BRF	**Brown-Forman Wines International** kate_sweet@b-f.com	020 7323 9332	020 7323 5316
BUC	**Buckingham Vintners**	01753 521 336	01753 576 748
BWC	**Berkmann Wine Cellars** susannah@berkmann.co.uk	020 7609 4711	020 7607 0018
BWL	**Bibendum Wine Ltd** cwilson@BIBENDUM-WINE.CO.UK	020 7722 5577	020 7692 2710
BXT	**32° South** bayexportuk@btinternet.com	020 7987 1241	020 7536 9721
CAX	**Caxton Wines** aluckes@caxton-wines.co.uk	020 8538 4000	020 8538 4545
CDL	**California Direct** laura@californiadirect.co.uk	020 7207 1944	020 7207 1972
CEB	**Croque-en-Bouche** mail@croque-en-bouche.co.uk	01684 565 612	0870 706 6282
CHN	**Charles Hawkins** charleshawkins@charleshawkins.demon.co.uk	01572 823 030	01572 823 040
CON	**Codorniu** info@codorniu.co.uk	0208 410 4480	0208 410 4490

		Tel	Fax
COO	Chandos Deli info@chandosdeli.com	0117 974 3275	0117 973 1020
CPR	Capricorn Wines ciaranl@capricornwines.co.uk	0161 908 1360	0161 908 1365
CPW	Christopher Piper Wines Ltd jok@christopherpiperwines.co.uk	01404 814 139	01404 812 100
CRE	F&M Cressi Ltd fmcressi@cressis.com	020 8607 6110	020 8570 9129
CRI	Chalié, Richards & Co Ltd michael.veale@chalie-richards.co.uk	01403 250 500	01403 250 123
CTL	CWF Ltd cwfeurofast@compuserve.com	01484 538 333	01484 544 734
CWS	The Co-op (CWS Ltd) carole.nicholson@co-op.co.uk	0161 827 5492	0161 827 5117
CYT	MBW Business Exchange Oxford clopez@conchaytoro.cl	+01865 338 013	+01865 338 113
D&D	D&D Wines International Ltd ddwi@ddwinesint.com	01565 650 952	01565 755 295
D&F	D & F Wine Shippers Ltd FFernandes@dandfwines.fsnet.co.uk	0208 838 4399	0208 838 4500
DBO	Boyar International Ltd steve.abrahams@domaineboyar.co.uk	020 7537 3707	020 7537 9377
DOU	CVBG UK uk@cvbg.com	020 7720 6611	020 7720 2670
DUL	Duval-Leroy UK Ltd rd@duval-leroy.co.uk	020 8982 4216	020 8982 4326
DVY	Davy & Co Ltd	020 7407 9670	020 7407 5844
DWI	Dedicated Wine Importers Ltd chrislake@dedicatedwines.fsbusiness.co.uk	01865 343 395	01865 343 355
DWL	Darlington Wines Ltd sales@darlingtonwines.co.uk	020 8453 0202	020 8961 9163
E&J	Ernest & Julio Gallo Winery jason.duggan@ejgallo.com	01895 813 444	01895 818 048
ECA	Edward Cavendish & Sons Ltd sales@ecavendish.co.uk	01794 835 800	01794 512 213
EGE	Embassy of Georgia gsulka@cs.com	020 7937 8233	020 79384 108
EHL	Ehrmanns Ltd iwc@ehrmanns.co.uk	020 7418 1800	020 7359 7788
ENO	Enotria Winecellars Ltd marketing@enotria.co.uk	020 8961 4411	020 8961 8773
EUW	Eurowines marketing@eurowines.co.uk	020 8747 2109	020 8994 8054
FDB	First Drinks Brands Ltd julie_herring@first-drinks-brands.co.uk	02380 312 000	02380 370 100
FEE	Free Run Wines Ltd charles@freerunwines.com	+01672 540 990	+01672 541 015
FTH	Forth Wines Ltd enquiries@forthwines.com	01577 866 001	01577 866 020
FXT	Freixenet (DWS) Ltd prowles@freixenet.co.uk	01344 758 500	01344 758 510
G2W	Grape-2-Wine charlotte@grape2wine.co.uk	01531 670 100	01531 670 802
GCF	Les Grands Chais de France	01962 622 067	01962 622 066
GDF	Grands Vins Selection SA	+33 4 74 66 57 24	+33 4 74 66 57 25
GGW	Great Gaddesden Wines ggwcl@nildram.co.uk	01582 760 606	01582 760 505
GON	Gauntleys of Nottingham rhone@gauntleywine.com	0115 911 0555	0115 911 0557
GRT	Great Western Wine Company Ltd philipa@greatwesternwine.co.uk	01225 322 800	01225 442 139

		Tel	**Fax**
GYW	Guy Anderson Wines louise.a@guyandersonwines.co.uk	01935 817 617	01935 817 611
H&H	H&H Bancroft	0207 627 8700	0207 627 8766
HAE	Halewood International Ltd admin@halewood-int.com	0151 480 8800	0151 489 0690
HBJ	Heyman, Barwell Jones Ltd paul.gow@heyman.co.uk	01473 232 322	01473 280 381
HBR	BRL Hardy Wine Company Ltd brett_fleming@brlhardy.co.uk	01372 473 000	01372 473 099
HBV	High Breck Vintners hbvrichanl.freeserve.co.uk	020 8340 1848	020 8340 5162
HFI	Hill International Wines (UK) Ltd	01283 217 703	01283 550 309
HMA	Hatch Mansfield Agencies Ltd hollinraker@hatch.co.uk	01344 871 800	01344 871 871
HOH	Hallgarten Wines Ltd cliff@vitisvinifera.demon.co.uk	01582 722 538	01582 723 240
HOT	House of Townend info@houseoftownend.co.uk	01482 326 891	01482 587 042
HWL	HWCG Wine Growers wine@hwcg.co.uk	01279 506 512	01279 657 462
HWL	HWCG Wine Growers wine@hwcg.co.uk	01279 506 512	01279 657 462
IWS	International Wine Services iws@intwine.co.uk	01494 680 857	01494 676 567
J&B	Justerini & Brooks claire.roberts@udv.com	020 7484 6400	020 7484 6499
JBF	Julian Baker Fine Wines julianbaker@supanet.com	01206 262 358	01206 263 574
JEF	John E Fells & Sons info@fells.co.uk	01442 870 900	01442 878 555
JSM	Sainsbury Supermarkets Ltd cewhi@tao.sainsburys.co.uk	020 7695 6000	020 7695 7610
KOM	Kingston Estate Wines (UK) admin@kingstonestatewines.fsnet.co.uk	01344 668 001	01344 668 125
KWS	Kingsland Wines & Spirits sarah.gilmore@lingsland-wines.com	0161 333 4300	0161 333 4301
L&S	Laymont & Shaw Ltd info@laymont-shaw.co.uk	01872 270 545	01872 223 005
L&T	Lane & Tatham nick@lanetat.demon.co.uk	01380 720 123	01380 720 111
L&W	Lay & Wheeler Ltd hugo.rose@laywheeler.com	01206 764 446	01206 560 002
LAU	Gresham International gresham@btconnect.com	01372 720 345	01372 720 346
LIB	Liberty Wines luciann@libertywine.co.uk	0207 720 5350	0207 720 6158
LNA	Bodegas Lan SA bodegaslan@fer.es	+34 9 41 45 09 50	+34 9 41 45 05 67
LUV	Lovico International Ltd paulscaife@lovico.co.uk	01494 511 234	01494 511 234
M&M	Italian Wine Service nl1steriws@aol.com	01235 813 815	01235 819 619
MAC	Makro UK kevin.wilson@makro.co.uk	0161 786 2256	0161 786 2260
MAX	Maxxium UK susan.ralston@maxxium.com	0178 643 0500	0178 643 0600
MCD	Marne & Champagne Ltd info@m-c-d.fr	+33 3 26 78 50 50	020 7408 0841
MCT	Matthew Clark iriso'loughlin@matthewclark.co.uk	01275 890 678	01275 890 285
MER	Meridian Wines sales@meridianwines.co.uk	0161 908 1350	0161 908 1355

		Tel	Fax
MHV	**Booker Belmont Wholesale Ltd** peter.j.taylor@bbw-booker.co.uk	01933 371 363	01933 371 304
MIS	**Mistral Wines**	020 7262 5437	020 7402 7957
MKV	**McKinley Vintners** info@mckinleyvintners.co.uk	020 7928 7300	020 7928 4447
MMD	**Maisons Marques et Domaines** bo.round@mmdltd.co.uk	020 8332 2223	020 8334 5900
MMD	**Maisons Marques et Domaines** bo.round@mmdltd.co.uk	020 8332 2223	020 8334 5900
MOR	**Moreno Wine Importers** christopher@moreno-wines.co.uk	020 8960 7161	020 8960 7165
MTW	**Montana Wines Ltd** anna_lawrence@seagram.com	020 8250 1325	020 8250 1752
MWW	**Majestic Wine Warehouses Ltd** agilson@majestic.co.uk	01923 298 200	01923 819 105
MYL	**Myliko International (Wines) Litd** aruna@myliko.co.uk	01204 392 222	01204 392 244
MZC	**Mentzendorff & Co Ltd** lwhetman@mentzendorft.co.uk	020 7840 3600	020 7840 3601
NEG	**Negociants UK Ltd** neguk@negociants.com	01582 462 859	01582 462 867
NID	**Not Sure of Submitter Check Stockists**		
NTD	**Nisa Today's** boozeline@nisa-todays.com	01724 282 028	01724 289 045
NWG	**New World Wines Ltd** matt@newworldwines.co.uk	020 7720 0371	020 7720 6001
NYW	**Noel Young Wines** noel.young@dial.pipex.com	01223 566 744	01223 844 736
PAT	**Patriarche Père et Fils Ltd** felicity@patriarchewines.com	020 7381 4016	020 7381 2023
PBA	**Paul Boutinot Agencies** db@paul-boutinot.co.uk	0161 908 1370	0161 908 1375
PEF	**Southcorp Wines Europe Ltd** toni.paterson@southcorp.co.uk	020 8917 4600	020 8917 4610
PFC	**Percy Fox & Co** alison.park@udv.com	01279 633 863	01279 633 769
PFT	**Parfrements** gerald@parfrements.co.uk	02476 503 646	02476 506 406
PLB	**Private Liquor Brands** daniel.brennan@plb.co.uk	01342 318 282	01342 314 023
POL	**Pol Roger Ltd** polroger@polroger.co.uk	01432 262 800	01432 262 806
POR	**Portland Wine Company (Manchester)** portwineco@aol.com	0161 928 0357	0161 905 1291
PRG	**Paragon Vintners Ltd** welcome@paragonvintners.co.uk	020 7887 1800	020 7887 1810
REN	**Renvic Wines Ltd**	01763 852 470	01763 852 470
RHC	**Reh Kendermann UK** richardnjones@btinternet.com	01295 760 000	01295 760 050
ROS	**Rosemount Estate Wines Ltd** melanie.owens@rosemountestates.co.uk	01483 211 466	01483 211 717
RSS	**Raisin Social Ltd** clare@raisin-social.com	020 8686 8500	020 8681 7939
RUK	**Ruinart UK Ltd**	020 7416 0592	020 7416 0593
SAF	**Safeway Stores Plc**	020 8970 3506	020 8756 2910
SCK	**Seckford Wines Ltd** meg@seckfordwines.co.uk	01394 446 629	01394 446 633
SEA	**Seagram UK Ltd** jenny_stewart@seagram.com	020 8250 1018	020 8250 1913
SGL	**Stevens Garnier Ltd** chantal.bryant@stevensgarnier.co.uk	01865 263 300	01865 791 594

		Tel	Fax
SMF	Somerfield Stores Ltd nicola.anthony@somerfield.co.uk	0117 935 9359	0117 978 0629
STB	Stokes Brothers (UK) Ltd bobstokes@sbltd.fsnet.co.uk	01303 252 178	01303 244 214
STG	Tony Stebbings daniellecaroll@tonystebbings.co.uk	01372 468 571	01372 467 949
SWS	Stratford's Wine Agencies hayley@stratfordwine.co.uk	01628 810 606	01628 810 605
T&W	T&W Wines contact@tw-wines.co.uk	01842 765 646	01842 766 407
THA	Dourthe UK uk@tw-wines.co.uk	020 7720 6611	020 7720 2670
THI	Thierry's Wine Services lsteer@thierrys.co.uk	01794 507 100	01794 516 856
THW	Southern Wine Brands Ltd swbltd@aol.com	01484 608 898	01484 609 495
TOS	Tesco Stores Ltd nicki.walden@uk.tesco.com	0800 505 555	01992 649 420
TVD	English Wines	01580 763 033	01580 765 333
UNS	The Unwins Wine Group brolfe@unwins.co.uk	01322 272 711	01322 294 469
VEX	Vinexports Ltd ho@vinexports.co.uk	01584 811333	01584 811544
VIC	Vica Wines Ltd	01273 477 132	01273 476 612
VIN	Chris Loveday's Wines loveday@vinum.co.uk	020 8840 4070	020 8840 6116
VNF	Vinfruco Ltd milmanl@capespan.co.uk	01753 712 473	01753 818 821
VNO	Vinoceros (UK)Ltd enquiries@vinoceros.com	01209 314 711	01209 314 712
VRA	Vranken UK Limited lefevre.vrankenuk@cclgb.co.uk	020 7304 7012	020 7304 7013
VRT	Vintage Roots info@vintageroots.co.uk	0118 976 1999	0118 976 1998
VTS	Vinites UK shinnie@globalnet.co.uk	0207 924 4974	0207 228 6109
VVI	Vinus Vita UK courtenay-clack@vmusvita.com	01225 322 813	01225 442 139
WAV	Waverley Wines & Spirits elaine.willis@waverly-group.co.uk	01738 472029	01738 630338
WAW	Waterloo Wine Co sales@waterloowine.co.uk	020 7403 7967	020 7357 6976
WBU	Wine Bureau winebureau@lineone.net	01403 256 446	01403 256 447
WFB	Beringer Blass Wine Estates Ltd lesley@mildarablasseurope.co.uk	020 8947 4312	020 8944 1041
WRC	Wine Rack (First Quench) jonathon.butt@firstquench.co.uk	01707 387 263	01707 387 350
WRT	Winerite Ltd jeni.bailey@winerite.co.uk	0113 283 7654	0113 283 7694
WSG	Walter S Siegel Ltd davidwright@walter-siegel.co.uk	01256 701 101	01256 701 518
WST	Western Wines Ltd manager@western-wines.com	01746 789 411	01746 789 501
WTS	Waitrose Ltd julian_brind@waitrose.co.uk	01344 424680	01344 825255
XXANG	Anglo American Farms T/A Vergelegen eturner@vergelegen.co.za	27 21 847 1334	27 21 847 1608
XXANT	Angerhof Tschida	+43 21 75 31 50	+43 21 75 31 50
XXBDC	Champagne Beaumont des Crayeres champagne-beaumont@wanadoo.fr	+33 3 26 55 29 40	+33 3 26 54 26 30

		Tel	Fax
XXBEJ	S.C.A. Jacques Beaujeau chateau.la.variere@wanadoo.fr	+33 2 41 91 22 64	+33 2 41 91 23 44
XXCCC	Casa Cortes de Cima Lda wine@cortesdecime.pt	+35 12 84 46 31 19	+35 12 84 46 32 92
XXCPN	Champagne Pannier	+33 3 23 69 51 30	+33 3 23 69 51 31
XXDIL	Distell ctorr@dist.co.za	+27 2 18 09 81 78	+27 2 18 83 96 51
XXDIS	Tokaj Domaine de Disznoko disznoko@mail.matav.hu	+36 47 36 13 71	+36 47 36 91 38
XXDOV	SA Domaines Virginie emile.geli@domains-virginie.fr	+33 4 67 49 85 85	+33 4 67 49 38 39
XXDPJ	Manoel D Poças Junior-Vinhos SA export@poças.pt	+35 12 23 77 10 70	+35 12 23 77 10 79
XXFRS	Weingut Friedrich Seiler georg.seiler@gmx.at	+43 2 68 56 44 90	+43 2 68 56 44 94
XXFVS	Farnese Vini SRL farnesevini@tin.it	39 8 59 06 73 88	39 8 59 06 73 89
XXGAL	Weingut Hans Gangl	02175 3131	02175 3131
XXGAP	Gapsted Wines gapstedwines@netc.net.au	+61 3 57 51 19 92	+61 3 57 51 13 68
XXGBB	Gibbston Valley Winery grant@gibbston-valley-wines.co.nz	+64 3 44 24 519	+64 3 44 26 909
XXGRO	Domaine Michel Gros Sarl domaine-mgros@wanadoo.fr	+33 3 80 61 04 69	+33 3 80 61 22 29
XXHAU	Familie Mad Wichelm office@wein-burgenland.at	+43 26 85 72 07	+43 26 85 71 77
XXJAC	Jackson-Triggs Vinters	+250 498 4981	+250 498 6505
XXJOH	AC Johnston Pty Ltd	+ 61 8 8323 8205	+ 61 8 8323 9224
XXKJW	Kendall Jackson Wine Estates jcaudil@kfmail.com	+1707 525 6229	+1707 569 0105
XXKOP	CN Kopke & Co Ltd info@porto-barros.pt	+351 22 375 23 20	+351 22 375 19 39
XXLUD	Weingut am Stein, Ludwig Knoll mailweingut-am-stein.de	0931 25 808	0931 25 880
XXMOM	Mommessin mathon@mommessin.com	+33 4 74 69 09 30	+33 4 74 69 09 29
XXMUA	Matua Valley Wines Ltd corey@matua.co.nz	+64 9 411 8301	+64 9 411 7982
XXQDI	Quinta Do Infantado qtainfantado@mail.telepac.pr	+351 22 610 0865	+351 22 610 0151
XXSCH	Scheiblhofer scheiblhofer@netway.at	+43 2176 26104	
XXSDM	Sandeman & Ca SA ligia_marques@seagram.com	+351 2 23 74 05 00	+351 2 23 74 05 99
XXSSU	Schmitt Sohne Gmbh Weinkellrei schmitt-soehne@t-online.de	+49 65 02 40 90	49 65 024 09 36
XXVDA	Vinos de Argentina	+54 61 29 22 13	+54 61 29 22 13
XXVJH	Vinhos Justino Henriques, Filhos, Lda justinos@justinosmadeira.com	+351 291 934 257	+351 291 934 049
XXVOR	Weingut Skoff walter.evelyn@weingut-skoff.com		+43 3453 4243-17
XXVTS	Vinedos Terranoble SA terranob@ctcreuna.cl	(56-2) 2033360	(56-2) 2033361
XXWHF	Weingut Hermann Fink hermannfink@utanet.at	43 26 82 64 376	43 26 82 64 376
XXWHW	Willow Heights Winery willow.heights@sympatico.ca	+1 905 562 4945	+1 905 562 5761
YVM	Tony Stebbings / Yvon Mau tony@tonystebbings.co.uk	01372 468 571	01372 467 949
YWL	Yates Brothers Ltd julie.waterfield@yates-bros.co.uk	01204 391 777	01204 393 666

RETAILERS

WHAT THIS CHAPTER CONTAINS

The following chapter has been conceived in order to help you to find almost everything – short of a congenial companion – you are likely to need to enjoy wine. If you are looking for a good local retailer, a wine from a specific region/country, or perhaps a wine course/school, vacation, tour, cellar, rack, or chiller, this is the place to look.

MAIN LIST OF RETAILERS

W.M. Addison ★★★★
Village Farm, Lilleshall, Newport, Shropshire TF10 9HB
☎ 01952 670200
FAX 01952 677309
@ sales@addisonwines.com
W www.addisonwines.com
Credit cards, delivery, tastings, en primeur, cellarage, mail order.
Following a national trend by expanding their New World listing while retaining all their Old World wines. So the range of classic French wines has now been joined by some good examples from Australia.

Adnams ★★★★★
Sole Bay Brewery, East Green, Southwold, Suffolk IP18 6JW
☎ 01502 727222
FAX 01502 727223
@ wines@adnams.co.uk
W www.adnams.co.uk
Credit cards, accessories, delivery, tastings, en primeur, glass hire, mail order.
Brilliantly eclectic, innovative and imaginative brewer and wine merchant. Only sell wines they like and have a money-back refund policy on all the wine they sell.

Amps Fine Wines ★★★★
6 Market Place, Oundle, Peterborough PE8 4BQ
☎ 01832 273502
FAX 01832 273502
@ info@ampsfinewines.co.uk
W www.ampsfinewines.co.uk
Credit cards, accessories, delivery, tastings, glass hire/loan, mail order, internet sales.
Traditional merchant whose wines are personally tasted and selected by staff members.

The Antique Wine Co. ★★★★
Portland House, Station Road, Ballasalla, Isle of Man IM99 6AB
☎ 01624 824771
FAX 01624 824837
@ info@antique-wine.com
W www.antique-wine.com
Mail order only, credit cards, accessories, delivery, tastings, cellarage, en primeur, internet sales.
Long established specialist in fine and rare wines. Specialists in anniversary wines with a unique gift presentation. GiantBottles.com is their large format bottle supply arm that specializes in French and Italians.

John Armit Wines ★★★★★
5 Royalty Studios, 105 Lancaster Road, London W11 1QF
☎ 020 7727 6846
FAX 020 7727 7133
@ info@armit.co.uk
W www. armit.co.uk
By the case only, mail order only, credit cards, free delivery, tastings, en primeur, cellarage, internet sales.
Superb clarets, Burgundies and Italians. Specialized wine events for women.

Asda Stores ★★★★
Asda House, Southbank, Great Wilson Street, Leeds LS11 5AD
☎ 0113 241 9172
FAX 0113 241 7766
W www.asda.co.uk
Credit cards, selected delivery, tastings, glass loan, Internet sales.
US-owned supermarket with a focus on value-for-money wines. Surprisingly, the range of top class wines has grown recently too and there are some very worthwhile bottles on offer. Six big-saver lines are available by the case only.

Australian Wine Club ★★★★★
Kershaw House, Great West Road,
Hounslow, Middx. TW5 0BU
- ℂ 020 8538 0718
  Order line: 0800 856 2004
- FAX 020 8572 5200
- @ orders@austwine.co.uk
- W www.austwine.co.uk

Mail order only, by the case only, credit cards,
delivery, tastings, internet sales.
Pioneers of Australian wines in the UK.

Averys of Bristol ★★★★
Orchard House, Southfield Road,
Nailsea, Bristol BS48 1JN
- ℂ 08451 283797
- FAX 01275 811 101
- @ averywines@aol.com

Credit cards, delivery, tastings, en primeur,
cellarage, glass hire/loan, mail order.
*Great wines from traditional as well
as up-and-coming areas.*

Bacchus Fine Wines ★★★★
Warrington House Farm, Warrington,
Olney, Buckinghamshire MK46 4HN
- ℂ 01234 711140
- FAX 01234 711199
- @ wine@bacchus.co.uk
- W www.bacchus.co.uk

By the case only, credit cards, delivery, tastings,
glass hire/loan, mail order, interent sales.
*Specializes in wines of the Burgenland in
Austria, close to the Hungarian border.*

Ballantynes of Cowbridge ★★★★
3 Westgate, Cowbridge, Vale of
Glamorgan, Wales CF71 7AQ
- ℂ 01446 774 840
- FAX 01446 775 253
- @ richard@ballantynes.co.uk
- W www.ballantynes.co.uk

Credit cards, accessories, delivery, tastings, en
primeur, cellarage, glass loan, mail order.
*Dynamic list, featuring Italy, Australia,
Burgundy and the Languedoc, with some
serious Californian wines.*

Balls Brothers ★★★★
313 Cambridge Heath Road,
London E2 9LQ
- ℂ 020 7739 6466
- FAX 020 7729 0258
- @ sales@ballsbrothers.co.uk
- W www.ballsbrothers.co.uk

Credit cards, delivery, tastings, glass hire/loan,
mail order, internet sales.
Good French wines.

H & H Bancroft ★★★★★
East Bridge Office North, New Covent
Garden Market, London SW8 5JB
- ℂ 020 7627 8700
- FAX 020 7627 8766
- @ mail@hhfinewines.co.uk
- W www.hhfinewines.co.uk

Credit cards, accessories, delivery, en primeur.
*Restaurant suppliers with a selection of
wines from France, Italy, and Australia.*

Bennetts Fine Wines ★★★★★
High Street, Chipping Campden,
Glos GL55 6AG
- ℂ 01386 840 392
- FAX 01386 840 974
- @ charlie@bennettsfinewines.com
- W www.bennettsfinewines.com

Credit cards, accessories, delivery, tastings, en
primeur, glass hire/loan, mail order.
*Specializing in the top end of the market
with a terrific selection of classic French
and Italian wines.*

Berkmann Wine Cellars ★★★★★
10/12 Brewery Road, London N7 9NH
- ℂ 020 7609 4711
- FAX 020 7607 0018
- @ karenm@berkmann.co.uk
- W www.berkmann.co.uk

Credit cards, delivery, glass hire/loan, mail order.
*Focus on France, plus good Italian and
South African wines.*

Berry Bros. & Rudd ★★★★★
3 St. James's Street, London SW1A 1EG
- ℂ 0870 900 4300
- FAX 0870 900 4301
- @ orders@bbr.com
- W www.bbr.com

Credit cards, accessories, delivery, en primeur,
cellarage, tastings, glass hire, mail order worldwide,
internet sales.
*Award-winning wine merchant with
fantastic French and New World wines.*

Bibendum ★★★★★
113 Regents Park Road,
London NW1 8UR
- ℂ 020 7916 7706
- FAX 020 7916 7705
- @ sales@bibendum-wine.co.uk
- W www.bibendum-wine.co.uk

By the case only, mail order only, credit cards,
delivery, tastings, glass loan, en primeur, cellarage,
internet sales.
*Excellent range of individual Old and
New World wines.*

Booths Supermarkets ★★★★★
4–6 Fishergate, Preston PR1 3LJ
☎ 01772 251 701
FAX 01772 255 642
Credit cards, accessories, tastings, glass hire/loan.
*One of Britain's most enterprising
supermarket groups.*

Bordeaux Index ★★★★★
1st Floor, 3–5 Spafield Street,
London EC1 4QB
☎ 020 7278 9495 and 7278 9795
FAX 020 7278 9707
@ sales@bordeauxindex.com
W www.bordeauxindex.com
By the case only, credit cards, delivery, en primeur,
cellarage, mail order.
*Young, dynamic merchants who also have
an excellent Burgundy range.*

Bottoms Up ★★★★
Enjoyment Hall, Bessemer Road,
Welwyn Garden City, Herts AL7 1BL
☎ 01707 387263
FAX 01707 387200
W www.enjoyment.co.uk
Credit cards, delivery, tastings, glass hire/loan.
*Oddbins-lookalike under same ownership
as Thresher and Victoria Wine.*

La Bouteille d'Or ★★★★
Queens Lodge, Queens Club Gardens,
London W14 9TA
☎ 020 7385 3122
FAX 020 7385 3122
@ labouteilledor@newbury.net
By the case only, mail order, delivery, tastings.
Focus on Champagne from small growers.

The Burgundy Shuttle ★★★★
168 Ifield Road, London SW10 9AF
☎ 020 7341 4053
FAX 020 7244 0618
@ peter@burgundyshuttle.ltd.uk
W www.burgundyshuttle.co.uk
By the case only, credit cards, accessories, en
primeur, cellarage, glass loan, delivery, internet sales.
Excellent Burgundy specialist.

The Butlers Wine Cellar ★★★★
247 Queens Park Road, Brighton,
East Sussex BN2 2XJ
☎ 01273 698724
FAX 01273 622761
W www.butlers-winecellar.co.uk
Credit cards, accessories, delivery, tastings, glass
hire/loan, mail order, internet sales.
Great range from the classic to the eclectic.

Anthony Byrne ★★★★★
Ramsey Business Park, Stocking Fen
Road, Ramsey, Huntingdon,
Cambs PE26 2UR
☎ 01487 814 555
FAX 01487 814 962
@ anthony@abfw.co.uk
W www.abfw.co.uk
Delivery, en primeur, cellarage, tastings, by the
case only, internet sales.
*Fine wines from Alsace, Burgundy and
South Africa.*

Cave Cru Classé ★★★★
Unit 13, Leathermarket, Weston Street,
London SE1 3ER
☎ 020 7940 5112
FAX 020 7378 8544
W www.cave-cru-classe.com
By the case only, accessories, cellarage, credit cards,
delivery, en primeur, tastings.
*Top vintages of top wines from Rhône,
Bordeaux and Burgundy.*

Les Caves de Pyrene ★★★★
Pew Corner, Old Portsmouth Road,
Artington, Guildford, Surrey GU3 1LP
☎ 01483 538820
FAX 01483 455068
W www.lescavesdepyrene.com
By the case only, credit cards, delivery, tastings and
wine dinners, mail order, internet sales.
*Quirky and traditional French wines with
some good New World fare.*

The Cellar d'Or ★★★★
37 St Giles, Norwich NR2 1JN
☎ 01603 626246
FAX 01603 626256
@ wine@cellardor.co.uk
W www.cellardor.co.uk
Credit cards, accessories, delivery, tastings,
en primeur, cellarage, glass hire/loan, mail order,
internet sales.
*A dynamic and constantly evolving wine
selection from around the world. Their
fine and rare wine branches trade as The
Antique Wine Company of Great Britain.*

Charterhouse Wine co. ★★★★
82 Goding Street, London SE11 5AW
☎ 020 7587 1302
FAX 020 7587 0982
@ norman@charterhousewine.co.uk
Credit cards, delivery, en primeur, cellarage, tastings,
glass loan, mail order.
*Good wines from Australia, Chile,
and Spain.*

Brian Coad Fine Wines ★★★★
Grape Expectations Wine Warehouse,
Stray Park, off Park St., Ivybridge,
Devon PL21 9DW
☎ 01752 896 545
FAX 01752 691 160
@ briancoadfinewines@lineone.net
Mail order, by the case only, credit cards, delivery,
tastings, en primeur (port only), glass loan.
Gems here include great Loires.

Cockburns of Leith ★★★★
7 Devon Place, Edinburgh,
Scotland EH12 5HJ
☎ 0131 346 1113
FAX 0131 313 2607
@ jhogg@winelist.co.uk
W www.winelist.co.uk
Credit cards, delivery, tastings, en primeur, glass loan,
cellarage, mail order, internet sales.
*Reliable, traditional merchant. Good for
Claret and Burgundy.*

Compendium Merchants ★★★★
Alanbrooke Road, Castlereagh, Belfast,
N. Ireland BT6 9PR
☎ 028 9079 1197
FAX 028 9079 8001
@ info@compendiumwines.com
W www.compendiumwines.com
Credit cards, delivery, glass loan/hire, tastings,
mail order, internet sales.
*An exciting portfolio and an
approachable manner. Australian range is
particularly impressive.*

Corkscrew Wines ★★★★
Arch 5, Viaduct Estate,
Carlisle CA2 5BN
☎ 01228 543033
FAX 01228 543033
@ wines@corkscrewwines.demon.co.uk
W www.corkscrew-wines.com
Credit cards, delivery, tastings, en primeur,
glass hire/loan, mail order.
*Small merchant with a big list. Good
Australian wines across the board.*

Corney and Barrow ★★★★
12 Helmet Row, London EC1V 3TD
☎ 020 7539 3200
FAX 020 7608 1373
@ wine@corbar.co.uk
W www.corneyandbarrow.com
Credit cards, accessories, delivery, en primeur,
cellarage, glass hire/loan, tastings, mail order.
*Fine wine specialists with an eye for the
world's most desirable wines.*

Croque-en-Bouche ★★★★★
221 Wells Road, Malvern Wells,
Worcester WR14 4HF
☎ 01684 565612
FAX 0870 7066282
@ mail@croque-en-bouche.co.uk
W www.croque-en-bouche.co.uk
By the case only, credit cards, delivery, cellarage.
*Great restaurant-cum-wine merchant.
A list packed with delights.*

Define Food & Wine ★★★★★
Chester Road, Sandiway,
Cheshire CW8 2NH
☎ 01606 882101
FAX 01606 888407
@ office@definefoodandwine.com
Credit cards, accessories, delivery, tastings,
cellarage, glass loan.
Merchants bursting with enthusiasm.

Direct Wine Shipments ★★★★★
5/7 Corporation Square, Belfast,
N. Ireland BT1 3AJ
☎ 028 9050 8000
FAX 028 9050 8004
@ enquiry@directwine.co.uk
W www.directwine.co.uk
Credit cards, accessories, delivery, tastings, en
primeur, cellarage, glass hire/loan, mail order.
*Merchant offering tastings and courses.
Generally very recommendable but
especially strong on Spain and Australia.*

Domaine Direct ★★★★★
10 Hardwick Street, London, EC1R 4RB
☎ 020 7837 1142
FAX 020 7837 8605
@ info@domainedirect.co.uk
W www.domainedirect.co.uk
By the case only, credit cards, delivery, cellarage,
tastings, en primeur.
*A serious list with brilliant Burgundy
and New World estates (e.g., Leeuwin)
often at surprisingly competitive prices.*

English Wine Centre ★★★★
Alfriston, East Sussex BN26 5QS
☎ 01323 870141
FAX 01323 870005
@ bottles@englishwine.co.uk
W www.englishwine.co.uk
credit cards, accessories, delivery, tastings, glass
hire/loan, mail order, internet sales.
*Home to the English Wine Museum, with
daily tastings of a good range of wines
from various parts of the UK. Wines from
other countries are available too.*

Farr Vintners ★★★★★
19 Sussex Street, Pimlico,
London SW1V 4RR
☎ 020 7821 2000
FAX 020 7821 2020
@ sales@farr-vintners.com
W www.farr-vintners.com
By the case only (min. order 500), cellarage,
en primeur, internet sales, worldwide shipping.
*The reference point for the world's finest
and rarest wines.*

Fine & Rare Wines ★★★★★
Unit 17–18 Pall Mall Deposit, 124–128
Barlby Road, London W10 6BL
☎ 020 8960 1995
FAX 020 8960 1911
@ wine@frw.co.uk
W www.frw.co.uk
Mail order, delivery, en primeur.
*Specialists in the world's fine and rare
wines; from en primeur to the oldest
vintages.*

Irma Fingal-Rock ★★★★
64 Monnow Street, Monmouth,
Wales NP25 3EN
☎ 01600 712372
FAX 01600 712372
@ irmafingalrock@msn.com
W www.pinotnoir.co.uk
Credit cards, delivery, tastings, glass hire/loan,
mail order.
*Originally a food shop, wine now
80 per cent of turnover. Emphasis is on
Burgundy with some good Chablis.*

Forth Wines ★★★★
Crawford Place, Milnathort,
Kinross-shire, Scotland KY13 9XF
☎ 01577 866000
FAX 01577 866010
@ enquiries@forthwines.com
W www.forthwines.com
By the case only, credit cards, delivery, en primeur,
glass loan/hire, mail order.
*Wines from first rate producers in the
old as well as the New World.*

Fortnum & Mason ★★★★★
181 Piccadilly, London WIA IER
☎ 020 7734 8040
FAX 020 7437 3278
@ info@fortnumandmason.co.uk
W www.fortnumandmason.co.uk
Credit cards, delivery, tastings,en primeur, mail order.
*Ultra-smart store with classic wines and
a 24 hour UK-wide delivery service.*

Four Walls Wine Co. ★★★★★
1 High Street, Chilgrove, Nr Chichester,
W. Sussex PO18 9HX
☎ 01243 535360
FAX 01243 535418
@ fourwallswine@compuserve.com
Credit cards, accessories, delivery, en primeur,
tastings, cellarage, glass hire/loan.
*A super list of 3,500 blue-chip Bordeaux,
Burgundies, Germans, and Loires.*

Frank Stainton Wines ★★★★
3 Berry's Yard, Finkle Street, Kendal,
Cumbria LA9 4AB
☎ 01539 731886
FAX 01539 730396
@ admin@stainton-wines.co.uk
Credit cards, delivery, tastings, mail order.
*Broad range. Good Rieslings, Bordeaux,
New World, and half-bottles.*

Gauntleys ★★★★★
4 High Street, Exchange Arcade,
Nottingham NG1 2ET
☎ 0115 911 0555
FAX 0115 911 0557
@ rhone@gauntleywine.com
W www.gauntleywine.com
Credit cards, accessories, delivery, en primeur,
mail order.
*Superb on Alsace, Rhône, and Loire,
expanding into Germany, Spain, Italy.*

Goedhuis & Co. ★★★★★
6 Rudolf Place, Miles Street,
London SW8 IRP
☎ 020 7793 7900
FAX 020 7793 7170
@ goedhuis@btinternet.com
W www.goedhuis.com
By the case only, delivery, en primeur, cellarage,
glass hire/loan.
*Source of Old and New World wine. En
primeur, Bordeaux, and Burgundy.*

Gordon & MacPhail ★★★★
58–60 South Street, Elgin, Moray,
Scotland IV30 1JY
☎ 01343 545 110
FAX 01343 540 155
@ info@gordonandmacphail.com
W www.gordonandmacphail.com
Credit cards, accessories, delivery, tastings, en
primeur (ports), glass hire/loan, mail order.
*Brilliant malt whisky from your birth
year, a good range of French country
wines and some first class examples
from the New World.*

Great Northern Wine Co. ★★★★
The Warehouse, Blossomgate, Ripon,
N. Yorks. HG4 2AJ
- **C** 01765 606767
- **FAX** 01765 609151
- **@** info@greatnorthernwine.com
- **w** www.greatnorthernwine.com

Credit cards, accessories, delivery, tastings, en
primeur, glass loan, mail order, internet sales.
*One of the best merchants between
Edinburgh and Watford. Friendly service.*

Great Western Wine Co. ★★★★
Wells Road, Bath BA2 3AP
- **C** 01225 322800
- **FAX** 01225 442139
- **@** davidl@greatwesternwine.co.uk
- **w** www.greatwesternwine.co.uk

By the case only, accessories, credit cards, delivery,
tastings, cellarage, glass loan, en primeur, mail order,
internet sales.
*Great range, especially good French
country wines. Plenty of half-bottles, too,
and an enticing diary of tastings.*

Greek Wine Centre ★★★★
48 Underdale Road, Shrewsbury,
Shropshire SY2 5DT
- **C** 01743 364636
- **FAX** 01743 367960
- **@** email@greekwinecentre.co.uk
- **w** www.greekwinecentre.co.uk

Delivery, tastings, by the case only, mail order
and internet sales only.
Exciting new-wave wines from Greece.

Alexander Hadleigh ★★★★
19 Centre Way, Lock's Heath,
Southampton, Hampshire SO31 6DX
- **C** 01489 885959
- **FAX** 01489 885960

sales@alexanderhadleigh.sagehost.co.uk
Credit cards, accessories, delivery, tastings, glass
hire/loan, mail order.
*Good stock of organic wines, Armagnacs,
Cognacs and malts, and gourmet food.*

Roger Harris ★★★★★
Loke Farm, Weston Longville,
Norfolk NR9 5LG
- **C** 01603 880 171
- **FAX** 01603 880 291
- **@** sales@rogerharriswines.co.uk
- **w** www.beaujolaisonline.co.uk

Mail order only, by the case only, credit cards,
delivery, internet sales.
*The best of Beaujolais and the Mâconnais
with the promise of next-day delivery.*

Harrods Ltd ★★★★★
87–135 Brompton Road, Knightsbridge,
London SW1X 7XL
- **C** 020 7730 1234
- **FAX** 020 7225 5823
- **@** food.halls@harrods.com
- **w** www.harrods.com

Credit cards, accessories, delivery, en primeur,
tastings, mail order.
*State-of-the-art wine shop, with some
1,600 wines in stock. Still, predictably,
hot on the classics of the Old World, but
there are plenty of big-name New World
stars too.*

Haynes Hanson & Clark ★★★★
25 Eccleston Street,
London SW1W 9NP
- **C** 020 7259 0102
- **FAX** 020 7259 0103
- **@** london@hhandc.co.uk

Credit cards, accessories, delivery, tastings,
en primeur, glass loan, mail order.
*France is the area of focus here, and
Burgundy the particular strength.*

Hedley Wright ★★★★
Twyford Business Centre, London Road,
Bishops Stortford, Herts CM23 3YT
- **C** 01279 465818
- **FAX** 01279 465819

Credit cards, delivery, tastings, en primeur,
cellarage, glass loan, mail order.
*A good country merchant offering classy
Chileans and Old World stars.*

Douglas Henn-Macrae ★★★★
61 Downs View, Burnham, Rochester,
Kent ME1 3RR
- **C** 01634 669394
- **FAX** 01634 683096
- **@** drhm@clara.co.uk
- **w** www.drhm.clara.co.uk

By the case only, delivery, tastings, mail order.
*German specialists with a good selection
of US wines, including examples from
hard-to-find regions*

Heyman Barwell Jones ★★★★
24 Fore Street, Ipswich, Suffolk IP4 1JU
- **C** 01473 232322
- **FAX** 01473 212237
- **@** paul.gow@heyman.co.uk
- **w** www.heyman.co.uk

By the case only, credit cards, delivery, tastings, en
primeur, mail order.
*A very good range from all corners of the
globe. Especially interesting Burgundy.*

George Hill ★★★★
59 Wards End, Loughborough,
Leicestershire LE11 3HB
☎ 01509 212717
FAX 01509 236963
@ sales@georgehill.co.uk
W www.georgehill.co.uk
Credit cards, en primeur, cellarage, glass hire/loan,
delivery, tastings, mail order.
Informative, easy to follow list.

House of Townend ★★★★
Red Duster House, 101 York Street,
Hull HU2 0QX
☎ 01482 586582
FAX 01482 218796
@ sales@houseoftownend.co.uk
W www.hotwines.co.uk
Credit cards, accessories, delivery, en primeur, mail
order, cellarage, glass loan, tastings, internet sales.
*Burgundy, Champagne, and Australia
are particular strengths.*

Ian G. Howe ★★★★
35 Appletongate, Newark,
Nottinghamshire NG24 1JR
☎ 01636 704366
FAX 01636 610502
@ howe@chablis-burgundy.co.uk
W www.chablis-burgundy.co.uk
Credit cards, accessories, delivery, tastings,
glass hire/loan, mail order.
*Exclusive Chablis and Burgundy
specialists, plus a little Champagne.*

Inspired Wines ★★★★
West End, High Street, Cleobury
Mortimer, Shropshire DY14 8DR
☎ 01299 270064
FAX 01299 270064
@ info@inspired-wines.co.uk
W www.inspired-wines.co.uk
Credit cards, accessories, delivery, tastings,
glass hire/loan, mail order, internet sales.
*A warehouse with a good US and Italian
wines and an expanding internet service.*

Jeroboams ★★★★
8–12 Brook Street, London W1Y 2BH
☎ 020 7288 8888
FAX 020 7495 3314
@ sales@jeroboams.co.uk
W www.jeroboams.co.uk
Credit cards, accessories, delivery, en primeur,
cellarage, delivery, glass hire, tastings, mail order,
internet sales.
*Specialists in wine and cheese from claret
to Caerphilly. Now incorporates Laytons.*

Michael Jobling Wines ★★★★
Baltic Chambers, 3–7 Broad Chare,
Newcastle-upon-Tyne NE1 3DQ
☎ 0191 261 5298
FAX 0191 261 4543
@ mjw@michaeljoblingwines.co.uk
W www.michaeljoblingwines.co.uk
By the case only, credit cards, delivery, tastings,
glass loan, mail order.
*Well-chosen wines backed up with
personal advice, tastings, and dinners.*

S.H. Jones & Co. ★★★★
27 High Street, Banbury,
Oxon OX16 8EW
☎ 01295 251179
FAX 01295 272352
@ sh.jones@btconnect.com
Credit cards, delivery, tastings, en primeur, cellarage,
glass loan, mail order.
*Dependable for Spanish, South American,
and south Italian wines. Top end French
are good.*

Justerini & Brooks ★★★★★
61 St. James's Street, London, SW1A 1LZ;
45 George Street, Edinburgh EH2 2HT
☎ 020 7484 6400
FAX 020 7484 6499
@ ruth.white@vdv.com
Credit cards, accessories, delivery, tastings,
en primeur, cellarage, glass loan, mail order.
*Second-to-none in the quality of the
range and in the service offered.*

Laithwaites ★★★★★
New Aquitaine House, Exeter Way,
Theale, Reading, Berkshire RG7 4Pl
☎ 0870 444 8383
FAX 0870 444 8182
@ orders@laithwaites.co.uk
W www.laithwaites.co.uk
Credit cards, accessories, delivery, glass hire/loan,
en primeur, tastings, mail order, internet sales.
*Highly innovative mail-order sister-firm
to the Sunday Times Wine Club.*

Lay & Wheeler ★★★★★
Gosbecks Park, Gosbecks Road,
Colchester, Essex CO2 9JT
☎ 01206 764446
FAX 01206 560002
@ sales@laywheeler.com
W www.laywheeler.com
Credit cards, accessories, delivery, tastings, en
primeur, cellarage, glass loan, mail order.
*One of the best regional and mail-order
sources of Old and New World classics.*

Laymont & Shaw ★★★★★
The Old Chapel, Millpool, Truro,
Cornwall TR1 1EX
℡ 01872 270 545
FAX 01872 223 005
@ info@laymont-shaw.co.uk
W www.laymont-shaw.co.uk
Mail order, by the case only, delivery,
tastings, glass loan.
*A treasure trove of both new wave and
traditional wines from Spain and
Portugal that are often hard to find.*

Lea & Sandeman ★★★★★
170 Fulham Road, London SW10 9PR
℡ 0207 2440522
FAX 0207 2440533
@ sales@leaandsandeman.co.uk
Credit cards, accessories, delivery, en primeur,
cellarage, tastings, glass loan, mail order.
*First class London merchant with shops
in Fulham, Notting Hill, and Barnes.
Good, across the board.*

Liberty Wines
Unit A53, New Covent Garden Food
Market, London SW8 5EE
℡ 020 7720 5350
FAX 020 7720 6158
@ order@libertywine.co.uk
By the case only, credit cards, delivery, mail order.
*One of the leading Italian specialists in
London, with a growing range from
France and Australia.*

O.W. Loeb & Co. ★★★★
82 Southwark Bridge Road,
London SE1 0AS
℡ 020 7928 7750
FAX 020 7928 1855
@ sales@owloeb.com
W www.owloeb.com
Credit cards, delivery, by the case only, en primeur,
tastings, cellarage, mail order.
*A well-chosen list with some superstars
from Burgundy, Germany and the Rhône.
Alsace is also worth a look.*

Magnum Fine Wines ★★★★
43 Pall Mall, London SW1Y 5JG
℡ 020 7839 5732
FAX 020 7321 0848
@ wine@magnum.co.uk
W www.magnum.co.uk
Credit cards, delivery, en primeur, tastings, cellarage,
mail order.
*Impressive selection of French fine wines,
especially Bordeaux.*

Majestic Wine ★★★★★
Majestic House, Otterspool Way,
Watford, Herts WD25 8WW
℡ 01923 298200
FAX 01923 819105
@ info@majestic.co.uk
W www.majestic.co.uk
By the (mixed) case only*, credit cards, accessories,
delivery, tastings, en primeur, glass loan, mail order,
internet sales.
*A generally good range of wines,
with bargain one-off purchases and
the opportunity to taste before you buy.
*The Vinopolis shop (020 7940 8313)
also sells by the bottle.*

Marks & Spencer ★★★★
46–47 Baker Street, London W1A 8EP
℡ 020 7935 4422
W www.marksandspencer.com
Credit cards, delivery, tastings, mail order.
*New World and Champagne are the
stars in this limited but reliable range.*

Martinez Fine Wines ★★★★
35 The Grove, Ilkley,
W. Yorks LS29 9NJ
℡ 01943 603241
FAX 01943 816489
@ martinez@martinez.co.uk
W www.martinez.co.uk
Credit cards, accessories, delivery, tastings,
en primeur, cellarage, glass hire/loan.
*Independent merchant specializing
in small botique wineries.*

Mayfair Cellars ★★★★
Minivier House, 19–20 Garlick Hill,
London EC4V 2AL
℡ 020 7329 8899
FAX 020 7329 8880
@ sales@mayfaircellars.co.uk
Mail order only, credit cards, delivery, tastings,
en primeur, cellarage.
*Small mail order, fine wine merchant
which, like, Berry Bros, boasts an office
in Hong Kong.*

The Moffat Wine Shop ★★★★
8 Well Street, Moffat, Dumfriesshire,
SW Scotland DG10 9DP
℡ 01683 220 554
@ moffwine@aol.com
W www.moffattown.com
Credit cards, accessories, delivery, tastings, cellarage,
glass loan, mail order.
*Independent merchant with a unique
range. Interesting wines from Uruguay.*

Montrachet ★★★★★
59 Kennington Road, Waterloo,
London SE1 7PZ
C 020 7928 1990
FAX 020 7928 3415
@ sales@montrachetwine.com
W www.montrachetwine.com
By the case only, by mail only, credit cards,
delivery, tastings, en primeur, internet sales.
*Superb domaine Burgundies, the best
German estates, and classic Bordeaux.*

Moreno Wine Merchants ★★★★★
11 Marylands Road, London W9 2DU
C 020 7286 0678
FAX 020 7286 0513
@ morenowi@dialstart.net
Credit cards, glass loan, tastings, delivery, mail order.
*Dynamic Spanish and South American
specialist. A good Fine and Rare Wine list
with some of the finest Spanish wines
available from as far back as the 1800s.*

Morris & Verdin ★★★★★
10 The Leathermarket, Weston Street,
London SE1 3ER
C 020 7357 8866
FAX 020 7357 8877
@ sales@m-v.co.uk
W www.morris-verdin.co.uk
By the case only, delivery, tastings, en primeur,
cellarage, mail order, internet sales.
*Brilliant Burgundies, sublime sherries,
and "new classic" Californians. Recent
developments include a passion for Riesling
from Alsace, Austria, and the Mosel.*

Morrisons Supermarkets ★★★
Hilmore House, Thornton Road,
Bradford, West Yorkshire BD8 9AX
C 01924 875234
FAX 01924 875300
Credit cards, accessories, glass hire/loan.
*Unashamedly discount-focused
supermarket chain (with special offers
on up to half the wines). Good affordable
US wines.*

New Zealand Wines Direct ★★★★
PO Box 476, London NW5 2NZ
C 020 7482 0093
FAX 020 7267 8400
W www.fwnz.co.uk
By the case only, credit cards, delivery, tastings,
mail order, internet sales.
*Exclusive New Zealand specialist
who arranges wine tours to the area.
Wines that are otherwise hard to find.*

Harvey Nichols ★★★★★
109–125 Knightsbridge,
London, SW1X 7RJ
C 020 7201 8537
FAX 020 72355020
Credit cards, accessories, delivery, tastings, mail order.
*A great collection of both Old World and
New World classics which can also be
enjoyed in the fifth-Floor restaurant.*

James Nicholson ★★★★★
27a Killyleagh Street, Crossgar, Co.
Down, Northern Ireland BT30 9DQ
C 028 44 830091
FAX 028 44 830028
@ info@jnwine.com
W www.jnwine.com
Credit cards, accessories, delivery, cellarage,
tastings, en primeur, wine club, glass loan,
mail order, internet sales.
*Superb growers' wines from California.
List is expanding with some good French
Country and Rhône wines.*

Nicolas UK ★★★★
Unit 1, Gateway Trading Estate,
Hythe Road, London NW10 6RJ
C 020 8964 5469
FAX 020 8962 9829
W www.nicolas-wines.com
Credit cards, delivery, cellarage, tastings, glass hire,
en primeur, cellarage.
*Reliable range from little-known French
regional wines to top-flight clarets.*

Noble Rot ★★★★
18 Market Street, Bromsgrove,
Worcs B61 8DA
C 01527 575 606
FAX 01527 833 133
@ info@nrwinewarehouse.co.uk
W www.nrwinewarehouse.co.uk
Credit cards, delivery, tastings, glass loan, wine club.
Majestic-style warehouse emporium.

Oddbins ★★★★★
31–33 Weir Road, Wimbledon,
London SW19 8OG
C 020 8944 4400
FAX 020 8944 4411
W www.oddbins.com
Credit cards, accessories, delivery, tastings,
glass loan, mail order, internet sales.
*A great range with wine-mad staff.
Those wanting more should try Oddbins
Fine Wine shops. Also now in Calais.
Also half of tasteforwine.co.uk (qv).
Changed hands in 2001.*

Ceci Paolo ★★★★
The New Cook's Emporium, 21 High Street, Ledbury, Herefordshire HR8 1DS
C 01531 632976
FAX 01531 631011
@ patriciaharrison@compuserve.com
W www.cecipaolo.com
Credit cards, accessories, delivery, tastings, mail order.
Italian specialists with a Caffe Bar where you can choose wines off the shelf to drink with your lunch.

Thos. Peatling ★★★★
Westgate House, Westgate Street, Bury St Edmunds, Suffolk IP33 1QS
C 01284 755948
FAX 01284 714483
Credit cards, accessories, cellarage, en primeur, delivery, glass loan, tastings, mail order.
Bordeaux specialist stocking over 50 malt whiskies. Under new ownership which has seen over 300 new wines introduced to their existing list.

Penistone Court Cellars ★★★★
The Railway Station, Penistone, South Yorkshire S36 6HP
C 01226 766037
FAX 01226 767310
@ pcwc@dircon.co.uk
By the case only, credit cards, accessories, delivery, glass loan, mail order.
Austrian specialists with a short list of well-chosen wines.

Philglas & Swiggot ★★★★
21 Northcote Road, Battersea, London SW11 1NG
C 020 7924 4494
FAX 020 7642 1308
@ karen@philglasandswiggot.co.uk
Credit cards, accessories, tastings, delivery, glass loan, mail order.
Antipodean specialists par excellence; great Italians and good Spanish wines.

Terry Platt ★★★★★
Council St. West, Llandudno, Conwy, Wales LL30 1ED
C 01492 874099
FAX 01492 874788
@ plattwines@clara.co.uk
W www.terryplattwines.co.uk
Credit cards, accessories, delivery by the case, tastings, glass hire/loan.
A range to satisfy bargain-seekers and enthusiasts alike.

Playford Ros ★★★★
Middle Park House, Sowerby, Thirsk, North Yorkshire YO7 3AH
C 01845 526777
FAX 01845 526888
@ sales@playfordros.com
W www.playfordros.com
By the case only, credit cards, accessories, delivery, tastings, en primeur, ceelarage, glass hire/loan, mail order, internet sales.
Good Bordeaux, Burgundy, Australian.

Le Pont de la Tour ★★★★★
Butlers Wharf Building, 36d Shad Thames, Butlers Wharf, London SE1 2YE
C 020 7403 2403
FAX 020 7403 0267
@ emmanuels@conranrestaurants.co.uk
W www.conran.com
Credit cards, accessories, delivery, tastings, glass loan, mail order.
The Pont de la Tour restaurant's excellent and in some cases exclusive wine list.

Raeburn Fine Wines ★★★★★
21/23 Comely Bank Road, Edinburgh, Scotland EH4 1DS
C 0131 343 1159
FAX 0131 332 5166
@ raeburn@netcomuk.co.uk
W www.raeburnfinewines.com
Credit cards, delivery, tastings, en primeur, glass hire/loan, cellarage, mail order.
Still enjoying a cult following both sides of the border. The list includes enticing names from the Mosel and Burgundy.

Reid Wines ★★★★★
The Mill, Marsh Lane, Hallatrow, Bristol BS39 6EB
C 01761 452 645
FAX 01761 453 642
Credit cards, delivery, tastings, glass loan, mail order.
Eccentric merchant with a witty list brimming with classic and rare wines.

La Réserve ★★★★★
56 Walton Street, Knightsbridge, London SW3 1RB
C 020 7589 2020
FAX 020 7978 4934
@ realwine@la-reserve.co.uk
W www.la-reserve.co.uk
Credit cards, accessories, delivery, tastings, en primeur, cellarage, glass loan, mail order.
Impeccable Burgundies and top wines from most other regions.

Howard Ripley ★★★★★

25 Dingwall Road, London SW18 3AZ

☏ 020 8877 3065

FAX 020 8877 0029

@ info@howardripley.com

W www.howardripley.com

By the case only, delivery, tastings, en primeur,
mail order and internet service only.

Dentist-turned-specialist wine merchant.
Lists 50 of the best Burgundy domaines.

Roberson Wine Merchant ★★★★★

348 Kensington High Street,
London, W14 8NS

☏ 020 7371 2121

FAX 020 7371 4010

@ wines@roberson.co.uk

W www.roberson.co.uk

Credit cards, delivery, tastings, cellarage,
glass loan, mail order.

An eclectic range of young and mature
wines from all over the world. A good
selection of "antique wines".

Irvine Robertson ★★★★

10–11 North Leith Sands,
Edinburgh, Scotland EH6 4ER

☏ 0131 553 3521

FAX 0131 553 5465

@ irviner@nildram.co.uk

W www.irwines.co.uk

By the case only, credit cards, delivery,
glass loan, mail order.

Traditional Scottish independent
merchant with a wide range.

Safeway ★★★★

6 Millington Road, Hayes,
Middlesex UB3 4AY

☏ 020 8970 3821

FAX 020 8756 2910

W www.safeway.co.uk (e-commerce:
www.safewaywinesdirect.co.uk)

Credit cards, accessories, tastings, glass loan,
internet sales.

Offering a range of good-value wines
in all sectors.

Sainsbury ★★★★

Stamford House, Stamford Street,
London SE1 9LL

☏ 020 7695 7416

FAX 020 7695 6416

W www.sainsburys.co.uk

Credit cards, accessories, en primeur, glass hire/loan.

Improving and increasingly
customer focused chain. Now
half of tasteforwine.co.uk (qv).

Satchells of Burnham Market
★★★★

North Street, Burnham Market,
Norfolk PE31 8HG

☏ 01328 738272

FAX 01328 730727

@ satchellswines@btinternet.com

Credit cards, accessories, delivery, tastings,
glass hire/loan, mail order.

Small traditional merchant with over
1,000 lines and a new wine club.

Savage Selection ★★★★

The Ox House, Market Place,
Northleach, Cheltenham,
Gloucestershire GL54 3EG

☏ 01451 860896

FAX 01451 860996

@ savage.selection@virgin.net

W www.savageselection.co.uk

Credit cards, accessories, delivery, tastings,
en primeur, cellarage, glass hire/loan, mail order.

Wines selected at source from individual
producers for their originality.

Scatchard ★★★★

Kings Dock Street, Wapping,
Liverpool L1 8JS

☏ 0151 709 7073

FAX 0151 709 1500

@ info@scatchard.com

Credit cards, accessories, delivery, tastings,
cellarage, glass loan, mail order.

Spain is the specialist subject.
Good French and Italians too.

Sebastopol Wines ★★★★

Sebastopol Barn, London Road,
Blewbury, Oxfordshire OX11 9HB

☏ 01235 850 471

FAX 01235 850 776

@ infosebastopol@aol.com

By the case only, credit cards, accessories,
en primeur, delivery, glass hire.

Australia and Bordeaux specialists
with some good fine and rare wines.

Seckford Wines ★★★★

Dock Lane, Melton, Suffolk IP12 1PE

☏ 01394 446622

FAX 01394 446633

@ marcus@seckfordwines.co.uk

W www.seckfordwines.co.uk

By the case only, credit cards, delivery, en primeur,
cellarage, mail order and internet sales only.

A fine range of classic wines, plus some
exciting new wines from South Africa
and Australia.

Edward Sheldon ★★★★

New Street, Shipston on Stour,
Warks CV36 4EN
C 01608 661409
FAX 01608 663166
@ finewine@edward-sheldon.co.uk
W www.edward-sheldon.co.uk
Credit cards, accessories, delivery, tastings,
en primeur, cellarage, glass loan, mail order.
Strong on Bordeaux and Burgundy.

Somerfield ★★★

Somerfield House, Whitchurch Lane,
Bristol BS14 OTJ
C 01179 359359
FAX 01179 357826
W www.somerfield.co.uk
Credit cards, accessories, delivery, tastings.
Price-conscious supermarket chain.

Sommelier Wine Co. ★★★★

The Grapevine, 23 St. George's
Esplanade, St. Peter Port,
Guernsey GY1 2BG
C 01481 721 677.
FAX 01481 716 818.
Credit cards, accessories, delivery, tastings,
glass hire/loan, mail order.
*Great New World and sweet wines
available. Individually described and –
agreeably – VAT-free.*

Stevens Garnier ★★★★

47 West Way, Botley, Oxford OX2 0JF
C 01865 263303
FAX 01865 791594
@ sales@stevensgarnier.co.uk
W www.stevensgarnier.co.uk
Credit cards, accessories, delivery, glass loan,
tastings, mail order.
*A good range (Loire, Burgundy, Portugal,
South Africa, South America) benefits
from this firm's other role as an importer-
wholesaler. Look for "niche" wines from
places like Savoie and Ontario.*

Stratford's Merchants ★★★★

High St, Cookham-on-Thames,
Berks SL6 9SQ
C 01628 810606
FAX 01628 810605
@ sales@stratfordwine.co.uk
W www.stratfordwine.co.uk
Credit cards, accessories, delivery, tastings, glass loan,
mail order, internet sales.
*A good international range, with some
particularly inspiring bottles from Chile
and Australia.*

The Sunday Times Wine Club
★★★★

New Aquitaine House, Exeter Way,
Theale, Reading, Berks RG7 4PL
C 0870 220 0010
FAX 0870 220 0030
@ orders@wine-club.co.uk
W www.sundaytimeswineclub.co.uk
Credit cards, accessories, delivery, tastings, en primeur,
cellarage, glass hire/loan, mail order, internet sales.
Laudable firm linked to Laithwaites (qv).

Tanners Wines ★★★★★

26 Wyle Cop, Shrewsbury,
Shropshire SY1 1XD
C 01743 234455
FAX 01743 234501
@ sales@tanners-wines.co.uk
W www.tanners-wines.co.uk
Credit cards, accessories, delivery, tastings, en
primeur, glass hire/loan, regional chain, mail order.
*Merchant with strengths in France and
Germany, featuring small growers.*

Tasteforwine.co.uk ★★★★

FAX 0208 272 4210
@ sales@tasteforwine.co.uk
W www.tasteforwine.co.uk
Credit cards, mail order.
*Mail order and web-based offspring
of Oddbins and Sainsbury.*

Tesco Stores ★★★★

PO Box 18, Delemare Road, Cheshunt,
Herts EN8 9SL
C 0800 505555.
@ customer.service@tesco.co.uk
W www.tesco.co.uk
Credit cards, accessories, delivery, tastings, glass loan.
Ultra-dynamic supermarket chain.

Thresher Wine Shop ★★★★

Enjoyment Hall, Bessemer Road,
Welwyn Garden City, Herts AL7 1BL
C 01707 387263
FAX 01707 387350
Credit cards, delivery, tastings.
Britain's largest high-street chain.

Turville Valley Wines ★★★★★

The Firs, Potter Row, Great Missenden,
Bucks HP16 9LT
C 01494 868818
FAX 01494 868832
@ info@turville-valley-wines.com
W www.turville-valley-wines.com
Delivery, en primeur, cellarage, mail order.
Classic Bordeaux, Burgundy, and port.

Unwins Wine Merchants ★★★★
Birchwood House, Victoria Road,
Dartford, Kent DA1 5AJ
☎ 01322 272 711
FAX 01322 294 469
@ info@unwins.co.uk
W www.unwins.co.uk
Credit cards, delivery, tastings, en primeur,
glass hire/loan.
*Improving Home Counties chain now
making an impact on London with the
acquisition of Fullers' shops.*

Valvona & Crolla ★★★★★
19 Elm Row, Edinburgh, EH7 4AA
☎ 0131 556 6066
FAX 0131 556 1668
@ sales@valvonacrolla.co.uk
W www.valvonacrolla.co.uk
Credit cards, accessories, delivery, tastings,
glass hire/loan, mail order, internet sales.
*Stunning Italian wines and an expanding
range from elsewhere. Tutored tastings.*

Victoria Wine ★★★
Enjoyment Hall, Bessemer Road,
Welwyn Garden City, Herts AL7 1BL
☎ 01707 387263
FAX 01707 387350
Credit cards, delivery, glass loan.
*Once-dynamic part of the same First
Quench group as Thresher. Now, sadly,
short of personality.*

La Vigneronne ★★★★★
105 Old Brompton Road,
London SW7 3LE
☎ 020 7589 6113
FAX 020 7581 2983
@ lavig@aol.com
W www.lavigneronne.co.uk
Credit cards, accessories, delivery, tastings,
en primeur, mail order.
*Specialists in fine and rare wines from
around the world and French country
wines. Frequent, tastings and dinners.*

Villeneuve Wines ★★★★
One Venlaw Court, Peebles,
Scotland EH45 8AE
☎ 01721 722 500
FAX 01721 729 922
@ wines@villeneuvewines.com
W www.villeneuvewines.com
Credit cards, accessories, delivery, cellarage, tastings,
en primeur, glass loan, mail order, internet sales.
*Three shops, with a range including rare
vintages of Château Musar.*

Vin du Van ★★★★★
Colthups, The Street, Appledore, Kent
TN26 2BX
☎ 01233 758727
FAX 01233 758389
W www.vinduvan.com
By the case only, mail order only, delivery,
credit cards, glass loan.
*Wacky, unpretentious, yet informative
list. Superb portfolio of Aussie wines.*

Vinceremos Wine & Spirits ★★★★
19 New Street, Leeds LS18 4BH
☎ 0113 205 4545
FAX 0113 205 4546
@ sales@vinceremos.co.uk
W www.vinceremos.co.uk
By the case only, mail order only, glass loan, en
primeur, cellarage, credit cards, delivery, internet sales.
*One of the best sources for organic wines,
not to mention new Moroccan wines with
which to surprise your friends.*

Vino Vino ★★★★
Freepost, SEA 5662,
New Malden, Kent KT3 3BR
☎ 07703 436949
FAX 020 8942 4003
@ vinovino@appleonline.net
Mail order only, credit cards, delivery.
*Specializing in wonderful classic and
new Italian wines. A new Spanish list
is in its infancy. Regular, informative
mailings are welcome too.*

Vintage Roots ★★★★★
Farley Farms, Bridge Farm,
Reading Road, Arborfield RG2 9HT
☎ 0800 980 4992
FAX 0118 976 1998
@ info@vintageroots.co.uk
W www.vintageroots.co.uk
By the case only, mail order only, credit cards,
delivery, tastings, internet sales.
*All wines 100 per cent certified organic,
some biodynamic, all full of character,
and now on-line.*

Vintage Wines ★★★★
116–118 Derby Road,
Nottingham, NG1 5FB
☎ 0115 947 6565
FAX 0115 950 5276
W www.vintagewinesltd.co.uk
Credit cards, cellarage, en primeur, delivery, tastings,
glass hire/loan, mail order, internet sales.
*Good list to pick from. France, Germany,
and Australia are explored in some depth.*

The Vintry ★ ★ ★ ★
Park Farm, Milland, Liphook,
Hants GU30 7JT
☎ 01428 741 389
FAX 01428 741 368
W www.vintry.co.uk
By the case only, glass loan/hire, en primeur,
credit cards (internet only), delivery, tastings.
*Six exclusively French outlets, offering a
good general selection, including British-
made French wines such as Ch. Méaume.*

Waitrose ★ ★ ★ ★ ★
Duncastle Rd., Southern Industrial Area,
Bracknell, Berks RG12 8YA
☎ 01344 424680
FAX 01344 825255
W www.waitrose-direct.co.uk
Credit cards, accessories, delivery, tastings, en primeur,
cellarage, glass hire/loan, mail order, internet sales.
*A well balanced list with good traditional
wines and plenty of innovative bottles to
look out for. Waitrose Wine Direct is their
mail order arm.*

Waterloo Wine Co. ★ ★ ★ ★
61 Lant Street, London, SE1 1QN
☎ 020 7403 7967
FAX 020 7357 6976
@ sales@waterloowine.co.uk
W www.waterloowine.co.uk
Credit cards, delivery, tastings, glass hire/loan,
mail order.
*Focus on New Zealand. Great Loire,
German, and Midi offerings too.*

Waters of Coventry ★ ★ ★ ★ ★
Collins Road, Heathcote,
Warwick, CV34 6TF
☎ 01926 888889
FAX 01926 887416
@ rc@wildbunch.co.uk
W www.waters-wine-merchants.co.uk
Credit cards, delivery, tastings, mail order.
*Top Rhônes, Burgundies, Spanish. New
world offerings include fine olive oils.*

Weavers of Nottingham ★ ★ ★ ★
Vintner House, 1 Castle Gate,
Nottingham NG1 7AQ
☎ 0115 258 0922
FAX 0115 950 8076
@ weavers@weavers-wine.co.uk
W www.weaverswine.co.uk
Credit cards, accessories, delivery, tastings,
glass hire/loan, mail order, internet sales.
*Traditional merchant with wide range of
wines, accessories, malts, and liqueurs.*

Whitebridge Wines ★ ★ ★ ★
Unit 21, Whitebridge Estate, Stone,
Staffs ST15 8LQ
☎ 01785 817229
FAX 01785 811181
@ sales@whitebridgewines.co.uk
W www.whitebridgewines.co.uk
Credit cards, accessories, delivery, tastings,
cellarage, glass hire/loan, mail order.
*Good wines from Australia and France.
Note also the recently-launched Fine
Wine arm trading as The Peckwater
Wine Company.*

Whiteside's of Clitheroe ★ ★ ★ ★ ★
Shawbridge Street, Clitheroe,
Lancs BB7 1NA
☎ 01200 422281
FAX 01200 427129
@ wine@whitesideswine.co.uk
Credit cards, accessories, delivery, tastings,
cellarage, glass loan, mail order.
*A good New World selection with an
unusually fine range of whiskies and
Spanish wines.*

Wine Cellar ★ ★ ★ ★
PO Box 476, Loushers Lane,
Warrington, Cheshire WA4 6RR
☎ 01925 444 555
FAX 01925 415 474
@ sales@winecellar.co.uk
W www.winecellar.co.uk
Credit cards, accessories, delivery, tastings, en
primeur, cellarage, glass loan, mail order.
*Innovative, independently-owned chain
of shops, some of which boast cafés.*

The Wine Cellar ★ ★ ★ ★
10 Station Parade, Sanderstead Road,
South Croydon, Surrey CR2 OPH
☎ 020 8657 6936
FAX 020 8657 9391
@ woodgeraldine@aol.com
Credit cards, accessories, delivery, tastings,
en primeur, cellarage, glass loan, mail order.
*This independent merchant offers a
commendable selection, including a
great range of malts.*

Wine Rack ★ ★ ★ ★
Enjoyment Hall, Bessemer Road,
Welwyn Garden City, Herts AL7 1BL
☎ 01707 387263
FAX 01707 387350
Credit cards, delivery, tastings, glass hire/loan.
*Up-market, high-street face of the First
Quench (Thresher, Victoria Wine) group.*

Wine Raks (Scotland) ★★★★
21 Springfield Rd, Aberdeen AB15 7RJ
☎ 01224 311460
FAX 01224 312186
@ enq@wineraks.co.uk
W www.wineraks.co.uk
Credit cards, accessories, delivery, tastings,
en primeur, glass hire/loan, cellarage.
An interesting list of Old World growers'
wines and exciting New World wines.

The Wine Society ★★★★★
Gunnels Wood Road, Stevenage,
Hertfordshire, SG1 2BG
☎ 01438 740222
FAX 01438 761167
@ memberservices@thewinesociety.com
W www.thewinesociety.com
Mail order only, credit cards, delivery, tastings,
glass hire/loan, en primeur, cellarage.
Britain's best mail-order merchant?
Member-owned and offering French
classics, good daily-drinking wine, and
well-chosen mixed cases and en primeur.

The Wine Treasury ★★★★
69–71 Bondway, London, SW8 1SQ
☎ 020 7793 9999
FAX 020 7793 8080
@ julian@winetreasury.com
W www.winetreasury.com
By the case only, credit cards, en primeur, delivery,
tastings, mail order.
Premium Californian wines; top names
from Italy, Australia, and elsewhere.

Winefinds ★★★★
Unit A, Dinton Business Park, Dinton,
Wilts SP3 5SR
☎ 01722 716916
FAX 01722 716179
@ sales@winefinds.co.uk
W www.winefinds.co.uk
By the case only, mail order only, credit cards,
free delivery.
A team of Masters of Wine seeking out
treats from the Old and New Worlds.

Wines of Westhorpe
Marchington, Staffs ST14 8NX.
☎ 01283 820285.
FAX 01283 820631.
@ wines@westhorpe.co.uk
W www.westhorpe.co.uk
By the case only, credit cards, delivery, tastings,
mail order, internet sales.
Experts on Hungary, with good South
African and New World wines.

The Wright Wine Co. ★★★★
The Old Smithy, Raikes Road, Skipton,
N. Yorks BD23 1NP
☎ 01756 700886
FAX 01756 700886
@ bob@wineandwhisky.co.uk
W www.wineandwhisky.co.uk
Credit cards, accessories, delivery, cellarage, glass loan.
Great wines from Alsace, South Africa,
and Australia, including many halves.

Wrightson & Company ★★★★
Manfield Grange, Manfield, Darlington,
N. Yorks DL2 2RE
☎ 01325 374134
FAX 01325 374135
@ ed.wrightson.wines@onyxnet.co.uk
W www.thatwineclub.co.uk
By the case only, credit cards, accessories, delivery,
tastings, en primeur, cellarage, glass loan, mail order.
Independent specialist wine importer
expanding into mail order. Specialist
in South African wineries.

Peter Wylie Fine Wines ★★★★★
Plymtree Manor, Plymtree, Cullompton,
Devon EX15 2LE
☎ 01884 277 555
FAX 01884 277 557
@ peter@wylie-fine-wines.demon.co.uk
W www.wyliefinewines.co.uk
Mail order only (visitors by appointment), delivery
(worldwide), en primeur, cellarage, internet sales.
A veritable treasure-trove of rare and
fine wines.

Yapp Brothers ★★★★★
The Old Brewery, Mere,
Wiltshire BA12 6DY
☎ 01747 860423
FAX 01747 860929
@ sales@yapp.co.uk
W www.yapp.co.uk
Credit cards, delivery, tastings, cellarage,
glass hire/loan, mail order, internet sales.
Britain's most faithful and probably
best Loire and Rhône specialists.

Noel Young Wines ★★★★★
56 High Street, Trumpington,
Cambridge CB2 2LS
☎ 01223 844 744/566 744
FAX 01223 844 736
W www.nywines.co.uk
Credit cards, accessories, delivery, tastings,
en primeur, glass hire/loan, mail order.
Good broad range with some
brilliant Australian wines.

RETAILERS IN BRIEF

3D Wines
- 01205 820 745
- www.3dwines.com

A&A Wines
- 01483 274666
- www.spanishwinesonline.co.uk

A&B Vintners Ltd
- 01892 724 977
- www.abvintners.co.uk

Allez Vins!
- 0800 096 6587
- www.allezvins.co.uk

Arriba Kettle
- 01386 833 024

Barrels & Bottles
- 0114 2555511
- www.barrelsandbottles.co.uk

Booths of Stockport
- 0161 432 3309

The Bottleneck
- 01843 861095
- www.thebottleneck.co.uk

Cape Province Wines
- 01784 451860
- www.capewinestores.co.uk

The Celtic Vintner
- 01633 430 055

Châteaux Wines
- 01454 613 959
- www.chateauxwines.com

Colombier Vins Fins
- 01283 552552

Connolly's Wine Merchants
- 0121 236 9269
- www.connollyswine.co.uk

Rodney Densem Wines
- 01270 212200

Eckington Wines
- 01246 433 213

Edencroft Fine Wines
- 01270 629975

Evington's Wine Merchants
- 0116 254 2702

Ferrers Le Mesurier & Son
- 01832 732 660

John Frazier
- 0121 704 3415
- www.fraziers.co.uk

Friarwood
- 020 7736 2628
- www.friarwood.com

Garrards Merchants
- 01900 823592

Charles Hennings
- 01798 872 485

Hicks & Don
- 01380 831234
- www.hicksanddon.co.uk

High Breck Vintners
- 020 8340 1848

Hopton Wines
- 01299 270734

Richard Kihl
- 01728 454455
- www.richardkihl.ltd.uk

Mayor Sworder
- 020 8686 1155
- www.mayorsworder.co.uk

Mills Whitcombe Fine Wines
- 01873 860222

Thomas Panton
- 01666 503088
- www.wineimporter.co.uk

Parfrements
- 02476 503646
- www.parfrements.co.uk

Christopher Piper Wines
- 01404 814139

R.S. Wines
- 0117 963 1780

The Rogers Wine Co
- 01473 748 464

Ashley Scott
- 01244 520655

Selfridges
- 020 7318 3730

Springfield Wines
- 01484 864 929

John Stephenson & Sons
- 01282 614 618

Transatlantic Wines
- 01664 565013

Trout Wines
- 01264 781 472

Uncorked
- 020 7638 5998
- www.uncorked.co.uk

Vine Trail
- 0117 921 1770

El Vino Co.
- 020 7353 5384

Vintage Cellars
- 020 7630 5254
- www.vintagecellars.co.uk

Waxman Wine Company
- 01422 371811
- FAX 01422 374101

York Wines
- 01347 878 716.
- www.yorkwines.co.uk

COUNTRY & REGION SPECIALISTS

THE AMERICAS

NORTH AMERICA
Adnams (see page 372)
The Antique Wine Co (see page 372)
Asda Stores (see page 372)
Averys of Bristol (see page 373)
Bennetts Wines (see page 373)
Bibendum (see page 373)
Booths (see page 374)
The Bottleneck (see page 387)
Corkscrew Wines (see page 375)
Gordon and MacPhail
(see page 376)
Great Northern Wine Co.
(see page 377)
Charles Hennings
(see page 387)
Inspired Wines (see page 378)
Lea & Sandeman (see page 379)
Lay & Wheeler (see page 378)
Morris & Verdin (see page 380)
New Fine Wines (see page 277)
James Nicholson (see page 380)
Oddbins (see page 380)
Terry Platt (see page 381)
R.S. Wines (see page 387)
Raeburn Fine Wines
(see page 381)
Sommelier Wine Co.
(see page 383)
Stevens Garnier (see page 383)
Stratford's (see page 383)
The Wine Treasury
(see page 386)

SOUTH AMERICA
Booths of Stockport
(see page 387)
The Bottleneck (see page 387)
Charterhouse Emporium
(see page 299)
Ben Ellis Wines (see page 272)
Forth Wines (see page 376)
Hedley Wright (see page 377)
Moreno Wine (see page 380)
Stevens Garnier (see page 383)
The Wine Society
(see page 386)
The Wright Wine Co.
(see page 386)

AUSTRALIA
W.M. Addison (see page 372)
Adnams (see page 372)
Amps Fine Wines (see page 372)

Australian Wine Club
(see page 373)
Bennetts (see page 373)
Booths of Stockport
(see page 387)
The Bottleneck (see page 387)
Corkscrew Wines (see page 375)
Charterhouse Emporium
(see page 374)
Direct Wine Shipments
(see page 375)
Domaine Direct (see page 375)
Eckington Wines (see page 387)
Edencroft Fine Wines
(see page 387)
Great Northern Wine Co
(see page 377)
H.& H. Fine Wines
(see page 273)
Jeroboams (see page 378)
Mills Whitcombe (see page 387)
Philglas & Swiggott
(see page 381)
Christopher Piper (see page 387)
R.S. Wines (see page 387)
Vin du Van (see page 384)
Vintage Wines (see page 384)

AUSTRIA
Bacchus Fine Wines (see page 373)
Ben Ellis Wines (see page 272)
Forth Wines (see page 376)
Morris & Verdin (380)
Penistone Court (see page 381)
Noel Young Wines
(see page 386)

EASTERN EUROPE
Wines of Westhorpe
(see page 283)

ENGLAND
Stratford's Wine Shippers
(see page 383)

FRANCE

ALSACE
Amps Fine Wines (see page 372)
Ballantynes of Cowbridge
(see page 373)
Anthony Byrne (see page 374)
Gauntleys (see page 376)
O.W. Loeb (see page 379)
Scatchard Wines (see page 382)
Tanners Wines (see page 383)

Wine Rack (see page 385)
The Wine Society (see page 386)

BEAUJOLAIS
Berkmann Wine Cellars (see page 373)
Colombier Vins Fins (see page 387)
Roger Harris (see page 377)
Domaine Direct (see page 375)

BORDEAUX
W.M. Addison (see page 372)
The Antique Wine Co. (see page 372)
John Armit Wines (see page 372)
Averys of Bristol (see page 373)
Balls Brothers (see page 373)
Berry Bros. & Rudd (see page 373)
Bibendum (see page 373)
Bordeaux Index (see page 374)
The Butlers Wine Cellar
(see page 374)
Anthony Byrne (see page 374)
Cave Cru Classé (see page 374)
Brian Coad (see page 375)
Colombier Vins Fins (see page 387)
Connolly's (see page 387)
Corney and Barrow (see page 375)
Direct Wine Shipments
(see page 375)
Farr Vintners (see page 376)
Forth Wines (see page 376)
Fortnum & Mason (see page 376)
Four Walls Wine Co.
(see page 376)
Friarwood (see page 387)
Goedhuis & Co. (see page 376)
Harrods (see page 377)
Harvey Nichols (see page 380)
Justerini & Brooks (see page 378)
Richard Kihl (see page 387)
Laithwaites (see page 378)
Lay & Wheeler (see page378)
O.W. Loeb (see page 379)
Magnum Fine Wines (see page 379)
Montrachet (see page 380)
Nicolas (see page 380)
Oddbins Fine Wines (see page 380)
Thos. Peatling (see page 381)
Le Pont de la Tour (see page 381)
Reid Wines (see page 381)
Roberson (see page 382)
Edward Sheldon (see page 383)
Tanners Wines (see page 383)
Turville Valley Wines
(see page 383)
Wilkinson Vintners (see page 282)
The Wine Society (see page 311)
Peter Wylie Fine Wines
(see page 386)

Yapp Brothers (see page 386)

BURGUNDY
3D Wines (see page 387)
A & B Vintners (see page 387)
The Antique Wine Co. (see page 372)
John Armit Wines (see page 372)
Averys of Bristol (see page 373)
Bibendum (see page 373)
The Burgundy Shuttle
(see page 374)
The Butlers Wine Cellar
(see page 374)
Anthony Byrne (see page 374)
Cave Cru Classé (see page 374)
Brian Coad (see page 375)
Colombier Vins Fins (see page 387)
Connolly's (see page 387)
Corney and Barrow (see page 375)
Domaine Direct (see page 375)
Farr Vintners (see page 376)
Irma Fingal-Rock (see page 376)
Fortnum & Mason (see page 376)
Four Walls Wine Co. (see page 376)
Goedhuis & Co. (see page 376)
Harrods (see page 377)
Harvey Nichols (see page 380)
Haynes Hanson & Clark
(see page 377)
Heyman Barwell Jones (see page 377)
House of Townsend (see page 378)
Ian G. Howe (see page 378)
Jeroboams (see page 378)
Justerini & Brooks (see page 378)
Lay & Wheeler (see page 378)
Lea & Sandeman (see page 379)
O.W. Loeb (see page 379)
Montrachet (see page 380)
Morris & Verdin (see page 380)
James Nicholson (see page 380)
Oddbins Fine Wines (see page 380)
Christopher Piper (see page 387)
Le Pont de la Tour (see page 381)
Raeburn Fine Wines (see page 381)
Howard Ripley (see page 382)
Stevens Garnier (see page 383)
Turville Valley Wines (see page 383)
La Vigneronne (see page 384)
The Wine Press (see page 282)

CHABLIS
Ian G. Howe (see page 378)

CHAMPAGNE
3D Wines (see page 387)
Amps Fine Wines (see page 372)
W.M. Addison (see page 372)
Connolly's (see page 387)

Farr Vintners (see page 376)
Fortnum & Mason (see page 376)
Marks & Spencer
(see page 379)
Harrods (see page 377)
Majestic Wine (see page 379)
Oddbins (see page 380)

COUNTRY WINES
A & B Vintners (see page 387)
Allez Vins! (see page 387)
The Great Western Wine Co.
(see page 377)
Laithwaites (see page 378)
Mills Whitcombe (see page 387)

LOIRE
Brian Coad (see page 375)
Colombier Vins Fins (see page 387)
Corkscrew Wines (see page 375)
Four Walls Wine Co.
(see page 376)
Yapp Brothers (see page 386)

RHONE
A & B Vintners (see page 387)
Bibendum (see page 373)
Connolly's (see page 387)
Corkscrew Wines (see page 375)
Croque-en-Bouche (see page 375)
Farr Vintners (see page 376)
Gauntleys (see page 376)
Waters of Coventry (see page 385)
Yapp Brothers (see page 386)

GERMANY
Adnams (see page 372)
Four Walls Wine Co. (see page 376)
Justerini & Brooks (see page 378)
O.W. Loeb (see page 379)
Majestic Wine (see page 379)
Tanners Wines (see page 383)

ITALY
John Armit (see page 372)
Averys of Bristol (see page 373)
Berkmann Wine Cellars (see page 373)
Ceci Paolo (see page 381)
Colombier Vins Fins (see page 387)
Connolly's (see page 387)
Inspired Wines (see page 378)
Liberty Wines (see page 379)
Philglass & Swiggot (see page 381)
Valvona & Crolla (see page 384)
Vino Vino (see page 384)
Winefinds (see page 386)

NEW ZEALAND
Vin du Van (see page 384)
Waterloo Wine Co. (see page 385)

PORTUGAL
Forth Wines (see page 376)
Moreno Wine Importers
(see page 380)
Raeburn Fine Wines (see page 381)

SOUTH AFRICA
Cape Province (see page 387)
Forth Wines (see page 376)
Heyman Barwell Jones (see page 377)
Irvine Robertson (see page 382)

SPAIN
A & A Wines (see page 387)
Arriba Kettle (see page 387)
Direct Wine Shipments
(see page 375)
S. H. Jones (see page 378)
Laymont & Shaw (see page 379)
Moreno Wine Importers
(see page 380)
Oddbins (see page 380)
Scatchard (see page 382)
Waters of Coventry (see page 385)

FORTIFIED WINE SPECIALISTS

PORT & MADEIRA
Ballantynes of Cowbridge
(see page 373)
Farr Vintners (see page 376)
Fortnum & Mason (see page 376)
Moreno Wine Importers
(see page 380)
Thos. Peatling (see page 381)
Reid Wines (see page 381)
Turville Valley Wines
(see page 383)
Peter Wylie (see page 386)

SHERRY
Ballantynes of Cowbridge
(see page 373)
Fortnum & Mason (see page 376)
Laymont & Shaw (see page 379)
Lea & Sandeman (see page 379)
Martinez (see page 379)
Moreno Wine Importers
(see page 380)
Morris & Verdin (see page 380)
Reid Wines (see page 381)
Scatchard (see page 382)

BEER SPECIALISTS

Adnams (see page 372)
Majestic Wine (see page 379)
Mitchells Wine Merchants
(see page 387)

Oddbins (see page 380)
Unwins (see page 384)
Wine Cellar
(see page 385)

SPIRIT SPECIALISTS

ARMAGNAC & COGNAC

Justerini & Brooks (see page 378)
Nicolas (see page 380)

WHISKY

Berry Bros. & Rudd (see page 373)

Harrods (see page 377)
Charles Hennings (see page 387)
S.H. Jones (see page 378)
Oddbins (see page 380)
Pallant Wines (see page 387)
La Réserve (see page 381)

FINE AND RARE WINE SPECIALISTS

John Armit Wines (see page 372)
Bennetts Wines (see page 373)
Berry Bros. & Rudd
(see page 373)
Bibendum (see page 373)
Bordeaux Index (see page 374)
Anthony Byrne (see page 374)
Cave Cru Classé (see page 374)
Corney and Barrow
(see page 375)
Farr Vintners (see page 376)
Fine and Rare Wines
(see page 376)
Fortnum & Mason
(see page 376)
Four Walls Wine Co.
(see page 376)
Goedhuis & Co. (see page 376)
Harrods (see page 377)
Harvey Nichols (see page 380)
Lay & Wheeler (see page 378)
Nicolas (see page 380)
The Pavilion Wine Co.
(see page 387)
Oddbins Fine Wines
(see page 380)
Thos. Peatling (see page 381)
Raeburn Fine Wines
(see page 381)
Reid Wines (see page 381)
La Réserve (see page 381)
Roberson (see page 382)
Tanners Wines
(see page 383)
Turville Valley Wines
(see page 383)
Whiteside's of Clitheroe
(see page 385)

Peter Wylie Fine Wines
(see page 386)
Yapp Brothers (see page 386)
Noel Young Wines (see page 386)

LIVE AUCTIONEERS

Bigwood Auctioneers
(01789 269 415 FAX 01789 294 168
W www.bigwoodauctioneers.co.uk
Christie's
(020 7839 9060 FAX 020 7839 1611
W www.christies.com
Lithgow
(01642 710 158 FAX 01642 712 641
@ lithgows.auctions@onyxnet.co.uk

Morphets
(01423 530030 FAX 01423 500717
Phillips
(01225 310 609 FAX 01225 446 675
Sotheby's
(020 7293 6423 FAX 020 7293 5961
W www.sothebys.com
J. Straker Chadwick & Sons
(01873 852 624 FAX 01873 857 311

WINE COURSES

Association of Wine Educators
(+FAX 020 8995 2277
Challenge Educational Services
(01273 220 261 FAX 01273 220 376
@ enquiries@challengeuk.com
Christie's
(020 7839 9060 FAX 020 7839 1611
German Wine Institute
((0049) 6131 282918
Grape Sense
(+FAX 01359 270318
@ grapesense@aol.com
Kensington & Chelsea College
(020 7573 5333 FAX 020 8960 2693
Leicestershire Wine School
(0116 254 2702 FAX 0116 254 2702
Leith's
(020 7229 0177 FAX 020 7937 5257
@ info@leiths.com
Maurice Mason
(+FAX 020 8841 8732
North West Wine and Spirit Assoc.
(+FAX 01244 678 624

Plumpton College
(01273 890 454 FAX 01273 890 071
@ enquiries@plumpton.ac.uk
Scala School
(020 7281 3040 FAX 020 7281 3001
@ scalawine@cs.com
Sotheby's
(020 7293 6423 FAX 020 7293 5961
Vinform (0181 876 0110
Wensum Lodge
(01603 666 021 FAX 01603 765 633
Wine Associates Ltd. (in UK & France)
(01803 299292 (UK)
(0033 553 588 148 (France)
W www.wineassociates.co.uk
Wine & Spirit Education Trust
(020 7236 3551 FAX 020 7329 8712
@ wset@wset.co.uk
Wine Education Service
(020 8423 6338 FAX 020 8723 3751
@info@wine-education-service.co.uk
Wine Wise
(020 7254 9734 FAX 020 7249 3663

WINE HOLIDAYS

Allez France & Great Escapes
(01903 748 100 and 748 138
FAX 01903 745 044
Arblaster & Clarke Wine Tours
(01730 893 344 FAX 01730 892 888
@ sales@winetours.co.uk
Country Lanes
(01425 655 022 FAX 01425 655 177
DER Travel
(020 7290 1111 FAX 020 7629 7442
Edwin Doran Travel
(020 8288 1000 FAX 020 8288 2955
Fine Wine Travel Company
(020 7229 1243
Francophiles Discover France
(+FAX 01362 851 076

In the French Alps with Wink Lorch
(01494 677 728 FAX 01494 677729
HGP Wine Tours
(01803 299 292 FAX 01803 292 008
KD River Cruises Europe
(01372 742 033 FAX 01372 724 871
Moswin Tours
(0116 271 4982 FAX 0116 271 6016
Ski Gourmet and Winetrails
(01306 712 111 FAX 01306 713 504
The Sunday Times Wine Club Tours
(01730 895 353 FAX 01730 892 888
Tanglewood Wine Tours
(01932 348 720 FAX 01932 350 861
Wessex Continental Travel
(+FAX 01752 846 880

ACCESSORIES

GLASSES
Conran Shop (Riedel range)
📞 020 7589 7401
FAX 020 7823 7015
Dartington Crystal
📞 01805 626 262
FAX 01805 626 267
Equinox (Belfast) (Riedel range)
📞 01232 230 089
Oneida/Schott UK
📞 01753 212500

CORKSCREWS
Screwpull
📞 01264 343 900

STORAGE
Access Storage Space
📞 020 8991 9717
FAX 020 8991 9611
Consort Wine Care Systems
📞 01635 550055
FAX 01635 41733
Euro-cave
📞 020 8200 1266
FAX 020 8200 1792
W www.artofwine.co.uk
Smith & Taylor
📞 020 7627 5070
FAX 020 7622 8235
Vin-Garde
📞+FAX 01926 811 376

WINE RACKS
A.&W. Moore
📞 0115 944 1434
FAX 0115 932 0735

R.T.A Wine Racks
📞 01328 829 666
Spiral Cellars
📞 01372 279 166
The Wine Rack Company
📞+FAX 01243 543 253

ANTIQUES
Bacchus Gallery
📞 01798 342 844
FAX 01798 342 634

GENERAL WINE ACCESSORIES
Most independent wine merchants also
stock a good range of accessories.
Birchgrove Products Ltd.
📞 01483 533 400 FAX 01483 533 700
The Hugh Johnson Collection
📞 020 7491 4912 FAX 020 7493 0602

CHILLING DEVICES
Chilla
📞 0181 891 6464
Coolbags & Boxes UK
📞 0118 9333 331 FAX 0118 9333 579
Vacu Products
📞 01299 250 480 FAX 01299 251 559

BOOKS
Books for Cooks
📞 020 7221 1992
FAX 020 7221 1517
W www.booksforcooks.com
Cooking the Books
📞+FAX 01633 400 150
Richard Stanford
📞 020 7836 1321

WINE CLUBS

Académie du Vin
📞 01803 299 292
FAX 01803 292 008
@ hgpwine@aol.com
Alston Wine Club
📞 01434 381 338
Amersham
📞 01494 771 983
Association of Wine Cellarmen
📞 020 8871 3092
Barrels and Bottles
📞 0114 255 6611
FAX 0114 255 1010
Charlemagne
📞 020 8567 1733

Cirencester
📞 01285 641 126
Confrérie Internationale de St. Vincent
📞 0113 267 9258 FAX 0113 228 9307
@ asmalley@cwcom.net
Cornwall
📞 01872 223 570
Decant & Taste
📞 01507 605 758
Eastbourne
📞 01323 727675
Goring & Streatley
📞 01491 873 620
Guild of Sommeliers
📞 0161 928 0852

Harrogate Medical
(01423 503 129 FAX 01423 561 820
Herefordshire
(01432 275 656
Hextable Wine Club
(01732 823 345
Hollingworth
(01706 374 765
@ peter-l@msn.com
Ightham Wine Club
(01732 885 557
Institute of Wines & Spirits
(Scotland) (+FAX 01324 554 162
The Interesting Wine Club
(020 7272 2457 FAX 020 7272 4312
International Wine and Food Society
(020 7495 4191 FAX 020 7495 4172
@ iwandfs@aol.com
Leicester Evington
(0116 231 4760
FAX 0116 287 5371
Leicester Grand Union
(0116 287 1662
Lincoln Wine Society
(+FAX 01522 680 388
London Branch of IWFS
(0208 349 2260
FAX 0208 346 4360
Manchester
(01706 824 283
Moreno
(020 7286 0678

Myster Wine Club
(01633 893 485
Notting Hill
(020 8969 9668
Preston
(01772 254 251
FAX 01772 203 858
Rochester
(01634 848 345
Scottish
(0131 664 8855
Tanglewood Wine Society
(01932 348 720
FAX 01932 350 861
West Hampstead
(020 7794 3926
Windsor and Eton
(01753 790 188 FAX 01753 790 189
@ enquiries@etonvintners.co.uk
Wine and Dine
(020 8673 4439
FAX 020 8675 5543.
@ bensonwines@connectingbusiness.com
Wine Collectors (WineShare)
(01306 742 164
Wine Schoppen
(0114 255 6611
FAX 0114 255 1010
The Winetasters
(01753 889 702
York
(+FAX 01904 691 628

CROSS-CHANNEL SHOPPING

EastEnders Bulk Beer Warehouse
14 Rue Gustave Courbet, 62100 Calais,
France
((33) 3 21 34 53 33
FAX (33) 3 21 97 61 22
Normandy Wine Warehouse
(4 branches – 2 in Cherbourg, 2 in
Ouistreham) 71 Avenue Carnot, 50100
Cherbourg, France
((33) 2 33 43 39 79
FAX (33) 2 33 43 22 69
Oddbins
Cité Europe, 139 Rue de Douvres,
62901 Coquelles, Cedex, France
((33) 3 21 82 07 32
FAX (33) 3 21 82 05 83
Perardel Wine Market
Z.A. Marcel Doret, Calais, France
((33) 3 21 97 21 22
Sainsbury's Wine Store
Centre Commercial Auchon, Route de
Boulogne, Calais, France

((33) 3 21 82 38 48
FAX (33) 3 21 36 01 91
Le Tastevin
9 Rue Val, 35400 St.-Malo,
France
((33) 2 99 82 46 56
FAX (33) 2 99 81 09 69
Tesco Vin Plus
Espace 122, Boulevard du Kent, Cité
Europe, 62231 Coquelles, France
((33) 3 21 46 02 70
FAX (33) 3 21 46 02 79
The Wine & Beer Company
Rue de Judée, Zone Industrielle Marcel
Doret, 62100 Calais, France
((33) 3 21 97 63 00
FAX (33) 3 21 97 70 15
The Wine Society
1 Rue de la Paroisse, 62140 Hesdin,
France
((33) 3 21 86 52 07
FAX (33) 3 21 86 52 13

The world of wine online is changing so rapidly that the following list can only offer a snapshot of what you may find if you go looking for wine on the web. But it should give you a pretty good start.

ONLINE RETAILERS

Apart from the specialist online retailers listed here, you will also find websites for many of the companies profiled on pages 372–387.

www.a-bestfixture.com
Wine accessories, supplies, and gifts.
www.auswine.com.au
Australian wines shipped worldwide.
www.avalonwine.com
Wines from the Pacific Northwest.
www.bbr.co.uk
Traditional merchant. Worldwide delivery.
www.cawineclub.com
California wine club.
www.chateau-online.com
French wines shipped throughout Europe.
www.clarets.com
Not just claret. Ship worldwide.
www.connseries.com
US site with limited-production wines.
www.esquin.com
Superstore and wine club.
www.everywine.co.uk
UK site offering 35,000 wines.
www.evineyard.com
Ship to most US States.

www.finestwine.com
Global supply of collectable wines.
www.libation.com
Wine and beer delivered worldwide.
www.madaboutwine.com
Wine delivered worldwide.
www.planetwine.com
Australian-turned international site.
www.tinamou.com
Premium French wines and vintage port.
www.virginwine.com
Dynamic UK-based site.
www.wine.com
Wines, gifts, accessories, and wine links.
www.winebroker.com
Fine wine specialists.
www.thewinebrokers.com
Worldwide delivery and online wineclub.
www.winepros.com
Contributors include this guide's author.
www.winex.com
A good general catalog of wine.

ONLINE AUCTIONEERS

www.auctionvine.com
A central online auction site.
www.amazon.com
Online giant associated with Sotheby's.
www.brentwoodwine.com
Auction site with fixed price sales, too.
www.tcwc.com
The Chicago Wine Company.
www.internetauctionlist.com
Network of auction company web sites.
www.magnumwines.com
Speciality wines.

www.wine-auction-gazette.com
Calendar of wine auctions.
www.winebid.com
Fine wines and spirit auctions in the US, the UK, and Australia.
www.winetoday.com
An updated archive of articles on auctions with news, views, and reviews.
www.vines.netauctions.net.au
Five annual auctions in Australia.
www.winesonauction.com
Wine sold by producers.

ONLINE WINE EDUCATION

www.WineEducation.com
Certified Wine Educator, Stephen Reiss.
www.wine.gurus.com
Society of Wine Educators'
home page.

www.wine-school.com
An online diploma wine course.
www.wineprofessor.com
Food and wine pairing, wine labels, etc.

NEWS, REVIEWS, & GENERIC SITES

www.4wine.com
US-dominant link to worldwide wines.
www.ambrosiawine.com
A search engine to find almost any wine, clubs, and a live online chat feature.
www.decanter.com
The UK wine magazine online.
www.connectingdrinks.com
The route to WINE Magazine online.
www.drinkwine.com
All about wine.
www.food-and-drink.com
Links to food and drink sites.
www.foodandwine.com
Food and Wine Magazine online.
www.gangofpour.com
Loads of general information about wine. Reviews and tasting notes.
www.goodwineguide.com
The online partner to this guide.
www.grapevineweekly.com
An online magazine with lots of links.
www.hotwine.com
A link to winesites, plus poetic quotes.
www.interaxus.com/pages/wine.html
Wine reviews.
www.intlwinechallenge.com
The world's biggest wine competition's official website.
www.intowine.com
Winemaking and wine-and-the-Bible.
www.purplepages.com
Directory of wine-related websites.
www.orgasmicwines.com
News and wines to buy.
www.smartwine.com
Market news for the investor.
www.thewinenews.com
News and reviews.
www.vine2wine.com
Links to over 2,000 wine sites.

www.wineadvocate.com
The guru Robert Parker @ home.
www.winebrats.org
New-wave, emphatically unstuffy wine news and chat.
www.winecellar.com
A complete source of wine links.
www.wine-collector.com
Swap and chat about collectable bottles.
www.wineculture.com
A hip guide to wine on the web.
www.wineenthusiastmag.com
Articles and the latest news.
www.wineinfonet.com
A multilanguage portal.
www.wine-investor.com
How to spend your cash.
www.wineplace.com
Winemaking galore.
www.wineontheweb.com
The talking online wine magazine.
www.winepros.com
Experts including James Halliday and the author of this guide.
www.wineratings.com
Wine reviews and advice.
www.wine-searcher.com
Search the web for all aspects of wine.
www.winesense.com
Wine appreciation and women in wine.
www.winexwired.com
The online presence of the irreverent *Wine X* Magazine.
www.winetoday.com
News from the *New York Times*.
www.thewinenews.com
Features, reviews, recommendations.
www.winespectator.com
The *Wine Spectator's* online magazine.
www.worldwine.com
A website dedicated to wine links.

WINERIES

www.cawinemall.com
Comprehensive directory of California web wineries by region or grape variety.
www.champagnes.com
An introduction to Champagne.
www.edgamesandart.com/wine.html
A database of wine and wineries.
www.hiddenwineries.com
Lesser-known US wineries.
www.vinosearch.com
Wines and wineries across the globe.

www.winecollection.com
An online collection of France's wineries.
www.wines.com
An award-winning guide to wine and wineries.
www.winetoday.com
A comprehensive list of wineries.
www.wineweb.com
Wines and wineries across the world.
www.worldwine.com
Lots of links.

REGIONAL SITES

www.argentinewines.com
Argentina's new-wave wines.
www.barossa.com
Wines of the Barossa Valley.
www.bordeaux.com
A virtual tour of Bordeaux.
www.coonawarra.com
Australia's most famous region.
vino.eunet.es
The Spanish wine page.
www.germanwines.de
Multilingual official site.
www.indagegroup.com
Promoting India's wine.
www.ivp.pt
The Port Wine Institute's web site.
www.liwines.com
Long Island wine country.
www.napawine.com
Visit Napa wineries and wine sites.
www.madeirawine.com
All about Madeira's wines and history.
www.nywine.com
New York uncorked.

www.nzwine.com
The official site of New Zealand wine.
www.sonomawine.com
Sonoma County Wineries Association.
www.washingtonwine.org
All about wine in Washington.
www.wine.ch
The Swiss wine page.
www.wine.co.za
A guide to South African wines.
www.winecountry.com
The gateway to wines of California.
www.winesofchile.com
Ever-expanding guide to Chilean wines.
www.wineinstitute.com
Californian wineries with lots of links.
www.wine.it
Wines of Italy.
www.wines-france.com
User-friendly guide to French wines.
www.winetitles.com.au
A complete guide to wine Down Under.
www.winetour.com
A guide to Ontario's wineries.

ONLINE CHATROOMS & CLUBS

www.4wine.com
Lists a multitude of chat rooms.
www.auswine.com.au/cgi-bin/
auswine/browse
The Australian Wine Centre's virtual
shop provides a search feature, a forum,
and a chat room.
www.drinkwine.com
Bulletin board and extensive listing of
associations.
www.evineyard.com
Offers live talk and a lively wine club.
www.iglou.com/wine/chat
Join a crowd of other wine lovers and
compare notes.
www.nobilevineyards.com
International wine club and
chat room.
www.secretcellars.com
A virtual wine club that brings
California's small vineyards to your door.
www.vineswinger.com
Plentiful chat rooms and busy wine
forums.
www.winebrats.org
Access to various wine chat rooms.
www.wineculture.com
A resource of various chat rooms.

www.wineinstitute.org
Lists discussion groups and chat rooms
focusing on California wine.
www.wine-lovers-page.com
Wine chat room.
www.wine.rave.com
Website with its own wine chat room –
arguably the liveliest on the net.
www.wines.com
Bulletin board where questions can be
posed to wine experts.
www.winesite.com
Extensive list of links to international
wine clubs.
www.winespectator.com
Regular opportunities to interview wine
personalities.
www.zinfans.com
For lovers of the Zinfandel – in its every
form.

*To assist me in keeping these lists
up-to-date for future editions, please
email recommendations of other sites to
robertjoseph@goodwineguide.com
In return, I will send copies of my book*
French Wines *to senders of the most
useful tips.*

INDEX

This index can be used as a supplement to the A–Z of Wine (pages 97–294)

C

N

O

WINE ON THE WEB

Apart from our lists of recommended websites
on pages 16–17 and 395–397,
if you enjoy
Robert Joseph's Good Wine Guide
visit Robert Joseph's
Good Wine Guide
site on the World Wide Web at
www.goodwineguide.com
for news, competitions,
an electronic Wine Atlas, comment,
and links to over 200 wineries and
retailers throughout the world.

Visit
www.wine-school.com
www.robertjoseph.com
for interactive food and wine updates

and, of course,
www.dk.com
for details of other
Dorling Kindersley titles.